D0717386

THE COMPLETE BOOK OF
VEGETABLES, HERBS & FRUIT

THE COMPLETE
BOOK OF
VEGETABLES
HERBS
& FRUIT

THE DEFINITIVE BOOK ON
EDIBLE GARDENING

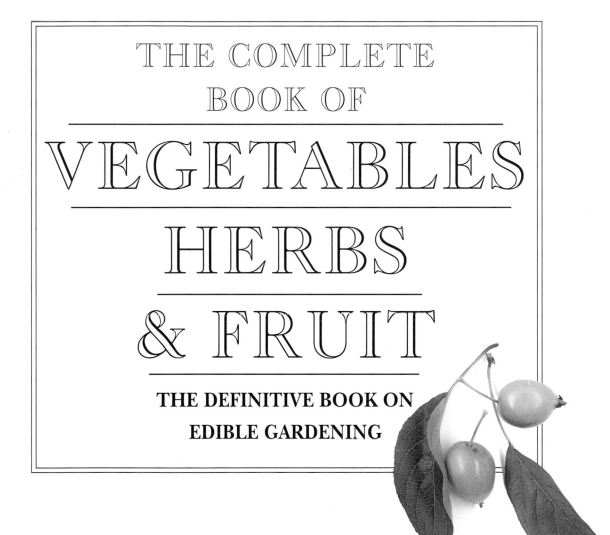

KYLE CATHIE LIMITED

To Henry John William and
Chloe Elizabeth
Matthew Biggs

To Mac, Hannah and Alistair
Jekka McVicar

To all those who helped make
our glorious fruits from such
humble beginnings
Bob Flowerdew

First published in Great Britain in 2002 by
Kyle Cathie Limited
122 Arlington Road
London NW1 7HP
general.enquiries@kyle-cathie.com
www.kylecathie.com

ISBN 1 85626 475 0

Text pages 14–193, 388–389, 502–505 © Matthew Biggs 1997,
2000, 2002
Text pages 196–387 © Jekka McVicar 1994, 1997, 1999, 2002
Text pages 392–501, 506–559 © Bob Flowerdew 1995, 1997,
2000, 2002

All rights reserved. No reproduction, copy or transmission
of this publication may be made without written
permission. No paragraph of this publication may be
reproduced, copied or transmitted save with written
permission or in accordance with the provision of the
Copyright Act 1956 (as amended). Any person who does
any unauthorised act in relation to this publication may be
liable to criminal prosecution and civil claims for damages.

Matthew Biggs, Jekka McVicar and Bob Flowerdew are
hereby identified as the authors of this work in accordance
with Section 77 of the Copyright, Designs and Patents
Act 1988.

Project editor: Jane Simmonds
Design: Geoff Hayes
Production: Lorraine Baird & Sha Huxtable

A Cataloguing in Publication record for this title is
available from the British Library.

Printed and bound in Singapore by Kyodo Printing Co.

Much of the material in this book is taken from *Matthew
Biggs's Complete Book of Vegetables*, *Jekka's Complete Herb Book*
and *Bob Flowerdew's Complete Fruit Book* first published in
1997, 1994 and 1995 respectively.

IMPORTANT NOTICE
**This book contains information on a
wide range of herbs and some fruits and
vegetables that can be used medicinally.
It is not intended as a medical reference
book, but as a source of information.
Before trying any herbal remedies, the
reader is recommended to sample a small
quantity first to establish whether there is
any adverse or allergic reaction.
Remember that some herbs that are
beneficial in small doses can be harmful
if taken in excess or for a long period.
The reader is advised not to attempt self-
treatment for serious or long-term
problems without consulting a qualified
medical herbalist. Neither the authors
nor the publisher can be held responsible
for any adverse reactions to the recipes,
recommendations and instructions
contained herein, and the use of any
plant or derivative is entirely at the
reader's own risk.**

CONTENTS

INTRODUCTION

A flourishing, productive garden, containing vegetables, herbs and fruit plants is a testament to diligent, imaginative gardening and a promise of a delicious harvest to come. The range of colour, texture, scent and flavour offered by these plants is unrivalled, and there is space in any garden – even in a window box – for a selection of edible and useful plants.

Vegetables, herbs and fruit have always been essential to humanity. They are the basis of the food chain – even for meat-eaters – and are a vital component in creating tempting, palatable meals, as well as providing unique flavouring and aromas. All provide essential vitamins and minerals for a balanced diet, and many herbs have the added dimension of being used medicinally.

Vegetables and herbs can be widely defined. Vegetables are those plants where a part, such as the leaf, stem or root, can be used for food. Herbs, similarly, are those plants that are used for food, medicine, scent or flavour. Fruits tend to be the sweet, juicy parts of the plants, containing the seed. There is considerable overlap between the three types of plant – one further distinction is that fruits are generally sweet, or used in sweet dishes, while vegetables are savoury, although this is by no means clear-cut.

For centuries throughout the world, productive gardens have been the focal point of family and community survival. Our earliest diet as hunter-gatherers must have included a wide range of seeds, fruits, nuts, roots, leaves and any moving thing we could catch. Gradually, over millennia, we learned which plants could be eaten and how to prepare them – as with the discovery that eddoes were edible only after washing several times and cooking to remove the injurious calcium oxalate crystals. Fruit trees and bushes sprang up at the camp sites of nomadic people and were waiting for them when they returned, growing prolifically on their fertile waste heaps. Vegetables and herbs were collected from the surrounding countryside, and gradually were domesticated. Cultivated wheat and barley have been found dating from 8000 to 7000 BC, and peas from 6500 BC, while rice was recorded as a staple in China by 2800 BC.

With domestication came early selection of plants for beneficial characteristics such as yield, disease resistance and ease of germination. These were the first cultivated varieties, or 'cultivars'. This selection has continued extensively and by the eighteenth century in Europe, seed selection had become a fine art in the hands of skilled gardeners. Gregor Mendel's work with peas in 1855–64 in his monastery garden at Brno in Moravia yielded one of the most significant discoveries, leading to the development of hybrids and scientific selection. Most development has centred on the major food crops. Minor crops, such as seakale, have changed very little, apart from the selection of a few cultivars. Others, like many fruits, are similar to their wild relatives, but have fleshier, sweeter edible parts. Herbs have in general had less intensive work done on selection; many of the most popular and useful herbs are the same as or closely related to plants found in the wild.

The Frugal Meal by Jozef Israels, 1824–1911

Food plants have spread around the world in waves, from the Roman Empire, which brought fruits such as peaches, plums, grapes and figs from the Mediterranean and North Africa to northern Europe, to the influx of plants such as potatoes and maize from the New World in the fifteenth century. In between, monasteries guarded fruits, vegetables and herbs for their own use and for their medicinal value. During the famine and winter dearth of the Middle Ages and beyond, the commonplace scurvy and vitamin deficiencies would have seemed to many people almost miraculously cured by monks' potions containing little more than preserved fruits, vegetables or herbs full of nutrients and vitamin C. In 1597 John Gerard wrote his *Herbal*, detailing numerous plants, their uses, and giving practical advice on how to use them.

Productive gardening developed on several levels. The rich became plant collectors and used the latest technology to overwinter exotic plants in hothouses and stovehouses. Doctors followed on in the traditions of the monasteries and had physic gardens of medicinal herbs. Villagers had cottage gardens filled with fruit trees and bushes, underplanted with vegetables and herbs.

In the 20th century, the expense of labour and decrease in the amount of land available meant that productive gardening declined. Home food production revived during the Second World War, but the availablility of ready-made foods afterwards again hit edible gardening at home. The later years of the century saw a reaction against the blandness and cost of mass-produced food. There was also an increasing awareness of the infinite variety of herbs, and their use in herbalism, cosmetics and cooking all over the world.

A well-kept vegetable garden is a source of pride

The Vegetable Garden, Coombe by **Paul Riley, 1988**

The wider realization that we had polluted our environment and destroyed much of the ecology of our farms, countryside and gardens was to bring about a real revolution. A mass revulsion against chemical-based methods was mirrored in the rise of organic production and the slowly improving availability of better foods. Vegetarianism also increased as many people turned away from meat, in part because of factory farming. These trends mean that there is an increased demand for fruits and vegetables, often organically produced or with a fuller flavour, and supermarkets now offer a huge range all year round.

But there is also a move by people towards growing their own. The health benefits, ecology and economy of gardening appeal to a greener generation. An increased awareness of alternative medicine, including herbalism and aromatherapy, have revived interest in a range of herbs. With food processors, juicers and freezers, it is easier than ever to store and preserve what we harvest. In addition, the genetic richness represented by the huge range of food plants has been recognized and organizations such as the Henry Doubleday Research Association in the

UK, Seed Savers in the USA and Seed Savers International are working to safeguard and make available the old and rare varieties.

The availability of different gardening techniques also offers great opportunities at home. Dwarfing fruit rootstocks, varieties that store well or resist disease, glass or plastic cover, and controlled heating in greenhouses give us scope to grow a huge variety of crops, even in a small garden. The earlier and later seasons, combined with gardening under cover, also mean that we can be planting and harvesting for a larger proportion of the year.

This book is intended to guide the reader in choosing which vegetables, herbs and fruit to grow, and then in producing a crop successfully. The vegetable and herb sections are arranged alphabetically by the botanical Latin name. The fruit section is grouped into five chapters covering different types of fruit plants – Orchard Fruits, Soft, Bush and Cane Fruits, Tender Fruits, Shrub and Flower Garden Fruits, and Nuts – according to how they are usually grown in temperate gardens.

Under each plant, after a brief introduction covering origins and history, the most useful and recommended varieties are given, followed by details of cultivation, including propagation, growing under glass and in containers, a maintenance calendar, pruning and training (if needed), dealing with pests and diseases, companion planting and harvesting and storing. Information and ideas are given for using the plant, including recipes and medicinal and cosmetic uses. If any part of the plant is toxic or harmful in any way, a detailed warning is given. If the plant is of particular ornamental or wildlife value in the garden, this is indicated. Hardy, half-hardy and tender plants are covered, with detailed growing guidelines for the best results in a temperate climate. The fruit and vegetable sections cover some of the more exotic tropical and sub-tropical crops that can, with variable success, be grown under cover.

The end section of the book covers the practical aspects of making a productive garden, including planning your plot and preparing the soil, creating an ornamental edible

garden, crop rotation, pollination, propagation, protected cropping and growing in containers, maintenance, companion planting and pests, diseases and weeds. A yearly calendar details the tasks in the productive garden month by month, although precise dates for these will vary according to frost times in different regions.

There is nothing more satisfying to the soul, eye and stomach than a garden well stocked with produce. This book will help you to grow what you want with confidence, and perhaps to experiment and try out new plants and flavours.

A Note on Botanical Names

While common names are widely used, one plant may have several common names, or a common name in different parts of the world refers to different plants. Botanical names arc vital for clearly identifying plants. The system of botanical names used today is known as the Binomial System and was devised by the 18th-century Swedish botanist Carl Linnaeus (1707–78). In this system, each plant is classified by using two words in Latin form. The first word is the name of the genus (e.g. *Thymus*) and the second the specific epithet (e.g. *vulgaris*): together they provide a universally known name (e.g. *Thymus vulgaris*).

The Linnaean system of plant classification has been developed so that the entire plant kingdom is divided into a multi-branched family tree according to each plant's botanical characteristics. Plants are gathered into particular families according to the structure of their flowers, fruits or seeds. A family may contain one genus or many. The Asteraceae family, for example, contains over 800 genera, including *Achillea*, *Arnica*, *Artemisia* to name a few, and over 13,000 species.

Plants are cultivated for the garden from the wild to improve their leaf or their flower or their root. This can be done either by selection from seedlings or by spotting a mutation. Such plants are known as cultivars (a combination of 'cultivated varieties'). Propagation from these varieties is normally done by cuttings or division. Cultivars are given vernacular names, which are printed within quotes, e.g. *Thymus* 'Doone Valley', to distinguish them from wild varieties in Latin form appearing in italics i.e. *Thymus pulegioides*. Sexual crosses between species, usually of the same genus, are known as hybrids and are indicated by a multiplication sign e.g. *Thymus* x *citriodorus*.

Finally, a problem that seems to be getting worse. Many plants are undergoing reclassification and long-established names are being changed. This is the result of scientific studies and research whereby it is found either that a plant has been incorrectly identified or that its classification has changed. This book uses the latest information available. Where there has been a recent change in the botanical name, this is shown in brackets.

VEGETABLES

Abelmoschus esculentus (syn. *Hibiscus esculentus*). *Malvaceae*

OKRA

Also known as Lady's Fingers, Bhindi, Gumbo. Annual grown for its edible pods. Tender. Value: rich in calcium, iron, potassium, vitamin C and fibre.

The okra, a close relative of the ornamental hibiscus, with slender edible pods, has been cultivated for centuries. It is thought to have originated in northern Africa around the upper Nile and Ethiopia, spreading eastwards to Saudi Arabia and to India. One of the earliest records of it – growing in Egypt – describes the plant, its cultivation and uses. It was introduced to the Caribbean and southern North America by slaves who brought the crop from Africa; the name 'gumbo' comes from a Portuguese corruption of the plant's Angolan common name.

The red forms lose their strong coloration when cooked

VARIETIES

'Artist', with purple-red pods, crops early and turns green when cooked. **'Burgundy'** grows about 1.5m (5ft) tall, with wonderful rich red pods, which are excellent in salads. The colour, however, is lost on cooking. This tolerates cooler growing conditions than most. **'Clemson Spineless'** is a popular, reliable variety with high yields of dark, fleshy pods over a long period. It grows well under cover. **'Dwarf Green Long Pod'** is only about 90cm (3ft) tall, but crops well, producing dark green, spineless pods. **'Mammoth Spineless Long Pod'** is vigorous and high-yielding with pods that stay tender for a long time. It is excellent fresh or bottled.

'Pure Luck', in spite of the name, is one of the best varieties for growing under cover in cooler climates. Harvest when the pods are about 5cm (2in) long. **'Red Velvet'**, another spectacular red variety, is vigorous, reaching 1.2–1.5m (4–5ft). **'Star of David Heirloom'** is

A defoliated plant with several upward-pointing fruits

an Israeli variety growing to 1.8–2.5m (6–8ft) tall, well flavoured and high-yielding. The pods grow to 23cm (9in) long, but are better eaten when small.

CULTIVATION

A garden plant for the tropics and warm temperate climates, okra can be tried outdoors in cooler climates during hot summers, though success is better guaranteed if it is sown under cover.

Propagation

Soak the seeds in warm water for 24 hours before planting. My friend Robert Fleming, who gardens in Memphis, Tennessee, has been successful with several other methods that reduce germination time from 15 down to 5 days: soak the

seed in bleach for 45–60 minutes, rinse, then plant; pour boiling water over seed, soak overnight, then plant; or place 3 seeds in each section of an ice-cube tray, allow to freeze for a few hours, then plant.

When soil temperatures are about 16°C (60°F), sow seeds in rows about 60cm (24in) apart, leaving the same distance between plants. Alternatively, sow in 'stations' 20–30cm (8–12in) apart, thinning to leave the strongest seedling. Plant seedlings grown in trays or modules into 7.5cm (3in) pots when they are large enough to handle and later harden them off ready for transplanting when they are about 10–15cm (4–6in) tall.

Growing

Okra needs a rich, fertile, well-drained soil, so incorporate organic matter several weeks before sowing. Put a stake in place before transplanting and tie in the plant as it grows, pinching out the growing tip on the main stems when plants are around 23–30cm (9–12in) tall to encourage bushy growth. Apply a general liquid fertilizer until plants become established, then change to a liquid high-potash feed every 2 weeks or scatter sulphate of potash around the plant base.

In cool temperate conditions, warm the soil for several days before planting outdoors, spacing plants 60cm (24in) apart once the danger of frost has passed.

Maintenance

Spring Sow seeds under cover or outdoors in warmer climates when the soil is warm enough. Pinch out the growth tips as they appear.
Summer Water, feed and tie in plants to their supporting stakes. Keep crops weed-free. Harvest young pods.
Autumn Protect outdoor crops in cooler climates to extend the cropping season.
Winter Prepare the ground for the following season.

Protected Cropping

In cooler climates, plant okra in heated greenhouses or polythene tunnels from early spring, waiting until mid-spring if heat is not provided. Plant them about 60cm (24in) apart in beds or borders. Insert a supporting cane before planting.

Temperatures should be a minimum of 21°C (70°F) with moderate humidity. Feed plants every 2 weeks with a liquid general fertilizer, changing to a high-potash fertilizer once they are established.

Container Growing

Okra can be grown in 25cm (10in) pots or growbags, in peat-substitute compost, under cover or outdoors. Water regularly and feed every 2 weeks with a high-potash liquid fertilizer during the growing season.

Harvesting and Storing

Harvest with a sharp knife or scissors while seed pods are young, picking regularly for a constant supply of new pods. Handle gently: the soft skin marks easily. Pods keep for up to 10 days wrapped in a polythene bag in the salad drawer of the fridge.

Pests and Diseases

Precautions should be taken against heavy infestations of aphids, which weaken and distort growth, and powdery mildew, which stunts growth and, in severe cases, causes death. This is more of a problem when plants are underwatered. Whitefly can cause yellowing, stickiness and mould formation on the leaves. They form clusters on the leaf undersides and fly into the air when the foliage is disturbed.

COMPANION PLANTING

Okra flourishes when it is grown with melons and cucumbers, as it enjoys the same conditions.

Growing in Brazil; bright yellow flowers are followed by the developing pods

MEDICINAL

The mucilage from okra is effectively used as a demulcent, soothing inflammation.

In India, infusions of the pods are used to treat urino-genital problems as well as chest infections.

Okra is also added to artificial blood plasma products.

CULINARY

Okra is used in soups, stews and curries, can be sautéed or fried and eaten to accompany meat or poultry. To deep-fry, remove the stalks, trim round the 'cone' near the base, simmer for about 10 minutes, drain and dry each pod, then deep-fry until crisp. In the Middle East pods are soaked in lemon juice and salt, then fried and eaten as a vegetable. In Indian cooking, bhindi is used as a vegetable or as a bhagee to accompany curries.

Okra should not be cooked in iron, brass or copper pans, otherwise it will discolour.

Overcooked, the pods become very slimy. Any 'gluey' texture can be overcome by adding a little lemon juice to the pan and the fine, velvety covering over the pod can easily be removed by scrubbing the pod gently under running water.

Okra can also be eaten raw in salads or used as a 'dip'. Wash pods, carefully trimming off the ends. To reduce stickiness, soak them for about 30 minutes in water with a dash of lemon juice, then drain, rinse and dry.

Okra seed oil is also used in cookery.

Gumbo
Serves 4

This spicy Creole dish is known for its good use of okra.

500g (18oz) okra
1 tablespoon olive oil
250g (8oz) home-cooked ham, cubed
175g (6oz) onion, finely sliced
175g (6oz) celery, chopped
1 red pepper, deseeded and chopped
½ tablespoon tomato purée
500g (18oz) tomatoes, skinned and chopped
1 dried chilli, chopped small
Salt and freshly ground black pepper

Trim the stalk ends of the okra to expose the seeds, then soak for 30 minutes in acidulated water.

In the meantime, heat the oil and gently cook the ham, onion, celery and pepper until the onion begins to colour. Add the tomato purée and the tomatoes, mix in well, and cook over a high heat for a minute or so.

Stir in the drained okra and season well. Cover and cook gently until stewed. Add a little water if the mixture gets dry.

Serve with plain grilled chicken.

Gumbo

Allium cepa. Alliaceae

ONION

Biennial; grown as annual for swollen bulbs. Half hardy. Value: small amounts of most vitamins and minerals.

A vegetable of antiquity, the onion was cultivated by the Egyptians not only as food, but also to place in the thorax, pelvis or near the eyes during mummification. Pliny recorded six varieties in ancient Rome. The onion was highly regarded for its antiseptic properties, but many other legends became attached to it. In parts of Ireland it was said to cure baldness: 'Rub the sap mixed with honey into a bald patch, keep on rubbing until the spot gets red. This concoction if properly applied would grow hair on a duck's egg.' Many varieties have been bred over the centuries; some, like 'The Kelsae', are famous for their size, while newer varieties have incorporated hardiness, disease resistance and colour.

'First Early'

VARIETIES

Varieties of *Allium cepa* fall into several different groups according to their colour, shape and use. The bulb or common onion has brown, yellow or red skin and is round, elongated or spindle-shaped, or flattened. (Grouped with these are Japanese onions, a type of the perennial *Allium fistulosum*, which are grown as an annual for overwintering.) Spring or bunching onions are harvested small for salads, and pickling varieties (also known as 'silverskin', 'mini' or 'button' onions) are allowed to grow larger before harvesting.

Bulb or Common Onions
'Ailsa Craig', an old favourite, is a large variety, round and straw-coloured with a mild flavour. 'Albion' is a round onion with a white bulb of medium size. 'Buffalo' is high-yielding, for sowing in summer and harvesting the following year. The round, firm bulbs are well flavoured. 'Express Yellow O-X' is a Japanese onion for sowing in summer and harvesting the following year. 'Marshalls Giant Fen Globe' is an old, heavy-cropping variety with a mild flavour. 'Red Baron' is a

gorgeous dark red-skinned onion with a strong flavour and red outer flesh to each ring. Good for storing. 'Rijnsberger' is large, pale yellow and round; this is an excellent keeper. 'Senshyu Semi-Globe Yellow' is a Japanese onion with a deep yellow skin. 'Sturon', an old, high-yielding variety, has straw-coloured skin and an excellent resistance to running to seed. 'Stuttgarter Giant' is a reliable variety with flattened bulbs and a mild flavour. A good keeper and slow to bolt. 'The Kelsae', a large, round onion with mild flesh, does not store well. 'Torpedo' is a spindle-shaped onion that is mild-flavoured, but does not store well.

'Torpedo', or 'Red Italian'

Bunching, Spring or Salad Onions
'Beltsville Bunching' is a vigorous, mild-tasting variety, tolerant of both winter cold and hot, dry weather. 'Ishikura', a cross between a leek and coarse chives, is prolific, tender and a rapid grower with upright, white stems and dark green leaves. It can be left in the ground to thicken and still retains its taste. 'Kyoto Market' is mild, easy to germinate and excellent for early sowings. 'Redmate' is a colourful variety which is red towards the base, and is ideal for livening up salads. This can be thinned to 7.5cm (3in) apart for mild bulb onions. 'Santa Claus', another red variety, is ready from about 6 weeks, keeps its taste well and can

Spring onions add bite to salads

be harvested until the size of a leek. The colour is stronger during cold weather, and when they are earthed up. **'White Lisbon'** is a tasty, popular and reliable variety. It is fast-growing and very hardy. **'Winter-Over'** is a well-flavoured, extremely hardy variety for sowing in autumn. **'Winter White Bunching'** has slim stalks, stiff leaves and a mild flavour. It is hardy and overwinters well.

Pickling Onions
'Brown Pickling SY300' is a pale brown-skinned early variety. It stores well and remains firm when pickled. **'Paris Silverskin'** is a popular, excellent 'cocktail' onion, which grows rapidly and thrives in poor soil. Sow from mid-spring and lift when about the size of your thumbnail. **'Shakespear'** is a tasty, small brown onion which is perfect for pickling.

Onions for pickling should be peeled thoroughly before storing.

CULTIVATION

Onions require an open, sunny site, fertile soil and free drainage. 'Sets' (immature bulbs that have been specifically grown for planting) are more tolerant than seedlings and do not need a fine soil or such high levels of fertility. Pickling onions tolerate poorer soil than other types. Rotate crops annually.

Propagation
For a constant supply, two plantings or sowings are needed, one in spring and another in autumn, when old varieties or newer hardy Japanese varieties are used.

Onion sets have several advantages over seed. They are quick to mature, are better in cooler areas with shorter growing seasons, they grow well in poorer soils and are not attacked by onion fly or mildew. They are easy to grow and mature earlier, but are more expensive and prone to run to seed. (Buying modern varieties and heat-treated sets about 2cm (¾in) in diameter reduces that risk.) There is a greater choice of varieties when growing from seed. If planting is delayed, spread out sets in a cool, well-lit place to prevent

premature sprouting. It is possible to save your own sets from bulbs grown the previous year. Plant onion sets when the soil warms from late winter to mid-spring. Sets that have been heat-treated should not be planted until late spring. Plant in shallow drills or push them gently into the soil until only the tips are above the surface. For medium-sized onions, plant 5cm (2in) apart in rows 25cm (10in) apart; for larger onions space sets 10cm (4in) apart in the rows.

Sow seed indoors in late winter at 10–16°C (50–60°F) in seed trays, pots or modules (about 6 seeds in each module). Harden off the seedlings carefully by gradually increasing ventilation, then plant out in early spring when the seedlings have 2 true leaves. When transplanting those raised in modules and pots, ensure that the roots fall down into the planting hole and that the base of the bulb is about 1 cm (½in) below the surface.

Onions can also be sown outdoors in a seedbed in early to mid-spring in cool temperate zones. Use cloches or polythene to ensure the soil is warm, as cold, wet soil leads to poor germination and disease. Use treated seed to protect against fungal disease.

When the soil is moist and crumbly, rake in a general

'Sturon' drying. Check stored onions regularly, removing any that are diseased or damaged.

fertilizer about 2 weeks before sowing and walk over the plot to create a firm seedbed, then sow onions 12–20mm (½–¾in) deep in rows 30cm (12in) apart. Once they germinate, thin to 4cm (1–1½in) apart for medium-sized onions and 7.5–10cm (3–4in) for large onions. Thin when the soil is moist to deter onion fly. Plant multi-sown blocks 25–30cm (10–12in) apart. Plant firmly.

Sowing times for Japanese onions are critical; sown too early, they run to seed; sown too late, they are too weak to survive the winter. To cover for losses over winter, sow seeds about 2.5cm (1in) apart in rows 30cm (12in) apart. Top-dress with nitrogen in mid-winter.

Sow pickling onions in spring, either broadcast or in drills the width of a hoe and about 10cm (4in) apart. Thin according to the size of onions required and harvest them when the leaves have died back.

Sow salad or bunching onions thinly, watering the drills before sowing in dry weather. Rows should be 10cm (4in) apart; thin to a final spacing of 1–2.5cm (½–1in) when the seedlings are large enough to handle for good-sized onions. For a regular supply sow at 2 to 3 week intervals through late spring and early summer, watering thoroughly during dry weather.

'Senshyu', a very attractive and reliable variety

Growing

Dig thoroughly during early winter, incorporating liberal quantities of well-rotted manure or compost if needed. Do not grow on freshly manured ground. Lime acid soils. Before planting, rake the surface level, removing any debris and adding a general granular fertilizer to it at 60g/sq m (2oz/sq yd). In summer pull back the earth or mulch from around the bulb to expose it to the sun.

Maintenance

Spring Plant sets or seeds. Keep weed-free, particularly in the early stages of growth. *Summer* Mulch to reduce water loss and weeds. Watering is only vital during drought. *Autumn* Lift early autumn. *Winter* Push back any sets that have been lifted by frost or birds.

Protected Cropping

Onions do not need protection, although early sowings in cold weather and overwintering onions benefit from clocking or from horticultural fleece in exceptionally cold or wet weather.

Early sowings of salad or bunching onions can be made in late summer or early autumn and protected with cloches during severe weather for harvesting the following spring.

Container Growing

Bulb onions can be grown in containers, but yields will be small and not really worth the trouble.

Harvesting and Storing

Harvesting commences when the tops bend over naturally and the leaves begin to dry out. Do not bend the leaves over. Allow the bulbs and leaves to dry out while still in the ground during fine weather; wait until the dried foliage rustles before lifting. In adverse weather, spread out the bulbs on sacking or in trays in cold frames, cloches or a shed, turning them regularly. Handle bulbs carefully to avoid damage and disease. Before storing, be sure to remove any damaged, soft, spotted or thick-necked onions and use

them immediately. Onions can be stored in trays, net bags or tights, or tied to a length of cord as onion ropes in a cool place.

Harvest salad or bunching onions before the bases swell. During dry weather, water before harvesting to make pulling easier.

Making an Onion Rope

Storing onions on a rope enables the air to circulate, reducing the possibility of diseases. It is attractive and a convenient method of storage. You can plait the stems to form a rope as with garlic, but they are usually too short and are better tied to raffia or strong string.

Firmly tie in 2 onions at the base, then wind the leaves of each onion firmly round the string, with each bulb just resting on the onions below. When you reach the top of the string, tie a firm knot around the bulbs at the top, then hang them up to dry. Cut onions from the rope as they are needed.

Pests and Diseases

If birds are a nuisance, protect plants with black thread or netting.

The larvae of onion fly tunnel into bulbs, causing the stems to wilt and become yellow. Seedlings and small plants may die. Cultivate the ground thoroughly over winter; grow under horti-cultural fleece; grow sets. Remove and destroy affected plants and rotate crops.

White rot can be a problem, particularly on salad onions. White mould like cotton-wool,

dotted with tiny, black spots, appears round the base. Leaves turn yellow and die. It is almost impossible to eradicate. Remove affected onions with as much of the soil round them as possible, dispose of plants and any debris – do not put them on the compost heap. Do not grow onions or their relatives on the area for 8 years. 'Norstar' has some resistance.

When attacked by stem eelworm, bulbs become distorted, crack, soften, then die. Grow plants from seed; rotate crops; in severe cases do not grow in the same place again. Dispose of plant debris thoroughly and remove any affected plants.

COMPANION PLANTING

Parsley sown with onions is said to keep onion fly away.

MEDICINAL

Used as an antiseptic and diuretic, the juice is good for coughs and colds. The bulbs and stems were applied as poultices to carbuncles.

The traditional way of storing onions is also highly decorative

CULINARY

So indispensable are onions for flavouring sauces, stocks, stews and casseroles that there is hardly a recipe that does not start with some variant of 'fry [or sauté or sweat] the onion in the oil or fat until soft…' They also make a delicious vegetable or garnish in their own right: roasted or boiled whole, cut into rings, battered and deep-fried, or sliced and slowly softened into a meltingly sweet 'marmalade'. Finely chopped raw onion adds zing to dishes like rice salad; you can also use the thinnings to flavour salads.

'Bunching' onions are perfect for salads, pastas, soups and flans. In France they are chopped, sautéed in butter and added to chicken consommé with vermicelli.

Pickled onions are an excellent accompaniment to bread, strong cheese and pickled beetroot – the traditional 'Ploughman's Lunch'. Besides being pickled, pickling varieties can be used fresh in salads and stir-fries, added to stews or else threaded on to kebab skewers for barbecuing.

Onion and Walnut Muffins
Makes 20

This wonderful recipe comes from chef Wally Malouf's *Hudson Valley Cookbook*.

1 large onion
250g (8oz) unsalted butter, melted
2 large eggs
6 tablespoons sugar
1 teaspoon sea salt
1 teaspoon baking powder
300g (10oz) shelled walnuts, coarsely crushed
350g (12oz) plain flour

Preheat the oven to 220°C/425°F/gas mark 7. Peel the onion, cut it into quarters and purée it finely in a food processor. Measure the purée to achieve 250g (8oz). Beat together the butter, eggs and sugar and add the onion purée. Stir in the remaining ingredients one by one and mix thoroughly. Fill the muffin tins almost full. Bake them for 20 minutes, or until they are puffed and well browned. Serve warm.

Onion and Walnut Muffins

Onion Tart
Serves 4

This Alsatian dish is full of flavour and very filling. Enjoy it with a simple fresh green salad.

90g (3oz) lard or olive oil
1 kg (2lb) onions, sliced into rings
90g (3oz) smoked bacon, diced
240ml (8fl oz) double cream
3 eggs, lightly beaten
Salt and freshly ground black pepper
Shortcrust pastry to line a 20–23cm (8–9in) tart tin

In a heavy pan, heat the lard or oil and sauté the onions until soft but not browned. Drain well on kitchen paper. Add the bacon to the pan and cook briskly for a couple of minutes, then drain off the fat. Next, mix the cream and the eggs and season well. Then stir in the onions and the bacon and fill the pastry case.

Bake in a preheated oven at 220°C/425°F/gas mark 7 for 10–15 minutes, turning the heat down to 190°C/375°F/gas 5 for a further 15 minutes, or until the filling is set. Serve warm.

Onion Tart

Allium cepa Aggregatum Group. *Alliaceae*

SHALLOT

Small onion, grown as an annual, forming several new bulbs. Hardy. Value: small amounts of most vitamins and minerals.

Shallots are hardy, mature rapidly, are good for colder climates, tolerate heat and will grow on poorer soils than common onions. Sets are more expensive than seed and are inclined to bolt unless they are heat-treated; buy virus-free stock which is higher-yielding and vigorous, or save healthy bulbs of your own for the following year.

VARIETIES

'Atlantic' can be sown early and produces heavy yields of moderate to large bulbs which are crisp, tasty and store well. 'Creation' F₁, a seed-grown variety, is delicious, highly resistant to bolting and stores well. 'Drittler White Nest', an old variety, produces tasty bulbs of variable size. 'Giant Yellow Improved' is well worth considering. The bulbs have yellow-brown skins, are consistently large and high-yielding. 'Golden Gourmet' is a mild-tasting shallot for casseroles and salads. It is reliable and high-yielding, stores well and produces good edible shoots. 'Hative de Niort' is an extremely attractive variety with elongated, pear-shaped bulbs, dark brown skins and white flesh. 'Pikant' is prolific and resistant to bolting. Its skin is dark reddish-brown, the flesh strongly flavoured and firm. 'Red Potato Onion' is extremely hardy, with bronze-red skin and pink flesh, which keeps well. 'Sante' is large and round with brown skin and pinkish-white flesh, which is packed with flavour. Yields are high and it stores well. However, it is inclined to bolt and should only be planted from mid- to late spring when conditions improve. 'Topper' is a mild-tasting, vigorous, golden-yellow variety for planting from late winter. It stores well.

CULTIVATION

Propagation
The ideal size for sets is about 2cm (¾in) diameter, which will result in a high yield of good-sized shallots; larger sets will produce a greater number of smaller shallots.

Plant from late winter or early spring, as soon as soil conditions are suitable. Shallots can also be planted from late autumn to midwinter for early crops. Cover the soil with cloches, fleece or polythene about 2 weeks before planting to warm the soil. If the weather is unfavourable, bulbs can be planted in 10cm (4in) pots of compost and transplanted when conditions improve.

Space sets 23cm (9in) apart with 30–38cm (12–15in) between the rows. Make small holes with a trowel rather than pushing bulbs into the ground (the compaction this causes, particularly in heavier soils, can act as a barrier to young roots). Leave the tips of the bulbs just above the soil. Alternatively, plant in drills, 1cm (½in) deep, 18cm (7in) apart, then cover with soil.

F₁ hybrids that are grown from seed produce one bulb, rather than several. From early to mid-spring, as soon as soil conditions allow, sow seed thinly 1cm (½in) deep in broad drills, the width of a hoe, thinning until there is 2.5–5cm (1–2in) around each plant. If spaced farther apart, clusters of bulbs are more likely to form.

Undersized shallots can be grown for their leaves, or you can pick a few leaves from those being grown for bulbs. Plant from autumn to spring under cloches for earlier crops, in seed trays or pots of compost under cover and outdoors when the soil becomes workable. Each bulb should be about 2.5cm (1in) apart.

Growing
Shallots flourish in a sheltered, sunny position on moist, free-draining soil, preferably one that has been manured for the previous crop.

Alternatively, double dig the area in early autumn, incorporating plenty of

Shallots are small and mild enough to be added whole to casseroles

Unlike onions, shallots develop in small clusters

well-rotted organic matter into the lower spit.

Before planting, level the soil and rake in a general fertilizer at 110g/sq m (4oz/sq yd). If you are sowing sets, a rough tilth will suffice, but seeds need a seedbed of a finer texture.

Water during dry periods and keep crops weed-free, particularly while becoming established. Use an onion hoe with care, as damaged bulbs cannot be stored.

Maintenance
Spring Plant sets when soil conditions allow. Sow seed when the soil warms up.
Summer Keep crops weed-free. Water during dry periods.
Autumn Dig in well-rotted organic matter if needed. Plant sets for early crops.
Winter Plant sets from late winter onwards.

Protected Cropping
Shallots are extremely hardy, but benefit from temporary protection under cloches or fleece in periods of severe winter weather, particularly if the soil is poorly drained.

Container Growing
Shallots will grow in large pots or containers of soil-based compost. Add slow-release fertilizer to the mix and put a good layer of broken crocks or polystyrene in the bottom of the pot, for drainage. Keep plants well watered in dry periods.

Harvesting and Storing
From midsummer onwards, as the leaves die back, carefully lift the bulbs and in dry weather leave them on the surface for about a week to dry out; otherwise dry them as onions. Do not cut off the green foliage as this may cause fungal infection, spoiling the bulbs for storage. Break up the bulbs in each clump, remove any soil and loose leaves, then store them in a dry, cool, well-ventilated place. Store on slatted trays, in net bags or in a pair of old tights. Shallots grown for their foliage should be harvested when the leaves are about 10cm (4in) high.

Pests and Diseases
Shallots are usually free of pests and diseases. Bolting may be a problem in early plantings or if temperatures fluctuate. Use resistant varieties for early plantings.

Bulbs infected with virus are stunted and yields are poor. Use disease-free stock. If mildew is a problem, treat as for onions.

Birds can be a nuisance, pulling sets from the ground. Sprinkling a layer of fine soil over the tips can help; otherwise protect the crop with humming wire or similar bird scarers.

Bulbs lifted by frost should be carefully replanted immediately.

Eelworms and onion fly should be treated in the same way as for onions.

COMPANION PLANTING

Shallots make good companions for apples and strawberry plants; storing sulphur, they are believed to have a fungicidal effect.

CULINARY

Shallots have a milder taste than onions; generally, the yellow-skinned varieties are larger and keep better, while red types are smaller and have the best flavour. The bulbs can be eaten raw or pickled and the leaves used like spring onions.

Shallots can be finely chopped and added to fried steak just before serving. Do not brown them, as it makes them bitter. Béarnaise sauce is made by reducing shallots and herbs in wine vinegar before thickening with egg and butter.

Shallots keep better than ordinary onions

Allium porrum. Alliaceae

LEEK

Biennial grown as annual for blanched leaf bases. Hardy. Value: good source of potassium and iron, smaller amounts of beta carotene and vitamin C, particularly in green leaves.

The Bible mentions 'the cucumbers, and the melons, and the leeks, and the onions and the garlic' which grew in Egypt, where the leek was held as a sacred plant and to swear by the leek was the equivalent to swearing by one of the gods. This ancient crop still stirs passions. Giant leek contests have been held in pubs and clubs throughout the north-east of England since the mid-1880s. At one show in 1895, W. Robson was awarded a second prize of £1 and a sheep's heart; now the world championships have a first prize of over £1,300. Alongside the daffodil, the leek is one of the national symbols of Wales. Currently the European Community produces over 7 million tonnes per year and France is the chief grower.

VARIETIES

Older varieties are divided into two main groups, long thin and short stout types. In many modern cultivars, such differences are less obvious. There are also early, mid-season and late varieties.

'King Richard' is a high-yielding, mild-tasting, early variety with a long shank. Good for growing at close spacing for 'mini leeks'.

'Prelina' is harvested in early autumn and has a moderate-length shank. 'Autumn Giant – Cobra' is a mid- to late harvest, medium-length variety with good bolting resistance. 'Autumn Mammoth 2 – Argenta' and the similar 'Goliath' mature in late autumn and can be harvested until mid-spring. A high-yielding leek with a medium shank length and thick stems. 'Cortina' can be harvested through the winter and yields moderate crops. 'Bleu de Solaise', a French winter variety, can be harvested until spring.

CULTIVATION

Leeks flourish in a sunny, sheltered site on well-drained, neutral to slightly acid soil.

Propagation

Leeks need a minimum soil or compost temperature of at least 7°C (45°F) to germinate, so you will achieve more consistent results, particularly with early crops, when they are sown under cover. For rapid germination, sow early varieties indoors during late winter at 13–16°C (55–60°F) in trays, pots or modules of seed compost. Pot on those grown in trays or pots, spacing them about 5cm (2in) apart, when two true leaves are produced or when they begin to bend over. Harden off gradually before planting out in late spring.

Leeks can also be sown in unheated glasshouses, in cold frames or under cloches. Sow seeds from late winter to early spring, pot on, harden off and transplant in late spring.

Although all varieties are suitable, later sowings of mid-season and later types are particularly successful in seedbeds. Warm the soil using cloches, black polythene or horticultural fleece and rake the seedbed to a fine tilth. Sow thinly in rows 15cm (6m) apart and 2.5cm (1in) deep, providing protection during cold spells. They can also be sown directly in the vegetable plot, 2.5cm (1in) deep in rows 30cm (12in) apart, thinning when seedlings have two or three leaves.

Sowing seeds in modules – either in pairs or singly – keeping the most vigorous of the two, and multi-sowing three to five per cell, avoids the necessity of 'pricking out' or thinning.

Growing

Fertile, moisture-retentive soil is essential, so dig in plenty of organic matter the winter before planting, particularly on light soils. On heavy soils, add organic matter and horticultural sand to improve drainage as crops are poor on heavy or waterlogged soil. Rake, level and firm the soil before planting in spring. As they are a long-term, high-nitrogen crop, apply a general fertilizer, fish, blood and bone or ammonium sulphate at 60–90g/sq m

A fine display of leeks grown in a deep raised bed for showing

Leek flowers are invaluable for attracting beneficial insects

Leeks grown in tile drains for early lifting

(2–3oz/sq yd) 1 or 2 weeks before planting.

Transplant leeks when they are 15–20cm (6–8in) tall. Trim the leaf tips back if they drag on the ground, but not the roots, as is often recommended. If the soil is dry, water the area thoroughly before planting. Planting 15cm (6m) apart in rows 30cm (12in) apart provides a high yield of moderately sized leeks. Planting them 7.5–10cm (3–4in) apart in rows gives a high yield of slim leeks. A spacing of 15–17.5cm (6–7in) each way provides a reasonable crop of medium-sized leeks. Leeks grown in modules should be planted 23cm (9in) apart each way.

There are two methods of planting to ensure well-blanched stems. I find the first method better, as deeply planted leeks are more drought-resistant and soil is less likely to fall down between the leaves. Make a hole 15–20cm (6–8in) deep with a dibber, drop the plant into it and fill the hole with water (this washes some soil into the bottom of the hole), but do not fill any further.

Alternatively, plant leeks 7.5cm (3in) deep and several times through the season pull the earth up around the stems, 5–7.5cm (2–3in) at a time, with a draw hoe. Stop earthing up when the plants reach maturity and make sure that the soil does not fall down between the leaves. Earthing up is easier on light soil.

Whichever method you use, after planting, water gently with a seaweed-based fertilizer. If there is a dry period after planting, water leeks daily until the plants are well established and thereafter only during drought conditions. Hand weed or hoe carefully to keep down weeds, using an onion hoe around younger plants to avoid any damage. In poorer soils, feed weekly in summer with a liquid seaweed or comfrey fertilizer.

Maintenance
Spring Pot on leeks grown under glass; sow seed outdoors.
Summer Transplant seedlings, water and feed. Keep crops weed-free by hoeing or mulching.
Autumn Harvest crops as required.
Winter Harvest mid- and late-season crops. Sow seed under glass in late winter.

Protected Cropping
Apart from early sowings in the greenhouse or cold frame or under cloches and horticultural fleece, leeks are an extremely hardy outdoor crop.

Harvesting and Storing
Early varieties are ready for lifting from early to mid-autumn, mid-season types from early to mid-winter and lates from early to mid-spring. Lift leeks carefully with a garden fork and ensure that you dispose of any leaf debris to reduce the risk of disease in the future. Late varieties taking up space in the vegetable garden that is needed for spring planting, can be stored for several weeks in a shallow, angled trench 15–20cm (6–8in) deep; cover them lightly with soil and leave the tops exposed. If inclement weather is likely to hinder harvest, they can be lifted and packed closely together in a cold frame. The top should be raised to provide ventilation on warmer days.

PESTS AND DISEASES

Leeks share many diseases with their close relatives, onions. Leek rust appears as orange pustules on the leaves during summer and is worse in wet seasons. Foliage developing later in the season is healthy. Feed with high-potash fertilizer, remove infected plants and debris. Improve drainage; do not plant leeks on the site for 4 to 5 years; grow partially resistant varieties like 'Autumn Mammoth', 'Titan' or 'Gennevilliers-Splendid'. Slugs can be damaging. Collect them at night, use biological control, set traps or use aluminium sulphate pellets. Mature leeks usually survive slug damage. Stem eelworm causes swelling at the base and distorted leaves. Destroy affected plants immediately and rotate crops. Leaf rot is common during periods of high humidity, particularly on high-nitrogen soils. White spots appear on the leaf tips, followed by shrivelling leaf tips. Spray with fungicide, increase the spacing between plants to improve air circulation and apply high-potash fertilizer.

COMPANION PLANTING

Leeks grow well with celery. When planted with onions and carrots they discourage onion and carrot fly. Grow leeks in your rotation programme alongside garlic, onions and shallots. Leeks are a useful crop after early potatoes and if they are grown at a 30cm (12in) spacing, their upright growth makes them ideal for intercropping with lettuces like 'Tom Thumb', land cress or winter purslane.

The blue-tinged 'Bleu de Solaise' is ideal for the ornamental border

CULINARY

Leeks can be boiled or steamed, made into terrines, cooked in casseroles, added to pasta dishes, wrapped in suet pastry and baked. They are a useful addition to soups and an important ingredient in 'Cock-a-leekie' soup and in French Vichyssoise. Braise in stock with a little wine added and bake in a moderate oven. Partially cook trimmed leeks in boiling water, drain well and roll in slices of good country ham and lay them in a dish; cover with a well-flavoured cheese sauce and bake in a hot oven until well browned. Slice or chop young leeks and use raw as a spring onion substitute in salads.

Leek and Ricotta Pie
Serves 4

4 largish leeks, trimmed
2 tablespoons olive oil
2 cloves garlic, finely chopped
225g (8oz) ricotta
2 tablespoons pine nuts
3 tablespoons raisins, softened
* in warm water*
1 egg
Salt and freshly ground black
* pepper*

For the pastry:
90g (3oz) butter
175g (6oz) plain flour
3 tablespoons water
Pinch salt

Make the pastry by crumbling the butter into the flour and then adding water to make a dough. Add the salt and sprinkle with flour. Wrap in cling film and chill in the fridge for 30 minutes.

Roughly chop the leeks. Steam gently for about 10 minutes and drain well.

Preheat the oven to 190°C/375°F/gas mark 5. In a heavy frying pan heat the oil and gently fry the garlic. Then add the leeks and stir to coat well with oil; allow them to cook for about 5 minutes, stirring occasionally.

Remove from the heat. In a bowl mix the ricotta with the pine nuts and raisins, and bind with an egg. Add the leeks, mix well and season.

Gently roll out the pastry to fit a 20cm (8in) tart tin. Prick the base and bake blind for 10–15 minutes. Fill the tart with the leek and ricotta mixture and continue cooking for 30 minutes.

Serve the pie with a green salad.

Leeks wrapped in country ham and baked with a covering of cheese sauce

Barbarea verna. Brassicaceae

LAND CRESS

Also known as American cress. Biennial or short-lived perennial grown as annual for young leaves. Hardy.
Value: low in calories, good source of iron, calcium, beta carotene and vitamin C.

The genus *Barbarea* was known as *herba Sanctae Barbarae*, the 'herb of St Barbara', patron saint of miners and artillerymen and protectress from thunderstorms! Land cress is a fast-growing, hardy biennial with a rosette of deeply lobed, shiny leaves and yellow flowers. Native to south-western Europe, it has been grown as a salad crop since the seventeenth century; by the eighteenth century, extensive cultivation had died out in England, though plants became naturalized and are still common in the wild. In America it is still a popular annual crop. The peppery-tasting leaves make a fine substitute for watercress – and are a good deal more practical for most gardeners to grow.

CULTIVATION

Land cress grows in wet shady conditions, but is best in moist fertile soil; in summer plant in light shade, under deciduous trees.

Propagation
Sow immediately the soil becomes workable, in early spring to early summer for a summer crop and in mid- to late summer for autumn to spring crops. Sow in seed trays or modules for transplanting when large enough to handle, or in drills 1cm (½in) deep, thinning the seedlings to 15–20cm (6–8in). Germination takes about 3 weeks in spring but in mid-summer half that time. If a few plants are left to run to seed in late spring to early summer the following year, they will seed freely; transplant seedlings into rows and water well.

Growing
Before sowing, dig in well-rotted manure or compost. Transplant seedlings sown in late summer under glass. In heat and drought they run to seed, so water often. Pick flower stalks as they appear.

Maintenance
Spring Sow seed, water well.
Summer Water as necessary so plants do not run to seed.
Autumn Sow winter crops and transplant plantlets under glass.
Winter Prepare beds for spring sowing; harvest protected crops.

Protected Cropping
Improve the quality of autumn and winter crops by growing in an unheated greenhouse or cold frame, or under cloches.

Container Growing
Grow in moisture-retentive, peat-substitute compost, water well and feed with a dilute general liquid fertilizer every 3 weeks.

Harvesting
Harvest after 7 weeks when plants are 7–10cm (3–4in) long. Pick or cut the tender young leaves about 2.5cm (1in) above ground. Do not harvest heavily until the plant is established. Soak in water to loosen dirt, then wash it off.

Pests and Diseases
Flea beetle may affect plants; dust seedlings with derris or grow under fleece.

COMPANION PLANTING

Makes a good edging plant for borders. Can be grown between taller crops, e.g. sweetcorn and brassicas.

CULINARY

Use its peppery-tasting leaves as a watercress substitute – as a garnish, in salads and sandwiches. Or cook them like spinach and make into soup. Good in rice, pasta salads and stir-fries.

Cress, Anchovy and Barley Salad
Serves 4

300g (10oz) pearl barley
4 tablespoons virgin olive oil
2 tablespoons white wine vinegar
2 tablespoons finely chopped dill
4 anchovy fillets, roughly chopped
350g (12oz) cress, washed and dried
1 cucumber, diced
Salt and freshly ground pepper

Cook the barley in boiling water until tender and drain. Set aside. Make the dressing: mix the oil and vinegar with the dill and seasoning. In a separate bowl, mix the barley with the anchovy, add the cress and cucumber, and pour over the dressing. Toss well.

Plants flower in early spring

Allium sativum. Alliaceae

GARLIC

Perennial grown as annual for strongly aromatic bulbs. Half hardy. Value: contains small quantities of vitamins and minerals.

Prized throughout the world for its culinary and medicinal properties, garlic, now known only as a cultivated plant, is thought to have originated in western Asia. It has been grown since Egyptian times and for centuries in China and India. Its reputation as a 'cure all' has been endorsed by modern science. The Egyptians placed it in their tombs and gave it to the slaves who built the pyramids to ward off infection, while Hippocrates prescribed it for uterine tumours. In medieval Europe it was hung outside doors to deter witches. Today almost 3 million tonnes per annum are produced globally.

VARIETIES

Many garlic clones exist that are adapted to regional variations in climate and day length. Buy cloves that are compatible with your area. **'California Late'** is very reliable in Mediterranean conditions. It keeps well. **'Cristo'** is an excellent, large, long-dormancy variety producing up to 15 cloves per bulb. **'Germidor'** crops early, producing large cloves and purple bulbs. **'Elephant'** garlic is sweet and mild; bulbs up to 10cm (4in) diameter.

Allium sativum var. *ophioscordon* is sold as **'Rocambole'** and is also called 'Serpent Garlic' on account of its coiled, bulbil-producing stem. The bulbs are red in colour. **'Long Keeper'** is well adapted to a cool temperate climate. The bulbs are white-skinned and firm. **'Solent Wight'**, a new variety producing large cloves with a mild flavour, is heavy-cropping.

CULTIVATION

Propagation
Garlic is usually grown from healthy, plump bulb segments ('cloves') saved from a previous crop. Where possible, buy nematode and virus-resistant stock.

Plant cloves, a minimum of 13mm (½in) diameter, in late autumn or early spring, at a depth of 2.5cm (1in) and 10cm (4in) apart, with the rows 15–20cm (6–8in) apart.

Garlic is surprisingly hardy and needs a cold, dormant period of 1 or 2 months when temperatures are 0–10°C (32–50°F) to yield decent-sized bulbs; for this reason it is generally better planted in late autumn. A long growing period is also beneficial for the ripening process.

In areas with heavy soil, cloves can be planted any time over winter in pots or modules containing loam-based compost with added horticultural sand, and can be planted out as soon as soil conditions are favourable. Plant cloves vertically with the flattened base plate at the bottom, twice the depth of the clove with at least 2.5cm (1in) of soil above the tip. On good soils, planting up to 10cm (4in) deep increases the yield. When planting, you should handle the cloves lightly: do not press them into the soil as this reduces root development.

The amount of leaf growth dictates the size of the mature bulb which develops during long summer days.

Growing
Garlic favours an open, sunny position on light, well-drained soil. On heavier soil, grow in ridges or improve the drainage by working horticultural sand or grit in to the topsoil.

Garlic is less successful in areas of heavy rainfall. On poor soils, it is beneficial to rake in a general fertilizer about 10 days before planting. Garlic can be grown on soil manured for the previous crop as well as limed acid soils.

Rotate the crop and do not grow in sites where onions have been planted the previous year. Keep the bulbs weed-free throughout the growing season.

Maintenance
Spring Mulch to suppress weeds. Water if necessary.
Summer Keep weed-free.
Autumn Plant cloves.
Winter Plant cloves in containers for planting out in spring.

Protected Cropping
Garlic can be grown in an unheated greenhouse for an early crop.

Container Growing
Garlic can be grown in pots, windowboxes or containers, in a moisture-retentive, free-draining compost. Water

Garlic 'Solent Wight'

regularly to produce decent-sized bulbs and place the container in a sunny position to allow the bulbs to develop.

Harvesting and Storing

From mid- to late summer, as soon as the leaves and stems begin to yellow, lift the bulbs carefully with a fork and leave them to dry off in the sun. Delaying harvest causes the bulbs to shrivel and increases the possibility of disease during storage. Handle them delicately as they are easily bruised.

In inclement weather, dry them under cover on trays. Store them in cool, dry conditions indoors or in a shed or garage. Hang them in bunches tied by the leaves, in string bags or plait the stems together. Plants that have gone to seed can still produce usable bulbs for the kitchen.

PESTS AND DISEASES

Onion fly lay their eggs around the base of garlic, the larvae tunnel into the bulb and the plant turns yellow and dies. Rotate crops, dig the plot over winter, grow under horticultural fleece and apply chemicals to the soil before sowing.

Downy mildew is a common problem in wet seasons. Grey patches appear on the leaves. White rot, a grey fungus on the roots, turns the leaves yellow. Lift and destroy infected plants, and do not grow garlic, onions or shallots on the site for 8 years.

Stem and bulb eelworm seedlings become blunted, bloated and distorted, and stems rot. Lift and destroy affected plants. Rotate crops.

Planting garlic in Thailand

COMPANION PLANTING

Planted beside rose bushes, garlic controls greenfly. Good companions are lettuce, beetroot, summer savory, Swiss chard and strawberries. It should not be planted with peas and beans.

MEDICINAL

Garlic has powerful anti-viral, anti-bacterial and anti-fungal properties, and is effective for digestive complaints, bowel disorders and insect stings. It contains 2 chemicals which combine to form the bactericide allicin, which gives it the characteristic odour. Modern herbalists believe a cold will be cured by rubbing garlic on the soles of feet. What a combination of odours! Current research indicates its ability to reduce blood cholesterol levels and the chance of heart attack. There is also a lower incidence of colonic and other types of cancer where it is part of the daily diet.

CULINARY

Garlic is used almost exclusively as a seasoning in a range of dishes from curries and stews to pasta. For the daring, the whole immature plants can be added to salads.

La Gasconnade
Serves 6–8

Jeanne Strang gives this recipe from Gascony in *Goose Fat and Garlic:*

1 leg lamb
12 anchovy fillets
500g (1lb) garlic
175ml (6fl oz) bouillon

The *gigot* (lamb) is spiked not only with the usual few cloves of garlic but with anchovy fillets as well. You will need to cut them into small pieces in order to slide them into the slits in the meat.

Lay the fillets across the top of the roast. During the cooking they will melt over the meat and give it the same effect as if it were roasted revolving on a spit.

Cook the joint in a pre-heated oven, 230°C/450°F/gas mark 8 for 20 minutes, then reduce the heat to 180°C/350°F/gas

4. Allow to cook for 15 minutes per 500g (1lb) from start to finish.

While the joint is cooking, peel the rest of the garlic and blanch in boiling water until the cloves are almost cooked, then throw them into cold water for 20 seconds and drain. Heat the *bouillon* in a saucepan, add any pan juices and the garlic and reduce the sauce until it is nearly a purée. Serve as a garnish to the *gigot.*

Pestou

This is a version of the classic garlic and basil butter, which is extremely good over pasta and which the Italians eat with fish. For 50g (2oz) butter, have 2 plump cloves garlic, 5–6 sprigs of fresh basil, 2 tablespoons Parmesan and a pinch of salt. Pound the garlic in a mortar, tear the basil leaves roughly, then add to the garlic with the butter and cheese. Pound to mix.

Aioli

Mayonnaise flavoured with garlic enriches many delicious soups and stews such as *Bouillabaisse.* Pound 2 cloves of garlic in a mortar, stir in the yolks of 2 eggs, pour into a blender and add 300ml (½pt) oil drop by drop at first, faster as the mixture begins to thicken. This will make just over 400ml (²/₃pt).

La Gasconnade

Alpinia galanga (syn. *Langaas galanga*). *Zingiberaceae*

GREATER GALANGAL

Also known as Galangal languas, Siamese Ginger. Herbaceous perennial;
rhizomatous rootstock used as flavouring. Tender.
Value: negligible nutritive value.

Two species, greater and lesser galangal, have been grown for centuries for their pungent, aromatic roots, which are used as spices and medicinally. The earliest records date from around AD 550, while Marco Polo noted its cultivation in southern China and Java in the thirteenth century. In the Middle Ages it was known as 'galangale', a name also used for the roots of sweet sedge, whose violet-scented rhizomes are used in perfumery.

The word galangal came from the Chinese, meaning 'a mild ginger from Ko', a region of the Canton province. It is an essential ingredient of many Malaysian and Thai dishes. The spicy rhizomes have a somewhat different use in the Middle East, where they have been used to 'spike' horses!

CULTIVATION

The plant is a herbaceous perennial with pale orange-flushed cream bulbous rhizomes. Stems grow to 2m (6ft) tall, with dark green lance-shaped leaves to 50cm (20in) long. Flowers are pale green and white with pink markings; the fruit a round red capsule. There are many different races in cultivation, including types with red and white rhizomes. Lesser galangal is regarded as superior as it is more pungent and aromatic, but is uncommon in cultivation.

Propagation
Sow fresh seed in pots of peat-substitute compost at 20°C (68°F). Keep the compost moist using tepid water and transplant seedlings when they are large enough to handle. In tropical and sub-tropical regions they can be sown outdoors in a seedbed (for ground preparation, see 'Growing').

Divide rhizomes in spring when the young shoots are about 2.5cm (1in) long. Remove young, vigorous sections from the perimeter of the clump using a sharp knife, dust the cuts with fungicide and transplant just below the soil or compost surface. Soak thoroughly with tepid water and maintain high humidity and temperatures.

Growing
Galangal grows outdoors in tropical or sub-tropical climates, thriving in sunshine or partial shade. It needs a rich, free-draining soil, so dig in plenty of well-rotted compost and allow the ground to settle for a few weeks before planting. Allow 90cm (36in) between plants. Keep crops weed-free and water during dry periods. Mulch with well-rotted compost when plants are well established.

Container Growing
Plants can be grown in containers under cover in a compost mix of 2 parts each of loam and leafmould, 1 part horticultural grit or sharp sand and 3 parts medium-grade bark. Repot and divide in spring when the rhizomes outgrow their allotted space.

Protected Cropping
In temperate zones, plants can be grown in a heated polythene tunnel or greenhouse in bright filtered light, with a minimum temperature of 15°C (58°F). Maintain high humidity by misting plants with tepid water and 'damping down' paths. Prepare borders as for 'Growing' and allow 90cm (36in) between plants. Keep the compost constantly moist with tepid water and reduce watering in lower temperatures. After flowering reduce watering as the foliage gradually becomes yellow and dies back. The compost should remain slightly moist throughout the dormant period. Increase watering when new shoots emerge the following spring.

Feed regularly with a liquid general fertilizer every 2 weeks while the plant is actively growing. Mulch plants grown in borders annually in spring with well-rotted manure.

Harvesting and Storing

Rhizomes are ready to harvest after 3–4 years. Lift plants towards the end of the growing season and remove mature rhizomes, retaining younger ones for transplanting. It is a good idea to divide and replant a few each year to ensure a constant supply.

Galangal are better used immediately after harvest but will keep for at least a week in a cool place. Alternatively, they can be frozen whole in a polythene bag and segments removed as required. Keep dried roots in airtight containers in a cool dark place.

PESTS AND DISEASES

Red spider mite can be a problem under glass. Check plants regularly, as small infestations are easily controlled. Speckling, mottling and bronzing of the leaf surface are the usual symptoms; in later stages, fine webbing appears on leaves and stems. They prefer hot, dry conditions. Control by maintaining high humidity or spray with derris or a similar insecticide.

MEDICINAL

Plants contain cineol, an aromatic, antiseptic substance. The essential oil acts as a decongestant and respiratory germicide and digestive aid. In India it is used as a breath purifier and deodorant, and a paste is made from the rhizomes to treat skin infections. It is also said to be an aphrodisiac. Infusions are taken after childbirth.

CULINARY

Before use scrape or peel off the skin. The raw chopped or minced root is used in Malaysian and Indonesian dishes with bean curd, meat, poultry, fish, curries and sauces. It is also used as a marinade to flavour barbecued chicken. The fruits are a substitute for cardamom, the buds can be pickled and the flowers are eaten raw with vegetables or pickles in parts of Java. In Thai cooking it is preferred to ginger. In medieval England a sauce was made from bread crusts, galangal, cinnamon and ginger pulverized and moistened with stock. It was heated with a dash of vinegar and strained over fish or meat.

Galangal Soup
Serves 4

There are many variations on this soup, the recipe for which comes from Vietnam. First, make a stock from the following:

1 litre (1¾pt water)
1 chicken carcass
4 bulbs lemon grass, bruised
12cm (5in) galangal, peeled and sliced
1 onion, roughly sliced
2 red dried chillies
6 kaffir lime leaves
Salt and freshly ground black pepper

Then strain the stock through some fine muslin. Reheat in a heavy saucepan, adding the meat from the chicken carcass, chopped finely, together with 1 tablespoon of fish sauce and 4 tablespoons of lime juice. Simmer for 5 minutes and then add 125g (4oz) shi-itake mushrooms, left whole. Simmer for a further 3 minutes before stirring in 125ml (¼pt) thick coconut milk. Do not allow to reboil, and check the seasoning. Serve hot.

OTHER USES

Roots of lesser galangal are used in Russia for flavouring tea and a liqueur called Nastoika. The rhizomes produce a yellow or yellow/green dye.

Kaempferia galanga
(Chinese keys)

The rhizomes, common in the markets of South-East Asia, produce a distinctive cluster of finger-like roots which are pale brown with bright yellow flesh and a pungent aroma. They have a very strong taste and should be used sparingly in green curry paste, sauces, soups and curries.

The rhizomes may be eaten raw when young, or steamed and eaten as a vegetable. Young shoots are cooked as a vegetable, pickled or eaten raw.

Chinese keys are used as a carminative, stomachic, expectorant, analgesic, and to treat dandruff and sore throats.

Apium graveolens var. *dulce. Apiaceae*

CELERY

Biennial grown as annual for fleshy leaf stems and leaves. Hardy. Value: low in carbohydrate and calories, high in potassium.

The species is a biennial plant, native to Europe and Asia. It is usually found on marshy ground by rivers, particularly where the water is slightly saline. Its Latin generic name *Apium* is derived from the Celtic *apon*, water, referring to its favoured habitat, while *graveolens* means heavily scented, alluding to its aroma. The stems of the wild plant are very bitter, distinguishing it from *var. dulce* – meaning sweet or pleasant – from which the culinary varieties have been bred. Celery became popular in Italy in the seventeenth century and during the following two hundred years spread throughout Europe to North America. 'Trench celery' (so called from the method used for blanching the stems) is very hardy and is harvested from late autumn to early spring, while the more recently developed self-blanching and American green types have a shorter growing season and are less hardy, cropping from mid-summer until mid-autumn. Less succulent, but full of flavour, is the smaller-stemmed 'cutting celery'.

VARIETIES

Trench celery
This is grouped into white, pink and the hardier red varieties:
'Giant Pink' is a hardy variety harvested from mid- to late winter. The crisp, pale pink stalks blanch easily. **'Giant Red'** is hardy and vigorous; the outer stalks turn shell-pink when blanched. **'Giant White'** is an old, tall, white celery variety with crisp stems and a solid, well-flavoured heart. It needs good growing conditions to flourish. **'Hopkins Fenlander'** is a late-maturing green celery with sticks of medium length and free from string. It has a good flavour. **'Standard Bearer'** red celery has the reputation of being the latest of all to reach maturity.

Self-blanching and American green celery varieties
These include: **'Celebrity'**, an early-maturing variety, has crisp, long stems and a nutty-flavoured heart. It has good bolting resistance and is one of the least stringy self-blanching varieties. **'Golden Self Blanching'** is compact

American green varieties do not need blanching

with firm golden-yellow hearts which are crisp and tasty. Does not become stringy. **'Greensleeves'**, a green variety, produces tasty green sticks. **'Ivory Tower'** has long white 'stringless' crisp stems. **'Lathom Self Blanching'** is a vigorous, well-flavoured early variety with crisp stems. **'Tall Utah Triumph'** has long, succulent, tender green stems. It crops from late summer to early autumn but the season can be extended by growing under cloches.

Leaf, cutting or soup celery
This produces leaves and stems over a long period and is very hardy. It is usually sold as seed mixes, but cultivars are available: **'French Dinant'** is excellent for drying and full of flavour. **'Soup Celery**

Celery maturing under glass

A healthy, well-grown row of celery is a tempting proposition

'd'Amsterdam' is aromatic and prolific, producing thin stems and lots of leaves. *Apium graveolens*, known as smallage or wild celery, is similar in appearance to cutting celery. It tastes bitter and has medicinal rather than culinary uses.

CULTIVATION

Celery is a crop for cool temperate conditions, flourishing at 15–21°C (59–70°F) on an open site. It requires rich, fertile soil which is constantly moist yet well drained and a pH of 6.5–7.5. Lime acid soils before planting if needed.

Propagation

Sow celery from mid- to late spring, in trays of moist seed compost, scattering the seed thinly over the surface; do not cover it with compost, as light is needed for germination. Keep the tray in a propagator or in a greenhouse at 13–16°C (55–60°F); germination can take several weeks, so be as patient as possible.

When two true leaves appear, transplant the seedlings into trays of moist seed compost about 6cm (2½in) apart or individually into 7.5cm (3in) pots and allow them to establish. Harden off before planting outdoors from late spring to early summer when they have 5 to 7 true leaves.

Low temperatures after germination sometimes cause bolting later in life; temperatures should not fall below 10°C (50°F) for longer than 12 hours until the seedlings have become established. They are particularly sensitive at transplanting size, so cover them with cloches and do not try to slow down the growth of advanced seedlings by putting them outdoors. It is much better to trim plants back to about 7.5cm (3in) with sharp scissors and keep them in the warm until outdoor temperatures are satisfactory. Cutting back also seems to lead to more successful transplanting. Planting in modules of seed compost lessens transplanting shock, which can also result in bolting. If you are unable to provide the necessary conditions, plantlets can always be bought.

Celery can also be sown *in situ* but germination is usually erratic and it is not worth the trouble. Celery's low germination rate can be improved by 'fluid sowing'. If possible, use treated seed to control celery leaf spot. Several sowings at 3-week intervals lengthens the harvesting season.

Sow cutting celery in trays of seed compost from late spring to late summer before hardening off and planting out 15cm (6in) apart each way. Alternatively, multi-sow in modules, about 6–8 seeds in each, and plant each module group 20cm (8in) apart. Leave a few plants to run to seed the following year, then transplant self-sown seedlings at the recommended spacing.

Growing

The planting method is different for 'trench celery' and self-blanching types. For the first, dig a trench 38–50cm (15–20in) wide and 30cm (12in) deep in late autumn or early spring and incorporate as much well-rotted manure or compost as you can find. If more than one trench is needed, their centres should be 120cm (4ft) apart. Trench celery can also be grown by filling in the trench to a depth of about 7.5–10cm (3–4in) and leaving the remaining soil alongside for earthing up. A week or 10 days before planting, rake in a balanced general fertilizer at rate of 60–90g/sq m (2–3oz/sq yd) into the bottom of the trench. Celery is easier to manage when planted in single rows with plants 30–45cm (12–18in) apart. If you plant in double rows, set the plants 23cm (9in) apart in pairs, rather than staggered. This makes blanching easier. Water thoroughly after planting.

Blanch by earthing up plants when they are about 30cm (12in) high. Before you start, tie the stems loosely, just below the leaves,

Where space is limited, celery can be grown in deep containers

using raffia or soft string and make sure the soil is moist, watering if necessary (or earth up after rain). Draw soil up the stems about 7.5cm (3in) at a time, repeating this two or three times at 3-week intervals until only the tops of plants are exposed. Do not earth up higher than the leaves, neither should you let soil fall into the heart of the plant. If heavy frosts are forecast in winter, place bracken, straw or other protective material over plants to keep in good condition for as long as possible.

Plants can also be blanched with 'collars'. Use 23–25cm (9–10in) strips of thick paper like newspaper, corrugated cardboard, brown wrapping paper or thick black polythene. (Ideally this should be lined with paper to prevent sweating.) I have also seen tile drainpipes and plastic guttering being used to good effect.

Begin blanching when plants are about 30cm (12in) high, tying the collar quite loosely around the plant to give it room to expand and leaving about one-third of the plant exposed. Further collars can be added every 2 to 3 weeks as the plants grow.

Remember to unwrap them periodically to remove any slugs hiding beneath. If collars are used in exposed sites, support them by staking with a cane. Cover the top of the cane with a flower pot, film case or ping-pong ball to avoid inflicting any damage to your eyes.

Labour-saving self-blanching types do not need earthing up. They also tolerate a wider range of soils, and are particularly good where the ground is heavy and trenching or waterlogging would be a problem. They are, however, shallow-rooted and should be fed and watered regularly throughout the growing season. Self-blanching celery is planted at ground level. Dig in generous amounts of well-rotted organic matter in spring before planting. The spacing varies according to your requirements and plants should be arranged in a square pattern, not staggered rows. Spacing about 15cm (6in) apart gives a high yield of very tender, small-stemmed sticks; 27cm (11in) apart each way, the optimum spacing, gives high yields of longer, well-blanched sticks and 23cm (9in) apart each way gives moderate stem growth. Plant with the crown at soil level and put straw around the outer plants when they mature to help blanching.

For good-quality crops celery must be watered copiously throughout the growing season and the soil should not be allowed to dry out. Apply up to 22 litres/sq m (5 gal/sq yd) per week during dry periods. Mulching with straw or compost once plants have established conserves moisture and suppresses weeds. Feed with a granular or liquid general fertilizer about 4 to 6 weeks after transplanting. Rotate crops, but do not plant next to parsnip, as both are attacked by celery fly. Avoid anything that checks plant growth throughout the season as this can cause bolting, so transplant the seedlings when the soil is warm, water and feed them regularly, and always mulch or hoe round the plants very carefully.

Maintenance
Spring Prepare the ground for planting. Sow seed and plant earlier crops out under cloches.
Summer Plant out in early summer, keep soil moist and weed regularly. Check for pests and diseases.
Autumn Harvest with care using a garden fork.
Winter Cover with straw, bracken or similar materials to allow harvest to continue during heavy frosts.

The dense foliage of maturing celery suppresses weed growth

Protected Cropping
Protect newly transplanted plantlets with cloches or horticultural fleece for several weeks after planting, until they become established. This is particularly necessary in cooler conditions.

Harvesting and Storing
Lift celery carefully with a garden fork, easing the roots from the ground. Bracken, straw or other protective material placed over trenches assists lifting in frosty weather.

Self-blanching celery can be harvested from mid-summer to early autumn. Before the first frosts, lift and store any remaining plants and put them in a cool, frost-free shed. They will keep for several weeks.

Harvest cutting celery regularly from about 5 weeks after planting.

Lush leaves top celery stems

MEDICINAL

Cultivated varieties are said to be beneficial in the treatment of rheumatism and as a diuretic.

PESTS AND DISEASES

Celery leaf miner or celery fly larvae tunnel through the leaves leaving brown blisters. Severe attacks check growth. Grow under horticultural fleece, pinch out affected leaves, do not plant seedlings which have affected leaves, or spray with systemic insecticide at the first signs of attack. Do not plant near to parsnips as they can be affected.

Slugs are a major problem, particularly on heavy soil. Use biological control, traps, hand pick or use aluminium-sulphate based slug pellets. Carrot fly attack the roots and stem bases, stunting growth. Rake insecticide into the soil before planting, grow under fleece or put fine mesh netting barriers 45–75cm (18–30in) high around the crop before or straight after transplanting. Celery leaf spot shows as brown spots on older leaves, spreading to younger ones. Severe attacks can stunt growth; use treated seed or spray with fungicide. Celery pale leaf spot (early blight) appears as tiny yellow spots on the leaf surfaces with accompanying grey mould in damp conditions. This disease spreads rapidly. Spray with Bordeaux mixture or similar fungicide. Destroy any plant debris at the end of the season.

COMPANION PLANTING

Celery helps brassicas by deterring damaging butterflies. It grows well with beans, tomatoes and particularly leeks. If left to flower, celery attracts beneficial insects.

CULINARY

Usually eaten raw rather than cooked, celery adds welcome crunchiness to salads, particularly in winter months. It is a key ingredient of Waldorf Salad, made with equal quantities of chopped red-skinned apples and celery, combined with walnuts and bound with mayonnaise.

Celery goes well with cheese – sticks filled with cream cheese or pâté are an appetizing 'nibble'. The 'heart' is particularly tasty. Cook celery in soups and stews, or stir-fry. Braise hearts by simmering in boiling water for 10 minutes, then cook in a covered dish for 45 minutes in a low oven to accompany roasts.

Add leaves to meat dishes, like parsley. Fresh or dried leaves flavour soups and stuffings. Cutting celery is a flavouring for salads, soups and stews; the seeds can also be used.

Celery will stay fresh in a polythene bag in the refrigerator for up to 3 days. Do not stand in water for long periods, or the freshness is lost.

Freeze celery by washing and cutting the sticks into 2.5cm (1in) lengths, blanch for 3 minutes, cool, drain and pack into polythene bags. Use frozen celery only in cooked dishes.

Celery and Courgette with Blue Cheese Dip
Serves 4

2 tablespoons olive oil
1 teaspoon chilli powder
½ teaspoon paprika
1 clove garlic, crushed
4 basil leaves, roughly chopped
4 courgettes, sliced lengthwise into quarters
4 stalks celery, cut into 7.5cm (3in) lengths
Chives, to garnish

For the dip:
4 tablespoons cottage cheese
2 tablespoons crumbled Roquefort cheese
50g (2oz) yoghurt
Salt and freshly ground pepper

In a heavy frying pan over a gentle heat, mix the oil with the chilli powder, paprika, garlic and basil. Turn up the heat and fry the courgette slices, cut side down, until browned and turn them to brown the second side.

In a small bowl mix together all the dip ingredients. On 4 small plates, arrange a fan of alternating courgette and celery sticks and fill the centre with the dip. Garnish with finely snipped chives and serve.

Apium graveolens var. *rapaceum. Apiaceae*

CELERIAC

(Celery Root) Biennial usually grown as annual for edible root. Hardy. Value: rich in potassium; moderate amounts of vitamin C.

If you have never grown this vegetable, do so immediately; it is absolutely delicious. This swollen-stemmed relative of celery has long been popular in Europe. It was introduced to Britain in the early eighteenth century by the writer and seedsman Stephen Switzer, who brought seed from Alexandria and wrote about the vegetable in his book, *Growing Foreign Kitchen Vegetables*. It is an excellent, versatile winter vegetable, hardier and more disease-resistant than celery, but with similar flavour and aroma.

VARIETIES

The lowest part of the stem, known as the 'bulb' is eaten; the roots that grow below are removed.

'Iram' is a medium-sized 'bulb', with few side shoots. It stores well and the flesh remains white when cooked. **'Marble Ball'**, a well-known variety, is medium-sized, globular and strongly flavoured. It stores well. **'Alabaster'** is a high-yielding variety with upright foliage, round bulbs and good resistance to running to seed. **'Tellus'** is a quick-growing variety which remains white after boiling. It has firm flesh and a smoother skin than many varieties. **'Balder'** has a good flavour with round medium-sized roots, which are excellent when cooked or raw. The 'bulb' of **'Brilliant'** is smooth with white flesh and does not discolour. **'Monarch'** is a popular variety with smooth skin and succulent flesh. 'Regent' produces large, firm roots with white flesh. It does not discolour when cooked.

CULTIVATION

Propagation
Celeriac needs a long growing season. Sow in late winter to early spring in a propagator at 18°C (65°F) or in mid- to late spring in a cold greenhouse, under cloches or in a cold frame. Plant seeds in peat substitute based compost either several to a pot or in seed boxes or modules. Germination is notoriously erratic. Pot on strong seedlings when they are about 1cm (½in) tall and large enough to handle. Plant them into single 7.5cm (3in) pots, modules or in seed trays at 6cm (2in) intervals, keeping the temperature at 13–16°C (55–60°F). Harden off when the weather becomes warm in late spring and plant outdoors once there is no danger of frost.

Celeriac is sensitive to cold at the transplanting stage; do not try to slow the growth of fast-growing seedlings by lowering the temperature, as this will encourage them to run to seed later in the season. Maintain the temperature and cut off the tops of the plants with sharp scissors to 8cm (3in) – the ideal size for transplanting.

Growing
Celeriac needs rich, fertile, moisture-retentive soil and is ideal for damper parts of the garden. In autumn, incorporate as much well-rotted manure or compost as possible. Space plants 30–38cm (12–15in) apart each way. Do not bury the crowns; they should be planted at ground level. Plant firmly and water thoroughly and continually. In midsummer remove the outer leaves to expose the crown and encourage the bulb to develop, and remove side shoots if they appear.

Maintenance
Spring Plant out seedlings – harden off. Keep weed free.
Summer Water in dry weather. Mulch to conserve moisture; feed weekly with a liquid manure, particularly in poorer soils.
Autumn Begin harvesting. Cover with straw.
Winter Prepare ground. Sow seeds under glass.

Protected Cropping
Celeriac only benefits from protection when it is at the seedling stage.

Celeriac 'Iram'

Harvesting and Storing

Celeriac can be harvested through the winter. Harvest when the plants are 7–13cm (3–5in) diameter, though they can be lifted when larger with no loss of flavour. Ideally they should remain in the ground until required. Before the onset of severe winter weather, protect plants with a layer of straw, bracken or with horticultural fleece to prevent the ground from freezing. If the soil is heavy, the site exposed or needed for another crop, lift and remove the outer leaves keeping the central tuft attached; cut off the roots and store in a cool shed in boxes of damp peat substitute or sand.

Alternatively, lift and 'heel in' or transplant the crop in another part of the garden, laying them close together in a trench and covering the bulbs with soil. They last for several weeks when stored in this manner.

Bulbs can be frozen; cut into cubes, blanch for 3 minutes, dry, store in polythene bags and put in the freezer. They will keep for a week in the salad drawer of a refrigerator.

PESTS AND DISEASES

Celeriac has the same problems as celery. Protect against slugs; use aluminium sulphate-based slug pellets, pick off slugs at night and encourage natural predators. Slugs congregate under lettuce leaves or wet paper; pick off and destroy. Carrot fly is often a pest when established on carrots. Rake insecticide into the soil before planting. Grow under fleece or place a barrier 75cm (2½ft) high of fine netting or polythene, erected before or just after sowing. Celery fly is less of a problem than on celery. Pick off any brown, blistered leaflets or grow under horticultural fleece.

COMPANION PLANTING

Celeriac grows well where legumes have been planted the previous year and benefits from being placed alongside beans, brassicas, leeks, tomatoes and onions.

MEDICINAL

Celeriac oil has a calming effect and is a traditional remedy for skin complaints and rheumatism. It is also said to restore sexual potency after illness! Celeriac is rich in calcium, phosphorus and vitamin C.

WARNING

Celeriac is a diuretic. Pregnant women and those with a kidney disorder should avoid eating it in large quantities.

CULINARY

Containing only 14 calories per 100g, celeriac is excellent for anyone on a diet.

Scrub the 'bulb' well to remove dirt before peeling. It discolours rapidly when cut; put immediately into acidulated water. Grated celeriac can be added raw to winter salads. Alternatively, blanch the slices or cubes in boiling water for a few seconds beforehand. In France it is cut into cubes and mixed with mayonnaise and Dijon mustard to make *Céleri-rave rémoulade.*

The 'bulb' adds flavour to soups or stews and is good with lamb or beef, puréed or seasoned with pepper, salt and butter, it is an ideal accompaniment for stronger-flavoured game.

The leaves are strongly flavoured and can be used sparingly to garnish salads or dried for use in cooking. The stems can be cooked and eaten like seakale.

Celeriac can be made into delicious chips: boil a whole, peeled root in salted water until just tender and then cut into chips and fry in a mixture of butter and oil until lightly browned. These chips make an excellent accompaniment to game or plain grilled steaks.

Boiled and sliced, celeriac can be covered with a cheese sauce well flavoured with French mustard. It also makes an excellent soup.

Monkfish with Celeriac
Serves 4

750g (1½lb) monkfish, cut into chunks
1 large onion, finely sliced
1 carrot, peeled and cut into julienne strips
50g (2oz) celeriac, cut into julienne strips
75g (3oz) butter
1 tablespoon flour
2 teaspoons French mustard
2 tablespoons Greek yoghurt
1 tablespoon double cream
Salt and freshly ground black pepper

Season the monkfish and prepare the vegetables. Heat half the butter in a heavy frying pan and cook the monkfish gently for about 7–8 minutes, turning it until just tender. Remove from the pan and keep warm. Using the rest of the butter, add the vegetables to the pan and sauté until soft. Stir in the flour and cook for a couple of minutes; then add the mustard, yoghurt and cream. Stir well and heat through gently. Put the fish pieces in, stir to coat well and serve piping hot.

Asparagus officinalis. Asparagaceae

ASPARAGUS

Long-lived perennial grown for slender young shoots and ornamental foliage. Half hardy. Value: high in potassium and folic acid, moderate source of beta carotene and vitamin E.

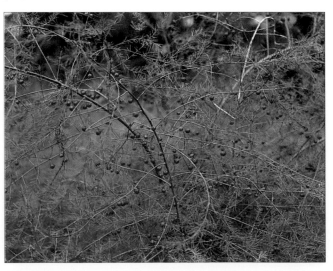

The genus *Asparagus* provides us with a range of robust foliage houseplants and one of the world's most desirable vegetables. The delicious taste, succulent texture and suggestive shape of the emergent shoots combine to create an eating experience verging on the decadent which has been celebrated for over 2,000 years. Pliny the Elder describes cultivation methods used by the Romans for producing plants with blanched stems, and mentions a cultivar of which three 'spears' weighed a pound. These spears were once believed to arise from rams' horns buried in the soil. Wild asparagus grows in Europe, Asia and north-west Africa, in habitats including dry meadows, sand dunes, limestone cliffs and volcanic hillsides.

VARIETIES

'Connover's Colossal', an early, heavy-cropping old variety producing large tasty spears, is suitable for light soils and freezes well. **'Franklim'** is heavy-cropping with thick spears. A few can be harvested from 2-year-old crowns. **'Giant Mammoth'**, with similar characteristics to 'Connover's Colossal', is more suitable for heavy soils. **'Lucullus'** crops heavily, and has long, slim, straight spears. **'Martha Washington'**, an established favourite in USA, crops heavily, has long spears and is rust-resistant.

The autumn fruits of 'Connover's Colossal'. Although the ripe fruits of female varieties are attractive, they tend to germinate more freely

CULTIVATION

Asparagus thrives in an open, sheltered position on well-drained soil. As a bed can be productive for up to 20 years, thorough preparation is essential.

Propagation

Asparagus can be grown from seed, though it is easier and less time-consuming to plant crowns. Soak seed for 2 days before sowing in mid-spring, 2.5cm (1in) deep in drills 45cm (18in) apart. Thin seedlings when they are 7.5cm (3in) tall until they are 15cm (6in) apart. Alternatively, sow indoors in late winter at 13–16°C

(55–60°F) directly into modules, pots or trays. Pot on, harden off and plant outdoors in early summer. Male plants are the more productive, so the following year, remove any females (identifiable by their fruits) before they shed their fruits. Transplant the remaining male crowns into their permanent position in mid-spring the following year.

Growing

The autumn or winter before planting, dig in plenty of well-rotted organic matter; lime acid soil to create a pH of 6.5–7.5. It is vital to remove perennial weeds. Fork over the soil 1 or 2 weeks before planting and rake in a general fertilizer at approximately 90g/sq m (3oz/sq yd).

One-year-old crowns establish quickly; 2- and 3-year-old crowns tend to suffer from a growth check after transplanting. Plant in mid-spring, once the soil is warm. The roots desiccate quickly and are easily damaged, so cover with sacking until ready to plant, then handle with care.

Either plant in single rows with the crowns 30–45cm (12–18in) apart or in beds with 2 or 3 rows 30cm (12in) apart. For several beds, set them 90cm (3ft) apart. Before planting dig a trench 30cm (12in) by 20cm (8in) and make a 4in (10cm) mound of soil in the base; plant crowns along the top, spreading out the roots, and cover them with 5cm (2in) of sifted soil. As the stems grow, gradually cover with soil; by autumn, the trench should be filled with soil. Keep beds weed-free by hand weeding or hoeing carefully to avoid damaging the shallow roots. On more exposed sites, support the 'ferns' when windy to avoid damage to the crown, and water during dry weather.

After harvesting, apply a general fertilizer to nurture stem growth and build up the plants for the following

Cutting off asparagus roots

year. In autumn, when stems have turned yellow, cut back to within 2.5–5cm (1–2in) of the surface and tidy up the bed. Ferns can be shredded and composted. Each spring apply a general fertilizer as growth begins. Mulching with manure has little value beyond suppressing weeds and conserving moisture.

Maintenance

Spring Sow seed and plant crowns. Harvest late spring.
Summer Keep weed-free and water as necessary. Stop harvesting by midsummer.
Autumn Cut back yellowing ferns and tidy beds.
Winter Prepare new beds: mix in organic matter and remove perennial weeds.

Protected Cropping

Protect the crowns from late frosts with horticultural fleece or cloches.

Harvesting and Storing

However tempting, do not cut spears until the third year after planting (except possibly with 'Franklim'). Harvesting lasts for 6 weeks in the first year and 8 weeks in subsequent years. Do not harvest after midsummer: it can result in thin spears the following year. When spears are 10–17.5cm (4–7in) long, cut them obliquely about 2.5–5cm (1–2in) below the surface with a sharp knife or a serrated asparagus knife.

Pests and Diseases

The black and yellow adults and small greyish larvae of asparagus beetles appear from late summer, stripping stems and foliage.

COMPANION PLANTING

Where growing conditions allow, asparagus is compatible with tomatoes, parsley and basil.

MEDICINAL

Asparagus is used to treat rheumatism, gout and cystitis. Anyone who lacks the enzyme to break down asparagin produces urine with a strong odour – a disconcerting but harmless phenomenon.

WARNING

The berries are poisonous.

CULINARY

Asparagus spears should be used as fresh as possible, preferably within an hour of harvesting. They can be refrigerated in a polythene bag for up to 3 days. To freeze, tie into bundles and blanch thick spears for 4 minutes, thin for 2. Freeze in a plastic container.

Asparagus is best eaten steamed or boiled and served hot with butter. Also good cold with vinaigrette, Parmesan or mayonnaise. Asparagus tips can be added to salads and pizza toppings.

To boil, wash spears, peel away the skin below the tips, and soak in cold water until all have been prepared. Sort into stalks of even length (perhaps 20 stalks if thin varieties and 6–8 if thicker-stemmed), and tie with soft string or raffia, one close to the base and another just below the tip. Stand bundles upright in boiling salted water, with the tips above water level. Cover and boil gently for 10–15 minutes until *al dente*, then drain and serve. Don't overcook: the tips should be firm, and the spears should not bend when held at the base. The water can be used in soup.

Asparagus Risotto
Serves 4

6 morels, fresh or dried
1 big bunch thin asparagus, cut into 2.5cm (1in) pieces
25g (1oz) unsalted butter
1½ tablespoons olive oil
2 red onions, finely chopped
300g (10oz) arborio rice
600ml (1pt) chicken stock, boiling
1 tablespoon fresh marjoram (or 1 teaspoon dried)
2 tablespoons mascarpone
Salt and freshly ground black pepper
Freshly grated Parmesan (optional)

Soak fresh morels in salted water for 10 minutes and wash thoroughly. Pat dry and cut each into several pieces. If using dried morels, soak in warm water for 30 minutes before cutting up.

Blanch the asparagus in boiling water for 1 minute, drain and set aside.

Heat the butter and oil in a heavy-bottomed pan and sauté the onion and morels until soft. Stir in the rice and coat it well with the oil and butter. Pour in a cup of the stock and the marjoram and cook over a low heat, stirring frequently, until the liquid is absorbed. Add more cupfuls of stock one at a time and continue cooking until the rice is just tender and the consistency is creamy. Stir in the asparagus and the mascarpone and season well. Serve with Parmesan.

Asparagus Risotto

Beta vulgaris subsp. *cicla. Chenopodiaceae*

SWISS CHARD

Also known as Silver Chard, Silver Beet, Seakale Beet. Biennial grown as annual for leaves and midribs. Hardy. Value: high in sodium, potassium, iron, and an exceptional source of beta carotene, the precursor of vitamin A.

Perpetual spinach is highly resistant to bolting

The umbrella name 'leaf beet' includes Swiss chard and also encompasses perpetual spinach or spinach beet. (The 'true' spinach and New Zealand spinach both belong to other genera.) A close relative of the beetroot, leaf beet is an ancient vegetable cultivated for its attractive, tasty leaves. Native to the Mediterranean, it was well known to the Greeks, who also ate its roots with mustard, lentils and beans. Aristotle wrote of red chard in the fourth century BC, and Theophrastus recorded both light and dark green varieties. The Romans introduced it to central and northern Europe and from there it slowly spread, reaching the Far East in the Middle Ages and China in the seventeenth century. The name 'chard' comes from the French *carde* and derives from the resemblance of the leaf stalks to those of globe artichokes and cardoons. In 1597 John Gerard wrote in his *Herbal*, '… it grew with me to the height of eight cubits and did bring forth his rough seeds very plentifully.' If the measurement is correct, his Swiss chard would be approximately 4m (12ft) tall. I wonder where that variety is today, was his yardstick wrongly calibrated, or had it simply bolted?

CULTIVATION

Though they tolerate a wide range of soils, the best growing conditions are sunny or lightly shaded positions in rich, moisture-retentive, free-draining soil. On impoverished soils, bolting can be a problem, so dig in plenty of well-rotted organic matter the winter before planting. The ideal pH is 6.5–7.5 and acid soils should be limed.

The ideal growing temperature is 16–18°C (60–65°F), though the range of tolerance is remarkably broad. They survive in winter temperatures down to about -14 °C (7°F) and are more tolerant of higher summer temperatures than true spinach, which is inclined to bolt.

Propagation
For a constant supply throughout the year, make two sowings, one in mid-spring for a summer harvest and another in mid- to late summer. The later crop is usually lower-yielding.

Sow 3–4 seeds in 'stations' 23cm (9in) apart, in drills 1–2cm (½–¾in) deep. Swiss chard needs 45cm (18in) between the rows, and perpetual spinach 38cm (15in). Thin seedlings when large enough to handle to

VARIETIES

Swiss chard has broad red or white leaf stems and midribs. **'Fordhook Giant'** has huge, glossy green leaves with white veins and stems. It is tasty and high-yielding, producing bumper crops even at high temperatures. **'Lucullus'** is vigorous and crops heavily, producing pale yellow-green leaves with fleshy midribs. Tolerant of high temperatures, it does not bolt. **'Rhubarb Chard'** (**'Ruby Chard'**) is noted for its magnificent bright crimson

The bright stems of 'Ruby Chard' are spectacular

leaf stalks and dark green puckered leaves. Ideal for the ornamental border or 'potager', it needs growing with care, as it is prone to bolting. **'Vulcan'** is another cultivar with beautiful red stems and dark green, sweet tasting leaves.

'Perpetual Spinach', or spinach beet, is similar but smaller, with narrower stems, dark, fleshy leaves and is very resistant to bolting. **'Erbette'**, an Italian variety, is well flavoured and has an excellent texture. It is good as a 'cut and come again' crop.

leave the strongest seedling. Alternatively, sow in modules or trays and transplant to their final spacing when they are large enough to handle. Swiss chard is particularly successful as a 'cut and come again' crop. Prepare the seedbed thoroughly and broadcast or sow seed in drills the width of a hoe.

Growing
Keep crops weed-free by hoeing or, preferably, mulching with well-rotted organic matter and keep the soil continually moist. In dry conditions, plants will need 9–13.5 litres (2–3 gal) per week, but are surprisingly drought-tolerant. A dressing of general granular or liquid fertilizer can be given to plants needing a boost.

Maintenance
Spring Sow the first crop in mid-spring in 'stations'; thin, leaving a strong seedling.
Summer Weed, water and feed as necessary. Sow a second crop in mid- to late summer. Harvest as needed.
Autumn Protect with cloches or fleece in late autumn for good-quality growth.
Winter Dig over the area where the following year's crop is to be planted. Harvest overwintering crops.

Protected Cropping
Though they are hardy enough to withstand winters outdoors, plants protected in cloches, cold frames, polythene tunnels or fleece produce better crops of higher-quality leaves.

Container Growing
Swiss chard can be grown in containers and makes a fine ornamental feature. Either transplant seedlings or sow directly into loam-based compost or garden soil, with added organic matter.

Harvesting and Storing
Seeds sown in mid-spring are ready to harvest from early to midsummer. Harvest the outer leaves first, working towards the centre of the plant and cutting at the base of each stem: snapping them off is likely to disturb the roots. Choose firm leaves and discard any that are damaged or wilted. Pick regularly to ensure a constant supply of tender regrowth, so harvest even if you are unable to use them – they are certain to be welcomed by friends.

They can also be grown as 'cut and come again' crops from seedling stage through to maturity. Cut seedlings when about 5cm (2in) tall. After 2–3 crops have been harvested, allow them to regrow to about 7.5cm (5in). Semi-mature plants are harvested leaf by leaf and mature plants can be cut about 2.5cm (1in) above the ground; from this, new growth appears.

Swiss chard and perpetual spinach are best eaten straight from the plant. Leaves (minus the stalks) keep in a refrigerator in the salad compartment or in polythene bags for 2–3 days.

Swiss chard is highly productive

PESTS AND DISEASES

They are relatively trouble-free, though beware of downy mildew when dense patches of seedlings are sown for 'cut and come again' crops. It appears as brown patches on leaves.

Birds sometimes attack seedlings, so protect crops; growing plants under brassicas or beans also gives them some protection.

COMPANION PLANTING

They grow well with all beans except runners, and flourish alongside brassicas, onions and lettuce. Herbs like sage, thyme, mint, dill, hyssop, rosemary and garlic are also compatible.

MEDICINAL

Leaves are vitamin- and mineral-rich with high levels of iron and magnesium. In folk medicine the juice is used as a decongestant; the leaves are said to neutralize acid and have a purgative effect. Beware of eating it in large quantities!

CULINARY

Perpetual spinach can be lightly boiled, steamed or eaten raw. Swiss chard takes longer to cook: try it steamed, served with butter or sorrel. Soup can be made from the leaves and its midribs cooked and served like asparagus, or added to pork pies. 'Rhubarb Chard' tastes milder than white-stemmed varieties.

Spinach Beet Fritters
Serves 4

These robust fritters go well with salmon or cod.

750g (1½ lb) spinach beet, well washed
Knob of butter
2 large eggs, separated
1 tablespoon grated Parmesan
1 teaspoon grated lemon peel
Olive oil, for frying
Salt and freshly ground black pepper
Pinch of nutmeg

Prepare the leaves, removing the midribs, and chop roughly. Cook in the water that clings to the leaves until wilted – 2–3 minutes – and drain well. Chop finely and return to the pan with the butter, cooking until all the liquid evaporates. Leave to cool for 5 minutes and stir in the egg yolks, Parmesan and lemon peel. When almost cold, fold in the stiffly beaten egg whites and season with salt, pepper and nutmeg to taste.

Drop spoonfuls into hot fat, heated in a heavy frying pan, and cook for a minute or two, turning halfway. Drain well and serve hot.

Beta vulgaris subsp. *vulgaris. Chenopodiaceae*

BEETROOT

Also known as Beet. Biennial grown as annual for swollen root and young leaves. Hardy. Value: slightly higher in carbohydrates than most vegetables, good source of folic acid and potassium.

Beetroot is a form of the maritime sea beet which has been selected over many centuries for its edible roots. From the same origin come mangold (a cattle fodder), the beet used for commercial sugar production and Swiss chard. Grown since Assyrian times, the vegetable was highly esteemed by the ancient Greeks and was used in offerings to Apollo. There were many Roman recipes for beetroot, which they regarded more highly than the greatly revered cabbage. It appeared in fourteenth-century English recipes and was first described as the beetroot we know today in Germany in 1558, though it was a rarity at that time in northern Europe. The typical red coloration comes from its cell sap, but there are also varieties in other colours.

VARIETIES

Beetroots are grouped according to shape – round or globe-shaped, tapered or long, and flat or oval. To reduce the amount of thinning needed, breeders have introduced 'monogerm' varieties.

Globe
'Boltardy' is a delicious, well-textured, smooth-skinned variety, an excellent early cropper as it is very resistant to bolting, and good in containers. **'Bonel'** has deep red, succulent, tasty roots and is high-yielding. It crops over a long period and is resistant to bolting. **'Detroit 2 Little Ball'** produces deep red, smooth-skinned 'baby

'Burpees Golden' is an especially tasty variety

beet', which are ideal for pickling, bottling or freezing. A good crop for late sowing and for storing. **'Detroit 2 Dark Red'** has dark red flesh, a good flavour and stores well. **'Monogram'** is dark red, well-flavoured and vigorous, with smooth skin and rich red flesh. It is a 'monogerm' variety. **'Monopoly'** is also a 'monogerm' and is resistant to bolting, with a good colour and rough skin. **'Regala'** has very dark roots and is quite small, even at maturity. An excellent variety for containers, and resistant to bolting.

Tapered
'Cheltenham Green Top' is a tasty, old variety with rough skin and long roots. It stores well. **'Cheltenham Mono'** is a tasty, medium-sized 'monogerm' which is resistant to bolting, good for slicing and stores well.

Others
'Albina Vereduna' (**'Snowhite'**) is a wonderful globe-shaped white variety, with smooth skin and sweet flesh; it has the advantage that it does not stain. The curly leaves can be used as 'greens' and are full of vitamins. It does not store

well and is prone to bolting. **'Barbabietola di Chioggia'** is a mild, traditional Italian variety. Sliced, it reveals unusual white internal 'rings'. It gives an exotic look to salads, certain to provoke comment. When cooked, it becomes pale pink. Sow from mid-spring. **'Burpees Golden'** has beautiful orange skin and tasty yellow flesh; it is better harvested when small. It looks great in salads, keeps its colour when cooked, does not bleed when cut and the leaves can be used as 'greens'. It stores well and has good bolting resistance. **'Egyptian Turnip Rooted'** (**'D'Egypte'**, **'Egyptian Flat'**) has smooth roots with deep red, delicious flesh. An American introduction, it was first grown around Boston about 1869. **'Forono'** is very tasty, with large, cylindrical roots, smooth skin and good colour. Slow to go woody, it is ideal for slicing, for summer salads, and stores well. Susceptible to bolting, it should be sown from mid-spring. **'Cylindrica'** has sweet-tasting, dark, oval roots with excellent keeping qualities and good flavour. Because of its shape, it is perfect for slicing and cooks well. Harvest when young.

Varieties of 'mini vegetables' include **'Pronto'**, **'Action'** and **'Monaco'**.

'Cylindrica' is ideal for slicing

'Boltardy' is a reliable variety

CULTIVATION

Propagation

In most varieties each 'seed' is a corky fruit containing 2 or 3 seeds, so a considerable amount of thinning is required. 'Monogerm' varieties, each containing a single seed, reduce such a work load. They also contain a natural inhibitor which slows or even prevents germination. Remove this by soaking seeds or washing them in running water for ½ to 1 hour before sowing.

At soil temperatures below 7°C (45°F) germination is slow and erratic. To overcome this, sow early crops in modules, 'fluid sow' or sow in drills or stations after warming the soil with cloches. These can be left in place after sowing until the weather warms tip. Use bolting-resistant varieties until mid-spring; after that, any variety can be used.

Sow the first crops under cloches from late winter to early spring 12mm–2cm (½–¾in) deep and 2.5cm (1in) apart with 23cm (9in) between rows. Thin to a final spacing of 10cm (4in) between plants. Alternatively sow 2–3 seeds at 'stations'

10cm (4in) apart, thinning to leave the strongest seedling when the first true leaf appears. 'Round' varieties can be 'multi-sown' in a cool greenhouse planting 3 seeds per module, thinning to 4–5 seedlings, then planting the modules 10cm (4in) apart when about 5cm (2in) high. Early crops can also be sown thinly in broad flat drills 12mm–2cm (½–¾in) deep, in a similar way to peas. Thin as soon as seedlings are touching and keep thinning as plants grow: those large enough can be used whole. If you grow beetroot under horticultural fleece or a similar cover (put in place once the seedlings have established), yields can be increased by up to 50%. Remove protection 4–6 weeks after sowing. From mid-spring, if the weather is warm seeds can be sown without the protection of cloches, thinning to 7.5–10cm (3–4in) apart.

Beetroot grown for pickling need to be about 5cm (2in) in diameter. Sowing in rows 7.5cm (3in) apart, thinning plants to 6.5cm (2½in) apart will give you the correct size.

From late spring to early summer sow the main crop, using any round or long variety. Harvest throughout the summer and for winter storing. Sow in drills or at

'stations', thinning to leave a final spacing of 7.5cm (3in) apart in rows 20cm (8in) apart or 12.5–15cm (5–6in) in and between the rows.

For a constant supply of beetroot, sow round cultivars under glass from late winter at 4-week intervals for mid-spring crops; and for a late autumn crop sow from early to midsummer in mild areas (for lifting during winter thin to 10cm/4in).

For winter storage sow in late May, early June.

Growing

Beetroot needs an open site with fertile, well-drained light soil which has been manured for the previous crop. The pH should be 6.5–7.5, so acid soils will need liming. Autumn-maturing varieties tolerate heavier conditions and long-rooted varieties require a deeper soil. The best quality grow in moderate temperatures around 16°C (61°F).

Scatter a slow-release general fertilizer at 30–60g/sq m (2–3oz/sq yd) 2–3 weeks before sowing, raking the seedbed to a fine tilth.

For good-quality beetroot, it is important to avoid any check in growth; at the onset of drought, water at a rate of 11 litres/sq m (2½ gal/sq yd) every 2 weeks. Do not over-water as this results in excessive leaf growth and small roots. If watering is neglected, yields are low, roots become woody and when it rains or you water

'Red Ace' is a vigorous grower

suddenly, the roots will split. Keep weed-free and hoe with care as damage causes the roots to bleed: use an onion hoe or mulch round the plants. Mulching with a 5cm (2in) layer of well-rotted compost or spent mushroom compost will conserve moisture.

Maintenance

Spring Sow early crops under glass or cloches. Mid-spring crops can be sown without protection.
Summer Sow successively every month, harvest earlier crops, keep the plot weed-free and water as required. Sow main crops.
Autumn Lift later crops and those for storage.
Winter In mild areas leave overwintering crops outdoors and protect with bracken, straw or similar materials. Alternatively, lift and store indoors.

Protected Cropping

Grow early crops under glass in modules and transplant under cloches. Alternatively, grow under cloches or crop covers and remove these about 6 weeks after sowing.

Container Growing

Unless growing for exhibition, grow only globe varieties in containers – about 20cm (8in) deep – or troughs or growbags. Sow seed thinly 1.2–2cm (½–¾in) deep from mid-spring to mid-summer, thinning to 10–12.5cm (4–5in) apart. Water regularly, harvest when the size of a tennis ball and keep weed-free.

Harvesting and Storing

Beetroot takes 60–90 days to mature. It must always be harvested before it becomes woody and inedible. Harvest salad beetroot from late spring to mid-autumn and maincrop varieties from midsummer onwards. Early varieties are best harvested when the size of a golf ball; when later crops reach that size, lift every other plant and use for cooking, leaving the rest for lifting when they reach cricket ball-size.

Lift roots carefully with a fork, shake off soil and twist off the leaves. Do not cut off the leaves: it causes bleeding and makes a terrible mess! Use any damaged roots immediately. Lift beet for storage by mid-autumn and put in stout boxes of moist peat substitute, sand or sawdust, leaving a gap between each root. Store in a cool, frost-free shed or garage. Roots should keep until mid-spring the following year but check regularly and remove any that deteriorate. The long-rooted types are traditionally grown for storage, but most varieties store successfully.

In mild areas and on well-drained soil they can be left over winter, but need a dense protective covering of straw or similar material before the frosts. This also makes lifting easier.

PESTS AND DISEASES

Beetroot are generally trouble-free but may suffer from the following problems:

Black bean aphid forms dense colonies on the leaves. Yellow blotches between the veins, the symptom of manganese deficiency, appear on older leaves first and can be a problem on extremely alkaline soil.

Rough patches on the surface of the root and waterlogged brown patches and rings at its centre are a sign of boron deficiency. There may also be corky 'growths' on the shoots and leaf stalks.

Make sure that beetroot seedlings are protected against birds.

Slugs make holes in leaves. The problem is worse in damp conditions.

COMPANION PLANTING

Beetroot flourish in the company of kohlrabi, carrots, cucumber, lettuce, onions, brassicas and most beans (not runners). Dill or Florence fennel planted nearby attracts predators. Because they combine well with so many other crops and small roots mature within 9–13 weeks, beetroots are good for intercropping and useful catch-crops.

OTHER USES

The foliage is attractive and ideal for inclusion in an ornamental border or 'potager', particularly varieties like 'Bull's Blood'. The leaf mineral content is 25% magnesium, making it useful on the compost heap.

MEDICINAL

Used in folk medicine as a blood tonic for gastritis, piles and constipation; mildly cardio-tonic. Recent research has shown that taking at least one glass of raw beetroot juice a day helps control cancer.

WARNING

The sap stains very badly and is difficult to remove from clothing and skin.

CULINARY

The roots are eaten raw – try them grated as a *crudité* – or cooked and served fresh or pickled. Young 'tops' can be cooked like spinach and used as 'greens'.

They add colour and flavour to salads, particularly the red, yellow, white and bi-coloured varieties. Bean and beetroot salad is particularly tasty. Wash in cold water, keeping root and stems intact: do not 'top and tail' or damage the skin, as bleeding causes loss of flavour and colour. Boil for up to 2 hours in saltwater, depending on the size, then carefully rub off the skin. It is delicious served hot as a vegetable, otherwise cool for pickling or for a fresh salad.

Beetroot can also be baked, and is the basis for borscht soup when cooked with white stock. It also makes excellent chutney and wine.

Freeze small beets which are no more than 5cm (2in) across. Wash and boil, skin and cool, then cut roots into slices or cubes and freeze in a rigid container. You should use within 6 months.

In a polythene bag or salad compartment of the fridge, they stay fresh for up to 2 weeks.

Spicy Beetroot Salad
Serves 4

750g (1½lb) beetroots, washed trimmed
Juice of half a lemon
½ teaspoon cumin
½ teaspoon cinnamon
½ teaspoon paprika pepper
1 tablespoon orange flower water
2 tablespoons olive oil
Salt and freshly ground black pepper
2 tablespoons chopped parsley
Lettuce (coloured varieties mixed with green leaves such as lamb's lettuce)

Cook the beetroots in a steamer for 20 or 30 minutes until tender. Peel and slice them when cool, reserving the liquid that accumulates on the plate.

Toss them in lemon juice and coat with the spices, orange-flower water and olive oil, together with the liquid. Season, cover and chill. To serve, toss with the parsley and arrange on individual plates on a bed of lettuce leaves.

Spicy Beetroot Salad

Brassica oleracea Gemmifera Group. *Brassicaceae*

BRUSSELS SPROUT

*Biennial grown as annual for leafy buds and 'tops'. Hardy.
Value: excellent source of vitamin C, rich in beta carotene,
folic acid, vitamin E and potassium.*

First recorded as a spontaneous sport from a cabbage plant found in the Brussels region of Belgium around 1750, this vegetable had reached England and France by 1800. The Brussels version may not have been the first occurrence: a plant described as 'Brassica capitata polycephalos' (a many-headed brassica with knob-like heads) was illustrated in D'Alechaps's *Historia Generalis Plantarum* in 1587. A stalwart among winter vegetables in cool temperate climates, sprouts are extremely hardy and crop heavily, but are rather fiddly to prepare. As with all vegetables, homegrown ones taste far better than those bought from a shop. If you have never eaten sprouts harvested fresh from the garden, try them: they are absolutely delicious.

Harvest the buttons while firm

VARIETIES

Sprouts are divided into early, mid-season and late varieties, harvested from early to mid-autumn, mid-autumn to mid-winter and mid-winter to early spring respectively. 'Earlies' are shorter and faster-growing than the hardier 'lates', which are taller with higher yields. To extend the season, grow one variety from each group if you have space; alternatively, grow mid-season and late types for mid-winter to early spring crops, when other vegetables are scarce.

Although older open-pollinated varieties are very tasty, it is generally accepted that the modern, compact F_1 hybrids are a better buy. They produce a heavy crop of uniform 'buttons' all the way up the stem, which remain in good condition for a long period without 'blowing'; plants are also less likely to fall over.

'**Citadel**' (mid-season) produces moderately sized dark green sprouts which freeze well. '**Falstaff**' is a vigorous, high-yielding red cultivar with tasty 'buttons'. The red coloration disappears when boiled, so steaming is a better method of cooking. '**Oliver**' (very early) is a high-yielding variety producing large tasty sprouts. Good resistance to powdery mildew. '**Peer Gynt**' (early to mid-season) produces medium-sized sprouts. Lower 'buttons' have a tendency not to open if mature sprouts are left on the plant. Harvest regularly. '**Rampart**' (late) has good-tasting sprouts that last for a long time before 'blowing' but tend to become bitter late in the season. Good resistance to powdery mildew and some resistance to ringspot. '**Rubine**', a red form, is worth a place in an ornamental border and produces small crops of tasty sprouts. '**Widgeon**' (mid-season) is a good-flavoured variety producing moderately sized sprouts.

'Rubine', a magnificent red variety, is an excellent ornamental plant

'Oliver' in full crop

CULTIVATION

Sprouts need a sheltered, sunny spot; wind rock can be a problem in exposed sites. Soil should be moisture-retentive yet free-draining, with a pH of 6.5.

Propagation

Sow early varieties from late winter to early spring, mid-season varieties from mid- to late spring and late varieties from mid-spring. Sow seeds thinly, 2cm (³⁄₄in) deep in a half tray of moist seed or multi-purpose compost and put them in an unheated greenhouse, cold frame or sheltered spot outdoors to germinate. Transplant seedlings when they are large enough to handle into a larger seed tray, in potting or multi-purpose compost, about 4–5cm (1½–2in) apart.

Sowing in modules reduces root disturbance when transplanting. Put 2 seeds in each module and retain the strongest after germination. Sow early varieties from late winter in a propagator at 10–13°C; (50–55°F) and transplant them into their permanent position after hardening off. Some taller varieties are prone to falling over when grown in modules, but when planted deeply, a long tap root develops.

The previous two methods are preferable to sowing in a seedbed, which takes up space that could be used for other crops, and leaves seedlings vulnerable to pests and diseases; I do not recommend it. If necessary, warm the soil with cloches or black polythene. Protect earlier sowings from cold weather; later sowings can be made without shelter. Water before sowing if the soil is dry. Level, firm and rake the seedbed to a fine tilth before sowing seed thinly, 2cm (³⁄₄in) deep in rows 20cm (8in) apart, thinning seedlings to 7.5–10cm (3–4in) apart when they are large enough to handle. Transplant into their final position when they are about 10–15cm (4–6in) tall.

Gradually harden off those grown under cover before planting them in their final positions.

Growing

Dig in plenty of well-rotted manure or compost several months before planting, particularly on light, poor or heavy soils. The ground should not be freshly manured, as excessive nitrogen causes sprouts to 'blow'.

Plant earlier, smaller varieties about 60cm (2ft) apart each way, those of moderate size 75cm (2½ft) apart and taller varieties 90cm (3ft) apart. Wider spacing encourages larger sprouts, improves air circulation and reduces fungal problems, while closer spacing means smaller, compact 'buttons' which will mature at the same time.

Plant with the lowest leaves just above the soil surface. Tug a leaf – if the whole plant moves it has not been planted firmly enough. On light soils, make a drill 7.5–10cm (3–4in) deep, plant sprouts in the bottom and refill it with soil. The extra support makes the plants more stable. Water immediately after transplanting for 3–4 weeks until plants have become established and, if available, mulch with straw to a depth of 5–7.5cm (2–3in).

Keep the beds weed-free. Watering is not normally needed once plants are established except during drought, when each plant can be given up to 142ml (½pt) per day to maintain the constant growth necessary for good cropping. Remove any diseased or yellowing leaves as they appear. Earthing up round the stem base to a depth of 7.5–12.5cm (3–5in) provides extra support against winter winds, although tall varieties will usually need staking. In exposed gardens, even dwarf varieties need staking.

'Stopping' by removing the growing point is only beneficial for autumn-maturing F_1 cultivars being grown for freezing. Plants can be stopped when lowest

Brussels sprouts at RHS Wisley, in the snow, proving their hardiness

'Falstaff – what would Shakespeare have thought?

sprouts reach 1cm (½in) diameter, to encourage even development of sprouts on the stem. When left unstopped, sprouts can be picked over a longer period.

Grow sprouts on a 3- or 4-year rotation, preferably following peas and beans (where they benefit from the nitrogen left in the soil). In late summer, feeding with a liquid high-potash fertilizer gives plants a useful boost. Plant small lettuces like 'Little Gem' between sprouts for summer and autumn cropping, and winter purslane or land cress for early winter crops.

Lift plants immediately after harvesting, put leaves on the compost heap and shred the stems.

Maintenance
Spring Sow outdoors in seedbeds, thin and keep weed-free.
Summer Transplant outdoors and water during drought.
Autumn Harvest early varieties; stake tall varieties if needed.
Winter Sow early varieties indoors. Harvest later crops.

Protected Cropping
Earlier sowings made outdoors in a seedbed should be protected with cloches or fleece. Continued protection with horticultural fleece provides a physical barrier against pests such as cabbage root fly, flea beetle, aphids and birds.

Harvesting and Storing
Pick sprouts when those at the base are walnut-sized and tightly closed. Snap them off with a sharp downward tug or cut with a knife, removing 'blown' sprouts and any yellow, diseased leaves. When harvest is over, the tops can be cooked as cabbage. During severe winter weather, lift a few plants to hang in a shed where they can be easily harvested. They will last for several weeks.

PESTS AND DISEASES

Sprouts are very robust yet subject to the usual brassica problems.

Downy mildew shows as yellow patches on the leaves, with patches of fluffy mould on the underside in humid conditions. Remove all affected leaves or spray with fungicide. If downy mildew appears on seedlings, improve ventilation and increase spacing.

Powdery mildew is a white powdery deposit over shoots, stems and leaves. In severe cases, plants become yellow and die. It is more of a problem when plants are dry at the roots. Water and mulch, remove diseased leaves and spray with fungicide.

Clubroot, affecting members of the family Brassicaceae, is a disease to be avoided at all costs. Roots swell and distort, young plants wilt on hot days but recover overnight, growth is stunted and crops ruined. It is more of a problem on poorly drained, acid soils. Spores remain in the soil for up to 20 years. Never buy brassicas from unknown sources: grow them yourself. Potting plants on into 10–15cm (4–6in) pots allows the roots to become established before they are planted out, which lessens the effects of clubroot. Improve drainage; lime acid soils to create a neutral pH. Earthing up often encourages new roots to form and reduces the effects. Remove all diseased plants, with the whole root system if possible, and destroy them.

Ringspot is worse in cool wet seasons and on well-manured land. It is most evident on older leaves as round brown spots with dark centres. Remove and burn any affected plants and rotate crops.

COMPANION PLANTING

When planted among maturing onions, sprouts benefit from their root residues and the firm soil.

CULINARY

Steam or boil sprouts briskly for the minimum time required to cook through – they should not turn mushy. Small sprouts can be shredded in salads – 'Rubine' and 'Falstaff' are particularly attractive.

They can be stored for up to 3 days in a polythene bag in the refrigerator. Freeze sprouts only if they are small. Blanch for 3 minutes, cool and drain before drying and packing them into polythene bags.

Stir-fried Sprouts
Serves 4
This can look quite spectacular made with a red variety such as 'Falstaff' or 'Rubine'.

2 tablespoons vegetable oil
2 tablespoons soya sauce
500g (1lb) Brussels sprouts, prepared and finely sliced
2 tablespoons hazelnuts, roughly ground
Salt and freshly ground black pepper

Heat the oil in a wok, stir in the soy sauce and, over a high heat, cook the sprouts for 2–3 minutes. Sprinkle over the hazelnuts. Season and serve.

Stir-fried Sprouts

Brassica napus Napobrassica Group. *Brassicaceae*

SWEDE

Also known as Rutabaga, Swedish turnip. Biennial grown as annual for swollen root and young leaves. Hardy. Value: small amounts of niacin (vitamin B) and vitamin C, low in calories and carbohydrates.

Swede is one of the hardiest of all root crops and is the perfect winter vegetable for cool temperate climates. An abbreviation of 'Swedish turnip', its name indicates its origins. Eaten in France and southern Europe in the sixteenth century, it came to Britain from Holland in 1755 and rapidly became popular as the 'turnip-rooted cabbage'. Along with the turnip, it was first used as winter fodder for sheep and cattle, improving milk production during a traditionally lean period. During times of famine, swedes were eaten by country folk and still have the reputation among many as 'peasant food'.

To despise them is your loss; they are robust, undemanding and one of the easiest vegetables to grow. New varieties are disease-resistant, tasty and a wonderful accompaniment to sprouts as a winter vegetable – particularly when mashed with butter, cream and spices.

CULTIVATION

Propagation

Swedes need a long growing season and should be sown from early spring in cooler climates to early summer where temperatures are warmer and germination and growth are rapid. Sow in drills 2cm (¾in) deep and 40–45cm (16–18in) apart, thinning seedlings to 23–30cm (9–12in). Thin when they are no more than 2.5cm (1in) high, when the first true leaves appear, to ensure that the roots develop properly. Firm the soil after thinning.

Growing

Swedes prefer a sheltered and open site in fertile, well-drained but moisture-retentive soil. Good drainage is essential. Summer sowings can be made in moderate shade, provided they receive sufficient moisture. Swedes prefer a pH of 5.5–7.0, so very acid soil will need liming. If the ground has not been manured for the previous crop, double dig in autumn, incorporate plenty of well-rotted organic matter and allow the soil to 'weather' over winter. About a week prior to sowing, remove any weeds or debris and rake general fertilizer into the soil at 60g/sq m (2oz/sq yd). In common with other brassicas, swedes grow poorly on loose soil, so rake the soil to a fine tilth and firm it with the head of a rake or by carefully treading. If the soil is dry, water thoroughly before sowing and stand on a planting board to avoid compacting the soil. Mark

VARIETIES

'Acme' has round roots with pale purple skin. Its tops are prone to powdery mildew. 'Angela' produces purple roots and is resistant to powdery mildew. 'Best of All' is a yellow-fleshed, purple-topped, globe-shaped cultivar with excellent texture and mild flavour. Very hardy. 'Lizzy' is a round variety with purple tops and yellow flesh, a soft texture and sweet, nutty flavour. Resistant to bolting and cracking. 'Marian' is purple with yellow flesh, very tasty and quick-growing. It produces large roots and has good resistance to clubroot and powdery mildew.

Correct spacing between plants is vital for vigorous growth

each row with canes or twigs, and label and date the crop.

Keep crops weed-free by hand weeding and careful hoeing. Swedes need a constant supply of water throughout the growing season, otherwise they tend to run to seed or produce small, woody roots. Sudden watering or rain after a period of drought causes the roots to split, so they will need up to 10 litres/sq m (2 gal/sq yd) per week in dry periods. This improves the size and quality but usually reduces the flavour.

Rotate swedes with other brassicas.

Swede tops can be blanched for eating raw as a winter salad vegetable. Lift a few roots in early to midwinter, cut back the leaves and plant the roots under the greenhouse staging, or stand them upright in boxes or wooden trays filled with peat substitute, humus-rich garden soil or with a thick layer of straw. Cover with upturned boxes or black polythene to exclude the light and put them in a cellar, garage or shed. After 3–4 weeks shoots will appear and can be cut when they are 10–12.5cm (4–5in) long.

Maintenance
Spring Warm soil under cloches for early sowings.
Summer Water crops and keep weed-free.
Autumn Harvest early varieties.
Winter Lift and store crops before severe weather starts.

Protected Cropping
Cover ground with cloches, fleece or black polythene for 2–3 weeks in late winter to early spring to warm the ground before sowing early crops. Seedlings should be protected until they are well-established.

Harvesting and Storing
Harvest begins any time from early to mid-autumn. Swedes are extremely hardy and can be left in the ground until needed,

though it is advisable not to leave them for too long or they will become woody. Lift when they are about the size of a grapefruit. They can be stored in boxes in a garage or cool shed. Twist off the leaves and place roots between layers of peat substitute, sawdust or sand in a stout box.

Smaller swedes are more tasty and succulent, so begin lifting as soon as the roots are large enough to use, before they reach their maximum size.

Pests and Diseases
Swedes are affected by the same problems as turnips.

Powdery mildew is common. It appears as a white powdery deposit over shoots, stems and leaves, causing stunted growth. In severe cases leaves become yellow and die. It is more of a problem when plants are dry at the roots and if it is cold at night and warm and dry in the day.

Swedes are susceptible to clubroot – a disease to be avoided at all costs. Roots swell and distort, young plants wilt on hot days but recover overnight, growth is stunted and crops ruined. It is more of a problem on poorly drained, acid soils. Spores remain in the soil for up to 20 years.

Flea beetles are 3mm (⅛in) long and black with yellow stripes. They nibble leaves of seedlings, checking growth.

'Acme', showing its subtle colour and extensive tap roots

COMPANION PLANTING

Swedes grow well with peas.

MEDICINAL

Swedes have been used in folk medicine for the treatment of coughs, kidney stones and whooping cough, though their efficacy has not been recorded.

CULINARY

Swedes can be sliced or cubed and roasted like parsnips, or added to casseroles and stews.

Otherwise, they are delicious mashed with potatoes and served with meat or fish.

To boil, peel off the outer 'skin', cut into slices or cubes and boil for 30 minutes. Drain thoroughly before serving.

Neeps, Tatties and Haggis

Neeps
Serves 4

This is the traditional accompaniment for haggis and tatties (mashed potatoes), washed down with plenty of whisky, on Burns Night in Scotland.

750g (1½lb) swedes
Salt and black pepper
Pinch nutmeg
Butter or olive oil

Clean the swedes, cut them up and boil in enough water to prevent them from burning until tender. Process in a blender or put through a sieve, discarding the juices. Season, and reheat with either butter or olive oil.

Brassica rapa Rapifera Group. *Brassicaceae*

TURNIP

Biennial grown as an annual for globular, swollen root and young leaves. Hardy. Value: low in calories and carbohydrate; small amounts of vitamins and minerals.

This ancient root crop was known to Theophrastus in 400 BC and many early varieties were given Greek place names. Pliny listed 12 distinct types under *rapa* and *napus* – which became *naep* in Anglo-Saxon, and together with the word 'turn' (meaning 'made round'), gave us the common name. Introduced to Canada in 1541, the turnip was brought to Virginia by the colonists in 1609 and was rapidly adopted by the native Americans. In Britain they have found a role in folklore. In Northern Ireland, turnips were made into lamps for Hallowe'en (31 October), and in the Shetland Islands of Scotland slices were shaped into letters and put into a tub of water for young revellers to retrieve with their mouths; they usually tried to pick the initial of someone they loved.

VARIETIES

Turnips are simple to grow and tasty. The leaves (turnip tops) are also delicious.

Earlies
'Purple Top Milan' produces flattish roots with purple markings and white flesh. Tender when young, early maturing and good for overwintering, it has an excellent flavour. **'Purple Top White Globe'** (**'Veitch's Red Globe'**) is an attractive old cultivar with round or slightly flattened roots. It is reddish-purple above ground and white below. 'Snowball' is a delicately flavoured, fast-maturing white variety with cut leaves. **'Tokyo Cross'** is an excellent F$_1$ hybrid that produces small tasty white globes and matures rapidly, in about 35–40 days. A 'mini vegetable' that is also tasty when larger, it is suitable as a late summer to early autumn crop.

'Purple Top Milan'

'Tokyo Cross' is reliable and has an unusual flavour

Maincrops
'Golden Ball' (**'Golden Perfection'** or **'Orange Jelly'**) is a small, round yellow variety that should be grown quickly to keep the flesh succulent. Tasty, hardy and excellent for storing. **'Manchester Market'** has round roots, green skin, white flesh and stores well. **'Green Globe'** is white-fleshed with round roots; excellent for turnip tops.

CULTIVATION

Turnips flourish at about 20°C (68°F) and prefer a sheltered, open site in light, fertile, well-drained but moisture-retentive soil. Summer sowings can be made in moderate shade provided they receive sufficient moisture. Turnips prefer a pH of 5.5–7.0; very acid soil will need liming.

Propagation
Sow early turnips in mid-spring, as soon as the ground is workable, or in late winter or early spring under cloches or fleece.

Prepare the seedbed carefully and sow early turnips thinly in drills about 2–2.5cm (¾–1in) deep, in rows 23cm (9in) apart. Then thin to a final spacing of 10–12.5cm (4–5in). They can also be grown in a grid pattern: mark 12.5cm (5in) squares in the ground with a cane and sow 3 seeds where the 'stations' cross, thinning after germination to leave the strongest seedling.

Sow maincrop varieties from mid- to late summer in drills 2cm (¾in) deep and 30cm (12in) apart, thinning to 15–23cm (6–9in) apart. It is important to thin seedlings when no more than 2.5cm (¾in) high, when the first true leaves appear, to ensure the roots develop properly. Firm the soil after thinning; do not thin turnips grown for tops.

When growing for their tops, prepare the seedbed and broadcast seed over a small area or sow thinly in rows 4–6in (10–15cm) apart as soon as soil conditions allow. Sow early cultivars in spring for summer cropping and hardy varieties in late summer or early autumn. Small seedlings of 'main-crops' overwinter and grow rapidly in spring, making them a useful early crop,

'Snowball', a popular variety

particularly when covered with cloches or fleece. To ensure a prolonged harvest, make successional sowings of 'earlies' from early spring until early summer.

Growing

If the ground has not been manured for the previous crop, double dig in autumn, working plenty of well-rotted organic matter into the soil and allowing it to weather over winter. About a week to 10 days before sowing, remove any weeds or debris and rake general fertilizer into the soil at 60g/sq m (2oz/sq yd). In common with other brassicas, turnips grow poorly on loose soil, so rake the soil to a fine tilth and firm it with the head of a rake or by carefully treading. If the soil is dry, water thoroughly before sowing and stand on a planting board to avoid compacting the soil. Mark each row with canes or twigs, and label and date the crop.

Keep crops weed-free by hand weeding or careful hoeing. Turnips must have a constant supply of water throughout the growing season, otherwise they tend to run to seed or produce small woody roots, while sudden watering or rain after a period of drought causes them to split. They will need up to 9 litres/sq m (2 gal/sq yd) per week during dry periods. This improves the size and quality of the crop, but usually reduces the flavour.

Turnips should be rotated with other brassicas.

Maintenance

Spring Prepare seedbed, sow early varieties under cloches. *Summer* Sow earlies every 2–3 weeks for successional cropping. Keep crops weed-free and water as necessary. From mid- to late summer, sow maincrop varieties. *Autumn* . Sow 'earlies' under cloches mid- to late autumn. Thin maincrop varieties. *Winter* Harvest and store maincrop turnips.

Protected Cropping

Cover ground with cloches, fleece or black polythene for 2–3 weeks in late winter to early spring to warm the ground before sowing early crops. In late summer protect sowings of early cultivars. Maincrop turnips grown for their tops can be grown under cloches after sowing in autumn and picked during winter.

Container Growing

Fast-maturing early varieties grow well in large containers of well-drained, soil-based compost with added organic matter. Water crops well.

Harvesting and Storing

Harvest early varieties when young and tender. Gather those to be eaten raw when they are the size of a golf ball; any time up to tennis ball-size if they are to be cooked. Hand pull them in the same way as radishes.

Maincrop turnips that are lifted in mid-autumn for winter use are much larger, hardier and slower to mature. To keep the flavour, harvest at maturity as they soon become woody and unpalatable. Turnips can be left in the soil and lifted as required using a garden fork. Keep them in a cool place and use within a few days. In cold wet climates, roots are better lifted to prevent deterioration. Twist off the leaves, remove any soil, put the roots between layers of dry peat substitute,

sawdust or sand in a box, then store in a cool shed.

Turnips grown for their tops can be harvested when about 10–15cm (4–6in) high, cutting about 2.5cm (1in) above ground level. Keep soil moist and they will resprout several times before finally running to seed.

Pests and Diseases

Flea beetle, 3mm (⅛in) long and black with yellow stripes, nibble holes in leaves of seedlings, checking growth. Large infestations of mealy aphid may kill young plants or cause black 'sooty mould' on leaves. Cabbage root fly larvae feed on roots; transplanted brassicas are particularly vulnerable. Powdery mildew, a white deposit over shoots, stems and leaves, causes stunted growth. In severe cases leaves yellow and die.

Glazed Turnips

CULINARY

Eat early turnips raw in salads or boiled, tossed in butter and chopped parsley.

Peel maincrop turnips before cooking. They are good mashed, roasted and in casseroles and soups.

COMPANION PLANTING

Growing with peas and hairy tares deters aphids. Turnips are useful for intercropping between taller crops and for catch-cropping.

MEDICINAL

The liquor from turnips sprinkled with demerara sugar was used in folk medicine to cure colds.

Glazed Turnips

Use small young turnips. Scrub them and cut into 1cm (½in) dice (or use whole). Drop into boiling water for 3 minutes. Drain. Melt a little butter and olive oil in a frying pan, add the turnips, sprinkled with a little sugar, and fry over a high heat, stirring constantly, until browned and caramelized. This is particularly delicious with the 'Snowball' variety.

Turnip Tops

Wash well, removing stringy stalks. Chop roughly into manageable pieces. Steam over boiling water until just tender. Serve warm, tossed in olive oil and lemon juice vinaigrette, sprinkled with a finely chopped garlic clove. Or cook like spinach: put the washed leaves in a pan, add salt, pepper and a small knob of butter and steam for 10 minutes in only the water remaining on the leaves. Drain thoroughly and serve immediately.

Brassica oleracea Acephela Group. *Brassicaceae*

KALE

Also known as Borecole, Collards, Colewort, Sprouts. Biennial grown as annual for young leaves and shoots. Hardy. Value: good source of calcium, iron, beta carotene, vitamins E and C.

Kales are exceptionally robust, making an ideal winter crop. In addition, they are untroubled by common brassica problems. A type of primitive cabbage, kales are among the earliest cultivated brassicas (the Romans grew several types), with many similarities to the wild *Brassica oleracea* on the western coasts of Europe. The Celtic 'kale' derives from 'coles' or 'caulis' used by the Greeks and Romans to describe brassicas; the German *Kohl* has the same origin. First recorded in North America by 1669, kales are thought to have been introduced much earlier.

VARIETIES

Varieties are classified into groups, including the true kale, Siberian kale and 'Collards'. These are popular in the southern states of America and other warm climates.

Kales vary in height from dwarf types, about 30–40cm (12–16in) high, to tall varieties growing to 90cm (3ft) and spreading to 60cm (24in). The novelty **'Jersey Kale'** ('Walking Stick Cabbage') is grown for its straight stems to 2.25m (7ft), which can be dried and made into walking sticks.

'Siberian Kale', 'Rape Kale' or 'Curled Kitchen Kale' (Brassica nalpus Pabularia Group)
This is a relative of the swede or rutabaga, grown for the leaves, not the roots. This is variable in form and colour, with broader leaves than kale, which are sometimes curled or frilled. This must be sown *in situ*, not transplanted, cropping when true kales have finished. **'Hungry Gap'** is a late variety, cropping mid- to late spring. **'Laciniato'**, an Italian variety, has deeply cut flat leaves. **'Ragged Jack'** has pink-tinged leaves and midribs. **'Red Russian'** has green/red frilly leaves; excellent flavour. **'True Siberian'** is fast-growing, with blue/green frilly leaves. Can harvest continually throughout winter.

Kale (Scotch Kale, Curly-leaved Kale or Borecole)
True kale usually has dark green or glaucous leaves with heavily frilled margins. **'Darkibor'** is exceptionally hardy with dark green curled leaves. **'Dwarf Blue Curled Scotch'** ('Dwarf Blue Curled Vates') is low-growing, with glaucous leaves, extremely hardy and slow to bolt. **'Dwarf Green Curled'** is compact, hardy and easy to grow; ideal for the small garden or windswept sites. **'Fribor'** is hardy, to about 45cm (18in), maturing from late autumn to late winter. **'Pentland Brig'**, a cross between curly and plain-leaved kale, is grown for the young leaves, side shoots and immature flower heads (which are cooked like broccoli). An excellent vegetable. **'Showbor'** is a 'mini vegetable'. **'Spurt'** produces tender, deep green, curly

'Ragged Jack' is appropriately named, its leaves an interesting contrast to curly-leaved kale

leaves. Ready to harvest 6–8 weeks after sowing, it crops for a long period. Grow as a 'cut and come again' crop. **'Tall Green Curled'** ('Tall Scotch Curled') is excellent for freezing, and shows good resistance to clubroot and cabbage root fly. **'Thousand Head'** is a plain-leaved, tall, old variety and exceptionally hardy. For harvesting through winter and spring.

Collards (or Greens)
These have smooth, thinner leaves than true kale, taste milder and are more heat-tolerant. **'Champion'** has dark green, cabbage-like leaves and is hardy, with good resistance to bolting. **'Georgia'** has glaucous, white-veined leaves; it tolerates poor soil and extreme heat. **'Hicrop Hybrid'** is mild, sweet and slow to bolt.

CULTIVATION

Propagation
Sow in early spring in trays of moist seed compost or modules, or outdoors in seedbeds in milder areas, for summer crops. Sow from late spring for autumn and winter crops. Alternatively, sow thinly in drills 1cm (½in) deep *in situ*, gradually thinning to final spacing, or sow 3 seeds in 'stations' at

The stout stem of curly-leaved kale, topped by its leaves, makes it look like a miniature tree

the final spacing, thinning to leave the strongest seedling. When 10–15cm (4–6in) high, water the rows the day before, then transplant in the early evening, keeping the lowest leaves just above the soil surface. Water well with liquid seaweed after planting and until they become established. The final spacing for dwarf varieties should be 45cm (18in) apart, with taller types 60–75cm (24–30in) apart.

Collards are sown in late spring in areas with cool summers and in late summer in hotter climates.

Sow Siberian kale thinly in early summer, *in situ*, in drills 45cm (18in) apart, thinning when large enough to handle to a final spacing of 45cm (18in) apart.

Growing
Kales are very hardy: some survive temperatures down to -15°C (5°F); others tolerate high summer temperatures. They grow in poorer soils than most brassicas, but flourish in a sunny position on well-drained soil with moderate nitrogen levels. Excessive nitrogen encourages soft growth, making plants prone to damage. Lime acid soils.

Prepare the seedbed when the soil is moist. Lightly fork the surface, remove any weeds, then firm (but do not compact) the soil.

Overwintering crops need top-dressing with high-nitrogen liquid or granular fertilizer at 60g/sq m (2oz/sq yd) in spring to encourage side shoots.

Keep crops weed-free, water thoroughly before the onset of dry weather, mulch with a 5cm (2in) layer of organic matter and in autumn, firm or earth up round the base of taller plants to prevent wind rock. On more exposed sites, they may need staking.

Kales are good where peas, early potatoes or very early crops have been grown. Rotate with brassicas.

'Tall Green Curled'

Maintenance
Spring Sow early crops under cover; in mid-spring sow in trays or modules, or outdoors in a seedbed.
Summer Transplant seedlings, feed and water well during dry spells. Keep weed-free. Harvest regularly.
Autumn Firm round plant bases; stake if necessary.
Winter Harvest regularly.

Protected Cropping
Make early sowings as a 'cut and come again' crop in the greenhouse border or in mild areas outdoors under cloches, from mid- to late winter. Sow in drills the width of a hoe, broadcast thinly, or sow sparingly in drills, thinning to 7.5cm (3in) apart.

Sow kale under cover in mid- to late winter for transplanting from mid-spring onwards when soil conditions are suitable.

Harvesting and Storing
Harvest by removing young leaves with a knife when they are 10–12.5cm (4–5in) long. Cut from several plants for an adequate picking.

Harvest regularly for constant young growth and a long cropping season; older shoots become bitter and tough. Harvest early sowings of 'cut and come again' crops when about 5–7.5cm (2–3in) high, or thin to 10cm (4in) and harvest when 12.5–15cm (5–6in) high.

Pests and Diseases
Kale is resistant to cabbage root fly and clubroot, and is usually ignored by pigeons.

Take necessary precautions against whitefly, cabbage caterpillar and flea beetle. Caterpillars eat irregular holes in the leaves: check regularly for eggs, squashing them. Beware of infestations of cabbage aphids, which check growth and may kill young plants.

COMPANION PLANTING

Kale can be planted with corn and peas.

CULINARY

Young leaves of later varieties taste better after being frosted.

Wash well and boil in 2.5cm (1in) of water for 8 minutes at most. Serve with butter or white sauce – an excellent accompaniment for poached eggs, fried fish, bacon and other fatty meats. Kale is also good with plain fish dishes such as salmon or cod. In parts of North America kale is served with hog jowls, and the juice is eaten with hot corn bread.

Kale can also be used in salads, soups and stews; it can be creamed, or braised with onions, parsley, spices and bacon or ham.

Before freezing, blanch young shoots for 1 minute, then cool, drain and chop. Kale stays fresh for about 3 days in the fridge or in a polythene bag.

Stir-fried Kale
Serves 4

750g (1½lb) young kale
3 tablespoons peanut or olive oil
Salt and freshly ground black pepper
Juice of half a lemon

Thoroughly wash and dry the kale in a salad spinner. Chop it roughly. Pour the oil in a wok or heavy frying pan over a high heat and, when the oil is steaming, toss in the kale and cook for 3 minutes, stirring constantly. Season and add the lemon juice, adding shavings of lemon peel for decoration if you wish. Serve piping hot with stews or roasted meats.

Stir-fried Kale

Brassica oleracea Botrytis Group. *Brassicaceae*

CAULIFLOWER

Annual or perennial grown for immature flowerheads. Hardy or half hardy.
Value: good source of vitamin C, traces of most other vitamins.

Cauliflowers are believed to have originated in Cyprus and the oldest record dates from the sixth century BC. One thousand years later they were still widely grown there, being known in England as 'Cyprus coleworts'. A Jewish-Italian traveller wrote from Cyprus in 1593 that cabbages and cauliflowers were to be found growing in profusion, and, 'For a quattrino one can get more almost than one can carry.' Gerard in his *Herbal* of 1597 calls them 'Cole flowery'. Moorish scholars in twelfth-century Spain described three varieties as introductions from Syria, where cauliflowers had been grown for over a thousand years and were much developed by the Arabs. Even in 1699, John Evelyn suggested that the best seed came from Aleppo (now Halab, in northern Syria). Cultivation methods improved after 1700, and by the end of the eighteenth century the cauliflower was highly regarded throughout Europe. Dr Johnson is said to have remarked, 'Of all the flowers in the garden, I like the cauliflower.' But Mark Twain wrote disdainfully, 'Cauliflower is nothing but cabbage with a college education.' This, of course, is a matter of opinion.

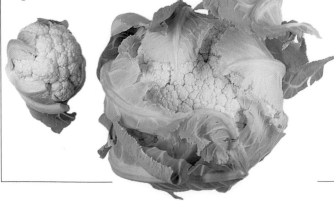

'Dok Elgon', a robust variety for autumn harvest

VARIETIES

There are four main groups for spring, summer, autumn and winter, but many overlap the seasons.

'All the Year Round' is sown in late autumn or spring for spring or summer harvest. Produces good-quality white heads. Excellent for successional sowing. **'Alverda'** has yellow-green heads. Sow late spring to midsummer for autumn cropping. **'Autumn Giant 3'** has beautiful white, firm heads. Excellent for late autumn and winter cropping. **'Castlegrant'** produces deep curds that are well protected from frost. **'Dok Elgon'** is a reliable variety for early and late autumn cropping with firm snow-white heads. **'Early Snowball'** is dwarf and compact, growing well in mild climates. Heads do not discolour in bad weather.

'Limelight' is an attractive soft green cauliflower for autumn harvest. **'Minaret'** has small, tasty, lime-green florets. Crops in late autumn. **'Orange Bouquet'** is pale gold and keeps its colour. **'Purple Cape'** is a hardy overwintering purple type cropping from late winter to mid-spring. Good raw or cooked; the head turns green when cooked. **'Snowball Self Blanching'** is high-yielding, and the leaves naturally blanch the curds. **'Snowcap'** is a very late variety, for harvest in mid- to late winter. **'Veitch's Autumn Giant'** is a huge plant with large leaves and massive heads to 30cm (12in) in diameter. Very tasty; stores well. **'Walcheren Winter 3 – Armardo April'** is an overwintering variety. Hardy, frost-resistant and tasty. **'Walcheren Winter 4 – Markanta'** is one of the hardiest of all overwintering varieties, with pure white heads. **'White Rock'** produces plenty of leaves to protect the curd. It is a very versatile variety.

CULTIVATION

Propagation

Start off crops as described in 'Protected Cropping' unless stated. Plants are ready for transplanting when they have 5–6 leaves; water before moving and retain as much soil as possible around the roots.

Sow successively to ensure regular cropping all year round.

Sow early summer crops in mid-autumn and leave them to overwinter under cover. Harden off in late winter, transplant from mid-spring as soon as the soil is workable and warm. Space plants 50cm (20in) apart with 60cm (24in) between the rows or with 50cm (20in) between the rows and plants. Protect with crop covers until established.

Sow summer cauliflowers in early spring under cover or in a seedbed outdoors if the soil is warm and workable, for transplanting in mid-spring and harvesting from midsummer to autumn. Spacing as above.

Sow early autumn cauliflowers in mid-spring for transplanting in early summer and harvesting from late summer to early autumn. Space 52cm (21in) apart in and between rows, or 50cm (20in) between plants and 60cm (24in) between rows.

Sow autumn cauliflowers in late spring for transplanting in mid-summer and harvesting from mid- to late autumn. Space plants 60cm (24in) apart in and between rows.

If you have available space, sow overwintering cauliflowers, but remember that they can be in the ground for almost a year. Sow in seedbeds outdoors and transplant in midsummer. Winter cauliflowers for harvesting from midwinter to early spring should be 65cm (26in) apart each way; those for cutting from mid-spring

Commercially grown cauliflowers harvested from Britain's Fenlands

to early summer should be spaced 60cm (24in) apart in and between the rows. Most varieties need frost protection to avoid damage to the heads.

Growing

Cauliflowers need a sheltered sunny site on deep, moisture-retentive, free-draining soil with a pH of 6.5–7.5. Dig in plenty of well-rotted organic matter in autumn before planting and lime acid soils where necessary. Avoid planting overwintering types in frost pockets. Rake over the area before planting: the ground should be firm, but not compacted.

Keep plants well watered from germination to harvest, as checks in growth spoil the quality of the heads. They need at least 22 litres/sq m (4 gal/sq yd) every 2 weeks.

Cauliflowers also need moderate nitrogen levels, though excessive amounts encourage soft leafy growth. Overwintering cauliflowers require low nitrogen levels, or they will be too soft to survive colder weather.

Keep crops weed-free with regular hoeing or mulching. Bend a few leaves over the heads of summer varieties to protect them from sunshine; do the same with winter crops to protect plants from frost and snow. Leaves can be easily tied in place with garden twine.

If the weather is hot and dry, mist plants every now and then to maintain humidity and cool temperatures. Unwrap heads occasionally to check for hiding pests. After cutting the head, feed with a general liquid fertilizer or scatter a granular general fertilizer at 15g/sq m (½oz/sq yd) to encourage the sideshoots to grow.

Rotate crops.

The dark florets of 'Purple Cape' do not affect the taste

A mass of leaves hug the developing curds

to handle. Ventilate on warm days, then harden off and transplant as required.

Harvesting and Storing

Harvest cauliflowers successively while they are small, rather than waiting until they all mature. If the heads become brown or if florets start to separate, it is too late: they should be cut. Harvest in the morning, except in frosty conditions when you should wait until midday.

Cauliflowers can be stored for up to 3 weeks by lifting whole plants, shaking the soil off the roots and hanging upside down in a cool shed; mist the heads occasionally to maintain freshness.

Freeze tight heads only. To prepare, divide into sprigs, blanch for 3 minutes in water with a squeeze of lemon juice. Cool, drain, pack carefully and freeze in polythene bags.

Cauliflowers will store, wrapped, in the salad drawer of a refrigerator for up to one week.

PESTS AND DISEASES

Beware of clubroot, cabbage root fly, caterpillars and birds.

COMPANION PLANTING

Plant with rosemary, thyme, sage, onions, garlic, beet and chards.

MEDICINAL

This is another vegetable reputedly good for reducing the risk of cancer, especially of the colon and stomach.

Maintenance

Spring Sow early crops under glass and outdoors in seedbeds. Keep well watered and weed-free. Transplant.
Summer Sow indoors or outdoors in seedbeds. Transplant, harvest.
Autumn Sow overwintering crops. Harvest.
Winter Prepare ground for the following year. Harvest.

Protected Cropping

Sow under a cold frame or under cloches and thin after germination to about 5cm (2in), or sow 2–3 seeds in 'stations' at the required spacing and thin to leave the strongest seedling. Grow on in the seedbed or transplant into small pots or modules. Alternatively, sow directly in small pots or modules and germinate in a propagator or an unheated greenhouse according to the time of year. Pot on when they are large enough

'All Year Round', a popular commercial variety

CULINARY

Separate into florets, boil or steam and serve with cheese or white sauce and grated nutmeg or flaked almonds. Alternatively, dip in batter, fry and eat as fritters.

Sprigs can be served raw with mayonnaise and other dips, or added to soups, soufflés and pickles.

Cauliflower with Chillies Black Mustard Seeds
Serves 4

In Indian cuisine, cauliflower can be cooked into curries but it is more often served dry, as in this recipe from southern India, given to me by the chef at Madras' Chola Hotel. For this dish, buy the washed or white dahl.

5 tablespoons vegetable oil
1/2 teaspoon asafetida
1 teaspoon whole black mustard seeds
1 teaspoon urad dhal
2 dried hot red chillies, left whole
6 fresh hot green chillies, left whole
750g (1 1/2 lb) cauliflower, broken into bite-size florets
Salt
2 tablespoons fresh coconut, grated

Either use a *karhari* or a heavy frying pan. Heat the oil over high heat and add the asafetida, then the mustard seeds. When the seeds pop, add the dhal; this will turn red, at which point add the chillies and cook until the red ones start to darken. Then stir in the cauliflower and cook for a minute or so. Add a tablespoon of water, season with salt and keep stirring, adding more water as necessary; you will probably need to cook for 4–5 minutes, using 4–5 tablespoons water. At this point, turn the heat right down and cook, covered, for a further 5 minutes, until all the liquid has evaporated. Take care not to let the cauliflower burn.

Stir in the coconut and serve, discarding the chillies unless you like really hot food. You have been warned!

Cauliflower with Chillies and Black Mustard Seeds

Cauliflower Soufflé
Serves 4

500g (1lb) cauliflower florets
1 tablespoon butter
1 tablespoon plain flour
150ml (1/4pt) milk
3 large eggs, separated
4 tablespoons grated cheddar
Pinch of nutmeg
Salt and freshly ground pepper

Steam or boil the cauliflower in salted water until just tender. Drain and dice finely. Keep warm. In a heavy saucepan, make a roux from the butter and flour and cook for 1 minute. Stir in the milk and bring to the boil, stirring constantly, to thicken the sauce. Then remove from the heat and stir in the egg yolks. Beat well and add the cheddar and cauliflower, seasoning well. Whisk the egg whites until stiff, then, using a metal spoon, fold into the cauliflower mixture.

Pour into a buttered soufflé dish and cook on the middle shelf of a preheated oven, 190°C/375°F/gas mark 5, until the top is gloriously browned.

This should take about 30–35 minutes. Serve the soufflé immediately.

Summer, autumn and winter cabbages need a dressing of fertilizer after transplanting and will benefit from a further granular or liquid feed in the growing season.

To increase stability, earth up spring and winter cabbages as they grow.

Provided growing conditions are good and plants healthy, you can produce a second harvest from spring or early summer varieties. After cutting the head, cut a cross shape 13mm (½in) deep in the stump, which will sprout a cluster of smaller cabbages.

Keep cabbages moist and weed-free with regular hoeing, hand weeding or mulching. Rotate cabbages with other brassicas.

Maintenance

Spring Sow and transplant summer, autumn and winter cabbage. Harvest.
Summer Sow spring cabbage. Harvest.
Autumn Transplant spring cabbage. Harvest.
Winter Sow summer cabbages. Harvest.

Harvesting and Storing

Spring cabbages are ready to harvest from mid- to late spring. Summer and autumn varieties are ready to harvest from midsummer to mid-autumn. Winter types can be harvested from late autumn to mid-spring.

Spring and summer varieties are eaten immediately after harvest. Dutch winter white cabbages and some red cabbages can be lifted for storing indoors. Choose those that are healthy and undamaged and dig them up before the first frosts for storage in a cool, slightly humid, frost-free place. Remove the loose outer leaves and stand the heads on a slatted shelf or a layer of straw on the shed floor. Alternatively, suspend them in nets.

They can also be stored in a spare cold frame if it is well ventilated to discourage

Spacing between cabbages directly determines the size of 'head'

rotting. They should store for up to 5 months.

Freeze only the best quality fresh crisp heads. Wash, shred coarsely, blanch for about 1 minute and pack into polythene bags or rigid plastic containers.

Wrapped in plastic cling film in a refrigerator, cabbages stay fresh for about a week.

PESTS AND DISEASES

Cabbages suffer from the common brassica problems, including cabbage root fly, clubroot, aphids and birds.

COMPANION PLANTING

Cabbages thrive in the company of herbs like dill, mints, rosemary, sage, thyme and chamomile. They also grow well with many other vegetables including onions, garlic, peas, celery, potatoes, broad beans and beets.

Like all brassicas, they benefit from the nitrogen left in the soil after legumes have been grown. The belief that they do not grow well with vines, oregano and cyclamen stems from Classical times. In the sixteenth century, it was well known that 'Vineyards where Coleworts grow, doe yeeld the worser Wines'.

MEDICINAL

Eating cabbage is said to reduce the risk of colonic cancer, stimulate the immune system and kill bacteria. Drinking the juice is alleged to prevent and heal ulcers.

Some active principles are partly destroyed on cooking, so cabbage is much more nutritious eaten raw.

According to folklore, placing heated cabbage leaves on the soles of the feet reduces fever; placed on a septic wound, they draw out pus or a splinter.

CULINARY

Traditionally cabbage is cooked by boiling – preferably as briefly as possible – in a small amount of water, to preserve the nutrients. Add the cabbage to boiling water, which should not stop boiling while you place the younger leaves from the heart on top of the older leaves below. Cover, cook briefly for 3 minutes, then drain. Or steam for about 6–8 minutes.

Stir-frying is an almost equally rapid method; alternatively, bake, braise or stuff. Use as a substitute for vine leaves in dolmades.

Eat shredded white or red cabbage raw in salads. Coleslaw is a mixture of shredded cabbage, carrot, apple and celery with French dressing or a mayonnaise/sour cream blend; its name derives from *cole*, the old name for cabbage, and the Dutch *slaw*, meaning salad.

Pickle red cabbage in vinegar and white cabbage in brine (as sauerkraut).

Czemona Kapusta
Serves 6

The Polish and Czechs are extremely keen on red cabbage. This dish combines subtle flavours to make a refreshing change from our usual ways of cooking the vegetable.

l kg (2lb) red cabbage, finely sliced
1 teaspoon salt
1 tablespoon butter
1 tablespoon plain flour
150ml (¼pt) red wine
2 teaspoons sugar
Pinch ground cloves
Pinch cinnamon
Freshly ground black pepper

Colcannon

Put the cabbage in a colander and sprinkle with salt; leave for 15 minutes and then rinse well under cold water. Transfer to a heavy pan of boiling water and simmer gently until the cabbage is just cooked. Drain and keep warm. Reserve a little of the liquid.

Heat the butter in a saucepan over a medium heat and mix in the flour to make a roux. Cook for 2 minutes without burning. Dilute with the cooking liquid to make a thick sauce and stir in the cabbage. Season and add the red wine, sugar, cloves and cinnamon. Mix well and simmer for a further 5 minutes. Serve.

Colcannon
Serves 4

Probably the most famous Irish dish, some believe this was traditionally made with kale but today it is commonly made with cabbage. Use a Savoy.

500g (1lb) potatoes, peeled cooked
1 leek, cleaned, sliced and cooked in a little cream or milk
500g (1lb) cabbage, sliced cooked
4 tablespoons butter
Salt and freshly ground black pepper

Mash the potatoes and season them before stirring in the slices of leek and juices in which they were cooked. Then add the cabbage and mix thoroughly over a low heat. Arrange on a warmed serving dish and make a hole in the centre. Keep warm. Partly melt the butter, season, and pour it into the cavity. Serve immediately, piping hot.

Czerwona Kapusta

Brassica oleracea Gongylodes Group. *Brassicaceae*

KOHLRABI

Biennial grown as annual for rounded, swollen roots. Hardy.
Value: rich in vitamin C, traces of minerals.

This odd-looking vegetable with a distinctive name has a rounded, swollen stem which, with the leaves removed, looks like a sputnik! Its common name, derived from the German *Kohl* meaning cabbage and *rabi*, turnip, accurately describes its taste when boiled. Raw, it has a fresh, nutty flavour. Found in northern Europe in the fifteenth century, it may already have existed for centuries, as a similar-sounding vegetable was described by Pliny around AD 70. This highly nutritious, tasty vegetable is more drought-resistant than most brassicas, succeeding where swedes and turnips fail. It deserves to be more widely grown and eaten.

VARIETIES

'Azur Star', a very early variety, has attractive deep blue skin and is resistant to bolting. 'Green Vienna', an early-maturing variety, is green-skinned with white flesh. 'Lanro' is a white-fleshed, green-skinned variety which does not deteriorate when harvested after maturity. 'Purple Vienna' is purple-skinned with white flesh, for late sowing and winter harvesting. 'Rowel' is juicy and sweet, with green skin, white flesh and a crisp texture. It does not become woody if allowed to grow larger than a tennis ball. 'Trero' is sweet, uniform, vigorous and slow to become 'woody'. 'White Vienna' has pale green skin and is delicately flavoured. Other varieties are especially well suited to growing as 'mini vegetables'.

'Purple Vienna', bizarrely shaped

CULTIVATION

Propagation

As a general rule, green varieties are sown from mid spring to midsummer for summer crops and the hardier purple-skinned types from midsummer to mid-autumn for winter use. Sow successionally for a regular harvest.

Early sowings in seed or multi-purpose compost in a propagator at 10–15°C (55–65°F) can be made during midwinter to early spring. Transplant after hardening off in mid-spring when they are no more than 5cm (2in) high; if you let them grow taller or sow seed when soil temperatures are below 10°C (50°F), they are liable to run to seed. Protect with cloches or horticultural fleece until the plants are established.

Water the drills before sowing and sow later crops thinly in drills 1cm (½in) deep in rows 30cm (12in) apart. Thin seedlings when they are about 2.5cm (1in) high and the first true leaves appear, to a final spacing 15–20cm (6–8in) apart. Prompt thinning is vital, as growth is easily checked. Alternatively, plant 3 seeds together in 'stations' 15cm (6in) apart and thin to leave the strongest seedling. Kohlrabi can also be grown successfully in modules and then transplanted at their final spacing.

Kohlrabi grown as a 'mini vegetable' is ideal for the small garden. Sow cultivars like 'Rolano', 'Logo', 'Korist' and 'Kolibra' and thin to about 2.5cm (1in) apart between the plants and rows. Harvest after 9–10 weeks when about the size of golf balls.

Growing

The ideal situation is a sunny position on light, fertile, humus-rich, well-drained soil. Incorporate organic matter the winter before planting if necessary and lime acid soils to create a pH of 6–7. The ground must be firm before planting, as (in common with other brassicas), kohlrabi does not grow well on loose soil. Lightly fork the area, removing any debris, then gently tread down the surface or firm it with the head of a rake. Finally, rake in a general fertilizer at 90g/sq m (3oz/sq yd) and level. Kohlrabi must receive a constant supply of water throughout the season. This is because if growth is checked they can become 'woody'. During drought periods, they need up to 8 litres/sq m (2gal/sq yd) of water per week. If growth slows down, liquid feed with a high-nitrogen fertilizer. Keep crops weed-free and mulch with compost to suppress weeds and retain moisture.

Rotate kohlrabi with brassicas.

Maintenance

Spring Prepare the seedbed and sow seed *in situ* under cloches.

Summer Sow regularly for successional cropping. Sow hardier purple varieties later in the season. Weed and water as necessary.

Autumn Sow in mid-autumn and protect with cloches for early winter harvest.

Winter From late winter, sow early crops in modules or trays. Prepare the ground for outdoor sowings.

Protected Cropping

Early and late outdoor crops should be protected with cloches or crop covers.

Container Growing

Kohlrabi are ideal for containers, particularly when grown as 'mini vegetables'. Plant in a loam-based compost with a moderate fertilizer content and maintain a regular supply of water. Feed every 2–3 weeks with a general liquid fertilizer.

Harvesting and Storing

Kohlrabi matures rapidly and is ready for harvest 2 months after sowing. Lift when plants are somewhere in size between a golf ball and a tennis ball. Larger 'bulbs' tend to become woody and unpalatable, but this is less of a problem with newer cultivars.

CULINARY

There is no need to peel tiny kohlrabi, but peel off the tough outer skin of older globes before cooking. Young ones can be trimmed, scrubbed and boiled whole or sliced for 20–30 minutes, then drained, peeled and served with melted butter, white sauce, or mashed.

Boiled kohlrabi can be made into fritters by frying with egg and breadcrumbs. Add kohlrabi to soups and stews, serve stuffed, cook like celeriac, or eat in a cheese sauce. It complements basil and is excellent steamed.

Kohlrabi globes can also be eaten raw, grated or sliced into salads, and the leaves are good boiled.

Kohlrabi Sautéed in Butter

Harvest as required. In particularly severe weather, they can be lifted and stored in boxes of sand or sawdust. Remove the outer leaves, retaining the central tuft of leaves to keep them fresh. Some flavour tends to be lost during storage.

'Rowel' is best harvested when small

PESTS AND DISEASES

As it matures quickly, kohlrabi is untroubled by many of the usual brassica problems, including clubroot.

Birds can cause severe damage, particularly to young plants. You should protect crops with netting, cages, humming wire or with bird scarers.

Flea beetles – 3mm (⅛in) long and black with yellow stripes – nibble holes in leaves of seedlings, checking growth. Dust plants and the surrounding soil thoroughly with derris or insecticide when symptoms appear. They can also be controlled by brushing a yellow sticky trap or piece of wood covered in glue along the tops of the plants: the insects jump out, stick to the glue and can be disposed of.

Cabbage root fly larvae cause stunted growth, wilting and death. Protect the seedlings when transplanting with 12.5cm (5in) squares of plastic, cardboard or rubberized carpet underlay, slit from edge to centre and fitted around the stems. This stops adults from laying eggs.

COMPANION PLANTING

Kohlrabi grows well with beet and onions.

Brassica oleracea Italica Group. *Brassicaceae*

BROCCOLI

Also known as Sprouting Broccoli, Calabrese. Perennial or annual grown for immature flowerheads. Hardy or half hardy. High in beta carotene, vitamin C, folic acid and iron. Moderate levels of calcium.

Said to have originated in the eastern Mediterranean, early forms of broccoli were highly esteemed by the Romans and described by Pliny in the first century AD. It spread from Italy to northern Europe, arriving in England in the eighteenth century. Philip Miller in his *Gardener's Dictionary* of 1724 called it 'Sprout Cauliflower' or 'Italian Asparagus'.

Broccoli is an Italian word, derived from the Latin *brachium*, meaning 'arm' or 'branch'. Calabrese, a similar plant with the same botanical origin, grown for its larger immature flowerheads, also takes its name from the Italian – meaning 'from Calabria'. This delicious vegetable was introduced to France by Catherine de Medici in 1560, spreading from there to the rest of Europe. 'Green broccoli' was first mentioned in North American literature in 1806, but was certainly in cultivation long before that. It is said to have been introduced by Italian settlers and is extensively grown around New York and Boston.

VARIETIES

Old varieties of perennial broccoli are still available; outstanding among them all is **'Nine Star'**, a multi-headed variety with small white heads. Cropping improves if unused heads are removed before they go to seed.

Sprouting broccoli
This excellent winter vegetable produces a succession of small flowerheads for cropping over a long season from early winter to late spring. It is an excellent crop for poor soils and cold areas. 'Purple' varieties are hardier than the 'white', which have a better taste, crop later, but tend to be less productive.

'Christmas Purple Sprouting' appears early during good weather, ready for your Christmas dinner! **'Purple Sprouting'** crops heavily from early to mid-spring. **'Purple Sprouting Early'** is easy, prolific and extremely hardy. Ready for harvesting from late winter. **'Purple Sprouting Late'** is similar, but ready for picking from mid-spring. **'White Sprouting'** is delicious, with shoots like tiny cauliflowers. **'White Sprouting Early'** is the white equivalent of **'Purple Sprouting'**. **'White Sprouting Late'** is ready to harvest from mid-spring.

Calabrese
Also known as American, Italian or green sprouting broccoli, this produces a large central flowerhead surrounded by smaller sideshoots, which develop after the main head has been harvested. Maturing about 3 months after sowing, it crops from summer until the onset of the first frosts.

'Broccoletto' is quick-maturing and sweet, with a single head. **'Citation'** is an early to mid-season variety with tasty blue-green 'heads'. It is resistant to downy mildew but prone to hollow stems and tends to flower prematurely. **'Early Emerald Hybrid'** produces rich green-blue heads over a season. **'Green Comet'** is early with a large dark-green flowerhead and masses of sideshoots. **'Green Sprouting'**, an old Italian variety, matures early. **'Mercedes'** matures rapidly, producing high-quality, blue-green stems with large flat heads. **'Ramoso'** (**'DeCicco'**), an old Italian variety for spring or autumn

Calabrese should be eaten before the buds turn yellow and flowers emerge

cropping, produces heads over a long period. Tasty, tender and freezes well. **'Romanesco'** is tender with an excellent flavour and lime-green heads. Steam and serve it like asparagus.

CULTIVATION

Propagation

Prepare the seedbed for sprouting broccoli by raking the soil to a fine texture. Sow over several weeks from mid- to late spring, planting the earlier varieties first. Sow thinly in drills in a seedbed, 30cm (12in) apart and 1 cm (½in) deep, thinning to 15cm (6in) apart before transplanting at their final spacing. Alternatively, sow 2–3 seeds in 'stations' 15cm (6in) apart, thinning to leave the strongest seedling.

For early spring crops, sow early maturing cultivars indoors in trays from late summer to early autumn. Transplant seedlings when they are about 13cm (5in) tall into a unheated greenhouse or cold frame. Harden off and transplant outdoors from late winter to mid-spring. Alternatively, sow 2 seeds per module and thin to leave the stronger seedling. The final spacing for plants should be about 68–75cm (27–30in) apart in and between the rows. It is worth noting that they take up a lot of space and have a long growing season!

Calabrese can be sown successively from mid-spring to midsummer for cropping from early summer to autumn. It does not transplant well and is better sown *in situ*. Sow 2–3 seeds at 'stations', thinning to leave the strongest seedling. Close spacing suppresses side shoots and encourages small terminal spears to form, which are useful for freezing. Wider spacing

The popular and prolific **'Purple Sprouting'** broccoli

Calabrese 'Romanesco' is outstanding for its unusual lime-green florets

means higher yields. While they can be as close as 7.5cm (3in) apart with 60cm (24in) between rows, the optimum spacing is 15cm (6in) apart with 30cm (12in) between the rows.

Growing

Sprouting broccoli thrives in a warm, sunny position. Soil should be deep, moisture-retentive and free-draining. Nitrogen levels should be moderate; excessive amounts encourage soft, leafy growth. You should avoid shallow or sandy soils and windy sites.

Sprouting broccoli tends to be top-heavy, so earth up round the stem to a depth of 7.5–13cm (3–5in) to prevent wind rock, or stake larger varieties. Firm stems loosened by wind or frost.

Keep crops weed-free with regular hoeing or mulch with a 5cm (2in) layer of organic matter. Water crops regularly before the onset of dry weather: do not let them dry out. Calabrese needs at least 22 litres/sq m (4 gal/sq yd) every 2 weeks, though a single thorough watering 2–3 weeks before harvesting is a useful option for those under watering restrictions!

Feed with a general liquid fertilizer, or scatter and water in 15g/sq m (½oz/sq yd) of granular fertilizer after the main head has been removed to encourage the side shoots to grow.

Maintenance

Spring Sow early broccoli indoors and later crops in seedbeds. Sow calabrese.
Summer Water crops and keep weed-free. Feed calabrese after harvesting the terminal bud.
Autumn Harvest calabrese, remove and dispose of crop debris.
Winter Harvest broccoli.

Harvesting and Storing

Cut sprouting broccoli when the heads have formed, well before the flowers open, when the stems are 15–20cm (6–8in) long. Regular harvesting is essential, as this encourages side-shoot formation and should ensure a 6–8 week harvest. Never strip the plant completely, or let it flower, as this stops the side shoots forming and makes existing 'spears' woody and tasteless.

Sprouting broccoli can be stored in a polythene bag in the refrigerator. It will keep for about 3 days.

To freeze, soak in salted water for 15 minutes, rinse and dry. Blanch for 3–4 minutes, cool and drain. Pack it in containers and then freeze.

Cut the mature central heads of calabrese with a sharp knife, while still firm and the buds tight. This encourages growth of side shoots within about 2–3 weeks. Pick regularly as for sprouting broccoli.

Calabrese can be stored in the refrigerator for up to 5 days, and freezes well.

PESTS AND DISEASES

Pollen beetle, pigeons and mealy aphids are frequently a problem.

Check regularly for caterpillars.

COMPANION PLANTING

Plant with rosemary, thyme, sage, onions, garlic, beet and chards.

Broccoli makes a magnificent plant for the potager

CULINARY

Remove any tough leaves attached to the stalks and wash florets carefully in cold water before cooking. For the best flavour cook immediately after picking in boiling salted water for 10 minutes, or steam by standing spears upright in 5cm (2in) of gently boiling water for 15 minutes with the pan covered. Drain carefully and serve hot with white, hollandaise or béarnaise sauce, melted butter, or vinaigrette. An Italian recipe book recommends braising calabrese in white wine or sautéing it in oil and sprinkling with grated Parmesan cheese. In Sicily it is braised with anchovies, olives and red wine. Broccoli fritters are dipped in batter, then deep-fried.

Stir-fried florets can be blanched for 1 minute and fried with squid and shellfish. On a more mundane (but practical) level, broccoli and calabrese can be used as a fine substitute in cauliflower cheese.

Penne with Broccoli, Mascarpone and Dolcelatte
Serves 4

500g (1lb) broccoli florets
150g (5oz) mascarpone
200g (7oz) dolcelatte
2 tablespoons crème fraîche
1 tablespoon balsamic vinegar
1 tablespoon dry, white wine
450g (14oz) penne
2 tablespoons capers
4 tablespoons black olives
1 tablespoon hazelnuts, crushed
Salt and freshly ground black
  pepper

Steam the broccoli florets over a pan of boiling water for 2–3 minutes. Run under cold water and set aside. In a heavy pan, gently heat the mascarpone, dolcelatte, crème fraîche, vinegar and wine. Add the broccoli florets. Cook the pasta until it is just tender and drain well. Pour over the hot sauce, sprinkle with the capers, olives and hazelnuts and toss well. Adjust the seasoning and serve.

Brassica rapa Pekinensis Group. *Brassicaceae*

CHINESE CABBAGE

Also known as Chinese leaves, Celery cabbage, Pe Tsai, Peking cabbage. Annual or biennial grown as annual for edible leaves, stems and flowering shoots. Half hardy. Value: moderate folic acid and vitamin C levels.

Chinese cabbage was first recorded in China around the fifth century AD, and has never been found in the wild. It is thought to have been a spontaneous cross in cultivation between the pak choi and the turnip. Taken to the East Indies and Malaya by Chinese traders and settlers who established communities and maintained their own culture, in the 1400s Chinese cabbage could be found in the Chinese colony in Malacca.

By 1751 European missionaries had sent seeds back home, but the vegetable was regarded as little more than a curiosity. Another attempt at introduction was made by a French seedsman in 1845, but the supply became exhausted and the seed was lost. In 1970 the first large-scale commercial crop was produced by the Israelis and distributed in Europe; about the same time it was marketed in the United States as the Napa cabbage, after the valley in California where it was grown. It has become a moderately popular vegetable in the West.

VARIETIES

There are many groups, but three have become popular: the 'tall cylindrical', the 'hearted' or 'barrel-shaped' and the 'loose-headed'.

The cylindrical type has long, upright leaves and forms a compact head, which can be loosely tied to blanch the inner leaves. It is slow-growing, takes about 70 days from sowing to harvest and is most susceptible to bolting. This type is sweet and stores well.

Hearted types have compact, barrel-shaped heads with tightly wrapped leaves and a dense heart. They mature after about 55 days and are generally slow to bolt.

Loose-headed types are lax and open-headed, often with textured leaves. The 'self-blanching' ones have creamy centres, beautifully textured leaves and look good in salads. They are less liable to bolt than headed types. **'Jade Pagoda'** is cylindrical with a firm, crisp head. It takes about 65 days to mature and is cold-tolerant. **'Kasumi'**, a barrel type, has a compact head and is resistant to bolting. **'Nerva'** is similar, maturing quickly, and has dark green leaves with dense heads. **'Ruffles'** is delicious and early-maturing, with lax, pale green heads and a creamy white heart. Early sowings are liable to bolt. **'Santo Serrated Leaved'**, a loose-headed variety, has attractively serrated leaves and makes a good seedling crop. It has good cold resistance. **'Shantung'** has a spreading habit, with tender, light green leaves and a dense heart. **'Tip Top'** is an early variety for spring planting and can be harvested around 70 days from sowing. It is vigorous and produces good-sized heads.

Chinese cabbage ready for picking, showing its open habit

CULTIVATION

Propagation

A cool-weather crop, Chinese cabbage is more likely to bolt in late spring and summer. Use resistant varieties or sow after mid-summer. The chance of bolting increases if young plants are subjected to low temperatures or dry conditions, or suffer from transplanting check.

Sow the main crop *in situ* from mid- to late summer, 2–3 seeds per 'station', spaced 30–35cm (12–14in) apart in and between the rows. Thin to leave the strongest seedling.

Alternatively, sow sparingly in drills and thin to the final spacing.

Otherwise it can be sown in modules or pots, transplanting carefully to avoid root disturbance when there are 4–6 leaves. If the soil is dry, water thoroughly.

Broadcast or sow loose-headed types as 'cut and come again' seedlings. Make first sowings in a cold greenhouse or cold frame in early spring, sow outdoors under cloches or fleece as the weather improves and the soil becomes workable. Summer sowings tend to grow too rapidly and become 'tough', unless it is a cool summer. Make the last sowing under cover in early autumn.

Cut seedlings when they have reached a few centimetres or inches tall, leaving them to resprout.

Seeds can also be sprouted, as for alfalfa.

Growing

Chinese cabbage needs a deep, moisture-retentive, free-draining soil with plenty of organic matter. Excessively light, heavy or poor soils should be avoided unless they are improved by incorporating organic matter or grit. Alternatively, grow in raised beds or on ridges. Dig the soil thoroughly before planting; acid soils should be limed, as the ideal pH is 6.5–7.0. Slightly more alkaline soils are advisable where there is a risk of clubroot.

Chinese cabbage prefers an open site, but tolerates some shade in midsummer.

Water crops thoroughly throughout the growing season; do not let them dry out. They are shallow-rooted and so need water little and often. Mulching is also advisable. Erratic watering can result in damage to the developing head, encouraging rots. Scatter general fertilizer around the base of transplants or feed with a general liquid fertilizer as necessary to boost growth – this is particularly important on poorer soils. Keep crops weed-free.

In late summer, tie up the leaves of hearting varieties with soft twine or raffia. (With self-hearting varieties, this is unnecessary.)

Rotate Chinese cabbage with other brassicas.

Maintenance

Spring Sow early 'cut and come again' seedling crops under cover. Sow later crops outdoors.
Summer Sow in drills from mid- to late summer. Water a little and often, mulch and keep weed-free. Harvest.
Autumn Sow quick-maturing varieties or 'cut and come again' crops outdoors; sow later crops under cover. Harvest.
Winter Harvest 'cut and come again' crops grown under cover.

Protected Cropping

Earlier crops can be achieved by sowing bolting resistant cultivars from late spring to early summer. They need temperatures of 20–25°C (68–77°F) for the first 3 weeks after germination to prevent bolting. Harden off,

Thai workers in evening light, harvesting crops grown on raised beds

transplant, then protect the plants with cloches or with crop covers.

Late summer-sown crops should be transplanted under cover. Space plants about 13cm (5in) apart and grow them as a semi-mature 'cut and come again' crop.

Container Growing

The fast-growing varieties give the best results. Use a 25cm (10in) pot or container and loam-based compost with added organic matter and a thick basal layer of drainage material. Sow seeds 1cm (½in) deep and 2cm (¾in) apart in shallow pots or modules in mid-spring. Transplant seedlings singly into pots when they have 3–4 leaves.

Harvesting and Storing

In autumn, cold-tolerant varieties stand outside for several weeks provided it is dry. Protect from wet and cold using cloches. Lift developing crops and replant in cold frames, or uproot and lay plants on straw, bracken or similar, covering them with the same material if temperatures fall below freezing. Ventilate on warm days.

Harvest as 'cut and come again' seedlings, semi-mature or mature plants and for the flowering shoots. Cut seedlings when they are 2.5–5cm (1–2in) tall. Semi-mature or mature plants can be cut with a sharp knife about 2.5cm (1in) above the ground and will then resprout; after several harvests they will send up a flower head. Harvest the flowering shoots when they are young, before the flowers open.

Harvest mature heads when they are firm.

Chinese cabbage keeps in the salad drawer of the fridge for several weeks. Wash thoroughly before storing. Heads can be stored in a cool, frost-free shed or cellar for up to 3 months. When storing, check plants every 3–4 weeks and remove any diseased or damaged leaves immediately.

PESTS AND DISEASES

Chinese cabbage can be affected by any of the usual brassica pests and diseases. You should take precautions in particular against flea beetle, slugs, snails, caterpillars, clubroot and powdery mildew. Crops grow well under horticultural fleece or fine netting.

COMPANION PLANTING

Plant with garlic and dill to discourage caterpillars. Main crops are ideal after peas, early potatoes and broad beans; late crops are good companions for Brussels sprouts. It is good for cropping between slower-growing vegetables.

Chinese cabbages are sometimes grown as sacrificial crops so that slugs, flea beetles and aphids are attracted to them rather than other crops. In the USA they are used among maize, as they attract corn worms.

Chinese cabbage crop growing near Kanchanaburi, Thailand

WARNING

To minimize the risk of listeria, you should never store Chinese cabbage in plastic bags.

CULINARY

Cook Chinese cabbage only lightly to retain the flavour and nutrients. Steam, quickly boil, stir-fry – or eat raw. (Seedlings are better cooked.) Leaves blend well in raw salads of lettuce, green pepper, celery, mooli and tomato. They also make a delicious warm salad, stir-fried and mixed with orange. Otherwise use in soups, cook with fish, meat, poultry and use in stuffing.

Outer stalks can be shredded, cooked like celery and tossed in butter. In Korea, China and Japan heads are used to make fermented and salted pickles.

Sweet and Sour Chinese Cabbage

Serves 4

2 tablespoons olive oil
1 onion or several shallots, sliced
2 tablespoons white wine vinegar
2 teaspoons sugar
6 tablespoons chopped tomatoes in their juices
750g (1½lb) Chinese cabbage, finely shredded
Salt and freshly ground black pepper

Heat the oil in a heavy-bottomed pan and cook the onions until soft. Stir in the vinegar, sugar and tomatoes and blend well. Add the Chinese cabbage and seasoning. Cook for 10 minutes with the lid on, stirring occasionally, until the cabbage is tender. Serve hot.

Sweet and Sour Chinese Cabbage

Capsicum annuum. Solanaceae

PEPPER & CHILLI

Also known as Sweet Pepper, Bell Pepper, Capsicum, Pimento. Annuals and short-lived perennials grown for edible fruits. Half hardy. Value: very rich in vitamin C and beta carotene.

Both hot and mild peppers come from one wild species, which is native to Central and South America. The name capsicum comes from the Latin *capsa*, meaning a box. It is thought that the hot types were the first to be cultivated; seeds have been found in Mexican settlements dating from 7000 BC, and the Aztecs are known to have grown them extensively. They are one of the discoveries made in the New World by Columbus. He thought he had discovered black pepper, which at the time was extremely expensive, and used the name 'pepper' for this new fiery spice. Spanish and Portuguese explorers then distributed the new kinds of peppers around the world.

Sweet peppers were introduced to Spain in 1493 and were known in England by 1548 and Central Europe by 1585. The Spanish use red sweet peppers to make the spice pimentón and for stuffing green olives. Chilli peppers are notorious for their fieriness. Their heat is caused by the alkaloid capsaicin, which is measured in Scoville Units. Mild chillies are around 600 units. Beware the 'Habanero' types, measured at between 200,000 and 350,000 units!

Peppers will keep for 14 days

VARIETIES

The larger, bell-shaped, mild-tasting sweet peppers eaten as vegetables are members of the *Capsicum annuum* Grossum Group. Green when immature, different cultivars ripen to yellow, orange, red or 'black'.

The smaller, hotter chillies used for flavouring are classed in the *C. a.* Longum Group.

Sweet peppers
'Big Bertha' is one of the largest bell peppers, growing to 18cm (7in) long by 10cm (4in) wide. Excellent for growing in cooler climates and for stuffing. **'Californian Wonder'** has a mild flavour, is good for stuffing and crops well over a long period. **'Calwonder Wonder Early'** grows well in short seasons. Prolific. **'Gypsy'** is an early cropper with slightly tapered fruits. Resistant to tobacco mosaic virus. **'Red Skin'** is compact and ideal for pots and growbags. **'Sweet Chocolate'** is an unusual chocolate-brown colour. Good when frozen whole.

Chilli peppers
'Anaheim' produces tapered, moderately hot fruits over a long period. **'Cayenne Long Slim'** is a hot pepper much used for flavouring. When kept for longer periods it becomes hotter. The moderately hot yellow fruits of **'Hungarian Yellow Wax Hot'** ripen to become crimson. Good for growing in cool areas. **'Italian White Wax'** has pointed fruits which pickle well and are mild-tasting when young. **'Jalapeno'** is extremely hot and can be harvested over a long period. **'Large Red Cherry'** is extremely hot, with flattened fruits ripening to cherry red. Good for drying and ideal in curries, pickles and sauces. **'Red Chili'** is a high-yielding extremely hot variety, for pickling or drying. Fruits are narrow and tapered. **'Ring of Fire'** is, not surprisingly, hot-fruited. Early cropping, producing short, thin cayenne-type peppers. **'Serrano'** is extremely hot with orange-red fruits. It is prolific and can be dried. **'Tabasco Habanero'** – as the name suggests – is lethal!

CULTIVATION

Propagation

Sow seed indoors from mid-
to late spring in trays,
modules or pots of moist
seed compost at 21°C
(70°F). Lower temperature
gradually after germination.
Transplant into 8–9cm
(3–3½in) pots when 3 true
leaves appear, repotting
again into 10–13cm (4–5in)
pots when sufficient roots
have been formed. Move
plants into their final
position when about 10cm
(4in) high and the first
flowers appear. Harden off
outdoor crops in cool
temperate zones and
transplant in late spring to
early summer when the soil
is warm and there is no
danger of frost.

Space standard varieties
38–45cm (15–18in) apart;
dwarf varieties should be
spaced 30cm (12in) apart.

Growing

Sweet peppers and chillies
flourish outdoors in warmer
climates. More successful
under cover in cooler zones,
they can be grown outside
in mild areas or warm
microclimates but benefit
from protection with
cloches or fleece. Chillies
tend to be more tolerant of
fluctuating temperatures
and high or low rainfall and

**Sweet peppers are best grown
under glass in cool climates**

grow in marginally less
fertile soil. Blossom drops
when night temperatures
fall below 15°C (60°F). Soil
should be moisture-retentive
and free-draining on
ground manured for the
previous crop. Alternatively,
dig in plenty of well-rotted
organic matter in autumn or
winter prior to planting.
Rake in a granular general
fertilizer at 135g/sq m
(4oz/sq yd) before planting.

Keep the soil moist and
weed-free; mulching is
recommended. Feed with a
general liquid fertilizer if
plants need a boost.
Excessive nitrogen can
result in flower drop.

If branches are weak and
thin, when the plant is
about 30cm (12in) tall
remove the growth tips from
the stems to encourage
branching. Normally, they
branch naturally. Support
with a cane if necessary.

Maintenance

Spring Sow seeds under
cover. Transplant when the
danger of frost is passed or
grow in an unheated
greenhouse.
Summer Keep crops weed-
free; damp down the
glasshouse in warm weather.
Harvest.
Autumn Cover outdoor
crops where necessary.
Harvest.
Winter Prepare the ground
for outdoor crops.

Protected Cropping

Crops are better grown
under glass, polythene, cold
frames or cloches in cool
temperate climates. In
glasshouse borders, prepare
the soil as for 'Growing'.
Keep it moist but not
waterlogged and mist with
tepid water to maintain
humidity and help fruit set.

Sow in mid-spring for
growing in a greenhouse
and in late spring for crops
under cloches. Ventilate well
during hot weather. If you
are growing dwarf varieties
on a sunny windowsill, you
should turn pots daily to
ensure even growth.

Peppers have the luxury of a choice of colours: here they are 'black'

Plants grown under
cloches may outgrow their
space: rigid cloches can be
turned vertically and
supported with canes.
Alternatively, use
polycarbonate sheeting.

Container Growing

Grow under cover or
outdoors. Plant in 20–25cm
(8–10in) pots of loam-based
compost with moderate
fertilizer levels or in
growbags. Dwarf varieties
can be grown successfully in
pots on windowsills. Keep
the compost moist but not
waterlogged and mist with
tepid water, particularly
during flowering to assist
fruit set.

Water frequently in warm
weather, less at other times.

Harvesting and Storing

Harvest with scissors or
secateurs when sweet
peppers or chillies are
green, or leave on the plant
for 2–3 weeks to ripen and
change colour. Picking them
when they are green
increases the yield.

Peppers may be stored in
a cool, humid place for up
to 14 days at temperatures
of 13–15°C (55–58°F).

Towards the end of the
season, uproot plants and
hang them by the roots in a
frost-free shed or green-
house; fruits will continue to
ripen for several months.

The heat of chillies
increases with the maturity of
the fruit. Fresh chillies keep
for up to 3 weeks in the
refrigerator in a paper bag.
Or store them in an airtight
jar in a dark cupboard.

Chillies can either be
dried and used whole or
ground into powder.

Both sweet peppers and
chillies freeze successfully.

**Chillies become hotter as they
mature**

PESTS AND DISEASES

Red spider mite can be a nuisance under cover. Slugs can damage seedlings, stems, leaves and fruits. Remove any decaying flowers or foliage immediately.

COMPANION PLANTING

The capsicum family grows well with basil, okra and tomatoes.

MEDICINAL

Capsaicin increases the blood flow and is used in muscle liniments. It is said to help the body metabolize alcohol, acts as expectorant, and prevents and alleviates bronchitis and emphysema. 10 to 20 drops of red-hot chilli sauce in a glass of water daily (or hot spicy meals 3 times a week) can keep airways free of congestion, preventing or treating chronic bronchitis and colds. It stimulates endorphins, killing pain and inducing a sense of wellbeing.

WARNING

Ventilate the kitchen when using chillies. If you have sensitive skin, wear rubber gloves to handle them and always avoid touching your eyes or other sensitive areas after handling.

CULINARY

Sweet peppers add both colour and taste to the table. They can be eaten raw in salads, roasted or barbecued, fried or stir-fried, stuffed with rice, fish or meat mixtures, and used in countless casseroles and rice dishes.

Chillies are used in chilli con carne, curries and hotpots. Removing the internal ribs and seeds reduces the heat intensity.

Paprika is the dried and powdered fruits of sweet peppers. Cayenne pepper is dried and ground powder made from chillies.

If chilli is too strong, it can cause intestinal burning – cucumber, rice, bread and beans are a good antidote. By coating the tongue, the fat content of yoghurt and butter soothes a chilli-burnt mouth. Water only makes things worse.

If you're uninitiated at eating chilli peppers, start with small doses and build up tolerance of heat. Excessively hot peppers can cause jaloproctitis or perianal discomfiture.

Mrs Krause's Pepper Hash
Serves 6

William Woys Weaver in *Pennsylvania Dutch Country Cooking* quotes this recipe from Mrs Eugene F. Krause of Bethlehem, who lived in the early part of the century and was renowned for her peppery hashes.

6 green peppers, deseeded finely chopped
6 red peppers, deseeded finely chopped
4 onions, finely chopped
2 small pods hot chilli peppers, deseeded and finely chopped
1½ tablespoons celery seeds
375ml (12fl oz) cider vinegar
250g (8oz) brown sugar
1½ teaspoons sea salt

Combine the peppers, onion, hot chilli peppers and celery seeds in a non-reactive preserving pan. Heat the vinegar in a non-reactive pan and dissolve the sugar and salt in it. Bring to a fast boil, then pour over the pepper mixture. Then cook over a medium heat for 15 minutes, or until the peppers begin to discolour.

Pack into hot sterilized preserving jars, seal, and place in a 15-minute water bath. Let the pepper hash mature in the jars for 2 weeks before using.

Duvec
Serves 4

This is a Croatian recipe and has subtle flavours. It makes an excellent one-dish supper and uses up leftovers as well.

1 onion, finely sliced
2 tablespoons olive oil
2 cloves garlic, crushed
3 sweet red, green or yellow peppers, deseeded and diced
500g (1lb) tomatoes, peeled and deseeded
100g (4oz) rice, cooked
500g (1lb) leftover cooked meat
450ml (¾pt) stock
Salt and freshly ground black pepper

Cook the onions in the oil in a heavy pan over medium heat until softened. Grease an ovenproof dish and put in a layer of onion and garlic, followed by one of peppers, then one of tomatoes, one of rice and bite-sized pieces of meat. Repeat the layers until all the ingredients are used up, seasoning as you go.

Pour in the stock, cover and bake in a preheated oven, 180°C/350°F/gas mark 4, for about 45 minutes.

Remove the covering and continue cooking for a further 15 minutes. Serve.

Mrs Krause's Pepper Hash

Cicer arietinum. Papilionaceae

CHICKPEA

Also known as Dhall, Egyptian Pea, Garbanzo, Gram. Annual grown for seed sprouts, seeds, young shoots and leaves. Tender. Value: high in protein, phosphorus, potassium, most B vitamins, iron and dietary fibre.

Chickpeas originated in the northern regions of the fertile crescent. Evidence of their ancient use as a domesticated crop was found at a site in Jericho and dated to around 6500 BC. Seeds excavated in Greece indicate that the chickpea must have been introduced to Europe with the first food crops arriving from the Near East. Today it is cultivated worldwide in sub-tropical or Mediterranean climates as a cool-season crop, needing about 4–6 months of moderately warm, dry conditions to flourish. It is the world's third most important pulse after peas and beans, and 80% of the crop is produced in India. It is eaten fresh or dried, made into flour, used as a coffee substitute and grown as a fodder crop. The plant grows about 30cm (12in) tall, with compound leaves of up to eight toothed leaflets. Its tiny white- or blue-tinged flowers are followed by a small flat pod containing one or two round seeds, each with a small 'beak' – hence the common name 'chickpea'.

6–10cm (2½–4in) deep with the rows 50cm (20in) apart, thinning to 25cm (10in) between plants after germination. Alternatively, sow 3–4 seeds in 'stations' 25cm (10in) apart and thin to leave the strongest seedling.

Growing

Dig over the area thoroughly before planting, adding organic matter to poor soils. Rake over the area to create a fine tilth and water well before sowing if the seedbed is dry. Alternatively, soak the seeds for an hour. Keep crops weed-free during the early stages; as plants mature, their spreading habit naturally stifles weed growth. Chickpeas are drought-tolerant, but watering just before flowering and as the peas begin to swell improves productivity. Rotate with other legumes and leave the roots in the ground after harvest to provide nitrogen for the following crop.

Chickpea in pod, showing the head and small 'beak'

VARIETIES

The smooth-seeded 'Kabuli' race is dominant throughout the Mediterranean and Near East and the wrinkled-seeded 'Desai' type in Ethiopia, Afghanistan and India. The following are Indian cultivars: **'Annegeri'** is a semi-spreading high-yielding variety with yellowish-brown seeds. It is deep-rooting and needs good soil, but a coarse tilth is adequate. **'Avrodhi'** has medium-sized brown seeds and is wilt-resistant. **'Bheema'**, a semi-spreading variety, has large, light brown smooth seeds and is suitable for drought-prone or low-rainfall areas.

CULTIVATION

Chickpeas need a light, fertile, well-drained soil in full sun.

Propagation

Seeds can be broadcast or sown in drills during winter in Mediterranean regions or after the rains in sub-tropical climates. Broadcasting is very simple. Prepare the soil using the 'stale seedbed' method, raking and levelling, allowing the weeds to germinate and hoeing them off before sowing. Then scatter the seed evenly, raking the soil twice – first in one direction, then again at 90° to ensure even coverage. Chickpeas can also be sown in drills

A lilac-flowered variety, growing in the USA

Maintenance

Spring Dig over the planting area, adding organic matter where needed.
Summer Keep crops weed-free. Water in prolonged drought, just before flowering and as the peas swell.
Autumn Harvest crops.
Winter Dig over the planting area, adding organic matter where needed.

Protected Cropping

In cooler climates, sow seeds in early spring into small pots of moist seed compost in a glasshouse or on a windowsill. Harden off in late spring and plant outdoors once there is no danger of frost. Growing crops in cloches or polythene tunnels increases the yield.

Container Growing

They can be grown in containers, but seed production levels do not make them a worthwhile proposition as a crop plant.

Harvesting and Storing

Crops are ready after about 4–6 months. Harvest when leaves and pods turn brown; don't leave it too late, or the seeds will be lost when the pods split. Cut the stems at the base and tie them together before drying upside down in a dry, warm place. Collect the dry seeds and store in airtight jars.

Peas can also be harvested fresh for cooking, but fresh ones deteriorate rapidly and should be used as soon as possible.

Sprouting Seeds

Always buy untreated chickpeas for sprouting, as seed sold for sowing is often treated with chemical dressings. Soak seeds overnight or for several hours in boiling water, tip into a sieve and rinse. Put several layers of moist paper towel or blotting paper in the base of a jar and cover with a layer of seed. Cut a square from a pair of tights or piece of muslin and cover the top, securing with a rubber band. Place in a bright position, away from direct sunshine, maintaining constant temperatures around 20°C (68°F). Rinse the seed 3–4 times a day by filling the jar with water and pouring off again. Harvest after 3–4 days when the 'sprouts' are about 12mm (½in) long.

Pests and Diseases

Plants can suffer from root rot. They turn black and finally dry up, leaves fall and the stems desiccate. Ensure the soil is well drained and destroy affected crops immediately. The acidic secretions from the glandular hairs are a good defence against most pests.
  Gram pod borer caterpillars feed on the crop from seedlings to maturity, damaging seedpods and the immature seeds. Spray with pyrethrum.

MEDICINAL

The leaves are astringent and used to treat bronchitis. They are also boiled and applied to sprains and dislocated bones; the exudate is used for indigestion, diarrhoea and dysentery. The seeds are a stimulant, tonic and aphrodisiac. In Egypt they are used to gain weight, and to treat headaches, sore throat and coughs. Powdered seed is used as a facepack and also in dandruff treatment.

WARNING

The whole plant and seed pods are covered with hairs containing skin irritants. You must always wear gloves when harvesting.

CULINARY

With a protein content of 20%, chickpeas are an important meat substitute and good for children and expectant and nursing mothers. Chickpeas are used fresh or dried. They are ground into 'gram flour' (used in vegan cooking), and the ground meal is mixed with wheat and used for chapatis. Whole chickpeas are fried, roasted (to eat as a snack) and boiled. To make hommous or hummus, grind boiled chickpeas into a paste, mix with olive or sesame oil, flavour with lemon and garlic and eat on pitta bread or crackers.

Chickpeas are also used to make dhall' and are found in spicy side dishes, vegetable curries and soups. The young shoots and leaves are used as a vegetable and cooked like spinach – boiled in soups, added to curries or fried with spices.

Puréed Chickpeas
Serves 4

300g (10oz) dried chickpeas, soaked overnight
2 tablespoons olive oil
1 onion, sliced finely
3 garlic cloves, crushed
300g (10oz) tomatoes, peeled, deseeded and chopped
Salt and freshly ground black pepper

Drain the chickpeas, put in a heavy-bottomed saucepan, cover with fresh water and cook until tender. This will take up to 1½ hours, depending on the age of the chickpeas. Drain. Purée through a *mouli légumes*.
  Heat the oil in a frying pan, sauté the onion until softened, add the garlic and cook for 30 seconds longer. Add the tomatoes and simmer for 5 minutes before adding the chickpea purée. Season well and serve immediately.

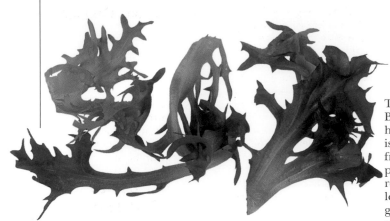

Cichorium endivia. Asteraceae

ENDIVE

Also known as Escarole, Batavian Endive, Grumolo. Annual or biennial grown as annual for blanched hearts and leaves. Value: rich in iron, potassium and beta carotene; moderate vitamin A and B complex.

The origins of this plant are obscure, but it was certainly eaten by the Egyptians long before the birth of Christ and is one of the bitter herbs used at Passover. Mentioned by Ovid, Horace, Pliny and Dioscorides, it was highly valued by the Greeks and Romans as a cultivated plant. It was introduced to England, Germany, Holland and France around 1548 and was described by several writers. The French at first used it primarily as a medicinal plant – to 'comfort the weake and feeble stomack' and to help gouty limbs and sore eyes. European colonists took it to America in 1806 and created a confusion that dogs transatlantic cookery books to this day. The French name of *chicorée frisée* – 'curly chicory' – must have travelled with it, so the USA calls the leafy green plants described here 'chicory'. (Even more confusingly, its forced 'Witloof' cousin, known as chicory in Britain, is *endive* in France and 'endive' or 'Belgian endive' in America.)

VARIETIES

There are two types. The Batavian, scarole or escarole has large, broad leaves and is an upright plant. Curly, or fringed frisée is a really pretty plant, with a low rosette of delicately serrated leaves. Curled varieties are generally used for summer cropping; the more robust broad-leaved types tolerate cold, are disease-resistant and grow well in winter.

'**Broad Leaved Batavian**' has tightly packed heads of broad, deep green leaves which become creamy-white when blanched. '**En Cornet de Bordeaux**', an old variety, is very tasty, extremely hardy and blanches well. '**Green Curled Ruffec**', a curly type, is easily blanched and makes a good garnish. Very hardy and cold resistant. '**Green Curled**' ('**Moss Curled**') produces compact heads of dark green, fringed leaves. '**Ione**' has light green finely cut leaves, with a creamy heart and mild taste. '**Limnos**' is a vigorous variety which is slow to bolt with broad upright leaves and a yellow heart. '**Riecia Pancalieri**' has very curly leaves with white, rose-tinged midribs. '**Salad King**' is prolific and extremely hardy, with large, dark green, finely cut leaves. '**Sanda**' is vigorous and resistant to tip burn, cold and bolting. '**Scarola Verde**' is broad-leaved with a large

Endive leaves are slightly bitter

Endive needs an open site

head and green and white leaves. It may bolt in heat. '**Très Fine Maraichère**' ('**Coquette**') has finely cut curled leaves. Mild and delicious, it grows well in most soils. '**Wallone Frisée Weschelkopf**' ('**Wallone**') has a large, tightly packed head with finely cut leaves. Vigorous and hardy.

CULTIVATION

Propagation
Sow thinly, 1cm (½in) deep *in situ* or in a seedbed, pots or modules to transplant. Allow 30–38cm (12–15in) between plants and rows.

Endive best germinates at 20–22°C, (68–72°F). Sow early crops under cover and shade summer crops.

Sow from early to mid-summer for autumn crops, in late summer for winter crops, using curled or hardy Batavian types. Sow all year round for 'cut and come again' seedlings or semi-mature leaves, making early and late sowings under glass.

Growing
Endive needs an open site, though slimmer crops tolerate a little shade. Soils should be light, moderately rich and free-draining; this

is particularly important for winter crops. If necessary, dig in plenty of well-rotted organic matter before planting. Excess nitrogen encourages lush growth and makes plants prone to fungal diseases.

Endive is a cool-season crop, flourishing between 10–20°C (50–68°F), yet it withstands light frosts; hardier cultivars withstand temperatures down to -9°C (15°F). Higher temperatures tend to encourage bitterness, though 'curled' types are heat-tolerant. Young plants tend to bolt if temperatures fall below 5°C (41°F) for long. Keep crops weed-free; mulch and water thoroughly during dry weather, as dryness at the roots can cause 'bolting'. Use a general liquid fertilizer to boost growth if necessary.

Blanch to reduce bitterness and make leaves more tender. Many newer cultivars have tight heads and some blanching occurs naturally. Damp leaves are likely to rot, so choose a dry period or dry plants under cloches for 2–3 days. Draw the outer leaves together and tie with raffia 2–3 weeks before harvest, placing a tile, piece of cardboard or dinner plate over the centre of the plant, and covering with a cloche to keep off the rain. Alternatively cover the

Fringed frisée is attractive

whole plant with a bucket or a flower pot with its drainage holes covered. Blanching takes about 10 days. Blanch a few at a time; they rapidly deteriorate afterwards.

Maintenance
Spring Sow early crops under glass or cloches. Harvest late crops under cover.
Summer Sow curly varieties outdoors in seedbeds for transplanting, or *in situ*. Keep early-sown crops weed-free and moist. Harvest.
Autumn Sow outdoors and under cover. Harvest.
Winter Sow under cover and harvest.

Protected Cropping
Sow hardy cultivars under cover in trays or modules at 20°C (68°F) in mid-spring for early summer crops and maintain a minimum temperature of 4°C (39°F) after germination for 3 weeks after transplanting to prevent bolting.

For winter and early spring crops, transplant in early autumn from seed trays or modules under cover. Sow 'cut and come again' crops under cover in early spring, and in early autumn.

Endive grows better than lettuce in low light and is also a useful crop for the greenhouse in winter.

Container Growing
Sow directly or transplant into large containers of loam-based compost with added well-rotted organic matter. Keep compost moist and weed-free. Use a general liquid fertilizer to boost growth if necessary.

The more tolerant 'Batavian'

Harvesting and Storing
Harvest endive from 7 weeks after sowing, depending on cultivar and season.

'Cut and come again' seedlings may be ready from 5 weeks. With some cultivars, only one or two cuts may be possible before they run to seed. Pick individual leaves as needed or harvest them using a sharp knife about 2cm (³/₄in) above the ground, leaving the root to resprout.

The whole plant can be lifted in autumn and put in a cool, dark place to blanch.

Leaves do not store well and are better eaten fresh. They last about 3 days in a polythene bag in the salad drawer of a refrigerator.

PESTS AND DISEASES

Protect plants from slugs and control aphids.

Keep winter crops well watered and mulched to prevent tip burn.

COMPANION PLANTING

Endive is good for inter-sowing and intercropping.

CULINARY

Endive is used mainly in salads with – or instead of – lettuce and other greens; the slightly bitter taste and crisp texture gives it more of a 'bite' than the usual lettuce combinations. It suits strongly flavoured dressings. Crisp lardons of bacon or croutons are often included. With mature endive, use the inner leaves for salads; the outer ones can be cooked as greens. Endive can also be braised. Try serving it shredded and dressed with hot crushed garlic, anchovy fillets and a little olive oil and butter.

Warm Red and Yellow Pepper Salad
Serves 6

The slightly bitter taste of curly endive (escarole or frisée) is ideal combined with other lettuces such as lamb's lettuce or watercress in winter months. The

sweetness of the peppers in this dish happily complements the endive.

1 large endive, washed roughly chopped
Big bunch lamb's lettuce, washed
2 large red peppers
3 tablespoons olive oil
3 cloves garlic, crushed
1 tablespoon fresh herbs
Salt and freshly ground black pepper

For the dressing:

3 tablespoons extra virgin olive oil
1 tablespoon white wine vinegar
Salt and freshly ground black pepper

Arrange the lettuces in a large bowl. Core and deseed the peppers and cut them into thin strips. Heat the oil in a heavy pan and sauté the peppers, stirring constantly. Add the garlic after 5 minutes and cook for a further minute.

Add the peppers to the salad. Make the dressing and toss in the herbs and seasoning. Serve the salad alongside plain grilled fish or chicken.

Cichonum intybus. Asteraceae

CHICORY

Also known as Witloof, Belgian Endive, Succory, Sugar Loaf Chicory, Radicchio. Hardy perennial grown as annual for blanched leaves or root. Very hardy. Value: moderate levels of potassium.

A native of Europe through to central Russia and western Asia, chicory has been cultivated for centuries. Pliny tells us that *cichorium* is a Greek adaptation of the Egyptian name; he also noted its medicinal use as a purgative and the blanching of leaves for salads.

Large-rooted varieties have long been used dried, ground and roasted as a substitute for coffee – particularly popular in England during the Napoleonic wars when a blockade of the French coast cut supplies. It has a distinctive fragrance and is often drunk by those who like the taste of coffee without caffeine. John Lindley in the nineteenth century recorded that roasted chicory was adulterated with a multitude of substances as diverse as marigolds, oak bark, mahogany sawdust and even baked horse liver!

Gibault in his *Histoire des Legumes* of 1912 tells of the accidental discovery in the 1840s that Witloof chicory could be blanched. The head gardener at Brussels Botanic Gardens wanted to bring on winter chicory in frames. He lifted several roots, chopped off the foliage and planted them. Soon small, tight shoots emerged through the soil. Next season he did the same. He kept his find a secret, but when he died his widow told her gardener, who passed it on and the technique is now widely practised. Perhaps it is due to this Brussels connection that the vegetable's American name is 'Belgian endive'.

VARIETIES

Chicory has a distinctive, slightly bitter flavour. Most varieties are hardy and make a good winter crop with colourful, attractive leaves. There are three types.

'Forcing' chicories like 'Witloof' (that is, whiteleaf) produce plump, leafy heads (known as 'chicons') when blanched. 'Red chicory' or 'radicchio' includes older cultivars which responded to the reduced daylength and lower temperatures of autumn by turning from green to red; newer cultivars are naturally red and heart earlier. 'Non-forcing' or 'sugarloaf' types produce large-hearted lettuce-like heads for autumn harvest.

'Brussels Widoof' ('Witloof de Brussels') is one of the most famous forcing types which is also grown for its root. 'Grumolo Verde' is non-forcing and very cold-hardy, with rounded leaves. 'Large Rooted Magdeburg' ('Magdeburg'), like 'Brussels Witloof', is grown mainly for its root, which matures after about 17 weeks. Young leaves can be harvested. 'Palla rossa Zorzi Precoce' is a radicchio with a tangy, delicate flavour. It colours better in cool weather. 'Rossa di Treviso', another radicchio, has crisp, green leaves that become deep red and veined with white in cooler conditions. Tolerates light frost. Dates back to the sixteenth century. 'Rossa di Verona' is a radicchio with a spreading habit that withstands considerable frost. 'Sugarhat' is a non-forcing sugarloaf variety that has sweet leaves. 'Witloof Zoom', a forcing chicory, produces tightly packed, high-quality leaves.

CULTIVATION

Propagation
Sow seed of forcing varieties thinly in late spring to early summer in drills 1cm (½in) deep and 23–30cm (9–12in)

'Red chicory', or 'radicchio'

Some varieties are very pretty

Sugarloaf' (non-forcing variety)

Maintenance

Spring Sow early radicchio under cover, transplant from mid-spring. Sow sugarloaf types as 'cut and come again' crops.
Summer Harvest early radicchio and sow maincrop. Sow sugarloaf outdoors for 'cut and come again' and autumn maincrop.
Autumn Harvest radicchio crops sown early to mid-summer; sow late crops for winter. Lift forcing types or force outdoors. Sow sugarloaf indoors.
Winter Force roots indoors successively until spring. Sow sugarloaf indoors.

Protected Cropping

Non-forcing varieties can be grown under glass, for early or late crops.

In autumn, cover outdoor crops of radicchio with cloches, fleece or similar to extend the growing season.

Container Growing

All chicories can be grown in large containers or beds of loam-based compost.

Forcing

Force 'chicons' indoors if soil is heavy, if winters are severe, or for earlier crops. In mid- to late autumn when the foliage dies down, lift

apart. Thin when the first true leaves appear to 20cm (8in) apart.

Sow early radicchio under cover in seed trays and modules before hardening off and transplanting from mid-spring for summer harvest, using early maturing types first. Sow for autumn harvest from early to mid-summer, and in mid- to late summer for transplanting under cover in autumn and cropping over winter. Thin to 23–38cm (9–15in) in and between the rows.

Non-forcing or sugarloaf types can be broadcast or sown in broad drills under cover in late winter. When the soil warms and the weather improves, sow successively outdoors until late summer. Sow the final crop during early autumn under cover.

Thin to a final spacing of 23–30cm (9–12in) in and between the rows. For a semi-mature 'cut and come again' winter crop, sow seed from mid- to late summer and transplant indoors in autumn.

Growing

Chicories prefer an open, sunny site, but tolerate a little shade. Soil should be fertile and free-draining, with organic matter added for the previous crop: avoid recently manured ground, as this causes the roots to fork.

Radicchio tolerates most soils except gravel or very heavy clay. The ideal pH is 5.5–7. Rake soil to a fine texture before sowing. Apply a general balanced fertilizer at 30g/sq m (1oz/sq yd).

Keep weed-free with regular hoeing or mulching. Water thoroughly during dry weather to prevent bolting.

Force appropriate varieties *in situ* if soil is light and winters are mild. In late autumn to early winter, cut back the leaves to 2.5cm (1in) above ground level. Form a ridge of friable soil 15–20cm (6–8in) high over the stumps and cover with straw or leaf mould. After about 8–12 weeks, when the tips are appearing, remove the soil and cut the heads off at about 2.5cm (1in) above the neck. Keep the compost moist while the 'chicons' are growing.

roots carefully, discard any forked or damaged ones and keep those that are at least 3–5cm (1½–2in) in diameter at the top.

Cut off the remaining leaves to within 1cm (½in) of the crown, trim back the side and main roots to about 20–23cm (8–9in). Pack horizontally in boxes of dry sand, peat substitute or sawdust and store in a cool, frost-free place.

For forcing, remove a few roots from storage at a time.

Plant about 5 to 6 roots in a 23cm (9in) pot of sand or light soil, ensuring that 1cm (½in) of the crown is above the surface. Surround the roots with moist peat or compost, leaving the crown exposed above ground.

Water sparingly and cover with a black polythene bag, an empty flower pot with the holes blocked up, or an empty box. Maintain temperatures of 10–15°C (50–60°F). They can also be blanched in a dark cellar or shed or under greenhouse staging (see 'Growing').

The blanched 'chicons' should be ready for cutting within 4 weeks, depending on the temperature.

Roots may resprout, producing several smaller shoots which can then be blanched.

Harvesting and Storing

Harvest chicories grown for roots after the first frost.

Cut heads of mature sugarloaf varieties with a sharp knife 2.5cm (1in) above the soil in late autumn; use immediately or store in a frost-free place.

Allow the plants to resprout as a 'cut and come again' crop under cloches.

Pick radicchio leaves as required, taking care not to over-harvest, as this weakens plants. Alternatively, cut the whole head and leave the roots to resprout.

'Chicons' can be stored in the refrigerator, wrapped in foil or paper to prevent them from becoming bitter. Non-forcing chicory will stay fresh for up to 1 month.

PESTS AND DISEASES

Though seldom troubled by pests and diseases, crops can rot outdoors in cold weather.

COMPANION PLANTING

The blue flowers of chicory are attractive in the ornamental border.

MEDICINAL

Chicory is said to be a digestive, diuretic and laxative, reducing inflammation. A liver and gall bladder tonic, it is used for rheumatism, gout and haemorrhoids. Culpeper suggests its use 'for swooning and passions of the heart'.

'Witloof' plants grown in the dark in stacked wooden racks to blanch for use as a vegetable

CULINARY

All types of chicory make a wonderful winter salad, particularly if you mix the colours of red, green and white. Add tomatoes or a sweet dressing to take away some of the bitter taste. Home-grown chicons stored in the dark tend to be less bitter.

For a delicious light supper dish, pour a robust dressing (made with lemon juice rather than vinegar) over the leaves, add some anchovy fillets, crumbled hard-boiled eggs and top with a handful of Kalamata olives.

As an accompaniment to cold meat and game, eat with sliced oranges, onion and chopped walnuts. With roast meats, braise chicory with butter, lemon juice and cream. Radicchio can also be braised, but loses its colour.

To make a chicory coffee substitute, dry roots immediately after harvest and grind.

Chicory with Ham and Cheese Sauce
Serves 4

4 heads chicory
8 slices smoked Bayonne ham
2 tablespoons butter
2 tablespoons plain flour
2 teaspoons Dijon mustard
150ml (¹/₄pt) milk
Enough single cream to mix to a smooth consistency
4 tablespoons Gruyère cheese
Salt and freshly ground black pepper

Bring a pan of salted water to the boil and drop in the chicory heads. Allow to blanch for 5 minutes, drain and gently squeeze as much water as you can out of them. Cut each

Chicory with Ham and Cheese Sauce

chicory in half and wrap in a slice of the ham. Then arrange in one layer in an ovenproof dish.

Preheat the oven to 200°C/400°F/gas mark 6. Make the cheese sauce: melt the butter in a heavy pan and stir in the flour. Cook for 2 minutes, then stir in the mustard. Pour in the milk gradually, stirring vigorously as the sauce thickens, then add the cream and cheese. Stir over a gentle heat for 5 minutes to let the cheese melt. Season to taste.

Pour the cheese sauce over the chicory wrapped in ham and cook in the oven for 20 minutes until nicely browned. Serve immediately.

Braised Chicory
Serves 4

The French, especially in the South-West and in Provence, braise chicory or Belgian endives and serve them with plain roasted meats such as lamb and beef.

2 tablespoons butter
1 red onion, finely chopped
2 rashers smoked bacon, diced
4 heads chicory, trimmed
150ml (¹/₄pt) chicken stock and white wine combined

Juice of half a lemon
Salt and freshly ground black pepper

Liberally coat the sides and bottom of a heavy, lidded casserole with half the butter and heat the remaining butter in a small pan over a medium flame. Gently fry the onion and bacon, and set aside.

Arrange the endives in the casserole. Add some of the stock and white wine, season with salt and pepper and

cover. Allow to sweat over a low heat until just turning colour. Roll them over and cook on the other side.

Add a little more liquid as required. The liquid should evaporate from the endives by the end, so that they are browned and tender (you may have to remove the lid for a short while). Add the onion and bacon and quickly heat up. Drizzle over the lemon juice, season and serve immediately.

Colocasia esculenta var. *esculenta. Araceae*

DASHEEN

Also known as Elephant's Ear, Arvi Leaves, West Indian Kale, Taro. Herbaceous perennial grown for its edible leaves, shoots and tubers. Tender. Value: tuber rich in starch; leaves high in vitamin A, good source of B2.

In cultivation for around 7,000 years, dasheen is said to have been first grown in India on terraces where rice now flourishes. The common name derives from '*de Chine*' (from China): the root was imported from South-East Asia following a competition organized by the Royal Geographical Society to find a cheap food source for the slaves on West Indian sugar plantations.

VARIETIES

Dasheen have a cylindrical main tuber with fibrous roots and a few side tubers. The upright stems up to 1.8m (6ft) tall are topped with large, heart-shaped leaves with prominent ribs on the underside. Cultivated types rarely flower and are grouped by the colour of their flesh, ranging from pink to yellow, and leaf stems of green, pinkish purple to almost black.

CULTIVATION

Propagation
Dasheen are propagated from 'tops' with a small section of tuber, small side tubers or 'suckers'. Plant 60cm (24in) apart with 100cm (40in) between rows, or 60–90cm (2–3ft) apart; add general fertilizer to the hole before planting.

Growing
Dasheen tolerate quite heavy, fertile, moisture-retentive soil rich in organic matter with a pH of 5.5–6.5. Dig in compost or well-rotted manure if necessary. As dasheen need plenty of water and tolerate waterlogging, they are ideal for areas by streams and rivers. Where the water table is high, mound or ridge planting is advised. Irrigate heavily during dry weather.

In well-manured soil, a second crop can be planted between the rows 12 weeks before the main crop is harvested.

Maintenance
Spring Plant pre-sprouted tubers with protection. *Summer* Keep crops well fed and watered and weed-free. *Autumn* Harvest crops. *Winter* Prepare for the following year.

Protected Cropping
Plant pre-sprouted tubers in spring into greenhouse borders. Keep temperatures around 21°C (70°F), and maintain high humidity by misting plants with soft tepid water or damping down the greenhouse floor. Do not worry about overwatering.

Feed every 3–4 weeks with a high-potash fertilizer; extra nitrogen may be needed if growth slows.

Growing in Paradise Park, Hawaii: the angle of the leaves allows accumulated water to be poured away

The true flowers are enclosed within the larger spath

Container Growing

Dasheen can be grown as a 'novelty' crop in 20–30cm (8–12in) pots of peat-substitute compost. Soak thoroughly after planting and stand the pot in a shallow tray of tepid water throughout the growing season. Treat as for 'Protected Cropping'.

PESTS AND DISEASES

Taro leaf blight causes circular water-soaked spots on leaves followed by collapse of the plant. Those grown under glass are susceptible to aphids. Red spider mite and downy mildew can also be a problem. Take the necessary precautions.

Dasheen is an important food crop in the humid tropics – seen here in Hawaii

CULINARY

Tubers can be roasted, baked or boiled, served with spicy sauces and in stews. Larger tubers, which tend to be dry and coarse, should be braised and cooked slowly.

Leaves (with midrib removed) can be stuffed, boiled or steamed and eaten with a knob of butter. Avoid particularly large leaves; they are often tough. In the West Indies, Callaloo Soup is made from dasheen leaves, okra, crab meat and coconut milk. Young blanched shoots can be eaten like asparagus.

Palusima

This is a Western Samoan or Polynesian dish.

Allow about 200g (7oz) dasheen per person. Peel and chop roughly, then parboil in plain salted water for 5–10 minutes. Drain, then boil until reduced in coconut milk (enough to come to half the height of the dasheen in the pan) until thickish. Mash.

Stuff the mashed dasheen into parboiled leaves and secure with a toothpick. (Alternatively, wrap it in banana leaves, and even spinach or cabbage.) Bake for 15 minutes in a lightly greased dish in a preheated oven at 180°C/350°F/gas mark 4. Serve with any good white fish such as cod.

Palusima

Harvesting and Storing

Dasheen take 7 to 11 months to mature. Harvest by lifting the main tuber, saving some of the small side tubers for eating and others for replanting. Undamaged tubers can be dried and stored for up to 4 weeks, while washed leaves keep for several days in a refrigerator.

WARNING

Although selection has, over the years, reduced calcium oxalate levels in the skin of dasheen, it is extremely important to wear gloves or to cover the hands with a layer of cooking oil. This prevents skin irritation when peeling the vegetables.

Always make sure dasheen are cooked thoroughly before eating.

Colocasia esculenta var. *antiquorum. Araceae*

EDDOE

Perennial grown as annual for edible tubers.
Tender. Value: rich in starch, magnesium,
potassium and vitamin C.

This variety of taro, native of India and South-East Asia, was first recorded by the Chinese 2,000 years ago. It is now grown throughout the humid tropics. Eddoes flourish in moist soil alongside rivers and streams. The central tuber is surrounded by clusters of smaller tubers which are harvested, making it different from the single-tubered dasheen. The brown, hairy tubers can weigh up to 2.2kg (5lb), and when they are sliced reveal flesh which is usually white but can also be yellow, pink or orange. Their taste is similar to a garden potato but with an attractive nutty flavour. Tubers should never be eaten raw as all varieties contain calcium oxalate crystals, a skin irritant.

VARIETIES

'Euchlora' has dark green leaves with violet margins and leaf stems. 'Fontanesii' produces leaf stems which are dark red-purple or violet. Its leaf blades are dark green with violet veins and margin.

CULTIVATION

Propagation
In the humid tropics, eddoes can be planted any time. In temperate climates, grow under glass or polythene at a minimum temperature of 21°C (70°F), and plant in spring. Plant small tubers or a tuber section containing some dormant buds in individual holes 60–75cm (25–30in) apart. Cuttings consisting of the top of a tuber with several

Eddoe cultivation

leaves and a growth point can be planted directly into the soil and will establish rapidly. Add general fertilizer to the planting hole.

Growing
Eddoes need humus-rich, slightly acid, moisture retentive soil, in sunshine or partial shade. Cultivate the soil before planting and remove any weeds.

Maintenance
Spring Plant tubers if protected cropping. *Summer* Feed every 3–4 weeks with a high potash fertilizer; additional nitrogen may be needed. During drier periods, irrigate as needed to ensure swelling of the tubers and earth up. Keep weed-free. *Autumn* Harvest as required. *Winter* Prepare beds for the following year's crop if growing in a greenhouse.

Protected Cropping
If you have space in a greenhouse or polythene tunnel, it is worth trying to grow eddoes. Plant pre-sprouted or chitted tubers in spring into growbags or 20–30cm (8–12in) pots containing peat substitute compost. Maintain heat and high humidity: damp down the glasshouse floor or mist plants with soft tepid water.

Harvesting and Storing
Eddoes take between 5 and 6 months to mature. Harvest when the stems begin to turn yellow and die back. Lift tubers carefully with a garden fork; select some for eating and save others for replanting. If they are undamaged and dried carefully, tubers can be stored for several months.

Health
The starch grains in tubers are among the smallest found in the plant kingdom, making them easy to digest.

Eddoe Soup

CULINARY

Tubers can be boiled, baked, roasted, puréed and made into soup. They can also be fried.

PESTS AND DISEASES

Eddoes grown outdoors are generally problem-free but when grown under glass they are susceptible to aphids and fungal leaf spots; red spider mite can also be a problem, particularly when humidity is low. Downy mildew can attack tubers after they have been lifted so it is important to ensure that they are dried well before being stored. Dispose of infected tubers and do not use them for propagation.

WARNING

When handling and peeling eddoes, be sure to wear gloves or cover the hands with a layer of cooking oil to prevent a nasty rash.

Cucumis sativus. Cucurbitaceae

CUCUMBER

Climbing or scrambling annual, grown for elongated or round succulent fruits. Tender. Value: moderate potassium and small amounts of beta carotene.

The smooth-skinned types can grow to well over 30cm (12in)

The wild species from central Asia is now rare in nature, yet the world-renowned salad crop has been cultivated for centuries. The first record was in Mesopotamia around 2000 BC in the earliest known vegetable garden, and cucumbers were grown in India a thousand years later. The Romans in the first century AD cultivated them in baskets or raised beds mounted on wheels so they could be moved around 'as the sun moved through the heavens'. When the day cooled, they were moved back under frames or into cucumber houses glazed with oiled cloth known as *specularia*. Tiberius found them tasty and was said to have eaten them every day of the year.

Early varieties were quite bitter and were boiled and served with oil, vinegar and honey. They were a common ingredient in soups, stews and as a cooked vegetable until the nineteenth century. Eighteenth-century English recipes include cucumbers stuffed with partly cooked pigeons (with head and feathers left on: the idea was to make the head appear attached to the cucumber); the whole was then cooked in broth and the heads garnished with barberries. Cooks in Georgian England must have had a rather bizarre sense of humour!

Columbus introduced cucumbers to the New World. They are recorded as being planted in Haiti in 1494 and grown by English settlers in Virginia in 1609. About the same time, French writers Estienne and Liébault warned: 'Beware that your seed be not olde, for if it be 3 years olde, will bring forth radishes.' Obviously their soil was as fertile as their imagination.

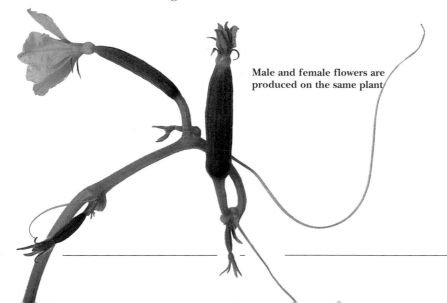

Male and female flowers are produced on the same plant

VARIETIES

Your seed catalogue will give an idea of the huge number of cultivars to choose from. There are 'greenhouse cucumbers' (though many indoor varieties can grow outdoors in a sheltered position in cooler climates and grow outdoors in warm zones); 'ridge' or outdoor types, which need protection as seedlings but can be grown outdoors in cool temperate climates; pickling cucumbers or gherkins; round varieties; Japanese climbing and bushy types.

Greenhouse or indoor cucumbers
'Crystal Apple', a small, yellow, round cucumber, is prolific and easy to grow. For the unheated greenhouse or outdoors. **'Danimas'** is a vigorous, 'all-female' mini-cucumber for a slightly heated or cold greenhouse. **'Telegraph'** is a popular, reliable variety with smooth skin and good-sized fruits. **'Telegraph Improved'** is tasty and prolific with long fruits. **'Yamato'** produces delicious long thin fruits.

Outdoor or ridge cucumbers
'Bianco Lungo di Parigi' fruits are moderately sized and have creamy-white skin. **'Burpless Tasty Green'** is tender, tasty and crisp,

resistant to mildew and tolerant of heat. **'Chicago Pickling'** is high-yielding and disease-resistant. **'Crystal Lemon'** fruits are tangy and the size of a lemon. They are perfect for pickling, slicing or stuffing. **'Long Green Improved'** is a robust, highly productive and reliable variety with large, tasty fruits. It can be also used for pickling. **'Marketmore'** is smooth, tasty and excellent for cooler conditions. It is resistant to powdery and downy mildew. **'Boothby Blond'** has been grown for generations by the Boothby family of Maine in USA, but it is not commercially available. Many older varieties were grown from seed saved from the previous year's crop.

Pickling cucumbers or gherkins **'Arena'** is a high-yielding hybrid for outdoors that produces good-quality dark green fruits. **'Athene'** is for outdoors or an unheated glasshouse or frame. **'Gherkin'** is fast-growing, with masses of small prickly fruits. **'Hokus'** is perfect for pickling and outdoor cultivation. **'Midget'** is a prolific and compact variety. **'National Pickling'** is short, blunt-ended with small, smooth fruits. It is vigorous and heavy-yielding. It was introduced in 1929 by the National Pickle Packers Association in Britain. **'Vert de Massy Cornichon'** is very tasty. Pickle when small, or allow to reach maturity.

CULTIVATION

Propagation

When growing outdoor cucumbers, sow 2 seeds edgeways 1–2cm (½–¾in) deep in a 5–7.5cm (2–3in) pot from mid-spring. Place in a propagator or heated greenhouse at 20°C (68°F). Retain the stronger seedling after germination, keep moist with tepid water and tie up small canes. Feed with a general liquid fertilizer to boost growth.

Give plants plenty of light and harden off before transplanting with care to avoid checks, when the danger of frost has passed. Allow 90cm (36in) between plants. Protect with cloches or horticultural fleece until established.

Sow successively to extend the cropping season.

Alternatively, pregerminate or sow 2–3 seeds, 1–2cm (½–¾in) deep *in situ* under jam jars or cloches from late spring to early summer when the soil temperature is around 20°C (68°F). Thin to leave the strongest seedling.

The second method is preferable as cucumbers do not transplant well.

Growing

'Ridge' cucumbers need rich, fertile, well-drained soil in a sunny, sheltered position. A few weeks before planting, dig out holes or longer ridges at least 45cm (18in) wide and 30cm (12in) deep. Half fill with well-rotted manure or good garden compost, then return the excavated soil, mounding it to about 15cm (6in) above ground level.

Better fruits are obtained when plants are grown against supports, though traditionally they are left to trail over the ground.

Once plants have produced 5–6 leaves, pinch out growing points of the stems, allow 2 laterals to form and pinch out the growing tips again. Ridge cucumbers are insect-pollinated, so do not remove male flowers as you would with greenhouse cultivars.

Grow gherkins like ridge cucumbers, or train them up some netting.

Train Japanese cultivars up trellis, cane tripods, wire or nylon netting. Nip out the growing point when stems reach the top of the support. Water regularly; feed with a high-potash fertilizer every 2 weeks when fruits are forming.

Keep crops weed-free and the soil moist.

'Boothby Blond', from the USA

Light-shading is essential, as with these 'Telegraph' types

Maintenance

Spring Sow under cover from mid-spring.
Summer Plant ridge cucumbers outdoors once frost is past. Maintain high temperatures and humidity indoors. Train and harvest.
Autumn Harvest.
Winter Store in a cool place.

Protected Cropping

Sow under cover or in a propagator from mid-spring at 21–25°C; (70–75°F). To avoid erratic germination, seeds can be pregerminated on moist kitchen towel in a covered plastic container, then placed in an airing cupboard or propagator. After about 3 days, when the seeds have germinated, sow in 7.5cm (3in) pots of seed compost.

Sow from late spring if no heat can be provided. Fill 8cm (3.5in) pots with seed compost and press the seed down edgeways into each pot about 1cm (½in) deep.

Greenhouse cucumbers need a humid atmosphere and temperatures around 20°C (70°F). Soils should be rich, moisture-retentive and free-draining, so incorporate well-rotted organic matter if you are planting in the greenhouse border. Even better, grow in 25cm (10in) pots of soil-based compost with added organic matter, in growbags, or in untreated straw bales with a bed of compost in the centre.

Insert a cane at the base of the plant and tie it into the roof structure of the greenhouse. Tie in the main stem and remove the growth tip when it reaches the roof, pinching out the laterals 2 leaves beyond each fruit.

Greenhouse cucumbers should not be pollinated or they become bitter: remove male flowers. Female flowers are identified by the swelling behind each one. Or choose 'all-female' cultivars.

Mist plants regularly with tepid water and keep the compost moist with tepid water. Feed every 2 weeks with high-potash fertilizer once fruits begin to swell.

Outdoor cucumbers can be grown in cold frames or a cold greenhouse in cooler climates. They are better trained above the ground. Ventilate well on warm days and mist regularly.

Container Growing

Sow indoor types in pots or growbags (see 'Protected Cropping'). Smooth-skinned varieties can be grown in a growbag or container 30cm (12in) wide by 20cm (8in) deep in a sunny position outdoors. Sow 3 seeds 2.5cm (1in) deep in late spring or early summer.

Thin out to leave the strongest seedling; pinch out growing tips when the plant develops 6–7 leaves. Train the side shoots on netting or canes. Keep soil moist. Feed with high-potash fertilizer when fruits form. 'Bush Champion' is ideal.

Harvesting and Storing

Fruits should never be harvested until they are fully ripe, and the sixteenth-century practice of leaving fruit on until they were mottled brown and yellow with a rich flavour may be to your taste!

Outdoor cucumbers crop mid-summer to early autumn: cut with a sharp knife when they are large enough to use. For maximum yields, you should pick fruit regularly.

Cucumbers last for several days in the salad drawer of a refrigerator. Cover the cut end with cling film and use as rapidly as possible. Or stand it stalk end down in a tall jug with a little water in the bottom. Like marrows, they can be stored in nets in a cool place.

PESTS AND DISEASES

Red spider mite, aphids, slugs and powdery mildew can be troublesome.

Cucumber mosaic virus shows as mottled, distorted leaves. Burn young infected plants and leaves from older plants. Older plants may recover, though yields will be lower.

COMPANION PLANTING

Ridge cucumbers thrive in the shade of maize or sunflowers, and grow well with peas and beans, beet or carrots.

Climbing cucumbers flourish scrambling over sweetcorn and beans.

MEDICINAL

Cucumbers were used by the Romans against scorpion bites, bad eyesight and to scare away mice.

Wives wishing for children wore cucumbers tied around their waists, and they were carried by midwives and thrown away once the child was born.

CULINARY

Eat while the stalk end is still firm. Some people remain adamant that peeled cucumbers are best: others think the flavour and appearance of the skin enhances the vegetable.

They are frequently sliced and eaten in salads, and are good in sandwiches with salmon. Mix with yoghurt and mint as a side dish to Middle Eastern dishes or curries. Make into a delicious cold soup.

To eat them as a vegetable, peel, seed, dice and stew them in a little water and butter for 20 minutes, until soft. Thicken with cream and serve with mild- or rich-flavoured fish.

Cucumber and Cream Cheese Mousse

Cucumber and Cream Cheese Mousse
Serves 4

Half a cucumber, in chunks
275g (10oz) cream cheese
1–2 tablespoons mint leaves
2 teaspoons white wine vinegar
2¹/₂ teaspoons gelatine
150ml (¹/₄pt) vegetable stock
Salt and freshly ground black pepper
Radicchio leaves and sprigs of mint, to serve

Put the cucumber into a blender with the cream cheese, mint and vinegar and purée until smooth. Dissolve the gelatine in a little stock over a low heat. Leave to cool, then stir in the balance of the stock. Add this to the cream cheese, season and blend.

Chill for at least 2 hours before serving, arranged individually with radicchio leaves, garnished with a few fine slices of cucumber and sprigs of mint.

Crambe maritima. Brassicaceae

SEAKALE

Perennial grown for its blanched young shoots. Hardy. Value: an excellent source of vitamin C.

Found on the seashores of northern Europe, the Baltic and the Black Seas, seakale was harvested from the wild and sold in markets long before it came into cultivation. In Victorian times it was seen as an aristocrat of the vegetable garden and widely cultivated by armies of gardeners in the enormous kitchen gardens attached to great houses. Today it is rarely grown, perhaps because the scale on which it was forced for Victorian tables gave it a reputation for being labour-intensive. However, it is easy to grow at home, and quite delicious; so it is high time it experienced a revival!

Seakale exposed to the sea breeze

VARIETIES

'Lily White' crops heavily, has a good flavour and pale stems. Unnamed selections of the wild species are also available from nurseries.

Seakale flowers in summer and is sweetly scented

CULTIVATION

Propagation

Seakale can be grown from seed, but it is usually propagated from crowns or root cuttings from the side roots, taken in autumn after the leaves have died back. These are called 'thongs'. Buy them from a nursery or select roots that are pencil-thick and 7.5–15cm (3–6in) long. Make a straight cut across the top of the root and an angled cut at the base (so top and bottom are distinguishable). Store in sand until planting.

Growing

Seakale needs a sunny position on deep, rich, well-drained light soil with a pH of around neutral. The winter before planting, dig in some well-rotted compost; on heavier soils, add horticultural sand or grit, or plant on a raised bed.

Seakale should crop for about 5–7 years before it needs replacing, so it is vital to prepare the ground thoroughly. Two weeks prior to planting, rake in a general fertilizer. Before planting, in early spring, rub off all the buds to leave the single strongest bud and plant thongs or crowns 45cm (18in) apart, covered with 2.5–5cm (1–2in) of soil.

Water regularly, feed occasionally, remove flower stems as they appear and keep weed-free. In autumn, cut down the yellowing foliage. From late autumn until midwinter, cover the crowns with a bucket, flower pot (cover the drainage holes) or seakale forcer and surround with manure, straw or leafmould.

Stop harvesting in late spring, rake in a general fertilizer and mulch with well-rotted manure or compost. Keep the beds weed-free and water well in dry periods. Delaying harvest until the second year lets plants become established.

Maintenance

Spring Force crops outdoors.
Summer Water in dry weather, feed occasionally, keep weed-free.
Autumn Remove the yellowing foliage.
Winter Lift crowns for forcing.

Protected Cropping

For an early crop, lift crowns after leaves die back, trim the main root to 15cm (6in) and remove the side shoots; plant 10cm (4in) apart in boxes or 3 per 23cm (9in) pot filled with rich soil from the seakale bed or loam-based compost with a high fertilizer content. Cover with upturned pots, polythene or

Seakale, after blanching, looks like a bizarrely twisted sculpture

anything opaque. Keep the compost moist. They should be ready in 5–6 weeks at temperatures of 10–13°C (48–55°F); from 16–21°C (60–70°F) they will be ready earlier. Keep them in a cellar, boiler house or under the greenhouse benches and maintain a constant supply by lifting crowns regularly. In frosty weather lift and store crowns in moist sand until required. Dispose of exhausted crowns after use.

Harvesting and Storing
When blanched sprouts are 7.5–20cm (3–8in) long, remove the soil from around the shoots and cut through the stems with a sharp knife, removing a tiny sliver of root. Crops forced outdoors can be harvested in late autumn to early spring. After harvesting, discard the exhausted roots of those forced indoors.

PESTS AND DISEASES

Do not plant in beds infected with clubroot. Flea beetle make round holes in the leaves; dust seedlings with derris.

OTHER USES

Seakale is attractive in the flower border. It forms a compact rosette of large, wavy-edged, glaucous leaves, with large bunches of white, honey-scented flowers towering above the foliage in summer.

Seakale with traditional terracotta forcing jars

CULINARY

Better eaten fresh, seakale lasts for 2–3 days in the salad compartment of the refrigerator.

Wash stems and tie them into bundles using raffia and steam or lightly boil them until tender – overcooking toughens the stems and makes them less palatable.

Victorians served seakale on folded napkins or toast, drenched in white sauce or melted butter.

Seakale is also delicious served as a starter with béchamel or hollandaise sauce, or covered in lemon-flavoured melted butter.

Young flowering shoots can be eaten once they are lightly boiled.

Seakale Gratinée
Serves 4

This is excellent served with baked ham.

750g (1½lb) well-washed seakale

For the béchamel sauce:
50g (2oz) butter
2 tablespoons flour
1 teaspoon French mustard
150ml (¼pt) milk or crème fraîche
4 tablespoons good strong Cheddar cheese
Salt and freshly ground black pepper

Rinse the seakale well, tie into bundles and cook until *al dente* in boiling salted water. Drain well. Arrange in an ovenproof dish.

Make the béchamel sauce, flavouring with the Cheddar cheese. Pour the sauce over the seakale and bake in a preheated oven, 200°C/ 400°F/gas mark 6 for 15 minutes. Serve hot.

Cucurbita maxima, Cucurbita moschata and *Cucurbita pepo. Cucurbitaceae*

PUMPKIN & SQUASH

MARROW, COURGETTE, ZUCCHINI, POTIRON

*Annuals grown for edible fruits, often colourful, which can be extremely large.
Tender. Value: high in beta carotene, moderate amounts of vitamin C and folic acid.*

On the coast of Coromandel
Where the early pumpkins blow
In the middle of the woods
Lived the Yonghy-Bonghy-Bo...
Edward Lear (1812–88)

The name 'pumpkin' appeared in the seventeenth century, shortly before Perrault wrote Cinderella, the tale about a poor girl whose fairy godmother turned a pumpkin into a golden coach which took her to a fabulous ball. 'Pumpkin' comes from the Greek word for melon – pepon or 'cooked by the sun' – while one French name, potiron, means 'large mushroom', from the Arabic for morel mushrooms. 'Squash' is an abbreviation of the native North American Indian word *askutasquash*, meaning 'eaten raw or uncooked'.

The squashes originated in the Americas and are believed to have been cultivated for between five and ten thousand years. Wild forms were originally gathered for their seeds and were only later found to have sweet flesh. Many varieties arrived in Europe soon after the discovery of the New World in the sixteenth century. Not only were they eaten, but the seeds were pounded in oatmeal and applied to the face, to bleach freckles and other blemishes. Estienne and Liébault wrote in 1570: 'To make pompions keep long and not spoiled or rotted, you must sprinkle them with the juice of a houseleek'. In the seventeenth century they were mashed to bulk up bread, or boiled and heavily buttered.

Winter squash

This group contains a wealth of edible and outstandingly ornamental fruits. One of the most beautiful sights in the kitchen garden is pumpkins ripening in golden sunshine during the fall.

'Crown of Thorns'

'Little Gem' comes from the same group as the courgette, but grows round rather than long

VARIETIES

Members of the genus *Cucurbita* are bushy or trailing annuals – sometimes extremely vigorous plants – bearing a wide range of edible and/or ornamental fruit. The fruits from all of these species are often grouped together according to their shape or time of harvest – crookneck, summer squash, winter squash and so on; in practice categories overlap and some are multi-purpose, being served differently when young and when mature. Additional confusion arises because of local variation in what is grown and what it is called. Here they are classed according to species.

The *Cucurbita maxima* group has large, variable fruits and includes most traditional pumpkins and winter squashes, containing several ornamentals like the banana, buttercup, hubbard and turban types. They tend to have hard skins when mature, and keep well; the yellow flesh needs cooking. They flourish in low humidity from 20–27°C (68–80°F), though some tolerate cooler conditions. **'Atlantic Giant'** is not for the faint-hearted – it can grow to 317 kg (700lb). **'Banana Pink'** is long, broad and curved, with pale pink skin. **'Big Max'** is a massive pumpkin with rough red-orange skin and bright flesh. It is excellent for pies, exhibitions and as a 'giant' vegetable. **'Buttercup'** is delicious with firm, dense, sweet flesh. The skin is dark green with pale narrow stripes. Good for soups, roasting and pumpkin pie. **'Crown Prince'** is small fruited with tender orange flesh. Tasty and keeps well.

'Queensland Blue', an attractive small variety with blue-grey skin, is very tasty. **'Turk's Turban'** (**'Turk's Cap'**), a wonderful ornamental squash, is orange with cream and green markings. The name aptly describes the shape. **'Warted Hubbard'** is a small, round fruit with extraordinary dark green warty skin, orange-yellow flesh. It keeps well. **'Whangaparoa Crown Pumpkin'**, a hard, grey-skinned variety with a pronounced crown and orange flesh, stores well.

Cucurbita pepo embraces summer squashes (including courgettes or zucchini and their larger version, the marrow), non-keeping winter pumpkins and ornamental gourds such as custard squash, plus straight and crook-necked types. The fruits are usually soft-skinned, especially when young, and may be served raw when small. One variety, **'Little Gem'**, is slow to mature, taking about 4 months. It may not be suitable for growing in cooler conditions.

Summer Squash
'Early Golden Summer Crookneck' is an early cropper with bright yellow fruits, excellent for eating. Harvest when 10cm (4in) long. **'Early Prolific Straight Neck'** is lemon-yellow with finely textured thick flesh. **'Vegetable Spaghetti'** (**'Spaghetti Squash'**) is pale yellow when mature. Boil or bake fruits whole; scoop out the flesh inside and it looks like spaghetti. **'White Patty Pan'** (**'White Bush Scallop'**) has an unusual flattened shape with a scalloped edge. It is better harvested and cooked whole when about 7.5cm (3in) in diameter. It is bushy and ideal for small gardens. **'Yellow Bush Scallop'** is an old variety with coarse, pale yellow flesh and a bright yellow skin.

Marrow
This elongated type of summer squash has long been popular in Britain.
'Long Green Trailing' is a prolific, long-fruited variety which is dark green with pale stripes. **'Tiger Cross'**, an early green bush type, crops well and has good-quality fruits. Resistant to cucumber mosaic virus. **'Tender and True'** is semi-trailing and matures early. Resistant to cucumber mosaic virus, it can be used as a courgette when young.

Courgette or Zucchini
Varieties of marrow bred for picking small, the following are all bush types and ideal for the smaller garden.

'Crown Prince' looks pale besides its brighter counterparts

an autumn decoration. **'Small Sugar'** has rounded orange fruits growing to 18cm (7½ in) diameter. The flesh is tender, yellow and excellent for pies. It matures from late autumn.

Cucurbita moschata includes the early butternut, butternut, Kentucky Field and crookneck squashes, harvested in autumn and winter. They are large, rounded and usually have smooth, tough skin. Possibly one of the earliest species in cultivation, they are widely grown and found throughout the tropics. Particularly heat-tolerant. **'Butternut'** has pale tan, stocky, club-shaped fruits with bright orange flesh. It

stores well and succeeds in cooler areas. **'Early Butternut'** is a curved, narrow fruit with a swollen tip. This bush variety matures rapidly and keeps well. **'Kentucky Field'** (**'Large Cheese'**) is flattened

with faintly ribbed, pale cream-coloured skin. **'Triple Treat'** is a bright orange round fruit. Its seeds are particularly good eaten raw, fried or roasted. It is easy to carve and is therefore a variety that is often grown for Halloween. **'Waltham Butternut'** has a smooth, pale tan skin, yellow-orange flesh and a nutty taste. It is very good for storing and yields extremely well.

CULTIVATION

Propagation

Sow *in situ* or in pots in cooler climates as seeds do not germinate if the soil is below 13°C (56°F).

From mid- to late spring, soak the seed overnight, then sow one seed edgeways about 2.5cm (1in) deep in a 7.5cm (3in) pot or module of moist multi-purpose or seed compost and place in a propagator or on a warm windowsill, preferably at 20–25°C (68–77°F). After germination transplant the seedlings when they are large enough to handle into 12.5cm (5in) pots, taking care not to damage the roots. Keep compost moist but not waterlogged. Harden off gradually and transplant from late spring to early summer when the danger of frost has passed. Protect with cloches until the plants are established.

'Ambassador' is high-yielding with dark green fruit and crops over a long period. **'Defender'** produces high yields of mid-green fruits. Harvest regularly. Resistant to cucumber mosaic virus. **'De Nice à Fruit Rond'**, a round variety, should be picked when the size of a golf ball. Delicious flavour. **'Gold Rush'**, a compact bush with yellow fruits, crops over a long period. **'Spacemiser'** is a compact and prolific gourmet variety. **'Supremo'** produces very tasty, dark green fruit.

Winter squash
These usually have white or pale yellow flesh, whereas pumpkins have coarse, orange flesh. **'Ebony Acorn'** (**'Table Queen'**) is an ancient early-cropping variety with thin, dark green skin and pale yellow, sweet flesh. It is a semi-bush, which is good for baking. **'Jack be Little'** is a miniature pumpkin with deep ribbed fruits about 5 x 7.5cm (2x3in) in diameter and orange skin. It is edible, but is more attractive simply as

The high-yielding 'Gold Rush'

Alternatively, sow *in situ* when the soil is warm and workable and there is no danger of frost, from late spring to early summer.

Dig out a hole at least 30–45cm (12–18in) square and half fill with well-rotted manure 7–10 days before planting. Sow 2–3 seeds 2.5cm (1in) deep in the centre of the mound and cover with a jam jar or cut the base from a plastic bottle and use as a crop cover. After germination, thin to leave the strongest seedling, remove the cover and mark the position with a cane so you know where to water the plant among the mass of stems. Alternatively, prepare the ground as described and transplant seedlings.

Space cultivars according to their vigour. Sow bush varieties on mounds or ridges, 60–90cm (24–36in) apart with 90–120cm (36–48in) between rows. Trailing varieties should be 120–180cm (48–72in) apart with 180–360cm (6–12ft) between rows.

Growing

Pumpkins and squashes need a sunny position in rich, moisture-retentive soil with plenty of well-rotted organic matter and a pH of 5.5–6.8.

It is a good idea to plant through a black polythene mulch laid over the soil with the edges buried to hold it in place. This warms the soil, suppresses weeds, conserves moisture and protects ripening fruit.

Outstandingly strange-looking, 'Turk's Turban' will store for several months

The 'White Patty Pan' looks like a flying saucer

A thick layer of straw or horticultural fleece are useful alternatives, or you can lay the ripening fruit on a roof tile, a piece of board or similar to protect it from the soil and prevent rotting.

Hand-pollination is recommended, particularly in cold weather when insect activity is reduced. Female flowers have a small swelling, the embryonic squash, immediately behind the petals, while male flowers have only a thin stalk.

When the weather is dry, remove a mature male flower, fold back or remove the petals and dust pollen on to the stigma of the female flowers. Alternatively, transfer the pollen with a fine paintbrush. Periods of hot weather can reduce the ratio of female to male flowers.

Plants need copious amounts of food and water, particularly when flowers and fruits are forming, up to 11 litres (2 gal) of water per week, but they should never be allow to become waterlogged.

Feed with a liquid general fertilizer every 2 weeks. Plants grown with a black plastic mulch also need an occasional foliar feed to boost growth.

Pinch out tips of main shoots of trailing varieties when they reach 60cm (2ft) to encourage branching and trim back those that outgrow their position.

Trailing types can also be trained over trellis or supports. Where space is limited, you can push a circle of pegs into the soil and trail the stems around the pegs.

To guarantee large fruits, allow only 2–3 to develop on each plant.

Keep crops weed-free.

Maintenance

Spring Sow seeds under glass or outdoors.
Summer Feed and water copiously; keep crops weed-free. Harvest courgettes and marrows.
Autumn Harvest pumpkins and winter squashes, allow to ripen and protect from frost.
Winter Store winter squashes until midwinter or later.

Protected Cropping

In cooler climates or to advance growth, sow seed indoors and transplant. Protect with cloches or crop covers until they are well established. Use bush varieties for earlier crops.

Container Growing

Courgettes, marrows, bush varieties of other squashes and those that are moderately vigorous can be grown in growbags or containers that are at least 35cm (14in) by 30cm (12in) deep. Use a loam-based compost with additional well-rotted organic matter. Sow indoors to transplant later or sow directly outdoors. Keep plants well watered and do not allow the compost to dry out.

Plants can be grown up strong canes 2m (6½ft) tall. Pinch out growing points when stems reach the top; tie the main stem and side shoots firmly to the supporting canes.

Hand-pollinate for successful cropping.

Harvesting and Storing

Pick courgettes or zucchini and summer squashes when they are about 10cm (4in) long and still young and tender. Marrows are harvested when they have reached full size. Push your thumbnail gently into the skin near the stalk; if it goes in easily then the marrow is ready for harvest. Cut them from the stem leaving a short stalk on the fruit and handle with care to avoid bruising. Harvest regularly for continual cropping. They can be stored in a cool place for about 8 weeks.

Courgettes can be kept in a polythene bag in the refrigerator and will stay fresh for about a week.

Courgettes are suitable for freezing. Cut into 1cm (½in) slices, blanch for 2 minutes, cool, drain and dry. Freeze in polythene bags. Flesh of winter squashes and pumpkins can be cooked then frozen, without any loss of flavour.

Towards the end of the growing season, remove any foliage that shades the fruits. Harvest pumpkins and winter squashes from late summer to autumn, though they must be brought into storage before the first heavy frosts. On maturity, the foliage rapidly dies, the skin hardens and stem starts to crack.

After harvest, leave them outdoors for about 14 days as cold weather improves the taste and sugar content, hardening the skin and sealing the stem. Protect from heavy frost with hessian, straw or similar.

In cooler areas they can be ripened in a greenhouse or on a sunny windowsill. Pumpkins will last until midwinter when stored in a frost-free shed.

Store winter squashes at a minimum temperature of 10°C (50°F); they last for up to 6 months, but may deteriorate earlier. Some Japanese varieties will last even longer.

Marrows are traditionally allowed to trail, but can also be grown on frames

The edible flowers of the marrow

COMPANION PLANTING

Grow courgette and marrow alongside sweetcorn for support and shade, and with legumes, which provide essential nitrogen.

PESTS AND DISEASES

If fruits show signs of withering, water and feed more often.

Aphids, powdery and downy mildew and slugs can be a problem.

Cucumber mosaic virus causes yellow mottling and puckering of the leaves and rotting of the fruit. Destroy infected plants immediately and control aphids which transmit this virus.

CULINARY

Flowers of all varieties can be used in salads or stuffed with rice or minced meat and fried in batter. Prepare the meat, rice and batter before picking the flowers as they wilt quickly. They can also be puréed and made into soup. Young shoots are steamed or boiled. Pumpkin flesh is used for pies; their seeds are deep-fried in oil, salted and are known as 'pepitos'.

The fruits can be stuffed, steamed, stir-fried, added to curries, made into jam or pickles.

Courgette Omelette
Serves 2

A particularly pretty omelette can be made with young courgettes; use a mixture of yellow and green ones to good effect.

5 eggs
300g (10oz) courgettes
4 tablespoons olive oil
1 tablespoon fresh basil leaves
* (purple for preference)*
1 tablespoon fresh thyme leaves
Salt and freshly ground black
* pepper*

Whisk the eggs with salt and pepper and set aside. Slice the courgettes in coarse dice. Heat half the oil and sauté the courgettes for a couple of minutes. Then remove from the heat.

In an omelette pan, heat the balance of the oil and pour in the eggs, courgettes and herbs. Stir gently over a low heat while the omelette sets. Turn it on to a plate and slide back into the pan to cook the second side for a minute or so until nicely browned. Serve as a refreshing Sunday supper dish.

Pumpkin Kibbeh
Serves 4

A centrepiece of many Middle Eastern meals, these 'balls' should be served warm, rather than hot. This recipe was given to me by Arto der Haroutunian.

200g (7oz) freshly boiled
* pumpkin flesh*
400g (14oz) bulgar wheat
150g (6oz) plain flour
1 onion, finely chopped
Salt and freshly ground black
* pepper*

For the filling:
2 shallots, finely chopped
250g (8oz) spinach, washed
150g (6oz) cooked chickpeas,
* drained*
50g (2oz) chopped walnuts
50g (2oz) dried apricots
1/4 teaspoon sumac
* (from Cypriot delis)*
1 tablespoon lemon juice
Salt and freshly ground black
* pepper*
Oil for frying

In a large bowl, purée the pumpkin using a fork. Sieve the bulgar and flour into the bowl and mix in the onion and seasoning. Leave in a cool place for 10–15 minutes. If the dough is too hard to handle, you may need to add a tablespoon of water and knead well.

To make the filling, sauté the shallots in the oil until they just turn brown. Mix in the spinach and allow to wilt, stirring constantly, for a couple of minutes. Then add the rest of the ingredients, mixing well.

Make the kibbehs with wet hands to prevent the mixture from sticking. Form the bulgar and pumpkin mixture into oval patties – they should be about 8cm (3in) long and just big enough to stuff. Create an opening at one end and fill each kibbeh with the spinach and apricot stuffing. Using your fingers, seal up the ends.

Fry the kibbehs in hot oil for a couple of minutes on each side and drain on

Acorn Squash with Balsamic Vinegar

kitchen paper. There should be enough to make between 20 and 24 kibbehs.

Acorn Squash with Balsamic Vinegar

Allow 100g (4oz) of acorn squash per person. Cut in half and remove the seeds and fibres. Place in a buttered, ovenproof dish and pour over 1 tablespoon balsamic vinegar, 2 tablespoons runny honey and 1 tablespoon lemon juice for each serving. Cook in a preheated oven, 180°C/ 350°F/gas mark 4 for 40 minutes, turning over halfway.

Custard Marrow with Bacon and Cheese

500g (1lb) custard marrow
2 tablespoons butter
1 small onion, finely sliced
75g (3oz) smoked back bacon,
* diced*
150ml (1/4pt) crème fraîche
4 tablespoons grated mature
* Cheddar*
Salt and freshly ground black
* pepper*

Cut the custard marrow into a rough dice and steam it until just tender. Remove from the heat and keep

warm. Make a sauce by heating the butter and cooking the onion until softened. Add the bacon and continue cooking for 5 minutes, stirring from time to time. mix in the crème fraîche, the custard marrow and seasoning and pour into a greased ovenproof dish. Top with the cheese and cook in a preheated oven, 225°C/425°F/gas mark 7, for 15 minutes.

OTHER USES

Pumpkins are hollowed out and made into Halloween 'Jack o'Lanterns'. Mature marrows can be used for wine making.

MEDICINAL

In Ethiopia seeds from squashes are used as laxatives and purgatives; they are used worldwide to expel intestinal worms. Eating winter squash and pumpkin is said to reduce the risk of cancer.

Cynara cardunculus. Asteraceae

CARDOON

**Also known as Cardon. Perennial grown as annual for
'heart' and blanched leaf midribs.
Half hardy. Value: rich in potassium.**

This close relative of the globe artichoke is found in the wild through much of the Mediterranean and North Africa. Cultivated versions are valued as a vegetable and in the ornamental garden. When grown as a food crop, the stems are blanched during autumn in a similar manner to celery. Its delights have been enjoyed for centuries; it was grown before the birth of Christ and was esteemed by the Romans, who paid high prices for it in their markets as an ingredient for stews and salads. Cardoons reached England by 1658 and North America by the following century, but never established themselves as a major crop despite their popularity in Europe. Today they are more likely to be found in the herbaceous border, where the bold angular foliage and tall candelabras of thistle-like purple flowers are outstanding.

VARIETIES

'**Gigante di Romagna**' is a reliable variety with long stalks. '**Plein Blanc Inerma Ameliora**' grows to 120cm (4ft) tall, with white ribs that are well textured and tasty. '**Tours**' is a large and vigorous variety. Beware of the large spines and protect yourself accordingly!

Cardoons make fine ornamentals

CULTIVATION

Cardoons need a sunny, sheltered site on light, fertile, well-drained soil.

Propagation

Sow *in situ* in mid-spring, planting 3–4 seeds 2.5cm (1in) deep in 'stations' 50cm (20in) apart with 1.5m (5ft) between rows. Thin after germination to retain the strongest seedling. In cooler areas or if spring is late and the soil is yet to warm up, sow indoors. Place 3 seeds in 7.5cm (3in) pots or modules of moist seed compost in a propagator or glasshouse at 13°C (55°F). Thin, leaving the strongest seedling, then harden off before planting outdoors in mid- to late spring, when there is no danger of frost. Water well after planting and protect from scorching sunshine until they have established.

Growing

The autumn or early spring before seed sowing or planting out seedlings, double dig the site, adding well-rotted organic matter. Alternatively, plant in trenches 38–50cm (15–20in) wide and 30cm (12in) deep; dig these in late autumn or early spring, incorporating plenty of rotted manure or compost into the base and refilling to 7.5–10cm (3–4in) below the surface. Leave the remaining soil alongside for earthing up. Before planting, rake in general fertilizer at 60g/sq m (2oz/sq yd).

In late summer to early autumn, on a day when the leaves and hearts are dry, begin blanching: pull stems into a large bunch (wear long sleeves and gloves for protection), and tie with raffia or soft string just below the leaves. Wrap cardoons with 'collars' of newspaper, corrugated cardboard, brown wrapping paper or black polythene tied firmly around the stems.

Tile drainpipes and plastic guttering are just as effective at excluding the light. Support collars with a stake, particularly on exposed sites. Alternatively, cardoons can be earthed up. Cover stems with dry hay, bracken or straw held firmly at several points with twine and cover with soil, banked at an angle of 45°. The first method is easier, cleaner and quicker.

Cardoons need a regular water supply from early summer through to early autumn, and liquid general fertilizer every 2 weeks. Keep weed-free by hand weeding, hoeing or, preferably, mulching with a 5cm (2in) layer of organic matter once plants are established.

Maintenance

Spring Sow seeds *in situ* or under glass.
Summer Feed and water regularly. Keep weed-free.
Autumn Harvest crops using a sharp knife. Prepare the planting bed.
Winter Store in a cool, dry place until required.

The flower heads are similar to those of globe artichokes

Protected Cropping

Protect transplants or seedlings under cloches or horticultural fleece if late spring frosts are forecast.

Container Growing

Grow in large containers of loam-based compost with added organic matter or in free-draining, moisture-retentive soil. Allow plenty of room for leaves to grow. Water and feed regularly: do not let the compost dry out. Blanch using 'collars'.

Harvesting and Storing

Blanching takes about 3–4 weeks. When ready to harvest, lift plants with a garden fork, trim off roots and remove outer leaves. Cardoons can remain in the ground until needed, but protect with bracken, straw or other insulating material in moderate frosts. If hard frosts are forecast, lift and store in a cool shed or cellar

Pests and Diseases

Cardoons are robust and have few problems. They can be affected by powdery mildew, which is worse when plants are dry at the roots and if nights are cold and days warm and dry.

Mice will eat the seeds. An old remedy is to dip the seeds in paraffin; otherwise buy humane traps or a cat!

CULINARY

The leaf midribs and thinly sliced hearts are eaten raw in salads, in soups and stews or as an alternative to fennel or celery. They can be boiled in salted water with a squeeze of lemon juice for about 30 minutes until tender. Once cardoons are cut, drop them into water with a squeeze of lemon juice as the cut surfaces do tend to blacken.

The dried flowers are used as a substitute for rennet in Spain and some parts of South America.

Lamb Tagine with Cardoons
Serves 4

Tagines (or stews) are popular in northern Africa. Cardoons give this traditional Moroccan dish a rich flavour.

750g (1½lb) chunks lamb
3 cloves garlic, crushed
1 teaspoon ground ginger
Pinch saffron
¼ teaspoon turmeric
2–3 tablespoons vegetable oil
2 tablespoons coriander
1 onion, peeled and sliced
750g–1kg (1½–2lb) cardoons
2 preserved lemons, quartered
4 tablespoons black olives
Juice of 2 lemons
Salt and freshly ground black pepper

Put the lamb, garlic, ginger, saffron, turmeric, oil, chopped coriander and onion in a heavy pan and mix well. Pour over a cup or two of water and bring to the boil.

Skim if needs be and then simmer, covered, for 1 hour, adding more water if necessary, to just cook the lamb. Then add the cleaned cardoons and enough water to cover them (this is important), and continue cooking for a further 30–40 minutes.

Stir in the preserved lemon quarters and the olives and enough lemon juice to taste, and ensure the tagine is well mixed. Taste and adjust the seasoning before serving piping hot.

Lamb Tagine with Cardoons

Cynara scolymus. Asteraceae

GLOBE ARTICHOKE

Also known as French artichoke, Green artichoke. Tall, upright perennial grown for edible flower buds. Half hardy. Value: 85% water; half carbohydrate indigestible inulin, turning to fructose in storage; moderate iodine and iron content.

Originating in the Mediterranean, globe artichokes were grown by the Greeks and Romans, who regarded them as a delicacy. The common name comes from the Italian *articoclos*, deriving from *cocali*, or pine cone – an apt description of the appearance of the flower bud. Artichokes waned in popularity in the Dark Ages, but were restored to favour when Catherine de Medici introduced them to France in the sixteenth century. From there they spread around the world. Globe artichokes reached the United States in 1806, travelling with French and Spanish settlers.

In Italy its bitter principle flavours the aperitif *cynar*, which is popular as a vermouth and definitely an acquired taste!

Growing to about 1.2–1.5m (4–5ft) tall, with a 90cm (3ft) spread, attractive leaves and large thistle–like flowers, globe artichokes always look wonderful in the flower border and make excellent dual-purpose plants.

VARIETIES

'**Green Globe**' has large green heads with thick, fleshy scales. It needs winter protection in cooler climates. '**Gros Camus de Bretagne**' is only suitable for warmer climates, but is worth growing for its large, well-flavoured heads. '**Purple Globe**' is hardier than the green form, but is not as tasty. '**Purple Sicilian**' has small, deep purple-coloured artichokes that are excellent for eating raw when they are very young. This variety is not frost-hardy. '**Vert de Laon**' is hardy with an excellent flavour. '**Violetta di Chioggia**', a purple-headed variety, is excellent in the flower border.

CULTIVATION

An immature flower head, just before harvesting

Artichokes need an open, sheltered site on light, fertile, well-drained soil.

Propagation
Artichokes can be grown from seed or divided, but are usually propagated from rooted 'suckers' – shoots arising from the plant's root system. Suckers are bought or removed from established plants in mid-spring. They should be healthy, about 20–23cm (8–9in) long and well rooted, with at least 2 shoots. Clear soil from around the roots of the parent plant and remove them with a sharp knife, cutting close to the main stem between the sticker and parent plant. Alternatively, divide established plants in spring by lifting the roots and easing them apart with 2 garden forks, a spade or an old knife and replanting the sections; these too should have at least 2 shoots and a good root system. To keep your stocks vigorous and productive, renew the oldest one-third of your plants every year. This extends the cropping season, too, as mature plants are ready for harvest in late spring to early summer and young plants in late summer.

You can grow from seed and select the best plants, but this is time-consuming, uses valuable space and is not recommended; it is far better to grow proven, named cultivars. If you have the time and inclination, then sow seed in trays of moist seed compost in an unheated glasshouse during late winter or outdoors in early spring. Thin to leave the strongest seedlings and harden off before planting out at their final spacing in late spring. Once flower buds have been produced, retain the best plants for harvest and for future propagation, discarding the rest.

Growing
If necessary, improve the soil by digging in plenty of well-rotted organic matter in spring or autumn before planting. This prevents summer drought and winter waterlogging, conditions that globe artichokes dislike. Before planting, rake in general fertilizer at 60g/sq m (2oz/sq yd).

Plant suckers or divisions 60cm (2ft) apart with 60–75cm (2–2½ft) between each row, trimming the leaves back to 12.5cm (5in), which helps to reduce water loss, and shading them from full sun until they are established. Water thoroughly after planting and during periods of dry weather, applying a high-potash liquid fertilizer every 2 weeks when the plants are actively growing.

Keep the beds weed-free and mulch with organic matter in spring. During autumn and winter, if heavy frosts are forecast, protect plants by earthing up with soil, then covering them with a thick layer of straw, bracken or other organic insulation. Remove the covering in spring.

Maintenance
Spring Divide or remove suckers from existing plants and replant.
Summer Keep weed-free and water thoroughly during drought.
Autumn In areas with moderate temperatures, retain leaves and stems as frost protection.
Winter If severe frost is forecast, remove the decayed leaves, earth up, and protect plants with insulating material. Remove the materials in spring before growth begins.

Harvesting and Storing
Each flowering stem normally produces one large artichoke at the tip and several smaller ones below. A few flower heads will be produced in the first year; these are best removed so that the energy goes into establishing the plant, but if you cannot resist the

Globe artichoke flowers, which are closely related to the cotton thistle, are attractive to pollinating insects

temptation, harvest in late summer. In the second and third years more stems will be produced and are ready for cutting in midsummer. Harvest when the scales are tightly closed, removing the terminal bud first with 5 or 7.5cm (2 or 3in) of stem, then the remaining side buds as they grow large enough. Alternatively, remove the lower artichokes for eating when they are about 4cm (1½in) long.

Once the scales begin to open, globe artichokes become inedible.

Pests and Diseases
Slugs attack young shoots and leaves – the problem is worse in damp conditions. Keep the area free of plant debris, use biological controls, scatter aluminium sulphate-based slug pellets around plants or make traps from plastic cartons half-buried in the ground and filled with milk or beer. Lay rooftiles, newspaper, old lettuce leaves or other tempting vegetation on the ground and hand pick

regularly from the underneath. Or put a barrier of grit around plants, or attract natural predators such as birds to the garden. Lettuce root aphid can be a problem. Creamy yellow aphids appear on the roots during summer, sucking sap and weakening plants. Water well in dry weather; apply systemic insecticide.

MEDICINAL

Artichokes are highly nutritious and are especially good for the liver, aiding detoxification and regeneration. They reduce blood sugar and cholesterol levels, stimulating the gall bladder and helping the metabolism of fat. Artichoke is also a diuretic and used to treat hepatitis and jaundice. It was used in folk medicine as a contraceptive and aphrodisiac, but its potency is not recorded!

Globe artichokes grow to 1.5m (5ft) high

CULINARY

Artichokes can be stored for up to a week in a polythene bag in a refrigerator.

The edible parts are the fleshy base of the outer scales, the central 'heart' and the bottom of the artichoke itself. Wash the artichoke thoroughly before use and sprinkle any cut parts with lemon juice to prevent them from turning black. Boil artichokes in a non-metallic pan of salted water with lemon juice for 30–45 minutes until soft. Check if they are ready by pushing a knife through the heart, or try a basal leaf to check it for tenderness.

Eat artichokes by hand, pulling off the leaves one by one and dipping the base in mayonnaise, hollandaise, lemon sauce, melted butter or plain yoghurt before scraping off the fleshy leaf base between your teeth. Pull off the hairy central 'choke', or remove it with a spoon, and then eat the fleshy heart.

Bottoms can be a garnish for roasts, filled with vegetables or sauces. Cook 'Cypriot-style' with oil, red wine and coriander seeds, or toss in oil and lemon dressing as hors-d'oeuvre. Make a salad of cubed artichoke bottoms and new potatoes (leftovers are suitable) and season well. Toss in mayonnaise and crumble over finely chopped hard-boiled egg and good-quality black olives. Sprinkle with chives and flat-leaved parsley. Whole baby artichokes can be battered and deep-fried or cooked in oil. Eat them cold with vinaigrette.

A seventeenth-century herbalist and apothecary wrote that even the youngest housewife knew how to cook artichokes and serve them with melted butter, seasoned with vinegar and pepper. Florence White, a founder of the English Folk Cookery Association and member of the American Home Economics Association, gives a recipe for artichokes in *Good Things in England* (1929) from the time of Queen Anne:

A Tart of Artichoke Bottoms

'Line a dish with fine pastry. Put in the artichoke bottoms, with a little finely minced onion and some finely minced sweet herbs. Season with salt, pepper and nutmeg. Add some butter in tiny pieces. Cover with pastry and bake in a quick oven. When cooked, put into the tart a little white sauce thickened with yolk of egg and sharpened with tarragon vinegar.'

Risotto with Artichokes
Serves 6

Rose Gray and Ruth Rogers give this recipe in their wonderful *River Café Cookbook*:

8 small globe artichokes, prepared and trimmed (chokes removed if at all prickly)
2 garlic cloves, peeled and finely chopped
3 tablespoons olive oil
Sea salt and freshly ground black pepper
1 litre (1³/₄pt) chicken stock
150g (5oz) butter
1 medium red onion, very finely chopped
300g (10oz) risotto rice
75ml (2¹/₂fl oz) extra dry white vermouth
175g (6oz) Parmesan, freshly grated

Cut the artichokes in half and slice as thinly as possible. Fry gently with the garlic in 1 tablespoon of the olive oil for 5 minutes, stirring continuously, then add 120ml (4fl oz) water, salt and pepper and simmer until the water has evaporated. Set aside.

Heat the chicken stock and check for seasoning. Melt 90g (3oz) of the butter in the remaining oil in a large heavy-bottomed saucepan and gently fry the onion until soft, about 15–20 minutes. Add the rice and, off the heat, stir for a minute until the rice becomes totally coated. Return to the heat, add 2 or so ladlefuls of hot stock or just enough to cover the rice, and simmer, stirring, until the rice has absorbed nearly all the liquid. Add more stock as the previous addition is absorbed. After about 15–20 minutes, nearly all the stock will have been absorbed by the rice; each grain will have a creamy coating, but will remain *al dente*.

Add the remaining butter in small pieces, then gently mix in the vermouth, Parmesan and artichokes, being careful not to overstir.

Risotto with Artichokes

Eruca vesicaria subsp. *sativa. Brassicaceae*

ROCKET

Rocket Salad, Roquette, Italian Cress, Rucola, Arugula. Annual grown for tender edible leaves. Hardy. Value: high in potassium and vitamin C.

Rocket has been cultivated since Roman times and is native to the Mediterranean and Eastern Asia, though it grows in many areas after 'escaping' from gardens. *Eruca* means 'downy-stemmed'; *vesicaria*, 'bladder-like', describes the slender seed pods. Introduced to North America by Italian settlers, the spicy leaves were particularly popular in Elizabethan England.

Flowering rocket in the herb garden

SPECIES

Eruca vesicaria subsp. sativa, an erect plant growing to lm (36in), has hairy stems, broadly toothed leaves and cross-shaped, creamy flowers with attractive purple veins. Cultivated plants, a separate subspecies, are larger than their wild counterparts and have paler flowers.

CULTIVATION

Propagation
Sow seed successively every 2–3 weeks, from mid-spring to early summer, in drills 12mm (½in) deep and 30cm (12in) apart. Thin when large enough to handle until 15cm (6in) apart. Rocket germinates at fairly low temperatures. In warmer climates sow in winter or early spring.

Growing
Rocket needs rich, moisture-retentive soil in partial shade. It may need extra shading in hot weather, otherwise it produces less palatable leaves. Keep weed-free and water regularly.

Maintenance
Spring Sow seeds from mid-spring; thin when large enough to handle.
Summer Continue sowing until midsummer. Water and feed as necessary. Harvest regularly to encourage tender growth and keep from 'bolting'.
Autumn Harvest, prepare the ground for the following year's sowing and sow seeds for protected crops.
Winter Harvest winter crops.

Protected Cropping
Although hardy, protect against severe frosts with cloches. Sow autumn/winter crops from late summer in a cool greenhouse, cold frame, or under cloches.

Container Growing
Rocket is not the perfect plant for pots, but it can be grown in a soil-based compost with low fertilizer levels with added peat-substitute compost. Sow seed *in situ*. Water thoroughly.

Harvesting
Plants are ready to harvest after 6–8 weeks. Pick frequently to encourage a regular supply of good-quality leaves and to prevent plants from running to seed in hot weather. Discard any damaged leaves. Either pull leaves as required or treat as a 'cut and come again' crop, cutting the plant 2.5cm (1in) above the ground.

Pests and Diseases
Rocket is usually trouble-free, but black flea beetle can damage seedlings. Treat and protect accordingly.

MEDICINAL

Young leaves are said to be a good tonic and are used in cough medicine. Dioscorides described rocket as 'a digestive and good for ye belly'.

CULINARY

The increasingly popular leaves are delicious in salads – younger leaves are milder. They can be lightly boiled or steamed, added to sauces, stir-fried, sautéed in olive oil and tossed with pasta. The flowers are edible and can decorate salads.

Penne with Merguez and Rocket
Serves 4

400g (14oz) penne
2 tablespoons olive oil
300g (10oz) merguez sausages, cut into bite-size pieces
1 red onion, thinly sliced
2 tablespoons dry while wine
12 cherry tomatoes, halved
85g (3oz) rocket leaves, washed and shredded
Salt and freshly ground black pepper
50g (2oz) Parmesan, freshly grated

Bring a pan of salted water to the boil and cook the penne. Meanwhile, heat the oil in a large frying pan, add the merguez and onion and fry for 2–3 minutes. Add the wine and simmer for 10 minutes. Then add the tomatoes. When the pasta is cooked, drain well and toss in the sauce with the rocket. Mix well, season and serve at once with Parmesan.

Daucus carota complex *sativus. Apiaceae*

CARROT

Swollen-rooted biennial grown as annual for edible orange-red roots. Hardy/half hardy. Value: extremely rich in beta carotene (vitamin A), small amounts of vitamin E.

'Sweetheart' produces good, uniform roots and is ideal for early cropping.

Though there are white, yellow, purple and violet carrots, most of us are more familiar with orange carrots, which have been known only since the eighteenth century. Domestication is thought to have occurred around the Mediterranean, Iran and the Balkans. The Greeks cultivated them for medicinal uses, valuing them as a stomach tonic. In Roman and early medieval times, carrots were branched, like the roots of wild types; the conical-rooted varieties seem to have originated in Asia Minor around AD 1000. Moorish invaders took them to Spain in the twelfth century; they reached North-West Europe by the fourteenth and England in the fifteenth century. Gerard mentions only one yellow variety, purple ones being most popular – even though when cooked they turned into a nasty brown colour.

The Elizabethans and early Stuarts used flowers, fruit and leaves as fashion accessories for hats and dresses and carrot tops were highly valued as a substitute for feathers, particularly when they coloured up in autumn.

European explorers took the carrot across the Atlantic soon after the discovery of the New World and it was growing on Margarita Island, off the coast of Venezuela, in 1565, arriving in Brazil before the middle of the seventeenth century. The Pilgrim Fathers took it to North America and it was grown by early colonists in Jamestown, Virginia in 1609. Said to make you see well in the dark and to make your hair curly, it is now highly valued as a rich source of vitamin A.

VARIETIES

There are several groups of carrots and the names indicate the root shape and time of maturity. With successional sowing it is possible to harvest carrots for up to 9 months of the year and still have supplies in store.

Paris Market types
These have small round or square roots and are ideal for difficult shallow, heavy or stony soils. Fast-maturing for early crops. **'Early French Frame'** is round-rooted, tasty and quick-maturing, ideal for forcing or sowing in succession outdoors. **'Little Finger'** is blunt-tipped with extremely sweet, bright orange round roots. **'Parmex'**, an early-maturing round carrot, is excellent for heavy, stony or shallow soil.

Amsterdam types
These varieties have small, stumpy, cylindrical roots. **'Amsterdam Forcing-3'** is early, slender-rooted and tasty. Ideal for freezing. **'Sweetheart'** has good colour and taste. Good for early crops and forcing.

Nantes types

These carrots are broader and longer. Mainly for forcing and early crops. **'Nantes Express'**, an early maincrop, is suitable for early sowing in frames. **'Navarre'** is tasty, sweet and well coloured. Crops heavily. **'Newmarket'** are good-quality, sweet-tasting, tender carrots.

Chantenay types

This group is stump-rooted and slightly tapered. A maincrop for summer. **'Red Cored Supreme'**, a smooth-skinned early maincrop, can be sown successively from spring to late summer. **'Red Cored-2'** is a richly coloured carrot with an excellent flavour and small core. **'Babyean'** is ideal for small carrots.

Berlicum types

These are cylindrical and stump-rooted, a late crop for storing. **'Camberly'** produces a high-quality, deep orange root with a smooth skin. **'Ingot'** is extremely tasty. Particularly high in beta carotene and vitamin C.

Chantenay type

Autumn King types

These are large and late-maturing. For winter use and storing. **'Autumn King'** is robust, substantial and well coloured. **'2 Vita Longa'** is late-harvesting, heavy-cropping and keeps well.

Other carrots worth growing are **'Flyaway'**, **'Sytan'** and **'Resistafly'** (all show considerable resistance to carrot fly) and **'Juared'**, also known as **'Juwarot'**. This is a medium to late variety, is extremely rich in vitamin A and is ideal for winter storage.

'Juared' has approximately double the quantity of vitamin A than regular varieties, and is ideal for juicing

CULTIVATION

Propagation

Germination is poor at soil temperatures below 7.5°C (45°F): warm the soil before sowing early crops. Another option is available for the small Paris Market varieties – sow 3–4 seeds per module and plant out after hardening off in mid-spring.

Carrot seed is very small and is easier to sow when mixed with sand or 'fluid sown'. Sow sparingly to reduce thinning and associated problems with carrot fly.

Seeds should be in drills 2cm (¾in) deep in rows 15cm (6in) apart; allow 10cm (4in) between plants in the rows for early crops and 4–6cm (1½–2¼in) apart for maincrops, depending on the size of roots you require.

Sow all but the Berlicum and Autumn King types from mid- to late spring for cropping from late summer to early autumn.

Sow Chantenay, Autumn King and Berlicum types from mid- to late spring for mid- to late autumn crops.

Sow Autumn King and Berlicum types in late spring for mid- to late winter harvesting.

Growing

Early carrots need an open, sheltered position; maincrops are less fussy. Soils should be deep, light and free-draining, warming early in spring, and with a pH of 6.5–7.5. Carrots are the ideal crop for light sandy soils – you should be able to push your index finger right down into the seedbed. Avoid walking on prepared ground to ensure maximum root growth.

Dig in plenty of well-rotted organic matter in the autumn before planting. On heavy or stony soils, grow round or short-rooted varieties, or plant in raised beds or containers.

Rake the seedbed to a fine texture about 3 weeks before sowing and use the 'stale seedbed' method, allowing the weeds to germinate and hoeing off before sowing.

Keep crops weed-free at first by mulching, hand weeding or careful hoeing to avoid damaging the roots. In later stages of growth the foliage canopy will suppress weed growth.

Keep the soil moist to avoid root splitting and bolting. Water at a rate of 14–22 litres/sq m (3–5 gal/sq yd) every 2–3 weeks, taking particular care with beds surrounded by barriers as a protection against carrot fly, as these create an artificial rain-shadow.

Maintenance

Spring Sow crops successively from mid-spring when the soil is workable.
Summer Harvest early crops, sow maincrops. Keep well watered.
Autumn Sow under cover for a mid-spring crop. Harvest.
Winter Harvest and store.

'Autumn King' ready for lifting

Protected Cropping

Sow Nantes types in an unheated greenhouse, under cloches or fleece in mid-autumn for a mid-spring crop. Sow Paris Market, Nantes and Amsterdam Forcing in mid-spring for early to mid-summer crops.

Container Growing

Choose short-rooted or round varieties for containers, window boxes or growbags. Sow in loam-based compost; keep moist throughout the growing season.

Harvesting and Storing

Early cultivars are ready to harvest after around 8 weeks, maincrops from 10 weeks. In light soils, roots can be pulled straight from

'Early Nantes' to the left; Autumn King' centre and right

the ground, but on heavier soils they should be eased out with a garden fork. Water the soil beforehand if it is dry.

On good soils, maincrop carrots can be left in the ground until required. Cover with a thick layer of straw, bracken or similar material before the onset of inclement weather to make lifting easier.

Alternatively, lift roots, cut or twist off foliage and store healthy roots in boxes of sand in a cool, dry, frost-free place for up to 5 months. Check regularly and remove any that are damaged.

Freeze finger-sized carrots in polythene bags. Top and tail, wash and blanch for 5 minutes. Cool and rub off the skins.

Carrots will stay fresh for about 2 weeks in a cool room or in a polythene bag in the refrigerator.

PESTS AND DISEASES

Carrot fly is the most serious problem. Attracted by the smell of the juice from the root, their larvae tunnel into the roots making them

inedible. Leaves turn bronze. Sow resistant cultivars, sow sparingly to avoid thinning, thin on a damp overcast day (or water before and after), pinch off the tops of thinnings just above the soil level and dispose of them in the compost heap. Lift and dispose of affected roots immediately. Lift 'earlies' by early autumn and maincrops by mid-autumn.

Since these pests do not fly very high, grow carrots under fleece or film, or surround with a barrier of fine netting or fleece 60cm (24in) high, or grow in raised beds or boxes.

Root and leaf aphids can also be a problem.

COMPANION PLANTING

Intercropping carrots with onions reduces carrot fly

attacks; leeks and salsify have also been used with some success.

Mixing with seeds of annual flowers also seems to discourage carrot fly.

Carrots grow well with lettuce, radishes and tomatoes and encourage peas to grow. They dislike anise and dill.

If left to flower, carrots attract hoverflies and other beneficial predatory insects to the garden.

MEDICINAL

Reputed to be therapeutic against asthma, general nervousness, dropsy, and skin disorders.

Recent research suggests that high intake of beta carotene slows cancerous growths. Beetroot and carrot juice is reported to prevent diarrhoea.

A bunch of carrots just waiting for Peter Rabbit to swipe them!

Carrot Juice

CULINARY

For eating raw, harvest young for maximum sweetness. Older carrots need to be peeled and the hard core discarded. Grated, they can be made into salads and are especially good mixed with raisins and a little chopped onion and then tossed in a good French dressing or mayonnaise thinned with a little virgin olive oil.

Try freshly plucked baby carrots, rinsed under the tap, topped and tailed, very lightly boiled in as little water as possible, then sprinkled with chopped parsley, a little sugar and freshly ground black pepper, or just a knob of butter. Add a sprinkling of sugar, a tablespoon of butter and a pinch of salt, cover and gently steam until tender. Cook in a cream sauce seasoned with tarragon, nutmeg and dill, or steam with mint leaves.

Cut into sticks as raw snacks, slice for stews and casseroles, pickle, stir-fry, use for jams, wine and carrot cake. Carrots are an essential ingredient in stocks, soups and many sauces.

Balkali Havuçi

Balkali Havuçi
Serves 4

Serve this Armenian-Turkish dish with pilav and salad; it can be topped with a dollop of yoghurt.

500g (1lb) broad beans, shelled
300ml (½pt) water
1 onion, chopped
2 cloves garlic, finely chopped
2 carrots, cut into rings 2.5cm (1in) thick
2 tablespoons dill or mint, chopped
1 teaspoon salt
Freshly ground black pepper
Pinch sugar
3 tablespoons virgin olive oil

Rinse the beans. Put the water into a large saucepan and bring to the boil; add the onion and beans, bring to the boil, cover and simmer until tender.

Stir in the remaining ingredients and cook until the vegetables are just tender, about 20 minutes more. Serve hot with chunks of good bread as a starter.

Carrot and Raisin Cookies

Carrot and Raisin Cake

This spicy dough mixture can equally be used to make cookies, in which case drop heaped tablespoonfuls of dough on to a lightly greased baking sheet 5cm (2in) apart and bake for 12–15 minutes until golden. Cool on a rack and store in tins in the refrigerator.

150g (6oz) plain flour
2 teaspoons baking powder
1 teaspoon cinnamon
Pinch mace
Pinch salt
2 heaped tablespoons seedless raisins
100g (4oz) carrots, grated
Grated zest of half an orange
2 tablespoons orange juice
100g (4oz) butter
125g (5oz) brown sugar
2 large eggs

Sift the flour, baking powder, spices and salt into a large bowl and set aside. Mix the raisins, carrots, orange zest and juice and set aside. Cream the butter and sugar thoroughly in a mixer and beat until light. Add the eggs, one at a time, with the blender on slow. Combine the batter with the flour and carrot mixtures and blend well.

Pour into a greased and lined 20cm (8in) tin and bake in a preheated oven (180°C/350°F/gas mark 4) for 40–60 minutes. Test with a skewer to ensure the cake is cooked and allow to cool in the tin for 15 minutes before turning out on a wire rack.

Dioscorea alata. Dioscoreaceae

YAM

Also known as Greater Yam, Asiatic Yam, White Yam, Winged Yam, Water Yam.
Twining climber grown for large edible tubers.
Tender. Value: rich in carbohydrate and potassium, small amounts of B vitamins.

The 'greater yam' is believed to have originated in east Asia and is widely cultivated as a staple crop throughout the humid tropics. It was said to have reached Madagascar by AD 1000 and by the sixteenth century Portuguese and Spanish traders had taken it to West Africa and the New World, often as a food on slave-trading ships. Christopher Columbus knew of the plant as *nyame* and the tubers were regularly used for ships' supplies because they stored for several months without deteriorating and were easy to handle. There are hundreds of different forms producing tubers with an average weight of 5–10kg (8–22lb), although specimens with massive tubers up to 62kg (136lb) have been recorded.

Yams maturing in paddy fields in Luazon, Philippines

VARIETIES

Dioscorea alata has square, 4-winged or angled twining stems with pointed, heart-shaped, leaves. Small bulbils are often produced on the stems. The tubers are brown on the outside with white flesh, vary in size and are usually produced singly. There is a great number of cultivars which vary in the colour and shape of the stems, leaves and tubers.

'White Lisbon', one of the most widely grown, is high-yielding, shallow-rooted and tasty; it will store for up to 6 months. 'Belep', 'Lupias', 'Kinbayo', and 'Pyramid' are also high-yielding.

Propagation
Yams are usually planted on banks, mounds or ridges at the end of the dry season while they are still dormant, as they need the long rainy season to develop. Small tubers, bulbils or sections with 2–3 buds or 'eyes' taken from the tops of larger tubers are used for propagation. The latter are preferable, as they sprout quickly and produce higher-yielding plants. They can be 'sprouted' in a shady position before planting 15cm (6in) deep and 30–90cm (12–36in) apart on mounds 120cm (48in) across or ridges 120cm (48in) apart. Spacing depends on the site, soil and the variety.

Growing
Yams need a humid, tropical climate, 150–175cm (60–70in) of rain in a 6–12 month growing season and a site in sun or partial shade. Soils must be rich, moisture-retentive and free-draining, as yams can survive drought but not waterlogging.

Dig in plenty of well-rotted organic matter before planting and grow plants up trellising, arbours, poles or netting at least 180cm (72in) high, or allow them to grow into surrounding trees.

Keep crops weed-free.

Tropical crops do not grow well below 20°C (68°F). Growth increases with temperature and the crucial time for rain is 14 to 20 weeks after planting, when food reserves are nearly depleted and the shoots are growing rapidly.

Maintenance
Spring Increase watering as new shoots appear when growing under cover.
Summer Maintain high temperatures and humidity.
Autumn Reduce watering as stems turn yellow.
Winter Keep compost slightly moist.

Protected Cropping
If you are able to provide an environment and cultural conditions similar to those described under 'Growing', yams can be grown indoors. The minimum temperature for active growth is 20°C

Yams drying in the sun

(68°F); damp down greenhouse paths and mist with tepid water during summer, and reduce watering during the resting season as the stems die back, gradually increasing the amount in spring when plants resume active growth.

Harvesting and Storing

Depending on the variety and weather conditions, tubers are ready to harvest from 7–12 months after planting as the leaves and stems die back. Lift them carefully, as damaged tubers cannot be stored.

Tubers are normally dried on a shaded vertical frame or in an open-sided shed before being stored in a dark, cool, airy place where they can last for several months. Do not store yams at temperatures below 10°C (50°F).

PESTS AND DISEASES

Leaf spot appears as brown or black spots on stems and leaves. Storage rot can be a serious problem and yam beetles feed on tubers and damage the shoots of newly planted sets. Scale insect also causes problems.

Yams need to be well spaced to flourish

COMPANION PLANTING

Grows well with taro, ginger, maize, okra and cucurbits.

MEDICINAL

Yams have been used as a diuretic and expectorant.

WARNING

All yams except *Dioscorea esculenta* contain a toxin, dioscorine, which is destroyed by thorough cooking.

CULINARY

Yam can be peeled and then boiled, mashed, roasted and fried in oil. In West Africa, they are pounded into *fufu* in a similar way to manioc, and are added to a thick soup made of spices, meat, oil, fish and vegetables. Yams are tasty cooked with palm oil, candied, casseroled with orange juice or curried.

They can be peeled and boiled in water with a pinch of salt, then brushed with melted butter and grilled or barbecued until brown; serve with more butter.

In China they are mashed with lotus root, wrapped in lotus leaves and steamed.

They can also be peeled, rubbed with oil and baked at 180°C/350°F/gas mark 4 for 1½ hours, then slit like a baked potato and eaten with seasoned butter or a similar filling.

Yellow Yam Salad
Serves 6

1.5kg (3lb) yellow yams
1 large onion, sliced
3 tablespoons chopped chives
1 sweet green pepper, deseeded diced

8 tablespoons mayonnaise
½ teaspoon cayenne pepper
Salt and freshly ground black pepper
4 hard-boiled eggs, chopped
1 tablespoon black olives, stoned and sliced

Clean the yams and cook in boiling salted water until tender but firm. Drain and allow to cool slightly, then cut into cubes. Add the onions, chives and pepper and mix well.

Season the mayonnaise with the cayenne, salt and pepper and stir into the yam mixture, folding in the eggs and olives carefully.

Check the seasoning. Chill for an hour before serving.

Foeniculum vulgare var. *dulce. Apiaceae*

FLORENCE FENNEL

Also known as Sweet Fennel, Finocchio.
Biennial or perennial grown as annual for pungent swollen
leaf bases, leaves and seeds. Half hardy. Value: good source
of potassium; small amounts of beta carotene.

This outstanding vegetable with a strong aniseed flavour, swollen leafbases (known as 'bulbs') the texture of tender celery, and delicate feathery leaves has been cultivated for centuries as an ornamental vegetable. Its close relative, wild fennel, which lacks the swollen base, is used as a herb. When Portuguese explorers first landed on Madeira in 1418, they found the air fragrant with the aroma of wild fennel, so the city of Funchal was named after *funcho*, the Portuguese name for the plant. Florence fennel was popular with the Greeks and Romans, whose soldiers ate it to maintain good health – while the ladies used it to ward off obesity. In medieval times, seeds were eaten during Lent to alleviate hunger, and dieters still chew raw stalks to suppress their appetite. The first records of its cultivation in England date from the early eighteenth century, when the 3rd Earl of Peterborough cultivated and ate it as a dessert.

In 1824 Thomas Jefferson received seeds from the American consul in Livorno and sowed them in his garden in Virginia. He enthused: 'Fennel is beyond every other vegetable, delicious … perfectly white. No vegetable equals it in flavour.' However, it has become a weed in those countries where conditions are particularly favourable.

VARIETIES

'**Cantino**' is ready to harvest from late summer and is resistant to bolting. '**Fino**' ('**Zefa Fino**') is particularly vigorous and ornamental, looking good in the flower border. It is resistant to bolting. '**Herald**', an old Italian variety, forms plump, sweet bulbs, is resistant to bolting and ideal for early and successional sowing. '**Perfection**', a French variety, has medium-sized bulbs and a delicate aniseed flavour. Resistant to bolting, it is ideal for early sowing. '**Sirio**', again from Italy, is compact with large, sweet white bulbs, and matures rapidly. '**Sweet Florence**' is moderately sized and should be sown from mid-spring to late summer. '**Tardo**' ('**Zefa Tardo**') is an early cropping, bolting-resistant variety.

'**Sweet Florence**', showing its developing bulbs and light, feathery foliage

CULTIVATION

Propagation
Fennel thrives in a warm climate and is inclined to bolt prematurely if growth is checked by cold, drought or transplanting. For early sowings choose cultivars that are bolt-resistant.

Grow successively from late spring to late summer for summer and autumn crops. Sow thinly in drills 1.5cm (½in) deep and 45–50cm (18–20in) apart, thinning when seedlings are large enough to handle to a final spacing of 23–30cm (9–12in) apart.

Where possible, fennel is better sown *in situ* to reduce problems with bolting. Modules are preferred for plants started under cover. Growing in trays is fine if transplants are treated carefully enough.

Growing
Fennel flourishes in temperate to sub-tropical climates, though mature plants can withstand light frosts. The largest bulbs are formed during warm, sunny summers. Plants should be grown as rapidly as possible, so incorporate a slow-release general fertilizer into the soil before planting at

30–60g/sq m (1–2oz/sq yd). Plants need a sunny, warm, sheltered position and well-drained, moisture-retentive, slightly alkaline soil. A light, sandy soil with well-rotted organic matter dug in the winter before planting is ideal. Stony soils and heavy clays should be avoided. Never allow the soil to dry out; mulch in spring and hand weed around bulbs to avoid damage.

When the stem bases start to swell, earth up to half their height to blanch and sweeten the bulbs. Or tie cardboard 'collars' round the base.

Maintenance

Spring Sow early crops under cover. Warm the soil with cloches before sowing early crops outdoors.
Summer Keep the soil constantly moist and weed-free. Harvest mature bulbs.
Autumn Cover later crops to prolong the growing season.
Winter Transplant later sowings for an early winter crop.

Protected Cropping

Cover early outdoor crops with cloches. Sow from mid spring, in modules or trays of seed compost at 16°C (60°F). Pot on seedlings grown in trays when very small, with a maximum of 4 leaves, into 7.5cm (3in) peat

Mature plant ready for harvest

The bulb is made up of swollen, overlapping leaf bases

pots. Transplant in the pots a month after hardening off.

Harden off and plant out those grown in modules at a similar size. Late sowings can be made for transplanting under cover in early winter. Plants do not always produce 'bulbs', but leaves and stems can be used in cooking.

Container Growing

Grow single plants in a container at least 25cm (10in) wide by 30cm (12in) deep containing loam-based compost with added sharp sand. Apply a general liquid fertilizer monthly from late spring to late summer.

Harvesting and Storing

Harvest about 15 weeks after sowing or 2–4 weeks after earthing up, when the bulbs are plump, about 5–7.5cm (2–3in) across and slightly larger than a tennis ball. Cut the bulb with a sharp knife, just above the ground, and the stump should resprout producing small sprigs of ferny foliage. Bulbs do not store and should be eaten when they are fresh.

Leaves can be harvested throughout summer and used fresh in salads, or deep-frozen.

Pests and Diseases

Slugs can damage young plants. Lack of water, fluctuating temperatures and transplanting check can cause bolting.

COMPANION PLANTING

Allow a few plants to flower; they are extremely attractive to a large number of beneficial insects which prey on garden pests.

Fennel has a detrimental effect on beans, kohlrabi and on tomatoes.

MEDICINAL

An infusion aids wind, colic, urinary disorders and constipation. Recent research indicates that fennel reduces the effects of alcohol.

Use in an eye bath or as a compress to reduce inflammation.

Chew to sweeten breath or infuse as a mouthwash or gargle for gum disease and sore throats, to alleviate hunger and ease indigestion.

WARNING

Do not take excessive doses of the oil; nor should it be given to pregnant women.

CULINARY

Use bulbs like celery, removing green stalks and outer leaves. For salads, slice inner leaf stalks and chill before serving. (To ensure that bulbs are crisp, slice and place in a bowl of water and ice cubes in the fridge for an hour.)

Fennel can be parboiled with leeks and is suitable for egg and fish dishes. Steam, grill or boil and serve with cheese sauce or butter. Infuse fresh leaves in oil or vinegar, add to a bouquet garni or snip as a garnish over soups or salads. Gives characteristic flavour to *finocchiona*, an Italian salami, and the French liqueur, *fenouillette*.

Fennel Sautéed with Peas and Red Peppers
Serves 4

2 tablespoons olive oil
2 sweet red peppers, deseeded cut into thin strips
500g (1lb) fennel, trimmed finely sliced
2 cloves garlic, crushed
250g (8oz) peas, shelled
Salt and freshly ground black pepper

In a wok or heavy-based frying pan heat the oil, add the peppers and fennel and cook for 10–15 minutes over a moderate heat until crunchy, stirring occasionally. Add the garlic and peas and continue cooking for 2 minutes. Season and serve.

Glycine max (syn. Glycine soja). Leguminosae

SOYA BEAN

**Also known as Soy Bean. Annual grown for seed sprouts and seeds. Half hardy.
Value: rich in potassium, protein, fibre, vitamins E, B and iron.
Seed sprouts are rich in vitamin C.**

One of the most nutritious of all vegetables, this native of Asia is thought to have been the plant that the Chinese emperor Shen Nung used to introduce people to the art of cultivation. It is mentioned in his *Materia Medica* from around 2,900 BC. Soya beans were first known in Europe through Engelbert Kaempfer, physician to the governor of the Dutch East India company on an island off Japan in 1690–92. The Japanese guarded their culture, but, by bribing the guards and picking plants along the route, Kaempfer was able to get his botanical specimens. Benjamin Franklin sent seeds back from France to North America in the late eighteenth century. In 1829 it was being grown at Cambridge, Massachusetts, where it was considered a luxury. One of the first Americans to be interested in soya beans was Henry Ford, who saw their potential for manufactured goods and is said to have eaten soya beans at every meal, had a suit made from 'soy fabric' and sponsored a 16-course soya bean dinner at the 1934 'Century of Progress' show in Chicago.

VARIETIES

Glycine max is a herb, usually with trilobed leaves and white to pale violet flowers. The pods containing 2–4 seeds are mainly on the lower parts of the stem. **'Black Jet'** is early-maturing; the seeds have a good flavour and it is ideal for a short growing season. **'Fiskeby V'** has yellow beans and is very hardy. **'Hakucho Early'**, an early dwarf Japanese variety, produces 3 small seeds per pod but is high-yielding. **'Lammer's Black'** is the best bean for short seasons, producing heavy crops of thin-skinned, tasty seeds. **'Maple Arrow'** is yellow, hardy and used in processed products. **'Prize'** is widely planted and good for sprouting.

Immature soya bean pods on plant, USA

CULTIVATION

Propagation
Sow when danger of frost has passed and the soil has warmed. Sow 2–3 seeds 2.5cm (1in) deep in heavy soil and 3cm (1½in) deep in lighter soils in 'stations' 7.5–10cm (3–4in) apart with 45–60cm (18–24in) between rows. After germination, thin, leaving the strongest seedling. Alternatively, sow thinly and thin to the final spacing when large enough.

Sprouting Seed
Seeds can also be sprouted. Use untreated seed and remove any that are damaged or mouldy. Soak overnight in cold water. The following morning rinse them thoroughly. Put a layer of moist kitchen roll over the base of a flat-bottomed bowl, tray or 'seed sprouter'. Spread over a layer of soya beans 1 cm (½in) deep and cover with clingfilm. Exclude light by putting the bowl in a dark cupboard or wrapping it in newspaper or tinfoil. Temperatures should be 20–25°C (68–75°F). Check that the absorbent layer stays damp, rinsing morning and night. They should be ready to harvest in 4–10 days when shoots are 2.5–5cm (1–2in) long. Remove sprouts from the shell, and rinse well before eating.

Growing
Soya beans flourish in an open site with rich, free-draining soil and a pH of 5.7–6.2, although there are now cultivars to suit most soils. Where necessary, lime soils and dig in well-rotted organic matter before planting. They are not frost hardy; they prefer 20–25°C (68–75°F); exceeding 38°C (100°F) may retard growth.

Keep plants well watered during drought and early stages of growth. Remove weeds regularly, or suppress by mulching in spring.

Maintenance
Spring Sow seeds under cover or outdoors when there is no danger of frost. *Summer* Keep crops weed-free. Water during drought. *Autumn* Harvest before the pods are completely ripe. *Winter* Hang in bunches in a cool shed and collect seed when the pods open.

Protected Cropping
In cooler climates, sow seeds in pots, modules or trays of seed compost, planting out when the soil is warm. Harden off before transplanting and protect under cloches until established. In cooler climates sow crops in a heated glasshouse.

Looking onto soya bean crop planted to match the field contours, Kansas, USA

Container Growing

This is only worth growing in containers as a 'novelty' crop. Use 20–25cm (8–10in) pots and loam-based compost with moderate fertilizer levels, adding well-rotted organic matter. Keep well watered and weed-free.

Harvesting and Storing

Soya needs a hot summer and fine autumn for the seeds to ripen. Harvesting should be carefully timed so that the seeds are ripe but the pods have not yet split. If conditions are unfavourable, pull up plants when the pods turn yellow and hang up to ripen in a dry place.

Do not harvest when plants are wet, as the seeds are easily bruised. Harvest for green beans as soon as pods are plump and the seeds are almost full size.

PESTS AND DISEASES

Fungal diseases can be a problem if plants are harvested when wet and pods are bruised or broken.

OTHER USES

Soya oil is used in a range of products including ice cream, margarine, soaps and paint; milk substitute is made from the crushed beans, and fermented they make soy sauce and tofu, and also Worcestershire sauce. Also firefighting foam and meat substitute. A valuable plant indeed!

MEDICINAL

Said to control blood sugar levels, lower cholesterol, regulate the bowels and relieve constipation.

WARNING

Soya beans should be cooked before drying; they can cause stomach upset.

CULINARY

Used mainly when green or sprouted for salads or stir-fries. Remove the shell by plunging into boiling salted water for 5 minutes, then allow to cool and squeeze out the seeds. Cook for 15 minutes, then sauté with butter. Juvenile pods can be cooked and eaten whole.

Soak dried beans before eating. A short-cut is to cover with water in a kettle, boil for 2 minutes, allow to stand for one hour, then cook until tender.

Soya Bean and Walnut Croquettes
Serves 4

112g (4oz) soya beans, soaked well rinsed
1 onion, finely chopped
1 clove garlic, crushed
28g (1 oz) butter
112g (4oz) walnuts, pulverized in the liquidizer
½ teaspoon dried thyme
56g (2oz) wholewheat breadcrumbs
1 tablespoon tomato purée
2 tablespoons chopped parsley
½ teaspoon grand mace
1 egg
Salt and freshly ground black pepper
Wholewheat flour
1 beaten egg
Dried breadcrumbs
Oil for shallow frying

Cook the beans until very tender, drain, then mash with a fork, enough to break them up. Fry the onion and garlic in the butter for 10 minutes, then remove from the heat and stir in the beans. Add the walnuts and thyme, together with the breadcrumbs, tomato purée, parsley, mace and egg. (You may need to add more liquid; otherwise use fewer breadcrumbs.) Mix well and season to taste.

Using your hands, shape into small croquettes, then roll in the flour, dip into the egg and roll in the crumbs. Fry in hot oil until crisp and drain on kitchen paper. Serve hot. These go particularly well with a spicy tomato sauce.

Helianthus tuberosus. Asteraceae

JERUSALEM ARTICHOKE

Also known as Girasole, Sunchoke. Tall perennial grown as annual for edible tubers. Hardy. Value: high in carbohydrate but mostly inulin, turning to fructose in storage; moderate vitamin Bl, B5, low in calories.

This vegetable is not from Jerusalem, nor is it any relative of the globe artichoke. Jerusalem' is said to be a corruption of the Italian *girasole* or 'sunflower' – a close relative; the nutty-flavoured tubers were thought to taste similar to globe artichokes, hence the adoption of that name. Frost-hardy, these tall, upright perennials are native to North America, where they grow in damp places. The tubers contain a carbohydrate which causes flatulence; in 1621 John Goodyear wrote that 'they stirre and cause a filthie loathsome wind within the bodie'. In the 1920s they were a commercial source of fructose and were expected to replace beet and cane as a source of sugar.

VARIETIES

'Boston Red' has large, knobbly tubers with rose-red skin. **'Dwarf Sunray'** is a short-stemmed, crisp, tender variety that does not need peeling. It flowers freely and is good for the ornamental border. **'Fuseau'** has long, smooth, white tubers. Plants are compact, reaching 1.5–1.8m (5–6ft). It is a traditional French variety. **'Golden Nugget'** has tapering, carrot-shaped tubers. **'Stampede'** is a quick-maturing variety with large tubers. **'Jacks Copperclad'** has dark coppery-purple tubers and small pretty sunflowers. Plants are tall, reaching 3m

(10ft). It is high yielding and has an excellent taste. **'Mulles Rose'** has large white tubers with rose-purple fleshed eyes. It is easy to grow and extremely tolerant of cold conditions. The tubers of **'Sun Choke'** have a fresh nutty flavour, and are excellent raw in salads, cooked or creamed.

CULTIVATION

Jerusalem artichokes prefer a sunny position, but will grow in shade. They tolerate most soils, though tubers are small on poor ground; the best are grown on sandy, moisture-retentive soil.

They will grow in heavy clay provided it is not extremely acid or subject to winter waterlogging. The fibrous root system makes them useful for breaking up uncultivated ground. The tall stems make excellent temporary screens or windbreaks in sheltered areas, but need staking in more exposed sites.

Propagation

Tubers bought from the greengrocer's can be used for planting. Choose tubers the size of hen's eggs, plant from early to late spring, when the soil becomes workable, 10–15cm (4–6in) deep, 30cm (12in) apart and 90cm (3ft) between rows; cover the tubers carefully. During harvest, save a few tubers to replant or leave some in the soil for the following year.

Growing

Incorporate organic matter in autumn or early winter before planting. Earth up the base of stems to improve stability when plants are 30cm (12in) high. Water during dry weather.

Remove flower buds as they appear. Shorten stems to 1.5–1.8m (5–6ft) in late summer to stop them from being blown over; on windy sites they may also need staking. On poor soil, feed with liquid general fertilizer every 2–3 weeks.

Maintenance

Spring Plant tubers.
Summer Keep weed-free, water and stake if necessary. Remove flower buds.

Jerusalem artichoke stems can make effective windbreaks

Autumn Cut back stems and begin harvesting.
Winter Save tubers for next year's crop.

Harvesting and Storing

In autumn, as the foliage turns yellow, cut back stems to within 7.5–15cm (3–6in) of the ground. Use the cut stems as a mulch to protect the soil from frost, making lifting easier; alternatively, cover with straw. Lift tubers from late autumn to midwinter. They keep better in the ground, but in cold climates or on heavy ground, lift in early winter and store for up to 5 months in a cool cellar in moist peat substitute or sand.

Pests and Diseases

Slugs tend to hollow out tubers. Set traps, aluminium sulphate pellets, pick off manually.

Sclerotinia rot causes stem bases to become covered with fluffy white mould. Lift and burn diseased plants; water healthy plants with fungicide.

Cutworms eat stems at ground level; damaged plants wilt. Keep crops weed-free, cultivate well or scatter an appropriate insecticide in the soil before planting.

MEDICINAL

The carbohydrate inulin is difficult to digest; tubers are low calorie and suitable for diabetics.

WARNING

Jerusalem artichokes can become an invasive weed. After harvesting, lift even the smallest tuber from the ground.

Artichoke Soup

CULINARY

Artichokes are versatile vegetables when the weather is cold: they can be kept in the ground until you want to cook them and then dug up root by root. Fresh tubers have a better flavour, but they become more digestible if stored; they will keep in a polythene bag in the salad drawer of the fridge for anything up to 2 weeks.

There is no need to peel them painstakingly unless you want a very smooth, creamy-white purée – the vitamins are, after all, just below the skin. (If you do want them peeled, steaming or boiling knobbly varieties makes the job easier.) To serve as a vegetable, scrub tubers immediately after lifting, boil for 20–25 minutes in their skins in water with a teaspoon of vinegar; peel before serving if desired. The addition of a little grated nutmeg always does wonders in bringing out the unusual flavour.

To make rissoles, form boiled, mashed artichokes into flat cakes and deep-fry. Jerusalem artichokes can also be fried, baked, roasted or stewed – or eaten raw.

Artichokes gratinéed in a sauce made with good, strong Cheddar make an excellent accompaniment to plain meat dishes such as baked ham or roast lamb. Parboil the artichokes and drain when they are just tender. Roughly slice and layer into a dish. Pour over a béchamel sauce flavoured with French mustard and well-matured cheese and bake in a hot oven (200°C/400°F/gas mark 6) until browned.

Artichoke Soup
Serves 4

500g (1lb) Jerusalem artichokes
2 tablespoons olive oil
2 large onions, sliced
1 large garlic clove, crushed
600ml (1pt) chicken stock
Strip of orange peel
Salt and finely ground black pepper
4 tablespoons thick cream

Scrub the artichokes, discard any hard knobs and roughly chop. Heat the oil in a heavy-based pan and add the onions. Cook until translucent, add the garlic, continue cooking for a couple of minutes and add the artichokes. Toss well to coat with oil and pour in the chicken stock. Bring to the boil, add the orange peel and season. Cover and simmer for 15–20 minutes, until cooked. Remove from the heat, discard the peel and blend in a food processor. Return to the pan, adjust the seasoning, stir in the cream and serve.

Ipomoea batatas. Convolvulaceae

SWEET POTATO

Also known as Kumara, Louisiana Yam, Yellow Yam. Trailing perennials grown as annuals for starchy tubers and leaves. Tender. Value: excellent source of beta carotene, rich in carbohydrates, moderate potassium and vitamins B and C. Yellow and orange types rich in vitamin A.

The 'sweet potato' is unrelated to the 'Irish' potato but is a relative of the bindweed, in the morning glory family. It was cultivated in prehistoric Peru and is now found throughout the tropics; it is also a 'staple' crop in Polynesia. Its arrival there is a mystery; some suggest it was taken there by Polynesians who visited South America, others think it arrived on vines clinging to logs swept out to sea. It was cultivated in Polynesia before 1250 and reached New Zealand by the fourteenth century. Captain Cook and Sir Joseph Banks found the Maoris of the North Island growing it when they landed in 1769.

It was grown in Virginia by 1648. Columbus introduced it to Spain and it was widely cultivated by the mid-sixteenth century, pre-dating the 'Irish' potato by nearly half a century. It reached England via the Canary Islands about the same time and was the 'common potato' in Elizabethan times, some even holding it to be an aphrodisiac.

VARIETIES

There are hundreds of sweet potato varieties worldwide. They are classified under three groups: dry and mealy-fleshed, soft and moist-fleshed, and coarse-fleshed types used as animal feed. White or pale types are floury with a chestnut-caramel flavour, while yellow and orange varieties are sweet and watery.

'Centennial' is vigorous, to 5m (16ft), with bright copper-orange skin and deep orange flesh. Prolific with high-quality tubers, it grows well in short seasons. 'Jewel', a vigorous, high-yielding variety, has excellent quality copper-coloured tubers with moist white flesh. Stores well and disease-resistant. 'Porto Rico Bush' has deep orange, sweet flesh. Excellent for baking. Does not need much space. 'Tokatoka Gold' is large, rounded and smooth-textured. Popular in New Zealand. 'Vardaman' does not 'vine', has golden-yellow skin and deep red-orange flesh. High-yielding.

CULTIVATION

Propagation
Take cuttings from healthy shoots 20–25cm (8–10in) long. Cut just below a leaf joint, remove basal leaves.

Alternatively, pack several healthy tubers in a tray of moist and sharp sand, vermiculite or perlite in a warm greenhouse, or plant into hotbeds. When shoots reach 23–30cm (9–12in), cut them off 5cm (2in) above the soil and take the cuttings as described above. Three potatoes should produce about 24 cuttings, enough for a 10m (25ft) row.

In the humid tropics and sub-tropics, cuttings are rooted *in situ* at the start of the rainy season. Plant on ridges 15–30cm (6–12in) high and 1–1.5m (3–4½ft) apart. Just below the ridge top, insert cuttings 23–30cm (9–12in) apart, leaving half of the stem exposed.

Or, instead of cuttings, plant small tubers 7.5–10cm (3–4m) deep along the top of the ridge. On sandy, free-draining soil plant cuttings and tubers on level ground.

Growing
Sweet potatoes thrive in a tropical or sub-tropical climate with an annual temperature of 21–26°C (70–77°F). Light frost kills leaves and damages tubers.

Ideal annual rainfall is 750–1200mm (30–50in), with wet weather in the growing period and dry conditions for the tubers to ripen. Tuber production is

Large-scale sweet potato crop in North Carolina, USA

fastest and sugar production highest when daylengths exceed 14 hours.

Soils should be moisture-retentive and free-draining with a pH of 5.5–6.5. If necessary, dig in well-rotted organic matter before planting. Watering is rarely needed if planted at the start of the rainy season.

Excessive nitrogen encourages stems to develop rather than tubers. Once established, scatter a high-potash granular fertilizer around plants. Occasionally lift vines from the ground to prevent rooting at the leaf joints. Rotate crops.

Maintenance
Spring Take cuttings under cover, keep warm and moist.
Summer Keep cuttings weed-free, water well and feed. Prune as necessary.
Autumn Harvest. Save some tubers for the next crop.
Winter Keep compost slightly moist.

Protected Cropping
Grow under cover in cool temperate climates at a minimum temperature of 26°C (77°F).

Take cuttings as normal from healthy shoots of mature plants, and insert about 4 cuttings round the outside of a 15cm (6in) pot filled with cuttings compost. Keep moist with tepid water. Transplant into a greenhouse border once a good root system has formed. Mist regularly. Prune stems longer than 60cm (24in) to encourage sideshoots and also late winter to thin out congested growth.

Container Growing
Grow in pots or containers 30cm (12in) deep and 37.5cm (15in) wide using loam-based compost with moderate fertilizer levels. Provide supports.

Harvesting and Storing
In good conditions, tubers ripen in 4–5 months. Lift when slightly immature; otherwise wait until vines

The flower is similar to that of the Morning Glory

begin to yellow. Lift carefully to avoid bruising. Use fresh or store once dried in a cool dark place for up to a week.

PESTS AND DISEASES

Leaves can suffer from leaf spot and sooty mould. Black rot appears at the base of the stem and brown rots on the tuber. Check stored tubers regularly. Also susceptible to whitefly or red spider mite under cover.

MEDICINAL

Sweet potatoes and their leaves contain anti-bacterial and fungicidal substances and are used in folk medicine. In Shakespeare's day they were sold in crystallized slices with sea holly ('eringo') as an aphrodisiac. In *The Merry Wives of Windsor*, Falstaff cries: 'Let the sky rain potatoes…hail kissing-comforts and snow eringoes'. The Empress Josephine introduced sweet potatoes to her companions, who were soon serving them to stimulate the passion of their lovers. The results are not recorded!

CULINARY

A sweet potato contains roughly one and a half times the calories and vitamin C of the 'Irish' potato. Before cooking, wash carefully and peel or cook whole. Parboil and cut into 'chips', grate raw and make into fritters or roast with a joint of meat.

Glazed with butter, brown sugar and orange juice, sweet potatoes accompany Thanksgiving dinner. In Latin America and the Caribbean they are used in spiced puddings, casseroles, soufflés and sweetmeats. The leaves can be steamed.

Tzimmes
Serves 4

This one-pot meal is based on Olga Phklebin's recipe from *Russian Cooking* but adapted to our ingredients.

1–2 sweet potatoes, depending on size
2 large potatoes
Olive oil
1kg (2lb) stewing steak, cubed
1 large onion, chopped
2 carrots, chopped
750ml (1¼pt) vegetable stock
3 tablespoons honey
½ teaspoon cinnamon powder
1 tablespoon plain flour
Chopped parsley, to garnish
Salt and freshly ground black pepper

Peel both sorts of potato and cut roughly. Heat the oil in a heavy pan and sauté the meat well to brown it on all sides. Remove from the pan and keep warm. Brown the onion, adding the carrots and the meat and sufficient stock to cover. Season with salt and pepper and bring to the boil, then simmer for 45 minutes.

Stir in the potatoes, the honey, cinnamon and more seasoning if required. Bring back to the boil and simmer for a further 45 minutes, covered. If the stew is too liquid, allow it to boil fast at this stage. Remove 5 tablespoons of the stock and mix with the flour. Pour this back into the pot, bring to the boil and cook for a further 30 minutes or until the meat is tender and the potatoes are cooked. Sprinkle with parsley and serve with a green salad.

Lactuca sativa. Asteraceae

LETTUCE

Annual grown for edible leaves. Half hardy to hardy. Value: rich in beta carotene, particularly outer leaves.

The garden lettuce is believed to be a selected form of the bitter-leaved wild species *Lactuca serriola*, which is found throughout Europe, Asia and North Africa. The ancient Egyptians were said to have been the first to cultivate lettuces and there are examples of tomb wall paintings depicting a form of Cos lettuce, which is said to have originated on the Greek island of the same name. They believed it was an aphrodisiac and also used its white sap and leaves in a concoction alongside fresh beef, frankincense and juniper berries as a remedy for stomach ache. The Romans, too, attributed medicinal properties to the lettuce and the Emperor Augustus erected an altar and statue in its honour; they believed that it upheld morals, temperance and chastity. The Romans were said to have introduced it to Britain with their conquering armies and even after many centuries it is still regarded as the foundation of a good salad.

Cos lettuce

'Lollo Rossa'

VARIETIES

The many cultivars are divided into three main categories – cabbage, leaf and Cos types. They can be grown all year round, and many modern cultivars are disease-resistant.

Cabbage Lettuce
More tolerant of drought and drier soils than the other kinds, this group includes Butterhead types, with soft buttery-textured leaves which are usually grown in summer, and Crisphead types, which have crisp leaves forming compact hearts.
   Butterhead: **'Action'** has thick, pale green leaves and is resistant to mosaic virus and downy mildew. **'All Year Round'** is tasty and compact with pale green leaves. It is slow to bolt and hardy. **'Avondefiance'** is an excellent, high-yielding, dark green lettuce which withstands drought and high temperatures. It is ideal for summer crops, particularly those sown from mid- to late summer, and is resistant to root aphid and downy mildew. **'Buttercrunch'** has compact, crisp, dark green heads and a beautiful 'buttery' heart. Slow to 'bolt' and heat-resistant. **'Dolly'** is a large lettuce for midsummer to mid-autumn cropping. It has good resistance to downy mildew and lettuce mosaic virus. **'Kwiek'**, a large-headed variety for winter cropping, is downy mildew-resistant. Sow in late summer for harvesting in midwinter or force as an early spring crop. **'Musette'** has dark green, succulent leaves and is resistant to root aphid, lettuce mosaic virus and downy mildew. **'Sabine'** is

'Lobioits Green' combines well with sorrel and can be made into soups

'Oak Leaf', an old variety, has several different colour forms

'Premier Great Lakes' is large, crisp and rapidly maturing. Heat- and 'tip-burn'-resistant. 'Saladin' is excellent for summer cropping and is resistant to 'tip burn'. 'Webb's Wonderful' is extremely popular, and rightly so. It is a good-quality lettuce which lasts well at maturity.

Salad Bowl or Leaf lettuce
These are loose-leaved varieties which sometimes form an insignificant heart. Cut to resprout, or remove single leaves as needed. They stand longer before bolting than other types and can be grown at any time of year; however, growth is slower in winter.
    'Grand Rapids' has crinkled pale green leaves

'Lollo Blonda'

has bronze-green to crimson leaves. 'Ruby' is crinkled and pale green with deep red tints. Has good heat resistance. 'Salad Bowl' was one of the first leaf lettuces with masses of green, deeply lobed leaves which are crisp but tender. Good resistance to bolting.

Cos or Romaine
These flourish in humus-rich, moist soil, take longer to mature than other varieties and are better in cooler weather. Some can overwinter outdoors or be grown as leaf lettuce if closely spaced. They are generally very tasty.
    'Bubbles' is similar to 'Little Gem', with crisp, crinkly leaves and a good

flavour. It is ideal for the small garden. 'Lobjoits Green' is a large, good-quality, tasty old variety which is deep green and crisp. It can be grown as closely as leaf lettuce. Subject to 'tip burn'. 'Little Gem' is a compact, quick-maturing, semi-Cos with a firm, sweet heart. Good as a catch crop, for early crops under cover and for small gardens. It has remained a popular variety since the late nineteenth century. 'Valmaine' is good for growing as a 'cut and come again' or for close planting and use as leaf lettuce. 'Winter Density' is very sweet-tasting and good for overwintering outdoors or for sowings under cover.

resistant to root aphid and downy mildew. The outer leaves of 'Sangria' are tinged red, the inner a pale green. Has some resistance to mildew and mosaic virus. 'Soraya' also has some resistance to downy mildew and lettuce mosaic virus. 'Valdor', which has firm, dark green hearts, is a hardy

'Rosa Pablo', showing its tightly packed habit

lettuce for overwintering outdoors.
    Crisphead: 'Avoncrisp' has some resistance to mildew and root aphid, but can suffer from 'tip burn'. 'Iceberg' has very crisp tender leaves with large ice-white hearts, ideal for spring or summer sowing. The heart has the best-quality leaves. 'Malika' grows very rapidly and should be harvested soon after it matures. It has some resistance to 'tip burn' and lettuce mosaic virus.

and is resistant to 'tip burn'. 'Lollo Blonda' is similar to 'Lollo Rossa', but with fresh pale green leaves and some resistance to lettuce root aphid. 'Lollo Rossa' adds colour to salads. The leaves are tinged red with serrated, wavy margins. Good mixed with Cos or Iceberg lettuces and attractive as an edging plant in the flower border or vegetable plot. 'Oak Leaf' has several different colour forms, from pale green to brown. It dates from the late eighteenth century and is tasty and ornamental. 'Red Salad Bowl'

'Webb's Wonderful'

CULTIVATION

Propagation

Germination is poor, particularly with Butterhead types, if soil temperatures exceed 25°C (77°F), with the critical period being a few hours after planting. During hot weather sow in late afternoon or evening when soil temperatures are lower, water after sowing to reduce soil temperature, shade before and after sowing, germinate in trays or modules in a cool place and transplant, or fluid sow. Lettuces do not transplant well in dry soil and hot weather; where possible, summer sowings are better made *in situ* or in modules.

Sow thinly in drills 1–1.5cm (½–¾in) deep; seeds sown too deeply are slow or fail to germinate. Thin to the final spacing when plants are large enough to handle (overcrowding checks growth and can cause bolting). In cool weather, thinnings can be transplanted if lifted with care to avoid root damage.

Sow those grown in trays or modules in loam-based potting compost to maintain strong growth and harden off before transplanting when they have 4 to 5 true leaves. Do not transplant when the weather is hot and dry, unless shading can be provided, and do not plant them too deeply.

Sow summer crops from mid-spring to midsummer. Sow winter-hardy varieties from late summer to early autumn, thinning to the final spacing in spring.

As they do not last long after maturity, maintain a continuous supply of lettuce by sowing successionally, about every 2 weeks, just as the seedlings from the previous sowing appear.

Thin when the seedlings are large enough to handle, where possible staggering them in a triangular pattern to make optimum use of the area.

Space small lettuces 20cm (8in) apart in and between the rows, Butterheads with about 28cm (11in) in and between the rows, or 25cm (10in) apart in rows 30cm (12in) apart. Crispheads should be planted 38cm (15in) apart or 30cm (12in) apart with the rows 38cm (15in) apart. Plant Salad Bowl or Cos about 35cm (14in) apart in and between the rows.

Leaf lettuce can also be grown as 'cut and come

'All Year Round' – ironically, for sowing only from spring to autumn

again' seedlings providing 2 or 3 harvests before bolting: summer crops tend to run to seed more rapidly. Make sure you sow thinly.

Cos varieties like 'Lobjoits Green' can be grown as leaf lettuce. Sow in rows 13cm (5in) apart, thinning to 2.5cm (1in). Sow weekly from late spring to early summer and again in 3 consecutive weeks from late summer. This technique was developed at Horticulture Research International, Wellesbourne, UK.

Growing

Lettuce prefer cool growing conditions, from 10–20°C (50–68°F), and need an open, sunny site on light, rich, moisture-retentive soil, with a pH of around neutral.

They struggle on dry or impoverished soil, so dig in plenty of well-rotted organic matter the autumn before sowing or grow on ground manured for the previous crop. Lightly fork in a base dressing of general fertilizer at 60g/sq m (2oz/sq yd) about 10 days before sowing and create a seedbed by raking to a fine tilth.

Hoe and hand weed regularly to remove weeds. A constant supply of moisture is vital for success.

Lettuce need 22 litres/sq m (4 gal/sq yd) per week in dry weather. Water in the mornings on sunny days so that the water on the leaves evaporates quickly, reducing the risk of disease. If water is scarce, apply only on the last 7–10 days before harvest.

Boost growth of winter-hardy outdoor crops with a liquid general fertilizer in mid-spring and use the same treatment for slow-growing crops at any time of year.

Rotate crops every 2 years to avoid the build up of pests and diseases.

Maintenance

Spring Sow crops under glass or outdoors under cloches in early spring. Sow later crops outdoors. Harvest early crops.
Summer Sow successionally and harvest overwintered crops. Keep crops weed-free, water as needed. Harvest.
Autumn Sow and protect crops under cloches. Harvest.
Winter Sow crops under cover. Harvest.

Protected Cropping

Sow from late winter to early spring in modules or trays for transplanting under cloches or cold frames from mid- to late spring.

It is worth growing the attractive 'Sangria' in ornamental borders

Alternatively, they can be sown *in situ* in cold frames or under cloches for growing on or transplanting outdoors in a protected part of the garden and covered with floating cloches.

Protect late spring and summer transplants under cloches until they become established and protect late summer sowings under cloches to maintain the quality of autumn crops.

Grow hardier varieties under floating cloches or in a glasshouse or a cold frame over winter, ideally with a gentle heat around 7°C (45°F).

Sow from late summer to mid-autumn for transplanting. Earlier sowings can be made outdoors in a seedbed for transplanting; others can be sown in modules or seed trays. Ventilate well to avoid disease problems.

Harvest from late autumn to mid-spring. Cover outdoor winter-hardy crops with glass or floating cloches to ensure a good-quality crop and provide protection during severe weather.

Sow early crops of 'cut and come again' seedlings under cover in late winter or spring, and also from mid-autumn.

Container Growing

Compact varieties are suitable for growing in pots, containers and window boxes. Use a soil-based compost, mix in a slow-release granular fertilizer and water regularly. Sow either *in situ* or in modules for transplanting.

Harvesting and Storing

Summer maincrop lettuce are ready to harvest from early summer to mid-autumn, around 12 weeks after sowing. Cos stand for quite a time in cool weather but Butterheads deteriorate within a few days of maturity. Crispheads last for about 10 days before deteriorating. Leaf lettuces can be picked over a long period. Harvest hardy overwintered outdoor crops from late spring to early summer.

Harvest 'cut and come again' seedlings about 4 weeks after sowing and Cos types grown as leaf lettuce about 2.5cm (1in) above the ground when they are 7.5–12.5cm (3–5in) high. A second crop can be harvested from 3 to 8 weeks later, depending on the growing conditions.

Cut mature lettuces at the base just below the lower leaves. Do not squeeze hearting lettuces to check if they are ready for harvesting as this can damage the leaves: press them gently but firmly with the back of your hand. Pull single leaves from leaf lettuce as required or cut 2.5cm (1in) above the base and allow to resprout.

Growing lettuce under black plastic sheeting warms the soil, suppresses weeds and conserves moisture

Store lettuce in the refrigerator in the salad drawer or a polythene bag for up to 6 days. Cos lettuce stores the longest.

PESTS AND DISEASES

Root aphids appear in clusters on the roots and are usually covered in a white powdery wax. The symptoms are stunted growth and yellowing leaves; plants may collapse in hot weather. They are less of a problem in cool, damp conditions. Pick and destroy affected plants or grow resistant varieties.

Aphids can also be a problem.

Leaf tips become brown and dry when affected by 'tip burn', caused by sudden water loss in warm weather. Water well and shade if necessary; do not allow lettuces to grow excessively large; grow resistant varieties where possible.

Botrytis or grey mould can be a problem in cool, damp conditions. Do not plant seedlings too deeply, handle transplants carefully to avoid damage, thin early, remove diseased material, improve ventilation, spray with systemic or copper-based fungicide. Grow resistant varieties.

Bolting or running to seed is caused by check during transplanting, drought, temperatures over 21°C (70°F), or long days; otherwise lettuces will only bolt after hearting. Grow resistant varieties or leaf lettuce.

Pigeons and sparrows can damage seedlings. Grow under horticultural fleece, tie thread between bamboo canes, use humming line or other deterrents.

Lettuce mosaic virus causes the leaves to become puckered and mottled, veins become transparent and growth is stunted. More of a problem on overwintering crops. Destroy those that are affected, control aphids, grow resistant varieties.

'Webb's Wonderful', a large-hearted lettuce, grows well in hot summers

COMPANION PLANTING

Lettuce grow well with cucumbers, onions, radishes and carrots. Dill and chervil protect them from aphids.

MEDICINAL

Lettuce is used as a mild sedative and narcotic, and lettuce soup is reported to be effective in treating nervous tension and insomnia. Lettuce sap dissolved in wine is said to make a good painkiller.

Lettuce soothes inflammation – lotions for the treatment of sunburn and rough skin are made from its extracts.

It can also be used as a poultice on bruises or taken internally for stomach ulcers and for irritable bowel syndrome.

It is also anti-spasmodic and can be used to soothe coughs and bronchial problems; it is reputed to cool the ardour.

CULINARY

Wash leaves thoroughly before use. Use fresh or wilted in salads, braise with butter and flavour with nutmeg or braise with peas and shallots and serve with butter. Stir-fry with onions and mushrooms, steam and add to chicken soup or make cream of lettuce soup and garnish with hardboiled eggs and a sprinkling of curry powder. Stalks can be sliced and steamed.

Braised Lettuce
Serves 4

Cos lettuces all seem to bolt at the same time, and braising them is an excellent way of ringing the changes from salads.

4–5 lettuce, trimmed
A little oil or butter
50g (2oz) bacon, roughly diced
1 carrot, roughly diced
1 red onion, sliced
300ml (½pt) well flavoured vegetable stock
2 tablespoons chopped thyme and parsley
Salt and freshly ground black pepper

In a saucepan of salted water, cook the lettuces for 5 minutes. Drain and refresh in cold water. Drain again and remove as much liquid as possible.

Grease an ovenproof dish and sprinkle the base with the bacon, carrot, onion and seasoning. Arrange the lettuces neatly in the dish and pour in the stock. Cover with buttered paper and braise in a preheated oven, 180°C/350°F/gas mark 4, for 30–40 minutes.

Remove the lettuces and other ingredients and keep hot. Then reduce the cooking liquid and pour it over the vegetables. Sprinkle with the fresh herbs and serve

Braised Lettuce

Lactuca sativa var. *augustana*. Asteraceae

CELTUCE

*Also known as Stem Lettuce, Asparagus Lettuce, Chinese Lettuce.
Annual grown for edible leaves. Value: little nutritive value;
low in carbohydrate and calories; a source of potassium.*

Introduced from China, where it has been grown for centuries, this 'oriental vegetable' consists of a short-stemmed mutation lettuce. It has been listed in European catalogues since 1885, but the name 'celtuce' was adopted by an American seed company who first offered seeds in 1942. It aptly describes its characteristics: the stems are used like celery; the leaves make a lettuce substitute.

VARIETIES

'Zulu' is a new variety for cooler climates, with narrow, dull-textured leaves. Others are sold in seed mixes of broad, dull, glossy or red-leaved varieties.

CULTIVATION

Celtuce needs well-drained, rich, fertile soil, with a pH of 6.5–7.5, around neutral. Celtuce tolerates a range of temperatures from light frosts to over 27°C (80°F). It tends to bolt prematurely in extremely hot conditions, but is still more heat-resistant than lettuce. Grow celtuce as a winter crop in mild areas.

Propagation
For successional cropping, sow every 2 weeks from mid-spring until midsummer in drills 1cm (¹⁄₂in) deep and 30cm (12in) apart. When large enough to handle, thin to 9cm (3¹⁄₂in).

Germination is poor in temperatures above 27°C (80°F). In hot summers, sow in seed trays or modules in a cool, partially shaded position. Modules tend to produce better plants than seed trays; weak seedlings rarely produce good stems. Transplant when 3–4 leaves have been produced, generally after 3–4 weeks. Mulch after planting to conserve moisture and suppress weeds; the shallow roots are very easily damaged by hoeing.

Growing
In poor soils add copious amounts of organic matter the winter before planting. Celtuce grows well on light soil, but develops a stronger root system and more robust plants on heavier soils.

Water well as leaves develop to keep them tender. As the stems develop, reduce watering, but take care to keep the supply steady: if the soil becomes too wet or too dry, the stems may crack. Feed with a liquid general fertilizer every 3 weeks.

Maintenance
Spring Sow seed.
Summer Water and remove weeds.
Autumn Transplant seedlings for winter crops.
Winter Grow under cover; harvest mature crops.

Protected Cropping
Grow in cloches, unheated glasshouses, tunnels or under horticultural fleece to extend the season. Raise early crops by sowing and planting under cover in early spring and late crops by transplanting summer-sown seedlings under cover in autumn.

Container Growing
Sow in containers or pots in a loam-based compost with moderate levels of added fertilizer.

Harvesting and Storing
Harvest 3–4 months after sowing, when 30cm (12in) high and 2.5cm (1in) diameter. Cut the stalks, pull up the plant or cut it off at ground level. Trim the leaves from the stem but do not touch the top rosette of leaves in order to keep the stem fresh.

Celtuce stems can be kept for a few weeks in cool conditions.

PESTS AND DISEASES

Celtuce is susceptible to the same problems as lettuce. Pick off slugs, set traps or use aluminium sulphate pellets. Downy mildew is worse in cool, damp conditions: treat with fungicide, and remove infected plants and debris at the end of the season.

COMPANION PLANTING

Plant with chervil and dill to protect from aphids. Interplant between slower-growing crops such as cauliflower, self-blanching celery or Chinese chives.

CULINARY

Celtuce is excellent raw and cooked. Prepare the stems by peeling off the outer layer. Cut into thin slices for salads (raw or cooked), or into larger pieces for cooking. Cook lightly, for 4 minutes at the most. Stir-fry with white meat, poultry, fish, other vegetables, or on its own seasoned with garlic, chilli, pepper, soy or oyster sauce.

Lagenaria siceraria. Cucurbitaceae

DOODHI

Also known as Bottle Gourd, Calabash Gourd, White, flowered Gourd, Trumpet Gourd. Vigorous annual climber grown for edible young fruits, shoots and seeds. Tender. Value: little nutritive value; a moderate source of vitamin C, small quantities of B vitamins and protein.

Early evidence for the cultivation of this versatile tropical gourd comes from South America around 7000 BC, though it is thought to have originated in Africa south of the Sahara or India. Some sources suggest that it may have dispersed naturally by floating on oceanic currents from one continent to another: experiments have found that seed will germinate after surviving over seven months in seawater. One of the earliest crops cultivated in the tropics, these gourds with their narrow necks have developed in many shapes and sizes, some reaching up to 2m (6ft) long. The young fruits are edible, but mature shells become extremely hard when dried and have been used to make bottles, kitchen utensils, musical instruments, floats for fishing nets and even gunpowder flasks. In the past *lagenaria* leaves were used as a protective charm when elephant hunting.

VARIETIES

Lagenaria sicerana is a vigorous annual, climbing or scrambling by means of tendrils to more than 10m (30ft). The leaves are broad and oval with wavy margins. Its solitary, fragrant, white flowers open in the evenings. Its fruits are pale green to cream or yellow, with a narrow 'neck', and contain white, spongy flesh and flat creamy-coloured seeds. The names of selected forms (like 'bottle', 'trumpet', 'club' or 'powderhorn' gourd) relate to their use and appearance.

CULTIVATION

They flourish in warm conditions, around 20–30°C (68–86°F) and plenty of sunshine, but will grow outdoors in warm temperate climates where humidity levels are moderate to high. Plants need to be trained over supporting structures.

Propagation

Soak seeds overnight in tepid water before sowing on mounds of soil about 30cm (12in) apart, containing copious amounts of well-rotted manure. Plant 3 seeds, edgeways, and thin to leave the strongest seedling. Seeds can be sown in a nursery bed and transplanted when they have 2 to 3 leaves. Seeds are usually sown at the start of the rainy season.

Growing

Doodhi needs fertile, well-drained soil, preferably with a pH of 7. Add a granular general fertilizer to the planting hole or scatter it around the germinated seedling. Train the stems into trees, or over fences, arbours or frames covered with 15cm (6in) mesh netting. Erect stakes or trellis on the beds or among the groups of mounds. Alternatively, grow plants in beds 120–180cm (48–72in) square, planting a seedling at each corner and training towards the centre. Pinch out the terminal shoots when they are 3–4cm (1¼–1½in) long to encourage branching. The best yields are obtained in warm-climate areas with rainfall around 80–120cm (28–48in) per annum, but they grow well in drier regions if they are kept well watered. Feed with a high-nitrogen fertilizer every 3 weeks during the growing season, keep crops weed-free and mulch with a layer of organic matter.

Plants can grow extremely rapidly in hot weather: 60cm (2ft) in 24 hours has been recorded. Where conditions are suitable they can be grown all year round. To grow outdoors in cooler climates, harden off under cloches or cold frames and plant in a sheltered, sunny position when the danger of frost has passed.

The chance of success is greater in hot summers; they should reach edible size, though they rarely have a long enough season to mature fully.

Maintenance
Spring Sow seeds under glass in warm conditions. *Summer* Train vines over trellis or netting. Water regularly, feed as necessary. Damp down the greenhouse to maintain humidity and harvest young fruits. *Autumn* In cooler climates harvest mature gourds for preserving, before the onset of the first frosts.

Protected Cropping
In cool temperate climates, sow seeds 6–8 weeks before the anticipated planting out time. Sow 2–3 seeds in a 15cm (6in) pot of peat-substitute compost in late winter or early spring at 21–25°C (70–75°F).

Germination takes 3–5 days. If the ideal temperatures cannot be achieved and maintained, delay sowing until mid- to late spring. Transplant when seedlings are 10–15cm (4–6in) high. They will grow at temperatures down to 10°C (50°F), but flourish at high temperatures and in humid conditions in bright filtered light.

Damp down the greenhouse floor at least twice a day, depending on outside weather conditions. Dig in plenty of well-rotted manure and horticultural grit or sharp sand into the glasshouse border, or grow in containers. Keep the compost constantly moist using tepid water and feed with a liquid general fertilizer every 2 weeks.

Train up a trellis, wires or netting. Flowers will appear from early summer and only 1 or 2 should be allowed to grow to maturity.

Doodhi growing in a Cypriot village garden

Container Growing
Pot on as plants grow until they are in 30cm (12in) pots, or grow in large containers of loam-based compost with added organic matter and horticultural grit or sharp sand to improve drainage. Keep the compost moist, with tepid water. Growth is better restricted when they are grown in pots and is preferable in the greenhouse border, increasing the chance of successful fruiting.

Stop the shoot tips when the stems are 1.5m (5ft) long and train the side stems along a wire. (It is worth noting that even with this method, plants still need a considerable amount of space.) Hand-pollination ensures a good crop. (Male and female flowers are on the same plant: females are recognized by the ovary at the back of the flower, covered in glandular hairs.) Once a flower has formed, allow 2 more leaves to appear, then pinch out the growing tip. If it is a male flower or a fruit is not going to form, cut the stem back to the first leaf. A replacement will be formed.

Harvesting and Storing
Vines begin to fruit 3–4 months after planting. Harvest immature fruits when a few centimetres (inches) long, 70–90 days after sowing. Mature fruits can be harvested and dried slowly as ornaments.

Pests and Diseases
This very robust plant is rarely troubled by disease. Whitefly can occasionally be a problem when plants are grown under cover. In warm, humid climates, anthracnose appears as pinhead-sized, water-soaked lesions on the fruits, combining to form a small black mass. Fruit rot can also be a problem. Spray with Bordeaux or Cheshunt compound and remove badly affected leaves. Harvest fruits carefully to avoid damage.

MEDICINAL USES

The fruit pulp around seeds is emetic and purgative and is sometimes given to horses! Juice from the fruit treats baldness; mixed with lime juice, it is used for pimples; boiled with oil, it is used for rheumatism. Seeds and roots are used to treat dropsy and the seed oil used externally for headaches.

CULINARY

Young fruits, which are rich in pectin, are popular in tropical Africa and Asia. They have a mild, somewhat bland taste, are peeled before eating and any large seeds removed. They can be cubed or sliced, sautéed with spices to accompany curries and other Indian dishes and added to stews or curries. Young shoots and leaves can be steamed or lightly boiled. Seeds are used in soups in Africa and are boiled in salt water and eaten as an appetizer in India. The seed oil is used for cooking.

Lens culinaris. Leguminosae

LENTIL

*Also known as Split Pea, Masur.
Annual herb grown for edible, flattened seeds. Tender.
Value: rich in protein, fibre, iron, carbohydrate, zinc and B
vitamins.*

'Lentille du Puy', a small seed French variety, in unripe pod

'Lentille du Puy', ready for harvest

Presumed to be native to south-west Europe and temperate Asia, lentils are one of the oldest cultivated crop plants. Carbonized seeds found in Neolithic villages in the Middle East have been dated at 7–6000 BC, and it is believed that they were domesticated long before that. By 2200 BC plants appeared in Egyptian tombs; they are referred to in the Bible as the 'mess of pottage' for which Esau traded his birthright (Genesis 25: 30, 34). The English 'lens', describing the glass in optical instruments, comes from their Latin name – its cross-section resembles a lentil seed. Christian Lent has the same origin, as it was traditionally eaten during the fast.

Grown throughout the world, lentils have become naturalized in drier areas of the tropics. Because of their relatively high drought tolerance, they are suitable for semi-arid regions. The quick-maturing plant is rarely more than 45cm (18in) tall and has branched stems forming a small bush. The white to rose and violet flowers lead to 2–3 seeded pods.

VARIETIES

Lentils have been selected over many centuries for their size and colour. Today many different races and cultivars exist. Two main races predominate: the larger, round-seeded types usually grown in Europe and North America, and the smaller, flatter-seeded types common in the East.

Frequently encountered is the **split red** or **Persian lentil**, which is extremely tender and quick to cook.

Among round-seeded types grown in Europe, the **'Lentille du Puy'**, a tiny green form, is the tastiest and tenderest. Similar but coarser is the **lentille blonde** or **yellow lentil** commonly grown in northern France, while **German** or **brown lentils** are coarser still and need lengthy cooking to make them tender. Of varieties grown in North America, **'O'Odham'** has flat grey-brown to tan-coloured seeds and **'Tarahumara Pinks'** from Mexico has mottled seeds and thrives well in semi-arid conditions.

CULTIVATION

Propagation
Prepare the seedbed by removing any debris from the soil surface and raking to a moderate texture. Sow in spring when the soil is warm in drills 2.5cm (1in) deep, thinning seedlings to 20–30cm (8–12in) apart with 45cm (18in) between rows. They can also be broadcast and then thinned after germination to 20–30cm (8–12in) apart.

Growing
Lentils are not frost-hardy but flourish in a range of climatic conditions. They prefer a warm, sunny, sheltered position on light, free-draining, moisture-retentive soil. Sandy soils with added well-rotted organic matter are ideal, though equally good crops are grown on silty soil. Keep crops weed-free and irrigate if necessary during periods of prolonged drought. Excessive watering can lead to over-production of leaves and poor cropping.

Lentils can be grown as a 'novelty' crop in cool temperate climates, but yields are not high enough to make it worthwhile on a large scale.

Growing in Idaho, USA

Maintenance

Spring Prepare the seedbed and sow when soil is warm.
Summer Keep crops weed-free and irrigate if necessary.
Autumn Harvest before the seeds split.
Winter Store seeds or pods in a cool dry place, for use as required.

Protected Cropping

In cool temperate climates sow seeds in spring in trays, pots or modules of seed compost. Keep compost moist and pot on when seedlings are large enough to handle. Harden off before planting outdoors when the soil is warm and workable and there is no danger of frosts. Protect plants under cloches until they are properly established.

Container Growing

Grow in containers of soil-based compost with moderate fertilizer levels. Water well and keep weed-free. To avoid the need for transplanting, seeds can be sown in a container which is then moved outdoors into a sunny spot after they have germinated.

Harvesting and Storing

Lentils take about 90 days to reach maturity. Harvest as foliage begins to yellow, before the pods split and the seeds are shed. Lift the whole plant and lay on trays or mats in the sunshine to air-dry or put them in an airy shed. When the pods dry and split, remove the seed and store in a cool, dry place.

CULINARY

As their protein content is about 25%, lentils are an important meat substitute. They also have the lowest fat content of any protein-rich food.

Soak overnight, drain and replace the water. Boil rapidly for 10 minutes, then simmer for 25 minutes until tender. Use in soups, thick broth or grind into flour.

Lentils are commonly used for 'dhal'. Seeds are moistened with water and oil and dried before milling 2–3 times, each time separating the 'chaff from the meal.

Puy Lentils with Roasted Red Peppers and Goat's Cheese
Serves 4

3 red peppers
175g (6oz) lentilles du Puy
1 red onion
1 carrot
Sprig each of parsley, marjoram and thyme
2 tablespoons sun-dried tomatoes, chopped
100g (4oz) crumbled goat's cheese
1 tablespoon freshly chopped herbs

for the dressing:
4 tablespoons extra-virgin olive oil
1¹⁄₂ tablespoons lemon juice
Salt and freshly ground black pepper

Roast the peppers on a baking tray in a pre-heated oven, 250°C/ 475°F/gas mark 9, for 30 minutes. Put them into a polythene bag in the fridge. When cooled, deseed and peel the peppers, then cut into strips. Set aside.

Wash the Puy lentils thoroughly and cook them, covered, with the whole onion, carrot and herbs. These lentils cook faster than other types and should be done in 15 minutes. Drain. Roughly chop the onion and add back into the lentils. Discard the carrot and herbs. While still warm, add the tomatoes and goat's cheese and stir gently. Season.

Make the dressing and toss the lentil mixture in it. Arrange the lentils with the slices of red pepper on individual plates. Sprinkle with the herbs and serve.

PESTS AND DISEASES

Lentils suffer from few pests and diseases. Leaf rust can occur; burn plants after harvest and use treated seed.

COMPANION PLANTING

Lentils can be grown as a 'green manure'.

OTHER USES

Dried leaves and stems are used as forage crops.

Lentils have also been used as a source of commercial starch in the textile and printing industries, the by-products being used as cattle feed. Plants are used fresh or dried as hay and fodder.

WARNING

Never eat lentils raw.

Lotus tetragonolobus (syn. Tetragonolobus purpureus). Papilionaceae

ASPARAGUS PEA

Also known as Winged Pea. Sprawling annual winged bean, ornamental but grown for edible pods. Half hardy. Value: small amounts of protein, carbohydrate, fibre and iron.

A wildflower of open fields and wasteland in Mediterranean countries, this plant may have arrived in Britain with imported grain. It has since become naturalized. Gerard records its cultivation before 1569 for its dark crimson, pea-like flowers; only later were its edible merits discovered, but it has never gained widespread popularity. The 1807 edition of Miller's *Gardener's Dictionary* notes: 'formerly cultivated as an esculent plant, for the green pods … it is now chiefly cultivated in flower gardens for ornament.'

The prominent winged pods illustrate the plant's other name

CULTIVATION

Propagation
Sow seed outdoors from mid- to late spring, once the soil warms and frosts are over. Drills should be 2cm (¾in) deep and 38cm (15in) apart; thin to 20–30cm (8–12in) apart once they are large enough to handle. In cooler areas, sow under cloches or in the glasshouse in trays or modules of moist seed compost. Harden off and transplant outdoors when plants are 5cm (2in) tall, spacing them about 20–30cm (8–12in) apart.

Growing
Asparagus peas flourish in an open, sheltered, sunny site on light, rich, free-draining soil. Keep weed-free and water as required.
As they are lax in habit, growing up pea sticks or a similar support saves space and makes harvesting easier. Rotate them with other legumes.

Maintenance
Spring Sow seed in mid- to late spring.
Summer Harvest regularly.
Autumn Harvest until early autumn.
Winter Prepare ground for the following year's crop.

Protected Cropping
In cooler areas sow under glass for transplanting later.

Harvesting and Storing
Harvest from midsummer to early autumn, when pods are 2.5cm (1in) long. Pick regularly to prolong the harvest. Longer, older pods are 'stringy' and inedible. Pods that do not bend easily are unsuitable for eating. Harvesting is easier in the evening, when the leaves close and the small green pods are more visible.

Pests and Diseases
Protect crops from birds using 'humming line' or similar bird scarers. They can also suffer from downy and powdery mildew.

CULINARY

The subtle flavour is similar to asparagus. Wash the pods, 'top and tail' if necessary, then steam for up to 5 minutes (check them after about 3 minutes, as they need only light cooking). Drain well before eating. Mix with butter and cream or serve on toast. Alternatively, cook in butter until tender, drain and serve.

Asparagus pea flowers are blood-red and tiny

Lycopersicon esculentum. Solanaceae

TOMATO

Also known as Love Apple. Short-lived perennial grown as annual for fleshy, succulent berry. Half hardy. Value: rich in beta carotene and vitamin C; some vitamin B.

The wild species is believed to have originated in the Andean regions of north and central South America, spreading to Central and North America along with maize during human migrations over 2,000 years ago. The fruits had been cultivated in Mexico for centuries when European explorers found them growing under local names including *tomati, tomatl, tumatle* and *tomatas*. When they were first brought to Europe around 1523, tomatoes were considered to be poisonous, due to their strong odour and bright white, red and yellow berries, and were grown only as ornamentals. Dodoens in his *Historie of Plants* of 1578 records, 'This is a strange plant and not found in this country, except in the gardens of some herborists…and is dangerous to be used.'

In Europe, it was first used for food in Italy. Like many vegetable introductions from the New World, it was considered to be an aphrodisiac. The Italian name *pommi dei mori* was corrupted during translation to the French *pomme d'amour* or 'apple of love', as it was thought to excite the passions. Not all believed it to have this effect. Estienne and Liébault wrote that tomatoes were boiled or fried, but gave rise to wind, choler and 'infinite obstructions' – hardly an inducement to romance!

The use of tomatoes by North American settlers was not recorded until after Independence, but they were regularly used as food by Italian immigrants to New England and French settlers living in New Orleans, who were making ketchup by 1779. Thomas Jefferson was certainly growing them in his garden in 1781 and they were introduced to Philadelphia eight years later.

'Tigerella' is unusual but worth growing for its flavour

VARIETIES

Most greenhouse varieties are 'indeterminate', with a main stem that can become several metres or yards long – these are usually grown as 'cordons'. Most of those grown outdoors are bush types which do not need supporting and can be grown under crop covers or cloches. Low-yielding, dwarf varieties are good for pots or window boxes.

As you will see from any seed catalogue, there are hundreds of tomato varieties. Those for cultivation under cover in a cold greenhouse and outdoor varieties are generally interchangeable. They range in size from the large ribbed, 'beefsteak' types to small 'cherry', 'pear-shaped' and 'currant' tomatoes in a great range of colours including mottled, dark skinned, pink and yellow.

'Ailsa Craig' grows well indoors/outdoors. It is a reliable, tasty, heavy-cropping variety. **'Alicante'**, another indoor/outdoor variety, crops heavily, producing smooth tasty fruit. Early maturing, it grows well in growbags. **'Black**

'Brandywine' can weigh up to 0.4kg (1lb) each

Plum' is a Russian variety found in specialist lists. The fruit are elongated, about 7.5cm (3in) long and deep mahogany to brown. 'Brandywine' is a delicious old variety; the fruit can become quite sizeable. The skin is rosy pink or tinged slightly purplish-red. Better in cooler climates. 'Cherry Belle', a tasty little 'cherry' tomato, is of good quality and high yielding. It has resistance to tobacco mosaic virus. 'Delicious' is a large 'beefsteak' variety with fruits weighing up to 0.4kg (1lb). They are tasty, succulent and store well. 'Dombito', also a 'beefsteak', is delicious, crops well and has resistance to tobacco mosaic virus and fusarium wilt. 'Gardener's Delight' is extremely popular, producing long trusses of delicious, sweet, 'cherry' tomatoes over a long period. Grows indoors/outdoors, is ideal for containers and generally trouble-free. 'Green Zebra' is a tasty tomato with unusual green fruits and yellow stripes. 'Marmande Super' is a delicious outdoor variety with deep red ribbed fruits. Early cropping and resistant to fusarium and verticillium wilt. 'Marvel Striped Traditional' is an old Mexican variety with large, tasty, juicy striped fruits. 'Minibel' is a bush tomato with tiny, tasty fruit. It grows well in pots and window boxes. 'Moneymaker' is a famous old variety for

indoors/outdoors. The succulent scarlet fruits are full of flavour. 'Oaxacan Pink' has small, flattened, pink fruits. 'Red Alert' is an early bush variety for the greenhouse or outdoors with small, sweet, oval fruits. 'Roma VF' is an outdoor bush 'plum' tomato for paste, ketchup, bottling, soups or juice. It crops heavily and has high resistance to fusarium and verticillium wilt. It sometimes needs supporting. 'San Marzano', another Italian tomato, is good for soups, sauces or garnishing salads. Crops heavily. 'Shirley' is grown commercially and has good quality, tender, tasty fruit. Withstanding lower temperatures than most types, it does not suffer from 'greenback', is highly resistant to tobacco mosaic virus, leaf mould and fusarium. An ideal tomato for organic growers. 'Siberia Tomato' crops extremely early, around seven weeks from transplanting. This bush variety sets fruit at temperatures down to 5°C (38°F), producing clusters of bright red berries. 'Super Beefsteak' is a huge old fleshy variety whose fruits are at least 0.4kg (1lb) in weight. Has resistance to wilt and root knot nematodes.

'Tigerella' produces tasty, small orange-red fruits with pale stripes. Crops well over a long period. 'Tiny Tim' is compact, bushy and ideal

for pots, window boxes and hanging baskets. Fruits are cherry-sized and tasty. 'Tumbler' was bred for hanging baskets. It has flexible, hanging stems, the bright red fruits ripen quickly and are sweet to the taste. 'Yellow Cocktail' produces large trusses of tiny, pear-shaped, golden-yellow fruits. Grow under glass. 'Yellow Pearshaped' are well described by their name. The dense clusters of fruit are sweet-tasting and have few seeds. Plants are vigorous and high-yielding. 'Yellow Perfection' is prolific with bright yellow fruits, early cropping and tasty. An excellent tomato.

Modern greenhouse varieties such as 'Aromata', 'Moravi' and 'Merlot' are significantly disease-resistant compared with older sorts.

CULTIVATION

Propagation
A minimum temperature of 16°C (60°F) is needed for germination, but seedlings can tolerate lower night temperatures if those during the day are above this level.

In cool climates, for growing in heated glasshouses, sow from midwinter. For growing outdoors or in an unheated greenhouse, sow seed indoors 2cm (¾in) deep in trays of seed compost, 6–8 weeks before the last frost is due or sow 2–3 seeds in 7.5cm (3in) pots or modules, thinning to leave the strongest seedling.

The popular and prolific 'Gardener's Delight'

Transplant tray- or module-grown seedlings into 7.5cm (3in) pots when 2–3 leaves have formed, keeping the plants in a light, well ventilated position. Harden off carefully and plant out when there is no danger of frost and air temperatures are at least 7°C (45°F) with soil temperatures at a minimum of 10°C (50°F).

Transplant, with the first true leaves just above the soil level, when the flowers on the first truss appear. Do not worry if your plants have become spindly; planting them deeply stimulates the formation of roots on the buried stems, making the plants more stable.

Tomatoes can also be fluid-sown from mid-spring *in situ* or in a cold frame for transplanting after warming the soil. Germinate on moist kitchen towel at 21°C (70°F), sowing when the rootlets are a maximum of 5mm (¼in) long (see advice on fluid sowing). Sow outdoors in drills and thin to leave the strongest seedling or in 'stations' at their final spacing. Cover the drills with compost and protect them with cloches until the first flowers appear.

When sowing in cold frames, sow seed in rows 12.5–15cm (5–6in) apart, thinning to 10–12.5cm (4–5in) apart in the rows. Transplant carefully when the plants are 15–20cm (6–8in) tall.

Alternatively, buy plants grown individually in pots rather than packed in boxes or trays, using a reliable supplier.

Plant 'cordon' types 38–45cm (15–18in) apart, or in double rows with 90cm (36in) between each pair of rows. Bush types should be planted 45–60cm (18–24in) apart and dwarf cultivars 25–30cm (10–12in) apart, depending on the variety.

Closer spacing produces earlier crops; wider spacing generally produces slightly higher yields.

Growing

Outdoor tomatoes need a warm, sheltered position, preferably against a sunny wall, in a moisture-retentive, well-drained soil. Add well-rotted organic matter where necessary and lime acid soils to create a pH of 5.5–7. If tomatoes are grown in very rich soil or are fed with too much nitrogen they produce excessive leaf growth at the expense of flowers and fruit. Fruit will not set at night temperatures below 12°C (55°F) and day temperatures above 33°C (90°F). Night temperatures around 25°C (76°F) may well cause blossom to drop.

Tomatoes should be fed with a liquid general fertilizer until established, then with a high-potash fertilizer to encourage flowering and fruiting. Excessive feeding and watering spoils the flavour.

Keep crops weed-free by hoeing and hand weeding, taking care not to damage the stems, or mulch with a layer of organic matter.

Keep them constantly moist but not waterlogged;

Plum tomatoes, grown primarily for cooking and tomato paste because of their fuller flavour

erratic watering causes the fruits to split and also encourages 'blossom end rot', particularly when plants are grown in containers or growbags. Use tepid water. In dry conditions or when the first flowers appear they need about 11 litres (2 gal) water each week.

Careful watering and feeding is essential, particularly near harvest time to ensure that the fruits are not excessively watery and have a good flavour. Feed with tomato fertilizer according to the manufacturer's instructions.

Cordons need supporting with canes, strings or a frame. Using a sharp knife or by pinching between the finger and thumb, remove sideshoots when they appear and 'stop' plants by removing the growing tip 2–3 leaves above the top truss when 3–5 trusses have been formed or when the plant has reached the top of the support. The number of trusses on each plant depends on the growing season: in shorter growing seasons, leave fewer trusses. Remove any leaves below the lowest truss to encourage good air circulation.

In seasons when ripening is slow, remove some of the leaves near to the trusses with a sharp knife, exposing fruits to the sunshine.

To keep the fruit clean and stop fruit from rotting, grow bush tomatoes on a mulch of straw, felt or crop covers laid over the soil. Black polythene or even a split bin liner (with the edges anchored by burying them in the soil) absorbs heat, warms the soil, conserves moisture and helps fruit to ripen.

Rotate crops annually.

Maintenance
Spring Sow crops under cover and, later, outdoors.
Summer Keep crops watered, fed and weed-free. Shade and ventilate as necessary. Remove sideshoots. Harvest.
Autumn Ripen later

'Pearshaped' and currant tomatoes

outdoor crops under cloches or indoors.
Winter Harvest crops in midwinter from cuttings taken in late summer.

Protected Cropping
In cooler climates, more reliable harvests can be achieved by growing tomatoes in an unheated greenhouse or polythene tunnels. Rotate crops to avoid the build-up of pests and diseases and sterilize or replace the soil every 2–3 years. Or use containers. To assist pollination and fruit set, particularly of plants grown indoors, mist occasionally and tap the trusses once the flowers have formed; do this around midday if possible. (It is not so important for outdoor crops, as wind movement assists pollination.) Shade glasshouses before the heat of summer and ventilate well in warm conditions.

A fairly recent innovation is the 'Wall-o-Water', a series of connected plastic tubes filled with water which absorbs heat during the day and warms by radiated heat at night. This is reusable

and offers protection down to -8°C (16°F), extending the growing season and warming the soil. Adding roughly 1 part bleach to 500 parts water will prevent the formation of algae on the inside of the tubes.

For tomatoes at Christmas, take cuttings in midsummer from sideshoots 13cm (5in) long and root them in a container of sharp sand or perlite and water. When roots appear they can be potted into 10cm (4in) pots and grown on under cover.

Protect newly planted outdoor tomatoes with cloches or floating crop covers until they become established. Once the first flowers are pushing against the cover, make slits along the centre; about 7–10 days later slit the remainder of the cover and leave as a shelter alongside the plants. 'Indeterminate' varieties can then be tied to canes.

Container Growing
Tomatoes are excellent for containers, pots or growbags, indoors or outside where they can be included in 'edible' displays

in window boxes, pots and hanging baskets.

Grow in 23cm (9in) pots of loam-based compost with high fertilizer levels. For requirements see 'Growing' and 'Protected Cropping'. Bushy varieties are ideal.

Plants in containers dry out rapidly, so careful feeding and watering is essential. Water regularly and remember to label your plants.

Harvesting and Storing
Harvest fruits as they ripen, about 7–8 weeks after planting for bush types and 10–12 weeks for cordon varieties. Lift and break the stem at the 'joint' just above the fruit. Outdoor crops should be harvested before the first frosts. Towards the end of the season, 'cordon' varieties with unripe fruit can be lifted by the roots and hung upside down in a frost-free shed to ripen. Alternatively, they can be detached from their support, laid on straw and covered with cloches or put in a drawer or a paper bag with a ripe banana or apple (the ethylene these produce

ripens the fruit). Bush and dwarf types can be ripened under cloches.

Tomatoes can be cooked and bottled in airtight jars. To freeze, skin and core when ripe, simmer for 5 minutes then sieve, cool and pack in a rigid container.

Tomatoes stay fresh for about a week in a polythene bag or the salad drawer of a refrigerator. To retain flavour they are better stored at 15°C (60°F).

Dry large 'meaty' tomatoes in the sun or the oven. Cut into halves or thirds and put skin side down on a tray and cover with a gauze frame as a protection from insects. Ideal drying conditions are in warm, dry windy weather, but they should be brought indoors at night if dew is likely to form. Humid conditions are not suitable for outdoor drying. Oven-dry just below 65°C (145°F) until tomatoes are dried but flexible. Stored in airtight containers in a cool place, they can last for up to 9 months. Before use put the tomatoes in boiling water or a 50:50 mix of boiling water and vinegar and allow them to stand until soft. Drain and marinate for several hours in olive oil with added garlic to suit your taste. They last in the marinade for about a month and are excellent with pasta and tomato sauce.

Pests and Diseases

Blossom end rot appears as a hard, dark flattened patch at the end of the fruit away from the stalk. This indicates a deficiency in calcium, usually caused by erratic watering. It is often a problem with plants grown in growbags. Water and feed regularly, particularly during hot weather. Erratic watering causes fruit to split, which may also happen with sudden growth after overcast weather. Pick and use split fruits immediately.

'Greenback', hard, green patches appearing near the stalk, caused by sun scorch and overheating, is more of a problem with plants growing under glass. Sometimes this becomes an internal condition known as 'whitewall'. Shade and ventilate well, water regularly and feed with a high-potash liquid fertilizer.

Curled leaves are caused by extreme temperature fluctuations between day and night. It is often a problem in greenhouses: shade, ventilate and damp down. Close ventilation before temperatures drop.

Whitefly, aphids and red spider mite can be a problem, as can potato blight in wet summers: dark blotches with lighter margins appear on the leaves. Spray with a copper fungicide before fruit set.

Plants with verticillium wilt droop during the day and usually recover overnight. Lower leaves turn yellow and cut stems have brown markings on the inside. Do not plant when the soil is cold, drench with a spray-strength solution of systemic fungicide, mist regularly and shade. Mounding moist compost round the stem encourages the formation of a secondary root system. The symptoms and control of fusarium wilt are similar.

Tobacco mosaic and other viruses show as mottling on the leaves, some of which may be misshapen; inside the fruit is browned and pitted and growth is stunted. Dispose of affected plants, wash your hands and sterilize tools by passing them through a flame. Grow the following year's plants in sterilized compost or in growbags.

Tomato moth caterpillars eat the fruit. They are about 4cm (1½in) long and green or brown with a pale lemon line along the body. They appear from late spring to early summer. Check the underside of leaves and squash the eggs. Also hand pick or spray plants with a biological control.

The symptoms of magnesium deficiency are yellowing between the leaf veins, older leaves being affected first. Spray, drench or scatter magnesium sulphate around the base. Where possible, grow disease-resistant varieties.

COMPANION PLANTING

Grow with French marigolds to deter whitefly.

Tomatoes grow well with basil, parsley, alliums, nasturtiums and asparagus.

MEDICINAL

Tomatoes are believed to reduce the risk of cancer and appendicitis.

In American herbal medicine tomatoes have been used to treat dyspepsia, liver and kidney complaints and are also said to cure constipation.

WARNING

Some doctors believe that tomatoes aggravate arthritis and may be responsible for food allergies. The leaves and stems are poisonous.

Cherry tomatoes underplanted with thyme

CULINARY

In salads, tomatoes are particularly good with mozzarella, basil, olive oil and seasoning. They are also good with chives. Some people prefer to peel them first, by immersing in boiled water for 1 minute to loosen the skins. Use in soups, stews, sauces, pasta and omelettes. Gazpacho is a spicy cold soup of tomatoes, peppers, cucumbers and onions and is delicious.

Tomatoes are wonderful grilled: cut them in half and cover the cut surface with olive oil, pepper and sugar. Grill for 5 minutes. Alternatively, glaze them with wine and brown sugar and grill.

Try a 'BLT' – a cold bacon, lettuce and tomato sandwich. Eat 'currant' and 'cherry' varieties as a snack.

Use larger 'beefsteak' varieties as a garnish with steak or hollow out and stuff with shrimps, potato salad, cold salmon, cottage cheese or mashed curried egg. Serve hot or cold.

Green tomatoes can be sliced, dipped in batter and then breadcrumbs, and fried in hot oil, or made into chutney or jam. They can also be added to orange marmalade.

Tomato and Red Onion Salad

Stuffed Tomatoes
Serves 4

In times gone by Catholics all over Europe ate these on fast days, when meat was not allowed.

4 large ripe tomatoes
350g (12oz) white breadcrumbs (day-old bread)
150ml (¹/₄pt) milk
2 eggs, lightly beaten
2 tablespoons chopped basil
2 tablespoons finely chopped parsley
2 cloves garlic, finely crushed
1 onion, finely chopped
2 tablespoons toasted breadcrumbs
5–6 tablespoons grated Gruyère
Olive oil
Salt and freshly ground black pepper

Remove a slice from the top of each tomato and scoop out the pulp. Season the insides of the tomatoes with salt and pepper, and arrange in a greased baking dish.

Preheat the oven to 180°C/ 350°F/gas mark 4. To make the stuffing, combine the white breadcrumbs with the milk and eggs in a bowl and add the garlic, herbs and onions. Season with salt and pepper and fill the tomatoes.

Sprinkle over the toasted breadcrumbs and Gruyère and drizzle over a little olive oil to prevent burning. Bake until the tomatoes are tender, about 30 minutes.

Manihot esculenta (syn. M. utilissima). Euphorbiaceae

CASSAVA

Also known as Tapioca, Yucca, Manioc.
Tall herbaceous perennial grown for edible tubers and leaves. Tender. Value:
mainly starch; small amounts of vitamin B, C and protein.

Mature cassava plants, Thailand

One of the most important food crops in the humid tropics, cassava is believed to have been cultivated since at least 2500 BC. Unknown as a wild plant, it may have originated in equatorial South America in the Andean foothills, the Amazon basin or regions of savannah vegetation. The earliest archaeological records, from coastal Peru, date from 1000 BC. Tubers contain highly toxic cyanide, which is removed by cooking; accounts tell of starving European explorers eating raw manioc and dying at the moment they thought sustenance had been found. The indigenous Indians tipped their arrows and blowpipe darts with its toxic sap; Arawak Indians committed suicide by biting into uncooked tubers rather than be tortured by the Conquistadors.

The Portuguese brought the crop to West Africa whence it quickly spread, reaching Sri Lanka in 1786, India in 1794 and Java by 1835. An estimated 62 million tonnes of cassava is produced annually, much of it in West Africa, where it is eaten as *fufu*.

VARIETIES

Manihot esculenta is tall and branched, its stems becoming woody with age. The leaves are long-stalked, with 5–9 lobes; toxic latex is present in all parts of the plant. The swollen tubers are cylindrical or tapering, forming a cluster just below the soil surface, and weigh 5–10kg (11–22lb).

There are two types. **'White cassava'** is sweet, soft and used as a source of starch; **'yellow'** varieties are bitter and usually grown as a vegetable. The more primitive bitter varieties contain larger quantities of cyanide, which is washed out by boiling in several changes of water before cooking. In recent selections of 'sweet' varieties, most of the toxin is in the skin, and tubers are edible after simple cooking.

There are well over 100 different forms with local names. **'Nandeeba'**, quick to mature, and **'Macapera'**, used for boiling, are both from Brazil.

Propagation
Take cuttings from mature stems 15–30cm (6–12in) long; plant 1.2m (4ft) apart in rows 1m (3ft) apart or 'pits' 90–105cm (3–3½ft) square in a grid pattern. Planting cuttings upright, leaving the top 5cm (2in) exposed, gives best results. Plant cuttings at the start of the rainy season.

Growing
Cassava flourishes where the warm rainy season is followed by a dry period. It has good resistance to drought; in a constantly wet climate, there is excessive

stem growth and tuber formation is poor. Soils should be deep, rich and free-draining. It is often grown on ridges or mounds as it dislikes waterlogging. Dig deeply before planting, adding well-rotted organic matter. Earth up as necessary. Cassava is a heavy feeder and cannot usually be grown for more than 3 years on the same ground.

Maintenance
Spring Dig in organic matter before planting. *Summer* Plant cuttings at the start of the rainy season. *Autumn* Keep weed-free. *Winter* Harvest at maturity.

Protected Cropping
In cool temperate zones, plants can be grown as a 'novelty crop' in a hothouse. Prepare the borders and cultivate as for 'Growing'. Water well during the growing season and reduce watering during winter.

Harvesting and Storing
Varieties are harvested from 8 months to 2 years after planting, depending on the locality and variety. Harvest when plants have flowered and the leaves are yellow. Lift the whole plant and carefully remove the tubers. They store for up to 2 years in the ground, but should be used within 4–5 days of lifting.

PESTS AND DISEASES

Whitefly and fungal diseases can be a problem. Bacterial diseases, scale and cassava mosaic are a severe problem in Africa.

Plants are highly resistant to locusts.

Harvesting cassava plants, Indonesia

OTHER USES

Cassava is also a source of starch for the manufacture of plywood, textiles, adhesives and paper.

WARNING

All parts of the plant contain toxic latex. Prepare tubers thoroughly before eating. Inhabitants of Guyana take chillies steeped in rum as an antidote to yucca poisoning, but do not rely on it!

CULINARY

The fresh root is equivalent in starch to 33.3% of its weight in rice and 50% in bread, but its nutritional value is unbalanced and high consumption often leads to protein deficiency.

Wash thoroughly and remove the skin and rind with a sharp knife or potato peeler. Boil in several changes of water and allow to dry before cooking.

It can be eaten mashed or boiled as a vegetable or made into dumplings and cakes. Mix with coconut and sugar to make biscuits. The juice from grated cassava is boiled down and flavoured with cinnamon, cloves and brown sugar to make 'cassareep', a powerful antiseptic and essential to the West Indian dish, Pepperpot. Tapioca flour is made from ground chips.

In Africa the fresh root is washed, peeled, boiled and pounded with a wooden pestle to make *fufu*. Cook cassava chunks in boiling water for 45–50 minutes, drain, cool, pound into dough and shape into egg-sized balls to add to soups and stews as a traditional African accompaniment.

Roots of 'sweet' forms can be roasted like sweet potato, baked or fried in slices.

Young leaves can be boiled or steamed and eaten with a knob of butter.

Cassava Chips (Singkong)

These thin, crispy wafers are perfect served as a snack or as a garnish. Allow 300g (10oz) per person to accompany a plain meat course.

Slice the cassava very thinly and leave to dry. Heat some peanut or vegetable oil (do not allow it to smoke) in a wok or a deep pan. Deep fry 1–3 slices at a time by immediately submerging each below the surface of the oil. Remove quickly from the heat and drain well on layers of paper towels.

Cooked Singkong can be stored in an airtight container for several weeks but is best served at once.

Medicago sativa. Papilionacae

ALFALFA

Also known as Lucerne, Purple Medick. Grown as annual or short-lived perennial for seed sprouts and young leaf shoots. Hardy. Value: good source of iron, and protein.

'Medick' comes from the Latin *Herba medica*, the Median or Persian herb, imported to Greece after Darius found it in the kingdom of the Medes. It was a vital fodder crop of ancient civilizations in the Near East and Mediterranean, and known in Britain by 1757. Today, alfalfa is valued by gardeners as a green manure as well as a nutritious vegetable. Its blooms in the wildflower meadow are rich in nectar, while the leaves are a commercial source of chlorophyll.

CULTIVATION

VARIETIES

The species *Medicago sativa* is a fast-growing evergreen legume with clover-like leaves; growing ultimately to 1m (3.5ft), it has spikes of violet and blue flowers. It produces quality crops on poor soils, as it is highly effective at fixing nitrogen in the root nodules.

Penetrating up to 6m (20ft) into the ground, the roots draw up nutrients and aerate the soil. Agricultural varieties are available. If you want to sprout alfalfa seeds, buy untreated seed; that sold for sowing as a crop is usually chemically treated.

Alfalfa can be grown as a short-lived perennial, a 'cut and come again' crop or as seedsprouts. It tolerates low rainfall and can be grown in any soil, in temperate to sub-tropical conditions or at altitude in the tropics.

Propagation
Sow in spring or from late summer to autumn. Thin those grown as perennials to 25cm (10in) apart when large enough to handle. Sow 'cut and come again' crops, spaced evenly, by broadcasting or in shallow drills 10–12.5cm (4–5in) wide.

Growing
Prepare seedbeds in winter, fork the area, remove debris and stones, rake level. Keep weed-free until established. Cut perennials to within a few inches of the base after flowering and renew every 3–4 years, as old plants become straggly.

Maintenance
Spring Sow seed outdoors.
Summer Harvest young shoots from perennials.
Autumn Sow protected crops.
Winter Prepare seedbed.

Protected Cropping
Sow under cloches, horticultural fleece or glass in late summer to autumn for winter cropping.

Container Growing
Sow 'cut and come again' crops in a bright open position in a loam-based compost with low fertilizer levels; water pots regularly.

Harvesting
Harvest 'cut and come again' crops when about 5cm (2in) long a few weeks after sowing. Cut back plants regularly to encourage new growth; they provide young growths for 4–5 years.

Sprouting Seeds
To sprout alfalfa, soak seeds overnight or for several hours, tip seeds into a sieve and rinse. Put several layers of moist paper towel or blotting paper in the base of a jar and cover with a 5mm (¼in) layer of seed. Cut a square from a pair of tights or piece of muslin to cover the top, securing with a band. Place in a bright position, away from direct sun, maintaining constant temperatures around 20°C (68°F). Rinse seed daily by filling the jar with water and pouring off again. Harvest shoots after 3–7 days, when they have nearly filled the jar. Wash and dry sprouts and use as required; do not store more than 2 days.

Pests and Diseases
Rabbits can be a problem.

CULINARY

Young shoot tips and sprouted seeds can be used raw in salads or cooked lightly.

For a tasty salad, try it with hard-boiled eggs (1 per person), anchovies and capers served on a bed of endive and radicchio leaves. To stir-fry, pour a little oil in a pan, add the alfalfa, stir briskly for 2 minutes; serve immediately.

COMPANION PLANTING

Alfalfa accumulates phosphorus, potassium, iron and magnesium; it keeps grass green longer in drought.

MEDICINAL

An infusion of young leaves in water is used to increase vitality, appetite and weight. The young shoots, rich in minerals and vitamin B, are highly nutritious and the seeds appear to reduce cholesterol levels.

Momordica charantia. Cucurbitaceae

KARELA

Also known as Bitter Gourd, Balsam Pear, Bitter Cucumber, Momordica. Annual climber grown for edible fruits and leaves. Tender. Value: fruit a good source of iron, ascorbic acid and vitamin C; leaves and young shoots contain traces of minerals.

This strange-looking fruit with skin the texture of a crocodile has been grown throughout the humid tropics for centuries. Rudyard Kipling's description in Mowgli's 'Song Against People' conveys the plant's vigour as it climbs to 4m (12ft) with the aid of tendrils:

I will let loose against you the feet footed vines,
I will call in the Jungle to stamp out your lines.
The roofs shall fade before it, the house-beams
*   shall fall;*
And the Karela shall cover it all.

The strongly vanilla-scented flowers are followed by the elongated fruit. When ripe, it splits at the tip into three sections, exposing brown or white flattened seeds surrounded by blood-red pulp. The fruits are better eaten young.

The odd-looking, slender fruit have a blistered, puckered skin

CULTIVATION

Male and female flowers are borne on the same plant. Male flowers are 5–10cm (2–4in) long; females are similar, but with a slender basal bract. The fruit can grow up to 25cm (10in) and ripens to become orange-yellow, though a white variety is grown in India and eastern Asia.

Propagation

In humid tropical climates sow at the start of the rainy season, placing 2–3 seeds outdoors in 'stations' 90cm (36in) apart, in and between the rows. Thin after germination, leaving the strongest seedling. Water plants as necessary.

The first flowers appear 30 to 35 days after sowing. In temperate zones, sow seed in early spring under glass at 20°C (68°F) in peat substitute compost. Keep the compost moist with tepid water and repot as necessary when the roots become visible through the drainage holes.

Growing

Karela flourish in moderate to high temperatures with sunshine and high humidity. Plant in beds or mounds of rich, moisture-retentive, free-draining soil. Dig in plenty of well-rotted manure or similar organic matter before sowing.

Pinch out the terminal shoots when they are 3–4cm (1¼–1½in) long to encourage branching, then train the stems into trees, or over fences, arbours, trellis or frames covered with 15cm (6in) mesh netting. Keep plants constantly moist and weed-free throughout the growing season.

Maintenance

Spring Sow seed under glass in peat-substitute compost.
Summer Keep plants well fed and watered.
Autumn When cropping finishes add leaves and stems to your compost heap
Winter Prepare the greenhouse border for the following year's crop.

Container Growing

Plants can be grown indoors in containers containing a rich, well-drained potting mixture of equal parts loam-based compost and well-rotted organic matter with added peat and grit.

Keep the compost moist with tepid water and feed every 2 weeks with a liquid general fertilizer.

Protected Cropping

Grow under cover in temperate zones. Plants need hot, humid conditions in bright light. When growing plants in the greenhouse border, prepare the soil as for 'Growing'.

Growth is better restricted in borders and containers. Stop the shoot tips when the main stems are 1.5m (5ft) long, training the lateral stems along wires or trellis.

Once a flower has formed, allow 2 more leaves to appear, then pinch out the growing tip. If it is a male flower or a flower does not form, cut the stem back to the first leaf to allow a replacement to form. Flowers should be hand-pollinated.

You should damp down the greenhouse floor regularly during hot weather.

Harvesting and Storing

The first fruits appear about 2 months after sowing and should be harvested when they are about 2cm (1in) long and are yellow-green in colour. They can be eaten when longer.

Fruits can be kept in a cool dark place for several days or stored in the salad drawer of a refrigerator for 4 weeks. Karela can also be sliced and dried for use out of season.

Ripe fruit showing crimson seeds

PESTS AND DISEASES

Fruit fly is common; spray with contact insecticide or protect the fruits with a piece of paper wrapped round the fruit and tied with string round the stalk. Red spider mite is a common pest under cover. Leaves become mottled and bronzed. Check plants regularly; small infestations are easily controlled – isolate young plants. The mite prefer hot, dry conditions, so keep humidity high. Spray with derris.

MEDICINAL

The fruits are said to be tonic, stomachic and carminative and are a herbal remedy for rheumatism, gout, and diseases of the liver and spleen. In Brazil, the seeds are used as an anthelmintic. Its fruits, leaves and roots are used in India and Puerto Rico for diabetes. In India, leaves are applied to burns and as a poultice for headaches and the roots used to treat haemorrhoids. In Malaya they are used as a poultice for elephants with sore eyes.

CULINARY

Remove the seeds from mature fruit, and remove any bitterness by salting. Young fruits do not need to be salted.

Karela are ideal diced in curries, Chop Suey or pickles, stuffed with meat, shrimps, spices and onions and fried or added to meat and fish dishes. Mature fruits can be parboiled before adding to a dish or cooked like courgettes and eaten as a vegetable.

Young shoots and leaves are cooked like spinach.

Pelecing Peria
Serves 4

Sri Owen gives this recipe in her marvellous book, *Indonesian Food and Cookery*. Some of the ingredients need determination to track down, but it is worth the trouble.

3–4 karela (peria)
Salt
6 cabé rawit (or hot red chillies)
3 candlenuts
2 cloves garlic
1 piece terasi (shrimp paste, available at Thai shops)
1 tablespoon vegetable oil
Juice of 1 lime

Cut the karela lengthwise in half, take out the seeds, then slice like cucumbers. Put the slices into a colander, sprinkle liberally with salt and leave for at least 30 minutes. Wash under cold running water before boiling for 3 minutes with a little salt.

Pound the cabé rawit, candlenuts, garlic and terasi in a mortar until smooth. Heat the oil in a wok or frying pan and fry for about 1 minute. Add the karela and stir-fry for 2 minutes; season with salt and lime juice. Serve hot or cold.

Oxalis tuberosa. Oxalidaceae

OCA

Also known as Iribia, cuiba, New Zealand yam. Perennial grown for tubers. Half hardy. Value: about 85% water; some carbohydrates; small amounts of protein.

This is common in the high-altitude Andes from Venezuela to northern Argentina, where it is second only to the potato in popularity. At the northern end of Lake Titicaca, more than 150 steep terraces dating from the Incas are still cultivated. Oca is grown in New Zealand, where it was introduced from Chile in 1869. Today it is rarely found in European or American gardens, though it was once grown as a potato substitute. Tubers form in autumn when day lengths are less than 9 hours.

VARIETIES

Oxalis tuberosa is bushy to 25cm (10in) tall, with tri-lobed leaves and orange-yellow flowers. It produces small tubers 5–10cm (2–4in) long which are yellow, white, pink, black or piebald.

CULTIVATION

Propagation
Plant single tubers or slice into several sections, each with an 'eye' or dormant bud and dust the cut surfaces with fungicide.

Plant 12.5cm (5in) deep and 30cm (1ft) apart with 30cm (1ft) between rows. In frost-free climates plant in mid-spring; in cooler areas propagate under cover in 12.5–20cm (5–8in) pots of compost before planting out once frosts have passed.

Growing
Oca flourish in deep fertile soils, so incorporate organic matter before planting. Earthing up before planting increases the yield.

Maintenance
Spring Plant tubers.
Summer Water as necessary.

Exposed tubers, New Zealand

Autumn Tubers can be lifted when needed.
Winter Store tubers in sand.

Protected Cropping
Where early or late frosts are likely, grow under cover to extend the harvest season. Plant in mid-spring in greenhouse borders. Harvest from mid-autumn to early winter. Extend outdoor cropping by protecting with horticultural fleece or cloches.

Container Growing
Oca grow well in containers, although yields are lower. Tubers should be planted in spring in 30cm (12in) pots in loam-based compost with moderate fertilizer levels, with added organic matter.

Regular watering is vital, particularly as tubers begin to form. Allow the compost surface to dry out before rewatering. An occasional feed with liquid fertilizer helps to boost growth.

Harvesting and Storing
About 8 months after planting, check to see if the tubers are mature, then lift carefully. Undamaged tubers can be stored in boxes of sand in a dry frost-free place.

Pests and Diseases
Slugs are often a problem.

COMPANION PLANTING

Oca grow well with potatoes and can be grown under runner beans, maize or crops of a similar height.

WARNING

Prepare tubers correctly before eating to remove calcium oxalate crystals.

CULINARY

Tubers have been selected over the centuries for flavour and reduced levels of calcium oxalate crystals, which otherwise render them inedible. Leave them for a few days to become soft before eating. In South America they are dried in the sun until floury and less acid. If dried for several weeks, they become sweet, tasting similar to dried figs.

The acidity can be removed by boiling in several changes of water. The flavour of tubers even improves once frozen.

Oca can be eaten raw, roasted, boiled, candied like sweet potato and added to soups and stews. Use leaves and young shoots in salads or cook them like sorrel.

Oca and Bacon

Clean 500g (1lb) oca and cut into cubes. Boil in salted water until just tender; drain and combine with 250g (½lb) smoked bacon which has been diced and fried. Coat with mayonnaise, sprinkle over fresh chives and season. Serve warm.

Pastinaca sativa. Apiaceae

PARSNIP

Biennial grown as annual for edible root. Hardy. Value: some carbohydrate, moderate vitamin E, smaller amounts of vitamins C and B.

This ancient vegetable is thought to have originated around the eastern Mediterranean. Exactly when it was introduced into cultivation is uncertain as references to parsnips and carrots seem interchangeable in Greek and Roman literature: Pliny used the word *pastinaca* in the first century AD when referring to both. Tiberius Caesar was said to have imported parsnips from Germany, where they flourished along the Rhine – though it is possible that the Celts brought them back from their forays to the east long before that. In the Middle Ages, the roots were valued medicinally for treating problems as diverse as toothache, swollen testicles and stomach ache. In sixteenth-century Europe parsnips were used as animal fodder, and the country name of 'madneps' or 'madde neaps' reflects the fear that delirium and madness would be brought about by eating the roots.

Introduced to North America by early settlers, they were grown in Virginia by 1609 and were soon accepted by the American Indians, who readily took up parsnip growing. They were used as a sweetener until the development of sugar beet in the nineteenth century; the juices were evaporated and the brown residue used as honey. Parsnip wine was considered by some to be equal in quality to Malmsey and parsnip beer was often drunk in Ireland. In Italy pigs bred for the best-quality Parma ham are fed on parsnips.

VARIETIES

Roots are 'bulbous' (stocky, with rounded shoulders), 'wedge' types (broad and long-rooted) or 'bayonet' (similar, but long and narrow in shape).

'**Alba**' has small, thin wedge- and bayonet-shaped roots and good canker resistance. '**All American**' has wedge-shaped roots and is sweet-tasting. '**Avonresister**' is small with bulbous roots, and excellent resistance to canker and bruising. It is sweet-tasting, performs well on poorer soil and grows rapidly. '**Cobham Improved Marrow**' is wedge-shaped, medium in size and well-flavoured. Resistant to canker. '**Exhibition Long**' is extra-long, with an excellent flavour. '**Gladiator**' produces large, vigorous, well-shaped and fine-flavoured roots with good canker resistance. '**Javelin**' is wedge- or bayonet-shaped, high-yielding and canker-resistant; 'fanging' rarely occurs. '**Hollow Crown**' has fine, mild, tender flesh and crops well. '**New White Skin**' has uniform, wedge-shaped roots and a pure white skin. Good canker resistance. '**Student**' has long slender roots and is very tasty. It originated around 1810 from a wild parsnip found in the grounds of the Royal Agricultural College, Cirencester, England. '**Tender and True**' is an old variety. Very tasty, tender and sweet, it has very little core. '**White Gem**' has wedge-shaped to bulbous smooth roots, with delicious flesh and good canker resistance. It is ideal for heavier soils.

Parsnips cultivated commercially are also rotated; seen growing here in Devon, England

CULTIVATION

Propagation

Parsnip seed must always be sown fresh, as it rapidly loses the ability to germinate. Seeds are also renowned for erratic, slow germination in the cold, wet conditions which often prevail early in the year when they are traditionally sown.

To avoid poor germination, sow later, from mid- to late spring, depending on the weather and soil conditions, when the ground is workable and temperatures are over 7°C (45°F).

Warm the soil with cloches or horticultural fleece a few weeks before sowing. Rake in a granular general fertilizer at 60g/sq m (2oz/sq yd) 1–2 weeks before sowing. Rake the seedbed to a fine texture before sowing.

Sow *in situ* on a still day so the light, papery seeds are not blown away. In dry conditions, water drills before sowing 2–3 seeds at the recommended final spacing in 'stations', thinning to leave the strongest seedling after germination. Sow radishes between the stations to act as a marker crop indicating where slower-germinating parsnip seeds are sown.

Alternatively, sow thinly in drills 5mm to 1cm (¼ to

'Hollow Crown Improved' lifted and washed, ready for use

½in) deep, sowing shorter-rooted varieties in rows 15–20cm (6–8in) apart, thinning to 5–10cm (2–4in), and larger types in rows 30cm (12in) apart, thinning to 13–20cm (5–8in).

In stony soil make a hole up to 90 × 15cm (36 × 6in) with a crowbar, fill with finely sieved soil or compost, sow 2–3 seeds in the centre of the hole and thin to leave the strongest seedling. Grow short-rooted varieties in shallow soils.

Growing

Parsnips thrive in an open or lightly shaded site on light, free-draining, stone-free soil which was manured the previous year.

Traditionally, parsnips are not grown on freshly manured soil as this causes 'fanging', or forking of the roots; however, recent research has not supported this. Dig the plot and add plenty of well-rotted organic matter in autumn or early winter the previous year. Deep digging is particularly important when growing long-rooted varieties.

The ideal pH is 6.5–7.0; lime where necessary, as roots grown in acid soil are prone to canker. Rotate with other roots.

Keep crops weed-free, by hoeing or hand weeding carefully to avoid damaging the roots, or by mulching with well-rotted organic matter. Do not let the soil dry out, as erratic watering causes roots to split. Water at 16–22 litres/sq m (3–4 gal/sq yd) every 2 weeks during dry weather when the roots are swelling.

Maintenance

Spring Rake the seedbed to a fine tilth, apply general fertilizer, sow seed in modules, 'fluid sow', or sow *in situ* when the soil is warm. *Summer* Keep crops weed-free by mulching, hand weeding or careful hoeing. *Autumn* Harvest crops. *Winter* Cover crops with straw or bracken before the

Wild parsnip bears little resemblance to its cultivated counterparts and is less tasty

onset of inclement weather. Dig the soil for the following year's crop.

Protected Cropping

Possible germination problems can be avoided by pre-germinating and fluid-sowing seed, or by sowing in modules under cover and transplanting before the tap root starts to develop.

Container Growing

Shorter-rooted varieties can be grown in large containers of loam-based compost. Longer types are grown in large barrels, making a deep hole in the compost as described above for stony soil. Make sure that containers are well drained.

Harvesting and Storing

Parsnips are a long-term crop and occupy the ground for around 8 months – a factor worth bearing in mind if your garden is small. Roots are extremely hardy and can remain in the ground until required.

Harvest from mid-autumn onwards, covering plants with straw, bracken or hessian for ease of lifting in frosty weather. Make sure you lift them carefully with a fork to avoid root damage.

Lift all your roots by late winter and store them in boxes of moist sand, peat substitute or wood shavings in a cool shed.

Parsnips have a better flavour when they have been

exposed for a few weeks to temperatures around freezing point. (This changes stored starch to sugar, increasing sweetness and improving the flavour.) Stored in a polythene bag in the refrigerator, they remain fresh for up to 2 weeks.

Wash, trim and peel roots, then cube and blanch in boiling water for 5 minutes before freezing them in polythene bags.

PESTS AND DISEASES

Parsnip canker is a black, purple or orange-brown rot, often starting in the crown, which can be a problem during drought, when the crown is damaged or the soil is too rich. There is no chemical control. Sow crops later, improve drainage, keep the pH around neutral, rotate crops and sow canker-resistant varieties. Carrot fly can also be a problem.

COMPANION PLANTING

Sow rapidly germinating radish and lettuces between rows. Parsnips grow well alongside peas and lettuce, providing they are not in the shade.

Plant next to carrots and leave a few to flower the following year as they attract beneficial insects.

MEDICINAL

In Roman times, parsnip seeds and roots were regarded as an aphrodisiac.

CULINARY

In seventeenth-century England there are records of parsnip bread and 'sweet and delicate parsnip cakes'. They were often eaten with salt fish and were a staple during Lent.

Scrub rather than peel parsnips, and use boiled, baked, mashed or roasted with beef, pork or chicken. They combine particularly well with carrots.

Parsnips can be lightly cooked and eaten cold. Parboil and fry like chips or slice into rings, dip in batter and eat as fritters. Grate into salads, add chopped and peeled to casseroles or soups. Or parboil, drain, then stew in butter and garnish with parsley. They are also good parboiled, then grilled with a sprinkling of Parmesan. Try steaming them whole, slicing them lengthways and pan-glazing with butter, brown sugar and nutmeg, or garnishing them with chopped walnuts and a dash of sweet sherry.

Purée of Parsnips

Boil some parsnips and mix them with an equal quantity of mashed potatoes, plenty of salt and freshly ground black pepper, a little grated orange rind, a splash of thick cream and enough butter to make a smooth dish. Sprinkle with chopped flat-leaf parsley and serve piping hot. (Puréed parsnips are also wonderful combined with carrots and seasoned with nutmeg.)

Curried Parsnip Soup
Serves 4–6

1kg (2lb) parsnips
1 large onion, sliced
1 tablespoon butter
2 cloves garlic, crushed
1 good teaspoon curry powder
1 × 400g (14oz) tin chopped tomatoes
1 litre (1³/₄pt) vegetable stock
1 bay leaf
Sprig each of thyme and parsley
4–6 teaspoons yoghurt
Salt and freshly ground black pepper
Chopped parsley, to garnish

Clean the parsnips and peel if old. Chop them roughly. Add the onion to a large soup pot with the butter and garlic and sauté over a medium heat until lightly browned (this helps to give the flavour of Indian cuisine). Stir in the curry powder and continue to cook for 1 minute, stirring constantly.

Then add the parsnips and stir, coating them well in the curry and onion mixture, and add the tomatoes, stock and herbs. Stir thoroughly. Season, bring to the boil and simmer, covered, for about 15–20 minutes, until the parsnips are tender.

Remove the herbs. Then liquidize the soup, adjust the seasoning and garnish with yoghurt and parsley. This is delicious served with crusty bread.

Curried Parsnip Soup

Petroselinum crispum var. tuberosum. Apiaceae

HAMBURG PARSLEY

The leaves look similar to those of flat-leaved parsley

Also known as Parsley Root, Turnip-rooted Parsley. Swollen-rooted biennial, usually grown as annual for roots and leaves. Hardy. Value: root contains starch and sugar; leaves high in beta carotene, vitamin C and iron.

Hamburg parsley is an excellent dual-purpose vegetable. The tapering white root looks and tastes similar to parsnip and can be eaten cooked or raw. The finely cut, flat, dark green leaves resemble parsley; they are coarser in texture, but contribute a parsley flavour and can be used as garnish. As an added bonus it grows in partial shade, is very hardy and an ideal winter vegetable.

Popular in Central Europe and in Germany, it is one of several vegetables and herbs known as *Suppengrun* or 'soup greens' which are added to the water when beef or poultry is boiled and later used for making sauce or soup. Introduced from Holland to England in the eighteenth century, this versatile vegetable enjoyed only a relatively brief period of popularity, but should certainly be more widely grown by Britain's gardeners.

CULTIVATION

Hamburg parsley needs a long growing season to develop good-sized roots. Grow it in moisture-retentive soil in an open or semi-shaded position.

Propagation

As seeds are sown early in the year, it may be necessary to cover the bed with cloches or polythene before sowing to warm up the soil. Sow from early to mid-spring in drills 1 cm (½in) deep and 25–30cm (10–12in) apart, thinning seedlings to a final spacing of 20cm (9in).

They can also be sown in 'stations', planting 3–4 seeds in clusters 23cm (9in) apart. Thin to leave the strongest seedling when they are large enough to handle.

Seeds can also be sown in modules, but should be planted in their final position before the tap root begins to form.

To extend the harvesting season, make a second sowing in midsummer, which will provide crops early the following year.

Growing

Dig in plenty of well-rotted organic matter the autumn before planting or plant in an area where the soil has been manured for the previous crop.

Rake the soil finely before sowing. Germination is often slow and it is important that the seedbed is kept free of weeds, particularly in the early stages.

Use a hoe with care as the plants become established to avoid damaging the roots. Mulching established plants is a sensible option as this stifles weed growth and conserves moisture. A 2.5cm (1in) layer of well-rotted compost will perform the task perfectly. Root splitting can occur if plants are watered after the soil has dried out, so water thoroughly and regularly during dry periods to maintain steady growth.

Maintenance

Spring Sow seeds outdoors, warming the soil if necessary. Seeds can also be sown in modules.
Summer Keep crops weed-free, water during drought and make a second sowing in midsummer for early crops the following year.
Autumn Harvest as required.
Winter Cover crops with bracken or similar protection to make lifting easier in severe weather.

Container Growing

Hamburg parsley can be grown in containers if they are deep enough not to dry out rapidly and provide sufficient space for the roots to form. Regular watering is vital and plants should also be kept out of scorching, bright sunshine.

Harvesting and Storing

This is such a hardy vegetable that it can remain in the ground until required any time from early autumn to mid-spring. When frosts are forecast, cover with straw, bracken or a similar material to make lifting easier. After removing the foliage, store in a box of sand or peat substitute in a cool shed or garage; some of the flavour is lost when roots are stored in this way, so they are better left in the ground if possible.

PESTS AND DISEASES

This tough vegetable is generally trouble-free, but it can suffer from parsnip canker. This appears as dark patches on the root. Control is impossible, but the following measures will help. Dig up and dispose of affected plants immediately, ensure that the soil is well drained, rotate crops and maintain the soil at a pH around neutral.

Hamburg parsley, showing its small parsnip-like roots – rarely seen in greengrocers in the UK

COMPANION PLANTING

When 'station sowing', fill the spaces by planting 'Tom Thumb' or a similar lettuce variety. Sowing radishes between 'stations' is also useful because their rapid germination indicates the position of the Hamburg parsley and prevents you accidentally removing any newly germinated seedlings when weeding.

WARNING

Hamburg parsley should not be eaten in large amounts by expectant mothers or those with kidney problems.

CULINARY

The flavour reminiscent of celeriac, Hamburg parsley is frequently used in Eastern European cooking.

Prepare for cooking by removing the leaves and fine roots, then gently scrubbing to remove the soil: don't peel or scrape. Try Hamburg parsley sliced, cubed and cooked like parsnips (sprinkle cut areas with lemon juice to prevent discoloration). It is delicious roasted, sautéed or fried like chips as well as boiled, steamed or added to soups and stews. It can also be grated raw in winter salads.

Dried roots can be used as a flavouring. Dry them on a shallow baking tray in an oven heated to 80°C (170°F); allow to cool before storing in an airtight jar, in a dark place. Wash the leaves and used as flavouring or garnish.

Croatian Hamburg Parsley Soup
Serves 8

500g (1lb) Hamburg parsley
1 turnip, peeled
1 large onion, peeled
1 good sized leek, cleaned
50g (2oz) butter
2½ litres (4pt) vegetable stock
Salt and freshly ground black pepper
4 tablespoons, sour cream
2 tablespoons each chives and dill
4 tablespoons croûtons

Chop all the vegetables coarsely. Heat the butter in a heavy-bottomed pan and sauté the vegetables until softened. Stir to prevent burning. Pour over the stock, season with salt and pepper and simmer until the vegetables are tender.

Put through a *mouli légumes* or liquidize and return to the pan. Stir in the sour cream and the herbs, allow to heat through again and adjust the seasoning. Do not allow to boil. Serve piping hot, with croûtons.

MEDICINAL

The leaves are a good source of vitamins A and C and contain similar properties to traditional garnishing parsley. They reduce inflammation, are used for urological conditions like cystitis and kidney stones, and help indigestion, arthritis and rheumatism. After childbirth the leaves encourage lactation; the roots and seeds promote uterine contractions. The leaves are also an excellent breath freshener – powerful enough to counter the effects of garlic!

Phaseolus aureus. Papilionaceae

MUNG BEAN

Also known as Green gram, Golden gram. Annual grown for its seed sprouts and seeds. Tender. Value: sprouts: rich in vitamins, iron, iodine, potassium, calcium; seeds: rich in minerals, protein and vitamins.

VARIETIES

Phaseolus aureus is a sparsely leaved annual to about 90cm (3ft) with yellow flowers and small, slender pods containing up to 15 olive, brown or mottled seeds.

CULTIVATION

Propagation

Rake in a general fertilizer at 60g/sq m (2oz/sq yd) about 10 days before sowing. Seeds can be broadcast or sown in drills on a well-prepared seedbed, thinning to 20–30cm (8–12in) apart with 40–50cm (16–20in) between the rows.

Growing

Mung beans flourish on rich, deep, well-drained soils and dislike clay. Add organic matter if necessary and lime to create a pH of 5.5–7.0. Water well throughout the growing season. Ideal growing conditions are between 30–36°C (86–97°F) and with moderate rainfall.

Sprouting Seeds

Use untreated seeds for sprouting, as those treated with fungicide are poisonous. Remove any that are discoloured, mouldy or damaged. Soak them overnight in cold water and the following morning, rinse in a colander. Place a layer of moist kitchen roll or damp flannel over the base of a flat-bottomed tray or 'seed sprouter', then spread a layer of mung beans about 1cm (½in) deep over the surface. Cover the container with polythene and put the bowl in a dark cupboard, or wrap it to exclude light.

   Temperatures of 13–21°C (55–70°F) should be maintained for rapid growth: an airing cupboard is ideal. Rinse the sprouts daily, morning and night.

   Make a 'seed sprouter' from a large yoghurt pot or a plastic ice cream tub with holes punched in the bottom and use the lid as a drip tray. This makes for

This major Indian pulse crop was introduced to Indonesia and southern China many centuries ago and is grown throughout the tropics and sub-tropics, being sown towards the end of the wet season to ripen during the dry season. The leaves and stems are used to make hay and silage and the seeds are used for cattle feed. Mung beans came to prominence in the West with an increased interest in Oriental cuisine: bean sprouts are an easy-to-grow major crop. Among other uses, their flour is a soap substitute and they serve as a replacement for soya beans in the manufacture of ketchup.

Young crop growing in a field in Thailand

Seedsprouts make great stir-fries

easier daily rinsing of the seedlings.

Maintenance

Outdoors Broadcast or sow seed in drills, water when needed, as the soil dries out. Harvest before the pods split. *Sprouting* Keep seeds moist. Harvest regularly.

Harvesting and Storing

Harvest shoots from 3 days onwards when they are about 2.5–5cm (1–2in) long. If the seed coats remain attached to the sprouts, soak them in water, then 'top-and-tailed', removing the seed and shoot tip. Store in the fridge. When growing for seed, gather before they split to prevent the seeds being lost.

Pests and Diseases

Powdery mildew is a problem when plants are dry at the roots. Mulch and water regularly, remove diseased leaves immediately, spray with a systemic fungicide or bicarbonate of soda and destroy plant debris at the end of the season.

MEDICINAL

The seeds are said to have a cooling and astringent effect on fever and an infusion is used as a diuretic when treating beriberi. In Malaya it is prescribed for vertigo.

WARNING

Do not let bean sprouts become waterlogged, as they rapidly become mouldy.

CULINARY

Bean sprouts can be eaten raw, in salads, with a suitable dressing or lightly cooked for about 2 minutes only in slightly salted water. (Be warned: overcooked shoots lose their taste.)

To stir-fry, use only a little oil, stirring briskly for about 2 minutes. In Oriental cooking, bean sprouts combine well with other vegetables, eggs, red meat, chicken and fish and can be used to stuff savoury pancakes, egg rolls and tortillas.

Stir-fried Mung Beans
Serves 2

1 bag mung beans
Groundnut oil, for frying
2 cloves garlic, crushed
250ml (8fl oz) chicken stock
1 tablespoon light soy sauce
1 heaped teaspoon cornflour
2–3 spring onions

Rinse the mung beans well. Heat the oil and the garlic in a wok, then add the mung beans. Fry for 1 minute, stirring constantly.

Cover with chicken stock and cook until tender and the liquid has evaporated. Then stir in the soy sauce and the cornflour. Cook for 2 minutes more.

Garnish with roughly chopped spring onions and serve with rice.

Dried beans just before soaking

Phaseolus coccineus. Papilionaceae

RUNNER BEAN

Also known as Scarlet Runner) Perennial climber grown as annual in temperate climates for edible pods and seeds. Half hardy. Value: moderate levels of iron, vitamin C and beta carotene.

A native of Mexico, the runner bean has been known as a food crop for more than 2,200 years. In the late sixteenth century, Gerard's *Herball* mentions it as an ornamental introduced by the plant collector John Tradescant the Elder: 'Ladies did not … disdain to put the flowers in their nosegays and garlands', and in the garden it was grown around gazebos and arbours. Vilmorin Andrieux commented in 1885: 'In small gardens they are often trained over wire or woodwork, so as to form summer houses or coverings for walks.' Philip Miller, keeper of Chelsea Physic Garden, is credited with being the first gardener to cook them.

It was the fashion in seventeenth-century England to experiment with soaking seeds. Mr Gifford, minister of Montacute in Somerset, noted in his diary: 'May 10th 1679, I steep'd runner beans in sack five days, then I put them in sallet-oyle five days, then in brandy four days and about noon set them in an hot bed against a south wall casting all liquor wherein they had been infused negligently about the holes, within three hours space, eight of the nine came up, and were a foot high with all their leaves, and on the morrow a foot more in height … and in a week were podded and full ripe.' You could try this for yourself – or perhaps you would prefer to stick to today's more conventional methods!

grown since the nineteenth century, has delicate red and white flowers and long pods.

Stringless types
'Butler' is vigorous and prolific, with tender pods. **'Desiree'** has white flowers and seeds, and is high-yielding and tasty. **'Kelvedon Marvel'** is tasty, matures early and crops heavily. It can also be grown along the ground. **'Polestar'** crops heavily with long, well-flavoured pods. **'Red Knight'**, with red flowers, crops heavily and is excellent for freezing; it is disease-resistant. **'Red Rum'** is very early, high-yielding, tasty and resistant to halo blight. It can also grow along the ground. **'Scarlet Emperor'** is a traditional variety with scarlet flowers and tasty pods.

Supports must be strong to take the weight of the heavy vines

VARIETIES

Older cultivars were rather stringy unless eaten young; newer varieties are 'stringless'. Besides the traditional tall-growing climbers, there is also a choice of dwarf varieties

that do not need supporting and are ideal for smaller gardens, early crops under cloches and in exposed sites.

Non-stringless types
'Bokki' has wonderful red flowers and pods. **'Enorma'** is equally ornamental, with red flowers. It has long pods and is very tasty. **'Liberty'** has good-quality pods to 45–50cm (18–20in) long. **'Painted Lady'**, a variety

Dwarf varieties
'Hammonds Dwarf Scarlet' is ideal for the small garden. Pods are easy to harvest. Tops may need to be pinched out. **'Pickwick'** is red-flowered, producing early heavy crops of juicy pods. No support needed.

CULTIVATION

Propagation
Runner beans are not frost-tolerant and need a minimum soil temperature of 10°C (50°F) to germinate. Sow from late spring to early summer 5–7.5cm (2–3in) deep, 15cm (6in) apart in double rows 60cm (24in) apart. To shelter pollinating insects they are better grown in blocks or several short rows rather than a single long one. Allow 1–1.75m (3–5ft) between rows for ease of harvesting, depending on the cultivar.

Climbing types can be encouraged to bush by pinching out the main stems when they are around 25cm (10in); the sideshoots can be pinched out at the second leaf joint for a bushy plant that does not need staking.

Seed sown outdoors crops in about 14–16 weeks, depending on climatic and cultural conditions.

Growing
Runner beans are not frost-hardy and are less successful in cooler areas unless you have a suitable microclimate. They flourish between 14–29°C (57–85°F), needing a warm, sheltered position to minimize wind damage and encourage pollinating insects.

Soil should be deep, fertile and moisture-retentive. Dig a trench at least 30cm (12in) deep and 60cm (24in) wide in late autumn to early winter before planting, adding plenty of well-rotted organic matter to the backfill. Before sowing, rake in 60–90g/sq m (2–3oz/sq yd) of granular general fertilizer.

Keep crops weed-free during early stages of growth. Mulch after germination or after transplanting. Watering is essential for good bud set: the traditional method of spraying flowers has little effect. As the first buds are forming and again as the first flowers are fully open plants need 5–11 litres/sq m (1–2 gal/sq yd). Crops should be rotated.

Climbers can be up to 3m (10ft) or more tall and a good sturdy support should be in place before sowing or transplanting. Traditionally, a 'wigwam' of canes, or a longer row of crossed canes, were used; these may need supporting strings at the end of each row, like tent guy ropes. Do improvise: I once saw a wonderful structure like a V-shaped frame designed so the beans would hang down and make picking easier. Use canes, strong wooden stakes, steel tubes, or make frameworks of netting. There should be one cane or length of strong twine for each plant.

Maintenance
Spring Sow crops under cover or outdoors in late spring. Erect supports.
Summer Keep crops weed-free and well watered. Harvest regularly.

'Pickwick' is stringless

Autumn Continue harvesting until the first frosts.
Winter Prepare the soil for the following year's crop.

Protected Cropping
For earlier crops and in cooler climates, sow in boxes or pots of seed compost under cover from mid-spring, harden off and plant out from late spring. Protect indoor and outdoor crops with cloches or horticultural fleece until they are established.

Container Growing
Runner beans can be grown in containers at least 20cm (8in) wide by 25cm (10in) deep, depending on the vigour of the cultivar.

Sow seeds 5cm (2in) deep and 10–13cm (4–5in) apart indoors in late spring, moving the container outdoors into a sunny site. Water frequently in warm weather, less often at other times. Feed with liquid general fertilizer if plants need a boost.

Stake tall varieties, pinching out growing points when plants reach top of supports. Otherwise use dwarf varieties.

Harvesting and Storing
Harvest from midsummer to mid-autumn. Regular picking is essential to ensure regular cropping, high yields and to avoid 'stringiness'.

Runner beans freeze well.

The seeds of 'Painted Lady' are a pink/brown colour

Beans growing over a frame

PESTS AND DISEASES

Slugs, black bean aphid and red spider mite may be troublesome.

Grey mould (*Botrytis*) and halo blight may cause problems in wet or humid weather. Mice may eat seeds.

Root rots may kill plants in wet or poorly drained soils. Rotate.

COMPANION PLANTING

Runner beans are compatible with all but the Allium family.

Grow with maize to protect the latter from corn army worms. Nitrogen-fixing bacteria in the roots improve soil fertility. After harvesting, cut off tops, leave roots in the soil or add to compost heaps. They thrive with brassicas; Brussels sprout transplants are sheltered and grow on once beans die back.

Late in the season, their shade can benefit celery and salad crops if enough water is available.

CULINARY

Wash, 'top and tail', pull off stringy edges, slice diagonally and boil for 5–7 minutes. Drain and serve with a knob of butter. Alternatively, cook whole and slice after cooking.

Runner Bean Chutney
Makes 1.5kg (3lb)

Clare Walker and Gill Coleman give this recipe in *The Home Gardener's Cookbook*:

1 kg (2lb) runner beans
500g (1lb) onions
300ml (½pt) water
1 level tablespoon salt
1 level tablespoon mustard seeds
75g (3oz) sultanas
1½ level teaspoons ground ginger
1 level teaspoon turmeric
6 dried red chillies, left whole
600ml (1pt) spiced vinegar
500g (1lb) demerara sugar

Wipe, top, tail and string the beans and cut them into small slices. Place in a preserving pan with the peeled and finely chopped onions. Add the water, salt and mustard seeds and simmer gently for 20–25 minutes until the beans are just tender.

Then add the sultanas, ginger, turmeric, chillies and spiced vinegar, bring back to the boil and simmer for a further 30 minutes, or until the mixture is fairly thick.

Stir in the sugar, allow to dissolve, then boil steadily for about 20 minutes until the chutney is thick. Pour into warm, dry jars, cover with thick polythene and seal with a lid, if available. Label and store in a cool, dry place for at least 3 months before using. The chillies can be removed before potting.

Runner Bean Chutney

Phaseolus vulgaris. Papilionaceae

FRENCH BEAN

Also known as Common, Kidney, Bush, Pole, Snap, String, Green, Wax Bean; Haricot;
Baked Bean; Flageolet; Haricot Vert.
Annual grown for edible pods and beans. Half hardy.
Value: moderate potassium, folic acid and beta carotene. Very rich in protein.

Evidence of the wild form, found in Mexico, Guatemala and parts of the Andes, has been discovered in Peruvian settlements from 8000 BC. Both bush and climbing varieties were introduced to Europe during the Spanish conquest in the early sixteenth century, though the dwarf varieties did not become popular for two more centuries. They were first referred to as 'kidney beans' by the English in 1551, alluding to the shape of their seeds.

Gerard in his *Herball* calls them 'sperage' beans and 'long peason', while Parkinson wrote: 'Kidney beans boiled in water and stewed with butter were esteemed more savory … than the common broad bean and were a dish more oftentimes at rich men's tables than at the poor.' Another writer commented in 1681: 'It is a plant lately brought into use among us and not yet sufficiently known.'

In Europe, 'haricot vert' was used in ships' stores in voyages of exploration during the early 1500s. When European colonists first explored the Americas, they found climbing beans planted with maize, providing starch and protein for indigenous tribes.

Beans are self-pollinating, so close spacing provides higher yields

VARIETIES

This group of beans contains considerable variety. Plants are dwarf (ideal for the smaller garden or containers) or climbing, pods are flat, oval or round in cross-section and are green, yellow (waxpods) or purple, or marbled.

The seeds are colourful and often mottled. As well as being grown for the immature pods, eaten whole, the seeds may be allowed to swell and ripen; seeds are eaten fresh as 'flageolets', or dried and known as 'haricots'.

Climbing types
'Borlotto Lingua di Fuoco' is an ornamental 'fire tongue' form, with red-marked green pods. **'Corona d'Oro'** is high-yielding with rounded, tender, golden-yellow pods. **'Hunter'** is flat-podded, and crops heavily over a long period. **'Kwintus'** produces tender, tasty pods. **'Musica'** can be sown early and is full of flavour. **'Or du Rhin'** is a yellow-podded, late maincrop type. It is delicious picked young. **'Romano'**, an old variety, is tender, tasty and prolific. Excellent for freezing.

Dwarf or bush types
'Annabel' is high-yielding, round and tasty – perfect for the patio. **'Chevrier Vert'**: this classic French flageolet from 1880 is tasty and tender. **'Forum'** is cold-tolerant. Yields high-quality beans. Resistant to halo blight and anthracnose. **'Masai'** has long thin pods, is robust, early and high-yielding, with good disease and cold tolerance. **'Purple Queen'** is delicious, producing heavy yields of glossy purple pods. **'Royal Burgundy'** germinates well

'Royalty', ideal for the 'potager'

in cold soil and has tasty, dark green pods. Resistant to pea and bean weevil. Freezes well. **'Royalty'** crops heavily. Delicately flavoured dark purple pods which turn green when cooked. The dark green pods of **'Sprite'** freeze well. **'Vibel'** is high-yielding, crops over a long period and is very tasty. A gourmet bean.

CULTIVATION

Propagation

French beans dislike cold wet soils and are inclined to rot; for successful germination, do not sow until the soil is a minimum of 10°C (50°F). For early sowings or in cold weather warm the soil first with cloches or black polythene 3–4 weeks before sowing.

Sow successively from mid-spring to early summer in staggered drills 4–5cm (1½–2in) deep with 22cm (9in) between the rows and plants for optimum yields.

Climbing varieties should be in double rows 15cm (6in) apart with 60cm (2ft) between rows.

Growing

French beans flourish in a sheltered, sunny site on a light, free-draining, fertile soil where organic matter was added for the previous crop. Alternatively, dig in plenty of well-rotted organic matter in late autumn or winter before planting.

The plants need a pH of 6.5–7.0; lime acid soils if necessary. Rake the soil to a medium tilth about 10–14 days before sowing, incorporating a balanced granular fertilizer at 30–60g/sq m (1–2oz/sq yd).

Keep crops weed-free or mulch when the soil is moist. Earth up round the base of the stems for added support and push twigs under mature bush varieties to keep pods off the soil, or support plants with pea sticks. Support climbing varieties in the same way as runner beans.

Keep well watered during drought; plants are particularly sensitive to water stress when the flowers start to open and as pods swell. Apply 13–18 litres/sq in (3–4 gal/sq yd) per week.

Maintenance
Spring Sow early crops under cover or outdoors in late spring. Support climbers. Transplant when 5–7.5cm (2–3in) tall.
Summer Keep crops weed-free, mulch, water in drought. Harvest regularly.
Autumn Continue harvesting until the first frosts. Protect later crops with cloches or fleece.
Winter Prepare the soil for the following year's crop.

Protected Cropping
For earlier crops and in cooler climates, sow in boxes, modules or pots of seed compost under cover from mid-spring. Warm the soil before transplanting. Harden off and plant out from late spring, depending on the weather and soil conditions. Protect crops sown indoors or *in situ* with cloches, polytunnels or with horticultural fleece until established.

For very early harvest, sow in pots in a heated greenhouse at 15°C (60°F) from late winter. Sow 4 seeds near the edge of a 23–25cm (9–10in) pot containing loam-based compost with moderate fertilizer levels.

Seeds can also be pre-germinated on moist kitchen towel in an airing cupboard or similar. Keep moist with tepid water, ventilate in warm weather, harvest in late spring.

Container Growing
French beans can be grown in containers that are at least 20cm (8in) wide by 25cm (10in) deep.

Sow seeds 4–5cm (1½–2in) deep indoors in mid-spring, moving the container outdoors into a sheltered, sunny site. Feed with liquid general fertilizer if necessary.

Stake climbing varieties; pinch out growing points when plants reach the top of supports.

Harvesting and Storing
Plants are self-pollinating, so expect a good harvest. Pick when pods are about 10cm (4in) long, when they snap easily, before the seeds are visible. Pick regularly for maximum yields. Cut them with a pair of scissors or hold the stems as you pull the pods to avoid uprooting the plant.

For dried or haricot beans, leave pods until they mature, sever the plant at the base and dry indoors. When pods begin to split, shell the beans and dry on paper for several days. Store in an airtight container.

French beans freeze well. Wash and trim young pods, blanch for 3 minutes, freeze in polythene bags or rigid

Climbing French beans

containers. You should use within 12 months.

They keep in a polythene bag in the refrigerator for up to a week and last about 4 days in a cool kitchen.

PESTS AND DISEASES

Slugs, black bean aphid and red spider mite can be troublesome. Grey mould (Botrytis) and halo blight may be problems in wet or humid weather. Mice may eat seeds. Root rots can kill plants in wet or poorly drained soils. Rotate crops.

COMPANION PLANTING

French beans do well with celery, maize, cucurbits, sweetcorn and melons. Intercrop with brassicas.

MEDICINAL

One cup of beans per day is said to lower cholesterol by about 12

French Bean, Roquefort and Walnut Salad

CULINARY

French beans, fresh from the garden, have such a delicate flavour that they hardly need more than boiling in water and serving as an accompaniment to meat and other dishes. Wash, 'top and tail' pods and cook whole in boiling salted water for 5–7 minutes, preferably within an hour of harvesting. Cut large flat-podded types into 2.5cm (1in) slices.

Alternatively, serve cold in salads or try them stir-fried with other vegetables.

For haricot beans, place fresh beans in cold water, bring to the boil, remove from the heat and allow to stand for an hour. Drain and serve as a hot vegetable, or in vinaigrette as a salad.

French Bean, Roquefort Walnut Salad
Serves 4

300g (10oz) French beans, topped and tailed
250g (8oz) Roquefort cheese
125g (4oz) walnuts
1 small radicchio
2 little gem lettuces
3 tablespoons extra virgin olive oil
1 tablespoon balsamic vinegar
1 clove garlic, crushed
Salt and freshly ground black pepper

Wash the beans and steam them over a pan of boiling water until just crunchy. Keep warm. Crumble the Roquefort and lightly crush the walnuts. Wash the lettuces. Make a dressing with the remaining ingredients.

Arrange the lettuces in a large bowl, top with the beans, walnuts and cheese, and pour over the dressing. Toss and serve while the beans are still warm.

Red Chilli Beef
Serves 4

3 or 4 ancho chillies
1–2 small red chillies, dried
1 tablespoon ground cumin
3 tablespoons vegetable oil
2 onions, finely sliced
3 cloves garlic, finely crushed
750g (1½lb) minced beef
300g (10oz) cooked red kidney beans
2 tablespoons tomato purée
Salt and freshly ground black pepper
300ml (½pt) good stock

Infuse the ancho chillies in hot water to soften them. Remove the stems and push the flesh through a fine sieve. Set aside. Then finely chop and deseed the dried chillies.

Put the cumin into a heavy frying pan over a medium heat and toast until the fragrance comes out, taking care not to burn it. Set aside.

Heat the oil in a large, heavy saucepan and cook the onions and garlic until just coloured. Add the meat and brown well. Add both sorts of chilli, the kidney beans, tomato purée and salt and pepper. Mix well.

Pour in the stock and cook for 40 minutes, covered, adding a little extra liquid if necessary. Serve hot with plainly cooked rice.

Pisum sativum. Papilionaceae

PEA

Also known as Garden Pea, English Pea. Climbing or scrambling annual grown for seeds, pods and shoot tips. Half hardy. Value: good source of protein, carbohydrates, fibre, iron and vitamin C.

'Early Onward', a robust, prolific variety

Like many legumes, peas are an ancient food crop. The earliest records are of smooth-skinned types, found in Mediterranean and European excavations dating from 7000 BC. The Greeks and Romans cultivated and ate peas in abundance and it was the Romans who were said to have introduced them to Britain. In classical Greece they were known as *pison*, which was translated in English to 'peason'; by the reign of Charles I they became 'pease' and this was shortened to 'pea' in the eighteenth century. During the reign of Elizabeth I types seen as 'fit dainties for ladies, they come so far, and cost so dear' were imported from Holland.

In England 'pease pudding', made from dried peas, butter and eggs, was traditionally eaten with pork and boiled bacon. It was obviously quite versatile, hence the nursery rhyme beginning, 'Pease pudding hot, pease pudding cold, pease pudding in the pot nine days old'. Peas were eaten dried or ground until the sixteenth century, when Italian gardeners developed tender varieties for cooking and eating when fresh. It took until the following century before this practice was accepted by the wealthy and fashionable in England.

They were the favourite vegetable of Thomas Jefferson, who held an annual competition among his friends to grow the first peas. The winner had the privilege of inviting others in the group to dinner celebrating their arrival. Invitations were issued saying, 'Come tonight, the peas are ready!'

some descriptions refer to the pea itself, or to the pod.

Earlier varieties are lower-growing than later types, which are taller and consequently higher-yielding. Smooth-seeded types are hardy and are used for early and late crops. Wrinkle-seeded varieties are less hardy and generally sweeter. 'Petit pois' are small and well flavoured. 'Semi-leafless' peas have more tendrils than leaves, becoming intertwined and self-supporting as they grow.

'Sugar peas' or 'mangetout' – varieties of *Pisum sativum* var. *macrocarpon* – are grown for their edible immature pods; of these, the 'Sugar Snap' type are particularly succulent and sweet. Some varieties can be allowed to mature and the peas eaten.

Early Peas
'Early Onward' is a heavy cropper, with large blunt pods and wrinkled seeds. **'Feltham First'** is an excellent early round-seeded variety with large, well-filled pods. **'Prince Albert'** is early and vigorous, producing bumper crops.

Maincrop peas
'Cavalier' produces huge crops and is highly resistant to mildew. Easy to harvest, with wrinkled seeds and fusarium resistance. **'Daisy'** is low-growing, to 60cm (2ft), producing good yields of excellent-quality peas.

VARIETIES

Peas are usually listed according to the timing of the crop – early, second early (or early maincrop) and maincrop types – but

A row of peas sitting snugly in the pod

'Feltham First', an early type, can be grown up pea sticks or netting

'Darfon' is a high-yielding 'petit pois' type, its pods packed with small peas. It resists downy mildew and fusarium. **'Hurst Green Shaft'** is sweet-tasting and heavy-cropping, maturing over a long period. Wrinkle-seeded. Downy mildew and fusarium-resistant. **'Bikini'** is a high-yielding semi-leafless type, which is good for freezing. Fusarium-resistant.

Sugar peas
'Oregon Sugar Pod' is sweet and tasty; harvest as the peas form. Fusarium-resistant. 'Reuzensuiker' is a compact plant, needing little support. Its pods are wide and fleshy, and very sweet. 'Sugar Snap' produces succulent, sweet edible pods or can be grown on for peas. Very sweet. Fusarium-resistant.

CULTIVATION

Propagation
Germination is erratic and poor on cold soils; do not sow outdoors when soil temperatures are below 10°C (50°F).

Sow earlies or second earlies successively every 14–28 days from mid-spring to midsummer. Avoid excessively hot times; these can affect germination.

According to the growing conditions, earlies mature after about 12 weeks, second earlies (or early maincrop) take 1–2 weeks longer, and maincrops take another 1–2 weeks longer again. As an alternative option, sow groups of earlies, second earlies and maincrops in mid- to late spring; the length of time taken for each type to reach maturity will give you a harvest over several weeks.

In midsummer, with at least 12 weeks before the first frosts are expected, sow an early cultivar for harvesting in autumn, and where winters are mild, sow earlies in mid- to late autumn for overwintering. Cloche protection may be necessary later in the season.

Peas can be sown in single V-shaped rows 2.5–5cm (1–2in) deep and 5cm (2in) apart, double rows 23cm (9in) apart or broad or flat drills 25cm (10in) wide.

The distance between the rows or pairs of rows should equal the ultimate height of the plant.

Peas can also be sown in strips 3 rows wide with the seeds 11 cm (4½in) apart in and between the rows and with 45cm (18in) between the strips.

They can also be sown in blocks 90–120cm (36–48in) wide with seeds 5–7.5cm (2–3in) apart.

Yields are higher when plants are supported. Use pea sticks made from brushwood or netting. Place supports down one side of a single row, on either side or down the centre of wide drills and around the outside of blocks of plants.

Growing
Peas are a cool-season crop flourishing at 13–18°C (55–65°F), so crops will be higher in cooler summer temperatures. They do not tolerate drought, excessive temperatures or waterlogged soil. Peas should be grown in an open, sheltered position on moisture-retentive, deep, free-draining soil with a pH of 5.5–7.0.

Incorporate plenty of organic matter in the autumn or winter prior to sowing or plant where the ground was manured for the previous year's crop.

Keep crops weed-free by hoeing, hand weeding or mulching (which also keeps the roots cool and moist). Earth up overwintering and early crops to provide extra support.

Unless there are drought conditions, established plants do not need watering until the flowers appear, then, for a good harvest, they will need 22 litres/sq m (4 gal/sq yd) each week until the harvest is complete.

Maintenance
Spring Sow early maincrops. *Summer* Sow maincrops early in the season. Harvest, keep weed-free and water. Sow earlies for autumn harvest. *Autumn* Sow early overwintering crops under cover. Prepare the ground for the following year. *Winter* Sow early crops under cover.

Protected Cropping
Warm the soil before sowing treated seed in spring. Sow the seed of dwarf cultivars under cover in early spring, removing the covers when the plants need supporting.

Early spring and late autumn sowings can be made under cover, as flowers and pods cannot withstand frost.

Container Growing
Sow early dwarf varieties successively through the season in large containers of loam-based compost with moderate fertilizer levels. Provide support, keep weed-free and well watered.

Harvesting and Storing
Harvest early types from late spring to early summer and maincrops from mid-summer to early autumn. Pick regularly to ensure a high yield when the pods are swollen. Harvest those grown for their pods when the peas are just forming.

If peas are to be dried, leave them on the plant as long as possible, lifting just before the seeds are shed; hang in a cool airy place or spread the pods out on trays to dry until they split and the peas can be harvested. Store in airtight containers.

Freeze young peas of any variety. Shell and blanch for 1 minute. Allow to drain, cool and freeze in polythene bags or containers. Use within 12 months.

Peas in a polythene bag in the refrigerator stay fresh for up to 3 days.

Evening light illuminating the foliage of young peas

Peas are one of the most popular frozen vegetables

Pests and Diseases

Birds and mice can be a problem: net crops.

Pea moths are common, their larvae eating the peas. Protect with crop covers at flower bud stage. Autumn, early and midsummer sowings often avoid problems; spray with pyrethrin-based insecticide 10 days after flowers open.

Pea thrips attack developing pods, making pods distorted and silvery; peas do not develop. Spray with derris or pyrethrum.

Mice may also be troublesome, eating seeds, particularly with over-wintered crops; trap them.

Powdery mildew, downy mildew and fusarium wilt can be a problem: sow resistant varieties.

COMPANION PLANTING

Peas grow well with other legumes, root crops, potatoes, cucurbits and sweetcorn.

MEDICINAL

Peas are said to reduce fertility, prevent appendicitis, lower blood cholesterol and control blood sugar levels.

CULINARY

Garden peas are eaten fresh or dried. When small and tender, they can be eaten raw in salads.

Peas are traditionally boiled or steamed with a sprig of mint. Eat with butter, salt and pepper or herbs. Serve in a cream sauce with pearl onions, with celery, orange, carrots, wine or lemon sauce.

Mangetout should be boiled for 3 minutes (or steamed), tossed in butter and served.

Young shoot tips can be cooked and eaten.

Pea and Pear Soup
Serves 4

An unusual combination and very refreshing in summertime when there is a glut of peas.

500g (1lb) peas, shelled weight
6–7 pears, very ripe, unpeeled
900ml (1½pt) chicken stock
Pinch cayenne pepper
2 tablespoons finely chopped fresh mint
Salt and freshly ground black pepper

Cook the peas in lightly salted water for 5 minutes or so. Drain. Quarter and core the pears. Liquidize them in a blender and, with the peas, the stock and the cayenne. Pour into a saucepan and stir in the mint and seasoning. Heat through and serve.

Pasta and Mangetout Salad

Pasta and Mangetout Salad
Serves 4

Mangetout or sugar peas from the garden are completely different from the tired beasts bought in the greengrocers. The quicker they are cooked, the better they taste.

500g (1lb) pasta – penne or fusilli
4 tablespoons olive oil
300g (10oz) mangetout, topped tailed
1 small onion, finely sliced
2 cloves garlic, crushed
250g (8oz) tuna, drained and flaked
2 tablespoons thick cream
2 tablespoons flat-leaf parsley
Salt and freshly ground black pepper

Cook the pasta in boiling salted water for 10 minutes, or until *al dente*, and drain. Drizzle over 1 tablespoon of the oil and toss well. Allow to cool.

Meanwhile, cook the mangetout in a steamer for 2–3 minutes; they should remain crunchy. In a separate pan, heat the oil and sauté the onion for a couple of minutes, then add the garlic and continue cooking for 1 minute. Remove from the heat and allow to cool.

Put the pasta into a large serving bowl and mix in all the ingredients. Taste for seasoning and serve.

Pea and Pear Soup

Portulaca oleracea subsp. *sativa. Portulacaceae*

PURSLANE

Also known as Summer Purslane. Annual grown for succulent shoot tips, stems and leaves. Half hardy. Value: rich in beta carotene, folic acid, vitamin C; contains useful amounts of essential fatty acids.

Purslane has been grown for centuries in China, India and Egypt, and is now widespread in the warm temperate and tropical regions of the world. It was once believed to protect against evil spirits and 'blastings by lightning or planets and burning of gunpowder'. Its name in Malawi translates as 'buttocks of the wife of a chief', referring to the plant's succulent, rounded leaves and juicy stems! The cultivated form has an erect habit and larger leaves than the wild species.

VARIETIES

Portulaca oleracea **var.** *sativa* is a vigorous, upright annual growing to 45cm (18in) tall with thick, succulent stems, spoon-shaped leaves and bright yellow flowers.

P. o. **var.** *aurea* is a yellow-leaved, less hardy form. It is more succulent, but has less flavour. Attractive in salads and as an ornamental.

CULTIVATION

Propagation

Sow in seed trays indoors in late spring and transplant seedlings into modules when large enough to handle. Harden off and plant when there is no danger of frost, 15cm (6in) apart. In frost-free climates or for later crops, sow directly, thinning to 15cm (6in) apart. Sow in late spring for a summer crop and in late summer for autumn cropping.

Mature purslane plant in flower

Growing
Easily cultivated, purslane thrives in a sunny, warm, sheltered site on light, well-drained soil. Add organic matter and sand to improve drainage if needed. Remove flowers as they appear.

Maintenance
Spring Sow protected crops, or *in situ* once the danger of frost is passed.
Summer Keep plants weed-free and water as necessary. Harvest regularly.
Autumn Cut back mature plants to allow regrowth.
Winter In late winter sow early crops under glass.

Protected Cropping
To extend the season, sow in early to mid-spring and early to mid-autumn under cover. Make earlier and late summer sowings under cover as a 'cut and come again' crop.

Container Growing
Plant seedlings or sow seed in pots or containers when there is no danger of frost, using a soil-based compost with a low fertilizer content. Continue to water regularly.

Harvesting
Pick young shoot tips, stems and leaves when about 3–5cm (1½–2in) long. 'Cut and come again' crops are ready to harvest after about 5 weeks. Regular picking encourages young growth. As older plants deteriorate towards the end of the growing season, cut them back to within 5cm (2in) of the ground, water well and they should resprout.

Pests and Diseases
Purslane is prone to slug damage, particularly when young. Damping off can be a problem if sown at low temperatures or in cold soil.

Medicinal
A traditional remedy for dry coughs, swollen gums and, infused in water, for blood disorders. Research indicates that its high levels of fatty acids can prevent heart attacks and stimulate the body's immune system.

CULINARY

Wash thoroughly; growing close to the ground, leaves can be gritty. It can be lightly cooked, although the taste is not memorable. Older leaves can be pickled.

Purslane Salad
Serves 4

Use young buds and stems as well as the leaves.

4 ripe nectarines or peaches
Hazelnut oil
Handful of purslane
15 hazelnuts, toasted
½ teaspoon of coriander
*   seeds, freshly crushed*

Slice the nectarines or peaches and arrange on a plate brushed with hazelnut oil. Add the purslane leaves. Trickle over a little more oil, sprinkle with the chopped nuts and season with crushed coriander.

WARNING

Expectant mothers and those with digestive disorders should not eat purslane in large quantities.

Raphanus sativus. Brassicaceae

RADISH

Annual or biennial grown for edible swollen roots, seed pods and leaves. Hardy. Value: low in calories, moderate vitamin C, small amounts of iron and protein.

Thought to be native to Asia, yet domesticated in the Mediterranean, this reliable little salad vegetable has been in cultivation for centuries. Depicted in the pyramid of Cheops, it was cultivated by the Egyptians in 2780 BC and Herodotus noted that labourers working on the pyramids received 'radishes, onions and garlic' as their rations. By 500 BC it was grown in China, reaching Japan 200 years later. Pliny records that 'models of turnips, beetroots and radishes were dedicated to Apollo in the temple at Delphi, turnips made of lead, beets of silver and radishes of gold,' while Horace wrote of 'lettuces and radishes such as excite the languid stomach.' John Evelyn, too, wrote: 'Radishes are eaten alone with salt only, as conveying their pepper in them.' The fiery flavour is due to the presence of mustard oil. Although radishes are usually red, there are also black, purple, yellow and green-skinned types.

VARIETIES

The fast-growing salad types are ready to harvest in about 4 weeks. Larger, slow-growing types, often with long cylindrical roots, include large overwintering varieties and the Oriental varieties known as 'mooli' or 'daikon'.

Salad and overwintering radishes
'Cherry Belle' is round, with crisp, white, mild flesh. Tolerant of poorer soils, it is slow to go woody and keeps well. Harvest 3 weeks after sowing. 'China Rose' is a well-flavoured winter variety with bright red roots and white flesh. 'D'Avignon' is rose-coloured with a white tip, crunchy and extremely hot. '18 Day' is a fast-growing French Breakfast type, crisp and mild. 'French Breakfast 3' is long, mild, sweet and tender. Harvest at maturity or they become hot and woody. 'Scarlet Globe' is justifiably popular for its mild flavour and good quality. Can be sown early under cover. 'Long Black Spanish', a winter variety, has wonderful dark skin and is extremely hot. 'Munchen Bier' is grown for its tasty green pods, which are eaten raw or stir-fried. 'Round

'Round Black Spanish'

Black Spanish' is similar to 'Long Black Spanish', but globe-shaped. 'Short Top Forcing' is a bright red variety, excellent for winter sowing under cover.

Mooli or daikon
'Mooli' and 'daikon' are general terms for a group of long, white radishes (*Raphanus sativus* var. *longipinnatus*) which need cool temperatures and short day lengths to flourish.
'April Cross' is crisp, juicy and mild. 'Long White Icicle' is tender with a pungent, almost nutty taste. 'Minowasa Summer', a Japanese variety, is long and mild. 'Mino Early' is a large Japanese variety. 'Summer Cross Hybrid' is fast-growing and ready to harvest when 15cm (6in) long.

CULTIVATION

Propagation
Radishes are one of the easiest and quickest vegetables to grow. Sow successively every 2 weeks from when the soil becomes workable in early to mid-spring to early autumn. Sow thinly in drills 1cm (1/2in) deep and 15cm (6in) apart, thinning to 2.5cm (1in) apart about 10 days after they appear. Alternatively, broadcast seed and thin to 2.5cm (1in) apart. Radishes dislike being overcrowded.

Sow overwintering radishes in summer, 2cm (¾in) deep in rows 23–30cm (9–12in) apart; depending on the cultivar, thin to 15–23cm (6–9in). Sow mooli/daikon from mid- to late summer.

Small radishes can be grown as 'cut and come again' seedlings. Harvest when seedlings are 5–7.5cm (2–3in) tall; if you allow them to grow to 20–22.5cm (8–9in), the leaves can be cooked like spinach.

Growing

As radishes are a cool-weather crop, grow earlier and later crops in an open site, but plant summer crops in light shade, surrounded by taller plants. They flourish in a light, moisture-retentive, free-draining soil which was manured for the previous crop, with a pH of 6.5–7.5. Dig the ground thoroughly before preparing the seedbed and remove any stones, particularly when growing longer-rooted varieties.

Rake a slow-release granular fertilizer into the seedbed at 30g/sq m (1oz/sq yd) before sowing the first crops and before planting winter varieties.

Rapid growth is essential for tasty, tender roots, so supply plenty of water and do not let the seedbed dry out. Overwatering encourages the production of leaves rather than roots and erratic watering causes roots to become woody or split. During drought, water weekly at 11 litres/sq m (2 gal/sq yd). Hoe and hand weed regularly.

Maintenance

Spring Sow crops outdoors when soil conditions allow.
Summer Sow successionally; keep crops well watered and weed-free. Sow winter crops.
Autumn Grow later crops under cover.
Winter Harvest over-wintering crops. Sow early crops under cover.

Protected Cropping

Grow early and late crops of summer varieties under cloches to extend the cropping season. Ventilate and water thoroughly.

Grow summer crops under floating cloches to protect them.

Radishes' pretty exterior belies their fiery taste

Container Growing

Radishes are easily grown in containers. These should be 15–30cm (6–12in) wide by 20cm (8in) deep. Use a loam-based compost or free-draining, moisture-retentive garden soil. Water well and liquid feed with general fertilizer if necessary. They can also be sown in growbags, thinning until they are 2.5–5cm (1–2in) apart.

Harvesting and Storing

Pull immediately they mature after 8 to 10 weeks, otherwise they will become woody or run to seed.

Later crops can be stored. Twist off leaves and store in boxes of dry sand or sawdust in a frost-free place. Overwintering types can be left in the ground and lifted as needed. Protect with straw or bracken. For ease of lifting, these can be allowed to grow over 35cm (15in) long without being coarse.

Kept in a polythene bag in the refrigerator, radishes stay fresh for about a week.

Pests and Diseases

Flea beetle, cabbage fly and slugs can be a problem.

COMPANION PLANTING

Radishes grow well with chervil, peas and lettuce and thrive with nasturtium and with mustard.

Because of their rapid growth, radishes make an excellent 'indicator crop'. Sown in the same row as slow-germinating crops like parsnips or parsley, they mark where the maincrop has been sown, make weeding easier, and can be harvested without disturbing the developing plants.

MEDICINAL

Radishes can be eaten to relieve indigestion and flatulence as well as being taken as a tonic herb and an expectorant.

'Cherry Belle', picked and packed

'Long Black Spanish'

Radish and Scallop Soup

CULINARY

Radishes are usually eaten raw, whole, grated or sliced into salads. Alternatively wash and trim the root, remove the leaves and all but the bottom 2.5cm (1in) of stalk to use as a 'handle' and enjoy it with rough bread, creamy butter, salt, cheese and a pint of good ale! (In Germany, you'll find them on the bar instead of peanuts.) They can also be sliced and used instead of onions in hamburgers.

Seedling leaves are eaten raw and older leaves are cooked like spinach.

Long white summer radishes and winter radishes can be eaten raw but are usually cooked and added to casseroles, stews or curries.

Winter varieties are also pickled. Peel, then cube or slice in slightly salted water for about 10 minutes. Drain thoroughly and serve tossed in butter.

Thin slices of winter varieties or larger summer types can be stir-fried.

For extra crispness, put them into a bowl of water with a few ice cubes for a couple of hours.

Slice radishes and tangerines, mandarins or oranges into small pieces, sprinkle lightly with salt, chopped fennel leaves and lemon juice. This interesting recipe is an acquired taste!

To make a 'radish rose', remove the stalk and make a number of vertical cuts from the stalk almost to the root. Place in iced water for 30 minutes; the petals open.

Immature green seed pods can be eaten raw, cooked or pickled. Pick when crisp and green. Scrape or peel and 'top and tail' mooli or daikon before use. In India they are eaten cooked or raw. In Japan shredded mooli is a traditional accompaniment to 'sashimi' (raw fish) and is eaten with 'sushi'.

As with summer radishes, a thin slice makes an excellent mustard substitute with a roast beef sandwich.

Radish and Scallop Soup
Serves 4

2 bunches radishes, topped and tailed
10 scallops, trimmed
2 spring onions, chopped
2 tablespoons butter
600ml (1pt) fish stock and milk combined
2 bay leaves
Pinch cayenne pepper
1 tablespoon parsley
4 tablespoons double cream

First wash the radishes thoroughly and cut them into small dice. Then cut the scallops in half and set to one side.

In a soup pot, cook the onions in the butter until soft, and then add the scallops. Cook them for 30 seconds on each side over a gentle heat and then add the radishes.

Pour over the stock and milk mixture. Add the bay leaves, cayenne and parsley and cook for 15 minutes over a gentle heat, just simmering.

Remove the soup from the heat. Take the scallops out of the soup with a slotted spoon; cut them into slivers and return them to the pan. Lastly, stir in the parsley and the cream and serve immediately.

Rheum x *cultorum. Polygonaceae*

RHUBARB

(Pieplant) Large perennial herb grown for pink edible stems. Half hardy. Value: very low in calories, contains small amounts of vitamins.

The earliest records of rhubarb date from China in 2700 BC and there are references to its cultivation in Europe in the early 1700s. It was originally grown for its medicinal use as a powerful purgative; the annual value of imports to England for this purpose was once estimated to be £200,000. It was first mentioned as a food plant in 1778 by the French, for making tarts and pies. Rhubarb was introduced to Maine from Europe around 1790; from there it spread to market gardeners in New England and Massachusetts. Forcing and blanching were discovered by chance at the Chelsea Physic Garden in 1817 after crowns were covered in debris when a ditch was cleared!

VARIETIES

A greater range of cultivars is to be found in specialist nurseries. **'Crimson Red'** has a distinctive sweet yet sharp flavour. **'Early Champagne'** (**'Early Red'**) produces long, delicious scarlet stalks which are excellent for winemaking and early forcing. **'Glaskin's Perpetual'** is vigorous and tasty, and crops over a long period. **'The Sutton'**, introduced by Suttons Seeds in 1893, is tasty and good for forcing. **'Timperley Early'** is very early, vigorous and suitable for forcing. **'Valentine'** is hardy and vigorous with tender, rose-coloured stalks. Perfect for pies and jams, it has a wonderful flavour. **'Victoria'**, a reliable old variety, is variable in size. Harvest from late spring. **'Zwolle Seedling'** has good flavour and fragrance and stays firm when cooked.

Rhubarb forced using traditional terracotta jars

CULTIVATION

Propagation

Rhubarb can be grown from seed, but the results are invariably poor. It is better to lift and divide mature crowns of known varieties or buy virus-free plants from a reputable nursery.

Plants should be divided every 2 or 3 years; if plants are any older, take divisions from the outer margins. Lift dormant crowns in winter after the leaves have died back and divide with a spade or knife. Each 'set' should be about 10cm (4in) across with plenty of fibrous roots and at least one bud.

Plants tend to establish more rapidly if transplanted into 25cm (10in) pots of multi-purpose compost for 3 months prior to planting out. Transplant, 75–90cm (2½–3ft) apart, from late autumn (the best time) to early spring, with the bud tip covered by 2.5cm (1in) of soil. Plant cultivars which have large buds with the buds slightly above ground to prevent rotting. Plants remain productive for several seasons, their decline is marked by the production of masses of thin stalks.

Alternatively, sow in drills about 2.5cm (1in) deep and 30cm (12in) apart, thinning to 15cm (6in). Plant out the strongest in autumn or the following spring.

Growing

Rhubarb flourishes in an open, sunny position in deep, fertile, well-drained soil with a pH of 5.0–6.0. It is ideal for cool temperate climates. It is very hungry, with deep roots, so ensure that the soil contains well-rotted manure or compost. On very heavy soils, plant on ridges or raised beds.

Mulch plants every winter with a good thick layer of well-rotted compost or manure. Do not allow them to flower unless you wish to save the seed, as this affects cropping the following year. Keep weed-free and watered, removing dead leaves instantly. In early spring, scatter a balanced general fertilizer around the crowns.

Maintenance

Spring Force early crops under a bucket or similar. *Summer* Harvest stems. *Autumn* When steins die back remove all plant debris. *Winter* Mulch with well-rotted compost or manure.

'Timperley Early', a popular variety for gardeners

Protected Cropping

For early crops lift a few crowns in late autumn, leave them above ground and let them be frosted, then bring indoors into a cool place for forcing. Put in a large container packed with soil or plant under greenhouse staging. Exclude light with an upturned box or bucket 38–45cm (15–18in) high to allow for stem growth. They can also be forced in bin liners. Keep compost moist. Dispose of exhausted forced crowns after harvest.

Alternatively, from late winter, cover *in situ* with a 15cm (6in) layer of straw or leaves or with an upturned bin, bucket or blanching pot covered with straw or strawy manure. Harvest in early to mid-spring. Do not harvest from a crown for at least 2 years after forcing.

Harvesting and Storing

Do not harvest until 12–18 months after planting, taking only a few 'sticks' in the second season and more in later years. Cropping can last from early spring to mid-summer. To harvest, hold the stems near the base and twist off. Avoid breaking the stems, as it can cause fungal problems. Do not over-pick; it can weaken the plant.

To freeze, chop the stems into sections and place on an open tray, freeze for 1 hour before packing into polythene bags. This prevents the sections from sticking together. They can be stored for up to a year.

PESTS AND DISEASES

Honey fungus may appear as white streaks in dead crown tissue; brown toadstools appear round base. Dig out and burn diseased roots.

Crown rot damages terminal buds and makes stems spindly. Dig out and burn badly infected plants. Do not replant in the area.

Virus disease has no cure. Dig up and burn.

COMPANION PLANTING

Rhubarb is reported to control red spider mite. A traditional remedy suggests putting rhubarb in planting holes to control clubroot. An infusion of leaves is effective as an aphicide and to check blackspot on roses.

CULINARY

Forced rhubarb is tender and needs less sugar. Cook stems slowly with sugar. Very little or no water is required; do not overcook them. Avoid using aluminium pans.

Rhubarb can be stewed for fruit pies, bottling or preserving, fools, mousses and rhubarb crumble, which is delicious. The flavour can be improved by adding orange juice, marmalade or cinnamon. It can also be puréed with apple. Claudia Roden's *Middle Eastern Food* demonstrates that it is unexpectedly wonderful stewed with beef or lamb in Persian *khoresh*.

Preserved Rhubarb

3.5kg (7lb) rhubarb
3.5kg (7lb) preserving sugar
Juice and grated peel of 2
* lemons*
50g (2oz) blanched almonds

Cut the rhubarb into 2.5cm (1in) lengths and cook gently in a preserving pan until the juices start to run. Add the sugar, lemon juice and peel and the almonds. Stir until the sugar dissolves, then boil until a good colour and thickened. Pot up into sterilized jars and seal.

Rhubarb Sorbet
Serves 4

400g (14oz) rhubarb
150g (5oz) caster sugar
Juice of half a lemon

Cut the rhubarb into 2.5cm (1in) lengths and put into a heavy-bottomed pan. Add 50ml (2fl oz) water. Warm gently until the juices run, then stir in the sugar and lemon juice and simmer, covered, until tender. Freeze, whisking several times as it freezes to break up the ice crystals. If you use a sorbetière, churn until smooth. Remove from the freezer 15 minutes before serving and leave in the fridge.

Rhubarb Sorbet

MEDICINAL

Rhubarb is an astringent, stomachic and potent laxative. Dioscorides recommended it for chest, stomach and liver complaints, and ringworm. By the sixteenth century, in western Europe, it was taken as an infusion with parsley as a cure for venereal disease.

WARNING

Do not eat the leaves, which are extremely poisonous!

Rorippa nasturtium-aquaticum. Brassicaceae (syn. Nasturtium officinale. Cruciferae)

WATERCRESS

Also known as Summer Watercress. Usually aquatic perennial grown for pungent, edible leaves and stems. Hardy. Value: excellent source of beta carotene, vitamins C and E, calcium, iron and iodine.

This highly nutritious aquatic herb, a native of Europe, North Africa and Asia, has been cultivated as a salad plant since Roman times and is grown throughout the world's temperate zones. It has become a weed in North America and New Zealand. Pliny records the Latin derivation of its original generic name as *Nasus tortus,* meaning 'writhing nose' – referring to its spicy taste and pungent odour; *officinale* is often applied to plants with medicinal uses. Watercress was listed as an aphrodisiac in Dioscorides' *Materia Medica* of AD77.

It was mentioned in early Irish poetry around the twelfth century – 'Well of Traigh Dha Bhan, Lovely is your pure-topped cress' and, 'Watercress, little green-topped one, on the brink of the blackbirds' well...' Early references to the shamrock are believed to be watercress. Evidence to support this comes from Ireland's County Meath and Shamrock Well, whose watercress was still remembered in the 1940s as 'the finest in the district'. Watercress was also known in Ireland as 'St Patrick's Cabbage'. The first records of commercial cultivation are from Germany around 1750, France between 1800 and 1811 and near Gravesend in England, around 1808.

CULTIVATION

Found in and alongside fast-flowing rivers and streams, watercress has fleshy, glossy leaves on long stalks with 5 to 10 leaflets. Its long stems creep or float on the surface and root easily. Small whitish-green flowers appear in flat-topped clusters from mid-spring to early autumn.

The best watercress is grown in pure, fast-flowing chalk or limestone streams with slightly alkaline water. This avoids the risk of contamination from pollution, which can cause stomach upsets.

Propagation
The easiest way to propagate watercress is from shop-bought material. Cuttings 10cm (4in) long take only about a week to root when placed in a glass of water.

If you live by a fast-flowing stream, plant rooted cuttings 15cm (6in) apart in the banks. Firm well to prevent them from being dislodged.

To grow watercress in the garden, dig a trench 60cm (2ft) wide and 30cm (12in) deep, put a 15cm (6in) layer of well-rotted farmyard manure or compost into the base. (Do not use sheep manure as it can carry dangerous liver fluke.) Mix in a little ground limestone if your soil is not alkaline, then cover with 7.5–10cm (3–4in) of soil. Plant cuttings 15cm (6in) apart in mid-spring. Alternatively, in spring, mark out an area and dig in well-rotted organic matter and ground limestone, firm and soak with water before scattering seed thinly on the surface. Water daily.

Seeds can also be sown indoors from mid- to late spring, in a propagator or trays of peat-substitute seed compost on a window sill. Cover the seeds with 3mm (1/8in) of compost, keep it constantly moist at around 10–15°C (50–60°F).

Transplant 3–4 seedlings into a 7.5cm (3in) pot when large enough to handle, then plant out 10–15cm (4–6in) apart from mid-spring onwards. When plants deteriorate replace them with fresh cuttings.

Growing
Plants grown in the garden need a bright, sheltered position away from direct sunshine; never allow it to dry out, or plants run to seed. As a cool-season crop, watercress grows most actively in spring and autumn, and during the winter in warmer climates.

Occasional feeding with a dilute high-nitrogen liquid fertilizer or liquid seaweed may be needed. Do not grow in stagnant or still water.

Maintenance
Spring Take cuttings or sow seed mid- to late spring.
Summer Do not let compost-grown plants dry out. Keep weed-free. Harvest as needed. Remove flower heads as they appear.
Autumn Continue to harvest.
Winter Protect with cloches for continuous growth.

Protected Cropping
Cover plants with cloches, fleece or polythene tunnels before the first frosts. Make a watercress bed in an unheated greenhouse over winter, or grow in pots.

Container Growing
Grow in large pots or containers of moist peat-

Wild watercress by a fast-flowing stream, Guernsey

substitute compost, with a layer of gravel in the base, spacing 10–15cm (4–6in) apart. Keep compost moist by standing the pot in a bowl of water which is replaced daily. Grow plants on a bright windowsill, but away from direct sunshine.

Harvesting and Storing

Younger leaves near the stem tips have the best flavour. Harvest lightly during the first season and annually towards autumn if plants are to be overwintered, cutting regularly for a constant supply of bushy shoots.

Use leaves fresh or store in the salad compartment of a refrigerator for 2–3 days.

PESTS AND DISEASES

Watercress is rarely troubled, but caterpillars of cabbage white butterfly may cause problems.

MEDICINAL

Watercress has been valued for its medicinal qualities since antiquity. It has been eaten to cure rheumatism, and used as a diuretic and as an expectorant for catarrh, colds and bronchitis; it is a stimulant, a digestive and a tonic to promote appetite, counteract anaemia and also to lower blood-sugar levels in diabetes.

Externally it is a hair tonic. Rubbed on the skin it is said to remove rashes. Culpeper recommended the bruised leaves or juice for clearing spots and freckles and a poultice was said to heal glandular tumours and lymphatic swellings.

Traditionally it was taken as a spring tonic. In the past, in isolated parts of the British Isles where the diet was predominantly shellfish and salt meat, it was often grown to prevent scurvy, and was so mentioned by Philip Miller in his *Gardener's Dictionary* of 1731.

Unless harvested regularly, watercress develops small white flowers. Once flowered, the leaves are less tender

WARNING

Gathering from streams is not recommended if sheep are grazing nearby, as there is a risk of liver fluke. Fluke can be destroyed by thorough cooking.

CULINARY

As with its relative the radish, the hot, spicy taste of watercress comes from mustard oil. Remove discoloured leaves and wash thoroughly, shaking off excess water. Eat in salads and stir-fries, or liquidize to make chilled soup. It makes a perfect garnish for sandwiches. Chop finely and add to butter, mashed potatoes, dumplings or a white sauce. Also sauté in butter for 10 minutes and serve as a vegetable.

Among her many tastebud-tingling recipes, Jane Grigson suggests cutting orange segments into quarters and mixing with watercress, olive oil vinaigrette and black pepper; add walnuts or black olives and eat as a salad with ham, duck or veal.

Salmon with Watercress Sauce
Serves 6

6 salmon fillets, trimmed
4 tablespoons butter
4 tablespoons finely chopped shallots
2 large bunches watercress, plus sprigs to garnish
150ml (1/4pt) double cream
Salt and freshly ground black pepper

Steam the salmon fillets, covered, on a steamer rack over boiling water until cooked; this should take 10 minutes or so.

Meanwhile, prepare the sauce by melting the butter in a heavy frying pan and sautéing the shallots until softened. Add the watercress and, constantly stirring, allow the watercress to wilt for about 2 minutes; it should retain its bright green colour. Stir in the cream and seasoning and bring to the boil. Remove from the heat and blend in a liquidizer until smooth. Then reheat gently.

Arrange the salmon fillets in the centre of individual plates and spoon sauce over each, garnishing with a little fresh watercress.

Crithmum maritimum. Apiaceae

SAMPHIRE

Also known as Rock Samphire, Sea Fennel, Sea Samphire. Low-growing maritime perennial. Half hardy. Value: good source of iron and vitamin C; moderate iodine.

Rock samphire is found on the shores and cliffs of Europe. Its name comes from 'sampiere', a contraction of the French *herbe de St Pierre* – the fisherman Saint's herb. Collected from the wild for centuries, by the English Tudor period it was widely cultivated in gardens. William Turner wrote: 'Creta marina groweth much in rockes and cliffes beside Dover.' This precarious habitat is mentioned in *King Lear*, where harvesters dangle over the cliffs from a rope. Robert Turner in 1664 described similar dangerous activities on the 200m (600ft) cliffs of the Isle of Wight, 'yet many adventure it though they buy their sauce with the price of their lives'. Samphire harvests were sent in casks of seawater to London, where wholesalers paid four shillings a bushell, but for the privilege of collecting it and gulls' eggs the Lord of the Manor exacted an annual rent.

VARIETIES

Crithmum maritimum has a woody base, with stems to 60cm (2ft) and lobed grey-green leaflets. The white/cream flowers, in flat clusters, are followed by small oval fruits. The leaves have an aromatic odour which has been likened to the smell of furniture polish!

CULTIVATION

Propagation
Plants are propagated from fresh seed sown in autumn or spring in a sheltered position. Transplant when large enough to handle, or divide plants in spring.

Growing
Its natural habitat is in sand; if you create a satisfactory habitat in a coastal garden, natural colonies may form. Plants often inhabit dry stone walls. They flourish in well-drained, sandy or gritty soil, which is constantly

Samphire flourishes in sea spray

moist and protected from full heat. An open east- or south-facing position is ideal. Mulch with seaweed, or burn seaweed and scatter with the sodium-rich debris. If possible, water with seawater or sea salt solution.

Maintenance
Spring Sow seed in gritty compost or in shallow drills.
Summer Keep soil moist with a saline solution. Harvest.
Autumn : Harvest. Protect crops during colder weather.
Winter Mulch with straw or leaves.

Protected Cropping
As a succulent plant, rock samphire needs frost protection. Cover with leaves, straw or cloches.

Container Growing
Grow in containers of gritty, loam-based compost. Water regularly in summer; in cooler climates, bring plants indoors during the winter.

Harvesting and Storing
Harvest young shoots and leaves by cutting or pulling. Young spring growth is the most tender. Do not harvest excessively from each plant. It is best eaten immediately after harvesting, but will last for up to 2 days in a fridge.

Pests and Diseases
Usually trouble-free.

CULINARY

Wash thoroughly in running water before use.
   Tender young shoots and leaves can be eaten fresh or cooked as a vegetable. They are added raw to salads or dressed with oil and lemon juice as an hors-d'oeuvre.
   Pickle young shoots, leaves and stems by filling a jar with samphire cut into 2.5cm (1in) lengths, add peppercorns and a little grated horseradish, pour over a boiling mixture of equal parts dry cider and vinegar, and infuse for an hour before sealing. Pickled, it is used as a garnish and as a caper substitute.
   In Italy it is known as 'Roscano'.

MEDICINAL

John Evelyn noted 'its excellent vertues and effects against the Spleen. Cleansing the Passages and sharpning appetite.' It was also recommended as a kidney, bladder and general tonic and as a treatment for 'stones'. It is said to be a diuretic, to improve digestion and has been used to encourage weight loss.

Scorzonera hispanica. Asteraceae

SCORZONERA

Also known as False Salsify, Spanish Salsify.
Grown as biennial for shoots, flower buds and flowers; annual for cylindrical tapering roots. Hardy. Value: contains indigestible carbohydrate inulin, which, when converted to fructose in storage, increases calorific content (27 calories per 100g); small amounts of vitamins and minerals.

Scorzonera is very similar to salsify, though scorzonera is perennial, not biennial, its skin is darker, the roots narrower and the flavour is not as strong. The name scorzonera may have come from the French '*scorzon*' or serpent, as the root was used in Spain to cure snake bites. Another interpretation suggests it comes from the Italian '*scorza*', bark, and '*nera*', black, describing the roots. Native to central and southern Europe through to Russia and Siberia, scorzonera was known by the Greeks and Romans, who took little interest in its cultivation; it arrived in England by 1560 and in North America by 1806. It is widely grown in Europe as an excellent winter vegetable. The leaves have been used as food for silkworms.

If allowed to grow, the bright yellow flowers make ideal ornamentals

'Russian Giant', one of the more commonly grown varieties

VARIETIES

'**Duplex**' produces long tasty roots. '**Flandria Scorzonera**' has long roots, growing to 30cm (12in), with strongly flavoured flesh. '**Habil**' is long-rooted with a delicious flavour. '**Lange Jan**' ('**Long John**') has long, tapering, dark brown roots. '**Long Black**' is similar, but with black roots. '**Russian Giant**' lives up to its name, with long roots and a subtle, delicate flavour.

CULTIVATION

Propagation
Sow fresh seed *in situ* from mid- to late spring, in drills 1–2cm (1/2–¾) deep with rows 15cm (6in) apart. Alternatively, sow 2 or 3 seeds in 'stations' 15cm (6in) apart, thinning to leave the strongest seedling when large enough to handle. Or sow in late summer for use early the following autumn.

Growing
It flourishes in a sunny position on a deep, light, well-drained soil which should have been manured for a previous crop. Do not grow on freshly manured or stony ground, as this causes 'forking'. A pH of 6.0–7.5 is ideal, so lime the soil if necessary. On heavy or stony soils, fill a narrow trench about 30cm (12in) deep with finely sieved soil or free-draining compost so that the roots grow straight. Dig the soil deeply and rake in 60–90g/sq m (2–3oz/sq yd) general balanced fertilizer 10 days before sowing.

Remove weeds around the plants by hand, as roots bleed easily when damaged by a hoe. Mulching once the roots have established helps to smother weeds, conserve moisture and reduces the risk of bolting during dry weather. Water at a rate of 16–22 litres/sq m (3–5 gal/sq yd) per week.

Scorzonera tends to be neglected by English gardeners, but is often found growing in Mediterranean countries

Roots can be left in the ground to produce 'chards' (edible shoots) the following spring. In autumn cut off old leaves, leaving 1–2.5cm (½–1in) above the soil. Earth up the roots to a depth of about 15cm (6in) so the developing shoots are blanched during the winter. In late spring, scrape away the soil and harvest when the shoots are 12–15cm (5–6in) long. They can also be blanched by covering to a similar depth with straw or leaves in early spring. Roots too small to harvest in the first year can be left to mature the following year.

Maintenance
Spring Sow thinly, from mid- to late spring. Thin when large enough to handle.
Summer Keep crops weed-free and water thoroughly as needed to keep soil moist.
Autumn Leave roots in the ground and lift carefully with a fork as needed.
Winter Continue harvesting. Prepare the ground for the next crop.

Protected Cropping
Scorzonera is hardy, but protection with straw or cloches before the onset of severe weather makes lifting much easier.

Container Growing
In shallow or stony soils plants can be grown in deep containers of loam-based compost. Water regularly.

Harvesting and Storing
Plants need at least 4 months to reach maturity and are ready to harvest from mid-autumn to mid-spring. In a good year the roots may grow to 40cm (16in) , but are more usually about 20cm (8in) long.
Roots can either be left in the ground until needed or lifted – with care, as they are easily damaged. Clean and store in boxes of sand or sawdust in a cool place. They last up to 1 week in a fridge.
Mature plants flower in spring or summer of the second year. The buds can be harvested with about 8cm (3in) of stem.
If, while lifting, you see that your crop has many forked roots, the remaining plants can be kept for their young shoots and buds.

PESTS AND DISEASES

Scorzonera rarely suffers from problems but may develop 'white blister', which looks like glistening paint splashes. Affected plants become distorted.

COMPANION PLANTING

Scorzonera repels carrot root fly and the flowers attract beneficial insects.

MEDICINAL

The name derived from the Spanish reflects its reputation as an antidote to snake venom, '...and especially to cure the bitings of vipers (of which there may be very many in Spaine and other hot countries),' wrote Gerard in his *Herball* of 1636. This has not been proven.

CULINARY

Roots can be baked, puréed, dipped in batter, sautéed and made into croquettes and fritters, deep-fried or served *au gratin* with cheese and breadcrumbs.
Boiling allows you to appreciate the flavour fully. They discolour when cut, so drop into water with a dash of lemon juice, then boil for 25 minutes in salted water with a tablespoon of flour added. Peel after boiling as you would a hard-boiled egg. Toss with melted butter and chopped parsley. Young 'chards' can be served raw in salads. The flower stalks are considered tastier than those of salsify.

Sautéed Scorzonera
Allow 150–175g (5–6oz) per person of cleaned scorzonera; it should not be peeled. Chop roughly and cook in a heavy frying pan in a little extra-virgin olive oil until *al dente*, turning to cook every side. Drain on kitchen paper and sprinkle with lemon juice mixed with 1 crushed garlic clove and 1 tablespoon finely chopped flat-leaf parsley.

Sautéed Scorzonera

Sechium edule. Cucurbitaceae

CHAYOTE

Also known as Choko, Chow Chow, Christophine. Vigorous, scrambling, tuberous rooted perennial, grown for edible fruit and seed. Tender. Value: 90 % water; low in calories; some vitamin C

In good conditions, this climber spreads to 15m (50ft) and produces huge tubers. It originated in central America; 'chayote' comes from the Aztec *chayotl*, while in the West Indies it is called 'christophine' after Columbus, who reputedly introduced it to the islands. The pear-shaped fruits contain a single nutty-flavoured seed, much prized by cooks.

VARIETIES

'Ivory White' is a small, pale-skinned variety.

CULTIVATION

Chayote needs rich, fertile, well-drained soil.

Propagation
Propagate cultivars from soft tip cuttings in spring at 18°C (65°F). Alternatively, plant the whole fruit laid on its side, at a slight angle, with the narrow end protruding from the soil.

Growing
Grow on mounds 30–40cm (12–14in) high and 90x90cm (3x3ft) apart; cover a shovel full of well-rotted manure with 15cm (6in) of soil. Lightly mulch.

Alternatively, grow on beds 3m (9ft) square; dig in organic matter, plant seeds in the corners and grow vines towards the centre. Or, plant in 90cm (3ft) wide ridges. Train the stems into trees, over trellising, fences, or 15cm (6in) mesh netting. Water regularly in dry weather; optimum growth is during the wet season. A day length of just over 12 hours is required for flowering.

In the humid tropics, it grows better in moderate temperatures at altitude.

Maintenance
Spring Sow seed or take cuttings.
Summer Feed and water.
Autumn Harvest.
Winter Store fruit for next year's crop.

Protected Cropping
In cool temperate regions, grow under glass in bright light with moderate temperatures and humidity. In warmer areas, start off indoors and plant when the danger of frost has passed. Grow in the greenhouse border or in containers.

Container Growing
Propagate in spring from seed or cuttings. Pot on into loam-based compost with a high fertilizer content, add well-rotted manure and grit to improve drainage. Water thoroughly, feed fortnightly with general liquid fertilizer and, once established, with a high-potash fertilizer. Train the growth on to a trellis.

Harvesting and Storing
In tropical climates, plants last for several years, fruiting from 3 to 4 months after sowing, all year round. Harvest by cutting the stalk above the fruit with a knife. Fruit reaches its maximum size 25–30 days after fruit set. It will keep up to 3 months in a cool place.

Pests and Diseases
Root knot nematode causes wilting; powdery mildew can appear on leaves and stems; and red spider mite affects plants grown under glass.

MEDICINAL

Chayote is good for stomach ulcers. It contains some trace elements.

CULINARY

This versatile vegetable can be made into soups, boiled, candied, puréed (spiced with chilli powder) or added to stews, curries and chutneys. Its seeds can be cooked in butter, the young leaves cooked like spinach, and the tuber eaten when young. Its flesh stays firm after cooking. It makes a good substitute for avocado in a salad and is ideal for those on a diet.

For a stuffing, try a well-flavoured bolognese sauce; add boiled chayote flesh and stuff back into halved chayote shells. Sprinkle with Cheddar and bake in an oven preheated to 180°C/350°F/gas mark 4, for 30 minutes.

Chayote in Red Wine
Serves 6

Jane Grigson gives a recipe for this pudding.

6 pear-sized chayotes, peeled and left whole
150g (5oz) sugar
300ml (1/2pt) water
150ml (1/4pt) red wine
5cm (2in) cinnamon stick
4 cloves
Lemon juice
Whipped cream and icing sugar

Use a pan that will hold the chayote in a single layer. Put the sugar and water on to dissolve and simmer for 2 minutes. Carefully add the chayote, then the wine and spices.

Cover and simmer until tender. Remove the chayote to a bowl and arrange upright like pears. Reduce the liquid until syrupy and add a little lemon juice to bring out the flavour. Strain the juice over the chayote and serve with whipped cream lightly sweetened with icing sugar.

Chayote in Red Wine

Stachys affinis. Lamiaceae

CHINESE ARTICHOKE

Also known as Japanese Artichoke, Crosne. Dwarf herbaceous perennial grown as annual for edible tubers. Hardy. Value: very high in potassium.

From the same family as mint, lavender and many other herbs, Chinese artichokes are not grown for their aromatic foliage but for the small, ridged tubers at the tips of creeping underground stems. A native of Japan and China, it has rough, oval leaves and white to pale pink flowers that appear in small spikes. It was introduced from Peking to France by a physician in the late nineteenth century. It has never been hugely popular, probably because a large area is needed for decent quantities, but it is worth trying, if only as a 'novelty' crop.

CULTIVATION

Chinese artichokes flourish in an open, sunny site on light, fertile yet moisture-retentive soil.

Propagation

For early crops, sprout the tubers in shallow trays or pots of potting compost in a moderately warm room, then plant out when soil is warm. Increase your stock by planting tubers individually in small pots of soil-based compost with added organic matter, transplanting as required. Place in 20–23cm (8–9in) pots for the rest of the growing season. Feed and water regularly.

Growing

In spring, plant the tubers vertically 4–7.5cm (1½–3in) deep; on light soils up to 15cm (6in) deep. Plant large tubers only, 30cm (12in) apart each way or 20cm (8in) apart in rows 40cm (16in) apart. When 30–60cm (1–2ft) high, earth up round the stems to about 7.5cm (3in). Keep weed-free at first; as the plants mature, the leaf canopy naturally suppresses weed growth. Feed with a liquid general fertilizer every 2 weeks and remove flowering spikes to concentrate energy into fattening the tubers. Trim back the foliage. Rampant growth make Chinese artichokes an ideal low-maintenance crop for a spare corner of the garden.

Maintenance

Spring Plant tubers when the soil has warmed.
Summer Keep crops weed-free, water and feed.
Autumn Harvest after the first frosts, or about 5 months.
Winter Protect crops with hessian, straw or sacking to enable harvesting to continue.

Harvesting and Storing

Harvest as required from mid-autumn to early spring, after the foliage has died back or when plants have

A mass of tubers

been in the ground for 5–7 months. Lift them just before use as they quickly shrivel. When forking through the ground during the final harvest, you should remove even the smallest tubers or they will rapidly become weeds.

PESTS AND DISEASES

Chinese artichokes are usually pest-free, but you should take precautions against lettuce root aphid, which can cause wilting.

CULINARY

The tubers have a delicate, nutty flavour. Only about 5cm (2in) long, they are rather fiddly to cook. Boiling is simplest, but they can also be fried, stir-fried, roasted, added to soup or eaten raw in salads.

Creamed Chinese Artichokes
Serves 4

Jane Grigson, in her *Vegetable Book*, quotes this recipe from *La Cuisine de Madame Saint-Ange*.

500g (1lb) Chinese artichokes
1 tablespoon butter
½ teaspoon lemon juice
300ml (½pt) double cream
Salt and freshly ground white pepper
Pinch nutmeg
Double cream, to serve

Boil the artichokes for about 5 minutes, drain, add the butter and lemon juice and cook gently for 5–7 minutes. Bring the cream to the boil, then add it to the artichokes, stirring in well. Season. Cover and leave for 15 minutes over a moderate heat, until the cream has reduced by a quarter. Just before serving, stir in 3 spoonfuls of double cream and quickly remove from the heat.

Solanum melongena. Solanaceae

AUBERGINE

Also known as Brinjal, Garden Egg, Eggplant, Guinea Squash, Pea Aubergine. Short-lived perennial grown as annual for fruits. Tender. Value: small amounts of most vitamins and minerals; very low in calories, with 3% carbohydrates and 1% protein.

Aubergine flowers reveal the family likeness to the potato

This glossy-skinned fruit was known to sixteenth-century Spaniards as the 'apple of love'. In contrast, many botanists of the time called it *mala insana* or 'mad apple', because of its alleged effects. The Chinese first cultivated aubergines in the fifth century BC and they have been grown in India for centuries, yet they were unknown to the Greeks and Romans. Moorish invaders introduced them to Spain and the Spaniards later took them to the New World. 'Aubergine' is a corruption of the Arabic name *al-badingan*.

VARIETIES

Fruits vary in shape from large, purple-skinned types to small, rounded white fruits 5cm (2in) in diameter. Most modern F1 hybrids are bushy and grow about 1m (3ft) tall. Unlike older varieties, they are almost spineless. **'Bambino'** is a small variety, grown as a 'mini vegetable'. **'Black Beauty'** produces dark purple fruits of good quality over a long period. It is high-yielding. **'Black Enorma'** has monstrous, dark, almost spherical fruit. Regular harvesting is advisable and a stout supporting stake is recommended, too! **'Easter Egg'**, despite its name, is not chocolate-coloured and sweet, but white, about the size of a large hen's egg. It should be harvested when it is about 12.5cm (5in) long. It ripens after 2 months in good growing conditions. **'Florida Market'** is oval, glossy purple-black and ideal for warm climates. Cropping over a long period, the fruits are rot-resistant and tasty. **'Long Purple'** produces good yields of dark purple fruits about 15cm (6in) long. **'Moneymaker'** is a superb early variety with tasty fruits. Tolerant of lower temperatures, it can be grown indoors as well as outside. **'Ova'** is delightful, producing masses of small, white-skinned fruits. It is decorative and ideal for unheated greenhouses. **'Short Tom'** is a small, early cropping variety. The fruits can be harvested when they are small or allowed to grow larger. It is ideal for containers. **'Violette di Firenze'** needs warmth to ripen fully. The unusual yet very attractive dark mauve fruits make this an ideal plant for growing in a 'potager'.

CULTIVATION

Aubergines need long, hot summers, and are the ideal crop for warm climates. In cooler regions, they will grow outside, but better harvests come from those protected indoors. Constant temperatures between 25–30°C (75–86°F) with moderate to high humidity are needed for optimum flower and fruit production. Below 20°C (68°F) growth is often stalled.

Propagation

Temperatures of 15–21°C (58–70°F) are needed for good germination. Sow seed in early spring, in trays, pots or modules of moist seed compost in a propagator or warm glasshouse or on a windowsill. Soaking seed in warm water for 24 hours before sowing helps germination. When 3 leaves appear, pot on plants grown in seed trays into 5–7.5cm (2–3in) pots, repotting as required until they are ready to plant outdoors or under cover. If you are growing aubergines outdoors, sow seeds 10–12 weeks before the last frosts are expected.

Growing

Aubergines flourish in a sunny, sheltered position on fertile, well-drained soil. Before planting, fork in a slow-release general fertilizer at 30–60g/sq m (1–2oz/sq yd), improve the soil with the addition of organic matter and, in cooler climates, warm the soil before planting and leave the cloches in place until the plants are established for 2–3 weeks, allowing them to 'harden off' before removing the cloches.

Space plants 50–60cm (20–24in) apart. 'Pinch out' the growth tip when plants are 40cm (16in) tall, or 23–30cm (9–12in) for smaller varieties. Stake the main stem or support branches with string if necessary as fruit begins to mature. Mulch outdoor plants to conserve moisture and suppress weeds.

Feed plants with a liquid general fertilizer until they are established, then water with a high-potash liquid feed every 10 days once the first fruits are formed. When the flowers begin to open a light spray with tepid water helps pollination; for large, high-quality fruits, allow only 4–5 to form on each plant, after which any new side shoots should be removed.

Maintenance
Spring Sow seeds under glass.
Summer Once frosts are over, transplant outdoors. Retain 4–6 fruits per plant, harvesting as they mature.
Autumn Protect outdoor crops from early frosts.
Winter Order seed for the following growing season.

Protected Cropping
When growing plants indoors, mist them regularly with tepid water or 'damp down' the paths on hot days. Keep the compost moist throughout the growing season but take care to avoid waterlogging.

Container Growing
Aubergines can be grown in 20–30cm (8–12in) pots or in growbags. Keep temperatures around 15–18°C (58–65°F); water regularly, keep the compost moist and feed with a half-strength high-potash fertilizer every other watering.

Harvesting and Storing
Harvest when the skin is shiny: overripe fruits have dull skin and are horribly bitter. Using a knife, cut the fruit stalks close to the stem. They will keep for 2 weeks in a cool, humid place or in a refrigerator.

PESTS AND DISEASES

Aubergines are susceptible to the typical problems of crops grown under glass.

Check plants for aphids, whitefly and red spider mite. Powdery mildew can stunt growth, and in severe cases leaves become yellow and die. Verticillium wilt turns lower leaves yellow; plants wilt but recover overnight.

COMPANION PLANTING

Aubergines flourish alongside thyme, tarragon and peas.

MEDICINAL

In Indian herbal medicine white varieties are used to treat diabetes and as a carminative. The Sanskrit *vatin-ganah* means 'anti-wind vegetable'. *Kama Sutra* prescribes it in a concoction for 'enlarging the male organ for a period of 1 month'. Neither claim has been proven!

WARNING

Always remove the fruit's bitter principle as it irritates the mucous membranes.

'Violette di Firenze', beautiful and unusual

CULINARY

The large 'berries' contain a bitter principle in the flesh. Slice large varieties, sprinkle with salt and leave for 30 minutes to leach out the bitterness, before rinsing. Small and newer varieties do not need this treatment. Rub cut surfaces with lemon juice to prevent discoloration.

Aubergines can be made into soups, puréed, stewed, stuffed, fried and pickled. Slices can be dipped in batter to make fritters, or drizzled with olive oil and grilled or roasted. In the Middle East the skin is burned off over a naked flame, giving the flesh a smoky flavour.

In Provence the vegetable stew *ratatouille* is made from aubergines, garlic, peppers, courgettes, onions and coriander seeds, all cooked in olive oil. The Greek *moussaka* contains minced meat and aubergines.

In the Caribbean small white varieties are stewed in coconut milk and sweet spices. Oriental aubergines have a sweetness that does not suit European cooking; use them in stir-fries.

Sautéed Aubergines with Mozzarella
Serves 4

This dish goes well with plain meats.

4 small, long, thin aubergines
1 clove garlic, crushed
1 tablespoon chopped parsley
Salt and freshly ground black pepper
50g (2oz) toasted breadcrumbs
3 tablespoons olive oil
100g (4oz) buffalo mozzarella, cut into 5mm (¼in) slices

Cut the aubergines in half lengthwise. Score the flesh deeply, but do not cut the skin. Arrange in a shallow pan, skin side down. Mix the garlic, parsley, salt and pepper, the breadcrumbs and half the olive oil and press this into the scored aubergines. Drizzle over the rest of the oil and place in a preheated oven (180°C/ 350°F/ gas mark 4) until tender, about 20 minutes.

Raise the heat to 200°C/ 400°F/ gas mark 6 and, as the oven warms, arrange the mozzarella on top of the aubergines. Return to the oven for 5 minutes. Serve this dish immediately the mozzarella melts.

Solanum tuberosum. Solanaceae

POTATO

Also known as Common Potato, Irish Potato. Perennial, grown as annual for edible starchy tubers. Half hardy. Value: rich in carbohydrates, magnesium, potassium; moderate amounts of vitamins B and C.

Then a sentimental passion of a vegetable fashion must excite your languid spleen.
An attachment à la Plato for a bashful young potato or a not too French French bean.
Sir William Gilbert (1836–1911)

The world's fourth most important food crop after wheat, maize and rice, the potato is a nutritious starchy staple grown throughout temperate zones. Hundreds of varieties have been developed since 5000 BC, when potatoes were first cultivated in Chile and Peru. The name derives from batatas, the Carib Indian name for the sweet potato, or from papa or patata, as it was called by South American Indians.

The Spaniards introduced potatoes to Europe in the sixteenth century and Sir John Hawkins is reputed to have brought them to England in 1563. Extensive cultivation did not start until Sir Francis Drake brought more back in 1586, after battling with the Spaniards in the Caribbean. Sir Walter Raleigh introduced them to Ireland and later presented some to Elizabeth I. Her cook is said to have discarded the tubers and cooked the leaves, which did not help its popularity!

In England and Germany potatoes were considered a curiosity; in France they were believed to cause leprosy and fever. However, in 1773 the French scientist Antoine Parmentier wrote a thesis extolling the potato's virtues as a famine food after eating them while a prisoner of war in Prussia. He established soup kitchens to feed the malnourished; potato soup is now known as *Potage*

Parmentier, and there is also *Omelette Parmentier*. He created 'French fries', which were served at a dinner honouring Benjamin Franklin, who was unimpressed; it was Thomas Jefferson who introduced French fries to America at a White House dinner.

Parmentier presented a bouquet of potato flowers to Louis XVI, who is said to have worn one in his buttonhole. Marie Antoinette wore them in her hair, which made it highly fashionable. By the early nineteenth century, the potato had become a staple in France.

Ireland's climate and plentiful rain produced large crops. Potatoes were propagated from small tubers which were passed from one household to another, so the whole crop came from a few original plants. These were susceptible to potato blight, and devastating crop failure in the 1840s caused the death of more than 1.5 million people. Almost a million others emigrated to North America. Without the potato famine, John Kennedy and Ronald Reagan may never have been presidents of the United States.

During the American Civil War, potatoes were sent to the prisons and front lines. By eating the potatoes in their skins, soldiers received adequate supplies of vitamin C. The common name 'spud' came from a tool which was once used to weed the potato patch.

VARIETIES

Potatoes are classified as 'first early', 'second early' (or 'mid-crop') and 'maincrop' varieties. Early and second early varieties grow rapidly, taking up less space for a shorter time than maincrops, so are better for small gardens. Yields are usually lower. They are also unaffected by some of the diseases afflicting maincrops. Second earlies are planted about a month after earlies. Maincrop are for immediate consumption or winter storage.

Potatoes come in a huge range of shapes, sizes, colours and textures. The skin may be red, yellow, purple or white and the flesh pale cream or yellow, mottled or blue. Their texture may be waxy or floury and shapes variously knobbly, round and oval. Because of government · legislation, some old varieties are only available from specialist societies, though many suppliers have a good range for sale. Choose varieties recommended for your area.

'Avalanche' can be grown as a second early or a maincrop. The round to oval white tubers have white flesh. They are uniform, productive and excellent for baking. 'Belle de Fontenay' is a very old, rare, French early variety which is excellent for salads. The yellow tubers are small and kidney-shaped, with a waxy texture and fine flavour. 'Concorde' is heavy-cropping and very early. The tubers are large and oval with pale yellow flesh, a waxy texture and excellent flavour. Suitable for most soils, showing resistance to late frosts. 'Desirée' is a popular maincrop with pink skin and pale yellow flesh. Crops well on most soils, but prefers medium to heavy. Good for chips and baking. Susceptible to mosaic and common scab. 'Famosa', a maincrop, has white-skinned long to oval tubers and pale yellow flesh. It has an excellent flavour and texture. 'Golden Wonder' is a variety well known to crisp eaters. This is a late maincrop with floury, yellow flesh, is good for baking and ideal for crisps, but usually disintegrates when boiled. It grows well in moist, humid climates, is resistant to scab but susceptible to slug

'King Edward', an old variety

damage and drought. 'Kennebec', a second early to maincrop, is smooth and white-skinned, with white flesh. A heavy cropper, it is easy to peel, good for boiling and keeps well. Resistant to blight and mosaic virus. 'King Edward', another famous high-yielding, good-quality maincrop, is good for

large, tasty tubers which are good for French fries. 'Navan' is a white-skinned, oval, high-yielding maincrop. First early 'Pentland Javelin' produces high yields of oval, white-skinned tubers with white waxy flesh. Resistant to common scab and golden eelworm. 'Pink Fir Apple' is a wonderful old late maincrop. The unusual elongated tubers are pink-skinned with

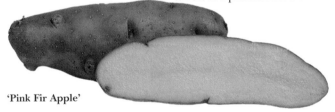

'Pink Fir Apple'

baking. Susceptible to blight, wart disease and drought. 'Maris Bard' is a very early 'first early', with white skin and white waxy flesh. It is high-yielding and good under cover. Excellent quality and good virus resistance. 'Maris Peer' is a second early. Its moderate yields of small white tubers are used for canning. It is scab- and skin spot-resistant, but susceptible to drought. 'Maris Piper' is a prolific second early with waxy flesh when cooked. 'Maxine' is a maincrop with round, smooth, red-skinned tubers. The white waxy flesh remains firm when cooked. It produces heavy crops of

pale yellow flesh. They are good in salads, remaining firm when cold, and make good chips. 'Red Norland' is an extra-early round potato with smooth red skin and white flesh. High-yielding, hardy, tasty and excellent for cooking. Good resistance to scab. 'Stroma' can be used as a second early or maincrop. It is oval with pink to red skin and pale yellow flesh. It is well flavoured and slug-resistant. 'Wilja' is a high-yielding second early with long white tubers and pale yellow waxy flesh. Good for salads and excellent for cooking. Resistant to blight, it has some resistance to scab and blackleg.

prouting seed potatoes, 'Maris Piper'

Potato crop in Oregon, USA

CULTIVATION

Propagation

Potatoes are normally grown from small tubers known as 'seed potatoes'. Buy 'certified' virus-free stock from a reputable supplier to be certain of obtaining a good-quality crop.

These are 'sprouted' (or 'chitted') about 6 weeks before planting to extend the growing season, which is particularly useful for early cultivars and in cooler climates. It is worth chitting second earlies and maincrops if they are to be planted late. Put a single layer of potatoes in a shallow tray or egg box with the 'rose end' (where most of the 'eyes' or dormant buds are concentrated) upwards, then put the tray in a light, cool, frost-free place to encourage growth. At 7°C (45°F) it takes about 6 weeks for shoots around 2.5cm (1in) long to form. At this stage, they are ready for planting. They can be planted when the shoots are longer, but need handling with care, as they are easily broken off. For a smaller crop but larger potatoes, leave 3 shoots per tuber on earlies; otherwise leave all of the shoots for a higher yield.

Plant earlies from mid-spring and maincrops from late spring, when there is no longer any danger of hard frosts and soil temperatures are 7°C (45°F).

Make trenches or individual holes 7–15cm (3–6in) deep, depending on the size of the tuber. Plant them upright with the shoots at the top and cover with at least 2.5cm (1in) of soil. Take care not to damage the shoots. Earlies can be planted a little deeper to give more protection from cooler weather. Ideally the rows should face north-south so that both sides of the row receive sunshine.

Plant earlies 30–38cm (12–15in) apart with 38–50cm (15–20in) between the rows and maincrops 38cm (15in) apart with 75cm (30in) between the rows. Alternatively, plant earlies 35cm (14in) apart and second earlies and maincrops 30–38cm (12–15in) apart in and between the rows. Spacing can be varied according to the size of the tubers and also to their subsequent cropping potential.

While the traditional method of propagation is very common, seed is also available, which is easy to handle and produces healthy crops. Seeds are sown indoors before potting on, hardening off and transplanting. 'Plantlets' produced by tissue culture are also available; these are healthy, virus-free and vigorous. These, too, will need growing on before hardening off and then transplanting.

Cutting large potatoes in half is not recommended; nor is the method I once saw being used – hollowing the tubers to leave a thin layer of flesh, then planting the skins only!

Growing

Potatoes flourish in an open, sunny, frost-free site on deep, rich, fertile, well-drained soil. They grow better in cool seasons, when temperatures are between 16–18°C (61–64°F), and are tolerant of most soils. Lighter soils are better for growing earlies. Add organic matter to sandy soils. Alkaline soils or heavy liming encourages scab. Grow resistant varieties and lime acid soils gradually to create a pH of 5–6, or cultivate in raised beds or containers. If necessary, dig in plenty of well-rotted organic matter in autumn, then rake to a rough tilth 10 days before planting, adding a general granular fertilizer at 90–120g/sq m (3–4oz/sq yd).

Potatoes are an excellent crop for new or neglected gardens; while the crop may not be large, the root system breaks up the soil and improves its structure. Keep crops weed-free until they are established, when the dense canopy of foliage suppresses weeds.

Potatoes are 'earthed up'; this prevents exposure to light, which makes them green and inedible, and also disturbs germinating weeds. When the plants are about 20–23cm (8–9in) tall, use a rake or spade to draw loose soil carefully around the stems to a depth of 10–15cm (4–6in). Alternatively, begin earthing up in stages when the plants are about 10cm (4in) tall, adding soil every 2–3 weeks.

To avoid having to earth up, plant small tubers about 12.5cm (5in) deep and 23–25cm (9–10in) apart on level ground. Wide spacing means tubers are not forced to the surface, yet still produce a moderate crop.

Potatoes need at least 500mm (20in) of rainfall over the growing season for a good crop. During dry weather water earlies every 12–14 days at 16–22 litres/sq in (3–4 gal/sq yd). Except when there are drought

Planting 'Baillie'

conditions, do not water maincrops until the tubers are the size of marbles (check their development by scraping back the soil below a plant). At this point, a single, thorough soaking with at least 22 litres/sq m (5 gal/sq yd) encourages the tubers to swell, increases the yield and makes them less prone to scab.

Potatoes need a constant supply of water; erratic watering causes malformed, hollow or split potatoes.

An organic liquid feed or nitrogenous top dressing helps plants to become established during the early stages of growth.

Early potatoes can be grown under black polythene, which also makes earthing up unnecessary. Prepare the soil, lay a sheet of black polythene over the area, anchor the edges by covering with soil and plant your potatoes through crosses cut in the polythene. Alternatively, plant the potatoes, cover them with plastic and when the foliage appears, make a cut in the polythene and pull through.

Where early frosts and windy conditions do not occur and the ground is excessively weedy or eelworm is a problem, potatoes can be grown in a bed of compost and straw. Clear the ground and cover the soil with a good layer of well-rotted manure or compost. Space the potatoes as required and cover them with a 5–7.5cm (2–3in) layer of straw or hay, adding more as the potatoes grow, to a maximum of 15cm (6in). At this point, spread a 3–4in layer of lawn mowings over the area to exclude light from the developing tubers.

Rotate earlies every 3 years and maincrops every 5 years.

Maintenance

Spring Chit potatoes before planting.
Summer Keep crops weed-free and water as necessary. Harvest and use or store.
Autumn Plant winter crops under cover. Prepare the soil for the following year.
Winter Harvest winter crops.

Protected Cropping

To advance early crops and protect them from frost, cover early potatoes with cloches or floating crop covers, anchored by burying the edges under the soil. When the shoots appear, cut holes in the plastic and pull the foliage through. After 3–4 weeks cut the cover, leaving it in place to allow the potatoes to become acclimatized.

Protect the foliage and stems ('haulm') from heavy frosts by covering them at night with a layer of straw, bracken or newspaper, or a thin layer of soil. Light frosts do not generally cause problems.

For winter crops of new potatoes, in warm areas, plant earlies in midsummer and cover with cloches in autumn. Alternatively, grow them in the borders of a frost-free greenhouse at 7–10°C (45–50°F). Provide warmth if necessary.

Container Growing

Potatoes can be grown in any container if it is at least 30cm (12in) wide and deep and has drainage holes. It is possible to buy a potato barrel for this purpose – some models have sliding panels for ease of harvesting – but an old dustbin, flower pot or similar is just as good. Potatoes can also be grown in black bin-liners! Wider containers can of course hold more potatoes.

Potatoes growing in a compost heap

Place a 10–12.5cm (4–5in) layer of compost or good garden soil in a container, stand 2–3 chitted potatoes on the surface and cover with a layer of compost about 10–15cm (4–6in) deep. When the shoots are about 15cm (6in) tall, cover with another 10–15cm (4–6in) layer of compost, leaving the tips showing. Continue earthing up until the shoots are 5–7.5cm (2–3in) below the rim of the container.

Winter crops of first earlies can also be grown in containers. Plant in mid-summer for harvesting at Christmas. Cover the 'haulms' in frosty weather or grow under glass.

Be sure to keep crops well fed and watered.

Harvesting and Storing

Earlies are ready to harvest from early to midsummer, second earlies from late summer to early autumn and maincrops mature from early to mid-autumn.

Harvest earlies when they are about the size of a hen's egg: their readiness is often indicated by the flowers opening. Remove some soil from the side of a ridge and check them for size before lifting the root. Insert a flat-tined fork into the base of the ridge and lift the whole plant, bringing the new potatoes up to the surface.

Harvest those grown under black polythene by folding back the sheeting: the crop of potatoes will be lying on the surface. Collect as required.

Scrape away compost from those grown in containers to check their size before harvesting them.

Leave healthy maincrop potatoes in the soil for as long as possible, but beware of slugs! In early autumn cut back the haulm to about 5cm (2in) above the soil, or wait until the foliage dies down naturally; leave the tubers in the ground for 2 weeks for the skins to harden before lifting.

Cut back the haulm and work along the side of each ridge, lifting the potatoes with a fork. Harvest on a dry sunny day when the soil is moderately moist, leave in the sun for a few hours to dry, then brush off the soil. If the weather is poor, dry them under cloches or on trays indoors. Store healthy tubers in paper or hessian sacks or boxes in a dark, cool, frost-free place. They should keep until spring. Check tubers weekly, removing those that are damaged or diseased.

When harvesting, ensure that all potatoes, however small, are removed from the soil to prevent future problems occurring with pests and diseases.

New potatoes do not store, but can be frozen. Blanch whole in boiling water for 3 minutes. Cool, drain, pack into rigid containers and freeze. Chips and French fries can also be frozen.

Digging up potatoes, Devon, England

PESTS AND DISEASES

Common potato scab shows as raised, corky scabs on the surface of the tuber. It does not usually affect the whole potato and can be removed by peeling. It is common in hot, dry summers, on light, free-draining and alkaline soils. Water well in dry conditions, add plenty of organic matter to the soil before planting, avoid excessive liming, or rotating after the soil has been limed for brassicas. Do not put infected potatoes or peelings on the compost heap. Grow resistant cultivars.

Potato blight appears on the leaves as brown patches, often with paler margins. The infection can spread to the stems and through the tuber, making it inedible. The disease spreads rapidly in warm, humid conditions and maincrops are more susceptible. Grow resistant cultivars, avoid overhead watering; before the problem appears apply a systemic fungicide every 2 weeks from midsummer. Alternatively use copper sulphate sprays such as 'Bordeaux mixture'. Earthing up creates a protective barrier, slowing the infection of tubers. Lift early potatoes as soon as possible and in late summer, cut back the 'haulms' of infected plants just above the ground and burn the infected material or put it in the dustbin. Leave tubers in the ground for 2 weeks before lifting.

Potato cyst eelworm ('golden nematode' or 'pale eelworm'). Growth is checked and yields can be severely reduced; badly affected plants turn yellow and die. Lift and burn infected plants, rotate crops, and do not grow potatoes or tomatoes in the soil for at least 6 years. Try to grow resistant varieties.

Wireworms are about 2.5cm (1 in) long and golden brown in colour. They tunnel into the tubers, making them inedible. They are fairly easy to control. Cultivate the soil thoroughly over winter to expose to the weather and birds, keep crops weed-free, and lift 'maincrops' as early as possible. Also rake in a soil insecticide.

Blackleg shows when the upper leaves roll and wilt and the stem becomes black and rotten at the base. The tubers may be rotten. It is more severe in wet seasons; do not plant on waterlogged land. Remove affected plants immediately, burn or put in the dustbin. Do not store damaged tubers.

Slugs can tunnel into the tubers; damage is more severe the longer they remain in the ground.

COMPANION PLANTING

Growing horseradish in large sunken pots near to potatoes controls some diseases. Plant with sweetcorn, cabbage, beans and marigolds. Grow with aubergines, which are a greater attraction to colorado beetle. Protect against scab by putting grass clippings and comfrey leaves in the planting hole or trench.

OTHER USES

Potatoes are made into flour and turned into bread. They can be boiled and the starch turned to glucose, which can be fermented to produce strong alcohol, like the poteen made in Ireland. In the past, they have also

Riddling and sorting potato crop under artificial lights

been a source of starch powder for whitening wigs. The juice of mature potatoes is particularly excellent for cleaning silks, cotton, wool and even furniture.

MEDICINAL

Potatoes are said to be good for rheumatism. One traditional cure for sciatica and lumbago is to carry a potato in your pocket.

The juice from a raw potato or the water in which potatoes have been boiled is said to relieve gout, rheumatism, lumbago, sprains and bruises.

Uncooked peeled and pounded potatoes are said to make a soothing plaster to scalds or burns when applied cold.

Potatoes contain little fat and provide more potassium *pro rata* than bananas, while the average potato contains as many kilojoules as most apples or a glass of orange juice and can be eaten by those on a diet.

WARNING

Green potatoes contain the toxic alkaloid solanine, which can cause vomiting and stomach upsets. Do not eat green potatoes. Beware that the tomato-like fruits and leaves of the plant are also poisonous.

CULINARY

There are more than 500 ways of serving potatoes. They can be boiled, steamed, baked, roasted, mashed, sautéed, fried and cooked *au gratin*.

In the past potatoes have been preserved and candied or mashed with butter, sherry, egg yolks, nutmeg and a little sugar and baked until brown.

Rub the skin from new potatoes under running water and boil for 12 minutes with a sprig of mint. Drain and toss in butter, then eat hot or cold in salads.

Scrape old potatoes; peeling removes much of the vitamin C just below the surface.

Cut potatoes into 1cm (½in) strips, wash in ice-cold water, drain and dry thoroughly. Fry until golden in a shallow frying basket in a pan one third full of oil at 125°C (250°F).

The difference between 'French fries' and 'chips' is their size and the method of cooking. French fries are very thinly sliced and deep-fried in oil. Chips are sliced thickly and were originally cooked in animal fat. Nowadays the only difference is the size.

Microwaving generally retains the flesh colour in unusual potatoes.

Mashed Potatoes with Olive Oil

For those on a diet, this at least has less calories than the traditional dish!

l kg (2lb) potatoes, peeled
8–10 cloves garlic, unpeeled
8 tablespoons olive oil, preferably extra-virgin
Salt and freshly ground black pepper

Put the potatoes and garlic cloves in a pan, cover with water and add salt. Bring to the boil and cook until tender, about 20 minutes, and then drain, reserving the potato cooking liquid. Boil this separately in the pan to reduce to roughly 250ml (8fl oz). Meanwhile peel the garlic cloves.

Mash the potatoes and garlic. Return the pan to a gentle heat and beat in the olive oil and enough potato liquid to give the potatoes the right texture. Season with salt and pepper.

To make the Irish champ add 115–175g (4–6oz) of cooked and roughly chopped cabbage or springy greens to the above.

Rösti
Serves 4

750g (1½lb) waxy potatoes
1 small onion, finely chopped
50g (2oz) smoked bacon, diced
6–8 tablespoons goosefat or olive oil
Salt and freshly ground black pepper

Clean the potatoes and boil them in lightly salted water until just tender. Drain and when cool enough to handle, peel. Grate coarsely

In a heavy pan, gently sauté the onion and bacon in half the fat. Fold this into the potatoes with the seasoning. Form the potatoes into one big 'cake In the same pan heat the balance of the fat and gently slide the potatoes into the pan. Cook over a high heat until the first side is browned. Place a plate over the pan and turn the potatoes onto the plate; then gently slide the 'cake' back into the pan to allow the second side to cook. Serve piping hot.

This classic Swiss dish can be eaten with Emmenthal melted on top (put the browned potatoes, covered with cheese slices, under the grill for a few minutes).

Rösti

Potato Salad with Goat's Cheese dressing
Serves 4

The South Americans have excellent ways of cooking potatoes, including this rich salad which makes a good summer first course.

750g (1½lb) potatoes, fairly small
½ red pepper, deseeded and diced
1 small onion, peeled and finely chopped
2 hard-boiled eggs, peeled and diced
Handful black olives, stoned
2 tablespoons flat-leaf parsley, chopped

For the dressing.
175g (6oz) well flavoured goat's cheese
2 cloves garlic, peeled
2 tablespoons yoghurt
2 tablespoons lemon juice
1 jalapeño pepper, de-seeded
¼ teaspoon turmeric
½ teaspoon ground cumin

Potato Salad with Goat's Cheese Dressing

Cook the potatoes in their skins in boiling water until tender, drain and peel.

Cut into generous dice and put into a serving dish. While the potatoes cook, mix the dressing ingredients in a blender, puréeing until smooth. Combine the potatoes with the red pepper and onion. Add the dressing and toss. Decorate the top with the crumbled eggs, olives and parsley.

Spinacia oleracea. Chenopodiaceae

SPINACH

Fast-growing annual, grown for highly nutritious leaves. Hardy. Value: high in iron, beta carotene and folic acid; rich in vitamins A and C.

Spinach is thought to be native to South-West Asia. Unknown to the Greeks and Romans, it was first cultivated by the Persians, was grown in China by the seventh century AD and reached Europe around 1100, after its introduction to Spain by the Moors. The prickly-seeded form was known in thirteenth-century Germany and by the following century it was commonly grown by European monastery gardens. Smooth-seeded spinach was first described in 1522. Its first mention in England comes in William Turner's *New Herball*, in the sixteenth century: 'An herbe lately found and not long in use.' The name comes from Old French *espinache*, derived from its Arabic and Persian name.

Children were encouraged to eat spinach because of its effect on Popeye the Sailor. The idea that it contains exceptional levels of iron originated from Dr E. von Wolf in 1870. His figures went unchecked until 1937, when it was discovered that the iron content was one-tenth that claimed by him as a result of a misplaced decimal point!

Harvest spinach regularly

VARIETIES

Traditionally there are two main groups. Prickly seeded varieties, which have lobed leaves, are regarded as hardier than the round, smooth-seeded types, which cope better with higher temperatures and are used for summer cropping. Modern cultivars are generally more adaptable. **'America'** has thick deep green leaves for spring sowing. It does not overwinter well. **'Bloomsdale'** (**'Bloomsdale Long Standing'**) is a savoy-leaved spinach with fleshy, tasty leaves. It is cold-tolerant, slow to bolt and crops over a long period. **'Dominant'** is a good all-rounder for spring or autumn sowing; it is thick-leaved, prolific and resistant to bolting. **'Giant Winter'**, a robust late autumn and winter variety, withstands some frost and is highly disease-resistant. **'Medania'** is for summer cropping. It withstands hot, dry weather and is resistant to downy mildew. **'Sigmaleaf'** is vigorous and tasty. Suitable for spring or autumn sowing. **'Space'** has smooth, dark green leaves and is resistant to downy mildew. Ideal for any season. **'Trinidad'**, for summer and autumn, has dark green leaves, is slow to bolt and shows good resistance to downy mildew.

CULTIVATION

Spinach grows best in cool conditions, at temperatures around 16–18°C (60–65°F). It thrives in a bright position, but is better in light shade and moist ground if your garden is hot and sunny.

Propagation

Soak seed overnight to speed up germination. My friend Robert Fleming wraps seed in a wet paper towel and places it in a sealed container in the fridge for 5 days before planting. Germination usually takes 5 days. As a cool-season plant, it will not germinate above 30°C (86°F).

Sow summer crops every 2–3 weeks from early to late spring for a summer harvest.

Sow in late summer, for cropping in winter until early summer. Sow *in situ* 2.5cm (1in) apart and 1–2cm (½–¾in) deep in rows 30cm (12in) apart. Thin when large enough to handle to 15–25cm (6–10in). It also works as a 'cut and come again' crop.

In colder areas it is better to sow in seed trays or modules for transplanting.

Sow thinly in broad drills the width of a hoe or in rows 10cm (4in) apart. Leave unthinned unless growth is slow, when they can be thinned to 5cm (2in) apart. Plants can be thinned to 10–12.5cm (4–5in) apart for larger leaves, though they are more inclined to bolt.

Growing

Spinach needs a rich, fertile, moisture-retentive soil, so where necessary, dig in well-rotted organic matter before planting. On poor soils leaves are stunted, bitter and prone to bolt. The ideal pH is 6.5–7.5; lime acid soils.

Never allow the soil to dry out. Water regularly before

the onset of dry weather and grow bolting-resistant cultivars. Water every 2 weeks with a high-nitrogen liquid fertilizer.

Maintenance
Spring Sow early crops successively.
Summer Keep the soil moist and weed-free. Sow winter crops from late summer.
Autumn Protect late crops under cloches, sow 'cut and come again' crops under glass.
Winter Protect winter crops under cloches or fleece or sow in cold frames.

Protected Cropping
Hardy varieties for winter and early spring cropping are better protected in cold frames, cloches or under horticultural fleece.

Container Growing
Spinach is ideal for containers 20–45cm (8–18in) wide and 30cm (12in) deep. Water regularly in dry weather. Avoid scorching sunshine.

Harvesting and Storing
Harvest from 5 weeks after sowing, cutting the outer leaves first. To harvest as a 'cut and come again' crop, remove the heads 2.5cm (1in) above the ground and allow them to resprout. Pick off the leaves carefully; the stems and roots are easily damaged. Alternatively, pull up whole plants and resow. Use the leaves fresh, or freeze. They can be washed and stored for up to 2 days in the refrigerator.

The leaves of 'Medania' are particularly thick

Pests and Diseases
Aphids and slugs can be troublesome, especially among seedlings. Downy mildew appears as yellow patches with fluffy mould on the underside of the leaf. Bolting caused by drying out or hot weather is most common cause of failure.

COMPANION PLANTING

Good with beans, peas, sweetcorn and strawberries.

MEDICINAL

Spinach is said to be good for anaemia, problems of the heart and kidney and in low vitality and general debility. Iron is in a soluble form, so any water left after cooking can be left to cool before drinking.

Research has shown that those who eat spinach daily are less likely to develop lung cancer. Of all the vegetable juices, spinach juice is said to be the most potent for the prevention of cancer cell formation.

OTHER USES

The water drained from spinach after cooking is said to make good matchpaper. It was used to make touchpaper for eighteenth- and nineteenth-century fireworks, as paper soaked in it smouldered well.

Spinach is packed with goodness

CULINARY

Wash leaves thoroughly. Eat immediately after harvesting. Use young leaves raw in salads, lightly cooked or steamed. Place spinach in a pan without adding water, cover and stand on moderate heat so the leaves do not scorch.

After 5 minutes, stir and cook over high heat for 1 minute. Drain in a colander and cut with a knife or fish-slice.

Spinach can also be cooked with olive oil, cheese, cream, yoghurt, ham, bacon and anchovies, besides being seasoned with nutmeg, pepper and sugar. All will bring out the flavour.

Scrambled Eggs with Raw and Cooked Spinach
Serves 6

1 kg (2lb) young spinach
2 tablespoons olive oil
Pinch grated nutmeg
2 tablespoons butter
12 eggs, lightly beaten with 1 tablespoon thick cream
1 tablespoon chopped chives
Salt and freshly ground black pepper

Wash the spinach and remove any tough stalks. Heat the oil in a heavy pan and then wilt most of the spinach, keeping back a couple of handfuls for decoration. Season with nutmeg, salt and pepper. Set aside and keep warm.

In the same pan, melt the butter and allow to just brown. Over a low flame, pour in the eggs and season. Stir constantly until just set (overcooked scrambled eggs are bad news!). Mound the eggs in the centre of individual plates and sprinkle with chopped chives. Arrange the cooked spinach around the outside, and then make a further ring from the raw spinach leaves. Serve hot.

Scrambled Eggs with Spinach

Tetragonia tetragonoides (syn. T. expansa). Aizoaceae

NEW ZEALAND SPINACH

Creeping perennial, usually grown as annual for edible leaves. Half hardy. Value: high in iron, beta carotene and folic acid.

This plant was unknown in Europe until 1771, when it was introduced to the Royal Botanic Gardens at Kew by the great botanist Joseph Banks after his voyage on board the *Endeavour* with Captain Cook. By 1820 it was widely grown in the kitchen gardens of Britain and France, but it did not appear in New Zealand literature until the 1940s, and there is no evidence of its use by the Maoris. It is unrelated to the true spinach, but its leaves are used in a similar manner – hence the borrowed name – though their flavour is milder than that of true spinach. A low-growing perennial with soft, fleshy, roughly triangular, blunt-tipped leaves, about 5cm (2in) long, it makes an attractive plant for edging and ground cover. It flourishes in hot dry conditions, without running to seed.

New Zealand spinach is seldom grown by gardeners, yet it is robust and a fine substitute for spinach

CULTIVATION

Propagation
The seed coat is extremely hard and germination is slow unless the seeds are soaked in water for 24 hours before sowing. Sow seeds individually, 2.5cm (1in) deep in 7.5cm (3in) pots indoors from mid- to late spring; repot as necessary. Plants are very cold-sensitive and so should be hardened off carefully before planting out once the danger of frost has passed.

Alternatively, sow seed *in situ* when there is no danger of frost, 1–2cm (½–¾in) deep in drills about 60cm (24in) apart, thinning to a similar distance between plants. Seeds can also be sown, 2 or 3 per 'station', 60cm (24in) apart, thinning to leave the strongest. Pinch out tips of young plants to encourage bushy growth.

Plants usually self-seed and appear in the same area the following year.

Growing
New Zealand spinach flourishes in an open site on light, fertile soil with low levels of nitrogen and grows well in dry, poor conditions. It tolerates high temperatures, but is very susceptible to frost.

Keep seedlings weed-free with regular hoeing. Once plants are established, their dense foliage will act as a ground cover and suppress weeds.

Water regularly during dry spells to encourage vigorous growth. It does not bolt in hot weather, but should be watered well to encourage growth. On poor soils, occasional feeding with a half-strength solution of general liquid fertilizer is beneficial, but take care not to over-feed.

The triangular leaves are striking

Maintenance

Spring Sow seed under cover for transplanting once frosts are over.

Summer Keep crops weed-free, water and harvest as required.

Autumn Protect plants to extend the growing season.

Winter Prepare the ground for planting in spring.

Protected Cropping

Protecting with cloches extends the harvesting season in cooler areas before frosts turn the plants into a soggy mess.

Container Growing

Crops can be grown in large containers of soil-based compost. Add grit to improve drainage. Water plants well throughout the growing season.

Harvesting and Storing

The first young leaves and shoots are ready to harvest from about 6 weeks after sowing. Pick regularly to maintain a constant supply of young growth and to extend the harvesting

The leaves can be eaten raw

CULINARY

The young leaves and shoots are steamed, lightly boiled and eaten with a knob of butter, or eaten raw in salads. They are better eaten fresh as the flavour deteriorates rapidly with age.

Cannelloni Stuffed with Chicken and New Zealand Spinach
Serves 4

500g (1lb) fresh New Zealand spinach
2 tablespoons butter
1 red onion, diced
2 tablespoons plain flour
450ml (³/₄pt) vegetable stock
1 bouquet garni
3 tablespoons thick cream
Salt and freshly ground black pepper
8 cannelloni shells
250g (8oz) cooked chicken, diced
100g (3oz) Parmesan, grated

Wash the spinach in several changes of water, place in a saucepan and cook for 3 minutes over high heat. Drain thoroughly and chop.

Melt the butter in a heavy pan, cook the onion until golden and stir in the flour to make a roux. Cook for 1–2 minutes. Stir in the stock, allow to boil and add the bouquet garni. Season and stir in the cream.

Simmer without boiling for 10 minutes.

Meanwhile, boil the cannelloni until *al dente* and drain, setting aside to cool. Combine the chicken and spinach and half the sauce and season well. Use a large piping bag to stuff each cannelloni shell with the chicken mixture and arrange in a shallow, greased ovenproof dish.

Preheat the oven to 200°C/ 400°F/gas mark 6. Reserve 1 tablespoon Parmesan and stir the balance into the remaining sauce. Pour this over the cannelloni and sprinkle with the reserved cheese. Cook for 20 minutes, until the top is browned and the dish hot through. Serve.

Cannelloni Stuffed with Chicken and New Zealand Spinach

season, which should last up to 4 months. Young leaves should be used immediately after cutting, can be stored for up to 2 days in a polythene bag in the fridge, or may be frozen. Wash, blanch for 2 minutes, allow to cool and drain before packing into polythene bags and placing in the freezer.

PESTS AND DISEASES

New Zealand spinach is very robust but **downy mildew** may be a problem.

COMPANION PLANTING

It is sometimes grown as a 'green manure' to improve the soil structure.

Tragopogon porrifolius. Asteraceae

SALSIFY

Also known as Oyster Plant, Vegetable Oyster, Goat's Beard. Grown as biennial for shoots, flower buds and flowers; annual for cylindrical tapering edible roots. Hardy. Value: contains inulin, turning to fructose in storage; small amounts of vitamins and minerals.

It is difficult to know whether to grow this plant for its delicious roots, or to grow it as a fragile ornamental by letting it flower (the flowers are also edible). Its Latin and common names are apt; *tragos* means goat and *pogon*, beard, describes the tuft of silky hairs on the developing seedheads; *porrifolius* means 'with leaves like a leek'. 'Salsify' comes from the old Latin name *solsequium*, from the way the flowers follow the course of the sun.

Salsify is a relatively recent crop. In the thirteenth century it was harvested from the wild in Germany and France. It was not cultivated until the early sixteenth century – in Italian gardens. The English plant collector John Tradescant the Younger recorded it in 1656. It was brought to North America in the late nineteenth century.

VARIETIES

The species *Tragopogon porrifolius* has a thin, creamy-white, tapering taproot up to 38cm (15in) long. It has narrow leaves and long, wand-like stems topped by beautiful dull purple flowers. These are followed by thistle-like seedheads. **'Geante Noire de Russie'** is an extremely long, black-skinned variety with white roots and a superb flavour. 'Giant' is consistently long-rooted with a delicate taste of oysters. 'Sandwich Island'

is a selected type with strongly flavoured roots and smooth skin.

CULTIVATION

Propagation
Always use fresh seed; its viability declines rapidly. Sow as early as possible, from early to mid-spring. Germination can be somewhat erratic, so it is better to sow 2–3 seeds in 'stations' 1–2cm (½–¾in) deep and 10cm (4in) apart with 30cm (12in) between the rows. After germination,

Salsify flowers vary from purple to near white

when the seedlings are large enough to handle, thin to leave the strongest seedling. Alternatively, sow the seeds in drills and thin to the above spacing.

Growing
Salsify thrives in an open situation on light, well-drained, stone-free soil which was manured for the previous crop (roots tend to fork when they are grown on freshly manured soil). On stony or heavy soils, dig a trench about 30cm (12in) deep and 20cm (8in) wide, filling it with finely sieved sandy soil or compost and sharp sand to give the roots room to grow. Lighten heavier soils by thoroughly digging over the area the autumn before planting, adding well-rotted organic matter and sharp sand. A pH of 6.0–7.5 is ideal; lime acid soils. Before sowing, rake the seedbed to a fine tilth and incorporate a slow-release general fertilizer at 60–90g/sq m (2–3oz/sq yd).

Regular watering ensures good-quality roots and, importantly, stops 'bolting' in dry conditions. It also prevents roots from splitting, which occurs after sudden rainfall or watering after a period of drought. Salsify should be kept weed-free, particularly during the early stages of growth. Hand weed, as the roots are easily damaged and inclined to 'bleed'. Alternatively, use an

onion hoe or mulch moist soil with a layer of organic matter to stifle weed growth and conserve moisture.

Roots can be left in the ground to produce edible shoots or 'chards' the following spring. In autumn, cut back the old leaves to within 1–2.5cm (½in) of the soil and earth up to about 12.5–15cin (5–6in). In mid-spring the following year, the shoots are ready to harvest when they appear. On heavier soils, 'chards' can be blanched with a covering of bracken, straw or dry leaves at least 12.5cm (5in) deep when new growth appears in spring. An upturned bucket or flower pots with the drainage holes covered work just as well.

Maintenance
Spring Rake over the seedbed, incorporating general fertilizer. Sow seeds in 'stations'.
Summer Keep the crop weed-free, mulch and water during dry periods.
Autumn Lift crops as required. Cut back the tops and cover those being grown for 'chards'.
Winter Dig over soil manured for the previous crop. Lift and store crops grown in colder areas.

Container Growing
Salsify can be grown in containers, but it is impractical to produce them in large quantities. However, if you are desperate, fill a large wooden box, tea chest

'Sandwich Island' is the most commonly grown form

Tragopogon dubius, **a relative of the cultivated plant**

Salsify seeds, like a giant dandelion clock

COMPANION PLANTING

Salsify grows well with mustard and, planted near carrots, discourages carrot fly.

MEDICINAL

Salsify is said to have an antibilious effect and to calm fevers. In folk medicine it is used to treat gall bladder problems and jaundice.

or plastic drum with sandy, free-draining soil or a loam-based compost with added sharp sand. Ensure there are sufficient drainage holes. Keep crops weed-free and water regularly.

Harvesting and Storing

Harvest from mid-autumn. Lift as required; protect roots with a layer of straw, bracken or a similar material before severe frosts or snow. They can be lifted in autumn and stored in boxes of peat substitute, sand or sawdust, in a cool, frost-free garage, shed or cellar. Lift carefully with a garden fork; the roots 'bleed' and snap easily.

If you begin lifting and find the crop misshapen, leave the roots in the ground and harvest the shoots and buds the following year. Next time, grow them in sieved soil.

Harvest 'chards' in early to mid-spring: scrape away the soil and cut the blanched shoots when they are 12.5–15cm (5–6in) long. Or lift when 15cm (6in) tall, without earthing up, though they are not as tender.

Pests and Diseases

Salsify is usually trouble-free but may suffer from white blister, which looks like glistening paint splashes and can distort plants. Spray with Bordeaux mixture and destroy any plants that are badly affected.

Aster yellows cause deformed new growth and the leaf veins or whole leaf become yellow. Control the aster leaf hopper which spreads the disease.

CULINARY

Salsify has a delicate oyster-like flavour and can be cooked in a variety of ways (there is bound to be a recipe that suits you). Peel after boiling until tender, 'skimming' under cold running water as you would a hard-boiled egg.

Cut roots discolour, so drop them into water with a dash of lemon juice, then boil for 25 minutes in salted water with lemon juice and a tablespoon of flour. Drain and skin, toss with melted butter and chopped parsley and indulge.

Try them with a light mornay sauce, deep-fried or served *au gratin* with cheese and breadcrumbs. Perhaps sautéing them in butter and eating with brown sugar is more to your liking?

Roots can also be baked, puréed, creamed for soup or grated raw in salads. They stay fresh in a refrigerator for about a week.

'Chards' can be served raw in salads or lightly cooked. Young flowering shoots can be eaten pickled, raw or cooked and eaten cold like asparagus with oil and lemon juice. The subtle flavour makes them an excellent hors d'oeuvre.

Pick flower buds just before they open with about 7.5cm (3in) of stem attached, lightly simmer and eat when they are cool.

Salsify in Batter
Serves 4

750g (1½lb) salsify, topped tailed, cleaned
Vegetable oil, for frying
Lemon wedges, to serve

For the batter:

110g (4oz) plain flour
1 teaspoon baking powder
1 egg
1 tablespoon olive oil
150ml (¼pt) water
¼ teaspoon harissa
½ teaspoon cumin
¼ teaspoon dried thyme
Salt and freshly ground black pepper

Cut salsify roots in half and boil in salted water for 30 minutes. Rinse under cold water. Peel and cut into 7.5cm (3in) pieces.

Make the batter: whizz all the ingredients in a food processor for 30 seconds.

Heat the oil in a large frying pan. Dip the salsify in the batter and fry in oil until crisp and golden, turning. Keep warm while cooking the remainder. Serve hot with lemon wedges.

Salsify in Batter

Salsify in Ham with Cheese Sauce
Serves 4

8 salsify, peeled and trimmed
8 slices cooked ham
2 tablespoons butter
2 tablespoons flour
1 teaspoon Dijon mustard
300ml (½pt) milk
4 tablespoons grated Gruyère
Pinch nutmeg
Salt and freshly ground black pepper

Boil the salsify for 5 minutes and drain. Cut into roughly 10cm (4in) lengths. When cool enough to handle, wrap each in a slice of ham and arrange in a greased baking dish.

Melt the butter in a heavy pan and stir in the flour to make a roux. Cook for a minute or two and stir in the mustard. Slowly add the milk, and then the Gruyère, and cook until the cheese is melted.

Season with nutmeg, salt and pepper and pour over the salsify. Bake in a preheated oven, 200°C/ 400°F/ gas mark 6, for 20 minutes, until browned.

Valerianella locusta (syn. Valerianella olitoria). Valerianaceae

LAMB'S LETTUCE

*Also known as Corn Salad, Mache, Lamb's Tongues.
Low-growing, extremely hardy annual grown for edible leaves. Value: good source of beta carotene, vitamin C and folic acid. Very few calories.*

'Jade' growing

In spite of its delicate appearance, lamb's lettuce is an extremely hardy plant, particularly valued as a nutritious winter salad crop. Its attractive bright green, rounded leaves have a slightly nutty taste. Depending on the authority, it was named lamb's lettuce because sheep are partial to it, or because it appears during the lambing season. Another name, corn salad, comes from its regular appearance as a cornfield weed.

Gerard wrote: 'We know the Lamb's Lettuce as loblollie; and it serves in winter as a salad herb among others none of the worst.' He also noted that 'foreigners using it in England led to its cultivation in our gardens'. It has been popular for centuries in France, where it is known as *salade de prêtre* (as it is often eaten in Lent), *doucette* ('little soft one', referring to the velvety leaves), and *bourcette*, describing their shape. In England it declined in popularity in the 1700s and a nineteenth-century commentator noted: '…. it is indeed a weed, and can be of no real use where lettuces are to be had.' Before the appearance of winter lettuce varieties, lamb's lettuce was the main winter salad; it was at one time classified in the same genus.

VARIETIES

There are two forms, the 'large' or 'broad-leaved' and the darker, more compact 'green' type, which is popular in western Europe, but less productive.
 'Cavallo' has deep green leaves and crops heavily. **'Elan'** is tender and mildew-resistant, as is the extremely robust **'Jade'**. **'Large Leaved'** is tender and prolific. **'Grote Noordhollandse'** is very hardy. **'Verte de Cambrai'**, a traditional French type, has small leaves and good flavour. **'Verte d'Etampes'** has unusual, attractive savoyed leaves. **'Vit'** is very vigorous with a mild flavour. **'Volhart'** is an old variety with bright green leaves.

CULTIVATION

Propagation
Lamb's lettuce can be grown as single plants or 'cut and come again' seedlings. Sow seeds successively from mid- to late spring for summer crops in drills 10–15cm (4–6in) apart and 1cm (½in) deep, thinning

when seedlings have 3–4 seed leaves to about 10cm (4in) apart. Sow winter crops successively from mid- to late summer.

Seeds can also be sown in broad drills, broadcast, or in seed trays or modules for transplanting. Leave a few plants to bolt, and transplant seedlings into rows.

Growing

Lamb's lettuce flourishes in a sheltered position in full sun or light shade and needs a deep, fertile soil for rapid and continuous growth. It tolerates most soils provided they are not waterlogged. Create a firm seedbed and rake in a slow-release general fertilizer at 30–60g/ sq m (1–2oz/sq yd) before sowing in spring and summer. Overwintered crops growing on the same site should not need it.

Keep crops weed-free, particularly during the early stages, and water thoroughly to encourage soft growth.

Maintenance

Spring Sow successively.
Summer Continue sowing and harvesting, keep crops weed-free and water well.
Autumn Sow crops under cover. Continue harvesting.
Winter When growth is slower, do not over-pick.

Protected Cropping

Although it is extremely hardy, growing lamb's lettuce under cloches, polythene tunnels or horticultural fleece, or in an unheated glasshouse,

Lamb's lettuce can fill any space in damp corners of the garden

The silver-blue flowers of lamb's lettuce are delicate and attractive

encourages better quality and higher productivity. Make the first sowings in early autumn.

Container Growing

Can be grown in 25cm (10in) pots of loam-based compost with a low fertilizer content. Sow seeds thinly 1cm (½in) deep every 3 weeks from early spring to early summer and again from early to mid-autumn, thinning to leave the strongest seedlings at a final spacing of 10cm (4in) apart.

Keep the compost moist when plants are growing vigorously; reduce watering in cooler conditions.

Harvesting and Storing

Harvest seedlings, pick leaves as required, or lift whole plants when they are mature – about 3 months after planting.

Do not weaken by removing too many leaves at one picking. This is particularly important with outdoor winter crops.

Leaves can be blanched for a few days before picking by covering with a box or pot to remove any bitterness.

Young flowers can be eaten in salads.

PESTS AND DISEASES

Some varieties are susceptible to mildew. Protect seedlings from birds and slugs.

COMPANION PLANTING

As plants take up very little space, lamb's lettuce is ideal sown between taller crops.

MEDICINAL

With its high beta carotene, vitamin C and folic acid content, it is regarded by many as a winter and early spring tonic, and is useful when other nutritional vegetables are scarce.

CULINARY

Thinnings can be used in salads. Wash the leaves thoroughly to remove grit and soil. In seventeenth-century Europe, lamb's lettuce was often served with cold boiled beetroot or celery. The leaves are used as a substitute for lettuce and combine well with it, also complementing fried bacon or ham and beetroot. Leaves can also be cooked like spinach.

Lamb's Lettuce and Prawn Salad
Serves 4

A mixture of winter salad leaves, such as lamb's lettuce, endive and radicchio
Large fresh prawns, peeled
Toasted sesame seeds

For the vinaigrette:
Lemon juice
Balsamic vinegar
Virgin olive oil
Mustard
Salt and freshly ground black pepper
Fresh herbs – sage, parsley and chives, chopped

Wash the salad leaves and arrange on individual plates.

Season the prawns with salt and pepper and coat generously with sesame seeds. (Allow 4 or 5 Dublin Bay or tiger prawns. per person) In a heavy-bottomed frying pan, gently cook them, turning after 3 minutes, when golden, to cook the other side. Arrange on the salad. Make the vinaigrette, sprinkle over and serve.

Vicia faba. Papilionaceae

BROAD BEAN

Also known as Fava Bean, Horse Bean, Windsor. Annual grown for seeds, young leaf shoots and whole young pods. Value: low protein, good source of fibre, potassium, vitamin E and C.

Thought to have originated around the Mediterranean, the oldest remains of domesticated broad beans have been dated to 6800–6500 BC. By the Iron Age they had spread throughout Europe. The Greeks dedicated them to Apollo and thought that overindulgence dulled the senses; Dioscorides wrote that they are 'flatulent, hard of digestion, causing troublesome dreams'.

They may be the origin of the term 'bean feast', being a major part of the annual meal given by employers for their staff to make merry. In the vernacular this has been changed to 'beano'. Britain has many folk sayings concerning the sowing date. Huntingdonshire country wisdom states: 'On St Valentine's Day, beans should be in clay', and it was generally accepted that four seeds were sown – 'One for rook, one for crow, one to rot, one to grow.' Flowers were considered to be an aphrodisiac – 'there ent no lustier scent than a beanfield in bloom' – while the poet John Clare wrote: 'My love is as sweet as a bean field in blossom, beanfields misted wi' dew.'

Hardy and prolific, they are the national dish of Egypt. An Arab saying goes, 'Beans have satisfied even the Pharoahs.' How about you?

VARIETIES

Broad beans are classified as Dwarf, with small, early-maturing pods which are excellent under cloches or in containers, Longpods, which are also hardy, and Windsors, with broad pods which usually mature later and have a better flavour. There are green- and white-seeded forms among the Longpods and Windsors. 'Aquadulce' is a reliable

hardy Longpod for autumn and spring sowing. 'Aquadulce Claudia' is similar, with medium to long pods and white seeds. Ideal for freezing, it is less susceptible to blackfly. 'Bonny Lad' is dwarf, 45cm (18in) high, and good for small gardens, cropping well. 'Express' is a fast-maturing early Longpod. Pods are plump and beans tasty. 'Imperial Green Longpod' produces pods around 38cm (15in) long with up to 9 large green beans. 'Masterpiece Green Longpod' is a good-quality, green-seeded bean. Freezes

well. 'Red Epicure' has beautiful deep chestnut-crimson seeds. Some of the colour is lost in cooking, but the flavour is superb. 'Sweet

The neatly spaced seeds of 'Red Epicure', a tasty variety

Lorane' is a delicious small-seeded, prolific bean. Cold-hardy. 'The Sutton', a Dwarf variety around 30cm (12in) high, is ideal for small gardens and under cloches. Excellent flavour, very prolific. 'Witkiem Vroma' is excellent for spring sowing, grows rapidly and has medium-sized pods.

CULTIVATION

Propagation
As they germinate well in cool conditions, broad beans can be sown from mid- to late autumn and overwintered outdoors for a mid-spring crop. Seedlings should be 2.5cm (1in) high when colder weather arrives. 'Aquadulce' cultivars are particularly suitable.

When the soil is workable sow every 3 weeks from late winter to late spring for successional cropping.

Plant seeds 5cm (2in) deep in rows or make individual holes with 30cm (12in) in and between the rows. Or grow in staggered double rows, with 23cm (9in) in and between the rows or in blocks 90cm (36in) square with 20–30cm (8–12in) between plants. Tall plants should be 30–45cm (12–18in) apart. Sow extra seeds at the end of rows, for use as transplants.

Growing
Broad beans flourish in an open, sunny site but overwintering crops need more shelter. Soils should be deeply dug, moisture-retentive and well-drained, having been manured for the previous year's crop. Alternatively, add well-rotted organic matter in late autumn before sowing. They need a pH of 6–7, so lime where necessary. Rotate with other legumes.

Rake a granular general fertilizer into the seedbed

1 week before sowing. Mulch, hoe or hand weed regularly, especially at first.

Watering should be unnecessary except in drought, but for good-quality crops, plants need 22 litres/sq m (4 gal/sq yd) per week from flower formation to harvest end.

Support taller plants with stakes. Planting several staggered rows allows plants to support one another. Dwarf types can be supported with brushwood.

Maintenance

Spring Sow early crops under glass followed by later sowings until late spring.
Summer Harvest from late spring to late summer. Keep crops weed-free and water after flower formation.
Autumn Sow outdoor crops for overwintering.
Winter Protect outdoor crops in severe weather.

Protected Cropping

Where plants cannot be overwintered outdoors, sow under cover in pots or boxes from midwinter. Harden off and plant out in mid-spring. Remove cloches from protected early crops when the beans reach the glass.

Container Growing

Grow dwarf cultivars in containers of low-fertilizer loam-based compost at least 20–45cm (8–18in) wide by 25cm (10in) deep. Sow seeds 5cm (2in) deep and 10–13cm (4–5in) apart. Water regularly in warm weather, less at other times.

Harvesting and Storing

Pick when the beans begin to show, before the pods are too large (and tough). Pull with a sharp downward twist or cut with scissors.

Pods harvested at 5–7.5cm (2–3in) long can be treated as snap peas and eaten whole, but picking at this stage reduces yields.

Broad beans freeze well, especially green-seeded varieties. Wash, blanch for 3 minutes, freeze in

'Masterpiece Green Longpod' produces a high yield of smaller, thinner beans

polythene bags or rigid containers. Use within 12 months. Keep them in a polythene bag in the refrigerator for 1 week.

PESTS AND DISEASES

Black bean aphid is the most common problem. Control by pinching off the top 7.5cm (3in) of stem when the first beans start to form. This also encourages an earlier harvest. Mice and jays steal the seeds.

COMPANION PLANTING

Plant with summer savory to discourage black bean aphid and among gooseberries to discourage gooseberry sawfly. The flowers are very attractive to bees. Broad beans are a good 'nurse' crop for developing maize and sweetcorn.

Interplant with brassicas, which benefit from the nitrogen-fixing roots. Dig in plant debris as a 'green manure' to increase soil fertility. Seedling beans protect early potato shoots from wind and frost.

CULINARY

Steam or lightly boil beans to eat with ham, pork and chicken. Eat with sautéed onions, mushrooms and bacon; dress with tomato sauce, warm sour cream or lemon butter and dill.

Bissara
Serves 4

An Algerian dish with subtle flavours, this recipe is based on one from the late, great foodie, Arto der Haroturian.

675g (1½lb) young broad beans, shelled weight
1 small green chilli, chopped
1 teaspoon paprika
1 teaspoon cumin seeds, pounded in a mortar
2 cloves garlic, peeled
8 tablespoons virgin olive oil
Juice of half a lemon
Salt and freshly ground black pepper

Garnish:
A little olive oil, lemon juice and paprika

Bissara

Boil the beans in lightly salted water until just tender. Drain and place in a food processor, together with the chilli, paprika, cumin and garlic. Purée by slowly drizzling in the oil and lemon juice. Season and pour into a bowl.

Garnish with a little olive oil, lemon juice and paprika. Serve bissara with warm bread.

Broad Beans with Summer Savory
Serves 4

A dish which reflects the pure tastes of summer.

500g (1lb) young broad beans, shelled weight
2 sprigs and 2 tablespoons summer savory
2 tablespoons butter
Salt and freshly ground black pepper

Put the beans into a pan of boiling, salted water with the sprigs of summer savory and cook until just done, about 3–5 minutes. Drain and put the pan back on a gentle heat. Add the butter and toss well as it melts. Season with more summer savory and salt and pepper.

Maintenance
Spring Sow seed under cover or outdoors.
Summer Sow seeds; keep crops weed-free and water. Harvest.
Autumn Harvest.
Winter Prepare the ground for next year's crop.

Protected Cropping
When soil temperatures are below 10°C (50°F), sow from mid-spring under cover in pots or modules at 55°F (13°C). Harden off and plant out once there is no danger of frost.

Harvesting and Storing
Each plant usually produces one or two cobs. Those sown *in situ* mature later than seed sown indoors.

When cobs are ready to harvest, the 'silks' wither and turn dark brown. Peel back the leaves and test for ripeness by pushing your thumbnail into a grain: if the liquid runs clear, it is unripe; if it is milky, it is ready to harvest; if it is thick, then it is over-mature and unsuitable for eating. To pick, hold the main stem in one hand and twist off the cob with the other.

After pollination the silks begin to turn brown, an indication that the cob is maturing.

Eat or freeze within 24 hours of picking, before the sugars in the seeds convert to starch. 'Supersweet' varieties hold their sugar levels longer.

To freeze, blanch cobs for 4–6 minutes, cool and drain, before wrapping singly in foil or cling film and placing in the freezer.

Cobs remain fresh for up to 3 days if they are stored in the refrigerator.

PESTS AND DISEASES

Birds can pull up the seedlings and attack the developing cobs. Slugs attack seedlings. Smut appears as large galls on the cobs and stalks in hot dry weather. Cut off and burn immediately, or they will burst open and release a mass of black spores. Burn plants and debris after harvesting and do not grow sweetcorn on the site for at least 3 years. Frit fly larvae bore into the growing points of corn seedlings, which then develop twisted and ragged leaves. Growth is stunted and cobs are undersized. Use 'dressed' seed and rake a granular insecticide into the soil. Mice enjoy newly planted seeds, especially 'supersweet' types. Trap, or buy a cat.

A well-grown cob, packed full of mature seeds

COMPANION PLANTING

Grow sweetcorn with or after legumes. Runner beans can be allowed to grow over sweetcorn plants. Intercrop corn with sunflowers, allowing cucurbits to trail through them.

The shade they provide is useful to cucumbers, melons, squashes, courgettes, marrows and potatoes. Brussels sprouts, kale, Savoy cabbages, swedes and broccoli can be interplanted. Grow lettuce and other salads, French beans and courgettes between the crops.

MEDICINAL

Corn is said to reduce the risk of certain cancers, heart disease and dental cavities. Corn oil is reported to lower cholesterol levels more successfully than other polyunsaturated oils.

In parts of Mexico corn is used to treat dysentery. It is also known in American folk medicine as a diuretic and mild stimulant.

Planting in blocks gives higher yields, as plants are wind-pollinated

CULINARY

To serve whole, strip off outer leaves, leaving 5–7cm (2–3in) of stalk on the ear. Pull off 'silks'. Boil in unsalted water, drain and eat hot with melted butter.

Roasted corn is a favourite with most children – it tastes wonderfully succulent compared with the sogginess of tinned corn.

Deep-fry spoonfuls of a mixture of mashed corn, salt, flour, milk and egg for 1–2 minutes or until golden brown to make corn fritters.

Seeds are ground, meal boiled or baked, cob can be roasted or boiled or fermented, maize meal is cooked with water to create a thick mash, or dough.

Tortillas are made by baking in flat cakes until they are crisp.

Dry-milling produces grits, from which most of the bran and germ are separated. Cornflakes are rolled, flavoured seeds. Multicoloured corn adds colour and flavour to sweet dishes and drinks.

Baby corns are particularly decorative and the perfect size for Oriental stir-fries, where they combine well with mangetout.

Polenta is made from ground maize.

Barbecued Corn on the Cob

This is the way to really taste the flavour of corn. Take 1 corn ear for each person. Boil them in salted water for 7–10 minutes and then drain.

Place each in the centre of a piece of foil. Use 1 tablespoon butter per corn ear and mix in

1 teaspoon fresh chopped herbs, sea salt and freshly ground black pepper; spread over the corn ears. Season well and then seal the foils.

Lay the corns on a medium-hot barbecue or in a charcoal grill (in which case keep it covered) and roast for 20 minutes, turning the cobs once halfway through the cooking.

Corn Maque Choux
Serves 4

Cajun cooking has become popular in recent years and this dish reveals the true taste of corn.

1 tablespoon butter
1 large onion, roughly chopped
1 green pepper, deseeded and diced
500g (1lb) corn, cooked and stripped from the cob

Succotash

2 tomatoes, peeled, deseeded and diced
1/2 teaspoon tabasco sauce
Salt and freshly ground black pepper

Heat the butter in a heavy pan and sauté the onion until softened. Add the pepper and continue cooking for 3–4 minutes. Toss in the corn and the remaining ingredients and, over a low heat, simmer for 10 minutes. Adjust the seasoning and serve.

Succotash
Serves 4

The American Indians cooked succotash, and many recipes still exist for it. 'Silver Queen' is a particularly good variety to use for this dish.

3–4 tablespoons unsalted butter
300g (10oz) broad beans, cooked

3 or 4 ears roasted corn, husked
250g (8oz) French beans, topped and tailed
1 medium red onion, finely chopped
300ml (1/2pt) vegetable stock
1/2 red pepper, finely diced
1 beef tomato, peeled, deseeded and chopped
Salt and freshly ground black pepper

Melt the butter in a heavy frying pan and sweat the broad beans, corn, French beans and onion over a medium heat for about 3 minutes.

Then add the stock and continue cooking for 5 minutes before stirring in the remaining ingredients.

Taste for seasoning, mix thoroughly and continue cooking for 5 minutes more. Serve hot.

Oyster mushrooms developing in a grow-bag, India

Pholiota nameko (nameko, viscid mushroom) is among the four most important fungi cultivated in Japan. Grows in clusters on tree trunks or wood chips. Orange-brown caps atop paler stems are 5–6cm (2–3 in) in diameter. It is pleasantly aromatic.

Pleurotus (or oyster mushroom) is a genus with a number of distinct species and strains. Popular in Japan and Central Europe, they are increasingly available in kit form, or can be grown from plugs of spawn. Eat when small, discarding the tough stem. Sauté in butter until tender, season, then add cream or yoghurt. The first two are fairly common in the wild and are also offered in seed catalogues.

Pleurotus ostreatus (oyster mushroom) has large fan-shaped caps ranging in colour from slate-blue to white and with white or pale straw-coloured gills; used coffee grounds (sterilized as the coffee is brewed) are becoming a popular medium for inoculating with the spawn.

P. cornucopiae (golden oyster) has a white stem with a cream cap turning to ochre-brown. Grows on the cut stumps of deciduous trees, usually elm or oak. Other species may be harder to find, and some need warmth to fruit.

P. ergyngii (king pleurotus) has a concave cap, whitish becoming grey-brown. It tastes sweet and meaty and grows in clusters on the decaying roots of plants in the carrot family. It can be grown on chopped straw. **P. flabellatus** is an oyster mushroom with pink caps. **P. pulmonarius** has brown or grey caps. **P. samoneus-tramineus** from Asia is pink-capped. **P. sajor-caju** has brown caps.

Stropharia rugosoannulata (king stropharia) is a brown-capped, violet-gilled fungus commonly cultivated in eastern Europe; it is claimed to be capable of growing in vegetable gardens. It requires a substrate of humus containing rotting hardwood or sawdust. Grow spawn from reputable sources: look-alikes include deadly *Cortinarius* species.

Volvariella volvaceae (Chinese or straw mushroom, paddy straw, padi-straw) has a grey-brown cap, often marked with black, and a dull brown stem. Grown on composted rice straw, it is regarded as an expensive delicacy in China and other Asian countries. Needs high temperatures and humidity to grow well. Harvest when it is immature.

Naturally occurring edible fungi
Many edible species of fungi may be found growing in your garden if it happens to provide the host trees or other conditions that form their natural habitat. In Continental Europe, fungi collected in the wild are often sold in markets; but local pharmacists or health inspectors are on hand to verify that those on sale are edible species.

NEVER EAT A FUNGUS UNLESS YOU HAVE FIRST HAD ITS IDENTITY CONFIRMED BY AN EXPERT

Agaricus arvensis (horse mushroom) and **A. campestris** (field mushroom) are cousins of the cultivated mushroom, found in clusters or rings in grazed or mown grassland. Dome-shaped white 'buttons' open to wide caps. Horse mushrooms can grow to soup-plate size with thick, firm flesh smelling of aniseed; the gills are pale greyish-pink darkening to chocolate-brown. Field mushrooms are smaller and rather more delicate in stature, with a 'mushroomy' smell; their deep pink gills become dark brown to black at maturity.

Boletus edulis (cep, penny bun) grows on the ground near trees, favouring pine, beech, oak and birch woodlands. The rounded, bun-like brown cap (often covered with a white bloom when young) sits on a bulbous whitish stem – also edible. Tube-like pores (rather than gills) beneath the cap are white, turning dull yellow at maturity. This delicious, fleshy fungus is highly prized in Continental markets and can be eaten fresh, pickled or dried. Related species of *Boletus* are also edible.

Cantharellus cibarius (chanterelle) is funnel-shaped; egg yolk-yellow caps, fading with age, are thick and fleshy with gill-like wrinkles running down from the cap underside into the stem. Has a mild peppery aftertaste when eaten raw; excellent flavour cooked. True chanterelles grow on soil in broad-leaved woodland: similar-looking species are highly toxic.

Oyster mushrooms growing on a tree trunk

Hirneola auricula judae, syn. **Auricularia auricula-judae** (Jew's ear, wood-ear) looks like a human ear and is date-brown, drying to become small and hard. Found on living and dead elder, beech and sycamore. Can be dried and reconstituted with water. Popular in Taiwan and China.

Hypholoma capnoides, syn. **Nematoloma capnoides**, is a gilled fungus found growing in clusters on conifer stumps. Caps 2–6cm (¾–2¼in) diameter are pale ochre with a buff-coloured margin. Check identity carefully: other *Hypholoma* species are suspect.

Laetiporus sulphureus, syn. **Polyporus sulphureus** (chicken of the woods) is a bracket fungus found on many hardwoods and softwoods, often on sweet chestnut, oak and beech. Has the flavour of chicken breast and is an orange to sulphur-yellow colour. Eat young, but only try a little the first time: it can cause nausea and dizziness in some people. The largest ever found weighed 45.4kg (100lb).

Langermannia gigantea (giant puffball) can be enormous: large and round with white skin, it sits on the ground like a giant soccer ball. The biggest ever recorded, according to the Guinness Book of Records, was 2.64m (8ft 8in) in circumference and weighed 22kg (over 48lb)! It is found on soil in fields, hedgerows, woodlands and gardens, often near nettles. Eat when young, while the flesh is pure white; it tastes good sliced, dipped in breadcrumbs and fried. Other related (and smaller) species of puffball are also edible while they remain white all through.

Lepista nuda (blewit, wood blewit, blue-stalk) is medium to large with a light

A basket of morel mushrooms

cinnamon-brown to tan cap; the gills and stems are violet to lavender. It is found in woodlands, parks and hedges. It can be grown in leaf debris around compost heaps. Better eaten young, it is well flavoured and particularly good in stews or fried. Never eat raw: cook thoroughly to remove traces of cyanic acid.

Marasmius oreades (fairy ring champignon) is found on lawns in a 'ring' of dark green grass with dying grass in the centre. Small with a bell-shaped light tan-coloured cap, matching gills and similar stem. Good in omelettes. Beware: similar looking species are toxic.

Morchella esculenta (common morel) is a delicious fungus that emerges annually in spring, earlier than most autumn-fruiters. The hollow cap has a surface covered in honeycomb-like pits and varies from round to conical in shape. (The many crevices of the cap often harbour dirt and insects – a rare instance when preparing by rinsing in water is advised.) Found on well-drained soils under deciduous trees, particularly in ash and elm woods, in gardens and near old hedges. Other edible species include **M. rotunda**, found on heavier soil, and **M. vulgaris**, on richer soil. Some similar-looking mushroom species are highly toxic.

Sparassis crispa (cauliflower mushroom, brain fungus) has a folded, rounded fruiting body, creamy-white when young, which looks more like a cauliflower than a conventional mushroom. It tastes nutty, with a spicy fragrance. Found at the base of pines and other conifers. As with morels, rinse to remove any debris.

Tuber melanosporum (the Perigord or black truffle), often found in oak woods, is highly desirable and the most valuable truffle. Pigs and trained dogs are used to sniff them out. Commercial growers are now developing truffle-inoculated trees; several closely related species are also edible – I have yet to try them!

CULTIVATION
(of *Agaricus* species)

Propagation

With the traditional commercial methods, indoor crops of *Agaricus* species are more reliable than those grown outdoors. Make a large heap of stable manure, preferably at least 150cm (60in) square, and moisten thoroughly. Cover until temperatures reach 45–60°C (140–160°F), turning once a week until it is crumbly and sweet-smelling. When it reaches that stage, fill boxes, buckets, containers or trays with a 23–30cm (9–12in) layer and firm. When the temperature falls to 25°C (75°F) and the surface is ready for spawning, push golfball-sized pieces about 2.5cm (1in) under the surface 30cm (12in) apart. After 2–3 weeks, white 'threads' appear on the surface. Spread a 5cm (2in) layer of 'casing' made from 2 parts peat substitute to 1 part chalk or ground limestone over the surface and keep it moist. When mushrooms start to appear reduce the temperature to 10–18°C (50–65°).

Two types of spawn are available – fungus-impregnated manure (block spawn) or impregnated rye (grain spawn). Block spawn is easier to use.

Alternatively, buy a bucket or bag of ready-spawned compost or a fungi-growing pack. Do not buy kits which have been in store for a long time and start the pack into growth within 3 weeks of buying it.

Growing

'Cultivated mushrooms' can be grown in or outdoors in the lawn or manure heap, though crops will be variable. Choose a shady position and enrich the ground with plenty of well-rotted organic matter. On a damp day in spring or autumn, 'plant' blocks of spawn, about the size of a golfball, 5cm (2in) below the soil and 30cm (12in) apart. A good crop of mushrooms often appears when spent mushroom compost is used as a mulch around other crops.

Maintenance

Indoor crops can be planted any time of the year. Plant spawn outdoors in spring or autumn.

Protected Cropping

Indoor crops grow well in an airy shed, cellar, greenhouse or cold frame. They do not need to be grown in the dark.

Container Growing

See 'Propagation'.

Harvesting and Storing

The first 'button' mushrooms are ready for harvesting 4–6 weeks after 'casing'; there may be another 2 weeks before the next 'flush'. Harvesting lasts for about 6 weeks. To harvest, twist and pull mushrooms upwards, disturbing the compost as little as possible, removing any broken stalks and filling the holes with 'casing'.

Mushrooms last in a ventilated polythene bag in the salad drawer of a refrigerator for up to 3 days.

Most species can be dried. Thread them on to a string and hang them over a radiator or in an airing cupboard, then store in a cool dry place. Reconstitute with water or wine.

After the final harvest, you can use the spent mixture as a mulch; you should never try to re-spawn for a second crop.

PESTS AND DISEASES

Mushroom fly can be a problem; pick mushrooms when young.

Shiitake mushrooms

MEDICINAL

Edible fungi lower blood cholesterol, stimulate the immune system and deactivate viruses. Shiitake mushrooms are particularly effective. Jew's ear has been used in herbal medicine for treating sore throats.

WARNING

If you gather wild mushrooms, be certain of their identity before eating. Best of all, collect with an expert. Those that are highly toxic are often similar to edible species. **Mistakes can be fatal.**

CULINARY

Fungi should always be eaten fresh as the flavour is soon lost and the quality deteriorates. Avoid washing most kinds: the fruit bodies absorb water, spoiling the texture and flavour. Simply clean the surface by wiping with a damp cloth or brushing off any dirt. Peel only when necessary.

Both caps and stems of *Agaricus* species can be eaten. With some other fungi, stems may be discarded as inedibly tough. Check for any special instructions on preparation: some fungi, for instance, are toxic unless cooked.

Harvested cultivated mushrooms at the 'button' stage can be eaten raw, added to salads; more mature caps can be baked, grilled or fried whole, or sliced and stir-fried, made into soups, pies or stuffings, added to stews or the stockpot, or used as a garnish. Other fungi can be prepared in many similar ways. Large fruit bodies can be stuffed.

Try frying in butter and a little lemon juice for 3–5 minutes. Brush with oil and seasoning and grill each side for 2–3 minutes. Add yoghurt or cream before serving, or dip in breadcrumbs and fry. Garlic mushrooms are especially delicious.

Mushroom Soup
Serves 4

This is particularly satisfying on a cold winter's day. Open-capped cultivated mushrooms make a good alternative to the wild variety.

75g (3oz) butter
4 shallots, finely chopped
1 clove garlic, crushed
500g (1lb) field mushrooms, cleaned and sliced
1 litre (1³/₄pt) chicken stock
1 tablespoon plain flour
Dash soya sauce
A little thick cream
Salt and freshly ground black pepper

Heat 50g (2oz) of the butter in a heavy bottomed pan and sauté the shallots until softened; add the garlic and cook for 1 minute more. Add the mushrooms and stir to coat well. Pour in the stock and bring to the boil. Season and cover, simmering for 10–15 minutes, until the mushrooms are cooked. Remove from the heat.

In a separate pan, heat the remaining butter and stir in the flour to make a roux. Cook for 2 minutes and remove from the stove. In a liquidizer, blend the roux with the soup (this may need to be done in 2 batches or more). Add the soya sauce and check the seasoning. Garnish with a little thick cream and serve.

Mushroom Mélange

Grilled Shi-itake Mushrooms
Serves 4

Allow 2 mushrooms per person for a first course to be served with Italian bread.

8–12 shi-itake mushrooms
6 tablespoons olive oil
1 sprig rosemary
1 tablespoon fresh thyme leaves
2 tablespoons balsamic vinegar
2 tablespoons Barolo wine
1 small onion, finely chopped
4 slices toasted Italian bread
1 tablespoon butter
1 clove garlic, crushed
Salt and freshly ground black pepper

Wash the shiitakes, ensuring the gills are free from dirt. Discard the stems and add to a stockpot. Dry the caps.

Leave the mushrooms in a marinade of oil, rosemary, thyme, vinegar, wine, onion and seasoning for 30–45 minutes, turning them occasionally.

Grill under a preheated grill for 5 minutes each side, brushing with the marinade juices. Serve on slices of toasted Italian bread, buttered and rubbed with garlic. Pour over a little of the juices on each helping.

Mushroom Mélange
Serves 4

500g (1lb) oyster mushrooms
500g (1lb) shi-itake mushrooms
4 tablespoons butter
2 cloves garlic, crushed
2 shallots, finely chopped
4 tablespoons white wine
150ml (¹/₄pt) double cream
4 tablespoons grated Parmesan
Salt and freshly ground black pepper

Wash the mushrooms well and chop them, including the stalks. Melt the butter in a heavy saucepan, add the garlic and shallots and allow to soften over a gentle heat. Add the mushrooms and stir well. Pour in the wine and the double cream and bring to simmering point. Then cover and leave to stew for 15 minutes.

Pour into a greased sauté pan, season with salt and pepper and sprinkle over the Parmesan. Put under a preheated grill on the highest setting for 3–5 minutes until the cheese is melted. Serve immediately.

Herbs

Achillea ageratum

ENGLISH MACE

From the family Asteraceae.

Native of Switzerland, now cultivated in northern temperate countries. This culinary herb is little known and under-used.

English mace belongs to the *Achillea* genus, named after Achilles, who is said to have discovered the medicinal properties of the genus. There is no direct historical record of English mace itself apart from the fact it was discovered in Switzerland in 1798.

English mace in spring
Achillea ageratum

SPECIES

Achillea ageratum
English Mace
Hardy perennial. Ht 30–45cm (12–18in) when in flower. Spread 30cm (12in). Clusters of small cream flowers that look very Victorian in summer. Leaves brightish green, narrow and very deeply serrated.

CULTIVATION

Propagation
Cuttings
This is the best method for the propagation of a large number of plants. Take softwood cuttings in late summer, protect from wilting as they will be very soft. Use the bark, peat mix of compost (see p.591). When well-rooted, harden off and plant out in the garden 30cm (12in) apart.

Division
If you require only a few plants it is best to propagate by division. Either divide the plant in early spring – it is one of the first to appear – or in autumn. Replant in the garden in a prepared site. As this is a hardy plant it will not need protection, but if you leave division until the frosts are imminent, winter the divided plants in a cold frame or cold greenhouse.

Pests and Diseases
Mace, in most cases, is free from pests and disease.

Maintenance
Spring Divide established plants.
Summer Cut back flowers. Take softwood cuttings.
Autumn Divide established plants if needed.
Winter Does not need protection.

Garden Cultivation
This fully hardy plant, which even flourishes on my heavy soil, prefers a sunny, well-drained site. It starts the season off as a cluster of low-growing, deeply serrated leaves and then develops long flowering stems in summer. Cut back after flowering for a fresh supply of leaves and to encourage a second flowering crop. When in flower this plant may need staking in a windy, exposed site.

Harvesting
Cut fresh leaves when you wish. For freezing – the best method of preserving – cut before flowering and freeze in small containers.

Pick the flowers during the summer. Collect in small bunches and hang upside down to dry.

Both flowers and leaves dry particularly well.

CULINARY

The chopped leaves can be used to stuff chicken, flavour soups, stews, and to sprinkle on potato salads, rice and pasta dishes. The leaf has a mild, warm, aromatic flavour and combines well with other herbs.

Chicken with English Mace in Foil

Serves 4

chicken breasts
tablespoons yoghurt
tablespoons Dijon mustard
alt and fresh ground black pepper
ouquet garni herb oil (or olive oil)
tablespoons of chopped English mace
ice of 1 lemon

Pre-heat oven to 190°C/ 375°F/ gas mark 5. Mix the yoghurt and mustard together and coat the chicken pieces on all sides. Sprinkle with salt and pepper. Cut 4 pieces of foil and brush with herb or olive oil. Lay the chicken breasts in the foil and scatter a thick layer of English mace on each piece. Sprinkle with lemon juice. Wrap in the foil, folding the ends very tightly so no juices can escape. Lay the packets on a rack in the oven, cook for 30 minutes. Serve with rice and a green salad.

OTHER USES

Flowers in dried flower arrangements.

CONTAINER GROWING

For a tall flowering plant this looks most attractive in a terracotta pot. Make sure it has a wide base to allow for its height later in the season. Use the bark, peat, grit mix of compost (see p.591).

Water regularly thoughout the growing season and give a liquid feed (according to manufacturer's instructions) in the summer months during flowering. Cut back after flowering to stop the plant from toppling over and encourage new growth. As this plant dies back in winter, allow the compost to become nearly dry, and winter the container in a cold greenhouse or cold frame.

English mace
Achillea ageratum

Achillea millefolium

YARROW

Also known as Nosebleed, Millefoil, Thousand Leaf, Woundwort, Carpenter's Weed, Devil's Nettle, Mille Foil, Soldier's Woundwort and Noble Yarrow. From the family Asteraceae.

Yarrow is found all over the world in waste places, fields, pastures and meadows. It is common throughout Europe, Asia and North America.

This is another very ancient herb. It was used by the Greeks to control haemorrhages, for which it is still prescribed in homeopathy and herbal medicine today. The legend of Achilles refers to this property – it was said that during the battle of Troy, Achilles healed many of his warriors with yarrow leaves. Hence the name, 'Achillea'.

It has long been considered a sacred herb. Yarrow stems were used by the Druids to divine seasonal weather. The ancient Chinese text of prophecy, *I Ching*, The Book of Changes, states that 52 straight stalks of dried yarrow, of even length, were spilled instead of the modern way of using 3 coins.

It was also associated with magic. In Anglo-Saxon times it was said to have a potency against evil, and in France and in Ireland it is one of the Herbs of St John. On St John's Eve, the Irish hang it up in their houses to avert illness.

There is an old superstition, which apparently still lingers in remote parts of Britain and the United States, that if a young girl tickles her nostrils with sprays of yarrow and her nose starts to bleed, it proves her lover's fidelity:

'Yarrow away, Yarrow away, bear a white blow?
If my lover loves me, my nose will bleed now.'

Yarrow *Achillea millefolium*

SPECIES

Achillea millefolium
Yarrow
Hardy perennial. Ht 30–90cm (1–3ft), spread 60cm (2ft) and more. Small white flowers with a hint of pink appear in flat clusters from summer to autumn. Its specific name, **millefolium**, means 'a thousand leaf', which is a good way to describe these darkish green, aromatic, feathery leaves.

Achillea millefolium 'Fire King'
Hardy perennial. Ht and spread 60cm (24in). Flat heads of rich, red, small flowers in flat clusters all summer. Masses of feathery dark green leaves. This has an upright habit and is a vigorous grower.

Achillea 'Coronation Gold'
Hardy perennial. Ht 1m (3ft), spread 60cm (2ft). Large flat heads of small golden flowerheads in summer that dry well for winter decoration. Masses of feathery silver leaves.

Achillea 'Moonshine'
Hardy perennial. Ht 60cm (24in), spread 50cm (20in). Flat heads of bright yellow flowers throughout summer. Masses of small feathery grey/green leaves.

CULTIVATION

Propagation
Seed
For reliable results sow the very small seed under cool protection in autumn. Use either a proprietary seeder or the cardboard trick and sow into prepared seed or plug trays. Leave the trays in a cool greenhouse for the winter. Germination is erratic. Harden off and plant out in the garden in spring. Plant 20–30cm (8–12in) apart, remembering that it will spread. As this is an invasive plant, I do not advise sowing direct into the garden.

Division
Yarrow is a prolific grower, producing loads of creeping rootstock in a growing season. To stop the invasion, divide by digging up a clump and replanting where required in the spring or early autumn.

Pests and Diseases
Yarrow is free from both.

Maintenance
Spring Divide established clumps.
Summer Dead-head flowers, and cut back after flowering to prevent self-seeding.
Autumn Sow seeds. Divide established plants.
Winter No need for protection, very hardy plant.

Garden Cultivation
Yarrow is one of nature's survivors. Its creeping rootstock and ability to self-seed ensure its survival in most soils.
It does well in seaside gardens, as it is drought-tolerant. Still, owners of manicured lawns will know it as a nightmare weed that resists all attempts to

Salad with Three Wild Herbs

eradicate it.
Yarrow is the plant doctor of the garden, its roots' secretions activating the disease resistance of nearby plants. It also intensifies the medicinal actions of other herbs and deepens their fragrance and flavour.

Harvesting
Cut the leaves and flowers for drying as the plant comes into flower.

CONTAINER GROWING

Yarrow itself does not grow well in containers. However, the hybrids, and certainly the shorter varieties, can look stunning. Use the bark, grit, peat mix of compost (see p.591) and feed plants with liquid fertilizer during the flowering season, following the manufacturer's instructions. Cut back after flowering and keep watering to a minimum in winter. No varietiy is suitable for growing indoors.

CULINARY

The young leaves can be used in salads. Here is an interesting salad recipe:

Salad made with Three Wild Herbs
Equal parts of yarrow, plantain and watercress
A little garlic
½ cucumber
Freshly chopped or dried chives and parsley
1 medium, boiled cold potato
Salad dressing consisting of lemon and cream, or lemon and oil, or lemon and cream and a little apple juice.

Select and clean herbs. Wash carefully and allow to drain. Cut the yarrow and plantain into fine strips. Cube cucumber and potato into small pieces. Leave watercress whole and arrange in bowl. Add herbs and other vegetables and salad dressing and mix well.

OTHER USES
Flowerheads may be dried for winter decoration.
This unassuming plant harbours great powers. One small leaf will speed decomposition of a wheelbarrow full of raw compost.
Infuse to make a copper fertilizer.

WARNING

Yarrow should always be taken in moderation and never for long periods because it may cause skin irritation. It should not be taken by pregnant women. Large doses produce headaches and vertigo.

MEDICINAL

Yarrow is one of the best known herbal remedies for fevers. Used as a hot infusion it will induce sweats that cool fevers and expel toxins. In China, yarrow is used fresh as a poultice for healing wounds. It can also be made into a decoction for wounds, chapped skin and rashes, and as a mouthwash for inflamed gums.

Aconitum napellus

MONKSHOOD

Also known as Friar's Cap, Old Woman's Night-cap, Chariots Drawn by Doves, Blue Rocket, Wolf's Bane and Mazbane. From the family Ranunculaceae.

Various species of monkshood grow in temperate regions. They can be found on shady banks, in deciduous woodlands and in mountainous districts. They are all poisonous plants.

One theory for the generic name, *Aconitum*, is that the name comes from the Greek akoniton, meaning 'dart'. This is because the juice of the plant was used to poison arrow tips and was used as such by the Arabs and ancient Chinese. Its specific name *napellus* means 'little turnip', a reference to the shape of the root. It was the name used by Theophrastus, the Greek botanist (370–285 BC), for a poisonous plant.

This plant has been known throughout history to kill both animals and humans. In the 16th century Gerard commented in his *Herbal* on its 'fair and good bluey flowers in shape like helmet which are so beautiful that man would think they were of some excellent virtue'. Appearances should not be trusted. 150 years later, Miller in his garden dictionary wrote, 'Monks Hood was in almost all old gardens and not to be put in the way of children less they should prejudice themselves therewith.'

As recently as 1993 a West Country flower seller had to be hospitalized after handling monkshood outside pubs in Salisbury and Southampton.

Monkshood *Aconitum napellus*

SPECIES

Aconitum napellus
Monkshood
Hardy perennial. Ht 1.5m (5ft), spread 30cm (1ft). Tall slender spires of hooded, light blue/indigo/blue flowers in late summer. Leaves mid-green, palm shaped and deeply cut. There is a white flowered version, **A. napellus 'Albiflorus'**, which grows in the same way.

Aconitum napellus subsp. napellus Anglicum Group
Monkshood
Hardy perennial. Ht 1.5m (5ft), spread 30cm (1ft). Tall slender spires of hooded, blue/lilac flowers in early/midsummer. Leaves mid-green, wedged shaped and deeply cut. One of a few plants peculiar to the British Isles, liking shade or half-shade along brooks and streams. Grows in only a few areas in south-west Britain. Probably the most dangerous of all British plants.

Monkshood *Aconitum napellus* **growing with dill**

CULTIVATION

Propagation
Seed
Sow the small seed under protection either in the autumn (which is best) or spring. Use prepared seed or plug trays. Cover with perlite. Germination can be erratic, an all-or-nothing affair. The seeds do not need heat to germinate. In spring, when the seedlings are large enough to handle, plant out into a prepared, shady site 30cm (12in) apart. Wash your hands after handling the seedlings; even better wear thin gloves. The plant takes 2–3 years to flower.

Division
Divide established plants throughout the autumn, so long as the soil is workable. Replant in a prepared site in the garden – remember the gloves. You will notice when splitting the plant that the tap root puts out tubicals or daughter roots with many rootlets. Remove and store in a warm dry place for planting out later.

Pests and Diseases
For obvious reasons this plant does not suffer from pests, and it is usually disease free.

Maintenance
Spring Plant out autumn-grown seedlings.
Summer Cut back after flowering.
Autumn Sow seeds, divide established plants.
Winter No need to protect. Fully hardy.

Garden Cultivation
In spite of the dire warnings this is a most attractive plant, which is hardy and thrives in most good soils.

Position it so that it is not accessible. Plant at the back of borders, or under trees where no animals can eat it or young fingers fiddle with it. It is useful for planting in the shade of trees as long as they are not too dense.

It is important always to teach people which plants are harmful, and which plants are edible. If you remove all poisonous plants from the garden, people will not learn which to respect.

Harvesting
Unless you are a qualified herbalist I do not recommend harvesting.

CONTAINER GROWING

Because of its poisonous nature, I cannot whole-heartedly recommend that it be grown in containers. But if you know you can control the situation, it does look very attractive in a large container surrounded by heartsease (**Viola tricolor**). Use the bark, peat, grit mix of compost (see p.591), water regularly throughout the summer months. Liquid feed in summer only.

WARNING

The symptoms of **Aconitum** poisoning are a burning sensation on the tongue, vomiting, abdominal pains and diarrhoea, leading to paralysis and death. Emergency antidotes, which are obtainable from hospitals, are atropine and strophanthin.

MEDICINAL

Aconitum is one of the most potent nerve poisons in the plant kingdom and is contained in proprietory analgesic medicines to alleviate pain both internally and externally. These drugs can only be prescribed by qualified medical practitioners. Tinctures of monkshood are frequently used in homeopathy.

Under no circumstances should monkshood ever be prepared and used for self-medication.

CULINARY

None

Agastache foeniculum

ANISE HYSSOP

Also known as Giant Hyssop, Blue Giant Hyssop, Fennel Hyssop,
Fragrant Giant Hyssop. From the family Lamiaceae.

Anise hyssop is a native of North America, the Mosquito Plant and *A. mexicana* '*Brittonastrum mexicana*' of Mexico, and *A. rugosa* is from Korea.

There are few references to the history of this lovely herb. According to Allen Paterson, Director of the Royal Botanical Garden in Ontario, it is a close cousin of the bergamots. It is common in North American herb gardens and is certainly worth including in any herb garden for its flowers and scent. The long spikes of purple, blue and pink flowers are big attractions for bees and butterflies.

SPECIES

Agastache cana
Mosquito Plant
Half-hardy perennial. Ht 60cm (2ft), spread 30cm (1ft). Pink tubular flowers in the summer with aromatic oval mid-green toothed leaves.

Agastache mexicana
'Brittonastrum mexicana'
(or 'Cedronella mexican')
Half-hardy perennial. Ht 1m (3ft), spread 30cm (1ft). In summer bears whorls of small tubular flowers in shades from pink to crimson. Leaves oval pointed, toothed and mid-green with a eucalyptus scent.

Agastache rugosa
Korean Mint
Hardy perennial. Ht 1m (3ft), spread 30cm (1ft). Lovely mauve/purple flower spikes in summer. Distinctly minty scented mid-green oval pointed leaves.

Anise hyssop
Agastache foeniculum

Agastache foeniculum
Anise Hyssop
Hardy perennial. Ht 60cm (2ft), spread 30cm (1ft). Long purple flower spikes in summer. Aniseed scented mid-green oval leaves.

CONTAINER GROWING

Not suitable for growing indoors. However, anise hyssop and Korean mint both make good patio plants provided the container is at least 25–30cm (10–12in) diameter. Use the bark, peat mix of compost (see p.591), and a liquid fertilizer feed only once a year after flowering. If you feed the plant beforehand, the flowers will be poor. Keep well watered in summer.

CULTIVATION

Propagation

Note: *A. mexicana* can only be propagated by cuttings.

Seed

The small fine seeds need warmth to germinate: 17°C (65°F). Use the cardboard method and artificial heating if sowing in early spring.

Use either prepared seed or plug trays or if you have only a few seeds directly into a pot and cover with perlite. Germination takes 10–20 days.

One can also sow outside in the autumn when the soil is warm, but the young plants will need protection throughout the winter months.

When the seedlings are large enough to handle prick out and pot on using a bark or peat mix of compost. In mid-spring, when air and soil temperatures have risen, plant out at a distance of 45cm (18in).

Cuttings

Take cuttings of soft young shoots in spring; when all the species root well. Use 50 per cent bark, 50 per cent peat mix of compost. After a full period of weaning cuttings should be strong enough to plant out in the early autumn.

Semi-ripe wood cuttings may be taken in late summer, use the same compost mix. After they have rooted, pot up, and winter in a cold frame or cold greenhouse.

Division

This is a good alternative way to maintain a short-lived perennial. In the second or third year divide the creeping roots either by the 'forks back-to-back' method, or by digging up the whole plant and dividing.

Pests and Diseases

Being an aromatic plant, pests keep their distance. Rarely suffers from disease, although seedlings can damp off.

Maintenance

Spring Sow seeds.
Summer Take softwood or semi-ripe cuttings late season.
Autumn Tidy up the plants by cutting back the old flower heads and woody growth. Sow seeds. Protect young plants from frost.
Winter Protect half-hardy species (and Anise hyssop below –6°C (20°F)) with either agricultural fleece, bark or straw.

Garden Cultivation

All species like a rich, moist soil and full sun, and will adapt very well to most ordinary soils if planted in a sunny situation. All are short-lived and should be propagated each year to ensure continuity.

Anise hyssop, although hardier than the other species, still needs protection below –6°C (20°F).

The Mexican half-hardy species need protection below –3°C (26°F).

Harvesting

Flowers
Cut for drying just as they begin to open.

Leaves
Cut leaves just before late spring flowering.

Seeds
Heads turn brown as the seed ripens. At the first sign of the seed falling, pick and hang upside down with a paper bag tied over the heads.

OTHER USES

Anise hyssop, Korean mint and *Agastache mexicana* all have scented leaves which makes them suitable for potpourris.

Korean mint tea

Summer fruit cup made with anise hyssop

CULINARY

The two varieties most suitable are –

Anise Hyssop
Leaves can be used in salads and to make refreshing tea. Like borage, they can be added to summer fruit cups. Equally they can be chopped and used as a seasoning in pork dishes or in savoury rice.

Flowers can be added to fruit salads and cups giving a lovely splash of colour.

Korean Mint
Leaves have a strong peppermint flavour and make a very refreshing tea, said to be good first thing in the morning after a night on the town. They are also good chopped up in salads, and the flowers look very attractive scattered over a pasta salad.

Alchemilla mollis

LADY'S MANTLE

From the family Rosaceae.

Lady's mantle is a native of the mountains of Europe, Asia and America. It is found not only in damp places but also in dry shady woods.

The Arab 'alkemelych' (alchemy) was thought to be the source of the herb's Latin generic name, *Alchemilla*. The crystal dew lying in perfect pearl drops on the leaves has long inspired poets and alchemists, and was reputed to have healing and magical properties, even to preserve a woman's youth provided she collected the dew in May, alone, in full moonlight, naked, and with bare feet as a sign of purity and to ward off any lurking forces.

In the medieval period it was dedicated to the Virgin Mary, hence lady's mantle was considered a woman's protector, and nicknamed 'a woman's best friend', and was used not only to regulate the menstrual cycle and to ease the effects of menopause, but also to reduce inflammation of the female organs. In the 18th century, women applied the leaves to their breasts to make them recover shape after they had been swelled with milk.

It is still prescribed by herbalists today.

Lady's mantle *Alchemilla mollis*

Alchemilla conjuncta
Lady's Mantle Conjuncta
Hardy perennial. Ht 30cm (12in), spread 30cm (12in) or more. Tiny, greenish-yellow flowers in summer. Leaves star-shaped, bright green on top with lovely silky silver hairs underneath. An attractive plant suitable for ground cover, rockeries and dry banks.

SPECIES

Alchemilla alpina L.
Alpine Lady's Mantle
Known in America as Silvery Lady's Mantle.
Hardy perennial. Ht 15cm (6in), spread 60cm (24in) or more. Tiny, greenish-yellow flowers in summer. Leaves rounded, lobed, pale green and covered in silky hairs. An attractive plant suitable for ground cover, rockeries and dry banks.

Alchemilla mollis
Lady's Mantle (Garden variety)
Hardy perennial. Ht and spread 50cm (20in). Tiny, greenish-yellow flowers in summer. Large, pale green, rounded leaves with crinkled edges.

Alchemilla xanthochlora (vulgaris)
Lady's Mantle (Wild flower variety)
Also known as Lion's Foot, Bear's Foot and Nine Hooks.

Hardy perennial. Ht 15–45cm (6–18in), spread 50cm (20in). Tiny, bright greenish-yellow flowers in summer. Round, pale green leaves with crinkled edges.

CULTIVATION

Propagation
Seed
Why is it that something that self-seeds readily around the garden can be so difficult to raise from seed? Sow its very fine seed in early spring or autumn into prepared seed or plug trays (use the cardboard method), and cover with perlite. No bottom heat required. Germination can either be sparse or prolific, taking 2–3 weeks. If germinating in the autumn, winter seedlings in the trays and plant out the following spring when the frosts are over, at a distance of 45cm (18in) apart.

Division
All established plants can be divided in the spring or autumn. Replant in the garden where desired.

Pests and Diseases
This plant rarely suffers from pests or disease.

Maintenance
Spring Divide established plants. Sow seeds if necessary.
Summer To prevent self-seeding, cut off flowerheads as they begin to die back.
Autumn Divide established plants if necessary. Sow seed.
Winter No need for protection.

Garden Cultivation
This fully hardy plant grows in all but boggy soils, in sun or partial shade. Seed can be sown in spring where you want the plant to flower. Thin the seedlings to 30cm (12in) apart.
  This is a most attractive garden plant in borders or as an edging plant, but it can become a bit of a nuisance, seeding everywhere. To prevent this, cut back after flowering and at the same time cut back old growth.

Early morning dew on
Alchemilla mollis

Harvesting
Cut young leaves after the dew has dried for use throughout the summer. Harvest for drying as plant comes into flower.

CONTAINER GROWING

All forms of lady's mantle adapt to container growing and look very pretty indeed. Use a soil-based compost, water throughout the summer, but feed with liquid fertilizer (following manufacturer's instructions) only occasionally. In the winter, when the plant dies back, put the container in a cold greenhouse or cold frame, and water only very occasionally. Lady's mantle can be grown in hanging baskets as a centrepiece.

MEDICINAL

Used by herbalists for menstrual disorders. It has been said that if you drink an infusion of green parts of the plant for 10 days each month it will help relieve menopausal discomfort. It can also be used as a mouth rinse after tooth extraction. Traditionally, the alpine species has been considered more effective, although this is not proven.

Leaves laid out for drying

CULINARY

Tear young leaves, with their mild bitter taste, into small pieces and toss into salads. Many years ago Marks & Spencer had a yoghurt made with lady's mantle leaves! I wish I had tried it.

OTHER USES
Excellent for flower arranging.
  Leaves can be boiled for green wool dye and are used in veterinary medicine for the treatment of diarrhoea.

Allium

WELSH AND TREE ONIONS

From the family Alliaceae.

These plants are distributed throughout the world. The onion has been in cultivation so long that its country of origin is uncertain, although most agree that it originated in Central Asia. It was probably introduced to Europe by the Romans. The name seems to have been derived from the Latin word 'unio', a large pearl. In the Middle Ages it was believed that a bunch of onions hung outside the door would absorb the infection of the plague, saving the inhabitants. Later came the scientific recognition that its sulphur content acts as a strong disinfectant. The juice of the onion was used to heal gunshot wounds.

SPECIES

There are many, many varieties of onion (see p.16); the following information concerns the two that have herbal qualities.

Allium fistulosum
Welsh Onion
Also known as Japanese Leek.
Evergreen hardy perennial. Ht 60–90cm (2–3ft). Flowers on second year's growth greenish yellow in early summer. Leaves, green hollow cylinders. This onion is a native of Siberia and extensively grown in China and Japan. The name Welsh comes from 'walsch' meaning foreign.

Welsh onion *Allium fistulosum*

Allium cepa Proliferum Group
Tree Onion
Also known as Egyptian Onion, Lazy Man's Onions. Hardy perennial. Ht 90–150cm (3–5ft). Small greenish-white flowers appear in early summer. It grows bulbs underground and then, at the end of flowering, bulbs in the air. Seeing is believing. It originates from Canada. It is very easy to propagate.

CULTIVATION

Propagation
Seed
Welsh onion seed loses its viability within 2 years, so sow fresh in late winter, early spring under protection with a bottom heat of between 15°C (60°F) and 21°C (70°F). Cover with perlite.
When the seedlings are large enough, and after a period of hardening off, plant out into a prepared site in the garden at a distance of 25cm (9in) apart.
The tree onion is not grown from seed.

Division
Each year the Welsh onion will multiply in clumps, so it is a good idea to divide them every 3 years in the spring.
Because the tree onion is such a big grower, it is a good idea to split the underground bulbs every 3 years in spring.

Bulbs
The air-growing bulbils of the tree onion have small root systems, each one capable of reproducing another plant. Plant where required in an enriched soil either in the autumn, as the parent plant dies back, or in the spring.

Pests and Diseases
The onion fly is the curse of the onion family especially in late spring, early summer. The way to try and prevent this is to take care not to damage the roots or leaves when thinning the seedlings and also not to leave the thinnings lying around, as the scent attracts the fly.
Another problem is downy mildew caused by cool wet autumns; the leaves become velvety and die back. Again, too warm a summer may encourage white rot. Burn the affected plants and do not plant in the same position again.
Other characteristic diseases are neck rot and bulb rot, both caused by a Botrytis fungus that usually occurs as a result of the bulbs being damaged either by digging or hoeing.
Onions are prone to many more diseases but, if you keep the soil fertile and do not make life easy for the onion fly, you will still have a good crop.

Maintenance

Spring Sow the seed, divide 3-year-old clumps of Welsh and tree onions. Plant bulbs of tree onions.
Summer Stake mature tree onions to stop them falling over and depositing the ripe bulbils on the soil.
Autumn Mulch around tree onion plants with well-rotted manure. Use a small amount of manure around the Welsh onions.
Winter Neither variety needs protection.

Garden Cultivation

Welsh Onions
These highly adaptable hardy onions will grow in any well-drained fertile soil. Seeds can be sown in spring after the frosts, direct into the ground. Thin to a distance of 25cm (9in) apart. Keep well watered throughout the growing season. In the autumn give the area a mulch of well-rotted manure.

Tree Onions
Dig in some well-rotted manure before planting. Plant the bulbs in their clusters in a sunny well-drained position at a distance of 30–45cm (12–18in) apart.
In the first year nothing much will happen (unless you are one of the lucky ones). If the summer is very dry, water well.
In the following year, if you give the plant a good mulch of well-rotted manure in autumn, it grows to 90–150cm (3–5ft) and produces masses of small onions.

Harvesting

Welsh onions may be picked at any time from early summer onwards. The leaves do not dry well but can be frozen like those of their cousin, chives. Use scissors and snip them into a plastic bag. They form neat rings; freeze them.

The little tree onions can be picked off the stems and stored; lay them out on a rack in a cool place with good ventilation.

CULINARY

Welsh onions make a great substitute for spring onions, as they are hardier and earlier. Pull and use in salads or stir-fry dishes, chop and use instead of chives.

Tree onions provide fresh onion flavour throughout the year. The bulbils can be pickled or chopped raw in salads (fairly strong), or cooked whole in stews and casseroles.

Pissaladière
Serves 4–6

4 tablespoons olive oil (not extra virgin)
20 tree onions, finely chopped
1 clove garlic, crushed
1 dessertspoon fresh thyme, chopped
Salt
Freshly ground black pepper
360g (³/₄lb) once-risen bread dough
250g (½lb) ripe tomatoes, peeled and sliced
60g (2oz) canned anchovy fillets, drained and halved lengthways
16 large black olives, halved and pitted

Heat the olive oil in a heavy frying pan, add the onions, cover the pan tightly and fry, gently stirring occasionally for 15 minutes. Add the garlic and the thyme and cook uncovered for 15 minutes, or until the onions are reduced to a clear purée. Season to taste and leave to cool. Pre-heat the oven to 200°C/400°F/gas mark 6.

Pissaladière

Roll the bread dough directly on the baking sheet into a circle 25cm (10in) diameter. Spread the puréed onions evenly over the dough, put the tomato slices on the onions and top with a decorative pattern of anchovy fillets and olives.

Bake for 5 minutes. Reduce the oven temperature to 190°C/375°F/ gas mark 5 and continue to bake for 30 minutes or until the bread base is well risen and lightly browned underneath.

Serve hot with a green herb salad.

OTHER USES

The onion is believed to help ward off colds in winter and also to induce sleep and cure indigestion. The fresh juice is antibiotic, diuretic, expectorant, antispasmodic, so useful in the treatment of coughs, colds, bronchitis, laryngitis and gastroenteritis. It is also said to lower the blood pressure and to help restore sexual potency that has been impaired by illness or mental stress.

CONTAINER GROWING

Welsh onions can be grown in a large pot using a soil-based compost, and making sure it does not dry out. Feed regularly throughout the summer with a liquid fertilizer.

Tree onions grow too tall for containers.

Allium schoenoprasum

CHIVES

From the family Alliaceae.

Chives are the only member of the onion group found wild in Europe, Australia and North America, where they thrive in temperate and warm to hot regions. Although one of the most ancient of all herbs, chives were not cultivated in European gardens until the 16th century.

Chives were a favourite in China as long ago as 3,000 BC. They were enjoyed for their delicious mild onion flavour and used as an antidote to poison and to stop bleeding. Their culinary virtues were first reported to the West by the explorer and traveller, Marco Polo. During the Middle Ages they were sometimes known as rush-leeks, from the Greek 'schoinos' meaning rush and 'parson' meaning 'leek'.

Chives *Allium schoenoprasum*

Chives
Allium schoenoprasum

SPECIES

Allium schoenoprasum
Chives
Hardy perennial. Ht 30cm (12in). Purple globular flowers all summer. Leaves green and cylindrical. Apart from being a good culinary herb it makes an excellent edging plant.

Allium schoenoprasum fine-leaved
Extra Fine-Leaved Chives
Hardy perennial. Ht 20cm (8in), Purple globular flowers all summer. Very narrow cylindrical leaves, not as coarse as standard chives. Good for culinary usage.

Allium schoenoprasum white
White Chives
Hardy perennial. Ht 20cm (8in). White globular flowers all summer. Cylindrical green leaves. A cultivar of ordinary chives and very effective in a silver garden. Good flavour.

Allium schoenoprasum 'Forescate'
Pink Chives
Hardy perennial. Ht 20cm (8in). Pink flowers all summer. Cylindrical green leaves. Also a cultivar of ordinary chives, its pink flowers can look a bit insipid if planted too close to the purple-flowered variety. Good in flower arrangements.

Garlic chive flower
Allium tuberosum

Allium tuberosum
Garlic Chives (Chinese chives)
Hardy perennial. Ht 40cm (16in). White flowers all summer. Leaf mid-green, flat and solid with a sweet garlic flavour when young. As they get older the leaf becomes tougher and the taste coarser.

CULTIVATION

Propagation

Seed

Easy from seed, but they need a temperature of 19°C (65°F) to germinate, so if sowing outside, wait until late spring for the soil to be warm enough. I recommend starting this plant in plug trays with bottom heat in early spring. Sow about 10–15 seeds per 3cm (1in) cell. Transplant either into pots or into the garden when the soil has warmed.

Division

Every few years in the spring lift clumps (made up of small bulbs) and replant in 6–10-bulb clumps, 15cm (6in) apart, adding fresh compost or manure.

Pests and Diseases

Greenfly may be a problem on pot-grown herbs. Wash off gently under the tap or use a liquid horticultural soap. Be diligent, for aphids can hide deep down among the bulbs.

Cool wet autumns may produce downy mildew; the leaves will become velvety and die back from the tips. Dig up, split and re-pot affected plants, at the same time cutting back all the growth to prevent the disease spreading.

Chives can also suffer from rust. As this is a virus it is essential to cut back diseased growth immediately and burn it. DO NOT COMPOST. If very bad, remove the plant and burn it all. Do not plant any rust prone plants in that area.

Maintenance

Spring Clear soil around emerging established plants. Feed with liquid fertilizer. Sow seeds
Summer Remove the flower stem before flowering to increase leaf production.

Autumn Prepare soil for next year's crop. Dig up a small clump, pot, bring inside for forcing.
Winter Cut forced chives and feed regularly.

Garden Cultivation

Chives are fairly tolerant regarding soil and position, but produce the best growth planted 15cm (6in) from other plants in a rich moist soil and in a fairly sunny position. If the soil is poor they will turn yellow and then brown at the tips. For an attractive edging, plant at a distance of 10cm (4in) and allow to flower. Keep newly transplanted plants well watered in the spring, and in the summer make sure that they do not dry out, otherwise the leaves will quickly shrivel. Chives die right back into the ground in winter, but a winter cutting can be forced by digging up a clump in autumn, potting it into a rich mix of compost (bark, peat mix, see p.591), and placing it somewhere warm with good light.

Harvesting

Chives may be cut to within 3cm (1in) of the ground 4 times a year to maintain a supply of succulent fresh leaves. Chives do not dry well. Refrigerated leaves in a sealed plastic bag will retain crispness for seven days. Freeze chopped leaves in ice cubes for convenience.

Cut flowers when they are fully open before the colour fades for use in salads and sauces.

MEDICINAL

The leaves are mildly antiseptic and when sprinkled onto food they stimulate the appetite and promote digestion.

CONTAINER GROWING

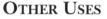

Chives grow well in pots or on a windowsill and flourish in a window box if partially shaded. They need an enormous quantity of water and occasional liquid feed to stay green and succulent. Remember too that, being bulbs, chives need some top growth for strengthening and regeneration, so do not cut away all the leaves if you wish to use them next season. Allow to die back in winter if you want to use it the following spring. A good patio plant, easy to grow, but not particularly fragrant.

CULINARY

Add chives at the end of cooking or the flavour will disappear. They are delicious freshly picked and snipped as a garnish or flavour in omelettes or scrambled eggs, salads and soups. They can be mashed into soft cheeses or sprinkled onto grilled meats. Add to sour cream as a filling for jacket potatoes.

COMPANION PLANTING

Chives planted next to apple trees prevent scab, and when planted next to roses can prevent black spot. Hence the saying, 'Chives next to roses creates posies'.

OTHER USES

Chives are said to prevent scab infection on animals.

Chive Butter

Use in scrambled eggs, omelettes and cooked vegetables and with grilled lamb or fish or on jacket potatoes.

100g/4oz/½cup butter
4 tablespoons chopped chives
1 tablespoon lemon juice
Salt and pepper

Cream the chives and softened butter together until well mixed. Beat in the lemon juice and season to taste. Cover and cool the butter in the refrigerator until ready to use; it will keep for several days.

Ajuga reptans

BUGLE

Also known as Common or Creeping Bugle, Bugle Weed, Babies' Shoes, Baby's Rattle, Blind Man's Hand, Carpenter's Herb, Dead Men's Bellows, Horse and Hounds, Nelson's Bugle, Thunder and Lightening and Middle Comfrey. From the family Lamiaceae.

The bugle found in Britain is a native of Europe. It is frequently found in mountainous areas and often grows in damp fields, mixed woodland and meadows. The bugle of North America is a species of *Lycopus* (gypsy weed).

Among the many folk tales associated with bugle is one that its flowers can cause a fire if brought into the house, a belief that has survived in at least one district of Germany.

SPECIES

Ajuga reptans
Bugle
Hardy evergreen perennial. Ht 30cm (1ft), spread up to 1m (3ft). Very good spreading plant. Blue flowers from spring to summer. Oval leaves are dark green with purplish tinge. It is this plant that has medicinal properties.

Ajuga reptans 'Atropurpurea'
Bronze Bugle
Hardy evergreen perennial. Ht 15cm (6in), spread 1m (3ft). Blue flowers from spring to summer. Deep bronze/purple leaves. Very good for ground cover.

Ajuga reptans 'Multicolor'
Multicoloured Bugle
Hardy evergreen perennial. Ht 12cm (5in), spread 45cm (18in). Small spikes of blue flowers from spring to summer. Dark green leaves marked with cream and pink. Good for ground cover.

CULTIVATION

Propagation
Seeds
Sow the small seed in autumn, or spring as a second choice. Cover only lightly with soil. Germination can be erratic and slow.

Division
This method is easy and the only one suitable for cultivars as bugle produces runners, each one having its own root system. Plant out in autumn or spring. Space 60cm (2ft) apart, as a single plant spreads rapidly.

Pests and Diseases
Nothing much disturbs this plant!

Maintenance
Spring Clear winter debris around established plants. Dig up runners and replant in other areas. Sow seeds.
Summer Control established plants by digging up runners. *Autumn* Sow seed, dig up runners of established plants, pot on, using the bark, peat compost, and winter in a cold frame, or replant in garden.
Winter No protection needed unless very cold -20°C (-6°F).

Garden Cultivation
It will grow vigorously on any soil that retains moisture, in full sun, and it also tolerates quite dense shade. It will even thrive in a damp boggy area near the pond or in a hedgerow or shady woodland area. At close quarters bugle is very appealing and can be used as a decorative ground cover. Guard against leaf scorch on the variegated variety.

Harvesting
For medicinal usage the leaves and flowers are gathered in early summer.

CONTAINER GROWING

Bugle makes a good outside container plant especially the variegated and purple varieties. Use the bark, peat mix of compost (see p.591). Also good in hanging baskets.

CULINARY

The young shoots of *Ajuga reptans* can be mixed in salads to give you a different taste. Not mine.

MEDICINAL

An infusion of dried leaves in boiling water is thought to lower blood pressure and to stop internal bleeding. Nowadays it is widely used in homeopathy in various preparations against throat irritation especially in the case of mouth ulcers.

OTHER USES

In some countries it is gathered as cattle fodder.

SPECIES

Aloe vera
Aloe vera
Half-hardy perennial. Grown outside: Ht 60cm (2ft), spread 60cm (2ft) or more. Grown as a house plant: Ht 30cm (12in). Minimum temperature 10°C (50°F). Succulent grey/ green pointed foliage, from which eventually grows a flowering stem with bell-shaped yellow or orange flowers.

Aloe arborescens 'Frutescens'
Half-hardy perennial. Grown outside: Ht, spread 2m (6ft). Minimum temperature 7°C (45°F). Each stem is crowned by rosettes of long, blue green leaves with toothed edges and cream stripes. Produces numerous spikes of red tubular flowers in late winter and spring.

Aloe variegata
Partridge-breasted Aloe
Half-hardy perennial. A house plant only in temperate climates. Ht 30cm (12in), spread 10cm (4in). Minimum temperature 7°C (45°F). Triangular, white marked, dark green leaves. Spike of pinkish-red flowers in spring.

CULTIVATION

Propagation
Seed
A temperature of 21°C (70°F) must be maintained during germination. Sow onto the surface of a pot or tray and cover with perlite. Place in a propagator with bottom heat. Germination is erratic – 4 to 24 months.

Division
In summer gently remove offshoots at the base of a

mature plant. Leave for a day to dry, then pot into 2 parts compost to 1 part sharp sand mix. Water in and leave in warm place to establish. Give the parent plant a good liquid feed when returning to its pot.

Pests and Diseases
Overwatering causes it to rot off.

Maintenance
Spring Give containerized plants a good dust! Spray the leaves with water. Give a good feed of liquid fertilizer.
Summer Remove the basal offshoots of a mature plant to maintain the parent plant. Re-pot mature plants if necessary.
Autumn Bring in pots if there is any danger of frost.
Winter Rest all pot-grown plants in a cool room (minimum temperature 5°C (40°F); keep watering to the absolute minimum.

Aloe vera

Aloe vera
From the family Aloaceae

There are between 250 and 350 species of aloe around the world. They are originally native to the arid areas of Southern Africa. In cultivation they need a frost-free environment. Aloe has been valued at least since the 4th century BC when Aristotle requested Alexander the Great to conquer Socotra in the Indian Ocean, where many species grow.

Garden Cultivation
Aloes enjoy a warm, frost-free position – full sun to partial shade – and a free-draining soil. Leave 1m (3ft) minimum between plants.

Harvesting
Cut leaves throughout the growing season. A plant of more than 2 years old has stronger properties.

CONTAINER GROWING

Compost must be gritty and well drained. Do not over water. Maintain a frost-free, light environment.

Aloe vera

MEDICINAL

The gel obtained by breaking the leaves is a remarkable healer. Applied to wounds it forms a clear protective seal and encourages skin regeneration. It can be applied directly to cuts, burns, and is immediately soothing. Rumour has it that the US Government is building up stocks for use in the event of a nuclear disaster.

COSMETIC

Aloe vera is used in cosmetic preparations, in hand creams, suntan lotions and shampoos.

WARNING

It should be emphasized that, apart from external application, aloes are not for home medication. ALWAYS seek medical attention for serious burns.

Aloysia triphylla (Lippia citriodora)

LEMON VERBENA

From the family Verbenaceae.

Lemon verbena grew originally in Chile. This Rolls Royce of lemon-scented plants was first imported into Europe in the 18th century by the Spanish for its perfume.

SPECIES

Aloysia triphylla (Lippia citriodora)
Lemon Verbena
Half-hardy deciduous perennial. Ht 1–3m (3–10ft), spread up to 2.5m (8ft). Tiny white flowers tinged with lilac in early summer. Leaves pale green, lance shaped and very strongly lemon scented.

CULTIVATION

Propagation
Seeds
The seed sets only in warm climates and should be sown in spring into prepared seed or plug trays and covered with perlite; a bottom heat of 15°C (60°F) helps. Prick out into 9cm (3¹/₂in) pots using the bark, peat, grit compost mix (see p.591). Keep in pots for the first 2 years before planting specimens out in the garden 1m (3ft) apart.

Cuttings
Take softwood cuttings from the new growth in late spring. The cutting material will wilt quickly so have everything prepared.
Take semi-hardwood cuttings in late summer or early autumn. Keep in pots for the first 2 years.

Pests and Diseases
If grown under protection you will have to contend with whitefly and red spider mite; spray both with a liquid horticultural soap.

Maintenance
Spring Trim established plants. Take softwood cuttings. In warm climates sow seed.
Summer Trim after flowering. Take semi-hardwood cuttings.
Autumn Cut back, but not hard. Bring in before frosts.
Winter Protect all winter.

Garden Cultivation
Likes a warm humid climate. The soil should be light, free draining and warm. A sunny wall is ideal. It will need protection against frost and wind, and temperatures below 4°C (40°F). If left in the ground, cover the area around the roots with mulching material.
In spring give the plant a gentle prune and spray with warm water to help revive it.
New growth can appear very late so never discard a plant until late summer. Once the plant has started re-shooting, remove the dead tips and prune gently to encourage new growth.

At the end of the growing season, cut the plant back again gently to restore some shape.

Harvesting
Pick the leaves any time before they start to wither and darken. Leaves dry very quickly and easily, keeping their colour and scent. Store them in a damp-proof container.

CONTAINER GROWING

Choose a container at least 20cm (8in) wide and use the bark, peat, grit mix of compost (see p.591). Place the container in a warm, sunny, light and airy spot. Water well throughout the growing season and feed with liquid fertilizer during flowering. Then trim the plant to maintain shape, and trim further during the autumn. In winter move the container into a cold greenhouse, and allow the compost to nearly dry out.

MEDICINAL

A tea last thing at night is refreshing and has mild sedative properties; it can also soothe bronchial and nasal congestion and ease indigestion. However, long-term use may cause stomach irritation.

CULINARY

Use fresh leaves to flavour oil and vinegar, drinks, fruit puddings, confectionery, apple jelly, cakes and stuffings. Infuse in finger bowls.
Add a teaspoon of chopped, fresh leaves to home-made ice cream for a delicious dessert.

OTHER USES

The leaves with their strong lemon scent are lovely in potpourris, linen sachets, herb pillows, sofa sacks. The distilled oil made from the leaves is an essential basic ingredient in many perfumes.

Althaea officinalis

MARSH-MALLOW

Also known as Mortification Root, Sweet Weed, Wymote, Marsh Malice, Mesh-mellice, Wimote, and Althea. From the family Malvaceae.

Marsh-mallow is widely distributed from Western Europe to Siberia, from Australia to North America. It is common to find it in salt marshes and on banks near the sea.

The generic name, *Althaea*, comes from the Latin 'altheo' meaning 'I cure'. It may be the althea that Hippocrates recommended so highly for healing wounds. The Romans considered it a delicious vegetable, used it in barley soup and in stuffing for suckling pigs. In the Renaissance era the herbalists used marsh-mallow to cure sore throats, stomach trouble and toothache.

The soft, sweet marshmallow was originally flavoured with the root of marsh-mallow.

SPECIES

Althaea officinalis
Marsh-Mallow
Hardy perennial. Ht 60–120cm (2–4ft), spread 60cm (2ft). Flowers pink or white in late summer/early autumn. Leaves, grey-green in colour, tear shaped and covered all over with soft hair.

CULTIVATION

Propagation
Seed
Sow in prepared seed or plug trays in the autumn.

Cover lightly with compost and winter outside under glass. Erratic germination takes place in spring. Plant out, 45cm (18in) apart, when large enough to handle.

Division
Divide established plants in the spring or autumn, replanting into a prepared site in the garden.

Pests and Diseases
This plant is usually free from pests and diseases.

Maintenance
Spring Divide established plants.
Summer Cut back after flowering for new growth.
Autumn Sow seeds and winter the trays outside
Winter No need for protection. Fully hardy.

Garden Cultivation
Marsh-mallow is highly attractive to butterflies. A good seaside plant, it likes a site in full sun with a moist or wet, moderately fertile soil. Cut back after flowering to encourage new leaves.

Harvesting
Pick leaves for fresh use as required; they do not preserve well.

For use either fresh or dried, dig up the roots of 2-year-old plants in autumn, after the flowers and leaves have died back.

MEDICINAL

Due to its high mucilage content (35 percent in the root and 10 percent in the leaf), marsh-mallow soothes or cures inflammation, ulceration of the stomach and small intestine, soreness of throat, and pain from cystitis. An infusion of leaves or flowers serves as a soothing gargle; an infusion of the root can be used for coughs, diarrhoea and insomnia.

The pulverized roots may be used as a healing and drawing poultice, which should be applied warm.

CULINARY

Boil the roots to soften, then peel and quickly fry in butter.

Use the flowers in salads, and leaves, too, which may also be added to oil and vinegar, or steamed and served as a vegetable.

DECOCTION FOR DRY HANDS

Soak 25g (1oz) of scraped and finely chopped root in 150ml (1/4pint) of cold water for 24 hours. Strain well. Add 1 tablespoon of the decoction to 2 tablespoons of ground almonds, 1 teaspoon of milk and 1 teaspoon of cider vinegar. Beat it until well blended. Add a few drops of lavender oil. Put into a small screw top pot.

Anethum graveolens

DILL

**Also known as Dillweed and Dillseed.
From the family Apiaceae.**

A native of southern Europe and western Asia, dill grows wild in the cornfields of Mediterranean countries and also in North and South America. The generic name 'Anethum' derives from the Greek 'Anethon'. 'Dill' is said to come from the Anglo-Saxon 'dylle' or the Norse 'dilla', meaning to soothe or lull. Dill was found amongst the names of herbs used by Egyptian doctors 5,000 years ago and the remains of the plant have been found in the ruins of Roman buildings in Britain.

It is mentioned in the Gospel of St Matthew, where it is suggested that herbs were of sufficient value to be used as a tax payment – oh that that were true today! 'Woe unto you, Scribes and Pharisees, hypocrites! for ye pay tithe of mint and dill and cumin, and have omitted the weightier matters of the law.'

During the Middle Ages dill was prized as protection against witchcraft. While magicians used it in their spells, lesser mortals infused it in wine to enhance passion. It was once an important medicinal herb for treating coughs and headaches, as an ingredient of ointments and for calming infants with whooping cough – dill water or gripe water is still called upon today. Early settlers took dill to North America, where it came to be known as the 'Meeting House Seed', because the children were given it to chew during long sermons to prevent them feeling hungry.

SPECIES

Anethum graveolens
Dill
Annual. Ht 60–150cm (2–5ft), spread 30cm (12in). Tiny yellow/green flowers in flattened umbel clusters in summer. Fine aromatic feathery green leaves.

CULTIVATION

Propagation
Seed
Seed can be started in early spring under cover, using pots or plug trays. Do not use seed trays, as it does not like being transplanted, and if it gets upset it will bolt and miss out the leaf-producing stage.

The seeds are easy to handle, being a good size. Place four per plug or evenly spaced on the surface of a pot, and cover with perlite. Germination takes 2–4 weeks, depending on the warmth of the surrounding area. As soon as the seedlings are large enough to handle, the air and soil temperatures have started to rise and there is no threat of frost, plant out 28cm (9in) apart.

Garden Cultivation
Keep dill plants well away from fennel, otherwise they will cross pollinate and their individual flavours will become muddled. Dill prefers a well-drained, poor soil in full sun. Sow mid-spring into shallow drills on a prepared site, where they will be harvested. Protect from wind. When the plants are

Dill *Anethum graveolens*

large enough to handle, thin out to a distance of 20cm (8in) to give plenty of room for growth. Make several small sowings in succession so that you have a supply of fresh leaves throughout the summer. The seed is viable for three years.

The plants are rather fragile and it may be necessary to provide support. Twigs pushed into the ground around the plant and enclosed with string or raffia will give better results than attempting to stake each plant individually.

In very hot summers, make sure that the plants are watered regularly or they will run to seed. There is no need to liquid feed, as this only promotes soft growth and in turn encourages pests and disease.

Pests and Diseases
Watch out for greenfly in crowded conditions. Treat with a liquid horticultural soap if necessary. Be warned slugs love dill plants.

Maintenance
Spring Sow the seeds successively for a leaf crop.
Summer Feed plants with a liquid fertilizer after cutting to promote new growth.
Autumn (early) Harvest seeds.
Winter Dig up all remaining plants. Make sure all the seed heads have been removed before you compost the stalks, as the seed is viable for 3 years. If you leave the plants to self-seed they certainly will, and they will live up to their other name of Dillweed.

Harvesting

Pick leaves fresh for eating at any time after the plant has reached maturity. Since it is quick-growing, this can be within 8 weeks of the first sowing

Although leaves can be dried, great care is needed and it is better to concentrate on drying the seed for storage.

Cut the stalks off the flower heads when the seed is beginning to ripen. Put the seed heads upside down in a paper bag and tie the top of the bag. Put in a warm place for a week. The seeds should then separate easily from the husk when rubbed in the palm of the hand. Store in an airtight container and the seeds will keep their flavour very well.

CONTAINER GROWING

Dill can be grown in containers, in a sheltered corner with plenty of sun. However, it will need staking. The art of growing it successfully is to keep cutting the plant for use in the kitchen. That way you will promote new growth and keep the plant reasonably compact. The drawback is that it will be fairly short-lived, so you will have to do successive sowings in different pots to maintain a supply. I do not recommend growing dill indoors – it will get leggy, soft and prone to disease.

MEDICINAL

Dill is an antispasmodic and calmative. Dill tea or water is a popular remedy for an upset stomach, hiccups or insomnia, for nursing

mothers to promote the flow of milk, and as an appetite stimulant. It is a constituent of gripe water and other children's medicines because of its ability to ease flatulence and colic.

CULINARY

Dill is a culinary herb that improves the appetite and digestion. The difference between dill leaf and dill seed lies in the degree of pungency. There are occasions when the seed is better because of its sharper flavour. It is used as a flavouring for soup, lamb stews and grilled or boiled fish. It can also add spiciness to rice dishes, and be combined with white wine vinegar to make dill vinegar.

Dill leaf can be used generously in many dishes, as it enhances rather than dominates the flavour of food.

Before it sets seed, add one flowering head to a jar of pickled gherkins, cucumbers and cauliflowers for a flavour stronger than dill leaves but fresher than seeds. In America these are known as dill pickles.

Gravlax – the traditional Scandinavian dish of salmon and dill

Gravlax
Salmon marinaded with dill

This is a traditional Scandinavian dish of great simplicity and great merit. Salmon treated in this way will keep for up to a week in the refrigerator.

420 800g (1¹/₂–2lb) salmon, middle cut or tail piece
1 heaped tablespoon sea salt
1 rounded tablespoon caster sugar
1 teaspoon crushed black peppercorns
1 tablespoon brandy (optional)
1 heaped tablespoon fresh dill

Have the salmon cleaned, scaled, bisected lengthways and filleted. Mix remaining ingredients together and put some of the mixture into a flat dish (glass or enamel) large enough to take the salmon. Place one piece of salmon skin side down on the bottom of the dish, spread more of the mixture over the cut side. Add the second piece of salmon, skin up, and pour over the remaining mixture. Cover with foil and place a plate or wooden board larger than the area of the salmon on top. Weigh this down with

weights or heavy cans. Put in the refrigerator for 36–72 hours. Turn the fish completely every 12 hours or so and baste (inside surfaces too) with the juices.

To serve, scrape off all the mixture, pat the fish dry and slice thinly and at an angle. Serve with buttered rye bread and a mustard sauce called Gravlaxsas:

4 tablespoons mild, ready-made Dijon mustard
1 teaspoon mustard powder
1 tablespoon caster sugar
2 tablespoons white wine vinegar

Mix all the above together, then slowly add 6 tablespoons of vegetable oil until you have a sauce the consistency of mayonnaise. Finally stir in 3 to 4 tablespoons of chopped dill.

Alternatively, substitute a mustard and dill mayonnaise.

OTHER USES

Where a salt-free diet must be followed, the seed, whole or ground, is a valuable replacement. Try chewing the seeds to clear up halitosis and sweeten the breath. Crush and infuse seeds to make a nail-strengthening bath.

Dill vinegar

Angelica archangelica

ANGELICA

**Also known as European Angelica, Garden Angelica and Root of the Holy Ghost.
From the family Apiaceae.**

Angelica in its many forms is a native of Europe, Asia and North America. It is also widely cultivated as a garden plant. Wild angelica is found in moist fields and hedgerows throughout Europe. American angelica is found in similar growing conditions in Canada and north-eastern and northern central states of America.

'Angelica' probably comes from the Greek *angelos*, meaning 'messenger'. There is a legend that an angel revealed to a monk in a dream that the herb was a cure for the plague, and traditionally angelica was considered the most effective safeguard against evil, witchcraft in particular. Certainly it is a plant no self-respecting witch would include in her brew.

Angelica is an important flavouring agent in liqueurs such as Benedictine, although its unique flavour cannot be detected from the others used. It is also cultivated com-mercially for medicinal and cosmetic purposes.

SPECIES

Angelica archangelica
Angelica
Biennial and short-lived perennial (about 4 years). Ht 1–2.5m (3–8ft), spread 1m (3ft) in second year. Dramatic second-year flowerheads late spring through summer, greenish-white and very sweetly scented. Bright green leaves, the lower ones large and bi- or tri-pinnate; the higher, smaller and pinnate. Rootstock varies in colour from pale yellowish beige to reddish-brown.

Angelica sylvestris
Wild Angelica
Also known as Ground Ash, Jack Jump About, Water Kesh.
Biennial. Ht 1.2–1.5m (4–5ft). White flowers in summer often tinged with pink; smaller than flowers of **A. archangelica**. Lower leaves are large, pinnate and sharply toothed. Stems often have a purple tinge. Rootstock is thick and grey on the outside.

Angelica atropurpurea
American Angelica (left)
Also known as Bellyache Root, High Angelica, Masterwort, Purple Angelica and Wild Angelica.
Biennial. Ht 1.2–1.5m (4–5ft). Flowers resemble those of **A. archangelica** – white to greenish white, late spring through summer. Leaves large and alternately compound. Rootstock purple. The whole plant delivers a powerful odour when fresh.

Angelica sinensis
Chinese Angelica
Also known as Dang Gui, Women's Ginseng.

CULTIVATION

Propagation
Seed
Angelica can only be grown from seed but, as it loses viability after 3 months, sow preferably when fresh, in the autumn. (If for some reason this cannot be done, store in a refrigerator and sow in the spring in tiny pinches.) As seedlings do not transplant well, sow in planting position and thin out all but the best plants once germination has occurred. If transplanting is unavoidable, do it when seedlings are small, before the tap roots are established.

When planting out or thinning seedlings leave 1m (3ft) between plants.

If maintaining for another season mark spot as the plant will die back fully during the winter.

If the plant has flowered and seeded, cut back and dig up roots. If you want thousands more angelicas compost the flower head; if not, bin it.

Pests and Diseases
Blackfly can be removed easily with liquid horticultural soap.

Angelica in seed
Angelica archangelica

Maintenance

Spring Clear ground around existing plants. Plant out autumn seedlings. Sow seed.
Summer Cut stems of second year growth for crystallizing. Cut young leaves before flowering to use fresh in salads or to dry for medicinal or culinary uses. It cannot be stressed often enough that angelica needs plenty of water and if in summer the leaves turn a yellowish green, it is usually a sign that the plant needs more water.
Autumn Seed sowing time.
Winter No need for protection.

Garden Cultivation

Angelica dislikes hot humid climates and appreciates a spot in the garden where it can be in shade for some part of every day. But it can be a difficult plant to accommodate in a small garden, as it needs a lot of space. Site at the back of a border, perhaps near a wall where the plant architecture can be shown off. Make sure that the soil is deep and moist. Add well-rotted compost to help retain moisture. Note that angelica dies down completely in winter but green shoots appear quickly in the spring. Angelica is a biennial plant forming a big clump of foliage in the first summer and dramatic flowers the second, dying after the seed is set. A plant will propagate itself in the same situation if allowed to self-seed. But by cutting back in the autumn, and preventing the flower-head from seeding, the same plant can be maintained as a short-lived perennial for approximately 4 years.

Harvesting

Harvest leaves for use fresh from spring onwards; for drying, from early summer until flowering. Wild angelica is harvested in early autumn. Pick flowers in early summer for dried flower arrangements. Collect seeds when they begin to ripen.

Harvest roots for use medicinally in the second autumn immediately after flowering and dry.

CONTAINER GROWING

Angelica is definitely not an indoor plant, though if the container is large enough it can be grown as such. Do not over-fertilize and be prepared to stake when in flower. Be wary of the pot toppling over as the plant grows taller.

CULINARY

Young leaves of wild angelica can be used as an aromatic in salads and the seeds are used by confectioners in pastry.

Candied Angelica

Angelica is now best known as a decorative confectionery for cakes. There is a bright emerald, apparently plastic, specimen sold commercially as angelica, which cannot compare with home-made, pale green candied angelica; this tastes and smells similar to the freshly bruised stem or crushed leaf of the plant.

Angelica stems
Granulated sugar
Water
Caster sugar for dusting

Choose young tender springtime shoots. Cut into 8–10cm (3–4in) lengths. Place in a saucepan with just enough water to cover. Simmer until tender, then strain and peel off the outside skin. Put back into the pan with enough water to cover and bring to the boil, strain immediately and allow to cool.

When cool, weigh the angelica stalks and add an equal weight of granulated sugar. Place the sugar and angelica in a covered dish and leave in a cool place for 2 days.

Put the angelica and the syrup which will have formed back into the pan. Bring slowly to the boil and simmer, stirring occasionally, until the angelica becomes clear and has good colour.

Strain again discarding all the liquid, then sprinkle as much caster sugar as will cling to the angelica.

Allow the stems to dry in a cool oven (100°C/200°F/ gas mark ¼). If not thoroughly dry they become mouldy later.

Store in an airtight container between grease-proof paper.

Candied angelica

Stewed rhubarb

If when you cook rhubarb or gooseberries you add young angelica leaves, you will need to add less sugar. It is not that the angelica actually sweetens the fruit but its muscatel flavour cuts through the acidity of the rhubarb.

900g (2lb) rhubarb
225g (8oz) angelica stems
1 orange juice and rind
150ml (5fl oz) water
50g (2oz) sugar

MEDICINAL

Angelica stimulates the circulation. It also has anti-bacterial and anti-fungal properties.

Young leaves can be made into a tea, the flavour resembling China tea. Drink last thing at night for reducing tension, good for nervous headaches, indigestion, anaemia, coughs and colds. The tea made from the root is soothing for colds and other bronchial symptoms made worse by damp, cold conditions.

Externally it is used in bath preparations for exhaustion and rheumatic pain. Crushed leaves freshen the air in a car and help prevent travel sickness.

American angelica can be used much as you would its European relatives, but its most common use is medicinal, for heartburn and flatulence.

Chinese angelica is a blood tonic used in Chinese herbal prescriptions.

WARNING

Large doses first stimulate and then paralyse the central nervous system. The tea is not recommended for those suffering from diabetes. Wild angelica can also be used medicinally, though large doses have the effect of depressing the central nervous system.

Wild angelica can be confused with water hemlock, also known as water-dropwort (*Oenanthe crocata*), which is poisonous. Beware.

Anthriscus cerefolium

CHERVIL

From the family Apiaceae.

Chervil *Anthriscus cerefolium*

Native to the Middle East, South Russia and the Caucasus, chervil can be cultivated in warm temperate climates. It is now occasionally found growing wild.

Almost certainly brought to Britain by the Romans, chervil is one of the Lenten herbs, thought to have blood-cleansing and restorative properties. It was eaten in quantity in those days, especially on Maundy Thursday.

Gerard, the Elizabethan physician who superintended Lord Burleigh's gardens, wrote in his *Herbal* of 1597, 'The leaves of sweet chervil are exceeding good, wholesome and pleasant among other salad herbs, giving the taste of Anise seed unto the rest.'

SPECIES

Anthriscus cerefolium
Chervil
Hardy annual (some consider it to be a biennial). Ht 30–60cm (1–2ft), spread 30cm (12in). Flowers, tiny and white, grow in clusters from spring to summer. Leaves, light green and fern-like, in late summer may take on a purple tinge. When young it can easily be confused with cow parsley. However, cow parsley is a perennial and eventually grows much taller and stouter, its large leaves lacking the sweet distinctive aroma of chervil.

Anthriscus cerefolium crispum
Chervil curly leafed
Hardy annual. Grows like the ordinary chervil except that, in my opinion, the leaf has an inferior flavour.

CULTIVATION

Propagation
Seed
The medium-size seed germinates rapidly as the air and soil temperatures rise in the spring provided the seed is fresh (it loses viability after about a year). Young plants are ready for cutting 6–8 weeks after sowing, thereafter continuously providing leaves as long as the flowering stems are removed.

Seed in prepared plug trays if you prefer, and cover with perlite. Pot on to containers with a minimum 12cm (5in) diameter. But as a plant with a long tap root, chervil does not like being transplanted, so keep this to a minimum. It can in fact be sown direct into a 12cm (5in) pot, growing it, like mustard and cress, as a 'cut and come again' crop.

Pests and Diseases

Chervil can suffer from greenfly. Wash off gently with a liquid horticultural soap. Do not blast off with a high-pressure hose, as this will damage the soft leaves.

Maintenance

Spring Sow seeds.
Summer A late sowing in this season will provide leaves through winter, as it is very hardy. Protect from midday sun.
Autumn Cloche autumn-sown plants for winter use.
Winter Although chervil is hardy, some cloche protection is needed to ensure leaves in winter.

Garden Cultivation

The soil required is light with a degree of moisture retention. Plant spacing 23–30cm (9–12in). Semi-shade is best, because the problem with chervil is that it will burst into flower too quickly should the weather become sunny and hot and be of no use as a culinary herb. For this reason some gardeners sow between rows of other garden herbs or vegetables or under deciduous plants to ensure some shade during the summer months.

Harvesting

Harvest leaves for use fresh when the plant is 6–8 weeks old or when 10cm (4in) tall, and all the year round if you cover with a cloche in winter. Otherwise, freezing is the best method of preservation, as the dried leaves do not retain their flavour.

CONTAINER GROWING

When grown inside in the kitchen chervil loses colour, gets leggy and goes floppy, so unless you are treating it as a 'cut and come again' plant, plant outside in a large container that retains moisture and is positioned in semi-shade.

Chervil looks good in a window box, but be sure that it gets shade at midday.

MEDICINAL

Leaves eaten raw are rich in Vitamin C, carotene, iron and magnesium. They may be infused to make a tea to stimulate digestion and alleviate circulation disorders, liver complaints and chronic catarrh, and fresh leaves may be applied to aching joints in a warm poultice.

CULINARY

It is one of the traditional 'fines herbes', indispensable to French cuisine and a fresh green asset in any meal, but many people in Britain are only now discovering its special delicate parsley-like flavour with a hint of aniseed. This is a herb especially for winter use because it is easy to obtain fresh leaves and, as every cook knows, French or otherwise, 'Fresh is best'.

Use its leaf generously in salads, soups, sauces, vegetables, chicken, white fish and egg dishes. Add freshly chopped towards the end of cooking to avoid flavour loss.

In small quantities it enhances the flavour of other herbs. Great with vegetables.

OTHER USES

An infusion of the leaf can be used to cleanse skin, maintain suppleness and discourage wrinkles.

Chervil with broad beans

Armoracia rusticana (Cochlearia armoracia)

HORSERADISH

From the family Brassicaceae.

Native of Europe, naturalized in Britain and North America. Originally the horseradish was cultivated as a medicinal herb. Now it is considered a flavouring herb. The common name means a coarse or strong radish, the prefix horse often being used in plant to donate a large, strong or coarse plant. In the 16th century it was known in England as Redcol or Recole. In this period the plant appears to have been more popular in Scandinavia and Germany, where they developed its potential as a fish sauce. In Britain horseradish has become strongly associated with roast beef.

SPECIES

Armoracia rusticana (Cochlearia armoracia)
Horseradish
Hardy perennial. Ht 60–90cm (24–35in), spread infinite! Flowers white in spring (very rare). Leaves large green oblongs. The large root, which is up to 60cm (24in) long 5cm (2in) thick and tapering, goes deep into the soil.

Armoracia rusticana 'Variegata'
Hardy perennial. Ht 60–90cm (24–35in), spread also infinite. Flowers white in spring (rare in cool climates). Leaves large with green/cream variegation and oblong shape. Large root which goes deep into the soil. Not as good flavour as **A. rusticana**.

Roast beef is traditionally served with horseradish

CULTIVATION

Propagation
Root Cuttings
In early spring cut pieces of root 15cm (6in) long. Put them either directly into the ground, at a depth of 5cm (2in), at intervals of 30cm (12in) apart, or start them off in individual pots. These can then be planted out when the soil is manageable.

Division
If you have a perpetual clump it will need dividing; do this in the spring. Remember small pieces of root will always grow, so do it cleanly, making sure that you have collected all the little pieces of root. Replant in a well-prepared site.

Pests and Diseases
Cabbage white caterpillars may feed on the leaves during late summer. The leaves may also be affected by some fungus diseases but this should not be a problem on vigorous plants and leaves should be simply removed and burnt.

Maintenance
Spring Sow seeds. Plant cuttings in garden.
Summer Liquid feed with seaweed fertilizer.
Autumn Dig up roots if required when mature enough.
Winter No need for protection, fully hardy.

Garden Cultivation
Think seriously if you want this plant in your garden. It is invasive. Once you have it you have it. It is itself a most tolerant plant, liking all but the driest of soils. But for a good crop it prefers a light, well-dug, rich, moist soil. Prepare it the autumn before with lots of well-rotted manure. It likes a sunny site but will tolerate dappled shade.

If large quantities are required, horseradish shoul be given a patch of its own where the roots can be lifte and the soil replenished after each harvest. To produce strong, straight roots I found this method in an old gardening book. Make holes 42cm (15in) deep with a crow bar, and drop a piece of horseradish

5–8cm (2–3in) long with a crown on the top into the hole. Crown up. Fill the hole up with good rotted manure. This will produce strong straight roots in 2–3 years, some of which may be ready in the first year.

Harvesting

Pick leaves young to use fresh, or to dry.

If you have a mature patch of horseradish then the root can be dug up any time for use fresh. Otherwise dig up roots in autumn. Store roots in sand and make sure you leave them in a cool dark place for the winter.

Alternatively, wash, grate or slice and dry. Another method is to immerse the whole washed roots in white wine vinegar.

COMPANION PLANTING

Grow near potatoes to improve their disease resistance. Be careful it does not take over.

Horseradish root

CULINARY

The reason horseradish is used in sauces, vinegars, and as an accompaniment rather than cooked as a vegetable is that the volatile flavouring oil which is released in grating evaporates rapidly and becomes nothing when cooked. Raw it's a different story. The strongest flavour is from root pulled in the autumn. The spring root is comparatively mild. Fresh root contains calcium, sodium, magnesium and vitamin C, and has antibiotic qualities useful for preserving food.

It can be used grated in coleslaw, dips, pickled beetroot, cream cheese, mayonnaise and avocado fillings.

The young leaves can be added to salads for a bit of zip.

Make horseradish sauce to accompany roast beef, and smoked oily fish.

Avocado Pear with Horseradish Cream

Fresh horseradish root (approx. 15cm (6in) long); preserved horseradish in vinegar can be substituted. If it is, leave out the lemon juice.
1 tablespoon butter
3 tablespoons fresh breadcrumbs
1 apple
1 dessertspoon yoghurt
1 teaspoon lemon juice
Pinch of salt and sugar
1 teaspoon chopped fresh chervil
1/2 teaspoon each of fresh chopped tarragon and dill
3–4 tablespoons double cream
2 avocado pears (ripe) cut in half with the stones removed

Peel and grate the horseradish, melt the butter and add the breadcrumbs. Fry until brown, and add grated horseradish. Remove from heat and grate the apple into the mixture. Add yoghurt, lemon juice, salt, sugar and herbs. Put aside to cool. Chill in refrigerator.

Just before serving gently fold the cream into the mixture and spoon generously into the avocado pear halves. Serve with green salad and brown toast.

MEDICINAL

Horseradish is a powerful circulatory stimulant with antibiotic properties.

As a diuretic it is effective for lung and urinary infections. It can also be taken internally for gout and rheumatism.

Grate into a poultice and apply externally to chilblains, stiff muscles, sciatica, rheumatic joints, to stimulate blood flow.

Its sharp pungency frequently has a dramatic effect and has been known to clear the sinuses in one breath.

WARNING

Overuse may blister the skin. Do not use it if your thyroid function is low or if taking thyroxin. Avoid continuous dosage when pregnant or suffering from kidney problems.

OTHER USES

Chop finely into dog food to dispel worms and improve body tone.

Make an infusion 600ml (1 pint) water, 25g (1oz) horseradish roots and dilute 4:1. Spray on apple trees to protect against brown rot.

The roots and the leaves produce a yellow dye for natural dyeing.

Slice and infuse in milk for a lotion to improve skin clarity.

Arnica montana

ARNICA

Also known as Mountain Tobacco, Leopards Bane, Mountain Arnica, Wolfsbane and Mountain Daisy. From the family Asteraceae.

It is found wild in the mountainous areas of Canada, North America, and in Europe, where it is a protected species. Bees love it.

The name 'arnica' is said to be derived from the word 'ptarmikos', Greek for sneezing. One sniff of arnica can make you sneeze.

The herb was known by Methusalus and was widely used in the 16th century in German folk medicine. Largely as a result of exaggerated claims in the 18th century by Venetian physicians, it was, for a short time, a popular medicine.

SPECIES

Arnica montana
Arnica
Hardy perennial. Ht 30–60cm (1–2ft), spread 15cm (6in). Large, single, scented yellow flowers throughout summer. Oval, hairy, light green leaves.

CULTIVATION

Propagation
Seed
Sow the small seed in spring or late summer in either a pot, plug or seed tray, and cover with perlite. Place trays in a cold frame as heat will inhibit germination. The seed is slow to germinate, even occasionally as long as two years! Once the seedlings are large enough, pot up and harden off in a cold frame.

You can get a more reliable germination if you collect the seed yourself and sow no later than early autumn. After potting up, winter the young plants under protection. They will die back in winter. Plant out in the following spring, when the soil has warmed up, 30cm (1ft) from other plants.

Division
Arnica's root produces creeping rhizomes, which are easy to divide in spring. This is much more reliable than sowing seed.

Pests and Diseases
Caterpillars and slugs sometimes eat the leaves.

Maintenance
Spring Sow seeds. Divide creeping rhizomes.
Summer Dead head if necessary. Harvest plant for medicinal use.
Autumn Collect seeds and either sow immediately or store in an airtight container for sowing in the spring.
Winter Note the position in the garden because the plants die right back.

Garden Cultivation
Being a mountainous plant it is happiest in a sandy acid soil, rich in humus, and in a sunny position. Arnica is a highly ornamental plant with a long flowering season. It is ideally suited for large rock gardens, or the front of a border bed.

Harvesting
Pick flowers for medicinal use in summer, just before they come into full flower. Pick in full flower, with stalks, for drying.

Collect leaves for drying in summer before flowering.

Dig up roots of 2nd/3rd year growth after the plant has fully died back in late autumn/early winter for drying.

MEDICINAL

Arnica is a famous herbal and homeopathic remedy. A tincture of flowers can be used in the treatment of sprains, wounds and bruises, and also to give relief from rheumatic pain and chilblains, if the skin is not broken. Homeopathic doses are effective against epilepsy and sea sickness, and possibly as a hair growth stimulant. It has also been shown to be effective against salmonella.

WARNING

Do not take arnica internally except under supervision of a qualified herbalist or homeopath. External use may cause skin rash or irritation. Never apply to broken skin.

OTHER USES

Leaves and roots smoked as herbal tobacco, hence the name Mountain Tobacco.

Artemisia abrotanum

SOUTHERNWOOD

Also known as Lad's Love and Old Man. From the family Asteraceae.

This lovely aromatic plant is a native of southern Europe. It has been introduced to many countries and is now naturalized widely in temperate zones.

The derivation of the genus name is unclear. One suggestion is that it honours Artemisia, a famous botanist and medical researcher, sister of King Mausolus (353 BC). Another is that it was named after Artemis or Diana, the Goddess of the Hunt and Moon.

In the 17th century, Culpeper recommended that the ashes of southernwood be mingled with salad oil as a remedy for baldness.

Southernwood *Artemisia abrotanum*

SPECIES

Artemisia abrotanum
Southernwood
Deciduous or semi-evergreen hardy perennial. Ht and spread 1m (40in). Tiny insignificant clusters of dull yellow flowers in summer. The abundant olive green feathery leaves are finely divided and carry a unique scent.

wintered as a rooted cutting, when it sheds its leaves and is dormant. Keep the cuttings on the dry side, and in early spring slowly start watering. Plant out 60cm (24in) apart after the frosts have finished.

Pests and Diseases
It is free from the majority of pests and disease.

Maintenance
Spring Cut back to maintain shape. Take cuttings.
Summer Take cuttings.
Autumn Trim any flowers off as they develop.
Winter Protect the roots in hard winters with mulch.

Garden Cultivation
Southernwood prefers a light soil containing well-rotted organic material in a sunny position. However tempted you are by its bedraggled appearance in winter (hence its name, Old Man) NEVER cut hard back as you will kill it. This growth protects its woody stems from cold winds. Cut the bush hard in spring to keep its shape, but only after the frosts have finished.

Harvesting
Pick leaves during the growing season for use fresh. Pick leaves for drying in midsummer.

CULTIVATION

Propagation
Seed
It rarely flowers and sets seeds, except in warm climates.
Cuttings
Take softwood cuttings in spring from the lush new growth, or from semi-hardwood cuttings in summer. Use the bark, peat, grit mix of compost (see p.591). Roots well. It can be

CULINARY

The leaves can be used in salads. They have a strong flavour, so use sparingly. It does also make a good aromatic vinegar.

MEDICINAL

It can be used for expelling worms and to treat coughs and bronchial catarrh. A compress helps to treat frost bite, cuts and grazes.

OTHER USES

The French call it Garde Robe, and use it as a moth repellent. It is a good fly deterrent, too – hang bunches up in the kitchen, or rub it on the skin to deter mosquitoes.

WARNING

No product containing southernwood should be taken during pregnancy.

Artemisia absinthium

WORMWOOD

Also known as Absinthe and Green Ginger. From the family Asteraceae.

A native of Asia and Europe, including Britain, it was introduced into America as a cultivated plant and is now naturalized in many places. Found on waste ground, especially near the sea in warmer regions.

Legend has it that as the serpent slithered out of Eden, wormwood first sprang up in the impressions on the ground left by its tail. Another story tells that in the beginning it was called 'Parthenis absinthium', but Artemis, Greek goddess of chastity, benefited so much from it that she named it after herself – 'Artemisia absinthium'. The Latin meaning of 'absinthium' is 'to desist from', which says it all.

Although it is one of the most bitter herbs known, it has for centuries been a major ingredient of aperitifs and herb wines. Both absinthe and vermouth get their names from this plant, the latter being an 18th century French variation of the German 'wermut', itself the origin of the English name Wormwood.

Wormwood was hung by the door where it kept away evil spirits and deterred night-time visitations by goblins. It was also made a constituent of ink to stop mice eating old letters.

It was used as a strewing herb to prevent fleas, hence:

'White wormwood hath seed, get a handful or twaine,
to save against March, to make flea to refrain.
Where chamber is sweeped and wormwood is strewn,
no flea for his life, dare abide to be knowne.'

This extract comes from Thomas Tusser's *Five Hundred Pointes of Good Husbandrie*, written in 1573.

Finally, wormwood is believed to be the herb that Shakespeare had in mind when his Oberon lifted the spell from Titania with 'the juice of Dian's bud', Artemis being known to the Romans as Dian or Diana.

Wormwood *Artemisia absinthium*

SPECIES

Artemisia absinthium
Wormwood
Partial-evergreen hardy perennial. Ht 1m (40in), spread 1.2m (4ft). Tiny, insignificant, yellow flowerheads are borne in sprays in summer. The abundant leaves are divided, aromatic and grey/green in colour.

Artemisia absinthium 'Lambrook Silver'
Evergreen hardy perennial. Ht 80cm (32in), spread 50cm (20in). Tiny, insignificant, grey flowerheads are borne in long panicles in summer. The abundant leaves are finely divided, aromatic and silver/grey in colour. May need protecting in exposed sites.

Artemisia pontica
Old Warrior
Evergreen hardy perennial. Ht 60cm (24in), spread 30cm (12in). Tiny, insignificant, silver/grey flowerheads are borne on tall spikes in summer. The abundant, feathery, small leaves are finely divided, aromatic and silver/grey in colour. This can, in the right conditions, be a vigorous grower, spreading well in excess of 30cm (12in).

Artemisia 'Powis Castle'
Evergreen hardy perennial. Ht 90 cm (36in) spread 1.2m (4ft). Tiny insignificant, greyish yellow flowerheads are borne in sprays in summer. The abundant leaves are finely divided, aromatic and silver/grey in colour.

CULTIVATION

Propagation
Seed
Of the species mentioned above, only wormwood is successfully grown from seed. It is extremely small and best started off under protection. Sow in spring in a prepared seed or plug tray, using the bark, peat, grit mix of compost (see p.591). Cover with perlite and propagate with heat, 15–21°C (60–70°F). Plant out when the seedlings are large enough to handle and have had a period of hardening off.

Cuttings
Take softwood cuttings from the lush new growth in early summer; semi-hardwood in late summer. Use the bark, peat, grit mix of compost.

Division
As they are all vigorous growers, division is a good idea at least every 3 to 4 years to keep the plant healthy, to stop it becoming woody and to prevent encroaching. Dig up the plant in spring or autumn, divide the roots and replant in a chosen spot.

Pests and Diseases
Wormwood can suffer from a summer attack of blackfly. If it gets too bad, use a liquid horticultural soap, following manufacturer's instructions.

Maintenance
Spring Sow seeds. Divide established plants. Trim new growth for shape. Take softwood cuttings.
Summer Take semi-hardwood cuttings.
Autumn Prune back all the species mentioned to within 15cm (6in) of the ground. Divide established plants.
Winter Protect in temperatures below –5°C (23°F). Cover with agricultural fleece, straw, bark, anything that can be removed in the following spring.

Garden Cultivation
Artemisias like a light well-drained soil and sunshine, but will adapt well to ordinary soils provided some shelter is given. Planting distance depends on spread.
Wormwood is an overpoweringly flavoured plant and it does impair the flavour of dill and coriander so do not plant nearby.

Harvesting
Pick flowering tops just as they begin to open. Dry.
Pick leaves for drying in summer.

CONTAINER GROWING

Artemisia absinthium 'Lambrook Silver' and *Old Warrior* (**Artemisia pontica**) look very good in terracotta containers. Use the bark,

Left: Artemisia 'Powis Castle'

peat, grit mix of compost. Only feed in the summer; if you feed too early the leaves will lose their silvery foliage and revert to a more green look. In winter keep watering to the absolute minimum and protect from hard frosts.

OTHER USES

It can produce a yellow dye.

Antiseptic vinegar
This vinegar is known as the 'Four Thieves' because it is said that thieves used to rub their bodies with it before robbing plague victims.

1 tablespoon wormwood
1 tablespoon lavender
1 tablespoon rosemary
1 tablespoon sage
1.1l (1³/4) pints vinegar

Put the crushed herbs into an earthenware container. Pour in the vinegar. Cover the container and leave it in a warm sunny place for two weeks. Strain into bottles with tight-fitting, non-metal lids. This makes a very refreshing tonic in the bath, or try sprinkling it on work surfaces in the kitchen.

Wormwood vinegar

Moth-Repellent
Wormwood or southern-wood can be used for keeping moths and other harmful insects away from clothes. The smell is sharp and refreshing and does not cling to your clothes like camphor moth-balls.

Wormwood moth-repellant

Bug Ban Recipe
2 tablespoons dried wormwood or southernwood
2 tablespoons dried lavender
2 tablespoons dried mint

Mix the ingredients well and put into small sachets.

MEDICINAL

True to its name, wormwood expels worms especially round- and thread- worms.

WARNING

Not to be taken internally without medical supervision. Habitual use causes convulsions, restlessness and vomiting. Overdose causes vertigo, cramps, intoxication and delirium. Pure wormwood oil is a strong poison, although with a proper dosage there is little danger.

Artemisia dracunculus

TARRAGON

Also known as Estragon. From the family Asteraceae.

A native of southern Europe, tarragon is now found in dry areas of North America, Southern Asia and Siberia.

Dracunculus means little dragon. Its naming could have occurred (via the Doctrine of Signatures) as a result of the shape of its roots, or because of its fiery flavour. Whatever, it was certainly believed to have considerable power to heal bites from snakes, serpents and other venomous creatures.

In ancient times the mixed juices of tarragon and fennel made a favourite drink for the Kings of India.

In the reign of Henry VIII, tarragon made its way into English gardens, and the rhyme, 'There is certain people, and certain herbs, that good digestion disturbs,' could well be associated with tarragon. I love, too, the story that Henry VIII divorced Catherine of Aragon for her reckless use of tarragon.

SPECIES

Artemisia dracunculus
French Tarragon
Half-hardy perennial. Ht 90cm (3ft), spread 45cm (18in). Tiny, insignificant, yellow flowerheads are borne in sprays in summer but rarely produce ripe seed sets except in warm climates. The leaves are smooth dark green, long and narrow, and have a very strong flavour.

Artemisia dranunculus dracunculoides
Russian Tarragon
Hardy perennial. Ht 1.2m (4ft), spread 45cm (18in). Tiny, insignificant, yellow flowerheads borne in sprays in summer. The leaves are slightly coarser and green in colour, their shape long and narrow. This plant originates from Siberia, which explains why it is so hardy.

CULTIVATION

Propagation
Seed
Only the Russian variety produces viable seed. A lot of growers are propagating and selling it to the unsuspecting public as French tarragon. If you really want Russian tarragon sow the small seed in spring into prepared seed or plug trays, using the bark, peat, grit compost (see p.591). No extra heat required. When the young plants are large enough to handle, transfer to the garden, 60cm (24in) apart.

Cuttings
Both French and Russian tarragon can be propagated by cuttings.
Dig up the underground runners in spring when the frosts are finished, pull them

apart; do not cut. You will notice growing nodules, these will reproduce in the coming season. Place a small amount of root – 8–10cm (3–4in) – each with a growing nodule, in a 8cm (3in) pot, and cover with compost. Use the bark, grit, peat mix and place in a warm, well-ventilated spot. Keep watering to a minimum. When well rooted, plant out in the garden after hardening off, 60cm (24in) apart.

It is possible to take softwood cuttings of the growing tips in summer. You will need to keep the leaves moist, but the compost on the dry side. It works best under a misting unit with a little bottom heat 15°C (60°F).

Division
Divide established plants of either variety in the spring.

Pests and Diseases
Recently there has been a spate of rust developing on French tarragon. When buying a plant, look for tell-tale signs – small rust spots on the underneath of a leaf. If you have a plant with rust, dig it up, cut off all foliage carefully, and bin the leaves. Wash the roots free from soil, and pot up into fresh sterile soil. If this fails, place the dormant roots in hot water after washing off all the compost. The temperature of the water should be 40–46°C (105–115°F); over 46°C will damage the root. Leave the roots in the hot water for 5 minutes then replant in a new place in the garden.

Maintenance
Spring Sow Russian tarragon seeds if you must. Divide established plants. Take root cuttings.
Summer Remove flowers.
Autumn: Pot up pieces of French tarragon root as insurance.
Winter Protect French tarragon. As the plant dies back into the ground in winter it is an ideal candidate for either

agricultural fleece, straw or a deep mulch.

Garden Cultivation
French tarragon has the superior flavour of the two and is the most tender. It grows best in a warm dry position, and will need protection in winter. It also dislikes humid conditions. The plant should be renewed every 3 years because the flavour deteriorates as the plant matures.

Russian tarragon is fully hardy and will grow in any conditions. There is a myth that it improves the longer it is grown in one place. This is untrue, it gets coarse. It is extremely tolerant of most soil types, but prefers a sunny position, 60cm (2ft) away from other plants.

Harvesting
Pick sprigs of French tarragon early in the season to make vinegar.

Pick leaves for fresh use throughout the growing season. For freezing it is best to pick the leaves in the midsummer months.

CONTAINER GROWING

French tarragon grows well in containers. Use the bark, grit mix of compost (see p.591). As it produces root runners, choose a container to give it room to grow so that it will not become pot bound. At all times make sure the plant is watered, and in the daytime, not at night. It hates having wet roots. Keep feeding to a minimum; overfeeding produces fleshy leaves with a poor flavour; be mean. In winter, when the plant is dormant, do not water, keep the compost dry and the container in a cool, frost-free environment.

CULINARY

Without doubt this is among the Rolls Royces of the culinary herb collection. Its flavour promotes appetite and complements so many dishes – chicken, veal, fish, stuffed tomatoes, rice dishes, and salad dressings, and of course is the main ingredient of sauce béarnaise.

Chicken Salad with tarragon and grapes
Serves 4–6

1 1.3 kg (3lb) cooked chicken
150ml (5fl oz) mayonnaise
75ml (3fl oz) double cream
1 heaped teaspoon fresh chopped tarragon (½ teaspoon dried)
3 spring onions, finely chopped
100g (4oz) green grapes (seedless or de-pipped)
1 small lettuce
A few sprigs watercress
Salt and pepper

Remove the skin from the chicken and all the chicken from the bones. Slice the meat into longish pieces and place in a bowl.

In another bowl mix the mayonnaise with the cream, the chopped tarragon, and the finely chopped spring onions. Pour this mixture over the chicken and mix carefully together. Arrange the lettuce on a dish and spoon on the chicken mixture. Arrange the grapes and the watercress around it.

Serve with jacket potatoes or rice salad.

MEDICINAL

No modern medicinal use. Formerly used for toothache. If nothing else is available, a tea made from the leaves is said to overcome insomnia.

Red Orach
Atriplex hortensis var. *rubra*

Atriplex hortensis

ORACH

From the family Chenopodiaceae.

The garden species of orach, *Atriplex hortensis*, originated in Eastern Europe and is now widely distributed in countries with temperate climates. In the past it was called mountain spinach and grown as a vegetable in its own right.

The red form, *Atriplex hortensis* var. *rubra*, is still eaten frequently in Continental Europe, particularly with game, and was used as a flavouring for breads.

The common orach, *Atriplex patula*, was considered a poor man's pot herb, which is a fact worth remembering when you are pulling out this invasive annual weed.

SPECIES

Atriplex hortensis
Orach
Hardy annual. Ht 1.5m (5ft), spread 30cm (12in). Tiny greenish (boring) flowers in summer. Green triangular leaves.

Atriplex hortensis var. rubra
Red Orach
Hardy annual. Ht 1.2m (4ft), spread 30cm (1ft). Tiny reddish (boring) flowers in summer. Red triangular leaves.

Atriplex patula
Common Orach
Hardy annual. Ht 90cm (3ft), spread 30cm (12in). Flowers similar to orach, the leaves more spear shaped and smaller.

CULTIVATION

Propagation
Seed
If you wish to have a continuous supply of leaves, start off under protection in early spring, sowing the flat seeds directly into prepared plug trays. Cover with perlite. When the seedlings are large enough, and after hardening off, plant out in a prepared site in the garden 25cm (10in) apart.

Pests and Diseases
In the majority of cases this herb is pest and disease free.

Maintenance
Spring Sow seeds.
Summer Cut flowers before they form.
Autumn Cut seeds off before they are fully ripe to prevent too much self-seeding.
Winter. Dig up old plants.

Garden Cultivation
This annual herb produces the largest and most succulent leaves when the soil is rich. So prepare the site well with well-rotted manure. For red orach choose a site with partial shade as the leaves can scorch in very hot summers. The seeds can be sown in rows 60cm (2ft) apart in spring when the soil has warmed. Thin out to 25cm (10in) as soon as the seedlings are large enough. Water well throughout the growing season.

As this plant is a very rapid grower, it is as well to do 2 sowings to ensure a good supply of young leaves. The

Orach
Atriplex hortensis

Orach makes an excellent container plant

Red Orach Soup

450g (1lb) potatoes
225g (8oz) young red orach
   leaves
50g (2oz) butter
900ml (1½pt/3¾ cups)
   chicken stock
1 clove garlic, crushed
Salt and black pepper
4 tablespoons sour cream

Peel the potatoes and cut
them into thick slices. Wash
the orach and cut up
coarsely. Cook the potatoes
for 10 minutes in salted
water, drain. Melt the butter
in a saucepan with the
crushed garlic and slowly
sweeten; add the red orach
leaves and gently simmer for
5–10 minutes until soft (if
the leaves are truly young
then 5 minutes will be
sufficient). Pour in the
stock, add the parboiled
potatoes and bring to the
boil; simmer for a further 10
minutes. When all is soft,
cool slightly then purée in a
blender or liquidize. After
blending, return the soup to
a clean pan, add salt and
pepper to taste and heat
slowly (not to boiling). Stir
in the sour cream, and serve.

CONTAINER GROWING

The red-leaved orach looks
very attractive in containers,
provided you don't let it get
too tall. Nip out the growing
tip and the plant will bush
out, and do not let it flower.
Use the peat, bark mix of
compost (see p.591). Keep
the plant in semi-shade in
high summer and water well
at all times. If watering in high
sun be careful not to splash
the leaves as they can scorch,
especially the red variety.

MEDICINAL

*This herb is no longer used
medicinally. In the past it
was a home remedy for sore
throats, gout and jaundice.*

Red Orach Soup

red varieties look very
attractive grown as a hedge.
Remove flowering tips as
soon as they appear. This
will help maintain the shape
of the plant.
   If seed is not required,
pick the flowers off as soon
as they appear. To save the
seed, collect before it is fully
ripe, otherwise you will have
hundreds of orach babies all
over your garden and next
door.

Harvesting

Pick young leaves to use
fresh as required. The herb
does not dry or freeze
particularly well.

CULINARY

The young leaves can be
eaten raw in salads, and the
red variety looks most
attractive. The old leaves of
both species ought to be
cooked as they become
slightly tough and bitter. It
can be used as a substitute
for spinach or as a
vegetable, served in a white
sauce. It is becoming more
popular in Europe, where it
is used in soups.

Ballota nigra

BLACK HOREHOUND

Also known as Stinking Horehound, Dunny Nettle, Stinking Roger and Hairy Hound.
From the family Lamiaceae.

Black horehound comes from a genus of about 25 species mostly native to the Mediterranean region. Some species have a disagreeable smell and only a few are worth growing in the garden. Black horehound is found on roadsides, hedge banks and in waste places throughout most of Europe, Australia and America.

Ballota nigra, the black horehound, was originally called 'ballote' by the ancient Greeks. It has been suggested that this comes from the Greek word 'ballo' which means 'to reject', 'cast', or 'throw', because cows and other farm animals with their natural instincts reject it. The origin of the common name is more obscure, it could come from the Anglo-Saxon word 'har' which means 'hoar' or 'hairy'.

SPECIES

Ballota nigra
Black Horehound
Hardy perennial. Ht 40–100cm (16–40in), spread 30cm (12in). Purple-pink attractive flowers in summer. The leaves are green and medium-sized, rather like the stinging nettle. All parts of the plant are hairy and have a strong, disagreeable smell and taste.

Ballota pseudodictamnus
Half-hardy perennial. Ht 60cm (24in), spread 30cm (12in). White flowers with numerous purple spots in summer. Leaves white and woolly. This plant originated from Crete. The dried calyces look like tiny furry spinning tops; they were used as floating wicks in primitive oil lamps.

Black horehound *Ballota nigra*

CULTIVATION

Propagation
Seed
Sow the seeds direct into the prepared garden in late summer, thinning to 40cm (16in) apart.

Division
Divide roots in mid-spring.

Pests and Diseases
Rarely suffers from any pest or diseases.

Maintenance

Spring Dig up established plants and divide; replant where required.

Summer When the plant has finished flowering, cut off the dead heads before the seeds ripen, so preventing it seeding itself in the garden.

Autumn Sow seed.

Winter No need to protect.

Garden Cultivation

Black horehound will grow in any soil conditions, though it prefers water-retentive soil – in fact I have seen it growing in hedgerows throughout England. In the garden, place it in a border. The bees love it and the flowers are attractive. Make sure it is far enough back so that you do not brush it by mistake because it does stink.

Harvesting

As this is a herbalist's herb, the leaves should be collected before flowering and dried with care.

CONTAINER GROWING

Not recommended, as it is such an unpleasantly smelling plant.

MEDICINAL

Black horehound was used apparently in the treatment of bites from mad dogs. A dressing was prepared from the leaves and laid on the infected part. This was said to have an anti-spasmodic effect.

This is not a herb to be self administered. Professionals use it as a sedative, anti-emetic and to counteract vomiting during pregnancy.

Black horehound *Ballota nigra*

Calendula officinalis

MARIGOLD

Also known as Souci, Marybud, Bulls Eye, Garden Marigold, Holligold, Pot Marigold and Common Marigold. From the family Asteraceae.

Native of the Mediterranean and Iran. Distributed throughout the world as a garden plant.

This sunny little flower – the 'merrybuds' of Shakespeare – was first used in Indian and Arabic cultures, before being 'discovered' by the ancient Egyptians and Greeks.

The Egyptians valued the marigold as a rejuvenating herb, and the Greeks garnished and flavoured food with its golden petals. The botanical name comes from the Latin 'calendae', meaning the first day of the month.

In India wreaths of marigold were used to crown the gods and goddesses. In medieval times they were considered an emblem of love and used as chief ingredient in a complicated spell that promised young maidens knowledge of whom they would marry. To dream of them was a sign of all good things; simply to look at them would drive away evil humours.

In the American Civil War, marigold leaves were used by the doctors on the battlefield to treat open wounds.

SPECIES

Calendula officinalis
Marigold
Hardy annual. Ht and spread 60cm (24in). Daisy-like, single or double flowers, yellow or orange: from spring to autumn. Light green, aromatic, lance-shaped leaves.

Marigold
Calendula officinalis

CULTIVATION

Propagation
Seeds
Seeds can be sown in the autumn under protection directly into prepared pots or singly into plug trays, covering lightly with compost. They can be wintered in these containers and planted out in the spring after any frost, 30–45cm (12–18in) apart.

Pests and Diseases
Slugs love the leaves of young marigolds. Keep

night-time vigil with a torch and a bucket, or lay beer traps. In the latter part of the season, plants can become infested with blackfly. Treat this in the early stages by brushing off the fly and cutting away the affected areas, or later on by spraying with a horticultural soap. Very late in the season, the leaves sometimes become covered with a powdery mildew. Cut off those affected and burn them in case it spreads.

Maintenance

Spring Sow seeds in garden.
Summer Dead head flowers to promote more flowering.
Autumn Sow seeds under protection for early spring flowering.
Winter Protect young plants.

Garden Cultivation

Marigold is a very tolerant plant, growing in any soil that is not waterlogged, but prefers, and looks best in, a sunny position.

The flowers are sensitive to variations of temperature and dampness. Open flowers forecast a fine day. Encourage continuous flowering by dead heading. It self-seeds abundantly but seems never to become a nuisance.

Harvesting

Pick flowers just as they open during summer, both for fresh use and for drying. Dry at a low temperature. You can make a colourful oil.

Pick leaves young for fresh use; they are not much good preserved.

CULINARY

Flower petals make a very good culinary dye. They have been used for butter and cheese, and as a poor man's saffron to colour rice. They are also lovely in salads and omelettes, and make an interesting cup of tea.

Young leaves can be added to salads.

Sweet Marigold Buns

Makes 18

100g/4oz softened butter
100g/4oz caster sugar
2 eggs, size 1 or 2
100g/4oz self-raising flour
1 teaspoon baking powder
2 tablespoons fresh marigold petals

Put the butter, sugar, eggs, sifted flour and baking powder into bowl, and mix together until smooth and glossy. Fold in 1½ tablespoons of marigold petals. Turn the mixture into greased bun tins or individual paper cake cases. Sprinkle a few petals onto each bun with a little sugar. Bake in an oven 160°C/325°F/gas mark 3 for approximately 25–30 minutes.

CONTAINER GROWING

Marigolds look very cheerful in containers and combine well with other plants. Well suited to window boxes, but not so in hanging baskets, where they will become stretched and leggy.

Use the bark, peat compost (see p.591). Pinch out the growing tips to stop the plant from becoming too tall and leggy. Dead head flowers to encourage more blooms.

OTHER USES

There are many skin and cosmetic preparations that contain marigold. Infuse the flowers and use as a skin lotion to reduce large pores, nourish and clear the skin, and clear up spots and pimples.

MEDICINAL

Marigold flowers contain antiseptic, anti-fungal and anti-bacterial properties that promote healing. Make a compress or poultice of the flowers for burns, scalds, or stings. Also useful in the treatment of varicose veins, chilblains and impetigo. A cold infusion may be used as an eyewash for conjunctivitis, and can be a help in the treatment of thrush.

The sap from the stem has a reputation for removing warts, corns and calluses.

Marigold skin lotion

Carum carvi

CARAWAY

From the family Apiaceae.

Caraway is a native of Southern Europe, Asia and India and thrives in all but the most humid warm regions of the world. It is commercially and horticulturally cultivated on a wide scale, especially in Germany and Holland.

Both the common and species names stem directly from the ancient Arabic word for the seed, 'karawya', which was used in medicines and as a flavouring by the ancient Egyptians. In fact fossilized caraway seeds have been discovered at Mesolithic sites, so this herb has been used for at least 5,000 years. It has also been found in the remains of Stone Age meals, Egyptian tombs and ancient caravan stops along the Silk Road.

Caraway probably did not come into use in Europe until the 13th century, but it made a lasting impact. In the 16th century when Shakespeare, in *Henry IV*, gave Falstaff a pippin apple and a dish of caraways, his audience could relate to the dish, for caraway had become a traditional finish to an Elizabethan feast. Its popularity was further enhanced 250 or so years later when Queen Victoria married Prince Albert, who made it clear that he shared his countrymen's particular predilection for the seed in an era celebrated in England by the caraway seed cake.

No herb as ancient goes without magical properties of course, and caraway was reputed to ward off witches and also to prevent lovers from straying, a propensity with a wide application – it kept a man's doves, pigeons and poultry steadfast too!

SPECIES

Carum carvi
Caraway
Hardy biennial. Ht in first year 20cm (8in), second year 60cm (24in); spread 30cm (12in). Flower white/pinkish in tiny umbellate clusters in early summer. Leaves feathery, light green, similar to carrot. Pale thick tapering root comparable to parsnip but smaller. This plant is not particularly decorative.

Caraway *Carum carvi*

CULTIVATION

Propagation
Seed
Easily grown; best sown outdoors in early autumn when the seed is fresh. Preferred situation full sun or a little shade, any reasonable, well-drained soil. For an acceptable flavour it must have full sun.

If growing caraway as a root crop, sow in rows and treat the plants like vegetables. Thin to 20cm (8in) and keep weed free. These plants will be ready for a seed harvest the following summer; the roots will be ready in their second autumn. Caraway perpetuates itself by self-sowing and can, with a little control, maintain the cycle.

If you want to sow in spring, do it either direct in the garden into shallow drills after the soil has warmed, or into prepared plug trays to minimize harmful disturbance to its tap root when potting up. Cover with perlite. Pot up when seedlings are large enough to handle and transplant in the early autumn.

Pests and Diseases

Caraway occasionally suffers from carrot root fly. The grubs of these pests tunnel into the roots. The only organic way to get rid of them is to pull up the plants and bin them.

Maintenance

Spring Weed well around autumn-sown young plants. Sow seed.
Summer Pick flowers and leaves.
Autumn Cut seed heads. Dig up 2nd-year plants. Sow seeds.
Winter Does not need much protection unless it gets very cold.

Garden Cultivation

Prepare the garden seedbed well. The soil should be fertile, free draining and free of weeds, not least because it is all too easy to mistake a young caraway plant for a weed in its early growing stage. Thin plants when well established to a distance of 20cm (8in).

Harvesting

Harvest the seeds in summer by cutting the seed heads just before the first seeds fall. Hang them with a paper bag tied over the seed head or over a tray in an airy place. It was once common practice to scald the freshly collected seed to rid it of insects and then dry it in the sun before storing. This is not necessary. Simply store in an airtight container.
Gather fresh leaves when young for use in salads. They are not really worth drying.
Dig up roots in second autumn as a food crop.

CONTAINER GROWING

Caraway really is not suitable for growing in pots.

CULINARY

When you see caraway mentioned in a recipe it is usually the seed that is required. Caraway seed cake was one of the staples of the Victorian tea table. Nowadays caraway is more widely used in cooking, and in savouries as well as sweet dishes. The strong and distinctive flavour is also considered a spice. It is frequently added to sauerkraut, and the German liqueur, Kummel, contains its oil along with cumin.
Sprinkle over rich meats, goose, Hungarian beef stew – as an aid to digestion. Add to cabbage water to reduce cooking smells. Add to apple pies, biscuits, baked apples and cheese.

Serve in a mixed dish of seeds at the end of an Indian meal to both sweeten the breath and aid digestion.
Caraway root can be cooked as a vegetable, and its young leaves chopped into salads and soups.

Caraway and Cheese Potatoes
Serves 4

4 large potatoes
100gm/4oz/1 cup grated Gruyère cheese
2 teaspoons caraway seeds

Scrub but do not peel the potatoes. Cut them in half length-wise. Wrap in a boat of greaseproof foil and sprinkle each half with some of the grated cheese and a little caraway. Pre-heat the oven to 180°C/350°F/gas mark 4 and cook for 35–45 minutes, or until the potatoes are soft.

Caraway seeds

Caraway and Cheese Potatoes

MEDICINAL

The fresh leaves, roots and seeds have digestive properties.
Chew seeds raw or infuse them to sharpen appetites before a meal, as well as to aid digestion, sweeten the breath, and relieve flatulence after the meal. Safe for children.
An infusion can be made from 3 teaspoons of crushed seeds with ½ cup of water.

OTHER USES

Pigeon fanciers claim that tame pigeons will never stray if there is baked caraway dough in their coot.

Cedronella canariensis (triphylla)

BALM OF GILEAD

Also known as Canary Balm. From the family Lamiaceae.

Although this herb originates from Madeira and the Canary Islands, as indicated by its species name, balm of Gilead is now established in many temperate regions of the world. Many plants have been called balm of Gilead, the common link that they all have a musky, eucalyptus, camphor-like scent.

The Queen of Sheba gave Solomon a balm of Gilead, which was *Commiphora opobalsamum*, an aromatic desert shrub found in the Holy Land. Today this plant is rare and protected, its export prohibited.

The balm of Gilead mentioned in the Bible ('Is there no balm in Gilead; is there no physician there?') was initially held to be *Commiphora meccanensis,* which was an aromatic shrub. However some now say it was oleo-resin obtained from *Balsamodendron opobalsamum*, a plant now thought to be extinct. Whatever is the case, the medicinal balm of Gilead is *Populus balsamifera*. This is balsam poplar, a tree found growing in several temperate countries, which smells heavenly in early summer, while the herb now known as balm of Gilead is *Cedronella canariensis*. This is said to have a similar scent to the Biblical shrubs, perhaps the reason for its popular name.

Balsam poplar *Populus balsamifera*

SPECIES

Cedronella canariensis (triphylla)
Balm of Gilead
Half-hardy perennial, partial evergreen. Ht 1m (3ft), spread 60cm (2ft). Leaves with strong eucalyptus scent, 3 lobes and toothed edges, borne on square stems. Pink or pale mauve, two-lipped flowers throughout summer. Black seed heads.

CULTIVATION

Propagation
Seed

The fairly small seeds should be sown directly on the surface of a prepared pot, plug or seed tray. Cover with a layer of perlite.

It is a temperamental germinator so bottom heat of 20°C (68°F) can be an asset. If using heat remember not to let the compost dry out, and only water with a fine spray when needed. The seedlings will appear any time between 2–6 weeks. When 2 leaves have formed, prick out and plant in position 1m (3ft) apart.

Cuttings

More reliable than seed. They take readily either in early summer before flowering on new growth or in early autumn on the semi-ripe wood. Use the bark, peat, grit mix of compost (see p.591).

Pests and Diseases

Being aromatic, aphids and other pests usually leave it alone, but the seedlings are prone to damping off.

Maintenance

Spring Sow seeds under protection. In a warm garden a mature plant can self-seed; rub the leaves of any self-seedlings to see if it is balm of Gilead or a young nettle (but don't get stung!). At this stage their aroma is the only characteristic that tells them apart.

Plants overwintered in containers should be repotted if root-bound and given a liquid feed.

Summer Cut back after flowering to keep it neat and tidy, and also to encourage new growth from which late cuttings can be taken.

Autumn Take stem cuttings. Collect seed heads.

Winter Protect from frost.

Balm of Gilead
Cedronella canariensis

Garden Cultivation

Balm of Gilead grows happily outside in sheltered positions. Plant in a well-drained soil in full sun, preferably against a warm, wind-protecting wall. The plant has an upright habit but spreads at the top, so planting distance from other plants should be approximately 1m (3ft).

It is a tender plant that may need protection in cooler climates. If you get frosts lower than –2°C (29°F) protect the plant for the winter, either by bringing it into a cool greenhouse or conservatory or by covering in an agricultural fleece.

Harvesting

Pick leaves for drying before the flowers open, when they will be at their most aromatic.

Either pick flowers when just coming into bloom and dry, or wait until flowering is over and collect the black flower heads (good for winter arrangements).

Seeds are ready for extraction when you can hear the flower heads rattle. Store in an airtight container to sow in the spring.

CONTAINER GROWING

Balm of Gilead makes an excellent container plant. A 23–25cm (9–10in) pot will be required for a plant to reach maturity. Use a free-draining compost with bark and grit. Liquid feed a mature plant monthly throughout summer.

When grown in a conservatory, the scent of the leaves perfumes the air especially when the plant is watered or the sun shining on it. Flowers are long lasting and give a good show during the summer. Keep watering to the absolute minimum in the winter months.

MEDICINAL

Crush the leaves in your hand and inhale the aroma to clear your head.

Rub the leaves on skin to stop being bitten by mosquitoes.

Said to be an aphrodisiac when applied....no comment.

OTHER USES

Dried leaves combine well in a spicy or woody potpourri with cedarwood chippings, rosewood, pineneedles, small fir cones, cypress oil and pine oil.

Add an infusion of the leaves to bath water for an invigorating bath.

White Foxglove *Digitalis purpurea* f. *albiflora*

If you live in a cold climate -10°C (14°F) protect during the first winter. Use agricultural fleece, straw, bracken or pine needles. In areas where the soil is damp and cold, it is advisable to lift the plants for the first winter and keep them in a cold frame, replanting the following spring.

Harvesting
This is not advised unless you are a herbalist or a pharmacist.

MEDICINAL

Foxgloves are grown commercially for the production of a drug the discovery (a major medical breakthrough) of which is a classic example of a productive marriage between folklore and scientific curiosity. Foxgloves contain glycosides which are extracted from second-year leaves to make the heart drug digitalis. For more than 200 years digitalis has provided the main drug for treating heart failure. It is also a powerful diuretic. Although a synthetic form of the drug has been developed, the plant is still grown commercially for the drug industry.

CULTIVATION

Propagation
The seed is very small and fine. Sow in either spring or autumn as carefully as possible, using the cardboard method, either directly onto the prepared ground, or into pots or plug trays. Sow on the surface; do not cover with perlite, but with a piece of glass, which should be removed as soon as the seedlings appear. No bottom heat required.

Remember, they will not flower the first season.

Pests and Diseases
Foxgloves, on the whole, are pest and disease free.

Maintenance
Spring Sow seeds. Plant out first-year plants.
Summer Remove main flowering shoot after flowering.
Autumn Check round second-year plants for self-sown seedlings, thin out if over-crowded, remove if not required. Pot up a few in case of an exceptionally hard winter.
Winter In the majority of cases no protection needed.

See 'Garden Cultivation' for the exceptions.

Garden Cultivation
This is one of the most poisonous plants in the flora. Foxgloves will grow in most conditions, even dry exposed sites, but do best in semi-shade and a moist but well-drained acid soil enriched with leaf mould. The rosettes and leaves are formed the first year and the flower spike the second. The plant then dies but usually leaves lots of self-sown babies nearby. Water well in dry weather and remove the centre spike after flowering to increase the size of the flowers on the side shoots.

CONTAINER GROWING

These tall elegant plants do not honestly suit growing in containers. It is possible, but care has to be taken that the plant is not damaged in winds. Use a soil-based compost. Water regularly.

Echium vulgare

VIPER'S BUGLOSS

Also known as Bugles, Wild Borage, Snake Flower, Blue Devil, Blueweed, Viper's Grass and Snakeflower. From the family Boraginaceae.

This plant originates from the Mediterranean region and is now widespread throughout the northern hemisphere, being found on light porous stones on semi-dry grassland, moorlands, and waste ground. It is regarded as a weed in some parts of America. To many American farmers this will seem an understatement; they consider it a plague.

The common name, Viper's Bugloss, developed from the medieval Doctrine of Signatures, which ordained that a plant's use should be inferred from its appearance. It was noticed that the brown stem looked rather like a snake skin and that the seed is shaped like a viper's head. So, in their wisdom, they prescribed it for viper bites, which for once proved right; it had some success in the treatment of the spotted viper's bite.

SPECIES

Echium vulgare
Viper's Bugloss
Hardy biennial. Ht 60–120cm (2–4ft). Bright blue/pink flowers in the second year. The leaves are mid-green and bristly.

CULTIVATION

Propagation
Seed
Viper's bugloss is easily grown from seed. Start it off in a controlled way in spring by sowing the small seed into a prepared seed or plug tray. Cover the seed with perlite. When the seedlings are large enough to handle, and after a period of hardening off, plant out into a prepared site in the garden, 45cm (18in) apart.

Pests and Diseases
It rarely suffers.

Maintenance
Spring First year, sow seeds; second year, clear round plants.
Summer Second year, pick off flowers as they die so that they cannot set seed.
Autumn First year, leave well alone. Second year, dig up plants and bin. Do not compost unless you want thousands of viper's bugloss plants appearing all over your garden.
Winter No need to protect first-year plant.

Garden Cultivation
This colourful plant is beautifully marked. Sow the seed in spring directly into the garden. It will grow in any soil and is great for growing on dry soils and sea cliffs. With its long tap root, the plant will survive any drought but cannot easily be transplanted except when very young. The disadvantage is that it self-seeds and is therefore invasive.

Harvesting
Gather flowers in summer for fresh use.

CONTAINER GROWING

Because it is a rampant self-seeder, it is quite a good idea to grow it in containers. For the first year it bears only green prickly leaves and is very boring. However, the show put on in the second year is full compensation. Use a soil-based compost; no need to feed. Over-feeding

Viper's bugloss Echium vulgare

will prohibit the flowering. Very tolerant of drought; nevertheless do water it regularly. Dies back in winter of first year – leave the container somewhere cool and water occasionally.

CULINARY

The young leaves are similar to borage, but they have lots more spikes. It is said you can eat them when young, but I have fought shy of this. The flowers look very attractive in salads. They can also be crystallized.

MEDICINAL

The fresh flowering tips can be chopped up for making poultices for treating whitlows and boils. Infuse lower leaves to produce a sweating in fevers or to relieve headaches.

OTHER USES

At one time, a red colouring substance for dyeing fabrics was extracted from the root.

Equisetum arvense

HORSETAIL

Also known as Mare's Tail, Shave Grass, Bottle Brush, Pewter Wort, Snake's Pie, Fairy Spindle, Paddock's Pipes, Cat's Tail and Joint Grass. From the family Equisetaceae.

Horsetail *Equisetum arvense*

This plant is a native of the temperate regions, although some species are found in the tropics where they can grow to a considerable size.

When I first started herb farming I suddenly noticed all these spiky things growing all over the floor of one of my polythene tunnels. Subsequently I discovered it was a very worthy herb, not an invasive weed.

The horsetail is a plant left over from prehistoric times. By the evidence of fossil remains, it has survived almost unchanged since the coal seams were laid. It does not flower but carries spores as do ferns, to which it is related. The fronds have a harsh feel to them, this is because, uniquely, the plant absorbs large quantities of silica from the soil. The Romans always used horsetail to clean their pots and pans, not just to make them clean but also, thanks to the silica, to make them non-stick. The plant was used in the Middle Ages as an abrasive by cabinet makers and to clean pewter, brass and copper, and for scouring wood containers and milk pans.

No plant, having survived so long, could escape myth and magic. This herb has been associated far and wide with various goblins, toads and snakes, and the Devil.

SPECIES

Equisetum arvense
Horsetail
Hardy perennial. Ht 45cm (18in). The plant does not flower. It grows on a thin creeping rhizome producing 20cm (8in) long grey/brown fertile shoots with 4–6 sheaths in spring. The shoots die off and the spores are spread just like ferns.

CULTIVATION

Propagation
I am not sure that this is necessary, but if you do require a supply of horsetail it may be of merit.

Cuttings
Each piece of horsetail root is capable of reproducing. In summer place small pieces in a seed or plug tray

Use the peat, bark mix of compost (see p.591). Plant out the following spring when the cuttings are well rooted.

Pests and Diseases

For a plant to have survived so long, it has to be pest- and disease-free.

Maintenance

Spring Make sure the plant is well contained and not wandering off.
Summer Cut back plants that are beginning to die back to stop the spores spreading.
Autumn After harvest, cut down to the ground, again to stop the spores spreading.
Winter No protection necessary; very hardy.

Garden Cultivation

If grown in open ground unconfined, horsetail becomes a permanent inhabitant and is only eradicated with great difficulty. Its root systems have been found to extend down a cliff face 12m (40ft), and breaking the rhizomes stimulates buds on the remainder to sprout and produce more growth.
If horsetail is to be introduced into the garden at all, and to be honest I do not recommend it, it is best confined to a strong container partially sunk into the ground. Leave the rim

visible so that the rhizomes cannot penetrate or creep over the top.

Harvesting

The green/brown shoots look almost like minute Christmas trees and these are the parts that can be collected during the summer months. Dry them.

CONTAINER GROWING

The only sane way to grow horsetail is in a container. But be sure to cut it back in the summer to prevent spread by the spores. No need to feed, and it requires little watering. It can look attractive!

CULINARY

It has been eaten as a substitute for asparagus, but I do not recommend it unless you are stuck on a desert island and there is no other food available.

COSMETIC

Horsetail Nail Strengthener

A simple method of improving easily broken nails is to immerse the finger tips in a decoction made by simmering 50g (2oz) of dry or fresh herb in 900ml/1½ pints/3¾ cups of water for 20 minutes.

Horsetail Hair Rinse and Tonic

Horsetail provides a good, all-round conditioner and helps the hair to a natural shine.

*About 8 horsetail stems
15–20cm (6–8in) long
600ml (1 pint) of boiling water*

Bruise the horsetail stems with a spoon before adding boiling water to make an infusion. Cover and leave until lukewarm then strain off the liquid. After shampooing and rinsing, pour the infusion over the hair and massage into the scalp. Blot up excess moisture with a towel and comb through your hair. Cover your head with a warm towel and wait for 10 minutes before drying your hair in the usual way.

Horsetails look like minute Christmas trees

MEDICINAL

This plant is a storehouse of minerals and vitamins, so herbalists recommended it in cases of amnesia and general debility. The tea enriches the blood, hardens fingernails and revitalizes lifeless hair. Its astringent properties help to strengthen the walls of the veins, tightening up varicose veins and help guard against fatty deposits in the arteries. It is also useful when white spots occur on the nails, which indicate a calcium imbalance in the body, as the silica encourages the absorption and use of calcium by the body.

WARNING

It is advised that, if you wish to use horsetail, you do so with consultation from a herbalist.

OTHER USES

Stems have a high silica content and can be used after drying to scour metal and polish pewter and fine woodwork.
The whole plant yields a yellow ochre dye.

Filipendula

MEADOWSWEET

Also known as Bridewort, Meadow Queen, Meadow-Wort, and Queen of the Meadow. From the family Rosaceae.

Meadowsweet can be found growing wild in profusion near streams and rivers, in damp meadows, fens and marshlands, or wet woodlands to 1,000m (3,300ft) altitude.

It is a native of Europe and Asia that has been successfully introduced into, and is naturalized in, North America.

The generic name, *Filipendula*, comes from 'filum', meaning thread, 'pendulus' meaning hanging. This is said to describe the root tubers that hang, characteristically of the genus, on fibrous roots.

The common name, meadowsweet, is said to be derived from the Anglo-Saxon word 'medesweete', which itself owes its origin to the fact that the plant was used to flavour mead, a drink made from fermented honey.

It has been known by many other names. In Chaucer's *The Knight's Tale* it is Meadwort and was one of the ingredients in a drink called 'save'. It was also known as Bridewort, because it was strewn in churches for festivals and weddings and made into bridal garlands. In Europe it took its name Queen of the Meadow from the way the herb can dominate a low-lying, damp meadow. In America, it became Gravelroot or Joe Pie Weed (*Eupatorium purpureum*).

In the 16th century, when it was customary to strew floors with rushes and herbs (both to give warmth underfoot and to overcome smells and infections), it was a favourite of Queen Elizabeth I. She desired it above all other herbs in her chambers.

The sap contains a chemical of the same group as salicylic acid, an ingredient of aspirin. It was isolated for the first time in the 19th century by an Italian professor. When the drug company Bayer formulated acetylsalicylic acid, they called it aspirin after the old botanical name for meadowsweet, *Spirea ulmaria*.

SPECIES

Filipendula ulmaria
Meadowsweet
Hardy perennial. Ht 60–120cm (2–4ft), spread 60cm (2ft). Clusters of creamy-white flowers in mid-summer. Green leaf made up of up to 5 pairs of big leaflets separated by pairs of smaller leaflets.

Filipendula ulmaria 'Aurea'
Golden Meadowsweet
Hardy perennial. Ht and spread 30cm (12in). Clusters of creamy-white flowers in midsummer. Bright golden yellow, divided leaves in spring that turn a lime colour in summer. Susceptible to sun scorch.

Filipendula ulmaria 'Variegata'
Variegated Meadowsweet
Hardy perennial. Ht 45cm (18in) and spread 30cm (12in). Clusters of creamy-white flowers in mid-summer. Divided leaf, dramatically variegated green and yellow in spring. Fades a bit as the season progresses.

Filipendula vulgaris
Dropwort
Hardy perennial. Ht 60–90cm (2–3ft), spread 45cm (18in). Summertime clusters of white flowers (larger than meadowsweet). Fern-like green leaves.

CULTIVATION

Propagation
Seed
Sow in prepared seed or plug trays in the autumn. Cover lightly with compost (not perlite) and winter outside under glass. Check from time to time that the compost has not become dry as this will inhibit germination. Stratification is helpful but not essential. Germination should take place in spring. When the seedlings are large enough to handle, plant out, 30cm (12in) apart, into a prepared site.

Division
The golden and variegated forms are best propagated by division. This is easily done in the autumn. Dig up established plant and tease the plantlets apart; they separate easily. Either replant in a prepared site, 30cm (12in) apart, or, if it is one of the decorative varieties, pot up using the bark, peat mix of compost (see p.591).

Pests and Diseases
Meadowsweet rarely suffers from these.

Maintenance
Spring Sow seeds if required.
Summer Cut back after flowering.
Autumn Divide established plants, sow seed for wintering outside.
Winter No need for protection.

Garden Cultivation
Meadowsweet adapts well to the garden, but does prefer sun/semi-shade and a moisture-retentive soil. If your soil is free-draining, mix in plenty of well-rotted manure and/or leaf mould, and plant in semi-shade.

Harvesting
Gather young leaves for fresh or dry use before flowers appear. Pick flowers just as they open and use fresh or dry.

MEDICINAL

The whole plant is a traditional remedy for an acidic stomach.

The fresh root is used in homeopathic preparations and is effective on its own in the treatment of diarrhoea.

The flowers, when made into a tea, are a comfort to flu victims.

Golden meadowsweet
Filipendula ulmaria 'Aurea'

CULINARY

A charming, local vet who made all kinds of vinegars and pickles gave me to try meadowsweet vinegar. Much to my amazement it was lovely, and combined well with oil to make a different salad dressing, great when used with a flower salad.

I am not a fan of meadowsweet flower fritters so mention them only in passing. The flowers do however make a very good wine, and add flavour to meads and beers. The flowers can also be added to stewed fruit and jams, introducing a subtle almond flavour.

Young leaves can be added to soups, but are not recommended for the faint-hearted!

OTHER USES

A black dye can be obtained from the roots by using a copper mordant.

Use dried leaves and flowers in potpourris.

CONTAINER GROWING

Golden and variegated meadowsweet look very attractive in containers, but use a soil-based compost to make sure moisture is retained. Position in partial shade to inhibit drying out and prevent sun scorch. The plant dies back in winter so leave it outside in a place where the natural weathers can reach it. If you live in an extremely cold area, protect the container from damage by placing in a site protected from continuous frost, but not warm. Liquid feed only twice during flowering.

Meadowsweet dye

Meadowsweet *Filipendula ulmaria*

Galium odoratum (Asperula odorata)

SWEET WOODRUFF

Also known as New Mowed Hay, Rice Flower, Ladies in the Hay, Kiss Me Quick, Master of the Wood, Woodward and Woodrowell. From the family Rubiaceae.

This is a native of Europe and has been introduced and cultivated in North America and Australia. It grows deep in the woods and in hedgerows.

Records date back to the 14th century, when woodruff was used as a strewing herb, as bed-stuffing and to perfume linen.

On May Day in Germany, it is added to Rhine wine to make a delicious drink called 'Maibowle'.

SPECIES

Galium odoratum (Asperula odorata)
Sweet Woodruff
Hardy perennial. Ht 15cm (6in), spread 30cm (12in) or more. White, star-shaped flowers from spring to early summer. The green leaves are neat and grow in a complete circle around the stem. The whole plant is aromatic.

CULTIVATION

Propagation
Seed
To ensure viability only use fresh seed. Sow in early autumn into prepared seed or plug trays, and cover with compost. Water in well. Seeds require a period of stratification (see p.590). Once the seedlings are large enough, either pot or plant out as soon as the young plants have been hardened off. Plant 10cm (4in) apart.

Root Cuttings
The rootstock is very brittle and every little piece will grow. The best time is after flowering in the early summer. Lay small pieces of the root, 2–4cm (1–1½in) long, evenly spaced, on the compost in a seed tray. Cover with a thin layer of compost, and water. Leave in a warm place, and the woodruff will begin to sprout again. When large enough to handle, split up and plant out.

Pests and Diseases
This plant rarely suffers from pests and diseases.

Maintenance
Spring Take root cuttings before flowering.
Summer Dig up before the flowers have set, to check spreading.
Autumn The plant dies back completely in autumn. Sow seeds.
Winter Fully hardy plant.

Garden Cultivation
Ideal for difficult places or underplanting in borders, it loves growing in the dry shade of trees right up to the trunk. Its rich green leaves make a dense and very decorative ground cover, its underground runners spreading rapidly in the right situation.

It prefers a rich alkaline soil with some moisture during the spring.

Harvesting
The true aroma (which is like new mown hay) comes to the fore when it is dried. Dry flowers and leaves together in early summer.

CONTAINER GROWING

Make sure the container is large enough, otherwise it will become root-bound very quickly. The compost should be the bark, peat mix (see p.591). Only feed with liquid fertilizer when the plant is flowering. Position the container in semi-shade and do not over-water.

CULINARY

Add the flowers to salads. Main ingredients for a modern day May Wine would be a bottle of hock, a glass of sherry, sugar, and strawberries, with a few sprigs of woodruff thrown in an hour before serving.

MEDICINAL

A tea made from the leaves is said to relieve stomach pain, act as a diuretic, and be beneficial for those prone to gall stones.

Sweet woodruff tea

WARNING

Consumption of large quantities can produce symptoms of poisoning, including dizziness and vomiting.

Glycyrrhiza glabra

LIQUORICE

Also known as Licorice, Sweet Licorice and Sweetwood.
From the family Papilionaceae.

This plant, which is a native of the Mediterranean region, is commercially grown throughout the temperate zones of the world and extensively cultivated in Russia, Iran, Spain and India. It has been used medicinally for 3,000 years and was recorded on Assyrian tablets and Egyptian papyri. The Latin name *Glycyrrhiza* comes from 'glykys' meaning sweet, and 'rhiza' root.

It was first introduced to England by Dominican friars in the 16th century and became an important crop. The whole of the huge cobbled courtyard of Pontefract Castle was covered by top soil simply to grow liquorice. It is sad that Pontefract cakes are made from imported liquorice today.

Liquorice sticks

SPECIES

Glycyrrhiza glabra
Liquorice
Hardy perennial. Ht 1.2m (4ft), spread 1m (3ft). Pea-like, purple/blue and white flowers borne in short spikes on erect stems in late summer. Large greenish leaves divided into oval leaflets.

CULTIVATION

Propagation
Seed
The seedlings often damp off. In cooler climates the seed tends not to be viable. Root division is much easier.

Division
Divide when the plant is dormant, making sure the root has one or more buds. Place into pots half filled with compost. Cover with compost. Water well and leave in a warm place until shoots appear. Harden off, then plant out in early spring or autumn. If the latter, winter in a cold greenhouse or cold frame.

Pests and Diseases
Largely pest and disease free.

Maintenance
Spring Divide established plants.
Summer Do nothing.
Autumn Divide established plants if necessary.
Winter In very cold winters protect first year plants.

Garden Cultivation
Liquorice needs a rich, deep, well-cultivated soil.
Plant pieces of the root, each with a bud, directly into a prepared site 15cm (6in) deep and 1m (3ft) apart in early spring or in autumn during the dormant season if the ground is workable and not frosty.
Liquorice does best in long, hot summers, but will need extra watering if your soil is very free draining.

Harvesting
Harvest roots for drying in early winter from established 3 or 4 year old plants.

CONTAINER GROWING

Never displays as well as in the garden. Use a soil-based compost. Feed throughout the growing season and water until it dies back.

CULINARY

Liquorice is used as a flavouring in the making of Guinness and other beers.

MEDICINAL

The juice from the roots provides commercial liquorice. It is used either to mask the unpleasant flavour of other medicines or to provide its own soothing action on troublesome coughs. The dried root, stripped of its bitter bark, is recommended as a remedy for colds, sore throats and bronchial catarrh.

Liquorice is a gentle laxative and lowers stomach acid levels, so relieving heartburn. It has a remarkable power to heal stomach ulcers because it spreads a protective gel over the stomach wall and in addition it eases spasms of large intestine. It also increases the flow of bile and lowers blood cholesterol levels.

WARNING

Large doses of liquorice cause side effects, notably headaches, high blood pressure and water retention.

Helichrysum italicum

CURRY PLANT

From the family Asteraceae.

This plant is from southern Europe and has adapted well to damper, cooler climates. It is the sweet curry scent of its leaves that has caused its recent rise in popularity.

SPECIES

Helichrysum italicum (angustifolium)
Curry Plant
Hardy evergreen perennial. Ht 60cm (24in), spread 1m (3ft). Clusters of tiny mustard yellow flowers in summer. Narrow, aromatic, silver leaves. Highly scented. Planting distance for hedge 60cm (2ft).

Helichrysum italicum 'Dartington'
Curry Plant, Dartington
Hardy evergreen perennial. Ht 45cm (18in), spread 60cm (24in). Compact plant with clusters of small yellow flowers in summer. Grey green, highly scented, narrow leaves (half the size of **H. italicum**). Its compact upright habit makes this a good plant for hedges and edging in the garden. Planting distance for hedge 30cm (1ft).

Curry plant flowers

Helichrysum microphyllum (Willd.)
Curry Plant Dwarf
Hardy evergreen perennial. Ht 30cm (12in), spread 45cm (18in). Clusters of tiny mustard yellow flowers in summer. Narrow, aromatic, silver leaves. Ideal for formal hedging and knot gardens. Planting distance for hedge 30cm (1ft).

Helichrysum italicum subsp. serotinum
Curry Plant
Hardy evergreen perennial. Ht 60cm (24in), spread 1m (3ft). Broad clusters of small bright yellow flowers, produced on upright white shoots. Narrow, aromatic, sliver/grey leaves. Planting distance for hedge 60cm (2ft).

CULTIVATION

Propagation
Seed
I have not known **H. italicum** set good seed. For this reason I advise cuttings.

Cuttings
Take softwood cuttings in spring and semi-ripe ones in autumn.

Pests and Diseases
Pests give this highly aromatic plant a wide berth, and it is usually free from disease.

Curry plant *Helichrysum italicum*

Maintenance
Spring Trim established plants after frosts to maintain shape and promote new growth. Take softwood cuttings.
Summer Trim back after flowering, but not too hard.
Autumn Take semi-ripe wood cuttings.
Winter If the temperature falls below −10°C (14°F), protect from frost.

Garden Cultivation
The curry plant makes an attractive addition to the garden and it imparts a strong smell of curry even if untouched. It is one of the most silvery of shrubs and makes a striking visual feature all year round.
   Plant in full sun in a well-drained soil. Do not cut the curry plant as hard back as cotton lavender but it is worth giving a good hair cut after flowering to stop the larger ones flopping and to keep the shape of the smaller ones.
   If it is an exceptionally wet winter, and you do not have a free-draining soil, lift some plants, and keep in a cold greenhouse, or cold frame.

Harvesting
Pick leaves at any time for fresh use. Pick the flowers when fully open. Dry by hanging in small bunches upside down in an airy place.

CONTAINER GROWING

Dwarf and Dartington curry plants grow happily in large containers (at least 20cm (8in) in diameter). Place in the sun to get the best effect, and do not over-water.

CULINARY

There are not many recipes for the curry plant in cooking, and in truth the leaves smell stronger than they taste, but a small sprig stuffed into the cavity of a roasting chicken makes an interesting variation on tarragon.
   Add sprigs to vegetables, rice dishes and pickles for a mild curry flavour. Remove before serving.

OTHER USES

The bright yellow button flowers add colour to potpourris.

Hesperis matronalis

SWEET ROCKET

Also known as Damask Violet and Dame's Violet. From the family Brassicaceae.

This sweet-smelling herb is indigenous to Italy. It can now be found growing wild in much of the temperate world as a garden escapee. The old Greek name *Hesperis* was used by Theophrastus, the Greek botanist (370–285 BC). It is derived from 'hesperos', meaning evening, which is when the flowers are at their most fragrant.

Sweet rocket
Hesperis matronalis

SPECIES

Hesperis matronalis
Sweet Rocket
Hardy biennial; very occasionally it will be a perennial, sending out new shoots from the rootstock. Ht 60–90cm (2–3ft), spread 25cm (10in). The 4-petalled flowers are all sweetly scented and come in many colours – pink, purple, mauve and white – in the summer of the second year. The leaves are green and lance shaped.
There is a double-flowered form of this plant – *Hesperis matronalis* double. It can only be propagated by cuttings or division and needs a more sandy loam soil than sweet rocket.

CULTIVATION

Propagation
Seed
Sow the seed in the autumn in prepared seed or plug trays, covering the seeds with perlite. Winter the young plants in a cold greenhouse for planting out in the spring at a distance of 45cm (18in) apart. Propagated this way it may flower the first season as well as the second.

Pests and Diseases
This herb is largely free from pests and diseases.

Sweet rocket
Hesperis matronalis

Maintenance
Spring Sow seed outdoors.
Summer In the second year dead head flowers to prolong flowering.
Autumn Sow seed under protection.
Winter No need to protect.

Garden Cultivation
It likes full sun or light shade and prefers a well-drained fertile soil. The seed can be sown direct into a prepared site in the garden in late spring thinning to 30cm (12in) apart, with a further thinning to 45cm (18in) later on if need be.

Harvesting
Pick leaves when young for eating. Pick flowers as they open for using fresh or for drying.

CONTAINER GROWING

Sweet rocket is a tall plant. It looks attractive if 3 or 4 1-year-old plants are potted together, positioned to make the most of the scent on a summer evening. Use the bark, peat, grit mix of compost (see p.591) and water well in summer months. No need to feed.

CULINARY

Young leaves are eaten occasionally in salads. Use sparingly because they are very bitter. The flowers look attractive tossed in salads. They can also be used to decorate desserts.

OTHER USES

Add dried flowers to potpourris for pastel colours and sweet scent.

Humulus lupulus

HOPS

Also known as Hopbind and Hop vine. From the family Cannabaceae.

Native of the Northern temperate zones, cultivated commercially, especially in Northern Europe, North America and Chile.

Roman records from the 1st century AD describe hops as a popular garden plant and vegetable, the young shoots being sold in markets to be eaten rather like asparagus. Hop gardens did not become widespread in Europe until the 9th century. In Britain the hop was a wild plant and used as a vegetable before it became one of the ingredients of beer. It was not until the 16th century that the word hop and the practice of flavouring and preserving beer with the strobiles or female flowers of the *Humulus lupulus* were introduced into Britain by Flemish immigrants, and replaced traditional bitter herbs such as alehoof and alecost.

During the reign of Henry VIII, Parliament was petitioned against the use of the hop, as it was said that it was a wicked weed that would spoil the taste of the drink, ale, and endanger the people. Needless to say the petition was thrown out. The use of hops revolutionized brewing since it enabled beer to be kept for longer.

Hops have also been used as medicine for at least as long as for brewing. The flowers are famous for their sedative effect and were either drunk as a tea or stuffed in a hop pillow to sleep on.

Common hop
Humulus lupulus

Golden hop
Humulus lupulus
'Aureus'

Humulus lupulus
Common Hop
Hardy perennial, a herbaceous climber. Ht up to 6m (20ft). There are separate female and male plants. The male plant has yellowish flowers growing in branched clusters. They are without sepals and have 5 tepals and 5 stamen. The female plant has tiny greenish yellow, scented flowers, hidden by big scales. The scales become papery when the fruiting heads are ripe. These are the flowers that are harvested for beer. The mid-green leaves have 3 to 5 lobes with sharply toothed edges. The stems are hollow and are covered with tiny hooked prickles. These enable the plant to cling to shrubs, trees, or anything else. It always entwines clockwise.

Humulus lupulus 'Aureus'
Golden Hop
Hardy perennial, a herbaceous climber. Ht up to 6m (20ft), The main difference between this plant and the common hop is that the leaves and flower are much more golden, which makes it very attractive in the garden and in dried flower arrangements. It has the same properties as the common hop.

Common Hop *Humulus lupulus*

CULTIVATION

Propagation
Seed
Beer is made from the un-pollinated female flowers. If you grow from seed you will not know the gender for 2 to 3 years, which is the time it takes before good flowers are produced. Obtain seed from specialist seedsmen.

Sow in summer or autumn. The seed is on the medium to large side so sow sparingly; if using plug trays, 1 per cell. Push the seed in and cover it with the compost. Then cover the tray with a sheet of glass or polythene, and leave somewhere cool to germinate – a cold frame, a cold glasshouse, or a garage. Germination can be very erratic. If the seed is not fresh you may need to give the hot/cold treatment.

Warning: As the seed will be from wild hops these should not be grown in areas of commercial hop growing, because they might contaminate the crop.

Cuttings
Softwood cuttings should be taken in spring or early summer from the female plant. Choose young shoots and take the cuttings in the morning as they will lose water very fast and wilt.

Division
In the spring dig up and divide the root stems and suckers of established plants. Replant 1m (3ft) apart against support.

Pests and Diseases
The most common disease is hop wilt. If this occurs, dig up and burn. Do not plant hops in that area again.

Leaf miner can sometimes be a problem. Remove infected leaves immediately.

The golden variety sometimes suffers from sun scorch. If this occurs prune

to new growth, and change its position if possible the following season.

Maintenance
Spring Divide roots and separate rooted stems and suckers in spring. Re-pot container grown plants. Check trellising.
Summer Sow seed late in the season.
Autumn Cut back remaining growth into the ground. Give the plants a good feed of manure or compost. Bring containers into a cool place.
Winter No need for protection.

Garden Cultivation
For successful plants the site should be sunny and open, the soil needs to be rich in humus and dug deeply. It is not generally necessary to tie the plants if good support is at hand. A word of warning: you must dominate the plant. Certainly it will need thinning and encouraging to entwine where you want it to go rather than where it chooses. But remember that it dies back completely in winter. Cut the plant into the ground each autumn and then give it a good feed of manure or compost.

Harvesting
Pick young fresh side shoots in spring. Gather young fresh leaves as required.

Pick male flowers as required. Pick ripe female flowers in early autumn. Dry and use within a few months, otherwise the flavour becomes unpleasant.

CONTAINER GROWING

Hops, especially the golden variety, can look very attractive in a large container with something to grow up. Use a compost made up of the bark, peat mix (see

p.591), and feed regularly with a liquid fertilizer from late spring to midsummer. Keep well watered in the summer months and fairly dry in winter. It can be grown indoors in a position with good light such as a conservatory, but it seldom flowers. Provide some form of shade during sunny periods. During the winter months, make sure it has a rest by putting the pot in a cool place, keeping the compost on the dry side. Re-pot each year.

OTHER USES

The leaf can be used to make a brown dye. If you live close to a brewery it is worth chatting them up each autumn for the spent hops, which make either a great mulch or a layer in a compost heap.

WARNING

Contact dermatitis can be caused by the pollen of the female flower. Also, hops are not recommended in the treatment of depressive illnesses because of their sedative effect.

MEDICINAL

Hop tea made from the female flower only is recommended for nervous diarrhoea, insomnia and restlessness. It also helps to stimulate appetite, dispel flatulence and relieve intestinal cramps. A cold tea taken an hour before meals

Hop pillow

is particularly good for digestion.

It can be useful combined with fragrant valerian for coughs and nervous spasmodic conditions. Recent research into hops has shown that it contains a certain hormone, which accounts for the beneficial effect of helping mothers improve their milk flow.

To make a hop pillow, sprinkle hops with alcohol and fill a small bag or pillowcase with them (which all in all is bound to knock you out).

CULINARY

In early spring pick the young side shoots, steam them (or lightly boil), and eat like asparagus. The male flowers can be parboiled, cooled and tossed into salads. The young leaves can be quickly blanched to remove any bitterness and added to soups or salads.

Hyoscyamus niger

HENBANE

Also known as Devil's Eye, Hen Pen, Hen Penny, Hog Bean, Stinking Roger, Symphoniaca, Jusquiamus, Henbell, Belene, Hennyibone Hennebane, Poisoned Tobacco and Stinking Nightshade. From the family Solanaceae.

This native of Europe has become widely distributed worldwide and is found growing on waste ground or roadsides on well-drained sandy or chalk soils.

Two famous deaths are attributed to henbane. Hamlet's father was murdered by a distillation of henbane being poured in his ear, and in 1910 Dr Crippen used hyoscine, which is extracted from the plant, to murder his wife. Every part of the plant is toxic.

Henbane has been considered to have aphrodisiac properties and is the main ingredient in some love potions and witches' brews. It was also placed by the hinges of outer doors to protect against sorcery.

SPECIES

Hyoscyamus niger
Henbane
Annual/biennial. Ht up to 80cm (32in), spread 30cm (12in). Flowers bloom in summer, are yellow/brown or cream, funnel-shaped, and usually marked with purple veins. Leaves are hairy with large teeth, and the upper leaves have no stalks. The whole plant smells foul.

Hyoscyamus albus
White Henbane
Annual. Ht 30cm (12in), spread 30cm (12in). Its summer flowers are pale yellow marked with violet veins, funnel-shaped. Leaves are identical to **H. niger**.

CULTIVATION

Propagation
Seed
Sow the fairly small seeds on the surface of pots or trays in spring, and cover with perlite. Germination 10–15 days. If you want henbane to behave like a biennial, sow in early autumn, keeping the soil moist until germination (which can be erratic, but on average takes about 14–21 days). Winter the young plants in a cold frame or cold glasshouse. Plant out the following spring at a distance of 30cm (12in).

Pests and Diseases
This plant in the main is free from pests and diseases.

Maintenance
Spring Sow seed.
Summer Dead-head flowers to maintain plant (wear gloves).
Autumn Sow seed for second-year flowers.
Winter Protect young plants.

Garden Cultivation
Choose the site for planting henbane with care, because it is poisonous. It will tolerate any growing situation but shows a preference for a well-drained sunny site. Sow seeds in late spring. When the seedlings are large enough to handle, thin to 30cm (12in) apart. It can look striking in a mixed border.

Harvesting
Collect seed when the head turns brown and begins to open at the end.

CONTAINER GROWING

Inadvisable to grow such a poisonous plant this way.

MEDICINAL

This plant was used for a wide range of conditions which required sedation. The alkaloid hyoscine, which is derived from the green tops and leaves, is used as a hypnotic and brain sedative for the seasick, excitable and insane. It is also used externally in analgesic preparations to relieve rheumatism and arthritis. The syrup has a sedative effect in cases of Parkinson's disease.

WARNING

The whole plant is poisonous. Children have been poisoned by eating the seeds or seed pods. Use preparation and dosage strictly only under medical direction.

Hypericum perforatum

ST JOHN'S WORT

Also known as Warriors Wound, Amber, Touch and Heal, Grace of God and Herb of St John. From the family Clusiaceae.

This magical herb is found in temperate zones of the world in open situations on semi-dry soils.

Whoever treads on St John's Wort after sunset will be swept up on the back of a magic horse that will charge round the heavens until sunrise before depositing its exhausted rider on the ground.

Besides its magical attributes, *Hypericum* has medicinal properties and was universally known as the 'Grace of God'. In England it cured mania, in Russia it gave protection against hydrophobia and the Brazilians knew it as an antidote to snake bite. St John's Wort ('wort', incidentally, is Anglo-Saxon for 'medicinal herb') has been used to raise ghosts and exorcise spirits. When crushed, the leaves release a balsamic odour similar to incense, which was said to be strong enough to drive away evil spirits. The red pigment from the crushed flowers was taken to signify the blood of St John at his beheading, for the herb is in full flower on 24th June, St John's Day.

Division
Divide established plants in the autumn.

Pests and Diseases
Largely free from pests and diseases.

Maintenance
Spring Sow seeds.
Summer Cut back after flowering to stop self-seeding.
Autumn Divide established clumps.
Winter No need for protection, fully hardy.

Garden Cultivation
Tolerates most soils, in sun or light shade, but it can be invasive in light soils.

Harvesting
Harvest leaves and flowers as required.

OTHER USES

The flowers release a yellow dye with alum, and a red dye with alcohol.

WARNING

St John's Wort has sometimes poisoned livestock. Its use also makes the skin sensitive to light.

MEDICINAL

Oil extracted by macerating the flowers in vegetable oil and applied externally eases neuralgia and the pain of sciatica wounds, varicose veins, ulcers and sunburn. Only take internally under supervision.

SPECIES

Hypericum perforatum
St John's Wort
Hardy perennial. Ht 30–90cm (12–36in), spread 30cm (12in). Scented yellow flowers with black dots in summer. The small leaves are stalkless; covered with tiny perforations (hence **perforatum**), which are in fact translucent glands. This is the magical species.

CULTIVATION

Propagation
Seed
Sow very small seed in spring into prepared seed or plug trays, and cover with perlite. Germination is usually in 10–20 days depending on the weather. When the seedlings are large enough to handle and after a period of hardening off, plant out 30cm (12in) apart.

CONTAINER GROWING

Can be grown in containers, but it is a bit tall so you do need a large clump for it to look effective. Use a soil-based compost. Water in the summer months; only feed with liquid fertilizer twice during the growing season, otherwise it produces more leaf than flower.

'Purge me with Hyssop and I shall be clean'
(Psalm 51, verse 7).

Hyssopus officinalis

HYSSOP

From the family Lamiaceae.

Hyssop is a native of the Mediterranean region, where it grows wild on old walls and dry banks. It is found as a garden escapee elsewhere in Europe and has been cultivated in gardens for about the last 600 years. It was one of the herbs taken to the New World by the colonists to use in tea, in herbal tobacco and as an antiseptic.

There has been much to-ing and fro-ing about whether common hyssop is the one mentioned in the Bible. Some say it was oregano or savory. However, present thinking is that hyssop is flavour of the month especially since it has been discovered that the mould that produces penicillin grows on its leaf. This may have acted as an antibiotic protection when lepers were bathed in hyssop.

The Persians used distilled hyssop water as a body lotion to give a fine colour to their skin.

Hippocrates recommended hyssop for chest complaints, and today herbalists still prescribe it.

Hyssop *Hyssopus officinalis*

SPECIES

These are the common hyssops, readily available from nurseries and garden centres.

Hyssopus officinalis
Hyssop
Also known as Blue Hyssop
Hardy semi-evergreen perennial. Ht 80cm (32in), spread 90cm (36in). Blue flowers from summer to early autumn. Small, narrow, lance-shaped leaves, aromatic and darkish green.

Hyssop *Hyssopus officinalis*

Hyssopus officinalis f. albus
White Hyssop
Semi-evergreen hardy perennial. Ht 80cm (32in), spread 90cm (36in). White flowers from summer to early autumn. Small, narrow, lance-shaped leaves, aromatic, and darkish green in colour.

Hyssopus officinalis subsp. aristatus
Rock Hyssop
Hardy, semi-evergreen, perennial. Ht 30cm (12in), spread 60cm (24in). Dark blue flowers from summer to early autumn. Small, narrow, lance-shaped leaves, aromatic and darkish green.

Hyssopus officinalis 'Roseus'
Pink Hyssop
Hardy, semi-evergreen, perennial. Ht 80cm (32in), spread 90cm (36in). Pink flowers from summer to early autumn. Small, narrow, lance-shaped leaves, aromatic and darkish green.

Pink hyssop
Hyssopus officinalis 'Roseus'

CULTIVATION

Propagation
Seeds
In early spring sow the small seeds in plug or seed trays under protection, using the bark and peat mix of compost. Cover with perlite. If very early in spring, a bottom heat of 15–21°C (60–70°F) would be beneficial. When the seedlings are large enough, either pot up or transplant into the garden after a period of hardening off. Plant at a distance of 30cm (12in) apart. All varieties can be grown from seed with the exception of rock hyssop, which can only be grown from cuttings. However, if you want a guaranteed pink or white hyssop, cuttings are a more reliable method.

Cuttings
In late spring, early summer take softwood cuttings from the new lush growth and non-flowering stems.

Pests and Diseases
This genial plant rarely suffers from pests or diseases.

Maintenance
Spring Sow seeds. Trim mature plants. Trim hedges.
Summer Dead-head flowers to maintain supply, trim after flowering to maintain shape. Trim hedges.
Autumn Cut back only in mild areas.
Winter Protect in cold, wet winters and temperatures that fall below −5°C (23°F). Use agricultural fleece, straw, bracken, etc.

Garden Cultivation
This attractive plant, which has only recently become popular again, likes to be planted in conditions similar to rosemary and thyme, a well-drained soil in a sunny position. The seeds can be sown directly into the ground in very late spring or early summer, when the soil is warm. Thin to 30cm (12in) apart if being grown as specimen plants. If for hedging, 18cm (7in).

As all parts of the plant are pleasantly aromatic and the flowers very attractive, plant it where it can be seen and brushed against. The flowers are also attractive to bees and butterflies. For these reasons hyssop makes a very good hedge or edging plant. Trim the top shoots to encourage bushy growth. In early spring, trim the plant into a tidy shape with scissors. To keep the plant flowering in summer, remove the dead heads. Cut back to 20cm (8in) in autumn in mild areas, or trim back after flowering in cold areas. Keep formal edges well clipped during the growing season.

Harvesting
Cut young leaves for drying in summer. The flowers should be picked during the summer too, when they are fully opened. The scent is generally improved with drying.

MEDICINAL

An infusion is used mainly for coughs, whooping cough, asthma and bronchitis, and upper respiratory catarrh. It is also used for inflammation of the urinary tract. Externally it can be used for bruises and burns. It was once a country remedy for rheumatism.

COMPANION PLANTING
Grow near cabbages to lure away cabbage whiteflies. Plant near vines to increase yield.

WARNING

Hyssop should not be used in cases of nervous irritability. Strong doses, particularly those of distilled essential oil, can cause muscular spasms. This oil should not be used in aromatherapy for highly strung patients, as it can cause epileptic symptoms. Do not use continuously for extended periods. No form of hyssop should be taken during pregnancy.

Hyssop sugar syrup

CONTAINER GROWING

Hyssop is a lovely plant in containers. It is happy in plenty of sunshine and prefers a south-facing wall. It also likes dry conditions and its tough leaves are not affected by the fumes of city centres, making it ideal for window boxes. Equally, it is good on a patio as the scent is lovely on a hot summer's evening. Give it a liquid feed only during the flowering period. Cut back after flowering to maintain shape.

CULINARY

The flowers are delicious tossed in a green salad. In small amounts, leaves aid digestion of fatty foods but as they are somewhat pungent use them sparingly. The herb has a slightly bitter, minty taste and is therefore good flavouring in salads or as an addition to game, meats and soups, stews and stuffings. A good idea is to add a teaspoon of chopped leaf to a Yorkshire pudding batter. Hyssop is still used in Gascony as one of the herbs in bouquet garni and for flavouring a concentrated purée of tomatoes preserved for the winter. It is used in continental sausages and also added to American fruit pies, $\frac{1}{4}$ teaspoon hyssop being sprinkled over the fruit before the top crust goes on.

When making a sugar syrup for fruit, add a sprig of hyssop as you boil the sugar and water; it adds a pleasant flavour, and the sprig can be removed before adding the fruit. When making cranberry pie, use the leaves as a lining for the dish.

Basque-Style Chicken
Serves 6

1.5 kg (3lb 6oz) chicken
4 sweet peppers (2 red, 2 green)
Hyssop olive oil
5 tablespoons dry white wine
4 medium tomatoes, peeled and roughly chopped
6 onions
4 cloves of garlic
1 bouquet garni with a sprig of hyssop
salt and pepper

De-seed and slice the peppers into thin strips. Gently fry them in a small amount of oil until soft. Remove from pan and put to one side. Joint the chicken and gently fry in the oil, turning all the time. Transfer to a casserole, and season with salt and pepper, moisten with the wine, and leave over a gentle heat to finish cooking. Slice the onions and peel the garlic cloves, and soften without colouring in the olive oil in the frying pan. Then add the tomatoes, peppers and bouquet garni, and season. When reduced almost to a cream, turn into the casserole over the chicken and keep on a low heat until ready to serve, about a further 20–30 minutes.

Inula helenium

ELECAMPANE

Also known as Allecampane, July Campane, Elicompane, Dock, Sunflower, Wild Sunflower, Yellow Starwort, Elfdock, Elfwort, Horse Elder, Horse Heal and Scabwort. From the family Asteraceae.

Elecampane originates from Asia whence, through cultivation, it spread across Western Europe to North America and now grows wild from Nova Scotia to Ontario, North Carolina, and Missouri.

Sources for the derivation of the principal common name, Elecampane, and the generic/species name, *Inula helenium*, are not altogether satisfactory, but I have found three possible explanations.

Helen of Troy was believed to be gathering the herb when she was abducted by Paris, hence 'helenium'.

Down through the ages the herb was considered as good medicinally for horse or mule as for man; it was even sometimes called horselene. 'Inula' could come from 'hinnulus' meaning 'a young mule'.

Finally, the Romans called the herb *Enula Campana* (Inula of the fields) from which Elecampane is a corruption.

According to the Roman writer Pliny, the Emperor Julius Augustus enjoyed elecampane so much he proclaimed, 'Let no day past without eating some of the roots candied to help the digestion and cause mirth'. The Romans also used it as a candied sweetmeat, coloured with cochineal. This idea persisted for centuries, and in the Middle Ages, apothecaries sold the candied root in flat pink sugary cakes, which were sucked to alleviate asthma and indigestion and to sweeten the breath. Tudor herbalists also candied them for the treatment of coughs, catarrhs, bronchitis and chest ailments. Their use continued until the 1920s as a flavouring in sweets.

I have discovered an Anglo-Saxon ritual using elecampane – part medicinal, part magical. Prayers were sung of the Helenium and its roots dug up by the medicinal man, who had been careful not to speak to any disreputable creature – man, elf, goblin or fairy – he chanced to meet on the way to the ceremony. Afterwards the elecampane root was laid under the altar for the night and eventually mixed with betony and lichen from a crucifix. The medicine was taken against elf sickness or elf disease.

There is an ancient custom in Scandinavia of putting a bunch of elecampane in the centre of a nosegay of herbs to symbolize the sun and the head of Odin, the greatest of Norse gods.

Inula helenium **seed heads**

SPECIES

Inula helenium
Elecampane
Hardy perennial. Ht 1.5–2.4m (5–8ft) spread 1m (3ft) Bright yellow, ragged, daisy-like flowers in summer. The leaves are large, oval-toothed, slightly downy underneath, and of a mid-green colour. Dies back fully in winter.

Inula hookeri
Hardy perennial. Ht 75cm (30in) spread 45cm (18in). Yellowish green, ragged, daisy-like flowers slightly scented in summer. Lance-shaped hairy leaves, smaller than **I. magnifica**, and mid-green in colour. Dies back fully in winter.

Inula magnifica
Hardy perennial. Ht 1.8m (6ft), spread 1m (3ft). Large, ragged, daisy-like flowers. Lots of large, dark green lance-shaped rough leaves. May need staking in an exposed garden. This is often mistaken for **I. helenium**, the leaf colour is the biggest difference, and on average **I. magnifica** grows much larger. Dies back fully in winter.

CULTIVATION

Propagation
Seed
The seed is similar to dandelion; when the plant has germinated you can see the seeds flying all over the garden, which should be all the warning you need... Sow on the surface of a pot or plug tray. Cover with perlite. Germination is 2–4 weeks, depending on sowing season and seed viability. Prick out and plant 1–1.5m (3–5ft) apart when the seedlings are large enough to handle.

Root Division
If the plant grows too big for its position in the garden, divide in the autumn when the plant has died back. As the roots are very strong

choose the point of division carefully. Alternatively remove the offshoots that grow around the parent plant; each has its own root system, so they can be planted immediately in a prepared site elsewhere in the garden. This can be done in autumn or spring.

Pests and Diseases
It rarely suffers from disease, although if the autumn is excessively wet, as the leaves die back, they may suffer from a form of mildew. Simply cut back and destroy the leaves.

Maintenance
Spring Sow seed. Divide established plants.
Summer Remove flowerheads as soon as flowering finishes.
Autumn Cut back growth to stop self-seeding and to prevent the plant becoming untidy. Remove offshoots for replanting.
Winter The plant dies back so needs no protection.

Garden Cultivation
Plant in a moist, fertile soil, in full sun, sheltered from the wind (elecampane grows tall and would otherwise need staking). It can look very striking at the back of a border against a stone wall, or in front of a screen of deciduous trees. In a very dry summer it may need watering.

Elecampane *Inula helenium*

Harvesting
Dig up second- or third-year roots in the autumn, they can be used as a vegetable, or dried for use in medicine.
The flowers are good in autumn flower arrangements and dry well upside down if you cut them just before the seeds turn brown.

CONTAINER GROWING

Elecampane grows too big for most containers and is easily blown over.

CULINARY

Elecampane has a sharp, bitter flavour. Use dried pieces or cook as a root vegetable.

OTHER USES
Your cat may be interested to know that scientific research indicates that elecampane has a sedative effect on mice.

Seeds on a leaf in autumn

MEDICINAL

The main use is for respiratory complaints, at one time specifically for TB. It is still employed in folk medicine as a favourite constituent of cough remedies, and has always been popular both as a medicine and as a condiment.

In America, elecampane oil is used for respiratory, intestinal catarrh, chronic diarrhoea, chronic bronchitis and whooping cough.

A decoction of the root has long been used externally for scabies, herpes, acne and other skin diseases, hence its country name Scabwort.

Recent research shows that the lactines found in the roots are powerful agents against bacteria and fungi.

Elecampane oil

Iris

IRIS

From the family Iridaceae.

All those mentioned are native of the northern hemisphere and are cultivated in varying conditions, from dry light soil (orris – *Iris* 'Florentina') to damp boggy soils (blue flag iris – *Iris versicolor*).

The Greek word 'iris', meaning 'rainbow' and the name of the Greek goddess of the rainbow, was appended to describe the plant's variable colours. The iris is one of the oldest cultivated plants – it is depicted on the wall of an Egyptian temple dating from 1500 BC.

In this very large family, three stand out for their beneficial herbal qualities. Orris has a violet-scented root which has been powdered and used in perfumes since the ancient Egyptians and Greeks. The Latin *Iris* 'Florentina' depicts its association with Florence in the early Middle Ages. It is said to be the fleur de lys of French heraldry.

The blue flag iris is the common wetlands plant, native to eastern North America and exported from there to Europe. Employed by the Indians and early settlers as a remedy for gastric complaints, it was included in the United States Pharmacopeia and is still believed in folk medicine to be a blood purifier of use in eruptive skin conditions. Sometimes the plant is known as liver lily because of its purifying effect.

The root of the yellow flag iris, a native of the British Isles, was powdered and used as an ingredient in Elizabethan snuff. It was taken to America and Australia by the earliest settlers.

SPECIES

Iris 'Florentina'
Orris
Also known as Florentine Iris and Oris root. Hardy perennial. Ht 60cm–1m (2–3 ft). Spread indefinite. Large white flowers tinged with pale lavender and with a yellow beard appear early to mid-summer. Green, sword-shaped leaves. The root stock is stout and rhizomatous with a violet scent. Grows well throughout Europe and North America, except in the warm moist climate of Florida and the Gulf Coast.

Iris germanica
Purple Iris
Also known as Garden Iris, and Flag Iris. Hardy perennial. Ht 60–90cm (2–3ft), spread indefinite. The fragrant flowers are blue/violet, occasionally white, and form early to midsummer. Leaves are greyish-green and sword-shaped. The root is thickish rhizome. There are many cultivated varieties. It is grown commercially for the rhizomes and, like **Iris 'Florentina'**, is used in perfumery and pharmaceutical preparations.

Iris pseudacorus
Yellow Iris (Yellow Flag)
Perennial. Ht 40cm–150cm (16in–5ft), spread indefinite. Flowers are bright yellow with radiating brown veins and very slightly scented. They appear early to midsummer. The root is thick rhizome from which many rootlets descend.

Yellow iris *Iris pseudacorus*

Iris versicolor
Blue Flag Iris

Also known as Flag Lily, Fleur de Lys, Flower du Luce, Iris, Liver Lily, Poison Flags, Snake Lily, Water Flag and Wild Iris. Hardy perennial. Ht 30–100cm (12–39in), spread indefinite. Flowers claret-purple-blue in summer. Large, sword-shaped, green leaves. Root large and rhizomatous.

Purple iris *Iris germanica*

CULTIVATION

Propagation
Seed

All the irises produce large seeds, which take some time to germinate and often benefit from a period of stratification. As the seeds are of a good size, sow directly into an 8cm (3in) pot in autumn, using a peat, grit, bark mix of compost (see p.591). Water in well, and cover the pots with cling film (to stop the mice eating the seed). Put outside to get the weather. Check that the compost remains damp. If there is any danger of it drying out, stand the container in water. This is especially important for blue and yellow flag irises.

Division

Divide the rhizome roots in late spring or early autumn. This suits all the varieties. Replant immediately in a prepared site. Leave a decent distance between plants; spread is indefinite.

Pests and Diseases

The only major pest is the iris sawfly. The darkish grey larvae feed along the leaf-margins, removing large chunks. Pupation takes place in the soil beneath or near the host plants, and the adult sawflies are on the wing during early to mid-summer. Cut off infected leaves only if you find them unsightly – the plant will not be weakened. This is an annual pest and there is not much one can do to prevent it.

Maintenance

Spring Divide roots of mature plants.
Summer Collect the seeds as soon as ripe.
Autumn Sow seeds and leave outside.
Winter Fully hardy; no need for protection.

Garden Cultivation

Orris and common iris prefer a well-drained, rich soil and a sunny situation. When planting, make sure that part of the rhizomes are exposed.

Yellow and blue flag irises are marsh-loving plants, ideal for those with a pond or ditch or piece of boggy ground. They grow happily in semi-shade but need full sun in order to produce the maximum bloom. In deep shade it will not flower at all but will spread quickly by stout underground rhizomes. A measure of control will be necessary.

Harvesting

The full violet fragrance of orris will not be apparent until the roots are 2 years old. Dig up these rhizomes in autumn and dry immediately.

Gather yellow flag flowers and roots for use as a dye, in early summer and autumn respectively.

Dig up blue flag roots in autumn and dry.

CONTAINER GROWING

These irises grow on strong rhizomes, so make sure that the container is strong enough, large enough, and so shaped that it will accommodate the plant happily and not blow over.

For the bog lovers use more peat than usual in the compost mix – up the ratio to 75%, but put lots of gravel and broken crocks in the bottom of the container to make up for loss of weight. For the dry gang, use a soil-based compost. Do not let either compost dry out. They become pot-bound very quickly, so split and re-pot every year.

WARNING

Always wash your hands well after handling this plant as it can cause uncontrollable vomiting and violent diarrhoea. Large doses of the fresh root can cause nausea, vomiting and facial neuralgias.

Iris used as a fixative in a potpourri

OTHER USES

The violet-scented, powdered root of orris is used as a fresh scent to linen, a base for dry shampoos, a base for tooth powders, in face-packs, as a fixative in potpourris and as a dry shampoo.

Flowers of yellow flag make a good yellow dye, while the rhizomes yield a grey or black dye when used with an iron mordant.

MEDICINAL

Orris and yellow flag are rarely used medicinally nowadays. However, herbalists still use the blue flag as a blood purifier acting on the liver and gall bladder to increase the flow of bile, and as an effective cleanser of toxins. It is also said to relieve flatulence and heartburn, belching and nausea, and headaches associated with digestive problems.

CULINARY

Apparently, if you roast the seed of the yellow flag iris, they make an excellent coffee substitute. Apart from this little gem, I cannot find any culinary uses for irises.

Juniperus communis

JUNIPER

From the family Cupressaceae.

Juniper is widely distributed throughout the world and grows either as a shrub or a small tree. It is a native of the Mediterranean region, but also grows in the Arctic, from Norway to the Soviet Union, in the North and West Himalayas and in North America. It is found on heaths, moorlands, open coniferous forests and mountain slopes.

This widely distributed plant was first used by the ancient Greek physicians and its use has continued right up to modern days. It was believed to cure snake bites and protect against infectious diseases like the plague.

The English word 'gin' is derived from an abbreviation of Holland's 'geneva' as the spirit was first called. This in turn stems from the Dutch 'jenever' meaning juniper.

SPECIES

Juniper is a conifer, a group of trees and shrubs distinguished botanically from others by its production of seeds exposed or uncovered on the scales of the fruit. True to form, it is evergreen and has needle-like leaves.

There are many species and varieties available, **Juniperus communis**, being the main herbal variety. On the varieties detailed below, the flowers are all very similar: male flowers are very small catkins; female flowers are small, globose and berry-like, with usually 3–8 fleshy scales. Over a period of 3 years, these turn blue and then finally black as they ripen.

Irish Juniper
Juniperis communis 'Hibernica'

Juniperus communis 'Compressa'
Juniper Compressa
Hardy evergreen perennial tree. Ht 75cm (30in), spread 15cm (6in). The leaves are small and bluish-green, sharply pointed and aromatic. Very slow growing with an erect habit, ideal for rock gardens or containers.

Juniperus communis 'Hibernica'
Irish Juniper
Hardy evergreen perennial tree. Ht 3–5m (10–15ft), spread 30cm (12in). Leaves small and bluish/silvery-green, sharply pointed and aromatic. Columnar in shape and with a hint of silver in certain lights. Very slow growing.

Juniperus communis 'Hornibrookii'
Juniper Hornibrookii
Hardy evergreen perennial tree. Ht 50cm (20in), spread 2m (6ft). Leaves small and darkish green, sharply pointed and aromatic. A big carpeting plant.

Juniperus communis
Juniper
Hardy evergreen perennial. Ht 30cm–8m (1–25ft), spread 1–4m (3–12ft) – size of the plant very dependent on where it is growing. Leaves small and bright green, sharply pointed and aromatic.

Juniperus communis 'Prostrata'
Prostrate Juniper
Hardy evergreen perennial tree. Ht 20–30cm (8–12in), spread 1–2m (3–6ft). Leaves small and bluish-green, sharply pointed and aromatic. A smaller carpeting plant.

CULTIVATION

Propagation
Seed

All the species can be propagated by seed. Sow seeds taken from ripe berries in a cold greenhouse, cold frame or cold conservatory in early autumn. As junipers on the whole are extremely slow growing, it is best to grow the seedlings in a controlled environment for 1 or 2 years, before planting out in a permanent position in the garden. Start in seed or plug trays; then, when the seedlings are large enough, pot up into small pots using a soil-based compost. This method is the easiest but to be sure of the plant's gender and leaf colour, taking cuttings is more reliable.

Cuttings

It is quite easy to raise juniper from semi-hardwood cuttings taken from fresh current growth in spring or autumn.

Pests and Diseases

Various rusts attack juniper. If you see small rusty spores on the underside of the leaves, cut the branches out and burn them.

Honey fungus attacks many conifers, especially young plants. If this occurs, dig up the plant, making sure you have all the roots, burn it, and plant no further trees in that space.

Maintenance

Spring Plant out 2-year-old plants. Remove any leaders growing incorrectly in late spring/early summer.
Summer Take semi-hardwood cuttings.
Autumn Sow seeds.
Winter Winter young plants in cold frames, or provide added protection.

Garden Cultivation

Juniper likes an exposed sunny site. It will tolerate an alkaline or neutral soil. Both male and female plants are necessary for berry production. The berries, which only grow on the female bush, can be found in various stages of ripeness on the same plant. Their flavour is stronger when grown in warm climates.

To maintain the shape of the juniper, trim with secateurs to ensure that there is no more than one leader, the strongest and straightest. Remember, when trimming, that most conifers will not make new growth when cut back into old wood, or into branches that have turned brown.

Harvesting

Harvest the berries when ripe in late summer. Dry them spread out on a tray, as you would leaves.

CULINARY

Crushed berries are an excellent addition to marinades, sauerkraut and stuffing for guinea fowl and other game birds. Although no longer generally considered as a spice, it is still an important flavouring for certain meats, liqueurs, and especially gin.

Pork chops with juniper

Pork Chops Marinated with Juniper
Serves 4

Marinade
2 tablespoons olive oil
6 juniper berries, crushed
2 cloves of garlic, crushed
Salt and pepper

Mix the oil, juniper berries, garlic and seasoning together in a bowl.

4 pork chops
25g (1oz) plain flour
275ml (½ pint) dry cider

Lay the pork chops in the base of a shallow dish and cover them with the marinade, turning the chops over once to make sure they are covered. Leave for a minimum of 3 hours, if possible overnight. Remove the chops from the marinade, and reserve it. Heat a large frying pan and add the reserved marinade. When hot, add the pork chops and cook over a moderate heat for about 20 minutes turning the chops regularly. When all traces of pink have gone from the meat, remove from heat, and put the chops on a plate. Return the pan to the heat and stir the flour into the remaining juices. Add the cider and bring to the boil. Return the chops to the sauce in the pan. Heat through slowly, and serve with mashed potato and broccoli.

WARNING

Juniper berries should not be taken during pregnancy or by people with kidney problems. Internal use of the volatile oil must only ever be prescribed by professionals.

MEDICINAL

Juniper is used in the treatment of cystitis, rheumatism and gout. Steamed inhalations of the berries are an excellent treatment for coughs, colds and catarrh.

CONTAINER GROWING

Juniper is slow growing and can look most attractive in pots. Use a soil-based compost, starting off with a suitable-sized pot, only potting up once a year if necessary. If the root ball looks happy, do not disturb it. Do not over-water. As the plant is hardy and evergreen, the container will need more protection than the plant during the winter months. Feed during the summer months only with a liquid fertilizer as per manufacturer's guidelines.

Laurus nobilis

BAY

from the family Lauraceae

Bay is an evergreen tree native to southern Europe, and now found throughout the world.

That this ancient plant was much respected in Roman times is reflected in the root of its family name, Lauraceae, the Latin 'laurus' meaning 'praise', and in its main species name, *Laurus nobilis*, the Latin 'nobilis' meaning 'famous', 'renowned'. A bay wreath became a mark of excellence for poets and athletes, a symbol of wisdom and glory. The latin 'laureate' means crowned with laurels (synonym for bay), hence Poet Laureate, of course, and the French *baccalaureate*.

The bay tree was sacred even earlier – to Apollo, Greek god of prophecy, poetry and healing. His priestesses ate bay leaves before expounding his oracles at Delphi. As large doses of bay induce the effect of a narcotic, this may explain their trances. His temple had its roof made entirely of bay leaves, ostensibly to protect against disease, witchcraft and lightning. Apollo's son Aesculapius, the Greek god of Medicine, also had bay dedicated to him as it was considered a powerful antiseptic and guard against disease, in particular the plague.

In the 17th century, Culpeper wrote that 'neither witch nor devil, thunder nor lightening, will hurt a man in the place where a bay-tree is.' He also wrote that 'the berries are very effectual against the poison of venomous creatures, and the stings of wasps and bees.'

SPECIES

Laurus azorica (canariensis)
Canary Island Bay
Perennial evergreen tree. Ht to 6m (20ft). Reddish-brown branches, a colour that sometimes extends to the leaves.

Laurus nobilis
Bay
Also known as Sweet Bay, Sweet Laurel, Laurel, Indian Bay, Grecian Laurel. Perennial evergreen tree. Ht up to 8m (26ft), spread 3m (12ft). Small pale yellow waxy flowers in spring. Green oval berries turning black in autumn. The leaves may be added to stock, soups and stews and are among the main ingredients of bouquet garni. *L. nobilis* is the only bay used for culinary purposes.

Standard bay tree

Laurus nobilis 'Aurea'
Golden Bay
Perennial evergreen tree. Ht up to 5m (18ft). Small pale yellow waxy flowers in spring. Green berries turning black in autumn. Golden leaves can look sickly in damp, cooler countries. Needs good protection in winter especially from wind scorch and frosts. Trim in the autumn/spring to maintain the golden leaves.

Laurus nobilis f. angustifolia
Willow Leaf Bay
Perennial evergreen tree. Ht up to 7m (23ft). Narrow leafed variety, said to be hardier than *L. nobilis*. This is not strictly true.

Umbellularia californica
Californian Laurel
Perenial evergreen tree. Ht up to 18m (60ft). Pale yellow flowers in late spring. Very pungent/aromatic leaves. Can cause headaches and nausea when the leaves are crushed. NOT culinary.

CULTIVATION

Propagation
Seed
Bay sets seed in its black berries, but rarely in cooler climates. Sow fresh seed on the surface of either a seed or plug tray or directly into pots. Keep warm: 21°C (65°F). Germination is erratic, may take place within 10–20 days, in 6 months, or sometimes even longer. Make sure the compost is not too wet or it will rot the seeds.

Cuttings
Not a plant for the faint hearted. When I started propagating over 20 years ago I thought my bay cuttings were doing really well, but a year later not one had properly struck, and three-quarters of them had turned black and died. Out of 100 cuttings only one eventually turned into a tree!

A heated propagator is a great help and high humidity is essential. Use either a misting unit or cover the cutting in plastic and maintain the compost or perlite at a steady moisture. It may be an art but worth a try. Cuttings are taken in late summer 10cm (4in) in length.

Bay *Laurus nobilis* **in flower**

Division

If offshoots are sent out by
the parent plant, dig them
up or they will destroy the
shape of the tree.
Occasionally roots come
with them and these then
can be potted up, using the
bark, peat, grit mix of
compost (see p.591). Place a
plastic bag over the pot to
maintain humidity. Leave
somewhere warm and check
from time to time to see if
new shoots are starting.
When they do, remove the
plastic bag. Do not plant out
for at least a year.

Layering

Do it in spring. A good
method of propagating a
difficult plant.

Pests and Diseases

Bay is susceptible to sooty
black spots, caused by the
scale insect which sticks
both to the undersides of
leaves and to the stems,
sucking the sap. Get rid of
them by hand or use a
liquid horticultural soap.

Maintenance

Spring Sow seeds. Cut back
standard and garden bay
trees to maintain shape and
to promote new growth. Cut
back golden bay trees to
maintain colour. Check for
scale insect and eradicate at
first signs. Give container-
grown plants a good liquid
feed.
Summer Check that young
plants are not drying out too
much. In very hot weather,
and especially if you live in a
city, spray-clean container-

grown plants with water.
Propagate by taking stem
cuttings or layering in late
summer.
Autumn Take cuttings of
mature plants. Protect
container-grown plants and
young garden plants.
Garden plants can be
protected either by covering
in straw or bracken, if in a
sufficiently sheltered
position, or by agricultural
fleece.
Winter In severe winters the
leaves will turn brown but
don't despair. come the
spring, it may shoot new
growth from the base. To
encourage this, cut the plant
nearly down to the base.

Garden Cultivation

Bay is shallow rooted and
therefore more prone to
frost damage. Also, leaves
are easily scorched in
extremely cold weather or
in strong cold winds.
Protection is thus essential,
especially for bay trees
under two years old. When
planting out, position the
plant in full sun, protected
from the wind, and in a rich
well-drained soil at least 1m
(3ft) away from other plants
to start with, allowing more
space as the tree matures.
Mulch in the spring to
retain moisture throughout
the summer months.

Harvesting

Being evergreen, leaves can
be taken all year round. It is
fashionable now to preserve
bay leaves in vinegars.
   Berries are cultivated for
use in laurel oil and laurel
butter. The latter is a vital
ingredient of laurin
ointment, which is used in
veterinary medicine.

CONTAINER GROWING

Bay makes a good container
plant. Young plants benefit
from being kept in a
container and indoors for
the winter in cooler
climates. The kitchen
windowsill is ideal. Do not
water too much, and let the
compost dry out in the
winter months.
   Large standard bays or
pyramids look very effective
in half barrels or containers
of an equal size. Anything in
a container will need extra
protection in winter from
frosts and wind, so if the
temperature drops below
−5°C (25°F) bring the plants
in.
   To produce a standard bay
tree, start with a young
containerized plant with a
straight growing stem. As it
begins to grow remove the
lower side shoots, below
where you want the ball to
begin. Allow the tree to
grow to 20cm (8in) higher
than desired, then clip back
the growing tip. Cut the
remaining side shoots down
to about 3 leaves. When the
side shoots have grown a
further 4/5 leaves, trim
again to 2/3 leaves. Keep

repeating this until you have
a leafy ball shape. Once the
shape is established, prune
with secateurs in late spring
and again in late summer to
maintain it.

OTHER USES

Place in flour to deter
weevil. Add an infusion to a
bath to relieve aching limbs.

CULINARY

Fresh leaves are stronger in
flavour than dried ones. Use
in soups, stews and stocks.

Add leaves to poached fish,
like salmon.
Put on the coals of a
barbecue.
Put fresh leaves in jars of
rice to flavour the rice.
Boil in milk to flavour
custards and rice pudding.

Bouquet Garni
I quote from my
grandmother's cookbook,
Food for Pleasure, published
in 1950: 'A bouquet garni is
a bunch of herbs constantly
required in cooking.' The
essential herbs in a bouquet
garni are bay leaf, parsley
and thyme.

Bay bouquet garni

MEDICINAL

*Infuse the leaves to aid
digestion and stimulate
the appetite.*

Lavandula

LAVENDER

From the family Lamiaceae.

Native of the Mediterranean region, Canary Isles and India. Now cultivated in different regions of the world, growing in well-draining soil and warm, sunny climates.

Long before the world manufactured deodorants and bath salts, the Romans used lavender in their bath water; the word is derived from the Latin 'lava', to wash. It was the Romans who first introduced this plant to Britain and from then on monks cultivated it in their monastic gardens. Little more was recorded until Tudor times when people noted its fragrance and a peculiar power to ease stiff joints and relieve tiredness. It was brought in quantities from herb farms to the London Herb Market at Bucklesbury. 'Who will buy my lavender?' became perhaps the most famous of all London street cries.

It was used as a strewing herb for its insect-repellent properties and for masking household and street smells. It was also carried in nosegays to ward off the plague and pestilence. In France in the 17th century, huge fields of lavender were grown for the perfume trade. This has continued to the present day.

SPECIES

This is another big family of plants that are eminently worth collecting. I include here a few of my favourites.

Lavandula angustifolia (spica, officinalis)
Common/English Lavender
Hardy evergreen perennial. Ht 80cm (32in), spread 1m (3ft). Mauve/purple flowers on a long spike in summer. Long, narrow, pale greenish-grey, aromatic leaves. One of the most popular and well known of the lavenders.

Old English lavender
Lavandula x intermedia 'Old English'

Lavandula angustifolia 'Alba'
White Lavender
Hardy evergreen perennial. Ht 70cm (28in), spread 80cm (32in). White flowers on a long spike in summer. Long, narrow, pale greenish-grey, aromatic leaves.

Lavandula angustifolia 'Bowles' Early'
Lavender Bowles
Hardy evergreen perennial. Ht and spread 60cm (24in).

Light blue flowers on a medium size spike in summer. Medium-length, narrow grey-greenish, aromatic leaves.

Lavandula angustifolia 'Folgate'
Lavender Folgate
Hardy evergreen perennial. Ht and spread 45cm (18in). Purple flowers on a medium spike in summer. Leaves as above.

Lavandula angustifolia 'Hidcote'
Lavender Hidcote
Hardy evergreen perennial. Ht and spread 45cm (18in). Dark blue flowers on a medium spike in summer. Fairly short, narrow, aromatic, grey-greenish leaves. One of the most popular lavenders. Often used in hedging, planted at a distance of 30–40cm (12–16in).

Lavandula angustifolia 'Loddon Blue'
Lavender Loddon Blue
Hardy evergreen perennial. Ht and spread 45cm (18in). Pale blue flowers on a medium-length spike in summer. Fairly short, narrow grey-greenish, aromatic leaves. Good compact habit. There is another variety called 'Loddon Pink' – same size, same height, with pale pink flowers.

Lavandula angustifolia 'Munstead'
Lavender Dwarf Munstead
Hardy evergreen perennial. Ht and spread 45cm (18in). Purple/blue flowers on a fairly short spike in summer. Medium length, greenish-grey, narrow, aromatic leaves. This is now a common lavender and used often in hedging, planted at a distance of 30–40cm (12–16in).

Lavender Hidcote *Lavandula angustifolia* 'Hidcote'

Lavandula angustifolia 'Nana Alba'
Dwarf White Lavender
Hardy evergreen perennial. Ht and spread 30cm (12in). White flowers in summer. Green-grey narrow short leaves. This is the shortest growing lavender and is ideal for hedges.

Lavandula angustifolia 'Rosea'
Lavender Pink/Rosea
Hardy evergreen perennial. Ht and spread 45cm (18in). Pink flowers in summer. Medium length greenish-grey, narrow, aromatic leaves.

Lavandula dentata
Fringe Lavender
(sometimes called French Lavender)
Half-hardy evergreen perennial. Ht and spread 60cm (24in). Pale blue/mauve flowers from summer to early autumn. Highly aromatic, serrated, pale green, narrow leaves. This plant is a native of southern Spain and the Mediterranean region and needs protecting in cold damp winters. It is ideal to bring inside into a cool room in early autumn as a flowering pot plant.

Lavandula x intermedia Dutch group
Lavender Vera
Hardy evergreen perennial. Ht and spread 45cm (18in). Purple flowers in summer on fairly long spikes. Long greenish-grey, narrow, aromatic leaves.

Lavandula x intermedia 'Grappenhall'
Lavender Grappenhall
Hardy evergreen perennial. Ht and spread 1m (3ft). Large pale mauve flowers on long spikes in summer. The flowers are much more open than those of other species. Long greenish-grey, narrow, aromatic leaves.

Lavandula x intermedia 'Old English'
Old English Lavender
Hardy evergreen perennial. Ht and spread 60cm (24in). Light lavender-blue flowers on long spikes. Long, narrow, silver/grey/green, aromatic leaves.

French lavender
Lavandula stoechas

Lavandula x intermedia 'Seal'
Lavender Seal
Hardy evergreen perennial. Ht 90cm (3ft), spread 60cm (24in). Long flower stems, mid-purple. Long, narrow, silver/grey/green aromatic leaves.

Lavandula x intermedia 'Twickel Purple'
Lavender Twickel Purple
Hardy evergreen perennial. Ht and spread 50cm (20in). Pale purple flowers on fairly short spike. Medium length, greenish-grey, narrow, aromatic leaves. Compact grower.

Lavender Pedunculata
Lavandula stoechas subsp. *pedunculata*

Lavandula lanata
Woolly Lavender
Hardy evergreen perennial. Ht 50 cm (20in), spread 45cm (18in). Deep purple flowers on short spikes. Short, soft, narrow, silver-grey aromatic foliage.

Lavandula pinnata
Lavender Pinnata
Half-hardy evergreen perennial. Ht and spread 50cm (20in). The flower spikes are a mixture of **L. angustifolia** and **L. stoechas**, purple in colour. Leaves are fern-like, grey, and slightly aromatic. Could be easily mistaken for an **artemisia**. Protect in winter.

Lavandula stoechas
French Lavender
(sometimes called Spanish Lavender)
Hardy evergreen perennial. Ht 50cm (20in). Spread 60cm (24in). Attractive purple bracts in summer. Short, narrow, grey/green, aromatic leaves.

Lavandula stoechas f. leucantha
White French Lavender
As **L. stoechas** except white bracts in summer.

Lavandula stoechas subsp pedunculata
Lavender Pedunculata
(sometimes known as Papillon)
Half-hardy evergreen perennial. Ht and spread 60cm (24in). These attractive purple bracts have an extra centre tuft, which is mauve and looks like two rabbit ears. The aromatic leaves are very narrow, grey and longer than the ordinary **stoechas**. Protect in winter.

Lavandula viridis
Lavender Viridis
Half-hardy evergreen perennial. Ht and spread 60cm (24in). This unusual plant has green bracts with a cream centre tuft. The leaves are green, narrow, and highly aromatic. Protect in winter.

Lavenders – Small (grow to 45–50cm/18–20in)
Lavender Folgate, Lavender Hidcote, Lavender Lodden Pink, Lavender Lodden Blue, Lavender Dwarf Munstead, Dwarf White Lavender, Lavender Twickel Purple.

Lavenders – Medium (grow to 60cm/24in)
Lavender Bowles, Old English Lavender.

Lavenders – Big (70cm/28in and above)
Lavender Grappenhall, White Lavender, Lavender Seal.

Half-hardy Lavenders
Fringe Lavender (50cm/20in), Woolly Lavender (50cm/20in), Lavender Pinnata (50cm/20in), French Lavender (50cm/20in), White French Lavender (50cm/20in), Lavender Pendunculata (60cm/24in), Lavender Viridis (50cm/20in).

Fringe lavender
Lavandula dentata

Lavender viridis
Lavandula viridis

CULTIVATION

Propagation
Seed
Lavender can be grown from seed but it tends not to be true to species, with the exception of **Lavandula stoechas**.

Seed should be sown fresh in the autumn on the surface of a seed or plug tray and covered with perlite. It germinates fairly readily with a bottom heat of 4–10°C (40–50°F). Winter the seedlings in a cold greenhouse or cold conservatory with plenty of ventilation. In the spring, prick out and pot on using the bark, peat, grit mix of compost (see p.591). Let the young plant establish a good size root ball before planting out in a prepared site in the early summer. For other species you will find cuttings much more reliable.

Cuttings
Take softwood cuttings from non-flowering stems in spring. Root in bark, peat, grit mix of compost. Take semi-hardwood cuttings in summer or early autumn from the strong new growth. Once the cuttings have rooted well, it is better to pot them up and winter the young lavenders in a cold greenhouse or conservatory rather than plant them out in the first winter. In the spring, plant them out in well-drained, fertile soil, at a distance of 45–60cm (18–24in) apart or 30cm (12in) apart for an average hedge.

Layering
This is easily done in the autumn. Most hardy lavenders respond well to this form of propagation.

Pests and Diseases
One of the chief pests of lavenders are the cuckoo spit insects and the caterpillars of several types of moth. Cure cuckoo spit by spraying away the foamy white spit with water. Then use a horticultural liquid soap to remove the bugs and caterpillars (follow manufacturer's instructions).

The flowers in wet seasons may be attacked by grey mould (Botrytis). This can occur all too readily after a wet winter. Cut back the infected parts as far as possible, again remembering not to cut into the old wood if you want it to shoot again.

There is another fungus (**Phoma lavandulae**) that attacks the stems and branches causing wilting and death of the affected branches. If this occurs dig up the plant immediately and destroy, keeping it well away from any other lavender bushes.

Maintenance
Spring Give a spring hair cut.
Summer Trim after flowering. Take cuttings.
Autumn Sow seed. Cut back in early autumn, never into the old wood. Protect all the half-hardy lavenders. Bring containers inside.
Winter Check seedlings for disease. Keep watering to a minimum.

Garden Cultivation
Lavender is one of the most popular plants in today's herb garden and is particularly useful in borders, edges, as internal hedges, and on top of dry walls. All the species need an open sunny position and a well-drained, fertile soil. But it will adapt to semi-shade as long as the soil conditions are met, otherwise it will die in winter. If you have very cold winter temperatures, it is worth container growing.

The way to maintain a lavender bush is to trim to shape every year in the spring, remembering not to cut into the old wood as this will not re-shoot. After flowering, trim back to the leaves. In the early autumn trim again, making sure this is well before the first autumn frosts. Otherwise the new growth will be too soft and be damaged. By trimming this way, you will keep the bush neat and encourage it to make new growth, so stopping it becoming woody.

If you have inherited a straggly mature plant then give it a good cut back in autumn, followed by a second cut in the spring and then adopt the above routine. If the plant is aged, I would advise that you propagate some of the autumn cuts, so preserving the plant if all else fails.

Harvesting
Gather the flowers just as they open, and dry on open trays or by hanging in small bunches.

Pick the leaves any time for use fresh, or before flowering if drying.

Lavender sachets make good presents and can be used as moth repellent

CONTAINER GROWING

If you have low winter temperatures, lavender cannot be treated as a hardy evergreen. Treated as a container plant, however, it can be protected in winter and enjoyed just as well in the summer. Choose containers to set off the lavender; they all suit terracotta. Use a well-drained compost – the peat, bark, grit mix suits them well. The ideal position is sun, but all lavenders will cope with partial shade, though the aroma can be impaired.

Feed regularly through the flowering season with liquid fertilizer, following the manufacturer's instructions. Allow the compost to dry out in winter (not totally, but nearly), and slowly reintroduce watering in spring.

CULINARY

Lavender has not been used much in cooking, but as there are many more adventurous cooks around, I am sure it will be used increasingly in the future. Use the flowers to flavour a herb jelly, or a vinegar. Equally the flowers can be crystallized.

Lavender Biscuits

100g/4oz butter
50g/2oz caster sugar
175g/6oz self-raising flour
2 tablespoons fresh chopped lavender leaves
1 teaspoon lavender flowers removed from spike

Lavender biscuits

Cream the sugar and butter together until light. Add the flour and lavender leaves to the butter mixture. Knead well until it forms a dough. Gently roll out on a lightly floured board. Scatter the flowers over the rolled dough and lightly press in with the rolling pin. Cut into small rounds with cutter. Place biscuits on a greased baking sheet. Bake in a hot oven 450°F/230°C/gas mark 7 for 10–12 minutes until golden and firm. Remove at once and cool on a wire tray.

Lavender herb jelly

MEDICINAL

Throughout history, lavender has been used medicinally to soothe, sedate and suppress. Nowadays it is the essential oil that is in great demand.

The oil was traditionally inhaled to prevent vertigo and fainting. It is an excellent remedy for burns and stings, and its strong antibacterial action helps to heal cuts. The oil also kills diphtheria and typhoid bacilli as well as streptococcus and pneumococcus.

Add 6 drops of oil to bath water to calm irritable children and help them sleep. Place 1 drop on the temple for a headache relief. Blend for use as a massage oil in aromatherapy for throat infections, skin sores, inflammation, rheumatic aches, anxiety, insomnia and depression. The best oil is made from distillation, and may be bought from many shops.

OTHER USES

Rub fresh flowers onto skin or pin a sprig on clothes to discourage flies. Use flowers in potpourri, herb pillows, and linen sachets, where they make a good moth repellent.

Levisticum officinale

LOVAGE

Also known as Love Parsley, Sea Parsley, Lavose, Liveche, Smallage and European Lovage. From the family Apiaceae.

Lovage *Levisticum officinale*

This native of the Mediterranean can now be found naturalized throughout the temperate regions of the world, including Australia, North America and Scandinavia.

Lovage was used by the ancient Greeks, who chewed the seed to aid digestion and relieve flatulence. Knowledge of it was handed down to Benedictine monks by the Romans, who prescribed the seeds for the same complaints. In Europe a decoction of lovage was reputedly a good aphrodisiac that no witch worthy of the name could be without. The name is likely to have come from the Latin 'ligusticum', after Liguria in Italy, where the herb grew profusely.

Because lovage leaves have a deodorizing and antiseptic effect on the skin, they were laid in the shoes of travellers in the Middle Ages to revive their weary feet, like latter-day odour eaters.

SPECIES

Levisticum officinale
Lovage

Hardy perennial. Ht up to 2m (6ft), spread 1m (3ft) or more. Tiny, pale, greenish-yellow flowers in summer clusters. Leaves darkish green, deeply divided, and large toothed.

A close relation, **Ligusticum scoticum**, shorter with white clusters of flowers, is sometimes called lovage. It can be used in the same culinary way, but lacks its strong flavour and the growth.

CULTIVATION

Propagation
Seed

Sow under protection in spring into prepared plug or seed trays and cover with perlite; a bottom heat of 15°C (60°F) is helpful. When the seedlings are large enough to handle and after a period of hardening off, transplant into a prepared site in the garden 60cm (2ft) apart.

Division

The roots of an established plant can be divided in the spring or autumn. Make sure that each division has some new buds showing.

Pests and Diseases

Leaf miners are sometimes a problem. Watch out for the first tunnels, pick off the affected leaves and destroy them, otherwise broad dry patches will develop and the leaves will start to wither away. To control this, cut the plant right down to the ground, burning the affected shoots. Give the plant a feed and it will shoot with new growth. The young growth is just what one needs for cooking.

Maintenance

Spring Divide established plants.
Summer Clip established plants to encourage new shoots.
Autumn Sow seed in garden
Winter No need for protection.

Garden Cultivation

Lovage prefers a rich, moist but well-drained soil. Prior to first planting, dig over the ground deeply and manure well. The site can be either in full sun or partial shade. Seeds are best sown in the garden in the autumn. When the seedlings are large enough, thin to 60cm

(2ft) apart. It is important that lovage has a period of dormancy so that it can complete the growth cycle.

Lovage is a tall plant, so position it carefully. It will reach its full size in 3–5 years. To keep the leaves young and producing new shoots, cut around the edges of the clumps.

Harvesting

After the plant has flowered the leaves tend to have more of a bitter taste so harvest in early summer. I personally believe that lovage does not dry that well and it is best to freeze it (see p.611).

Harvest seed heads when the seeds start to turn brown. Pick them on a dry day, tie a paper bag over their heads, and hang upside down in a dry, airy place. Use, like celery seed, for winter soups.

Dig the root for drying in the autumn of the second or third season.

CONTAINER GROWING

Lovage is fine grown outside in a large container. To keep it looking good, keep it well-clipped. I do not advise letting it run to flower unless you can support it. Remember at flowering stage, even in a pot, it can be in excess of 1.5m (5ft) tall.

WARNING

As lovage is very good at reducing water retention, people who are pregnant or who have kidney problems should not take this herb medicinally.

CULINARY

Lovage is an essential member of any culinary herb collection. The flavour is reminiscent of celery. It adds a meaty flavour to foods and is used in soups, stews and stocks. Also add fresh young leaves to salads, and rub on chicken, and round salad bowls.

Crush seeds in bread and pastries, sprinkle on salads, rice and mashed potato. If using the rootstock as a vegetable in casseroles, remove the bitter-tasting skin.

Lovage Soup
Serves 4

25g (1oz) butter
2 medium onions, finely
  chopped
500g (1lb) potatoes, peeled and
  diced
4 tablespoons finely chopped
  lovage leaves
850ml (1¼ pints) chicken or
  vegetable stock
300ml (½ pint) milk or
  1 cup cream
Grated nutmeg
Salt and pepper

Melt the butter in a heavy pan and gently sauté the onions and diced potatoes for 5 minutes until soft. Add the chopped lovage leaves and cook for 1 minute. Pour in the stock, bring to the boil, season with salt and pepper, cover and simmer gently until the potatoes are soft (about 15 minutes). Purée the soup through a sieve or liquidizer

and return to a clean pan. Blend in the milk or cream, sprinkle on a pinch of nutmeg and heat through. Do not boil OR IT WILL CURDLE. Adjust seasoning. Delicious hot or cold. Serve garnished with chopped lovage leaves.

Lovage and Carrot
Serves 2

2 teaspoons chopped lovage
  leaves
3 carrots, grated
1 apple, grated
125g (5oz) plain yoghurt
2 tablespoons mayonnaise
1 teaspoon salt (if needed)
Lettuce leaves
1 onion sliced into rings
Chives

Toss together the grated carrots, apple, lovage, mayonnaise and yoghurt. Arrange the lettuce leaves on a serving dish and fill with the lovage mixture. Decorate with a few raw onions rings, chives and tiny lovage leaves.

Lovage as a Vegetable

Treat lovage as you would spinach. Use the young growth of the plant stalks and leaves. Strip the leaves from the stalks, wash, and cut the stalks up into segments. Bring a pan of water to the boil add the lovage, bring the water back to the boil, cover, and simmer for about 5–7 minutes until tender. Strain the water. Make a white sauce using butter, flour, milk, salt, pepper and grated nutmeg. Add the lovage. Serve and wait for the comments!

Lovage soup

MEDICINAL

Lovage is a remedy for digestive difficulties, gastric catarrh and flatulence. I know of one recipe from the West Country – a teaspoon of lovage seed steeped in a glass of brandy, strained and sweetened with sugar. It is taken to settle an upset stomach!

Infuse either seed, leaf or root and take to reduce water retention. Lovage assists in the removal of waste products, acts as a deodorizer, and aids rheumatism.

Its deodorizing and antiseptic properties enable certain skin problems to respond to a decoction added to bath water. This is made with 45–60g (1½–2oz) of rootstock in 600ml (1 pint) water. Add to your bath.

Lovage, brandy and sugar settle an upset stomach

Lonicera

HONEYSUCKLE

Also known as Woodbine, Beerbind, Bindweed, Evening Pride, Fairy Trumpets, Honeybind, Irish Vine, Trumpet Flowers, Sweet Suckle, and Woodbind. From the family Caprifoliaceae.

'Come into the garden, Maud,
I am here at the gate alone;
And the woodbine spices are wafted abroad,
And the musk of the rose is blown.'
Alfred Lord Tennyson (1809–1892)

Honeysuckle grows all over northern Europe including Britain and can also be found growing wild in North Africa, Western Asia and North America.

Honeysuckle, *Lonicera*, receives its common name from the old habit of sucking the sweet honey-tasting nectar from the flowers. Generically it is said to have been named after the 16th-century German physician, Lonicer.

Honeysuckle was among the plants that averted the evil powers abroad on May Day and took care of milk, the butter and the cows in the Scottish Highlands and elsewhere. Traditionally it was thought that if honeysuckle was brought into the house, a wedding would follow, and that if the flowers were placed in a girl's bedroom, she would have dreams of love.

Honeysuckle's rich fragrance has inspired many poets, including Shakespeare, who called it woodbine after its notorious habit of climbing up trees and hedges and totally binding them up.

'Where oxlips and the nodding violet grows
quite over-canopied with luscious woodbine . . .'

A Midsummer Night's Dream

The plant appeared in John Gerard's 16th-century *Herbal*; he wrote that 'the flowers steeped in oil and set in the sun are good to anoint the body that is benummed and grown very cold'.

SPECIES

There are many fragrant climbing varieties of this lovely plant. I have only mentioned those with a direct herbal input.

Lonicera x americana
American Honeysuckle
Deciduous perennial. Ht up to 7m (23ft). Strongly fragrant yellow flowers starting in a pink bud turning yellow and finishing with orangish pink throughout the summer. The berries are red, and the leaves are green and oval, the upper ones being united and saucer-like.

Lonicera caprifolium
Deciduous perennial. Ht up to 6m (20ft). The buds of the fragrant flowers are initially pink on opening; they then change to a pale white/pink/yellow as they age and finally turn deeper yellow. Green oval leaves and red berries, which were once fed to chickens. The Latin species name, **caprifolium**, means goats' leaf, reflecting the belief that honeysuckle leaves were a favourite food of goats. This variety and **Lonicera periclymenum** can be found growing wild in hedgerows.

Lonicera periclymenum
Deciduous perennial. This is the taller grower of the two common European honeysuckles, and reaches a height of 7m (23ft). It may live for 50 years. Fragrant yellow flowers appear mid-summer to mid-autumn, followed by red berries. Leaves are oval and dark green with a bluish underside.

Lonicera etrusca
Etruscan Honeysuckle
Semi-evergreen perennial. Ht up to 4m (12ft). Fragrant, pale, creamy yellow flowers which turn deeper yellow to red in autumn and are followed by red berries. Leaves oval, mid-green, with a bluish underside. This is the least hardy of those mentioned here, and should be grown in sun on a south-facing wall, and protected in winter where temperatures fall below –3°C (23°F).

Lonicera caprifolium

Lonicera japonica
Japanese Honeysuckle
Semi-evergreen perennial.
Ht up to 10m (33ft).
Fragrant, pale, creamy white
flowers turning yellow as the
season progresses, followed
by black berries. The leaves
are oval and mid-green in
colour. In the garden it is
apt to build up an
enormous tangle of shoots
and best allowed to clamber
over tree stumps or a low
roof or walls. Attempts to
train it tidily are a lost cause.
Still used in Chinese
medicine today.

CULTIVATION

Propagation
Seed
Sow seed in autumn thinly
on the surface of a prepared
seed or plug tray. Cover with
glass and winter outside.
Keep an eye on the compost
moisture and only water if
necessary. Germination may
take a long time, it has been
known to take 2 seasons, so
be patient. A more reliable
alternative method is by
cuttings.

Cuttings
Take from non-flowering,
semi-hardwood shoots in
summer and root in a bark,
grit, peat mix of compost (see
p.591). Alternatively, take
hardwood cuttings in late
autumn, leaving the cuttings
in a cold frame or cold
greenhouse for the winter.

Layering
In late spring or autumn
honeysuckle is easy to layer.
Do not disturb until the
following season when it can
be severed from its parent.

Pests and Diseases
Grown in too sunny or warm
a place, it can become
infested with greenfly,
blackfly, caterpillars and red
spider mites. Use a
horticultural soap, and spray
the pests according to the
manufacturer's instructions.

Maintenance
Spring Prune established
plants.
Summer Cut back flowering
stems after flowering. Take
semi-hardwood cuttings.
Autumn Layer established
plants. Lightly prune if
necessary.
Winter Protect certain
species in cold winters.

Garden Cultivation
This extremely tolerant,
traditional herb garden
plant will flourish vigorously
in the most unpromising
sites. Honeysuckle leaves are
among the first to appear,
sometimes mid-winter, the
flowers appearing in very
early summer and
deepening in colour after
being pollinated by the
insects that feed on their
nectar. Good as cover for an
unsightly wall or to provide
a rich summer evening
fragrance in an arbour.
   Plant in autumn or spring
in any fertile, well-drained
soil, in sun or semi-shade.
The best situation puts its
feet in the shade and its
head in the sunshine. A
position against a north or
west wall is ideal or on the
shady side of a support such
as a tree stump, pole or
pergola. Prune in early
spring, if need be. Prune
out flowering wood on
climbers after flowering.

MEDICINAL

*An infusion of the heavy
perfumed flowers can be
taken as a substitute for tea.
It is also useful for treating
coughs, catarrh and asthma.
As a lotion it is good for skin
infections.
   Recent research has proved
that this plant has an outstanding curative action in
cases of colitis.*

*Warning: The berries are
poisonous. Large doses cause
vomiting.*

Harvesting
Pick and dry the flowers for
potpourris just as they open.
This is the best time for
scent although they are
their palest in colour.
   Pick the flowers for use in
salads as required. Again the
best flavour is before the
nectar has been collected,
which is when the flower is
at its palest.

CULINARY

Add flowers to salads.

CONTAINER GROWING

This is not a plant that
springs to mind as a good
pot plant, certainly not
indoors. But with patience,
it makes a lovely mop head
standard if carefully staked
and trained; use an
evergreen variety like
Lonicera japonica. The
compost should be a soil-
based one. Water and feed
regularly throughout the
summer and in winter keep
in a cold frame or
greenhouse and water only
occasionally.

OTHER USES
Flowers are strongly scented
for potpourris, herb pillows
and perfumery. An essential
oil was once extracted from
the plant to make a very
sweet perfume but the yield
was extremely low.

Honeysuckle flowers in a fresh summer salad

Malva sylvestris

MALLOW

Also known as Billy Buttons, Pancake Plan, and Cheese Flower. From the family Malvaceae.

Native to Europe, Western Asia and North America, it can be found growing in hedgebanks, field edges, and on road sides and wastelands in sunny situations.

The ancient Latin name given to this herb by Pliny was 'malacho', which was probably derived from 'malachi', the Greek word meaning 'to soften', after the mallow's softening and healing properties. Young mallow shoots were eaten as vegetables, and it was still to be found on vegetable lists in Roman times. Used in the Middle Ages for its calming effect as an antidote to aphrodisiacs and love-potions. The shape of its seed rather than its flowers suggested the folk name.

SPECIES

Malva sylvestris
Common Mallow
Also known as High Mallow, Cheese Flower and Country Mallow. Biennial. Ht 45–90cm (18–36in), spread 60cm (24in). Flower, dark pink or violet form, early summer to autumn. Mid-green leaves, rounded at the base, ivy shaped at stem.

Malva rotundifolia
Dwarf Mallow
Also known as Cheese Plant, Low Mallow and Blue Mallow. Annual. Ht 15–30cm (6–12in), a creeper. Purplish-pink, trumpet-shaped flowers from early summer to mid-autumn. Leaves rounded, slightly lobed and greenish. North American native.

Malva moschata
Musk Mallow
Perennial. Ht 30–80cm (12–32in), spread 60cm (24in). Rose/pink flowers, late summer to early autumn. Mid-green leaves – kidney-shaped at base, deeply divided at stem – emit musky aroma in warm weather or when pressed.

CULTIVATION

Propagation
Seed
Sow in prepared seed or plug trays in the autumn. Cover lightly with compost (not perlite). Winter outside, covered with glass. Germination is erratic but should take place in the spring. Plant out seedlings when large enough to handle, 60cm (24in) apart.

Cuttings
Take cuttings from firm basal shoots in late spring or summer. When hardened off the following spring, plant out 60cm (24in) apart into a prepared site.

Pests and Diseases
Mallows can catch hollyhock rust. There is also a fungus that produces leaf spots and a serious black canker on the stems. If this occurs dig up the plants and destroy them. This is a seed-borne fungus and may be carried into the soil, so change planting site the following season.

Maintenance
Spring Take softwood cuttings from young shoots.
Summer Trim after flowering.
Autumn Sow seed.
Winter Hardy enough.

Garden Cultivation
Mallows are very tolerant of site, but prefer a well-drained and fertile soil (if too damp they may well need staking in summer), and a sunny position (though semi-shade will do). Sow where it is to flower from late summer to spring. Press gently into the soil, 60cm (24in) apart, and cover with a light compost. Cut back stems after flowering, not only to promote new growth, but also to keep under control and encourage a second flowering. Cut down the stems in autumn.

Harvesting
Harvest young leaves for fresh use as required throughout the spring. For use in potpourris, gather for drying in the summer after first flowering.

CONTAINER GROWING

Musk mallow is the best variety to grow in a large container. It can look very dramatic and smells lovely on a warm evening. Water well throughout the growing season, but feed only twice. Maintain as for garden cultivation.

CULINARY

Young tender tips of the common mallow may be used in salads or steamed as a vegetable. Young leaves of the musk mallow can be boiled as a vegetable.

Young leaves of the dwarf mallow can be eaten raw in salads or cooked as a spinach.

Musk mallow salad

MEDICINAL

Marshmallow (**Althaea officinalis**) is used in preference to the mallows (**Malva**) in herbal medicine. However, a decoction can be used in a compress, or in bath preparations, for skin rashes, boils and ulcers, and in gargles and mouth washes.

Marrubium vulgare

WHITE HOREHOUND

Also known as Horehound and Maribeum. From the family Lamiaceae.

Common throughout Europe and America, the plant grows wild everywhere from coastal to mountainous areas.

The botanical name comes from the Hebrew 'marrob' which translates as 'bitter juice'. The common name is derived from the old English 'har hune' meaning a downy plant.

SPECIES

Marrubium vulgare
White Horehound
Hardy perennial. Ht 45cm (18in), spread 30cm (12in). Small clusters of white flowers from the second year in midsummer. The leaves are green and wrinkled with an underside of a silver woolly texture. There is also a variegated version.

CULTIVATION

Propagation
Seed
The fairly small seed should be sown in early spring in a seed or plug tray, using the bark, grit, peat mix of compost (see p.591). Germination takes 2–3 weeks. Prick out into pots or transplant to the garden after a period of hardening off.

Cuttings
Softwood cuttings taken from the new growth in summer usually root within 3–4 weeks. Use the bark, grit, peat mix of compost. Winter under protection in a cold frame or cold greenhouse.

Division
Established clumps benefit from division in the spring.

Pests and Diseases
If it is very wet and cold in winter, the plant can rot off.

Maintenance
Spring Divide established clumps. Prune new growth to maintain shape. Sow seed.
Summer Trim after flowering to stop the plant flopping and prevent self-seeding. Take cuttings.
Autumn Divide only if it has dangerously transgressed its limits.
Winter Protect only if season excessively wet.

Garden Cultivation
White horehound grows best in well-drained, dryish soil, biased to alkaline, sunny and protected from high winds. Seed can be sown direct into a prepared garden in late spring, once the soil has started to warm up. Thin the seedlings to 30cm (12in) distance apart.

Harvesting
The leaves and flowering tops are gathered in the spring, just as the plants come into flower, when the essential oil is at its richest. Use fresh or dried.

CONTAINER GROWING

Horehound can be grown in a large container situated in a sunny position. Use a compost that drains well and do not overwater. Only feed after flowering, otherwise it produces lush growth that is too soft.

OTHER USES

Infuse the leaf as a spray for cankerworm in trees.

Mix the infusion with milk and put in a dish as a fly killer. Do not spray!

MEDICINAL

White horehound is still extensively used in cough medicine, and for calming a nervous heart; its property, marrubiin, in small amounts, normalizes an irregular heart beat. The plant has also been used to reduce fevers and treat malaria.

A Cold Cure
Finely chop 9 small horehound leaves. Mix 1 tablespoon of honey and eat slowly to ease a sore throat or cough. Repeat several times if necessary.

Cough Sweets

100g (4oz) of fresh white horehound leaves
½ teaspoon of crushed aniseed
3 crushed cardamom seeds
350g (12oz) white sugar
350g (12oz) moist brown sugar

Put the horehound, aniseed and cardamom into 600ml (1 pt) of water and simmer for 20 minutes. Strain through a filter. Over a low heat, dissolve the sugars in the liquid; boil over a medium heat until the syrup hardens when drops are put into cold water. Pour into an oiled tray. Score when partially cooled. Store in wax paper.

Horehound sweets

Melissa officinalis

LEMON BALM

Also known as Balm, Melissa, Balm Mint, Bee Balm, Blue Balm, Cure All, Dropsy Plant, Garden Balm and Sweet Balm. From the family Lamiaceae.

This plant is a native of the Mediterranean region and Central Europe. It is now naturalized in North America and as a garden escapee in Britain.

This ancient herb was dedicated to the goddess Diana, and used medicinally by the Greeks some 2,000 years ago. The generic name, *Melissa*, comes from the Greek word for bee and the Greek belief that if you put sprigs of balm in an empty hive it would attract a swarm; equally, if planted near bees in residence in a hive they would never go away. This belief was still prevalent in medieval times when sugar was highly priced and honey a luxury.

In the Middle Ages lemon balm was used to soothe tension, to dress wounds, as a cure for toothache, mad dog bites, skin eruptions, crooked necks, and sickness during pregnancy. It was even said to prevent baldness, and ladies made linen or silk amulets filled with lemon balm as a lucky love charm. It has been acclaimed the world over for promoting long life. Prince Llewellyn of Glamorgan drank Melissa tea, so he claimed, every day of the 108 years of his life. Wild claims apart, as a tonic for melancholy it has been praised by herbal writers for centuries and is still used today in aromatherapy to counter depression.

SPECIES

Melissa officinalis
Lemon Balm
Hardy perennial. Ht 75cm (30in), spread 45cm (18in) or more. Clusters of small, pale yellow/white flowers in summer. The green leaves are oval toothed, slightly wrinkled, and highly aromatic when crushed.

Melissa officinalis 'All Gold'
Golden Lemon Balm
Half-hardy perennial. Ht 60cm (24in), spread 30cm (12in) or more. Clusters of small, pale yellow/white flowers in summer. The leaves are all yellow, oval in shape, toothed, slightly wrinkled and aromatic with a lemon scent when crushed. The leaves are prone to scorching in high summer; also more tender than the other varieties.

left: **Lemon balm** *Melissa officinalis* and **variegated lemon balm** *Melissa officinalis 'Aurea'*

Melissa officinalis 'Aurea'
Variegated Lemon Balm
Hardy perennial. Ht 60cm (24in), spread 30cm (12in) or more. Clusters of small, pale yellow/white flowers in summer. The green/gold variegated leaves are oval, toothed, slightly wrinkled and aromatic with a lemon scent when crushed. This variety is as hardy as common lemon balm. The one problem is that in high season it reverts to green. To maintain variegation keep cutting back, this in turn will promote new growth, which should be variegated

Lemon balm *Melissa officinalis* **in flower**

Left: **Variegated lemon balm** *Melissa officinalis* 'Aurea'

CULTIVATION

Propagation
Seed
Common lemon balm can be grown from seed. The seed is small but manageable, and it is better to start it off under protection. Sow in prepared seed or plug trays in early spring, using the bark, grit, peat mix of compost (see p.591) and cover with perlite. Germination takes between 10 and 14 days. The seeds dislike being wet so, after the initial watering, try not to water again until germination starts. When seedlings are large enough to handle, prick out and plant in the garden, 45cm (18in) apart.

Cuttings
The variegated and golden lemon balm can only be propagated by cuttings or division. Take softwood cuttings from the new growth in late spring/early summer. As the cutting material will be very soft, take extra care when collecting it.

Division
The rootstock is compact but easy to divide (autumn or spring). Replant directly into the garden in a prepared site.

Pests and Diseases
The only problem likely to affect lemon balm is a form of the rust virus; cut the plant back to the ground and dispose of all the infected leaves, including any that may have accidentally fallen on the ground.

Maintenance
Spring Sow seeds. Divide established plants.
Summer Keep trimming established plants. Cut back after flowering to help prevent self-seeding.
Autumn Divide established plants, or any that may have encroached on other plant areas.
Winter Protect plants if the temperature falls below -5°C (23°F). The plant dies back, leaving but a small presence on the surface of the soil. Protect with a bark or straw mulch or agricultural fleece.

Garden Cultivation
Lemon balm will grow in almost any soil and in any position. It does prefer a fairly rich, moist soil in a sunny position with some midday shade. Keep all plants trimmed around the edges to restrict growth and encourage fresh shoots. In the right soil conditions this can be a very invasive plant. Unlike horseradish, the established roots are not difficult to uproot if things get out of hand.

Harvesting
Pick leaves throughout the summer for fresh use. For drying, pick just before the flowers begin to open when flavour is best; handle gently to avoid bruising. The aroma is rapidly lost, together with much of its therapeutic value, when dried or stored.

CULINARY

Lemon balm is one of those herbs that smells delicious but tastes like school-boiled cabbage water when cooked.
Add fresh leaves to vinegar. Add leaves to wine cups, teas and beers, or use chopped with fish and mushroom dishes. Mix freshly chopped with soft cheeses.
It has frequently been incorporated in proprietary cordials for liqueurs and its popularity in France led to its name 'Tea de France'.
It is used as a flavouring for certain cheeses in parts of Switzerland.

Lemon balm with cream cheese

MEDICINAL

Lemon balm tea is said to relieve headaches and tension and to restore the memory. It is also good to drink after meals to ease the digestion, flatulence and colic. Use fresh or frozen leaves in infusions because the volatile oil tends to disappear during the drying process.

The isolated oil used in aromatherapy is recommended for nervousness, depression, insomnia and nervous headaches. It also helps eczema sufferers.

OTHER USES
This is a most useful plant to keep bees happy. The flower may look boring to you but it is sheer heaven to them. So plant lemon balm around beehives or orchards to attract pollinating bees.

CONTAINER GROWING

If you live in an area that suffers from very cold winters, the gold form would benefit from being grown in containers. This method suits those with a small garden who do not want a takeover bid from lemon balm. Use the bark, peat, grit mix of compost. Only feed with liquid fertilizer in the summer, otherwise the growth will become too lush and soft, and aroma and colour will diminish. Water normally throughout the growing season. Allow the container to become very dry (but not totally) in winter, and keep the pots in a cool, protected environment.

Mentha

MINT

From the family Lamiaceae.

The *Mentha* family is a native of Europe that has naturalized in many parts of the world, including North America, Australia and Japan. Mint has been cultivated for its medicinal properties since ancient times and has been found in Egyptian tombs dating back to 1,000 BC. The Japanese have been growing it to obtain menthol for at least 2,000 years. In the Bible the Pharisees collected tithes in mint, dill and cumin. Charlemagne, who was very keen on herbs, ordered people to grow it. The Romans brought it with them as they marched through Europe and into Britain, from where it found its way to America with the settlers.

Its name was first used in Greek mythology. There are two different stories, the first that the nymph Minthe was being chatted up by Hades, god of the Underworld. His queen Sephony became jealous and turned her into the plant, mint. The second that Minthe was a nymph beloved by Pluto, who transformed her into the scented herb after his jealous wife took umbrage.

SPECIES

The mint family is large and well known. I have chosen a few to illustrate the diversity of the species.

Mentha arvensis var. piperascens
Japanese Peppermint
Hardy perennial. Ht 60cm–1m (2–3ft), spread 60cm (24in) and more. Loose purplish whorls of flowers in summer. Leaves, downy, oblong, sharply toothed and green-grey; they provide an oil (90 per cent menthol), said to be inferior to the oil produced by **M. x piperita**. This species is known as English mint in Japan.

Mentha aquatica
Water Mint
Hardy perennial. Ht 15–60cm (6–24in), spread indefinite. Pretty purple/lilac flowers, all summer. Leaves soft, slightly downy, mid-green in colour. The scent can vary from a musty mint to a strong peppermint. This should be planted in water or very wet marshy soil. It can be found growing wild around ponds and streams.

Mentha x gracilis (Mentha x gentilis)
Ginger Mint
Also known as Scotch Mint. Hardy perennial. Ht 45cm (18in), spread 60cm (24in). The stem has whorls of small, 2-lipped, mauve flowers in summer. The leaf is variegated, gold/green with serrated edges. The flavour is a delicate, warm mint that combines well in salads and tomato dishes.

Mentha longifolia
Buddleia Mint
Hardy perennial. Ht 80cm (32in), spread indefinite. Long purple/mauve flowers that look very like buddleia (hence its name). Long grey-green leaves with a musty minty scent. Very good plant for garden borders.

Mentha x piperita
Peppermint
Also known as Mentha d'Angleterre, Mentha Anglais, Pfefferminze and Englisheminze.
Hardy perennial. Ht 30–60cm (12–24in), spread indefinite. Pale purple flowers in summer. Pointed leaves, darkish green with a reddish tinge, serrated edges. Very peppermint scented. This is the main medicinal herb of the genus. There are 2 species worth looking out for – black peppermint, with leaves much darker, nearly brown, and white peppermint, with leaves green, tinged with reddish brown.

above: **Ginger mint**
Mentha x *gracilis*

Mentha x piperita f. citrata
Eau de Cologne Mint
Also known as Orange Mint and Bergamot Mint. Hardy perennial. Ht 60–80cm (24–32in), spread indefinite. Purple/mauve flowers in summer. Purple tinged, roundish, dark green leaves. A delicious scent that has been described as lemon, orange, bergamot, lavender, as well as eau de cologne. This plant is a vigorous grower. Use in fruit dishes with discretion. Best use is in the bath.

Mentha x piperita f. citrata 'Basil'
Basil Mint
Hardy perennial. Ht 45–60cm (18–24in), spread indefinite. Purple/mauve flowers in summer. Leaves green with a reddish tinge, more pointed than eau de cologne mint. The scent is unique, a sweet and spicy mint scent that combines well with tomato dishes, especially pasta.

Mentha x piperita f. citrata 'Lemon'
Lemon Mint
Hardy perennial. Ht 45–60cm (18–24in), spread indefinite. Purple whorl of flowers in summer. Green serrated leaf, refreshing minty lemon scent. Good as a mint sauce, or with fruit dishes.

Mentha pulegium
Pennyroyal
Hardy semi-evergreen perennial Ht 15cm (6in) creeper, spread indefinite. Mauve flowers in spring. Bright green leaves, very strong peppermint scent. There is so much to write about this plant, it has got its own section (see pp.296–7).

Mentha requienii
Corsican Mint
Also known as Rock Mint. Hardy semi-evergreen perennial. Ground cover, spread indefinite. Tiny purple flowers throughout the summer. Tiny bright green leaves, which, when crushed, smell strongly of peppermint. Suits a rock garden or paved path, grows naturally in cracks of rocks. Needs shade and moist soil.

Mentha spicata
Spearmint
Also known as Garden Mint and Common Mint. Hardy perennial. Ht 45–60cm (18–24in), spread indefinite. Purple/mauve flowers in summer. Green pointed leaves with serrated edges. The most widely grown of all mints. Good for mint sauce, mint jelly, mint julep.

Mentha spicata var. crispa
Curly Mint
Hardy perennial. Ht 45–60cm (18–24in), spread indefinite. Light mauve flowers in spring. When I first saw this mint I thought it had a bad attack of aphids, but it has grown on me! The leaf is bright green and crinkled, its serrated edge slightly frilly. Flavour very similar to spearmint, so good in most culinary dishes.

Apple mint *Mentha suaveolens*

Left: **Pineapple mint**
Mentha suaveolens 'Variegata'

Mentha spicata var. crispa 'Moroccan'
Moroccan Mint
Hardy perennial. Ht 45–60cm (18–24in), spread indefinite. White flowers in summer. Bright green leaves with a texture and excellent mint scent. This is the one I use for all the basic mint uses in the kitchen. A clean mint flavour and scent, lovely with yoghurt and cucumber.

Mentha suaveolens
Apple Mint
Hardy perennial. Ht 60cm–1m (2–3ft), spread indefinite. Mauve flowers in summer. Roundish hairy leaves. Tall vigorous grower. Gets its name from its scent, which is a combination of mint and apples. More subtle than some mints, so good in cooking.

Mentha suaveolens 'Variegata'
Pineapple Mint
Hardy perennial. Ht 45–60cm (18–24in), spread indefinite. Seldom produces flowers, all the energy going into producing very pretty cream and green, slightly hairy leaves that look good in the garden. Not a rampant mint. Grows well in hanging baskets.

Buddleia mint
Mentha longifolia

Mentha x villosa var. alopecuroides Bowles' mint
Bowles Mint
Hardy perennial. Ht 60cm–1m (2–3ft), spread indefinite. Mauve flowers, round, slightly hairy green leaves, vigorous grower. Sometimes incorrectly called apple mint. Has acquired reputation as the 'connoisseur's culinary mint'. Not sure I agree, but mint tastes do vary.

Above: **Corsican mint**
Mentha requienii

Pycnanthemum pilosum
Mountain Mint
Hardy perennial. Ht 90cm (3ft), spread 60cm (2ft). Knot-like white/pink flowers, small and pretty in summer. Leaves long, thin, pointed, and grey-green with a good mint scent and flavour. Not a **Mentha**, so therefore not a true mint, and does not spread. Looks very attractive in a border, and also appeals to butterflies. Any soil will support it provided it is not too rich.

Ginger mint
Mentha x *gracilis*

CULTIVATION

Propagation
Seed
The seed on the market is not worthwhile – leaf flavour is inferior and quite often it does not run true to species.

Cuttings
Root cuttings of mint are very easy. Simply dig up a piece of root. Cut it where you can see a little growing node (each piece will produce a plant) and place the cuttings either into a plug or seed tray. Push them into the compost (bark, peat mix, see p.591). Water in and leave. This can be done any time during the growing season. If taken in spring, in about 2 weeks you should see new shoots emerging through the compost.

Division
Dig up plants every few years and divide, or they will produce root runners all over the place. Each bit of root will grow, so take care.
Corsican mint does not set root runners. Dig up a section in spring and divide by easing the plant apart and replanting.

Pests and Diseases
Mint rust appears as little rusty spots on the leaves. Remove them immediately, otherwise the rust will wash off into the soil and the spores spread to other plants. One sure way to be rid is to burn the affected patch. This effectively sterilizes the ground.
Another method, which I found in an old gardening book, is to dig up the roots in winter when the plants are dormant, and clean off the soil under a tap. Heat some water to a temperature of 40–46°C (105°–115°F) and pour into a bowl. Place the roots in the water for 10 minutes. Remove the runners and wash at once in cold water. Replant in the garden well away from the original site.

Maintenance
Spring Dig up root if cuttings are required. Split established plants if need be.
Summer Give plants a hair cut to promote new growth. Control the spread of unruly plants.
Autumn Dig up roots for forcing. Bring in containers.
Winter: Sterilize roots if rust evident during growing season.

Garden Cultivation
Mint is one of those plants that will walk all over the plot if not severely controlled. Also, mint readily hybridizes itself, varying according to environmental factors.
If choosing a plant in a nursery or garden centre rub the leaf first to check the scent. Select a planting site in sun or shade but away from other mints. Planted side by side they seem to lose their individual scent and flavour.
To inhibit spread, sink a large bottomless container (bucket or bespoke frame) in a well-drained and fairly rich soil to a depth of at least 30cm (12in), leaving a small ridge above soil level. Plant the mint in the centre.

Harvesting
Pick the leaves for fresh use throughout the growing season. Pick leaves for drying or freezing before the mint flowers.

COMPANION PLANTING

Spearmint or peppermint planted near roses will deter aphids. Buddleia mint will attract hoverflies.

OTHER USES

Pick a bunch of eau de cologne mint, tie it up with string, and hang it under the hot water tap when you are drawing a bath. You will scent not only your bath, but the whole house. It is very uplifting (unless you too have a young son, who for some reason thinks it is 'gross').

Curly mint
Mentha spicata var. *crispa*

Chocolate mint mousse

CULINARY

With due respect to their cuisine, the French are always rude about our 'mint sauce with lamb'; they reckon it is barbaric. On the other side of the Channel they use mint less than other countries in cooking. But slowly, even in France, this herb is gaining favour.

Mint is good in vinegars and jellies. Peppermint makes a great tea. And there are many many uses for mint in cooking with fish, meat, yoghurt, fruit, and so on. Here is a recipe for chocoholics like me:

Chocolate Mint Mousse
Serves 2

100g (4oz) plain dark chocolate
2 eggs, separated
1 teaspoon instant coffee
1 teaspoon fresh chopped mint, either Moroccan, spearmint or curly
Whipped cream for decoration
4 whole mint leaves

Melt the chocolate either in a microwave, or in a double saucepan. When smooth and liquid, remove from heat. Beat egg yolks and add to the chocolate while hot (this will cook the yolks slightly). Add coffee and chopped mint.

Leave the mixture to cool for about 15 minutes. Beat the egg whites (not too stiff) and fold them into the cooling chocolate mixture. Spoon into containers. When you are ready to serve put a blob of whipped cream in the middle and garnish with whole leaves.

CONTAINER GROWING (AND FORCING)

Mint is good in containers. Make sure the container is large enough, use a soil-based compost, and do not let the compost dry out. Feed regularly throughout the growing season with a liquid fertilizer. Place the container in semi-shade.

One good reason for growing mint in containers is to prolong the season. This is called forcing. In early autumn dig up some root. Fill a container, or wooden box lined with plastic, with compost. Lay the root down its length and cover lightly with compost. Water in and place in a light, warm glasshouse or warm conservatory (even the kitchen windowsill will do). Keep an eye on it, and fresh shoots should sprout within a couple of weeks. This is great for fresh mint sauce for Christmas.

MEDICINAL

Peppermint is aromatic, calmative, antiseptic, anti-spasmodic, anti-inflammatory, anti-bacterial, anti-parasitic, and is also a stimulant. It can be used in a number of ways for a variety of complaints including gastro-intestinal disorders where anti-spasmodic, anti-flatulent and appetite-promoting stimulation is required. It is particularly useful for nervous headaches, and as a way to increase concentration. Externally, peppermint oil can be used in a massage to relieve muscular pain.

WARNING

The oil may cause an allergic reaction. Avoid prolonged intake of inhalants from the oil, which must never be used by babies.

Black peppermint tea

Mentha pulegium

PENNYROYAL

Also known as European Pennyroyal and Pudding Grass. From the family Lamiaceae.

This herb is a native of Europe including North Africa and now widespread in comparable climates.

Pulegium is derived from the Latin 'pulex', meaning flea because both the fresh plant and the smoke from the burning leaves were used to exterminate the insect.

Puliol was an old French name for thyme and this plant was designated Royal Thyme, thence Puliol Royale and the corruption Pennyroyal. Today the French name is La Mentha Pouliot, which reflects this history.

Long ago, the wise women of the village used pennyroyal to induce abortion. It has since been used to facilitate menstruation.

The Elizabethan Herbalist John Gerard called it Pudding Grass. He claimed it would purify corrupt water on sea voyages and that it would cure 'swimming in the head and the pains and giddiness thereof'.

Creeping pennyroyal　*Mentha pulegium*

SPECIES

Mentha pulegium
Pennyroyal
Also known as Creeping Pennyroyal.
Semi-evergreen hardy perennial. Ht 15cm (6in). A creeper, spread indefinite. Mauve flowers in late spring. Bright green leaves, very strong peppermint scent.

Mentha pulegium 'Upright'
Pennyroyal Upright
Semi-evergreen hardy perennial. Ht 30cm (12in). Spread indefinite. Flowers and leaves as *M. pulegium* and comes true to species, unlike most mints.
The American pennyroyal is **Hedeoma pulegioides** or Rock Pennyroyal. It has a similar aroma and usages to the European pennyroyal.

CULTIVATION

Propagation
Seed
Pennyroyal upright can be grown from seed. The seed is very fine, so sow under protection in prepared seed or plug trays in late spring, then cover with perlite. Germination is 10–20 days. You can leave the plant to become quite well established before planting out in early summer and leave at least 30cm (12in) space between the plants.

Cuttings

Both can be propagated by root cuttings. Unlike ordinary mint, which travels underground, the pennyroyals travel on the surface, and where the plant touches the soil there a small root system develops.

Dig up a plant in late spring and divide into small clumps. The miniature root systems are ideal for putting in prepared plug trays with the bark, peat, grit mix of compost (see p.591). Water in well; they will be fully rooted in 4 weeks.

Division

If the plant becomes invasive in the garden, simply remove a section.

Pests and Diseases

Pennyroyal can suffer from leaf-rotting mildew if too wet in winter or spring. Pick off any damaged leaves. If the plant is in a container and the weather is mild enough, put it outside and allow the air to get at it. Also, cut back on watering.

Maintenance

Spring Sow seed. Divide established plants.
Summer Cut back after flowering.
Autumn Divide plants. Dig up some plants to winter in a cold frame or greenhouse.
Winter Although this mint is hardy it hates wet winters followed by frosts. It will also suffer if the temperature falls consistently below -8°C (18°F). It is difficult to protect because if you lay a mulch over it the leaves will rot off. Therefore as a precaution, dig it up in the autumn and winter it in a cold frame or greenhouse.

Garden Cultivation

This mint prefers a rich but free-draining soil in a sunny spot, but – this may seem a contradiction – it does like water in summer, so water freely. The creeping pennyroyal can be grown as aromatic ground cover, but make sure that the ground is very free draining, does not get over wet in winter, and offers protection from hard frosts.

Harvesting

Pick leaves as required for use fresh. Pick either side of flowering for freezing purposes. Not worth drying.

CONTAINER GROWING

Both pennyroyals are good in containers. When the upright pennyroyal flowers it sends out long branches covered in little circles of mauve flowers. Use the bark, peat, grit mix of compost. Feed during flowering with a liquid fertilizer.

MEDICINAL

It has long been considered dangerous to use when pregnant because it is abortive. However, it has now been found that only the oil produced from the plant is active in this way. This oil, which is highly toxic, also leads to irreversible kidney damage. Therefore it should only be prescribed by a professional.

In a hot infusion this herb has always been a favourite remedy for colds as it promotes sweating.

American Pennyroyal, *Hedeoma pulegioides, has similar properties and uses. It is also an anti-spasmodic and calmative, and is used in minor gastric disturbances, flatulence, nausea, head-aches and menstrual pain.*

An excellent insect repellent, pennyroyal can be used to divert the path of ants, too

CULINARY

This mint has a very strong peppermint scent and flavour, so use sparingly in dishes.

It makes a strong mint sauce, and is a good substitute for peppermint in water ice.

WARNING

Not to be used in pregnancy or if suffering from kidney disease. May cause contact dermatitis.

OTHER USES

If you rub pennyroyal in the path of an army of ants, it will re-route them.

More practically, if you grow pennyroyal outside the kitchen door, it will prevent ants entering the house.

If you rub leaves on to bare skin it acts as a very good insect repellent. Equally, if you rub a leaf on a mosquito or horsefly bite, the itch will disappear. I have rubbed it on a wasp sting and it has brought relief.

Monarda

BERGAMOT

Also known as Oswego Tea, Bee Balm, Blue Balm, High Balm, Low Balm, Mountain Balm and Mountain Mint. From the family Lamiaceae.

This beautiful plant with its flamboyant flower is a native of North America and is now grown horticulturally in many countries throughout the world.

The species name *Monarda* honours the Spanish medicinal botanist Dr Nicholas Monardes of Seville who, in 1569, wrote a herbal on the flora of America. The common name, bergamot, is said to have come from the scent of the crushed leaf which resembles the small bitter Italian Bergamot orange (*Citrus bergamia*), from which oil is produced that is used in aromatherapy, perfumes and cosmetics.

The wild or purple bergamot (*Monarda fistulosa*) grows around the Oswego river district near Lake Ontario in the United States. The Indians in this region used it for colds and bronchial complaints as it contains the powerful antiseptic, thymol. They also made tea from it, hence Oswego tea, which was drunk in many American households, replacing Indian tea, following the Boston Tea Party of 1773.

SPECIES

There are many species and cultivars of bergamot, too many to mention here, so I have included some from each of the species.

Monarda 'Beauty of Cobham'
Bergamot Beauty of Cobham
Hardy perennial. Ht 75cm (30in), spread 45cm (18in). Attractive dense 2-lipped pale pink flowers throughout summer. Toothed mid-green aromatic leaves.

Monarda 'Blaustrumpf'
Bergamot Blue Stocking
Hardy perennial. Ht 80cm (32in), spread 45cm (18in). Attractive purple flowers throughout summer. Aromatic, green, pointed foliage.

Monarda 'Cambridge Scarlet'
Bergamot Cambridge Scarlet
Hardy perennial. Ht 1m (3ft), spread 45cm (18in). Striking rich red flowers throughout summer. Aromatic, slightly hairy leaves of a mid-green colour.

Monarda didyma
Bergamot (Bee Balm Red)
Hardy perennial. Ht 80cm (2.5ft), spread 45cm (18in). Fantastic red flowers throughout summer. Aromatic, mid-green foliage.

Monarda 'Schneewittchen'
Bergamot Snow Maiden
Hardy perennial. Ht 80cm (2.5ft), spread 45cm (18in). Very attractive white flowers throughout summer. Aromatic, mid-green, pointed leaves.

Monarda 'Croftway Pink'
Bergamot Croftway Pink
Hardy perennial. Ht 1m (3 ft), spread 45cm (18in). Soft pink flowers throughout summer. Aromatic green leaves.

**Monarda
'Prärienacht'**
Bergamot Prarie Night
Hardy perennial. Ht 1m
(3ft), spread 45cm (18in).
Attractive purple flowers
throughout summer.
Aromatic, mid-green,
pointed leaves.

CULTIVATION

Propagation
Seed
Only species will grow true
from seed. Cultivars (i.e.
named varieties) will not.
Sow the very small seed
indoors in the spring on the
surface of either seed or
plug trays or on individual
pots. Cover with perlite.
Germination is better with
added warmth 21°C (65°F).
Thin or transplant the
strongest seedlings when
large enough to handle.
Harden off. Plant in the
garden at a distance of
45cm (18in) apart.

Cuttings
Take first shoots in early
summer, as soon as they are
7.5–10cm (3–4in) long.

Division
Divide in early spring. Either
grow on in pots, or replant
in the garden, making sure
the site is well prepared with
well-rotted compost.
Planting distance from
other plants 45cm (18in).

Pests and Diseases
Bergamot is prone to
powdery grey mildew. At the
first sign remove leaves. If it
gets out of hand cut the
plant back to ground level.
Young plants are a *bonne
bouche* for slugs!

Maintenance
Spring Sow seeds of species.
Divide roots. Dig up 3-year-
old plants, divide and
replant.
Summer Take cuttings of
cultivars and species, if
desired.

Autumn Cut back to the
ground, and give a good
feed with manure or
compost.
Winter All perennial
bergamots die right back in
winter. In hard winters
protect with a mulch.

Garden Cultivation
Bergamot is a highly
decorative plant with long-
lasting, distinctively fragrant
flowers that are very
attractive to bees, hence
the country name bee balm.
All grow well in moist,
nutrient-rich soil, preferably
in a semi-shady spot;
deciduous woodland is ideal.
However, they will tolerate
full sun provided the soil
retains moisture. Like many
other perennials bergamot
should be dug up and
divided every three years, and
the dead centre discarded.

Harvesting
Pick leaves as desired for use
fresh in the kitchen. For
drying, harvest before the
flower opens.
Cut flowers for drying as
soon as fully opened. They
will dry beautifully and keep
their colour.
It is only worth collecting
seed if you have species
plants situated well apart in
the garden. If near one
another, cross-pollination
will make the seed variable –
very jolly provided you don't
mind unpredictably mixed
colours. Collect the flower
heads when they turn
brown.

CONTAINER GROWING

Bergamot is too tall for a
window box, but it can look
very attractive growing in a
large pot, say 35–45 cm
(14–18in) across, or tub as
long as the soil can be kept
moist and the plant be given
some afternoon shade.

CULINARY

Pick the small flower petals
separately and scatter over a
green salad at the last
moment. Put fresh leaf in
China tea for an Earl Grey
flavour, and into wine cups
and lemonade. The
chopped leaves can be
added sparingly to salads
and stuffings, and can also
be used in jams and jellies.

Pork Fillets with Bergamot Sauce
Serves 2

2 large pork fillets
75g (3oz/6 tablespoons) butter
2 shallots, very finely chopped
40g (1½oz/2½ tablespoons)
   flour
4 tablespoons dry white wine
3½ tablespoons chopped
   bergamot leaves
Salt, black pepper
1 tablespoon double cream

Pre-heat the oven to
200°C/400°F/gas mark 6.
Wash the fillets of pork.
Pat dry, season and smear
with half the butter.
Roast in a shallow greased
tin for 25 minutes. Allow to
rest for 5 minutes before
slicing. Arrange slices in
warmed serving dish.
Prepare this sauce while
the fillets are in the oven.
Sweat the shallots in half the

butter until soft. Stir in the
flour and cook for about a
minute, stirring all the time.
Whisk in the stock. Simmer
until it thickens, stirring
occasionally. Then slowly
add the wine and 3
tablespoons of the chopped
bergamot. Simmer for
several minutes then season
to taste. Remove from heat,
stir in the cream, pour over
arranged pork slices garnish
with remaining chopped
bergamot.
Serve with mashed potato,
and fresh green broccoli.

OTHER USES
Because the dried bergamot
flowers keep their fragrance
and colour so well, they are
an important ingredient in
potpourris.
The oil is sometimes used
in perfumes, but should not
be confused with the
similarly smelling bergamot
orange.

MEDICINAL

*Excellent herb tea to relieve
nausea, flatulence,
menstrual pain and
vomiting.*
*Aromatherapists have
found bergamot oil good for
depression, as well as
helping the body to fight
infections.*

Myrrhis odorata

SWEET CICELY

Also known as Anise, Myrrh, Roman Plant, Sweet Bracken, Sweet Fern and Switch.
From the family Apiaceae.

Sweet Cicely was once cultivated as a pot shrub in Europe and is a native of this region and other temperate countries.

The Greeks called Sweet Cicely 'seselis' or 'seseli'. It is logical to suppose that 'Cicely' was derived from them, 'sweet' coming from its flavour.

In the 16th century John Gerard recommended the boiled roots as a pick-me-up for people who were 'dull'. According to Culpeper, the roots were thought to prevent infection by the plague.

In South Wales, Sweet Cicely is quite often seen growing in graveyards, planted around the headstones to commemorate a loved one.

In the Lake District, sweet bracken (Cicely) was not only used in puddings but also for rubbing upon oak panels to make the wood shine and smell good.

SPECIES

Myrrhis odorata
Sweet Cicely
Hardy perennial. Ht 60–90cm (2–3ft), spread 60cm (2ft) or more. The small white flowers appear in umbels from spring to early summer. The seeds are long, first green, turning black on ripening. The leaves are fern-like, very divided, and smell of aniseed when crushed.

The following plant is called Sweet Cicely in North America. It is unrelated to the European one, but used in a similar way.

Osmorhiza longistylis
Also known as Anise Root, Sweet Anise and Sweet Chervil.
Perennial. Ht 45–90cm (18–36in). Inconspicuous white flowers appear in loose compound umbels in summer. The leaves are oval to oblong and grow in groups of three. The whole plant has an aniseed odour. Its roots used to be nibbled by children for their anise liquorice flavour.

CULTIVATION

Propagation
Seed
Sow the seed when ripe in early autumn. Use prepared plug or seed trays and, as the seed is so large, sow only one per plug and cover with compost. Then cover the trays with glass and leave outside for the whole winter. The seed requires several months of cold winter temperatures to germinate. Keep a check on the compost, making sure it does not dry out. When germination starts bring the trays into a cold greenhouse. A spring sowing can be

Sweet Cicely *Myrrhis odorata*

successful provided the seed is first put in a plastic bag mixed with a small amount of damp sharp sand, refrigerated for 4 weeks, and then sown as normal in prepared seed or plug trays. When the seedlings are large enough to handle, which is not long after germination, and after the frosts are over, transplant to a prepared site in the garden, 60cm (2ft) apart.

Root Cuttings
The tap root may be lifted in spring or autumn, cut into sections each with a bud, and replanted either in prepared plug trays or direct into a prepared site in the garden at a depth of 5cm (2in).

Division
Divide the plant in autumn when the top growth dies down.

Pests and Diseases
Sweet Cicely is, in the majority of cases, free from pests and disease.

Maintenance
Spring Take root cuttings.
Summer Cut back after flowering, to produce new leaves and to stop self-seeding.
Autumn Sow seeds. Divide established plants. Take root cuttings.
Winter No need for protection.

Garden Cultivation
It is one of the first garden herbs to emerge after winter and is almost the last to die down, and is therefore a most useful plant.

If you have a light well-drained poor soil you may find that Sweet Cicely spreads all round the garden, and when you try to dig out established plants that the tap root is very long; even a tiny bit remaining will produce another plant. On the soil at my farm, which is heavy clay, it is a lovely plant, however, remaining just where it was planted in

a totally controlled fashion.

The situation it likes best is a well-draining soil, rich in humus, and light shade. If the seed is not wanted for propagation or winter flavouring, the whole plant should be cut down immediately after flowering. A new batch of leaves will soon develop.

Sweet Cicely is not suitable for growing in humid areas because it needs a good dormant period before winter to produce its root and lush foliage.

Harvesting
Pick young leaves at any time for fresh use.

Collect unripe seeds when green; ripe seeds when dark brown.

The foliage and seed do not dry or freeze, but the ripe seed stores well in a dry container.

Dig up roots for drying in autumn when the plant has died back.

CONTAINER GROWING

As this herb has a very long tap root it does not grow happily in a container. But it can be done. Choose a container that will give the root room to grow, and use the bark, peat mix of compost (see p.591). Place it in a semi-shady place and keep it well watered throughout the growing season.

MEDICINAL

This herb is now rarely used medicinally. The boiled root is said to be a tonic for the teenager and the elderly.

Sweet Cicely wine

CULINARY

The root can be cooked as a vegetable and served with butter or a white sauce, or allow to cool and chop up for use in salads. Alternatively, it can be eaten raw, or peeled and grated, and served in a French salad dressing. It is difficult to describe the flavour – think of parsnip, add a hint of aniseed. The root makes a very good wine.

Toss unripe seeds, which have a sweet flavour and a nutty texture, into fruit salads. Chop into ice cream. Use ripe seeds whole in cooked dishes such as apple pie, otherwise use crushed.

The leaf flavour is sweet aniseed. Chop finely and stir in salads, dressings and omelettes. Add to soups, stews and to boiling water when cooking cabbage.

Add to cream for a sweeter, less fatty taste. It is a valuable sweetener, especially for diabetics but also for the many people who are trying to reduce their sugar intake.

When cooking tart fruit, such as rhubarb, plums, gooseberries, red or black currants, add 2–4 teaspoons of dried Sweet Cicely. Or, as I do sometimes, mix a handful of large fresh leaves with some lemon balm and add to the boiling water in which the fruit is to be stewed. It gives a delightful flavour and helps to save almost half the sugar needed.

OTHER USES

This is one of the first nectar plants to appear in the spring, so it is valuable to the beekeeper.

Myrtus communis

MYRTLE

From the family Myrtaceae.

Myrtle *Myrtus communis*
in flower

SPECIES

Myrtus communis
Myrtle
Half-hardy evergreen
perennial. Ht and spread
2–3m (6–10ft). Fragrant
white flowers from spring to
midsummer, each with a
dense cluster of golden
stamens, followed by dark,
purple-black fruits. The
leaves are oval, glossy, dark
green and aromatic.

Myrtle communis 'Variegata'
Variegated Myrtle
Half-hardy evergreen
perennial. Ht and spread
1–2m (3–6ft). Fragrant white
flowers from spring to midsummer, each with a hint of
pink, and a dense cluster of
golden stamens, followed by
dark, purple-black fruits.
Leaves are oval and dark
green with silver variegation,
and a pink tinge in autumn.

Myrtle communis subsp. tarentina
Tarentina Myrtle
Half-hardy evergreen
perennial. Ht and spread
1–2m (3–6ft). Fragrant
white flowers from spring to
midsummer, each with a
dense cluster of golden
stamens, followed by dark,
purple-black fruits. Leaves
are small and oval, dark
green and aromatic. This
myrtle is a good hedge in
mild areas. Plant 60cm
(24in) apart.

Myrtus communis subsp. tarentina 'Microphylla Variegata'
Variegated Tarentina Myrtle
Half-hardy evergreen
perennial. Ht 1m (3ft),
spread 60cm (2ft). Fragrant
white flowers from spring to
midsummer, each with a
hint of pink and a dense
cluster of golden stamens,
followed by dark, purple-
black fruits. Leaves are
small, oval, and dark green
with silver variegation, and a
pink tinge in autumn.

I have included the
following two because they
have only recently been reclassified as **Luma** and are
worth looking out for.

Luma chequen (Myrtus chequen)
Half-hardy evergreen
perennial. Ht and spread
10m (30ft). Fragrant white
flowers from spring to midsummer, each with a dense
cluster of golden stamens;
followed by dark purple-
black fruits. The leaves are
more oblong with a point at
the end: glossy dark green
and aromatic.

Luma apiculata 'Glanleam Gold' (Myrtus 'Glanleam Gold')
Half-hardy evergreen
perennial. Ht and spread
10m (30ft). Fragrant white
flowers from midsummer to
mid-autumn, each with a
hint of pink and a dense
cluster of golden stamens,
followed by red fruits, which
darken to deep purple as
they ripen. Leaves oval,
bright green, edged with
creamy yellow.

Myrtle comes from a fragrant genus
that is widely distributed in warm
temperate and tropical regions of the world.
Myrtle is a direct descendant of the Greek
Myrtos, the herb of love. It has been
dedicated to Venus and was planted all
round her temples. The story goes that
Venus transformed one of her priestess
called Myrrh into myrtle in order to protect
her from an over-eager suitor. Also, Venus
herself wore a wreath of myrtle when she was
given the golden apple by Paris in
recognition of her beauty. When she arose
out of the sea she was carrying a sprig of
myrtle, and to this day it grows very well by
the sea, flourishing
in the salt air.
Subsequently it
was considered an
aphrodisiac, and brides
carried it in their
bouquets or
wore wreaths of it at
weddings to symbolize love and consistency.

Myrtle *Myrtus communis* **in berry**

Myrtle growing in a hedge

CULTIVATION

Propagation
Cuttings
Take softwood cuttings in spring, semi-hardwood cuttings in summer. As these are tender plants it is as well to grow them on in pots for the first 2 years at least. If you live in an area where the winter temperatures fall continuously below 0°C (32°F) – for variegated varieties 5°C (41°F) – it would be better to leave them in their pots for the winter. Use the bark, peat, grit mix of compost (see p.591).

Pests and Diseases
In the majority of cases myrtles are free from pests and diseases, but susceptible to root rot from over-watering.

Maintenance
Spring Trim back growth to regain shape. Take softwood cuttings.

Summer Take semi-hardwood cuttings.
Autumn Protect from early frosts.
Winter Protect in the winter if you live in a frost area.

Garden Cultivation
This lovely, tender, aromatic shrub will grow in fertile well-drained soil in full sun. Where your winters are borderline, plant against a south- or west-facing wall to restrict the amount of water it receives from rain, and protect it from the winds. If a frost is forecast, cover lightly with an agricultural fleece.
   Trim back growth (where possible) to maintain shape in mid-spring after the frosts have finished.

Harvesting
Pick leaves for sweetness and scent when myrtle is in flower; they can be used dried or fresh.
   Preserve the leaves in oil or vinegar for use in cooking.
   Pick flowers for drying just as they open.

CULINARY

*Leaves can be added to pork for the final 10 minutes of roasting, or to lamb when barbecuing. They have a spicy flavour.
   After drying, the berries can be ground and used like juniper as a spice for game and venison.*

MEDICINAL

The leaves have astringent and antiseptic properties. Rarely used medicinally, but a leaf decoction may be applied externally to bruises and haemorrhoids. Recent research has revealed a substance in myrtle that has an antibiotic action.

CONTAINER GROWING

This plant, when young, is well suited to containers. Use the bark, peat, grit mix of compost. As an evergreen plant, it looks attractive all year round. Place in a cold conservatory away from central heating. Water in the summer months, and allow the compost nearly to dry out in winter. Watch the watering at all times; if ever in doubt give it less rather than more. Feed with a liquid fertilizer during the flowering period.

OTHER USES

Every part of the shrub is highly aromatic and can be used dried in potpourris.

Myrtle potpourri

Nepeta

CATMINT

**Also known as Catnep, Catnip, Catrup, Catswart and Field Balm.
From the family Lamiaceae.**

Catmint *Nepeta racemosa*

Native to Europe and East and West Asia, catmint is now naturalized in other temperate zones.

The species name may have derived from the Roman town Nepeti, where it was said to grow in profusion.

The Elizabethan herbalist, Gerard, recorded the source of its common name: 'They do call it *herba cataria* and *herba catti* because cats are very much delighted herewith for the smell of it is so pleasant unto them, that they rub themselves upon it and wallow or tumble in it and also feed on the branches and leaves very greedily.'

This herb has long been cultivated both for its medicinal and seasoning properties, and in the hippie era of the late 1960s and 1970s for its mildly hallucinogenic quality when smoked.

SPECIES

Nepeta cataria, **Nepeta x faassenii** and **Nepeta racemosa** are all called catmint, which can be confusing. However the first is the true herb with the medicinal and culinary properties and, just to be more confusing, is known also as dog mint!

Nepeta racemosa (mussinii)
Hardy perennial. Ht and spread 50cm (20in). Spikes of lavender blue/purple flowers from late spring to autumn. Small, mildly fragrant, greyish leaves. Marvellous edging plant for tumbling out over raised beds or softening hard edges of stone flags. Combines especially well with old-fashioned roses.

Nepeta camphorata
Hardy perennial. Ht and spread 60–75cm (24–30in). Very different from ordinary catmint and very fragrant. Tiny white blooms all summer. Small, silvery grey, aromatic foliage. Prefers a poor, well-drained, dryish soil, not too rich in nutrients, and full sun. However, it will adapt to most soils except wet and heavy.

Nepeta x faassenii
Hardy perennial. Ht and spread 45cm (18in). Loose spikes of lavender blue flowers from early summer to early autumn. Small greyish-green aromatic leaves form a bushy clump.

Nepeta cataria
Dog mint, Nep-in-a-hedge.
Hardy perennial. Ht 1m (3ft), spread 60cm (2ft). White to pale pink flowers from early summer to early autumn. Pungent aromatic leaves. This plant is the true herb. In the 17th century it was used in the treatment of barren women.

CULTIVATION

Propagation
Seed
Sow its small seed in spring or late summer, either where the plant is going to flower or on to the surface of pots, plug or seed trays. Cover with perlite. Gentle bottom heat can be of assistance. Germination takes from 10–20 days, depending on the time of year (faster in late summer). Seed is viable for 5 years. When large enough to handle, thin the seedlings to 30cm (12in). The seed of **N. camphorata** should be sown in autumn to late winter. This seed will usually flower the following season.

Cuttings
Take softwood cuttings from new growth in late spring through to midsummer. Do not choose flowering stems.

Catmint 'Six Hills Giant'
Nepeta 'Six Hills Giant'

Catmint *Nepeta cataria*

Division
A good method of propagation particularly if a plant is becoming invasive. But beware of cats! The smell of a bruised root is irresistible. Cats have been known to destroy a specimen replanted after division. If there are cats around, protect the newly divided plant.

Pests and Diseases
These plants are aromatic and not prone to pests. However, in cold wet winters, they tend to rot off.

Maintenance
Spring Sow seeds.
Summer Sow seeds until late in the season. Cut back hard after flowering to encourage second flush.
Autumn Cut back after flowering to maintain shape and produce new growth. If your winters tend to be wet and cold, pot up and winter this herb in a cold frame.
Winter Sow seeds of **Nepeta camphorata**.

Garden Cultivation
The main problem with catmint is the love cats have for it. If you have ever seen a cat spaced-out after feeding (hence catnip) and rolling on it, then you will understand why cat lovers love catmint, and why cat haters who grow it get cross with cat neighbours. The reason why cats are enticed is the smell; it reminds them of the hormonal scent of cats of the opposite sex. With all this in mind, choose your planting site carefully.
Nepeta make very attractive border or edging subjects. They like a well-drained soil, sun, or light shade. The one thing they dislike is a wet winter, they may well rot off.
Planting distance depends on species, but on average plant 50cm (20in) apart. When the main flowering is over, catmint should be cut back hard to encourage a second crop and to keep a neat and compact shape.

Harvesting
Whether you pick to use fresh or to dry, gather leaves and flowering tops when young.

CULINARY

Use freshly picked young shoots in salads or rub on meat to release their mintish flavour. Catmint was drunk as a tea before China tea was introduced into the West. It makes an interesting cup!

MEDICINAL

Nepeta cataria is now very rarely used for medicinal purposes. In Europe it is sometimes used in a hot infusion to promote sweating. It is said to be excellent for colds and flu and children's infectious diseases, such as measles. It soothes the nervous system and helps get a restless child off to sleep. It also helps to calm upset stomachs and counters colic, flatulence and diarrhoea.
In addition, an infusion can be applied externally to soothe scalp irritations, and the leaves and flowering tops can be mashed for a poultice to be applied to external bruises.

COMPANION PLANTING

Planting **Nepeta cataria** near vegetables deters flea beetle.

CONTAINER GROWING

N. x faassenii and **N. racemosa** look stunning in large terracotta pots. The grey green of the leaves and the blue-purple of the flowers complement the terracotta, and their sprawling habit in flower completes the picture. Use a well-draining compost, such as a peat, grit, bark mix (see p.591). Note: both varieties tend to grow soft and leggy indoors.

OTHER USES

Dried leaves stuffed into toy mice will keep kittens and cats amused for hours.
The scent of catnip is said to repel rats, so put bunches in hen and duck houses to discourage them.
The flowers of **Nepeta x faassenii**, and **Nepeta racemosa** are suitable for formal displays.

Ocimum basilicum

BASIL

Also known as Common Basil, St Joseph Wort, and Sweet Basil. From the family Lamiaceae

Basil is native to India, the Middle East and some Pacific Islands. It has been cultivated in the Mediterranean for thousands of years, but the herb only came to Western Europe in the 16th century with the spice traders and to America and Australia with the early European settlers.

This plant is steeped in history and intriguing lore. Its common name is believed to be an abbreviation of Basilikon phuton, Greek for 'kingly herb', and it was said to have grown around Christ's tomb after the resurrection. Some Greek Orthodox churches use it to prepare their holy water, and put pots of basil below their altars. However, there is some question as to its sanctity – both Greeks and Romans believed that people should curse as they sow basil to ensure germination. There was even some doubt about whether it was poisonous or not, and in Western Europe it has been thought both to belong to the Devil and to be a remedy against witches. In Elizabethan times sweet basil was used as a snuff for colds and to clear the brain and deal with headaches, and in the 17th century Culpeper wrote of basil's uncompromising if unpredictable appeal – 'It either makes enemies or gains lovers but there is no in-between.'

SPECIES

Ocimum basilicum
Sweet Basil (Genovese)
Annual. Ht 45cm (18in). A strong scent. Green, medium-sized leaves. White flowers. Without doubt the most popular basil. Sweet basil comes from Genoa in the north of Italy, hence its local name, Genovese. Use sweet basil in pasta sauces and salads, especially with tomato. Combines very well with garlic. Do not let it flower if using for cooking.

Ocimum basilicum 'Cinnamon'
Cinnamon Basil
Annual. Ht 45cm (18in). Leaves olive/brown/green with a hint of purple, highly cinnamon-scented when rubbed. Flowers pale pink. Cinnamon basil comes from Mexico and is used in spicy dishes and salad dressings.

The distinctive leaves of green ruffles basil

Ocimum basilicum 'Green Ruffles'
Green Ruffles Basil
Annual. Ht 30cm (12in). Light green leaves, crinkly and larger than sweet basil. Spicy, aniseed flavour, good in salad dishes and combines well with stir-fry vegetables. But it is not, to my mind, an attractive variety. In fact the first time I grew it I thought its crinkly leaves had a bad attack of greenfly. Grow in pots and protect from any frost.

Cinnamon basil *Ocimum basilicum* 'Cinnamon'

Ocimum x citriodorum
Lemon Basil (Kemangie)
Annual. Ht 30cm (12in).
Light, bright, yellowish-green leaves, more pointed than other varieties, with a slight serrated edge. Flowers pale, whitish. Lemon basil comes from Indonesia, is tender in cooler climates, and susceptible to damping off. Difficult to maintain but well worth the effort. Both flowers and leaves have a lemon scent and flavour that enhance many dishes.

Ocimum minimum
Bush Basil
Annual. Ht 30cm (12in).
Small green leaves, roughly half the size of sweet basil. Flowers small, scented and whitish. Spread from Chile throughout South America, where, in some countries, it is believed to belong to the pagan Goddess Erzulie and is carried both as a powerful protector against robbery and by young ladies to keep a lover's eye from roving. Excellent for growing in pots on the windowsill. Delicious added whole to green salads; goes well with ricotta cheese.

Ocimum minimum 'Greek'
Greek Basil (Fine-leaved Miniature)
Annual. Ht 23cm (9in). This basil has the smallest leaves, tiny replicas of the bush basil leaves but, despite their size, they have a good flavour. As its name depicts it originates from Greece. It is one of the easiest basils to look after and is especially good grown in a pot. Use leaves unchopped in all salads and in tomato sauces.

Ocimum basilicum 'Napolitano'
Lettuce-leaved Basil
Annual. Ht 45cm (18in).
Leaves very large, crinkled, and with a distinctive flavour, especially good for pasta sauce. Originates in Naples region of Italy and needs a hot summer in cooler countries to be of any merit.

Ocimum basilicum var. purpurascens 'Purple Ruffles'
Purple Ruffles Basil
Annual. Ht 30cm (12in).
Very similar to straight purple basil (below), though the flavour is not as strong and the leaf is larger with a feathery edge. Flowers are pink. It can be grown in pots in a sunny position outside, but frankly it is a pain to grow because it damps off so easily.

Ocimum basilicum var. purpurascens
Purple Basil
Annual. Ht 30cm (12in)
Strongly scented purple leaves. Pink flowers. Very attractive plant with a perfumed scent and flavour that is especially good with rice dishes. The dark purple variety that was developed in 1962 at the University of Connecticut represents something of a breakthrough in herb cultivation not least because, almost exclusively, herbs have escaped the attentions of the hybridizers. The variety was awarded the All American Medal by the seedsmen.

The many diverse shapes and colours of basil

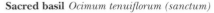
Sacred basil *Ocimum tenuiflorum (sanctum)*

Ocimum basilicum 'Horapha'
Horapha Basil (Rau Que)
Annual. Ht 42cm (15in).
Leaf olive/purplish. Stems red. Flowers with pink bracts. Aniseed in scent and flavour. A special culinary basil from Thailand. Use the leaves as a vegetable in curries and spicy dishes.

Ocimum tenuiflorum (sanctum)
Sacred Basil (Kha Prao Tulsi)
Annual. Ht 30cm (12in). A small basil with olive/purple leaves with serrated edges. Stems deep purple. Flowers mauve/pink. The whole plant has a marvellously rich scent. Originally from Thailand, where it is grown around Buddhist temples. Can be used in Thai cooking with stir-fry hot peppers, chicken, pork or beef. The Indian-related variety, *sanctum*, is considered kingly or holy by the Hindus, sacred to the gods Krishna and Vishnu. Being held in reverence it was the chosen herb upon which to swear oaths in courts of law. It was also used throughout the Indian subcontinent as a disinfectant where malaria was present.

CULTIVATION

Propagation
Seed
All basils can be grown from seed. Sow direct into pots or plug trays in early spring and germinate with warmth. Avoid using seed trays because basil has a long tap root and dislikes being transplanted. Plugs also help minimize damping off, to which all basil plants are prone (see below). Water well at midday in dry weather even when transplanted into pots or containers: basil hates going to bed wet. This minimizes the chances of damping off and will prevent root rot, a hazard when air temperature is still dropping at night.

Plant out seedlings when large enough to handle and the danger of frost has passed. The soil needs to be rich and well drained, and the situation warm and sheltered, preferably with sun at midday. However, prolific growth will only be obtained usually in the greenhouse or in large pots on a sunny patio. I suggest you plant basil in between tomato plants because:

1. Being a good companion plant, it repels flying insects
2. You will remember to use fresh basil with tomatoes
3. You will remember to water it
4. The situation will be warm and whenever you pick tomatoes you will tend to pick basil, which will encourage bushy growth and prevent it flowering, which in turn will stop the stems becoming woody and the flavour of its leaves bitter.

Pests and Diseases
Greenfly and whitefly may be a problem with pot-grown plants. Wash off with liquid horticultural soap.

Seedlings are highly susceptible to damping off, a fungal disease encouraged by overcrowding in overly wet conditions in seed trays or pots. It can be prevented by sowing the seed thinly and widely and guarding against an over-humid atmosphere.

Maintenance
Spring Sow seeds in early spring with warmth and watch out for damping off; plant out around the end of the season. Alternatively, sow directly into the ground after any frosts.
Summer Keep pinching out young plants to promote new leaf growth and to prevent flowering. Harvest the leaves.
Autumn Collect seeds of plants allowed to flower. Before first frosts, bring pots into the house and place on the windowsill. Dig up old plants and dig over the area ready for new plantings.

Garden Cultivation
Garden cultivation is only a problem in areas susceptible to frost and where it is not possible to provide for its great need for warmth and nourishment. In such areas plant out after the frosts have finished; choose a well-drained, rich soil in a warm, sunny corner, protected from the wind.

Harvesting
Pick leaves when young and always from the top to encourage new growth.

If freezing to store, paint both sides of each leaf with olive oil to stop it sticking to the next and to seal in its flavour.

If drying, do it as fast as you can. Basil leaves are some of the more difficult to dry successfully and I do not recommend it.

The most successful course, post-harvest, is to infuse the leaves in olive oil or vinegar. As well as being useful in your own kitchen, both the oil and the vinegar make great Christmas presents (see Preserving).

Gather flowering tops as they open in the summer and early autumn. Add fresh to salads, dry to potpourris.

CONTAINER GROWING

Basil is happy on a kitchen windowsill and in pots on the patio, and purple basil makes a good centrepiece in a hanging basket. In Europe basil is placed in pots outside houses to repel flies.

Water well at midday but do not overwater. If that is not possible, water earlier in the day rather than later and again do not over-water.

OTHER USES

Keep it in a pot in the kitchen to act as a fly repellent, or crush a leaf and rub it on your skin, where the juice repels mosquitoes.

MEDICINAL

Once prescribed as a sedative against gastric spasms and as an expectorant and laxative, basil is rarely used in herbal medicines today. However, leaves added to food are an aid to digestion and if you put a few drops of basil's essential oil on a sleeve and inhale, it can allay mental fatigue. For those that need a zing it can be used to make a very refreshing bath vinegar, which also acts as an antiseptic.

CULINARY

Basil has a unique flavour, so newcomers should use with discretion otherwise it will dominate other flavours. It is one of the few herbs to increase its flavour when cooked. For best results add at the very end of cooking.

Hints and ideas
1. Tear the leaves, rather than chop. Sprinkle over green salads or sliced tomatoes.
2. Basil combines very well with garlic. Tear into French salad dressing.
3. When cooking pasta or rice, heat some olive oil in a saucepan, remove from heat, add some torn purple basil, toss the pasta or rice in the basil and oil, and serve. Use lemon basil to accompany a fish dish – it has a sharp lemon/spicy flavour when cooked.
4. Add to a cold rice or pasta salad.
5. Mix low fat cream cheese with any of the basils and use in baked potatoes.
6. Basil does not combine well with strong meats such as goat or vension. However, aniseed basil is very good with stir-fried pork.
7. Sprinkle on fried or grilled tomatoes while they are still hot as a garnish.
8. Very good with French bread and can be used instead of herb butter in the traditional hot herb loaf. The tiny leaves of Greek basil are best for this because you can keep them whole.
9. Sprinkle on top of pizzas.
10. Basil makes an interesting stuffing for chicken. Use sweet basil combined with crushed garlic, breadcrumbs, lemon peel, beaten egg, and chopped nuts.

Pesto Sauce

One of the best known recipes for basil, here is a simple version for 4 people.

1 tablespoon pine nuts
4 tablespoons chopped basil leaves
2 cloves garlic
75g (3oz) Parmesan cheese
6 tablespoons sunflower oil or olive oil (not virgin)

Blend the pine nuts, basil and chopped garlic until smooth. Add the oil slowly and continue to blend the mixture until you have a thick paste. Season with salt to taste. Stir the sauce into the cooked and drained pasta and sprinkle with Parmesan cheese.

Pesto sauce will keep in a sealed container in the fridge for at least a week. It can also be frozen but it is important, as with all herbal mixtures, to wrap the container with at least two thicknesses of polythene to prevent the aroma escaping.

Pasta with purple ruffles basil

Oenothera

EVENING PRIMROSE

***Also known as Common Evening Primrose, Evening Star, Fever Plant, Field Primrose,
King's Cure-all, Night Willowherb, Scabish, Scurvish, Tree Primrose, Primrose, Moths
Moonflower and Primrose Tree. From the family Onagraceae.***

A native of North America it was introduced to Europe in 1614 when botanists brought the plant from Virginia as a botanical curiosity. In North America it is regarded as a weed, elsewhere as a pretty garden plant.

The generic name, *Oenothera*, comes from the Greek 'oinos' (wine) and 'thera' (hunt). According to ancient herbals the plant was said to dispel the ill effects of wine, but both plant and seed have been used for other reasons – culinary and medicinal – by American Indians for hundreds of years. The Flambeau Ojibwe tribe were the first to realize its medicinal properties. They used to soak the whole plant in warm water to make a poultice to heal bruises and overcome skin problems. Traditionally, too, it was used to treat asthma, and its medicinal potential is still evolving. Oil of evening primrose is currently attracting considerable attention worldwide as a treatment for nervous disorders, in particular multiple sclerosis. There may well be a time in the very near future when the pharmaceutical industry will require fields of this beautiful plant to be grown on a commercial scale.

The common name comes from the transformation of its bedraggled daytime appearance into a fragrant, phosphorescent, pale yellow beauty with the opening of its flowers in the early evening. All this show is for one night only, however. Towards the end of summer the flowers tend to stay open all day long. (It is called evening star because the petals emit phosphorescent light at night.) Many strains of the plant came to Britain as stowaways in soil used as ballast in cargo ships.

Evening primrose
Oenothera macrocarpa

SPECIES

Oenothera biennis
Evening Primrose
Hardy biennial. Ht 90–120cm (3–4ft), spread 90cm (3ft). Large evening scented yellow flowers for most of the summer. Long green oval or lance-shaped leaves. This is the medicinal herb, and the true herb.

Oenothera macrocarpa (missouriensis)
Hardy perennial. Ht 10cm (4in), spread 40cm (16in) or more. Large yellow bell-shaped flowers, sometimes spotted with red, open at sundown throughout the summer. The small to medium green leaves are of a narrow oblong shape.

Oenothera perennis (pumil
Hardy perennial. Ht 15–60cm (6–24in), spread 30cm (12in). Fragrant yello funnel-shaped flowers all summer. The green leaves a narrow and spoon-shaped

Evening Primrose
Oenothera biennis

CULTIVATION

Propagation
Seeds
Sow in early spring on the surface of pots or plug trays, or direct into a prepared site in the garden. Seed is very fine so be careful not to sow it too thick. Use the cardboard method. When the weather has warmed sufficiently, plant out at a distance of 30cm (12in) apart. Often the act of transplanting will encourage the plant to flower the first year. It is a prolific self-seeder. So once introduced into the garden, it will stay.

Pests and Diseases
This plant rarely suffers from pests or disease.

Maintenance
Spring Sow seed.
Summer Dead head plants to cut down on self-seeding.
Autumn Dig up old roots of second-year growth of the biennials.
Winter No need to protect.

Garden Cultivation
Choose a well-drained soil in a dry, sunny corner for the best results and sow the seeds in late spring to produce flowers the following year. Thin the seedlings to 30cm (12in) apart, when large enough to handle. After the seed is set, the plant dies. It is an extremely tolerant plant, happy in most situations, and I have known seedlings appear in a stone wall, so be forewarned.

Harvesting
Use leaves fresh as required. Best before flowering.
Pick the flowers when in bud or when just open. Use fresh. Picked flowers will always close and are no good for flower arrangements.

Collect the seeds as the heads begin to open at the end. Store in jar for sowing in the spring.
Dig up roots and use fresh as a vegetable or to dry.

CONTAINER GROWING

The lower-growing varieties are very good in window boxes and tubs. Tall varieties need support from other plants or stakes. None is suitable for growing indoors.

CULINARY

It is a pot herb – roots, stems, leaves, and even flower buds may be eaten. The roots can be boiled – they taste like sweet parsnips, or pickled and tossed in a salad.

MEDICINAL

Soon this plant will take its place in the hall of herbal fame.
It can have startling effects on the treatment of pre-menstrual tension. In 1981 at St Thomas's Hospital, London, 65 women with PMS were treated. 61 per cent experienced complete relief and 23 per cent partial relief. One symptom, breast engorgement, was especially improved – 72 per cent of women reported feeling better. In November 1982,

Evening primrose *Oenothera biennis*

an edition of the prestigious medical journal *The Lancet* published the results of a double-blind crossover study on 99 patients with ectopic eczema, which showed that when high doses of evening primrose oil were taken, about 43 per cent of the patients experienced improvement of their eczema. Studies of the effect of the oil on hyperactive children also indicate that this form of treatment is beneficial.
True to the root of its generic name, the oil does appear to be effective in counteracting alcohol poisoning and preventing hangovers. It can help withdrawal from alcohol, easing depression. It helps dry eyes and brittle nails and, when combined with zinc, the oil may be used to treat acne.
But it is the claim that it benefits sufferers of multiple sclerosis that has brought controversy. It has been recommended for MS sufferers by Professor Field, who directed MS research for the UK Medical Research Council.
Claims go further – that it is effective in guarding against arterial disease; the effective ingredient, gami-linolelic acid (GLA), is a powerful anti-blood clotter, that it aids weight-loss; a New York hospital discovered that people more

than 10 per cent above their ideal body weight lost weight when taking the oil. It is thought that this occurs because the GLA in evening primrose oil stimulates brown fat tissue... and that in perhaps the most remarkable study of all, completed in Glasgow Royal Infirmary in 1987, it helped 60 per cent of patients suffering from rheumatoid arthritis. Those taking fish oil, in addition to evening primrose oil, fared even better.
The scientific explanation for these extraordinary results is that GLA is a precursor of a hormone-like substance called PGEI, which has a wide range of beneficial effects on the body. Production of this substance in some people may be blocked. GLA has also been found in oil extracted from blackcurrant seed and borage seed, both of which are now a commercial source of this substance.

OTHER USES

Leaf and stem can be infused to make an astringent facial steam. Add to hand cream as a softening agent.

Origanum

OREGANO & MARJORAM

Also known as Wild Marjoram, Mountain Mint, Winter Marjoram, Winter Sweet, Marjolaine and Origan. From the family Lamiaceae.

Pot marjoram *Origanum onites*

For the most part these are natives of the Mediterranean region. They have adapted to many countries, however, and a native form can now be found in many regions of the world, even if under different common names. For example, *Origanum vulgare* growing wild in Britain is called wild marjoram (the scent of the leaf is aromatic but not strong, the flowers are pale pink); while in Mediterranean countries wild *Origanum vulgare* is known as oregano (the leaf is green, slightly hairy and very aromatic, the flowers are similar to those found growing wild in Britain).

Oregano is derived from the Greek 'oros' meaning mountain and 'ganos' meaning joy and beauty. It therefore translates literally as 'joy of the mountain'. In Greece it is woven into the crown worn by bridal couples.

According to Greek mythology, the King of Cyprus had a servant called Amarakos, who dropped a jar of perfume and fainted in terror. As his punishment the gods changed him into oregano, after which, if it was found growing on a burial tomb, all was believed well with the dead. Venus was the first to grow the herb in her garden.

Aristotle reported that tortoises, after swallowing a snake, would immediately eat oregano to prevent death, which gave rise to the belief that it was an antidote to poison.

The Greeks and Romans used it not only as scent after taking a bath and as a massage oil, but also as a disinfectant and preservative. More than likely they were responsible for the spread of this plant across Europe, where it became known as marjoram. The New Englanders took it to North America, where there arose a further confusion of nomenclature. Until the 1940s, common marjoram was called wild marjoram in America, bu is now known as oregano. In certain parts of Mexico and the southern states of America, oregano is the colloquial name for a totally unrelated plant with a similar flavour.

Sweet marjoram, which originates from North Africa, was introduced into Europe in the 16th century and was incorporated in nosegays to ward off the plague and other pestilence.

Wild marjoram
Origanum vulgare

SPECIES

Origanum amanum
Hardy perennial. Ht and spread 15–20cm (6–8in). Open, funnel-shaped, pale pink or white flowers borne above small heart-shaped, aromatic, pale green leaves. Makes a good alpine house plant. Dislikes a damp atmosphere.

Origanum x applii
Winter Marjoram
Half-hardy perennial. Ht 23cm (9in), spread 30cm (12in). Small pink flowers. Very small aromatic leaves which, in the right conditions, are available all year round. Good to grow in a container.

Origanum dictamnus
Ditany of Crete
Hardy perennial. Ht 12–15cm (5–6in), spread 40cm (16in). Prostrate habit, purplish pink flowers that appear in hop-like clusters in summer. The leaves are white and woolly and grow on arching stems. Pretty little plant, quite unlike the other **origanums** in appearance. Tea made from the leaves is considered a panacea in Crete.

Golden marjoram
Origanum vulgare 'Aureum'

Origanum 'Kent Beauty'
Hardy perennial. Ht 15–20cm (6–8in), spread 30cm (12in). Whorls of tubular pale pink flowers with darker bracts appear in summer on short spikes. Round, oval and aromatic leaves on trailing stems, which give the plant its prostrate habit and make it suitable for a wall or ledge. Decorative more than culinary.

Origanum laevigatum
Hardy perennial. Ht 23–30cm (9–12in), spread 20cm (8in). Summer profusion of tiny, tubular, cerise/pink/mauve flowers, surrounded by red/purple bracts. Aromatic, dark green leaves, which form a mat in winter. Decorative more than culinary.

Origanum laevigatum 'Herrenhausen'
Hardy perennial. Ht and spread 30cm (12in). Pink/mauve flowers which develop from deep purple buds in summer. Dark green, aromatic, slightly hairy leaves, with a pink tinge underneath. Decorative, and culinary when no other is available.

Greek oregano *Origanum vulgare* subsp. *hirtum* 'Greek'

Origanum majorana
Sweet Marjoram
Also known as Knotted Marjoram or Knot Marjoram Half-hardy perennial. Grown as an annual in cool climates. Ht and spread 30cm (12in). Tiny white flowers in a knot. Round pale green leaves, highly aromatic. This is the best variety for flavour. Use in culinary recipes that state marjoram. The leaf is also good for drying, retaining a lot of its scent and flavour.

Origanum onites
Pot Marjoram
Hardy perennial. Ht and spread 45cm (18in). Pink/purple flowers in summer. Green aromatic leaves that form a mat in winter. Good grower with a nice flavour. Difficult to obtain the true seed; grows easily from cuttings, however.

Origanum rotundifolium
Hardy perennial. Ht 23–30cm (9–12in), spread 30cm (12in). Prostrate habit. The pale pink, pendant, funnel-shaped flowers appear in summer in whorls surrounded by yellow/green bracts. Leaves are small, round, mid-green, and aromatic. Decorative more than culinary.

Origanum vulgare
Oregano
Also known as Wild Marjoram Hardy perennial. Ht and spread 45cm (18in). Clusters of tiny tubular mauve flowers in summer. Dark green, aromatic, slightly hairy leaves, which form a mat in winter. When grown in its native Mediterranean, it has a very pungent flavour, which bears little resemblance to that obtained in the cooler countries. When cultivated in the garden it becomes similar to pot marjoram.

Origanum vulgare subsp. hirtum 'Greek'
Greek Oregano
Hardy perennial. Ht and spread 45cm (18in). Clusters of tiny tubular white flowers in summer. Grey/green hairy leaves, which are very aromatic and excellent to cook with.

Origanum vulgare 'Aureum'
Golden Marjoram
Hardy perennial. Ht and spread 45cm (18in). Clusters of tiny tubular mauve/pink flowers in summer. Golden, aromatic, slightly hairy leaves, which form a mat in winter. The leaves have a warm aromatic flavour when used in cooking; combines well with vegetables.

Compact marjoram
Origanum vulgare 'Compactum'

Origanum vulgare 'Aureum Crispum'
Golden Curly Marjoram
Hardy perennial. Ht and spread 45cm (18in). Clusters of tiny tubular mauve/pink/white flowers in summer. Leaves, small, golden, crinkled, aromatic and slightly hairy, which form a mat in winter. The leaves have a slightly milder savoury flavour (sweeter and spicy) that combines well with vegetable dishes.

Origanum vulgare 'Compactum'
Compact Marjoram
Hardy perennial. Ht 15cm (6in), spread 30cm (12in). Lovely large pink flowers. Smallish green aromatic leaves, which form a mat in winter, have a deliciously warm flavour and combine well with lots of culinary dishes.

Origanum vulgare 'Gold Tip'
Gold Tipped Marjoram
Also known as Gold Splash Hardy perennial. Ht and spread 30cm (12in). Small pink flowers in summer. The aromatic leaves are green and yellow variegated. Choose the garden site carefully: shade prevents the variegation. The leaves have a mild savoury flavour.

Origanum vulgare 'Nanum'
Dwarf Marjoram
Hardy perennial. Ht 10cm (4in), spread 15cm (6in). White/pink flowers in summer. Tiny green aromatic leaves. It is a lovely, compact, neat little bush, great in containers and at the front of a herb garden. Good in culinary dishes.

CULTIVATION

Propagation
Seed
The following can be grown from seed: **Origanum vulgare**, **Origanum majorana**, **Origanum vulgare subsp. hirtum 'Greek'**. The seed is very fine, so sow in spring into prepared seed or plug trays. Use the cardboard trick. Leave uncovered and give a bottom heat of 15°C (60°F). Germination can be erratic or 100 per cent successful. Watering is critical when the seedlings are young; keep the compost on the dry side. As the seed is so fine, thin before pricking out to allow the plants to grow. When large enough, either pot on, using the bark, grit, peat mix of compost (see p.591), or if the soil is warm enough and you have grown them in plugs, plant into the prepared garden.

Cuttings
Apart from the 3 species mentioned above, the remainder can only be propagated successfully by cuttings or division.
Softwood cuttings can be taken from the new growing tips of all the named varieties in spring. Use the bark, grit mix of compost.

Division
A number of varieties form a mat during the winter. These lend themselves to division. In spring, or after flowering, dig up a whole clump and pull sections gently away. Each will come away with its own root system. Replant as wanted.

Pests and Diseases
Apart from occasional frost damage, marjorams and oreganos, being aromatic, are mostly pest free.

Maintenance
Spring Sow seeds. Divide established plants. Take softwood cuttings.
Summer Trim after flowering to prevent plants becoming straggly. Divide established plants in late summer.
Autumn Before they die down for winter, cut back the year's growth to within 6cm (2½in) of the soil.
Winter Protect pot-grown plants and tender varieties.

Garden Cultivation
Sweet marjoram and winter marjoram need a sunny garden site and a well-drained, dry, preferably chalk, soil. Otherwise plant them in containers. All the rest are hardy and adaptable, and will tolerate most soils as long as they are not waterlogged in winter. Plant gold varieties in some shade to prevent the leaves from scorching. For the majority, a good planting distance is 25cm (10in), closer if being used as an edging plant.

Harvesting
Leaves
Pick leaves whenever available for use fresh. They can be dried or frozen, or be used to make oil or vinegar.

Flowers
The flowers can be dried just as they open for dried flower arrangements.

CONTAINER GROWING

The **Origanum** species look great in containers. Use the bark, grit, peat mix of compost. Make sure that they are not over-watered and that the gold and variegated forms get some shade at midday. Cut back after flowering and give them a liquid fertilizer feed.

Red Mullet with Tomatoes and Oregano

CULINARY

Marjoram and oregano aid the digestion, and act as an antiseptic and as a preservative.
They are among the main ingredients of bouquet garni, and combine well with pizza, meat and tomato dishes, vegetables and milk-based desserts.

Red Mullet with Tomatoes and Oregano
Serves 4–6

*4–6 red mullet, cleaned
3 tablespoons olive oil
1 medium onion, sliced
1 clove garlic, chopped
500g (1lb) tomatoes, peeled and chopped
1 green or red pepper, seeded and diced
1 teaspoon sugar
1 teaspoon chopped fresh oregano or ½ teaspoon dried oregano
Freshly milled salt and pepper
Oil for baking or shallow frying*

Rinse the fish in cold water and drain on kitchen paper. Heat the olive oil in a pan and cook the onion and garlic slowly until golden brown; add the tomatoes, pepper, sugar and oregano, and a little salt and pepper.

Bring to the boil, then simmer for 20 minutes until thickened.
Bake or fry the fish. Brush them with oil, place in an oiled ovenproof dish and cook at a moderately hot temperature, 190°C/375°F/gas mark 5 for 7–8 minutes. Serve with the sauce.

MEDICINAL

This plant is one of the best antiseptics owing to its high thymol content.
Marjoram tea helps ease bad colds, has a tranquillizing effect on nerves, and helps settle upset stomachs. It also helps to prevent sea sickness.
For temporary relief of toothache, chew the leaf or rub a drop of essential oil on the gums. A few drops of essential oil on the pillow will help you sleep.

OTHER USES

Make an infusion and add to the bath water to aid relaxation.

Papaver

POPPY

From the family Papaveraceae

The poppy is widely spread across the temperate zones of the world. For thousands of years corn and poppy and civilizations have gone together. The Romans looked on poppy as sacred to their corn goddess, Ceres, who taught men to sow and reap.

The ancient Egyptians used poppy seed in their baking for its aromatic flavour.

The field poppy grew on Flanders fields after the battles of the First World War and became the symbol of Remembrance Day.

SPECIES

Papaver rhoeas
Field Poppy
Also known as Common Poppy, Corn Poppy, Blind Eyes, Blind Man, Red Dolly, Red Huntsmen, Poppet, Old Woman's Petticoat, Thunderbolt, and Wartflower
Hardy annual. Ht 20–60cm (8–24in), spread 45cm (18in). Brilliant scarlet flower with black basal blotch from summer to early autumn. The mid-green leaf has 3 lobes and is irregularly toothed.

Papaver somniferum
Opium Poppy
Hardy annual. Ht 30–90cm (12–36in), spread 45cm (18in). Large pale lilac, white, purple or variegated flowers in summer. The leaf is long with toothed margins and bluish in colour. There is a double-flowered variety, **P. paeoniaeflorum**.

Papaver commutatum
Ladybird Poppy
Hardy annual. Ht 30–90cm (12–36in), spread 45cm (18in). Red flowers in summer, each with black blotch in centre. Leaf oblong and deeply toothed. Native of Asia Minor.

Meconopsis cambrica
Welsh Poppy
Hardy perennial. Ht 30–60cm (12–24in). Yellow flowers in summer. The green leaves are divided into many leaflets. It differs from **Papaver** in that the seeds are released through slits in the seed heads and not through pepper-pot heads.

WARNING

All parts of the opium poppy, except the ripe seeds, are dangerous and should be used only by trained medical staff.

CULTIVATION

Propagation
Seed
Sow the very fine seed in autumn onto the surface of prepared seed or plug trays, using the bark, peat, grit mix of compost (see p.591). Cover with glass and leave outside for winter stratification. In spring, when seedlings are large enough, plant out into the garden in groups.

Pests and Diseases
Largely pest and disease free.

Maintenance
Spring Plant out in garden.
Summer Dead head flowers to prolong flowering and prevent self-seeding.
Autumn Sow seed. Dig up old plants.
Winter No need to protect.

Garden Cultivation
Poppies all prefer a sunny site and a well-drained fertile soil. Sow in the autumn in a prepared site, press seed into the soil but do not cover.

Thin to 20–30cm (8–12in) apart. Remove the heads after flowering to prevent self-seeding.

Harvesting
The ripe seeds can be collected from both field and opium poppies, the seed of which is not narcotic. It must however be ripe, otherwise it will go mouldy in store.

CULINARY

Sprinkle the ripe seeds on bread, cakes and biscuits for a pleasant nutty flavour. Add to curry powder for texture, flavour, and as a thickener.

CONTAINER GROWING

Use the bark, peat, grit mix of compost. Place in full sun out of the wind, and water well during the summer. Refrain from feeding as this will produce lots of soft growth and few flowers.

MEDICINAL

The unripe seed capsules of the opium poppy are used for the extraction of morphine and the manufacture of codeine.

OTHER USES

The oil extracted from the seed of the opium poppy is used not only as a salad oil, and for cooking, but also for burning in lamps, and in the manufacture of varnish, paint and soap.

Pelargonium

SCENTED GERANIUMS

From the family Geraniaceae.

These form a group of marvellously aromatic herbs which should be used more. Originally native of South Africa, they are now widespread throughout many temperate countries, where they should be grown as tender perennials.

The generic name, *Pelargonium*, is said to be derived from 'pelargos', a stork. With a bit of imagination one can understand how this came about: the seed pods bear a resemblance to a stork's bill.

Nearly all the species of scented geranium (the name is a botanical misnomer) came from the Cape of South Africa to England in the mid-17th century. The aromatic foliage found popular assent among Victorians, who used them as houseplants to scent the room. In the early 19th century the French perfumery industry recognized its commercial potential. Oil of geranium is now not only an ingredient of certain perfumes for men, but also an essential oil in aromatherapy.

SPECIES

There are many different scented geraniums. I am mentioning a few typical of the species that I have a soft spot for. They are very collectable plants.

Pelargonium 'Attar of Roses'
Half-hardy evergreen perennial. Ht 30–60cm (12–24in), spread 30cm (12in). Small pink flowers in summer. 3-lobed, mid-green leaves that smell of roses.

Pelargonium 'Atomic Snowflake'
Half-hardy evergreen perennial. Ht 30–60cm, (12–24in), spread 30cm (12in). Small pink flowers in summer. Intensely lemon-scented, roundish leaves with silver grey/green variegation.

Pelargonium capitatum
Half-hardy evergreen perennial. Ht 30–60cm (12–24in), spread 30cm (12in). Small mauve flowers in summer, irregular 3-lobed green leaves, rose scented. This is now mainly used to produce geranium oil for the perfume industry.

Pelargonium 'Chocolate Peppermint'
Half-hardy evergreen perennial. Ht 30–60cm (12–24in), spread 1m (3ft). Small white/pink flowers in summer. Large, rounded, shallowly lobed leaves, velvety green with brown marking and a strong scent of chocolate peppermints! This is a fast grower so pinch out growing tips to keep shape.

Pelargonium 'Clorinda'
Half-hardy evergreen perennial. Ht and spread 1m (3ft). Large pink attractive flowers in summer. Large rounded leaves, mid-green and eucalyptus-scented.

Pelargonium crispum
Half-hardy evergreen perennial. Ht and spread 30–60cm (12–24in). Small pink flowers in summer. Small 3-lobed leaves, green, crispy crinkled and lemon scented. Neat habit.

Pelargonium crispum 'Peach Cream'
Half-hardy evergreen perennial. Ht and spread 30–60cm (12–24in). Small pink flowers in summer. Small 3-lobed leaves, green with cream and yellow variegation, crispy crinkled and peach-scented.

A variety of scented geraniums

Pelargonium crispum 'Variegatum'

Half-hardy evergreen perennial. Ht and spread 30–60cm (12–24in). Small pink flowers in summer. Small 3-lobed leaves, green with cream variegation, crispy crinkled, and lemon scented.

Pelargonium denticulatum

Half-hardy evergreen perennial. Ht and spread 1m (3ft). Small pinky-mauve flowers in summer. Deeply cut palmate leaves, green with a lemon scent.

Pelargonium denticulatum 'Filicifolium'

Half-hardy evergreen perennial. Ht and spread 1m (3ft). Small pink flowers in summer. Very finely indented green leaves with a fine brown line running through, slightly sticky and not particularly aromatic, if anything a scent of balsam. Prone to whitefly.

Pelargonium Fragrans Group

Half-hardy evergreen perennial. Ht and spread 30cm (12in). Small white flowers in summer. Greyish green leaves, rounded with shallow lobes, and a strong scent of nutmeg/pine.

Pelargonium Fragrans Group 'Fragrans Variegatum'

Half-hardy evergreen perennial. Ht and spread 30cm (12in). Small white flowers in summer. Greyish green leaves with cream variegation, rounded with shallow lobes and a strong scent of nutmeg/pine.

Pelargonium 'Atomic Snowflake'

Pelargonium 'Lemon Fancy' in flower

Pelargonium graveolens
Rose Geranium

Half-hardy evergreen perennial. Ht 60cm–1m (24–36in). Spread up to 1m (3ft). Small pink flowers in summer. Fairly deeply cut green leaves with a rose/peppermint scent. One of the more hardy of this species, with good growth.

Pelargonium 'Lady Plymouth'

Half-hardy evergreen perennial. Ht and spread 30–60cm (12–24in) Small pink flowers in summer. Fairly deeply cut greyish green leaves with cream variegation and a rose/peppermint scent.

Pelargonium 'Lemon Fancy'

Half-hardy evergreen perennial. Ht 30–60cm (12–24in), spread 30–45cm (12–18in). Smallish pink flowers in summer. Small roundish green leaves with shallow lobes and an intense lemon scent.

Pelargonium 'Lilian Pottinger'

Half-hardy evergreen perennial. Ht 30–60cm (12–24in), spread 1m (3ft). Small whitish flowers in summer. Leaves brightish green, rounded, shallowly lobed with serrated edges. Soft to touch. Mild spicy apple scent.

Pelargonium 'Mabel Grey'

Half-hardy evergreen perennial. Ht 45–60cm (18–24in), spread 30–45cm (12–18in). Mauve flowers with deeper veining in summer. If I have a favourite, this is it: the leaves are diamond-shaped, roughly textured, mid-green and oily when rubbed and very strongly lemon-scented.

Pelargonium odoratissimum

Half-hardy evergreen perennial. Ht 30–60cm (12–24in) spread 1m (3ft). Small white flowers in summer. Green, rounded, shallowly lobed leaves, fairly bright green in colour and soft to touch, with an apple scent. Trailing habit, looks good in large containers.

Pelargonium 'Prince of Orange'

Half-hardy evergreen perennial. Ht and spread 30–60cm (12–24in). Pretty pink/white flowers in summer. Green, slightly crinkled, slightly lobed leaves, with a refreshing orange scent. Prone to rust.

Pelargonium quercifolium
Oak-Leafed Pelargonium

Half-hardy evergreen perennial. Ht and spread up to 1m (3ft). Pretty pink/purple flowers in summer. Leaves oak-shaped, dark green with brown variegation, and slightly sticky. A different, spicy scent.

Pelargonium 'Royal Oak'

Half-hardy evergreen perennial. Ht 38cm (15in) spread 30cm (12in). Small pink/purple flowers in summer. Oak-shaped, dark green leaves with brown variegation, slightly sticky with spicy scent. Very similar to **P. quercifolium**, but with a more compact habit.

Pelargonium 'Rober's Lemon Rose'

Half-hardy evergreen perennial. Ht and spread up to 1m (3ft). Pink flowers in summer. Leaves greyish green – oddly shaped, lobed and cut – with a rose scent. A fast grower, so pinch out the growing tips to maintain shape.

Oak-leafed pelargonium
Pelargonium quercifolium

Pelargonium tomentosum

Half-hardy evergreen perennial. Ht 30–60cm (12–24in), spread 1m (3ft). Small white flowers in summer. Large rounded leaves, shallow lobed, velvet grey-green in colour with a strong peppermint scent. Fast grower, so pinch out growing tips to maintain shape. Protect from full sun.

Pelargonium 'Chocolate Peppermint'

Pelargonium 'Attar of Roses'

CULTIVATION

Propagation
Seed
Although I have known scented geraniums to have been grown from seed, I do not recommend this method. Cuttings are much more reliable for the majority. However, if you want to have a go, sow in spring in a peat and grit compost (see p.591) at a temperature no lower than 15°C (59°F).

Cuttings
All scented geraniums can be propagated by softwood cuttings which generally take very easily in the summer. Take a cutting about 10–15cm (4–6in) long and strip the leaves from the lower part with a sharp knife. At all costs do not tear the leaves

off as this will cause a hole in the stem and the cutting will be susceptible to disease, such as black leg. This is a major caveat for such as **Pelargonium crispum 'Variegatum'**. Use a sharp knife and slice the leaf off, insert the cutting into a tray containing equal parts bark and peat. Water in and put the tray away from direct sunlight. Keep an eye on the compost, making sure it does not thoroughly dry out, but only water if absolutely necessary. The cuttings should root in 2 to 3 weeks. Pot up into separate pots containing the bark, peat, grit mix of compost. Place in a cool greenhouse or cool conservatory for the winter, keeping the compost dry and watering only very occasionally. In the spring re-pot into larger pots and water sparingly. When they start to produce flower buds give them a liquid feed. In early summer pinch out the top growing points to encourage bushy growth.

Pests and Diseases
Unfortunately pelargoniums do suffer from a few diseases.

1. Cuttings can be destroyed by blackleg virus. The cutting turns black and falls over. The main cause of this is too much water. So keep the cuttings as dry as possible after the initial watering.

2. Grey mould (Botrytis) is also caused by the plants being too wet and the air too moist. Remove damaged leaves carefully so as not to spread the disease, and burn. Allow the plants to dry out, and increase ventilation and spacing between plants.

3. Leaf gall appears as a mass of small proliferated shoots at the base of a cutting or plant. Destroy the plant, otherwise it could affect other plants.

4. Geraniums, like mint and comfrey, are prone to rust. Destroy the plant or it will spread to others.

5 Whitefly. Be vigilant. If you catch it early enough, you will be able to control it by spraying with a liquid horticultural soap. Follow manufacturer's instructions.

Maintenance
Spring Trim, slowly introduce watering, and start feeding. Re-pot if necessary.
Summer Feed regularly. Trim to maintain shape.
Autumn Take cuttings. Trim back plants. Bring in for the winter to protect from frost.
Winter Allow the plants to rest. Keep watering to a minimum.

Garden Cultivation
Scented pelargoniums are so varied that they can look very effective grown in groups in the garden. Plant out as soon there is no danger of frost. Choose a warm site with well-drained soil. A good method is to sink the re-potted, over-wintered geraniums into the soil. This makes sure the initial compost is correct, and makes it easier to dig up the pot and bring inside before the first frost.

Harvesting
Pick leaves during the growing season, for fresh use or for drying.
  Collect seeds before the seed pod ripens and ripen in paper bags. If allowed to ripen on the plant, the pods will burst, scattering the seeds everywhere.

CONTAINER GROWING

Scented pelargoniums make marvellous pot plants. They grow well, look good, and smell lovely. Pot up as described in 'Propagation'. Place the containers so that you can rub the leaves as you walk past.

CULINARY

Before artificial food flavourings were produced the Victorians used scented pelargonium leaves in the bottom of cake tins to flavour their sponges. Why not follow suit? When you grease and line the bottom of a 20cm (8in) sandwich tin, arrange approximately 20 leaves of either **'Lemon Fancy'**, **'Mabel Grey'**, or **'Graveolens'**. Fill the tin with a sponge mix of your choice and cook as normal. Remove the leaves with the lining paper when the cake has cooled. Scented pelargonium leaves add distinctive flavour to many dishes although, like bay leaves, they are hardly ever eaten, being removed after the cooking process. The main varieties used are **'Graveolens'**, **'Odoratissimum'**, **'Lemon Fancy'** and **'Attar of Roses'**.

Geranium Leaf Sorbet

Geranium Leaf Sorbet
12 scented Pelargonium graveolens leaves
75g/3oz/6 tablespoons caster sugar
300ml /¹/₂pint/1¹/₄ cups water
Juice of 1 large lemon
1 egg white
4 leaves for decoration

Wash the leaves and shake them dry. Put the sugar and water in a saucepan and boil until the sugar has dissolved, stirring occasionally. Remove the pan from the heat. Put the 12 leaves in the pan with the sugar and water, cover and leave for 20 minutes. Taste. If you want a stronger flavour bring the liquid to the boil again add some fresh leaves and leave for a further 10 minutes. When you have the right flavour, strain the syrup into a rigid container, add the lemon juice and leave to cool. Place in the freezer until semi-frozen (approximately 45 minutes) – it must be firm, not mushy – and fold in the beaten egg white. Put back into freezer for a further 45 minutes. Scoop into individual glass bowls, and decorate with a geranium leaf.

Rose Geranium Punch
1.2 litre/2 pints/5 cups of apple juice
4 limes
250g/8oz/1 cup sugar
6 leaves of graveolens
6 drops of green vegetable colouring (optional)

Boil the apple juice and sugar and geranium leaves for 5 minutes. Strain the liquid. Cool and add colouring if required. Thinly slice and crush limes, add to the liquid. Pour onto ice in glasses and garnish with geranium leaves.

Graveolens Geranium Butter
Butter pounded with the leaves makes a delicious filling for cakes and sweet biscuits. Spread on bread and top with apple jelly.

WARNING

None of the **crispums** should be used in cooking as it is believed that they can upset the stomach.

Rose Geranium Punch

OTHER USES

In aromatherapy, geranium oil is relaxing but use it in small quantities. Dilute 2 drops in 2 teaspoons of soy oil for a good massage, or to relieve pre-menstrual tension, dermatitis, eczema, herpes or dry skin.

Petroselinum

PARSLEY

Also known as Common Parsley, Garden Parsley and Rock Parsley. From the family Apiaceae.

Parsley in pots

Best-known of all garnishing herbs in the West. Native to central and southern Europe, in particular the Mediterranean region, now widely cultivated in several varieties throughout the world.

The Greeks had mixed feelings about this herb. It was associated with Archemorus, the Herald of Death, so they decorated their tombs with it. Hercules was said to have chosen parsley for his garlands, so they would weave it into crowns for victors at the Isthmian Games. But they did not eat it themselves, preferring to feed it to their horses. However, the Romans consumed parsley in quantity and made garlands for banquet guests to discourage intoxication and to counter strong odours.

It was believed that only a witch or a pregnant woman could grow it, and that a fine harvest was ensured only if the seeds were planted on Good Friday. It was also said that if parsley was transplanted, misfortune would descend upon the household.

Parsley *Petroselinum crispum*

SPECIES

Petroselinum crispum
Parsley
Hardy biennial. Ht 30–40cm (12–16in). Small creamy white flowers in flat umbels in summer. The leaf is brightish green and has curly toothed edges and a mild taste. It is mainly used as a garnish.

Petroselinum crispum French
French Parsley
Also known as Broad-Leafed Parsley.
Hardy biennial. Ht 45–60cm (18–24in). Small creamy white flowers in flat umbels in summer. Flat dark green leaves with a stronger flavour than **P. crispum**. This is the one I recommend for culinary use.

Petroselinum crispum var. tuberosum
Hamburg Parsley
Also known as Turnip-Rooted Parsley (see also pp.140–41). Perennial, grown as an annual. Root length up to 15cm (6in). Leaf, green and very similar to French parsley. This variety, probably first developed in Holland, was introduced into England in the early 18th century, but it was only popular for 100 years. The plant is still frequently found in vegetable markets in France and Germany.

Warning: In the wild there is a plant called Fool's Parsley, **Aethusa cynapium**, which looks and smells to the novice like French parsley. Do not be tempted to eat it as it is extremely poisonous.

French parsley
Petroselinum crispum French

CULTIVATION

Propagation
Seed
In cool climates, to ensure a succession of plants, sow seedlings under cover only in plug trays or pots. Avoid seed trays because it hates being transferred. Cover with perlite. If you have a heated propagator, a temperature of 18°C (65°F) will speed up germination. It takes 4–6 weeks without bottom heat and 2–3 weeks with. When the seedlings are large enough and the air and soil temperature have started to rise (about mid-spring), plant out 15cm (6in) apart in a prepared garden bed.

Pests and Diseases
Slugs love young parsley plants. There is a fungus that may attack the leaves. It produces first brown then white spots. Where this occurs the whole stock should be destroyed. Get some fresh seed.

Maintenance

Spring: Sow seed.
Summer: Sow seed. Cut flower heads as they appear on second-year plants.
Autumn: Protect plants for winter crop.
Winter: Protect plants for winter picking.

Garden Cultivation

Parsley is a hungry plant, it likes a good deep soil, not too light and not acid. Always feed the chosen site well in the previous autumn with well-rotted manure.

If you wish to harvest parsley all year round, prepare 2 different sites. For summer supplies, a western or eastern border is ideal because the plant needs moisture and prefers a little shade. For winter supplies, a more sheltered spot will be needed in a sunny position.

The seeds should be sown thinly, in drills 30–45cm (12–18in) apart and about 3cm (1in) deep. Germination is very slow. Keep the soil moist at all times, otherwise the seed will not germinate.

As soon as the seedlings are large enough, thin to 8cm (3in) and then 15cm (6in) apart. If at any time the leaves turn a bit yellow, cut back to encourage new growth and feed with a liquid fertilizer. At the first sign of flower heads appearing remove them if you wish to continue harvesting the leaves. Remember to water well during hot weather. In the second year parsley runs to seed very quickly. Dig it up as soon as the following year's crop is ready for picking, and remove it from the garden.

Hamburg or turnip parsley differs only in the respect that it is a root not a leaf crop. When the seedlings are large enough, thin to 20cm (8in) apart. Water well all summer. The root tends to grow more at this time of year, and unlike a lot of root crops the largest roots taste the best. Lift in late autumn, early winter. They are frost

Harvesting

Pick leaves during first year for fresh use or for freezing (by far the best method of preserving parsley).

Dig up roots of Hamburg parsley in the autumn of the first year and store in peat or sand.

CULINARY

Parsley is a widely used culinary herb, valued for its taste as well as its rich nutritional content. Cooking with parsley enhances the flavour of other foods and herbs. In bland food, the best flavour is obtained by adding it just before the end of cooking.

As so many recipes include parsley, here are some basic herb mixtures.

Fines Herbes

You will see this mentioned in a number of recipes and it is a classic for omelettes.

1 sprig parsley, chopped
1 sprig chervil, chopped
Some chives cut with scissors
1–2 leaves French tarragon

Chop up all the herbs finely and add to egg dishes.

Fish Bouquet Garni

2 sprigs parsley
1 sprig French tarragon
1 sprig fennel (small)
2 leaves lemon balm

Tie the herbs together in a bundle and add to the cooking liquid.

Boil Hamburg parsley as a root vegetable or grate raw into salads. Use in soup mixes; the flavour resembles both celery and parsley.

CONTAINER GROWING

Parsley is an ideal herb for containers, it even likes living inside on the kitchen windowsill, as long as it is watered, fed, and cut. Use the bark, peat mix of compost (see p.591). Curly parsley can look very ornamental as an edging to a large pot of nasturtiums. It can also be grown in hanging baskets, (keep well watered), window boxes (give it some shade in high summer), and containers. That brings me to the parsley pot, the one with six holes around the side. Do not use it. As I have already said, parsley likes moisture, and these containers dry out too fast, the holes in the side are small and make it very difficult to water, and the parsley has too big a tap root to be happy.

WARNING

Avoid medicinal use during pregnancy. There is an oil produced from parsley, but it should only be used under medical supervision.

MEDICINAL

All parsleys are a rich source of vitamins including vitamin C. They are also high in iron and other minerals and contain the antiseptic chlorophyll.

It is a strong diuretic suitable for treating urinary infections as well as fluid retention. It also increases mothers' milk and tones the uterine muscle.

Parsley is a well-known breath freshener, being the traditional antidote for the pungent smell of garlic. Chew raw, to promote a healthy skin.

Use in poultices as an antiseptic dressing for sprains, wounds and insect bites.

OTHER USES

A tea made from crushed seeds kills head lice vermin. Pour it over the head after washing and rinsing, wrap your head in a towel for 30 minutes and then allow to dry naturally. Equally, the seeds or leaves steeped in water can be used as a hair rinse.

Parsley tea

Phlomis fruticosa

JERUSALEM SAGE

From the family Lamiaceae.

Originates from the Mediterranean region but is now cultivated widely as a garden plant.

The generic name, *Phlomis*, was used by Dioscorides, a Greek physician in the first century whose *Materia Medica* was the standard reference on the medical application of plants for over 1,500 years.

SPECIES

Phlomis fruticosa
Jerusalem Sage
Hardy evergreen perennial. Ht and spread 1.2m (4ft). Whorls of hooded yellow flowers in summer. Grey/green oblongish leaves, slightly wrinkled.

Phlomis italica
Narrow-Leafed Jerusalem Sage
Hardy evergreen perennial. Ht 90cm (36in), spread 75cm (30in). Whorls of lilac pink flowers in midsummer, borne at the ends of shoots amid narrow, woolly, grey/green leaves.

CULTIVATION

Propagation
Seeds
Sow the medium-size seed in the autumn either into seed or plug trays and cover with a thin layer of compost. Winter in a cold greenhouse or cold frame. Does not need stratification nor heat, just cool temperature. Germination is erratic. When the seedlings are large enough to handle, prick out into pots using the bark, grit, peat mix of compost (see p.591). Plant the young plants into the garden when there is no threat of frosts.

Cuttings
Take softwood cuttings in summer from non-flowering shoots; they root easily.

Division
If an established plant has taken over its neighbour's spot, dig up and divide it in the spring; re-plant into a prepared site.

Pests and Diseases
In the majority of cases, this is free from pests and disease.

Maintenance
Spring Divide established plants if need be.
Summer Cut back after flowering to maintain shape.
Autumn Sow seeds.
Winter Protect outside plants if the winter temperature is persistently below −5°C (23°F).

Garden Cultivation
Jerusalem sage is an attractive plant, making a fine mound of grey-furred leaves, proof against all but the most severe winter. A prolific summer flowerer, happy in a dry, well-drained, sunny spot. Cut back each year after flowering (late summer) and you will be able to control and maintain its soft grey dome all year round. Do not trim in the autumn as any frost will damage and in some cases kill the plant.

Harvesting
Pick leaves for drying before planting flowers.

OTHER USES
The attractive, slightly aromatic leaves are a good addition to a potpourri.

CONTAINER GROWING

Jerusalem sage is happy if grown in a large container using a soil-based compost. Be mean on the feeding and watering as it is a drought-loving plant. Trim back especially after flowering to restrict its rampant growth. Protect during the winter in a cool greenhouse or conservatory. Keep watering to the absolute minimum.

CULINARY

Although not listed amongst culinary herbs, the leaves are pleasantly aromatic. In Greece the leaves are collected from the hillside and, once dried and bundled together with other related species, are hung up for sale. The dried leaves can be used in stews and casseroles.

Jerusalem sage *Phlomis fruticosa*

Phytolacca americana

POKE ROOT

Also known as Red Ink Plant, Virginia Poke Weed, Pigeon Berry, Coccum, Poke, Indian Poke, American Poke and Cancer Root. From the family Phytolaccaceae.

This herbaceous plant is a native to the warmer regions of America (especially Florida), Africa and Asia. It has been introduced elsewhere, particularly in the Mediterranean region.

Its generic name is derived from two Greek words: 'phyton' meaning plant and 'lac' meaning lake, referring to the purple/blue dye that flows from some of the *phytolaccas* when crushed.

The herb was introduced to European settlers by the Native Americans, who knew it as Pocan or Coccum, and used it as an emetic for a number of problems. It acquired a reputation as a remedy for internal cancers and was called cancer root.

SPECIES

Phytolacca americana (Phytolacca decandra)
Poke Root
Hardy perennial. Ht and spread 1.2–1.5m (4–5ft). Shallow, cup-shaped flowers, sometimes pink, flushed white and green, borne in terminal racemes in summer. They are followed by round fleshy blackish purple berries with poisonous seeds that hang down when ripe. Oval to lance-shaped mid-green leaves, tinged purple in autumn. There is a variegated form with green and white leaves.

Phytolacca polyandra
Hardy perennial. Ht and spread 1.2m (4ft). Clusters of shallow, cup-shaped, pink flowers in summer, followed by rounded blackish berries with poisonous seeds. Has brilliant crimson stems, oval to lance-shaped, mid-green leaves that turn yellow in summer through autumn. This plant is a native of China.

CULTIVATION

Propagation
Seed
Sow the seeds fresh in the autumn or spring in prepared seed or plug trays. Cover with perlite. If sown in the autumn, winter the young plants in a cold greenhouse or cold frame. In the spring, after a period of hardening off, plant them out in a prepared site in the garden, 1m (3ft) apart.

Division
Both species have large root systems that can be divided either in autumn or spring.

Pests and Diseases
Largely free from pests and diseases.

Maintenance
Spring Sow seeds. Divide established plants.
Summer Cut off the flowers if you do not want berries.
Autumn Sow seeds. Divide established plants.
Winter Dies back into the ground; no protection needed.

Garden Cultivation
Plant poke root in sun or shade in a moist, fertile soil, sheltered from the wind. Despite its poisonous seeds, this plant can look marvellous in a garden.

Harvesting
It can be used as a pot herb, the young shoots being picked in the spring. But because it is easy to confuse the identity of species, and toxicity varies among them, only do this if you really know what you are doing. So it is better to err on the side of caution and pick some nice fresh sorrel or red orach instead.

Poke root *Phytolacca americana*

CONTAINER GROWING

It is a tall plant, and when in berry is sufficiently heavy to unbalance even a large pot. Keep the poisonous berries out of reach of children.

If you choose to try it, use the bark, peat, grit compost (see p.591) and water well during the summer months.

MEDICINAL

Herbalists prescribe it for the treatment of chronic rheumatism, arthritis tonsillitis, swollen glands, mumps and mastitis.

An extract from the roots can destroy snails. This discovery is being explored in Africa as a possible means to control the disease bilharzia.

WARNING

POISONOUS. When handling either seeds, roots or the mature plant, gloves should be worn. It is toxic and dangerous. It should be used only by professional personnel.

Polemonium caeruleum

JACOB'S LADDER

Also known as Blue Jacket, Charity, Jacob's Walking Stick, Ladder to Heaven and Greek Valerian. From the family Polemoniaceae.

Jacob's ladder
Polemonium caeruleum

This European native species grows sparsely over the whole of the temperate regions of the northern hemisphere. It is not as prolific as some of the other closely related species in America.

It was known to the ancient Greeks as 'polemonium', and the root was once administered in wine in cases of dysentery, toothache, and on the bites of poisonous animals.

The leaf, being divided into many segments, has the appearance of a ladder, hence its common name – 'Jacob slept with a stone for a pillow and he dreamed and behold a ladder set upon the earth and the top of it reached to Heaven and behold the Angels of God ascending and descending on it' (Genesis 28, 12).

As late as the 19th century, it was known as 'Valeranae Graecae' or 'Greek Valerian' and was being used in some European pharmacies. It was predominantly used as an anti-syphilitic agent and in the treatment of rabies. To confuse things, the American Shakers called it 'Abscess' and used it for pleurisy and fevers.

SPECIES

Polemonium caeruleum
Jacob's Ladder
Hardy perennial. Ht and spread 45–60cm (18–24in). Clusters of attractive, cup-shaped, lavender-blue flowers in summer. The mid-green leaves are finely divided into small lance shapes.

Polemonium caeruleum subsp. caeruleum f. album
Jacob's Ladder
Hardy perennial. Ht and spread 45–60cm (18–24in). Cluster of attractive, cup-shaped, lavender-white flowers in summer. Leaves as **P. caeruleum**.

Polemonium reptans
Also known as False Jacob's Ladder or American Greek Valerian.
Hardy perennial. Ht 20–45cm (8–18in), spread 30cm (12in). Cluster of attractive, cup-shaped, blue flowers in summer. The silver/green leaves are finely divided into small lance shapes. The root of this species is bitter in flavour and is employed as an astringent and as an antidote to snake bites.

Other species worth looking out for (both native of western North America) –

Polemonium carneum
Hardy perennial. Ht and spread 45cm (18in). Cluster of attractive, cup-shaped, pink or purple/pink flower from early summer. Mid-green leaves are finely divided into small lance shapes.

Polemonium pulcherrimum
Hardy perennial. Ht 50cm (20in), spread 30cm (12in). Cluster of attractive, tubular blue/purple flowers in summer. The mid-green leaves are finely divided into small lance shapes.

CULTIVATION

Propagation

Seed

For flowering early the following spring, sow the fairly small seeds fresh in autumn into a prepared seed or plug tray. Cover with a thin layer of compost. Leave in a cool/cold greenhouse over winter. They will stay in their trays quite happily through the winter, as long as they are kept frost free. Prick out in spring when the threat of frosts is over and plant directly into the garden, after hardening off, at a distance of 30cm (12in) apart.

For flowering the following season, sow under protection in early spring, or direct in the garden in late spring.

Division

Named varieties must be propagated by division. Divide established plants in the spring. Dig up the whole plant and ease it in half. Replant in a prepared site in the garden.

Pests and Diseases

These plants rarely suffer from pests or disease.

Maintenance

Spring Sow seeds if not sown the previous autumn. Divide established plants if need be.
Summer Dead head flowers. After flowering, cut back to prevent self-seeding.
Autumn Sow seeds under protection.
Winter Established plants are hardy and should not need protection.

Garden Cultivation

This lovely short-lived perennial is not particular about site or soil, although it prefers a rich moisture-retaining soil with an addition of lime. It is not fussy about sun or shade, but looks prettier in the sun. In a long, hot summer, make sure the plant gets plenty of extra water. In an average summer it should not need extra watering.

The fairly short flowering season can be prolonged by dead heading. This is another plant beloved of cats, who seem to take a fancy to the young plants in particular. So, if you live in a catty area, give the young plants some protection.

Harvesting

Cut the flowers just as they open for drying. Dry either in small bunches or individual sprays.

CONTAINER GROWING

Jacob's ladder looks lovely in a container. Use a soil-based compost and do not allow to dry out. Place the container in a semi-shady place to protect if from over-heating in the midday sun. Feed with liquid fertilizer, following manufacturer's instructions, during the flowering period only.

CULINARY

I can find no record of this being used as a culinary herb, and the flowers do not add much flavour when added to salads.

OTHER USES

The dried flowers may not smell, but do look attractive in potpourris.

No longer used for medicinal purposes.

Jacob's ladder growing in a field

Polygonatum x hybridum

SOLOMON'S SEAL

Also known as David's Harp, Jacob's Ladder, Lady's Lockets, Lily of the Mountain, Drop Berry, Seal Root and Sealwort. From the family Convallariaceae.

A perennial plant that grows in thick woods and thickets in Europe, Asia and North America.

The plant's generic name, *Polygonatum*, is derived from 'poly', meaning many, and 'gonu', meaning a knee joint, which refers to its many-jointed rhizome.

King Solomon, wiser than all men, gave his approval to the use of its roots (said to resemble cut sections of Hebrew characters), as a poultice for wounds, and to help heal broken limbs.

In the 16th century Gerard cited its contribution in the soldering and gluing together broken of bones, when the root might be taken internally (in the form of ale) or applied externally as a poultice.

Solomon's seal
Polygonatum x *hybridum*

SPECIES

Polygonatum biflorum
Solomon's Seal
Hardy perennial. Ht 30–80cm (12–32in), spread 30cm (1ft). White waxy flowers tipped with green hang from arching stems in spring to summer. The berries are bluish-black. The leaves are oval to lance-shaped and mid-green in colour.

Polygonatum odoratum
Angular Solomon's Seal
Hardy perennial. Ht 60cm (24in), spread 30cm (12in). Produces pairs of fragrant, tubular, bell-shaped, green-tipped, white flowers in spring. The berries and leaves are as **P. multiflorum**. A variegated form called **Polygonatum odoratum 'Varigatum'**, which has creamy white striped leaves. Also a double-flowered one **Polygonatum odoratum 'Flore Pleno'**, has scented flowers that look rather like ballet dancers' skirts.

Polygonatum verticillatum
Whorled Solomon's Seal
Hardy perennial. Ht 1.2m (48in) spread 45cm (18in). The flowers are narrow and bell shaped, greenish white in colour, and appear in early summer. Its berries are first red, then dark blue.
The lance-shaped, mid-green leaves grow in whorls.

CULTIVATION

Propagation
Seed
Sow fresh seed in autumn into prepared seed or plug trays, cover with the compost, water in well, then cover with glass, and leave outside for the winter. Remove the glass as soon as germination starts in spring. When the seedlings are large enough plant out in a prepared site. Keep an eye on the watering throughout the first season – before they have developed their creeping rhizomes, young plants dry out quickly.

Division
The plant is best divided just after the stalks die down in autumn, although in dampish weather, division and transplanting can be undertaken any time of year. This method is easier and quicker than seeds.

Pests and Diseases
Sawfly caterpillar is a common pest, you will notice that the leaves have clean cut holes. This will no damage the plant but it can

look unsightly if you have a major attack. Spray with a liquid horticultural soap, at the first sign of attack. Complete eradication is difficult.

Maintenance
Spring Plant out seedlings.
Summer Make sure the soil does not dry out.
Autumn Sow fresh seeds. Divide established plants.

Winter Protect in the event of a prolonged frost below −10°C (14°F).

Garden Cultivation
This elegant graceful plant is sadly becoming scarce. Plant in groups on their own so that the tall and striking arching stems and waxy green-tipped flowers are shown off to their best. It requires a cool shady situation in fertile well-drained soil. Dig the soil over before planting with some leaf mould, and each winter top dress with extra leaf mould.

Harvesting
For medicinal use, dig up and dry the roots of a well-established 3-year-old-plant in the autumn after the foliage has died back.

OTHER USES

The plant has been employed cosmetically to clear freckles and as a skin tonic.

In Turkey the young shoots are harvested and cooked with asparagus.

Solomon's seal *Polygonatum biflorum* **in flower**

CONTAINER GROWING

Solomon's seal can be grown in large containers. Use a soil-based compost, and top dress in autumn with well-rotted manure or leaf mould. This will also protect it during winter. Position in semi-shade and water well throughout the summer.

WARNING

All parts of the plant are poisonous and should be taken internally only under supervision of a qualified medicinal or herbal practitioner. Large doses can be harmful.

MEDICINAL

The powdered roots and rhizomes make a good poultice for bruises, inflammation and wounds, and a good wash for skin problems and blemishes.

American Indians made a tea of the rootstock to take for women's complaints and general internal pains. They also used it as a wash to counteract the effect of poison ivy.

Polygonatum odoratum contains a substance that lowers the level of blood sugar and has long been used in the Orient for diabetes.

Solomon's seal makes a good skin wash

Primula veris

COWSLIP

Also known as Our Lady's Bunch of Keys, St Peter's Keys, Palsywort, Bunch of Keys, Covekeys, Cowflop, Cowstripling, Freckled Face, Golden Drops, Herb Peter, Hot Rod, Long Legs, Nook Maidens, Titsy Totsy, St Peters Herb, Paigale, Coweslop, Cowslap, Fair Bells, Fairy Cups and Keys of Heaven. From the family Primulaceae.

This traditional herb is native to Northern and Central Europe. It has naturalized elsewhere on porous, calcareous soils, meadows and pastures, to an altitude of 2,000m (6,500ft).

In America the plant that is called cowslip is in fact the English marsh marigold (*Caltha palustris*) and is not to be confused with the above.

'Cowslip' is a corruption of 'cowsslop' from the Old English 'cu-sloppe', from which cowslips sprang up in the meadow after a cow had lifted its tail.

The generic name *primula* is from the Latin 'primus', meaning first, after its early flowering in spring. A legend of northern Europe is that St Peter let his keys to Heaven drop when he learned that a duplicate set had been made. Where they fell the cowslip grew, hence the English, French and German common names 'Keys of Heaven', 'Clef de St Pierre' and 'Schlusselblumen'. The mediaeval *Regimen Sanitatis Salernitanum* recommended the cowslip as a cure for palsy or paralysis, a cure suggested perhaps by the trembling of its nodding flowers?

It is sadly no longer possible for country folk to go out and collect bushels of cowslip flowers to make cowslip wine. This once common grassland flower has now become relatively rare, a casualty of improved farming methods, which do not permit long grass and pastures to settle down and develop perennial flora. However, in East Anglia, where it retains the old alternative name 'paigale', it is beginning to re-establish itself on roadside verges and banked motorway edges in chalk and limestone areas, away from damaging pesticide sprays.

SPECIES

Primula veris
Cowslip

Hardy perennial. Ht and spread 15–20cm (6–8in). Tight clusters of fragrant, tubular, yellow flowers produced on stout stems in spring. Leaves, oval-shaped and mid-green, form a neat clump.

Cowslips are often mistaken for Oxlip (**P. elatior**), which is a hybrid of the cowslip and the primrose (**P. vulgaris**). The difference between the two is that oxlip have large pale yellow flowers in a one-sided cluster. Cowslip flowers are much deeper yellow, smaller and there are more in a cluster.

Cowslip *Primula veris*

CULTIVATION

Propagation
Seed
Better sown fresh. Collect the seeds heads in early autumn when the seeds are slightly succulent. Sow the fairly small seeds onto the surface of a prepared pot, seed or plug tray. Cover with glass. Put the container somewhere cool, like a cold frame, cold greenhouse or outside windowsill. Keep an eye on germination, which usually takes 4–6 weeks, and remove glass as soon as the seedlinsg emerge. If you sow in springtime, they will need cold then warm temperatures to break their dormancy – the frost treatment.

Plant into final position in the garden when the young plants are large enough to handle, or pot up for a spring display.

Division
Being a **primula**, cowslips divide easily. The best time for doing this is in the autumn. Dig up a clump and tease the plants apart. Replant *in situ* 15cm (6in) apart or pot up. Protect from frost until the roots have come down (this takes 4–6 weeks).

Pests and Diseases
The scourge of all **primula** plants is the vine weevil. I have known them decimate a complete stock of cowslips in a very short time.

Maintenance
Spring Early in year clear all the winter debris from established plants. Stratify seed if necessary and sow.
Summer Only dead head if you do not want the seed.
Autumn Collect seed. Divide established plants.
Winter No need to protect.

Cowslip wine

Garden Cultivation
Plant cowslips in semi-shade or sun, in a moist but well-drained soil. They prefer lime soil, but do adapt well. They look better grown in clumps rather than on their own, and are ideal for front of border in a spring garden, or for growing in the lawn, although you will have to mow round them until the seeds have set.

Harvesting
I am sure no reminder is necessary not to pick or dig up cowslips growing in the wild. This is prohibited in many European countries.

Pick leaves as required to use fresh. Not really worth drying.

Pick flowers as they open to use fresh.

Dig up roots in the autumn for drying.

CONTAINER GROWING

Essentially a wild plant, the cowslip does not thrive inside, but is happy in a container on a windowsill or patio. Use the standard bark, peat compost (see p.591), and do not let it dry out. Position the container where it gets some shade at midday.

WARNING

Some **primula** species can cause a form of contact dermatitis characterized by a violent vascular eruption in the fingers and forearms. Hyper-sensitive individuals should avoid these plants.

MEDICINAL

A tea from the flowers is a simple remedy for insomnia, nervous tension and headaches. Cowslip syrup was a country remedy for palsy and paralysis, hence its alternative name 'Palsywort'.

Cowslip roots are attributed with various medicinal propensities. One, owing to their high saponin content, is to treat whooping cough and bronchitis. Another, attributed to the salicylates present in the root, is to alleviate arthritis. For this reason, in many old herbals, cowslip roots are called **radix arthritica**.

CULINARY

Use leaves in salads and for meat stuffing. Use flowers in cowslip wine and salads.

Cowslip in salad

Primula vulgaris

PRIMROSE

Also known as Early Rose, Easter Rose, First Rose and May-Flower. From the family Primulaceae.

This herald of spring is a native of Europe.

The name primrose originates from the old Latin 'prima', meaning first, and 'rosa', meaning rose.

The polyanthus, which has been known in gardens since the 17th century, probably originates from crosses between coloured forms of the primrose and the cowslip.

In the Middle Ages concoctions were made from primroses which were used as a remedy for gout and rheumatism. The flowers were used in the preparation of love potions. An infusion of the roots was taken for nervous headaches.

The plant has become increasingly rare, in part due to the changing countryside. Legislation makes it illegal now to pick or dig up any wild plant and, with more sympathetic farming practices, one can see these plants beginning to re-establish in the hedgerows.

SPECIES

Primula vulgaris
Primrose
Hardy perennial. Ht and spread 15cm (6in). The fresh yellow, sweetly scented flowers with darker yellow centres are borne singly on hairy stems in early spring. Leaves are mid-green and wrinkled.

CULTIVATION

Propagation
Seed
In summer sow the fresh seed when it is still slightly green and before it turns darkish brown and becomes dry. Sow in a prepared seed or plug tray and cover with perlite. These fresh seeds usually germinate in a few weeks. Either winter in the plug trays, or prick out from seed trays when the seedlings are large enough and winter in pots for planting out into a prepared site the following spring.

The seed that one gets in seed packets should be sown in the autumn or early winter. Do not sow it directly into the ground where it can easily be lost. Water the seeds in; do not cover with

compost, but cover with glass or polythene. To help the seeds germinate, leave the trays outside for the winter so that the seeds get the frost (stratification). Sometimes they take 2 years to germinate from the dry state, so leave the seed trays until the following year if nothing appears in the spring, checking the compost occasionally to make sure it does not dry out. When the seedlings are large enough, plant out in a prepared site in the garden 15cm (6in) apart.

Division
Established clumps (from your own or friends' gardens, not from the wild) can be divided very easily in the autumn.

Pests and Diseases
The only major pest to attack the primrose is the

Primrose *Primula vulgaris*

Primrose *Primula vulgaris*

WARNING

Some **Primula** species can cause a form of contact dermatitis, characterized by a violent vascular eruption in the fingers and forearms. Hyper-sensitive individuals should avoid these plants.

MEDICINAL

Its medicinal use is really in the past, though it is still used occasionally as an expectorant for the treatment of bronchitis. A tisane, which is a mild sedative and good for anxiety and insomnia, can be made from the leaves and flowers.

Primrose salad

Primrose tisane

CULINARY

The flowers are lovely in green salads, and they can be crystallized to decorate puddings and cakes.

The young leaves make an interesting vegetable if steamed and tossed in butter.

vine weevil. Pollinated primrose flowers produce sticky seeds that attract ants; they then disperse them around the garden, which is why you sometimes see plants where you least expect them.

Maintenance

Spring Plant out young plants.
Summer Sow fresh seed.
Autumn Divide established plants.
Winter Sow dry seed that needs stratification. No need to protect plants, fully hardy.

Garden Cultivation

When planting primroses bear in mind that their natural habitat is in hedgerows and under deciduous trees and that therefore they prefer a moist soil, and will tolerate heavy soils, in semi-shade. Planted in a very well-sheltered site, they often open early in spring.

If you are growing primroses in a wild garden make sure you do not cut the grass until midsummer when the plants will have seeded themselves.

Harvesting

Pick flowers for fresh use any time. Pick young leaves to use fresh. In summer collect seed for immediate sowing.

CONTAINER GROWING

Primroses can be grown in containers and look very attractive and heartening especially if spring is damp and miserable. Use a soil-based compost. Keep the plant well watered and feed only occasionally with liquid fertilizer, once in the spring after flowering is sufficient. This is primarily a wild plant and does not benefit from over-feeding.

Prostanthera

PROSTANTHERA

Also known as Mint Bush. From the family Lamiaceae.

These highly attractive aromatic shrubs are natives of Australia.

I have fallen in love with these most generous of flowerers. When I was exhibiting one in flower at the Chelsea Flower Show some member of the public fell in love with it in equal measure and tried to liberate it from my display!

I can find no historical references other than in the RHS *Dictionary of Gardening*, which states that the generic name, *Prostanthera*, comes from 'prostithemi' to append, and anthera, meaning 'anther', the pollen-bearing part of the stamen. This therefore alludes to the appendages usually borne by the anthers.

Prostanthera cuneata

SPECIES

Prostanthera cuneata
Evergreen half-hardy perennial. Ht and spread 60–90cm (2–3ft). Very attractive white flowers with purple spots that look rather like little orchids; late spring, early summer. Round, dark green, slightly leathery and shiny, mint-scented leaves. Can withstand a minimum temperature of –2°C (28°F).

Prostanthera ovalifolia
Evergreen tender perennial. Reaches a height and spread of 1.2m (4ft) in its native country. Attractive purple flowers appear on short leafy racemes throughout the spring and summer. Dark green aromatic leaves. Can only withstand a minimum temperature of 5°C (41°F).

Prostanthera rotundifolia 'Rosea'
Evergreen half-hardy perennial. A small tree that reaches a height of 3m (10ft) in its native country; in cooler climates it's a lot smaller. Pretty mauve/purple flowers in spring that last a long time. The dark green leaves (not as dark as **P. cuneata**) are round and mint-scented. Can only withstand a minimum temperature of 0°C (32°F).

Prostanthera rotundifolia 'Rosea'

Prostanthera incisa
Evergreen tender perennial. Reaches a height of 2m (6ft), spread 1.5m (5ft) in its native country; in cooler climates it is a lot smaller. The green leaves are small (but larger than the other species mentioned), oval, and coarsely toothed, with a strong mint scent when crushed. Can only withstand a minimum temperature 5°C (41°F).

CULTIVATION

Propagation
Cuttings
Take cuttings in spring or late summer. Use the bark, peat, grit mix of compost (see p.591). When the cuttings are well rooted, 8–12 weeks, pot up again using the same mix and keep in containers for the first year.

Pests and Diseases
Over-watering young plants is a killer.

Maintenance
Spring Take cuttings.
Summer Cut back after flowering only if necessary.
Autumn Protect from frosts.
Winter Protect from hard frosts and excessive water.

Garden Cultivation
In cool climates with persistent frosts they are better grown in a container. However if your climate is mild, plant out in the spring in a warm corner, in a lime-free, well-draining soil at a distance of 60–90cm (24–35in) apart. Rain combined with frost is the killer in winter.

If you want to make a low hedge out of **Prostanthera cuneata** then plant specimens 45cm (18in) apart.

Harvesting
Pick leaves in the summer after flowering for drying and inclusion in potpourris.

CONTAINER GROWING

This is a real crowd puller when in flower, and even when not, makes a most attractive aromatic plant. Use the bark, peat, grit mix of compost. Keep young plants on the dry side, but water freely in the growing season.

MEDICINAL

I am sure that a plant that gives off as much scent, and has obviously so much oil in the leaf (**P. cuneata**), will one day have some use.

Prunella vulgaris

SELF HEAL

Also known as Carpenter's Herb, Sticklewort, Touch and Heal, All Heal, Woundwort, Hercules' Woundwort, Blue Curls, Brownwort and Hock Heal. From the family Lamiaceae.

This herb is found growing wild throughout all the temperate regions of the northern hemisphere, including Europe, Asia and North America. It is found on moist, loamy, well-drained soils, in grassland, pastures and open woodland, especially in sunny situations. Now introduced into China and Australia.

In strict 16th-century adherence to the Doctrine of Signatures, whereby it was believed that every plant bore an outward sign of its value to mankind, people noted that the upper lip of the flower was shaped like a hook, and as billhooks and sickles were a main cause of wounds in their agrarian society, they decided that the purpose of the herb was to heal wounds (hence Self Heal). They also saw the shape of the throat in the flower, which was why it was introduced to treat diseases of the throat such as quinsy and diphtheria, a propensity with a precedent in Ancient Greece, where physicians used it to cure sore throats and tonsillitis.

SPECIES

Prunella vulgaris
Self Heal
Hardy perennial. Ht 5–30cm (2–12in), spread 15–30cm (6–12in). Clusters of blue/purple flowers all summer. Oval leaves of a bright green.
There is a much rarer white-flowered species, **Prunella laciniata**, which has very deeply cut leaves.

CULTIVATION

Propagation
Seed
Sow the small seeds into prepared seed or plug trays in either spring or autumn and cover with perlite; no extra heat is required. If an autumn sowing, winter the young plants in a cold frame. In spring, when the plants are large enough, plant out 15–20cm (6–8in) apart.

Division
This plant grows runners that have their own small root systems and is, therefore, easy to divide. Dig up in the spring or autumn, and split and replant either in the garden or amongst grass.

Garden Cultivation
This plant, which is easy to establish, makes a colourful ground cover with attractive flowers. It is happy in full sun to semi-shade and will

Self heal *Prunella vulgaris*

grow in most soils, including those that are rather acid, though it does best if the soil is fertile. It can be grown in a lawn, and while the mower keeps its spread and height in check, it will still flower and be much visited by bees and butterflies.

Pests and Diseases
In most cases it is free from pests and disease.

Maintenance
Spring: Sow seed. Divide established plants.
Summer: Cut back after flowering to curtail self-seeding.
Autumn: Divide established plants. Sow seeds.
Winter: No need for protection, fully hardy.

Harvesting
Harvest for medicinal use only. Dry the leaves and flowers.

CONTAINER GROWING

Self heal can be grown in containers using a soil-based compost. However, as it looks a bit insipid on its own, it is better combined with plants like heartsease, poppies and cowslips.

Water well during the growing season, but only feed liquid fertilizer twice otherwise it will produce too lush a growth.

MEDICINAL

Used in herbal medicines as a gargle for sore throats and inflammation of the mouth. A decoction is used to wash cuts and to soothe burns and bruises.

Pulmonaria officinalis

LUNGWORT

Also known as Jerusalem Cowslip, Abraham, Isaac and Jacob, Adam and Eve, Bedlam, Cowslip, Beggar's Basket, Bottle of Allsorts, Children of Israel, Good Friday Plant, Lady's Milk, Lady Mary's Tears, Spotted Mary, Thunder and Lightning, Virgin Mary, Virgin Mary's Milkdrops and Virgin Mary's Tears, Spotted Bugloss, Jerusalem Sage, Maple Lungwort, Spotted Comfrey and Spotted Lungwort. From the family Boraginaceae.

Lungwort is a native plant of Europe and northern parts of the USA. It has naturalized in many countries in cool climates, where it grows in shady, moist areas and in woodlands. The markings on the leaves were attributed to the Virgin Mary's milk or her tears; however, the generic name, *Pulmonaria*, comes from 'pulmo' meaning lung, and the common name, Lungwort, conjures up a rather different image – of diseased lungs – to those blotched markings on the leaves. The Doctrine of Signatures, which held that all plants must be associated either by appearance, smell or habit with the disease which it was said to heal, used it for various lung disorders.

SPECIES

Pulmonaria angustifolia
Hardy perennial. Ht 23cm (9in), spread 20–30cm (8–12in). Flowers pink turning to bright blue in spring. Leaves lance-shaped and mid-green with no markings.

Pulmonaria longifolia
Hardy perennial. Ht 30cm (12in), spread 45cm (18in). The flowers start pinkish turning purplish-blue in spring. The leaves are lance-shaped, dark green, and slightly hairy with white spots.

Pulmonaria officinalis
Lungwort
Semi-evergreen hardy perennial. Ht 30cm (12in), spread 60cm (24in). Pink flowers turning blue in spring. Leaves oval with blotchy white/cream markings on a mid-green, slightly hairy surface.

Lungwort *Pulmonaria officinalis* **in flower**

Pulmonaria officinalis 'Sissinghurst White'
Semi-evergreen hardy perennial. Ht 30cm (12in), spread 45–60cm (18–24in). White flowers in spring. Leaves white-spotted, mid-green in colour, with a pointed oval shape.

Pulmonaria rubra 'Red Start'
Semi-evergreen hardy perennial. Ht 30cm (12in), spread 60cm (24in). Pink/red flowers in spring. The leaves are long ovals, velvety and mid-green with no markings.

Pulmonaria saccharata 'Mrs Moon'

Semi-evergreen hardy perennial. Ht 30cm (12in), spread 60cm (24in). Flowers start as pink and turn blue in spring. The green leaves are long pointed ovals with clear, creamy white, variable spots.

Note: The American native Virginian cowslip, **Mertensia virginica,** also known as smooth lungwort, belongs to the same Boraginaceae family as Lungwort. The flowers are purple/blue and the leaves lance-shaped. It is excellent for shady places. The foliage dies back very early in autumn and leaves a bare patch, so it is not suitable for front of border. Propagate in the same way as the **Pulmonarias**.

CONTAINER GROWING

Make sure the container is large enough to give the creeping rhizomes a chance to spread and so prevent the plant from becoming pot bound too quickly. Use a soil-based compost and a frost-hardy container, as these plants do not like coming inside even into a cold greenhouse, where the growth becomes soft and rots off. During the growing season keep the container in a shady spot and water well.

MEDICINAL

Lungwort is a soothing expectorant. The silica it contains restores the elasticity of the lungs. Externally it has been used for healing all kinds of wounds.

Lungwort potpourri

CULTIVATION

Propagation
Seeds
Lungwort seldom produces viable seed; increase your stock by division, but watch out in the garden, where it will self-seed erratically.

Division
Divide established plants either after flowering in late spring or in the autumn.

Pests and Diseases
Lungwort can suffer from powdery mildew when the leaves die back in autumn. Simply remove the damaged leaves and dispose of them.

Maintenance
Spring Dig up seedlings which mysteriously appear in odd parts of the garden.
Summer Do nothing.
Autumn Divide established plants. Cut back growth.
Winter No need to protect, fully hardy.

Lungwort
Pulmonaria officinalis

Garden Cultivation
This attractive, fully hardy plant prefers a moist but well-drained soil with added leaf mould or well-rotted manure. It is an ideal plant for shady parts of the garden but will tolerate most situations. Plant out 30cm (12in) apart in the autumn. Lungwort grows quickly and spreads to provide dense ground cover. Water freely in dry weather.

Harvesting
Pick the leaves after flowering in the summer and dry for medicinal use.

Rosmarinus

ROSEMARY

From the family Lamiaceae.

Rosemary is a shrub that originated in the Mediterranean area and is now widely cultivated throughout the temperate regions. The ancient Latin name means sea-dew. This may come from its habit of growing close to the sea and the dew-like appearance of its blossom at a distance. It is steeped in myth, magic and folk medicinal use. One of my favourite stories about rosemary comes from Spain. It relates that originally the blue flowers were white. When the Holy family fled into Egypt, the Virgin Mary had to hide from some soldiers, so she spread her cloak over a rosemary bush and knelt behind it. When the soldiers had gone by she stood up and removed her cloak and the blossoms turned blue in her honour. Also connected to the Christian faith is the story that rosemary will grow for 33 years, the length of Christ's life, and then die.

In Elizabethan days, the wedding couple wore or carried a sprig of rosemary as a sign of fidelity. Also bunches of rosemary were tied with coloured ribbon tipped with gold and given to guests at weddings to symbolize love and faithfulness.

Rosemary was burnt in sick chambers to freshen and purify the air. Branches were strewn in courts of law as a protection from gaol fever. During the plague people used to wear it in neck pouches to sniff as they travelled, and in Victorian times it was carried in the hollow handles of walking sticks for the same reasons.

SPECIES

Rosmarinus officinalis
Rosemary
Evergreen hardy perennial. Ht and spread 1m (3ft). Pale blue flowers in early spring to early summer and then sometimes in early autumn. Needle-shaped dark green leaves are highly aromatic.

Rosmarinus officinalis var. albiflorus
White Rosemary
Evergreen hardy perennial. Ht and spread 80cm (32in). White flowers in early spring to early summer and then sometimes in early autumn. Needle-shaped dark green leaves are highly aromatic.

Rosmarinus officinalis var. angustissimus 'Corsican Blue'
Corsican Rosemary
Evergreen hardy perennial. Ht and spread 80cm (32in). Blue flowers in early spring to early summer and then sometimes again in early autumn. The needle-shaped dark green leaves are highly aromatic. It is much bushier than the standard rosemary and has a very pungent scent. It is lovely to cook with.

Rosmarinus officinalis 'Aureus'
Golden Rosemary
Evergreen hardy perennial. Ht 80cm (32in), spread 60cm (24in). It hardly ever flowers, but if it does they are pale blue. The thin needle leaves are green splashed with gold. If you did not know better you would think the plant was suffering from a virus. It still looks very attractive.

Rosmarinus officinalis var. angustissimus 'Benenden Blue'
Benenden Blue Rosemary
Evergreen hardy perennial. Ht and spread 80cm (32in). Dark blue flowers in early spring to early summer and then sometimes again in early autumn. Leaves are fine needles and fairly dense on the stem, good aroma.

Prostrate rosemary *Rosmarinus officinalis* Prostratus Group

Miss Jessopp's Upright rosemary *Rosmarinus officinalis* 'Miss Jessopp's Upright'

Rosmarinus officinalis 'Fota Blue'
Fota Blue Rosemary
Evergreen hardy perennial. Ht and spread 80cm (32in). Very attractive dark blue flowers in early spring to early summer and then sometimes again in early autumn. Very well spaced narrow needle-like dark green leaves, the plant has a fairly prostrate habit.

Rosemary officinalis 'Majorca Pink'
Majorcan Pink Rosemary
Evergreen half-hardy perennial. Ht and spread 80cm (32in). Pink flowers in early spring to early summer and then sometimes again in early autumn. The needle-shaped dark green leaves are highly aromatic. This is a slightly prostrate form of rosemary.

Rosmarinus officinalis 'Miss Jessopp's Upright'
Miss Jessopp's Upright Rosemary
Evergreen hardy perennial. Ht and spread 2m (6ft). Very pale blue flowers in early spring to early summer and then sometimes again in early autumn. This rosemary has a very upright habit, making it ideal for hedges (see p.338). The leaves are dark green needles spaced closely together, making the plant very bushy.

Rosmarinus officinalis 'Primley Blue'
Primley Blue Rosemary
(Not Frimley which it has been incorrectly called for a few years.)
Evergreen hardy perennial. Ht and spread 80cm (32in). Blue flowers in early spring to early summer and then sometimes again in early autumn. The needle-shaped dark green leaves are highly aromatic. This is a good hardy bushy variety.

Rosmarinus officinalis Prostratus Group (lavandulaceus, repens)
Prostrate Rosemary
Evergreen hardy perennial. Ht 30cm (12in), spread 1m (3ft). Light blue flowers in early spring to early summer and then sometimes again in early autumn. The needle-shaped dark green leaves are highly aromatic. This is a great plant for trailing on a wall or bank.

Rosmarinus officinalis 'Roseus'
Pink Rosemary
Evergreen half-hardy perennial. Ht and spread 80cm (32in). Pink flowers in early spring to early summer and then sometimes again in early autumn. The needle-shaped dark green leaves are highly aromatic.

Rosmarinus officinalis 'Severn Sea'
Severn Seas Rosemary
Evergreen half-hardy perennial. Ht and spread 80cm (32in). Mid-blue flowers in early spring to early summer and then sometimes again in early autumn. The needle-shaped dark green leaves are highly aromatic. The whole plant has a slightly prostrate habit with arching branches.

Rosmarinus officinalis 'Sissinghurst Blue'
Sissinghurst Rosemary
Evergreen hardy perennial. Ht 1.5m (4½ft), spread 1m (3ft). Light blue flowers in early spring to early summer and then sometimes again in early autumn. The plant has an upright habit and grows very bushy. The needle-shaped dark green leaves are highly aromatic.

Rosmarinus officinalis 'Sudbury Blue'
Sudbury Blue Rosemary
Evergreen hardy perennial. Ht and spread 1m (3ft). Mid-blue flowers in early spring to early summer and then sometimes again in early autumn. Good hardy plant. The needle-shaped dark green leaves are highly aromatic.

Left to right: **White rosemary** *Rosmarinus officinalis* var. *albiflorus*, **Miss Jessopp's Upright rosemary** *Rosmarinus officinalis* 'Miss Jessopp's Upright', **Pink rosemary** *Rosmarinus officinalis* 'Roseus'

CULTIVATION

Propagation

Seed

Rosemary officinalis can, with care, be grown from seed. It needs a bottom heat of 27–32°C (80–90°F) to be successful. Sow in the spring in prepared seed or plug trays, using the bark, peat, grit compost (see p.591) and cover with perlite. Having got it to germinate, be careful not to over-water the seedlings as they are prone to damping off. Harden off the young plant slowly in summer and pot up. Keep it in a pot for the first winter, and plant out the following spring into the required position at a distance of 60–90cm (2–3 ft) apart.

Cuttings

This is a more reliable method of propagation and ensures that you achieve the variety you require.

Softwood: Take these in spring off the new growth. Cut lengths of about 15cm (6in). Use the bark, grit, peat mix of compost.

Semi-hardwood: Take these in summer from the non-flowering shoots, using the same compost as for softwood cuttings.

Layering

Rosemary lends itself to layering, especially as the branches of several varieties hang down. Layer established branches in summer.

Pests and Diseases

Being an aromatic plant, rosemary really does not suffer too much from pest and disease.

Maintenance

Spring Trim after flowering. Sow seeds of **Rosemary** **officinalis**. Take softwood cuttings.

Summer Feed container plants. Take semi-hardwood cuttings. Layer plants.

Autumn Protect young tender plants.

Winter Put a mulch, or straw, or agricultural fleece around all plants.

Garden Cultivation

Rosemary requires a well-drained soil in a sheltered sunny position. It is frost hardy but in cold areas it prefers to grow against a south or south-west facing wall. If the plant is young it is worth giving some added protection in winter. If trimming is necessary cut back only when the frosts are over; if possible leave it until after the spring flowering. Sometimes rosemary looks a bit scorched after frosts, in which case it is worth cutting the damaged plants to healthy wood in spring. Straggly old plants may also be cut back hard at the same time. Never cut back plants in the autumn or if there is any chance of frost, as the plant will be damaged or even killed. On average, despite the story about rosemary growing for 33 years, it is best to replace bushes every 5 to 6 years.

Harvesting

As rosemary is evergreen, you can pick fresh leaves all year round as long as you are not greedy. If you need large quantities then harvest in summer and either dry the leaves or make an oil or vinegar.

COMPANION PLANTING

If planted near carrot it repels carrot fly. It is also said to be generally beneficial to sage.

Golden rosemary *Rosmarinus officinalis* 'Aureus'

CONTAINER GROWING

Rosemary does well in pots and this is the preferred way to grow it in cold districts. The prostrate and less hardy varieties look very attractive and benefit from the extra protection offered by a container. Use the bark, grit, peat mix and make sure the compost is very well drained. Do not over-water, and feed only after flowering.

HEDGES

Rosemary certainly makes an effective hedge; it looks pretty in flower, smells marvellous and is evergreen. In fact it has everything going for it if you have the right soil conditions which, more importantly than ever, must be well drained and carry a bias towards lime. The best varieties for hedges are 'Primley Blue' and 'Miss Jessopp's Upright'. Both are upright, hardy and bushy. 'Primley Blue' has a darker blue flower and I think is slightly prettier. Planting distance 45cm (18in) apart. Again, if you need eventually to trim the hedge, do it after the spring flowering.

CULINARY

This is one of the most useful of culinary herbs, combining with meat, especially lamb, casseroles, tomato sauces, baked fish, rice, salads, egg dishes, apples, summer wine cups, cordials, vinegars and oils.

Vegetarian Goulash
Serves 4

2 tablespoons rosemary olive oil
2 medium onions, sliced
1 dessertspoon wholemeal flour
1 tablespoon paprika
275ml (10fl oz) hot water mixed with 1 teaspoon tomato purée
400gm (14oz) tin Italian tomatoes
2 sprigs 10cm (4in) long rosemary
225g (8oz) cauliflower sprigs
225g (8oz) new carrots, washed and cut into chunks
250g (8oz) new potatoes, washed and cut into halves
1/2 green capsicum, de-seeded and chopped
150ml (5fl oz) soured cream or Greek yoghurt
Salt and freshly milled black pepper

Vegetarian Goulash

Heat the rosemary oil in a flameproof casserole, fry the onion until soft, then stir in the ³/₄ of the paprika. Cook for 2 minutes. Stir in the water, tomatoes and sprigs of rosemary. Bring to the boil stirring all the time. Add all the vegetables and the seasonings. Cover and bake in the pre-heated oven (190°C/375°F/gas mark 5) for 30–40 minutes. Remove from oven, carefully take out the rosemary sprigs and stir in the soured cream or yoghurt, plus the remaining paprika. Serve with fresh pasta and/or garlic bread.

OTHER USES

Put rosemary twigs on the barbecue; they give off a delicious aroma. If you have a wood-burning stove, a few twigs thrown onto it makes the house smell lovely.

Rosemary is used in many herbal shampoos and the plant has a long reputation as a hair tonic. Use an infusion in the final rinse of a hair wash, especially if you have dark hair, as it will make it shine. (Use chamomile for fair hair.)

Rosemary infusion

MEDICINAL

Like many other essential oils, rosemary oil has anti-bacterial and anti-fungal properties, and it helps poor circulation if rubbed into the affected joints.

The oil may be used externally as an insect repellent. It also makes an excellent remedy for headaches if applied directly to the head.

Rosemary tea makes a good mouthwash for halitosis and is also a good antiseptic gargle. Drunk in small amounts it reduces flatulence and stimulates the smooth muscle of the digestive tract and gall bladder and increases the flow of bile. Put a teaspoon of chopped leaves into a cup and pour on boiling water; cover and leave it to stand for 5 minutes.

An antiseptic solution of rosemary can be added to the bath to promote heathy skin. Boil a handful in 475ml (16fl oz) of water for 10 minutes.

WARNING

The oil should not be used internally. Also, extremely large doses of the leaf are toxic, possibly causing abortion, convulsions and, very rarely, death.

Rumex

SORREL

Also known as Bread and Cheese, Sour Leaves, Tom Thumbs, A Thousand Fingers and Sour Sauce. From the family Polygonaceae.

Buckler Leaf Sorrel
Rumex scutatus

Sorrel is a native plant of Europe, Asia and North America . It has naturalized in many countries throughout the world on rich, damp, loamy, acid soils. The generic name, *Rumex*, comes from the Latin rumo 'I suck'. Apparently, Roman soldiers sucked the leaves to relieve thirst, and their doctors used them as a diuretic.

The name sorrel comes from the old French word 'surelle' meaning 'sour'. The Tudors considered the herb to be one of the best English vegetables; Henry VIII held it in great esteem. In Lapland, sorrel juice has been used instead of rennet to curdle milk.

SPECIES

Rumex acetosa
Sorrel
Also known as Broad Leafed, Common Sorrel, Garden Sorrel, Meadow Sorrel, and confusingly (see below), French Sorrel. Hardy perennial. Ht 60–120cm (2–4ft), spread 30cm (1ft). The flowers are small, dull and inconspicuous; colour greenish, turning reddish-brown as the fruit ripens. The mid-green leaves are lance-shaped with 2 basal lobes pointing backwards.

Rumex acetosella
Sheep's Sorrel
Hardy perennial. Ht 15–30cm (6–12in), spread indefinite (can be very invasive). The flowers are small, dull and incon-spicuous; colour greenish, turning brown as the fruit ripens. The mid-green leaves are shaped like a barbed spear. It grows wild on heaths and in grassy places, but is rarely found on chalky soil.

Rumex scutatus
Buckler Leaf Sorrel
Also known as French Sorrel.
Hardy perennial. Ht 15–45cm (6–18in), spread 60cm (24in). The flowers are small, dull and inconspicuous; colour greenish, turning brown as the fruit ripens. The mid-green leaves are shaped like squat shields.

CULTIVATION

Propagation
Seed
For an early crop start off under protection in early spring. Sow into prepared seed or plug trays, using the bark, peat compost and covering the seeds with perlite. Germination is fairly quick, 10–20 days without extra heat. When the seedlings are large enough and the soil has started to warm up, plant out 30cm (12in) apart.

Division
Sorrel is easy to divide and it is a good idea to divide broad leaf sorrel every other year to keep the leaves succulent. Autumn is the best time to do this, replanting in a prepared site.

Pests and Diseases
Wood pigeons, slugs and occasionally leaf miners attack sorrel, but should cause no problems with established plants. Remove the affected leaves, and put out traps for the slugs.

Maintenance
Spring Sow seed, under protection, in early spring and outdoors from mid-spring.
Summer Cut off flowers to maintain leaf production and prevent self-seeding. In a hot summer, water regularly to keep the leaves succulent.
Autumn Divide established plants.
Winter Fully hardy.

Sorrel *Rumex acetosa*

Garden Cultivation

This perennial herb likes a rich acid soil which retains moisture in full sun to partial shade. Sow the seeds in late spring into a prepared site. When germinated, thin seedlings out to a distance of 7.5cm (3in) and finally to a distance of 30cm (12in) apart. Can be grown under cloches to provide leaf throughout the year. The plant tends to run to seed quickly so, to keep the leaves fresh and succulent, remove flowerheads as they appear.

In really warm summers or generally warm climates, sorrel leaves tend to become bitter as the season progresses. A mulch will keep the soil cooler and, once the season cools down, the flavour will improve. Grow buckler leaf sorrel with its smaller leaf, as it is less susceptible.

If sorrel is causing a problem in your garden simply add some lime to eradicate it. It may need a few applications.

Harvesting

Pick young leaves throughout the growing season for fresh use and for freezing. Sorrel does not dry well.

CONTAINER GROWING

The buckler variety makes a good low-growing pot plant. Use the bark, peat mix of compost (see p.591), and make sure the container has room for the plant to spread. It is a very useful culinary herb, so for those with a small garden or who live on a chalk soil this makes an ideal container plant. Remember to keep cutting off flowers to keep leaves tender. Water well in the growing season, and feed with liquid fertilizer, especially if you are picking a lot.

Buckler leaf sorrel
Rumex scutatus

CULINARY

This is an excellent herb with which to experiment. Use sparingly in soups, omelettes, fish sauces, and with poultry and pork. It is useful for tenderizing meat. Wrap it around steaks or add pounded leaf to a marinade.

Eat leaves raw in salads, especially the buckler leaf sorrel, but reduce the vinegar or lemon in any accompanying dressing to compensate for the increased acidity.

Cook like spinach, changing the cooking water once to reduce acidity.

A Green Sauce

Wash a handful each of sorrel and lettuce leaves and a handful of watercress. Cook in a little water with a whole peeled onion until tender. Remove onion and discard. Allow the (mushy) leaves to cool then add 1 tablespoon (15ml) of olive oil, 1 tablespoon (15ml) of wine vinegar, pepper and salt. Stir until creamy. Serve with fish or cold poultry.

Sorrel and Lettuce Soup
Serves 4

100g (4oz) sorrel
100g (4oz) lettuce
100g (4oz) potatoes, peeled and sliced
50g (2oz) French parsley
50g (2oz) butter
600ml (1 pint) chicken stock
4 tablespoons thin cream

Wash the sorrel, lettuce and French parsley, pat dry and roughly chop. Heat the butter in a heavy pan and add the sorrel, lettuce, and parsley. Stew very gently for about 5 minutes, and then add the potato. Mix all together, pour over the heated stock, and simmer covered for 25 minutes. Put in a liquidizer, or, if you are a purist, through a coarse food mill. Return to the pan and heat gently (do not boil). Swirl in some cream just before serving.

OTHER USES

Sorrel is a good dye plant; with an alum mordant it makes a yellow or green dye.

Use juice of the leaf to remove rust, mould and ink stains from linen, wicker and silver.

Sorrel and Lettuce Soup

MEDICINAL

Sorrel is considered to have blood cleansing and blood improving qualities in a similar way to spinach, which improves the haemoglobin content of the blood. It also contains vitamin C.

A leaf may be used in a poultice to treat certain skin complaints, including acne.

WARNING

Care has to be taken that sorrel is not used in too great a quantity or too frequently. Its oxalic acid content may damage health if taken in excess. Very large doses are poisonous, causing severe kidney damage.

The herb should not be used medicinally by those predisposed to rheumatism, arthritis, gout, kidney stones or gastric hyperacidity.

The leaf may cause dermatitis.

Ruta graveolens

RUE

Also known as Herb of Grace and Herbygrass. From the family Rutaceae.

Rue is a native of Southern Europe, especially the Mediterranean region, and is found growing in poor, free-draining soil. It has established itself in North America and Australia in similar conditions. It has also adapted to cooler climates and is now naturalized in Northern Europe. Rue was known as Herb of Grace, perhaps because it was regarded as a protector against the Devil, witchcraft and magic.

It was also used as an antidote against every kind of poison from toadstools to snake bites. The Romans brought it across northern Europe to Britain, where it did not gain favour until the Middle Ages, when it was one of the herbs carried in nosegays by the rich as protection from evil and the plague. Also, like rosemary, it was placed near the judge before prisoners were brought out, as protection from the pestilence ridden gaols and gaol fever.

It was famous for preserving eyesight and was said to promote second sight, perhaps acting on the third eye. Both Leonardo da Vinci and Michelangelo are supposed to have said that their inner vision had been enhanced by this herb.

SPECIES

Ruta graveolens
Rue
Hardy evergreen perennial. Ht and spread 60cm (24in). Yellow waxy flowers with 4 or 5 petals in summer. Small rounded lobed leaves of a greeny blue colour.

Ruta graveolens 'Jackman's Blue'
Rue Jackman's Blue
Hardy evergreen perennial. Ht and spread 60cm (24in). Yellow waxy flowers with 4 or 5 petals in summer. Small rounded lobed leaves of a distinctive blue colour.

Ruta graveolens 'Variegata'
Variegated Rue
Hardy evergreen perennial. Ht and spread 60cm (24in). Yellow waxy flowers with 4 or 5 petals in summer. Small rounded lobed leaves with a most distinctive cream/white variegation, which is particularly marked in spring, fading in the summer unless the plant is kept well clipped. I have known people mistake the variegation for flowers and try to smell them, which shows how attractive this plant is. Smelling it at close quarters is not, however, a good idea as this plant, like other rues, can cause the skin to blister.

CULTIVATION

Propagation
Seed
In spring sow the fine seed using the cardboard trick in prepared plug or seed trays. Use the bark, peat mix of compost (see p.591) and cover with perlite. You may find that a bottom heat of 20°C (68°F) is helpful. Germination can be an all or nothing affair, depending on the source of the seed. Young seedlings are prone to damping off, so watch the watering, and just keep the compost damp, not wet.

Unlike many variegated plants, the variegated rue will be variegated from seed. When the seedlings are large enough, plant out into a prepared site in the garden at a distance of 45cm (18in).

Cuttings
Take cuttings of new shoots in spring or early summer. Jackman's Blue can only be propagated from cuttings. Use the bark, peat, grit mix of compost (see p.591) for the cuttings; again, do not over-water.

Rue *Ruta graveolens* **is said to have inspired the suit of clubs in playing cards**

Rue Jackman's Blue *Ruta graveolens* 'Jackman's Blue'

WARNING

Handling the plant can cause allergic reactions or phytol-photodermatitis. If you have ever seen a rue burn, it really is quite serious so do heed this warning.

To minimize this risk do not take cuttings off the plants either when they are wet after rain or when in full sun, as this is when the plant is at its most dangerous. Wait until the plant has dried out or the sun has gone in; alternatively wear gloves.

Must only be used by medical personnel and not at all by pregnant women, as it is abortive. Large doses are toxic, sometimes precipitating mental confusion, and the oil is capable of causing death.

Pests and Diseases

Rue is prone to whitefly followed by black sooty mould. Treat the whitefly with a liquid horticultural soap as soon as the pest appears, following manufacturer's instructions. This should then also control the sooty mould.

Maintenance

Spring Cut back plants to regain shape. Sow seed. Take softwood cuttings.
Summer Cut back after flowering to maintain shape.
Autumn The variegated rue is slightly more tender than the other two varieties, so protect when frosts go below -5°C (23°F).
Winter Rue is hardy and requires protection only in extreme conditions.

Garden Cultivation

All the rues prefer a sunny site with a well-drained poor soil. They are best positioned away from paths or at the back of beds where people won't brush against them accidentally, especially children, whose skin is more sensitive than adults. In the spring, and after flowering in the summer (not autumn), cut back all the plants to maintain shape, and the variegated form to maintain variegations.

Harvesting

Pick leaves for use fresh when required. No need to preserve.

CONTAINER GROWING

Rue can be grown in containers; use the bark, peat, grit mix of compost. Again position the container carefully so that one does not accidentally brush the leaves. Although it is a drought-tolerant plant, in containers it prefers to be watered regularly in summer. Allow to dry in winter, watering only once a month. Feed plants in the spring with liquid fertilizer following the manufacturer's instructions.

MEDICINAL

This ancient medicinal herb is used in the treatment of strained eyes, and headaches caused by eye strain. It is also useful for nervous headaches and heart palpitations, for treating high blood pressure and helping to harden the bones and teeth. The antispasmodic action of its oil and the alkaloids explains its use in the treatment of nervous digestion and colic. The tea also expels worms.

Variegated rue *Ruta graveolens* 'Variegata'

Rue tea

CULINARY

I seriously cannot believe that people enjoy eating this herb; it is incredibly bitter. It can be added finely chopped with discretion to egg, fish or cheese dishes.

Harvesting

Since sage is an evergreen plant, the leaves can be used fresh any time of the year. In Mediterranean-type climates, including the southern states of America, the leaves can be harvested during the winter months. In cooler climates this is also possible if you cover a chosen bush with agricultural fleece as this will keep the leaves in better condition. They dry well, but care should be taken to keep their green colour. Because this herb is frequently seen in its dried condition people assume it is easy to dry. But beware, although other herbs may lose some of their aroma or qualities if badly dried or handled, sage seems to pick up a musty scent and a flavour really horrible to taste – better to grow it in your garden to use fresh.

CONTAINER GROWING

All sages grow happily in containers. Pineapple sage is an obvious one as it is tender, but a better reason is that if it is at hand one will rub the leaves and smell that marvellous pineapple scent. Use the bark, grit, peat mix of compost (see p.591) for all varieties, feed the plants after flowering, and do not over-water.

COMPANION PLANTING

Sage planted with cabbages is said to repel cabbage white butterflies. Planted next to vines it is generally beneficial.

OTHER USES

The dried leaves, especially those of pineapple sage, are good added to potpourris.

MEDICINAL

For centuries, sage has been esteemed for its healing powers. It is a first-rate remedy as a hot infusion for colds. Sage tea combined with a little cider vinegar makes a gargle which is excellent for sore throats, laryngitis and tonsillitis. It is also beneficial for infected gums and mouth ulcers.

The essential oil, known as sage clary or muscatel oil, is obtained by steamed distillation of the fresh or partially dried flower stems and leaves. It is used in herbal medicine but more widely in toilet waters, perfumes and soap, and to flavour wine, vermouth and liqueurs.

CULINARY

This powerful healing plant is also a strong culinary herb, although it has been misused and misjudged in the culinary world. Used with discretion it adds a lovely flavour, aids digestion of fatty food, and being an antiseptic it kills off any bugs in the meat as it cooks. It has long been used with sausages because of its preservative qualities. It also makes a delicious herb jelly, or oil or vinegar. But I like using small amounts fresh. The original form of the following recipe comes from a vegetarian friend of mine. I fell in love with it and have subsequently adapted it to include some other herbs.

Hazelnut and Mushroom Roast
Serves 4

A little sage oil
Long grain brown rice (measured to the 150ml (5fl oz) mark on a glass measuring jug)
275ml (10fl oz) boiling water
1 teaspoon salt
1 large onion, peeled and chopped
110g (4oz) mushrooms, wiped and chopped
2 medium carrots, pared and roughly grated
½ teaspoon coriander seed
1 tablespoon soy sauce
110g (4oz) wholemeal breadcrumbs
175g (6oz) ground hazelnuts
1 teaspoon chopped sage leaves
1 teaspoon chopped lovage leaves
Sunflower seeds for decoration
A 900g (2lb) loaf tin, lined with greaseproof paper

Pre-heat the oven (180°C/350°F/gas mark 4).

Heat 1 dessertspoon of sage oil in a small saucepan, toss the rice in it to give it a coating of oil, add boiling water straight from the kettle and the teaspoon of salt. Stir, and let the rice cook slowly for roughly 40 minutes or until the liquid has been absorbed.

While the rice is cooking, heat 1 tablespoon of sage oil in a medium sized frying-pan, add the onions, mushrooms, carrots, the ground coriander seed and soy sauce. Mix them together and let them cook for about 10 minutes.

Combine the cooked brown rice, breadcrumbs, hazelnuts, sage and lovage; mix with the vegetables and place the complete mixture in the prepared loaf tin. Scatter the sunflower seeds on top and bake in the oven for 45 minutes. Leave to cool slightly in the tin. Slice and serve with a home-made tomato sauce and a green salad.

WARNING

Extended or excessive use of sage can cause symptoms of poisoning. Although the herb seems safe and common, if you drink the tea for more than a week or two at a time, its strong antiseptic properties can cause potentially toxic effects.

Broad-leaved sage *Salvia officinalis* broad-leaved

Tricolor Sage *Salvia officinalis* 'Tricolor'

Sambucus

ELDER

Also known as Boun-tree, Boon-tree, Dogtree, Judas Tree, Scores, Score Tree, God's Stinking Tree, Black Elder, Blackberried, European Elder, Ellhorne and German Elder. From the family Caprifoliaceae.

Elder grows worldwide throughout temperate climates. Its common name is probably derived from the Anglo Saxon 'Ellaern' or 'Aeld', which mean 'fire' or 'kindle', because the hollow stems were once used for getting fires going. The generic name, *Sambucus*, dates from ancient Greek times and may originally have referred to sambuke, a kind of harp made of elderwood. Pipes were made from its branches too, possibly the original Pan pipes. People thought that if you put it on the fire you would see the Devil. They believed it unlucky to make cradle rockers out of it, that the spirit of the tree might harm the child. Again, farmers were unwilling to use an elder switch to drive cattle and one folktale had it that elder would only grow where blood had been shed. Planting it outside the back door was a sure way of protecting against evil, black magic, and keeping witches out of the house, which would never be struck by lightning. It was thought that Christ's cross was made of elderwood.

Common elder
Sambucus nigra

Red elder *Sambucus racemosa*

SPECIES

Sambucus canadensis
American Elder
Also known as Black Elder, Common Elder, Rob Elder, Sweet Elder.
Deciduous hardy perennial. Ht 1.5–3.6m (5–12ft). Numerous small white flowers in flat cymes throughout summer. Berries are dark purple in early autumn; its leaves long, sharply toothed and bright green.
Caution: All parts of the fresh plant can poison. Children have even been poisoned by chewing or sucking the bark. Once cooked, however, flowers and berries are safe.
Some Native American tribes use a tea made from the root-bark for headaches, mucous congestion, and to promote labour in childbirth.

Sambucus canadensis 'Aurea'
Deciduous hardy perennial. Ht and spread 4m (12ft). Creamy white flowers in summer, red fruits in early autumn. Large golden yellow leaves.

Sambucus ebulus
Dwarf Elder
Also known as Blood Elder, Danewort, Wild Elder, Walewort.
Deciduous hardy perennial. Ht 60–120cm (2–4ft), spread 1m (3ft). White flowers with pink tips in summer. Black berries in early autumn. Its green leaves are oblong, lance-shaped, and toothed around the edges. Dwarf elder grows in small clusters in Europe and in Eastern and Central States of America.
Warning: All parts of the plant are slightly poisonous and children should be warned not to eat the bitter berries.
It has a much stronger action than its close relative, common elder (**S. nigra**). Large doses cause vertigo, vomiting and diarrhoea, the latter, denoted colloquially as 'the Danes', being the origin of Danewort. Nowadays dwarf elder is rarely used and should be taken internally only under strict medical supervision.

Sambucus nigra
Common Elder
Also known as European Elder, Black Elder, Bore Tree.
Deciduous hardy perennial. Ht 6–7m (20–23ft), spread 4.5m (15ft). Spreading branches bear flat heads of small, star-shaped, creamy-white flowers in late spring and early summer. These are followed in early autumn by drooping branches of purplish-black juicy berries.
The flowers and berries are used in industry for cosmetics, jams, jellies and liqueurs.
The leaves are purgative and should not be taken internally; decoctions have an insecticidal effect.
The wood from the adult plant is highly prized by craftsmen.

Sambucus nigra 'Aurea'
Golden Elder

Deciduous shrub. Ht and spread 6m (20ft). Flattened heads of fragrant, star-shaped, creamy-white flowers from early to mid-summer. Black fruits in early autumn. Golden yellow, oval, sharply toothed leaves usually in groups of five.

Sambucus racemosa
Red Elder

Deciduous hardy perennial. Ht and spread 3–4m (10–13ft). Brown bark and pale brown pith. Flowers arranged in dense terminal panicles of yellowish cream. 'Racemosa' refers to the flower clusters. The fruits are also distinct in being red in drooping clusters. It rarely fruits freely.

Red berried elder is native to central and southern Europe. It has naturalized in Scotland, the northern US and Canada. The fully ripe fruits are used medicinally. Bitter tasting, they may be used fresh or dried, and are high in vitamin C, essential oil, sugar and pectins. Fruits are a laxative and the leaves are a diuretic. This is the most edible and tasty of the elders.

Caution: The seeds inside the berries are poisonous before being cooked.

CULTIVATION

Propagation
Seed

Sow ripe berries 2cm (1in) deep in a pot outdoors. Plant seedlings in semi-shade in the garden when large enough to handle.

Cuttings

Take semi-hardwood cuttings in summer from the new growth. Use the peat, grit mix of compost (see p.591) and winter these cuttings in a cold frame or cold greenhouse. When rooted, either pot on or plant out into a prepared site 30cm (12in) apart.

Take hardwood cuttings of bare shoots in autumn and replant in the garden 30cm (12in) apart. The following autumn lift and replant.

Pests and Diseases
Rarely suffers from pests or diseases.

Maintenance
Spring Prune back golden and variegated elders.
Summer Take semi-ripe cuttings.
Autumn Take hardwood cuttings. Prune back hard.
Winter Established plants do not need protection.

Garden Cultivation
Elder tolerates most soils and **S. nigra** is very good for chalky sites. They all prefer a sunny position.

Elder grows very rapidly indeed and self-sows freely to produce new shoots 120cm (4ft) long in one season. It is short-lived.

It is important to dominate elder otherwise it will dominate your garden. Cut back in late autumn, unless it is gold or variegated, when it should be pruned in early spring before growth begins.

Harvesting
Handle flower heads carefully to prevent bruising, spread out to dry with heads down on a fine net without touching one another. Pick the fruits in autumn, as they ripen, when they become shiny and violet.

CONTAINER GROWING
Golden varieties of elder can look good in containers, as long as the containers are large enough and positioned to give the plants some shade, to stop the leaves scorching. Use a soil-based compost. Keep well watered, feed with a liquid fertilizer.

CULINARY

(Common Elder only)
Warning: Berries should not be eaten raw, nor fresh juice used. Be sure to cook very slightly first.

Elderflower Cordial
Pick flowers on a dry sunny day, as the yeast is mainly in the pollen.

4.5 litres/1 gallon of water
700g/1½lb sugar
Juice and thinly peeled rind of 1 lemon
30ml/2 tablespoons of cider or wine vinegar
12 elderflower heads

Bring the water to the boil and pour into a sterilized container. Add the sugar, stirring until dissolved. When cool add the lemon juice and the rind, vinegar and elderflowers. Cover with several layers of muslin and leave for 24 hours. Filter through muslin into strong glass bottles. This drink is ready after 2 weeks. Serve chilled.

OTHER USES
Elderflower water whitens and softens the skin, removes freckles.

The fruits make a lavender or violet dye when combined with alum.

Elderflower sorbet

MEDICINAL

Elderflowers reduce bronchial and upper respiratory catarrh and are used in the treatment of hay fever. Externally a cold infusion of the flowers may be used as an eye wash for conjunctivitis and as a compress for chilblains. A gargle made from elderflower infusion or elderflower vinegar alleviates tonsillitis and sore throats. Elderflowers have a mild laxative action and in Europe have a reputation for treating rheumatism and gout. The berries are a mild laxative and sweat inducing. 'Elderberry Rob' is traditionally made by simmering the berries and thickening with sugar as a winter cordial for coughs and colds.

Elderberry Conserve
(for neuralgia and migraine)

500g/1lb elderberries
500g/1lb sugar

Boil the elderberries with the least quantity of water to produce a pulp. Pass through a sieve and simmer the juice gently to remove most of the water. Add the sugar and stir constantly until the consistency of a conserve is produced. Pour into a suitable container. Take two tablespoons as required.

Sanguisorba minor

SALAD BURNET

Also known as Drumsticks, Old Man's Pepper and Poor Man's Pepper. From the family Rosaceae.

This herb is a native of Europe and Asia. It has been introduced and naturalized in many places elsewhere in the world, especially Britain and the United States. Popular for both its medicinal and culinary properties, it was taken to New England in the Pilgrim Fathers' Plant collection and called Pimpernel. It is found in dry, free-draining soil in grassland and on the edges of woodland. The name *Sanguisorba* comes from 'sanguis', meaning blood, and 'sorbere', meaning to soak up. It is an ancient herb, which has been grown in this country since the 16th century. Traditionally it was used to staunch wounds. In Tudor times salad burnet was planted along borders of garden paths so the scent would rise up when trodden on.

SPECIES

Sanguisorba minor
Salad Burnet
Evergreen hardy perennial. Ht 20–60cm (8–24in), spread 30cm (12in). Produces small spikes of dark crimson flowers in summer. Its soft mid-green leaves are divided into oval leaflets.

Sanguisorba officinalis
Great Burnet
Also known as Drumsticks, Maidens Hairs, Red Knobs, and Redheads. Perennial. Ht up to 1.2m (4ft), spread 60cm (2ft). Produces small spikes of dark crimson flowers in summer. Its mid-green leaves are divided into oval leaflets. This wild plant is becoming increasingly rare due to modern farming

Salad burnet
Sanguisorba minor

way. As an edging plant it should be planted at 20cm (8in) intervals.

Division
It divides very easily. Dig up an established plant in the early autumn, cut back any excessive leaves, divide the plant and replant in a prepared site in the garden.

Pests and Diseases
This herb is, in the main, free from pests and diseases.

Maintenance
Spring Sow seeds.
Summer Keep cutting to stop it flowering, if being used for culinary purposes.

CULTIVATION

Propagation
Seed
Sow the small flattish seed in spring or autumn into prepared seed or plug trays and cover the seeds with perlite; no need for extra heat. If sown in the autumn, winter the seedlings under protection and plant out in spring to a prepared site, 30cm (12in) apart. If spring sown allow to harden off and plant out in the same

Autumn Sow seeds if necessary. Divide established plants.
Winter No protection needed, fully hardy.

Garden Cultivation

This is a most attractive, soft-leaf evergreen and is very useful in both kitchen and garden. That it is evergreen is a particular plus for the herb garden, where it looks most effective as an edging plant. It also looks good in a wild flower garden, where it grows as happily as in its original grassland habitat.

The art with this plant is to keep cutting, which stops it flowering and encourages lots of new growth.

With no special requirements, it prefers chalky soil, but it will tolerate any well-drained soil in sun or light shade. It is deep rooting and very drought resistant.

Harvesting

Pick young tender leaves when required. Not necessary to dry leaves (which in any case do not dry well), as fresh leaves can be harvested all year round.

CONTAINER GROWING

Salad burnet will grow in containers, and will provide an excellent source of soft evergreen leaves throughout winter for those with no garden. Use a soil-based compost. Water regularly, but not too frequently; feed with liquid fertilizer in the spring only. Do not over-feed otherwise the leaf will soften and lose its cool cucumber flavour, becoming more like a spinach. For regular use the plant should not be allowed to flower. Cut back constantly to about 15cm (6in) to ensure a continuing supply of tender new leaves.

CULINARY

Leaves have a nutty flavour and a slight taste of cucumber. The young leaves are refreshing in salads and can be used generously – they certainly enhance winter salads. Tender young leaves can also be added to soups, cold drinks, cream cheeses, or used (like parsley) as a garnish or to flavour casseroles – add at the beginning of cooking. The leaves also make an interesting herbal vinegar.

Salad burnet combines with other herbs, especially rosemary and tarragon. Serve in a sauce with white fish.

Salad burnet *Sanguisorba minor*

OTHER USES

Because of its high tannin content, the root of great burnet can be used in the tanning of leather.

WARNING

Great burnet should never be taken in large doses.

This recipe is for a herb butter, which is lovely with grilled fish, either cooked under the grill or on the barbecue, and gives a cucumber flavour to the butter.

75g (3oz) butter
1¹/₂ tablespoons chopped salad burnet
1 tablespoon chopped garden mint (spearmint)
Salt and black pepper
Lemon juice

Mix the chopped herb leaves together. Melt the butter in a saucepan, add the herbs and simmer on a very low heat for 10 minutes. Season the sauce to taste with salt and pepper, and a squeeze (no more) of lemon. Pour over grilled fish (plaice or sole).

Salad burnet butter

MEDICINAL

Chewing the leaf assists digestion. An infusion of the whole plant is used for treating haemorrhoids and diarrhoea.

Santolina

Cotton Lavender

**Also known as Santolina and French Lavender.
From the family Asteraceae.**

Cotton lavender is a native of Southern France and the Northern Mediterranean area, where it grows wild on calcareous ground. It is widely cultivated, adapting to the full spectrum of European and Australian climates and to warm-to-hot regions of North America, surviving even an Eastern Canadian winter on well-drained soil.

The Greeks knew cotton lavender as 'abrotonon' and the Romans as 'habrotanum', both names referring to the tree-like shape of the flying branches. It was used medicinally for many centuries by the Arabs. And it was valued in medieval England as an insect and moth repellent and vermifuge.

The plant was probably brought into Britain in the 16th century by French Huguenot gardeners, who were skilled in creating the knot garden so popular among the Elizabethans. Cotton lavender was used largely in low clipped hedges, and as edging for the geometrical beds.

Cotton lavender Rosmarinifolia
Santolina rosmarinifolia ssp. *rosmarinifolia*

SPECIES

Despite its common name, this is not a member of the Lavandula family; rather it is a member of the daisy family.

Santolina chamaecyparissus
Cotton Lavender
Hardy evergreen perennial. Ht 75cm (2.5ft), spread 1m (3ft). Yellow button flowers from midsummer to early autumn, silver coral like aromatic foliage.

Cotton lavender
Santolina chamaecyparissus

Santolina chamaecyparissus 'Lemon Queen'
Cotton Lavender 'Lemon Queen'
As 'Edward Bowles', but feathery, deep-cut grey foliage.

Santolina pinnata subsp. neapolitana 'Edward Bowles'
Cotton Lavender 'Edward Bowles'
Hardy evergreen perennial. Ht 75cm (2.5ft), spread 1m (3ft). Cream button flowers in summer. Feathery, deep-cut, grey/green foliage.

Cotton lavender 'Lemon Queen'
Santolina chamaecyparissus
'Lemon Queen'

**Santolina pinnata subsp.
neapolitana**
Cotton Lavender 'Neopolitana'
As 'Edward Bowles'.

**Santolina rosmarinifolia
subsp. rosmarinifolia
'Primrose Gem'**
Cotton Lavender Primrose Gem
Hardy evergreen perennial.
Ht 60cm (2ft), spread 1m
(3ft). Pale yellow button
flowers in summer. Finely
cut green leaves.

**Santolina rosmarinifolia
subsp. rosmarinifolia**
*Cotton Lavender, Holy Flax,
Virens*
As 'Primrose Gem'. Bright
yellow button flowers in
summer. Finely cut, bright
green leaves.

Cotton lavender *Santolina
rosmarinifolia* subsp. *rosmarinifolia*

CULTIVATION

Propagation
Seed
Although seed is now
available, it is erratic and
not worth the effort as
germination is poor.

Cuttings
Take 5–8cm (2–3in) soft stem
cuttings in spring before
flowering, or take semi-ripe
stem cuttings from mid-
summer to autumn. They
root easily without the use
of any rooting compound.

Pests and Diseases
Compost or soil that is too
rich will attract aphids.

Maintenance
Spring Cut straggly old
plants hard back. Take
cuttings from new growth.
Summer I can not stress
enough that after flowering
the plants should be cut
back or the bushes will open
up and lose their attractive
shape.
Autumn Take semi-ripe
cuttings, protect them from
frost in a cold frame or
greenhouse.
Winter Protect in only the
severest of winters.

Garden Cultivation
This elegant aromatic
evergreen is ideal for the
herb garden as a hedging or
specimen plant in its own
right. Plant in full sun,
preferably in sandy soil. If
the soil is too rich the
growth will become soft and
lose colour. This is
particularly noticeable with
the silver varieties.
    Planting distance for an
individual plant 45–60cm
(18–24 in), for a hedging
30–38cm (12–15in). Hedges
need regular clipping to
shape in spring and
summer. Do not cut back in
the autumn in frosty
climates, as this can easily
kill the plants. If

temperatures drop below
–15° C (5°F) protect with
agricultural fleece or a layer
of straw, spruce or bracken.

Harvesting
Pick leaves and dry any time
before flowering. Pick small
bunches of flower stems for
drying, in late summer. They
can be dried easily by
hanging the bunches upside
down in a dry, airy place.

CONTAINER GROWING

Cotton lavender can not be
grown indoors, however as a
patio plant, a single plant
clipped to shape in a large
terracotta pot can look very
striking. Use a bark, peat
compost (see p.591). Place
pot in full sun. Do not over-
feed with liquid fertilizer or
growth will be too soft.

CULINARY

*Cotton lavender (***S.
chamaecyparissus***) makes an
interesting addition to
shortbread biscuits
instead of rosemary.
Interesting being the
operative word.

MEDICINAL

*Although not used much
nowadays, it can be applied
to surface wounds,
hastening the healing
process by encouraging scar
formation. Finely ground
leaves ease the pain of
insect stings and bites.*

OTHER USES
Lay in drawers, under
carpets, and in closets to
deter moths and other
insects, or make a herbal
moth bag.

Herbal Moth Bag

*A handful of wormwood
A handful of spearmint
A handful of cotton lavender
A handful of rosemary
1 tablespoon of crushed
    coriander*

Dry and crumble the
ingredients, mix together
and put in a muslin or
cotton bag.

Saponaria officinalis

SOAPWORT

Also known as Bouncing Bet, Bruisewort, Farewell Summer, Fuller's Herb, Joe Run By The Street, Hedge Pink. Dog's Clove, Old Maid's Pink and Soaproot. From the family Caryophyllaceae.

Soapwort, widespread on poor soils in Europe, Asia and Northern America, was used by medieval Arab physicians for various skin complaints. Fullers used soapwort for soaping cloth before it went on the stamps at the mill, and sheep were washed with a mixture of the leaves, roots and water before being shorn.

SPECIES

Saponaria officinalis
Soapwort
Hardy perennial. Ht 30–90cm (1–3ft), spread 60cm (2ft) or more. Compact cluster of small pretty pink or white flowers in summer to early autumn. The leaf is smooth, oval, pointed and mid-green in colour.

Saponaria officinalis 'Rubra Plena'
Double-Flowered Soapwort
Hardy perennial. Ht 90cm (3ft), spread 30cm (1ft). Clusters of red, ragged, double flowers in summer. The leaves are mid-green and oval in shape.

Saponaria ocymoides
Tumbling Ted
Hardy perennial. Ht 2.5–8cm (1–3in), spread 40cm (16in) or more. Profusion of tiny, flat, pale pink/crimson flowers in summer. Compact or loose sprawling mats of hairy oval leaves.

CULTIVATION

Propagation
Seed
Only soapwort and tumbling Ted can be grown from seed. Sow in autumn into prepared seed or plug trays and cover with compost. Place glass over container and leave outside over winter. Germination usually takes place in spring, but can be erratic. When large enough, plant 60cm (24in) apart.

Cuttings
Softwood cuttings of the non-flowering shoots can be taken from late spring to early summer.

Division
The creeping rootstock is easy to divide in the autumn.

Garden Cultivation
Plant it in a sunny spot, in a well-drained poor soil; rich garden soil makes its already undisciplined habit impossible. Soapwort can become very invasive. Do not plant soapwort around fish ponds because the creeping rhizomes excrete a poison.

Pests and Diseases
Soapwort is largely free from pests and disease.

Maintenance
Spring Take cuttings.
Summer Cut back after flowering to encourage a second flowering and to prevent self-seeding.
Autumn Divide established plants. Sow seed.
Winter Fully hardy.

Harvesting
Pick the leaves when required. Dig up the roots in the autumn and dry for medicinal use.

CONTAINER GROWING

Tumbling Ted is the best species for container growing. Use a soil-based compost. Water well during the growing season, but only feed twice. In winter keep in a cold greenhouse with minimum watering.

MEDICINAL

It has been used not only for treating skin conditions such as eczema, cold sores, boils, and acne, but also for gout and rheumatism. It is probably effective because of the anti-inflammatory properties of its saponins.

OTHER USES

The gentle power of the saponins in soapwort makes the following shampoo ideal for upholstery and delicate fibres.

Soapwort Shampoo
15gm (1/2oz) dried soapwort root or two large handfuls of whole fresh stems
3/4 litre (1 1/2 pints) water

Crush the root with a rolling pin or roughly chop the fresh stems. If using dried soapwort, prepare by soaking first overnight. Put the soapwort into an enamel pan with water and bring to the boil, cover and simmer for 20 minutes, stirring occasionally. Allow to stand until cool and strain through a fine sieve.

WARNING

This herb should only be prescribed by a qualified herbalist because of the high saponin content, which makes it mildly poisonous.

Satureja (Satureia)

SAVORY

From the family Lamiaceae.

Savory is a native of southern Europe and North Africa, especially around the Mediterranean. It grows in well-drained soils and has adapted worldwide to similar climatic conditions. Savory has been employed in food flavouring for over 2,000 years. Romans added it to sauces and vinegars, which they used liberally as flavouring. The Ancient Egyptians on the other hand used it in love potions. The Romans also included it in their wagon train to northern Europe, where it became an invaluable disinfectant strewing herb. It was used to relieve tired eyes, for ringing in the ears, indigestion, wasp and bee stings, and for other shocks to the system.

Winter savory *Satureja montana*

Summer savory
Satureja hortensis

SPECIES

Satureja hortensis
Summer Savory
Also known as Bean Herb. Half-hardy annual. Ht 20–30cm (8–12in), spread 15cm (6in). Small white/mauve flowers in summer. Aromatic leaves, oblong, pointed, and green. A favourite on the Continent and in America, where it is known as the bean herb. It has become widely used in bean dishes as it helps prevent flatulence.

Satureja coerulea
Purple-Flowered Savory
Semi-evergreen hardy perennial. Ht 30cm (12in), spread 20cm (8in). Small purple flowers in summer. The leaves are darkish green, linear and very aromatic.

Satureja montana
Winter Savory
Also known as Mountain Savory.
Semi-evergreen hardy perennial. Ht 30cm (12in), spread 20cm (8in). Small white/pink flowers in summer. The leaves are dark green, linear and very aromatic.

Satureja spicigera
Creeping Savory
Perennial. Ht 8cm (3in), spread 30cm (12in). Masses of small white flowers in summer. The leaves are lime greenish and linear. This is a most attractive plant and is often mistaken for thyme or even heather.

CULTIVATION

Propagation
Seed
Only summer and winter savory can be grown from seed, which is tiny, so it is best to sow into prepared seed trays under protection in the early spring, using the cardboard method. The seeds should not be covered as they need light to germinate. Germination takes about 10–15 days – no need to use bottom heat. When the seedlings are large enough, and after a period of hardening off (making quite sure that the frosts have finished), they can be planted out into a prepared site in the garden, 15cm (6in) apart.

Cuttings
Creeping, purple-flowered and winter savory can all be grown from softwood cuttings in spring, using a bark, peat, grit compost (see p.591). When these have rooted they should be planted out – 30cm (12in) apart for creeping savory, 15cm (6in) apart for the others.

Division
Creeping savory can be divided, as each section has its own root system similar to creeping thymes. Dig up an established plant in the spring after the frosts have finished and divide into as many segments as you require. Minimum size is only dependent on each having a root system and how long you are prepared to wait for new plants to become established. Replant in a prepared site.

Pests and Diseases

Being an aromatic plant savory is, in the main, free from pests and disease.

Maintenance

Spring Sow seed. Take softwood cuttings. Divide established plants.
Summer Keep picking and do not allow summer savory to flower, if you want to maintain its flavour.
Autumn Protect from prolonged frosts.
Winter Protect.

Garden Cultivation

All the above-mentioned savories like full sun and a poor, well-drained soil. Plant summer savory in the garden in a warm, sheltered spot and keep picking the leaves to stop it getting leggy. Do not feed with liquid fertilizer, otherwise the plant will keel over.

Winter savory can make a good edging plant and is very pretty in the summer, although it can look a bit sparse in the winter months. Again, trim it from time to time to maintain shape and promote new growth. Creeping savory does not like cold wet winters, or for that matter clay soil, so on this nursery I grow it in a pot (see below). If, however, you wish to grow it in your garden, plant it in a sunny rockery or a well-drained, sheltered corner.

Harvesting

For fresh use, pick leaves as required. For drying, pick those of summer savory before it flowers. They dry easily.

CONTAINER GROWING

All savories can be grown in containers, and if your garden suffers from prolonged cold wet winters

Savory is an important constituent of salami

it may be the only way you can grow this delightful plant successfully. Use the bark, peat, grit mix of compost. Pick the plants continuously to maintain shape, especially the summer savory, which can get straggly. If you are picking the plants a lot they may benefit from a feed of liquid fertilizer, but keep this to a minimum as they get ever eager when fed.

Summer savory, being an annual, dies in winter, creeping savory dies back, the winter savory is a partial evergreen. So, the latter two will need protection in winter. Place them in a cool greenhouse or conservatory. If the container cannot be moved, wrap it up in paper or agricultural fleece. Keep watering to the absolute minimum.

MEDICINAL

Summer savory is the plant credited with medicinal virtues and is said to alleviate the pain of bee stings if rubbed on the affected spot. Infuse as a tea to stimulate appetite and to ease indigestion and flatulence. It is also considered a stimulant and was once in demand as an aphrodisiac.

Winter savory is also used medicinally but is inferior.

CULINARY

The two savories used in cooking are winter and summer savory. The other varieties are edible but their flavour is inferior. Summer and winter savory combine well with vegetables, pulses and rich meats. These herbs stimulate the appetite and aid digestion. The flavour is hot and peppery, and so should be added sparingly in salads.

Summer savory can replace both salt and pepper and is a great help to those on a salt-free diet. It is a pungent herb and until one is familiar with its strength it should be used carefully. Summer savory also makes a good vinegar and oil. The oil is used commercially as a flavouring, as is the leaf, which is an important constituent of salami.

The flavour of winter savory is both coarser and stronger, its advantage is that it provides fresh leaves into early winter.

Beans with Garlic and Savory
Serves 3–4

200g (7oz) dried haricot beans
1 Spanish onion
1 carrot, scrubbed and roughly sliced
1 stick celery
1 clove garlic
3 tablespoons olive oil
1 tablespoon white wine vinegar
2 tablespoons chopped summer savory
2 tablespoons chopped French parsley

Soak the beans in cold water overnight or for at least 3–4 hours. Drain them and put them in a saucepan with plenty of water. Bring to the boil slowly. Add half the peeled onion, the carrot and celery, and cook until tender. As soon as the beans are soft, drain and discard the vegetables. Mix the oil, vinegar and crushed garlic. While the beans are still hot, stir in the remaining half onion (thinly sliced), the chopped herbs, and pour over the oil and vinegar dressing. Serve soon after cooling. Do not chill.

Beans with garlic and savory

Skullcap
Scutellaria galericulata

Scutellaria

Virginian skullcap
Scutellaria lateriflora

SKULLCAP

Also known as Helmet Flower, Mad Dog Weed, Blue Skullcap and Blue Pimpernel. From the family Lamiaceae.

The various varieties of skullcap are natives of different countries. They are found in America, Britain, India, and one grows in the rain forests of the Amazon.

The name *Scutellaria* is derived from 'scutella', meaning a small shield, which is exactly how the seed looks.

The American Indians used *Scutellaria lateriflora* as a treatment for rabies. In Europe it was used for epilepsy.

SPECIES

Scutellaria galericulata
Skullcap
Hardy perennial. Ht 15–50cm (6–20in), spread 30cm (12in) and more. Small purple/blue flowers with a longer spreading lower lip in summer. Leaves bright green and lance-shaped with shallow round teeth. This plant is a native of Europe.

Scutellaria minor
Lesser Skullcap
As **S. galericulata** except Ht 20–30cm (8–12in), spread 30cm (12in) and more. Small purple/pink flowers. Leaves lance-shaped with four rounded teeth. Found on wet land.

Scutellaria lateriflora
Virginian Skullcap
As **S. galericulata** except Ht 30–60cm (12–24in), spread 30cm (12in) and more. Leaves oval and lance-shaped with shallow, round teeth. Native of America.

CULTIVATION

Propagation
Seed
Sow the small seeds in autumn into prepared seed or plug trays and cover the seeds with compost. Leave the tray outside under glass. If germination is rapid, winter the young seedlings in a cold greenhouse. If there is no germination within 10–20 days leave well alone. The seed may need a period of stratification. In the spring, when the plants are large enough, plant out into a prepared site in the garden 30cm (12in) apart.

Root Cuttings
These produce a rhizomous root from which it is easy to take cuttings. In spring dig up an established clump carefully, for any little bits of root left behind will form another plant. Ensure each cutting has a growing node; place in a seed tray and cover with compost. Put into a cold greenhouse to root.

Division
Established plants can be divided in the spring.

Pests and Diseases
Skullcap is normally free from pests and disease.

Maintenance
Spring Divide established plants. Take root cuttings.
Summer Cut back to restrain.
Autumn Sow seeds.
Winter. No need for protection, fully hardy.

Garden Cultivation
Skullcap tolerates most soils but prefers a well-drained, moisture-retentive soil in sun or semi-shade. Make sure this plant gets adequate water.

Harvesting
Dry flowers and leaves for medicinal use only.

CONTAINER GROWING

This herb can be grown in containers but ensure its large root system has room to spread. Use a soil-based compost. Feed only rarely with liquid fertilizer or it will produce too lush a growth and inhibit flowering. Leave outside in winter in a sheltered spot, allowing the plant to die back.

MEDICINAL

The American skullcap is the best medicinal species; the two European species are a little less strong.

It is used in the treatment of anxiety, nervousness, depression, insomnia and headaches. The whole plant is effective as a soothing antispasmodic tonic and a remedy for hysteria and hydrophobia. Its bitter taste also strengthens and stimulates the digestion.

WARNING

Should only be dispensed by a trained herbalist.

Virginian skullcap
Scutellaria lateriflora

Sempervivum tectorum

HOUSELEEK

Also known as Bullocks Eye, Hen and Chickens, Jupiter's Eye, Jupiter's Beard, Live For Ever, Thunder Plant, Aaron's Rod, Healing Leaf, Mallow Rock and Welcome-Husband-Though-Never-So-Late. From the family Crassulaceae.

Originally from the mountainous areas of central and southern Europe, now found growing in many different areas of the world, including North America.

The generic name *Sempervivum* comes from the Latin 'semper vivo' meaning 'to live for ever'. The species name, *tectorum*, means 'of the roofs', there being records dating back 2,000 years of houseleeks growing on the tiles of houses. The plant was said to have been given to man by Zeus or Jupiter to protect houses from lightning and fire. Because of this the Romans planted courtyards with urns of houseleek, and Charlemagne ordered a plant to be grown on every roof. This belief continued throughout history and in medieval times the houseleek was thought to protect thatched roofs from fire from the sky and witchcraft. In the Middle Ages the plant was often called Erewort and employed against deafness. When the settlers packed their bags for America they took house-leek with them.

Houseleek *Sempervivum tectorum*

SPECIES

This genus of hardy succulents had 25 species 40 years ago. Now, due to re-classification, it has over 500 different varieties. As far as I am aware only houseleek has medicinal properties.

Sempervivum tectorum
Houseleek
Hardy evergreen perennial. Ht 10–15cm (4–6in) (when in flower) otherwise it is 5cm (2in), spread 20cm (8in). Flowers are star-shaped and pink in summer. The leaves, grey/green in colour, are oval, pointed and succulent.

Some other **Sempervivum** worth collecting:

Sempervivum arachnoideum
Cobweb Houseleek
Hardy evergreen perennial. Ht 10–12cm (4–5in), when in flower, otherwise it is 5cm (2in), spread 10cm (4in). Flowers are star-shaped and pink in summer. The leaves, grey/green in colour, are oval, pointed and succulent. The tips of the leaves are covered in a web of white hairs.

Sempervivum giuseppii
Hardy evergreen perennial. Ht 8–10cm (3–4in), when in flower, otherwise it is 2cm (1in), spread 10cm (4in). Flowers star-shaped, pink/red in summer. Leaves, grey/green in colour, are oval, pointed and succulent and grow into a very compact shape. This **Sempervivum** is a vigorous grower.

Sempervivum montanum
Hardy evergreen perennial. Ht 8–15cm (3–6in), when in flower, otherwise 5cm (2in), spread 10cm (4in). Flowers star-shaped and deep red in summer. Leaves grey/green in colour, oval, pointed and succulent.

Houseleek *Sempervivum tectorum* **in flower**

Summer Collect seeds if required from flowering plants.

Autumn Remove offsets if the plant is becoming too invasive, pot up for following season's display.

Winter No need for protection.

Garden Cultivation

Basically the soil should be well-drained and thin, as they prefer very little to no soil. They will grow anywhere, on weathered rocks and screes and of course rock gardens. Another good place to plant them is between paving stones, or in between other creeping plants like thymes. They can take many years to flower, and when they do they die, but by then there will be many offsets to follow.

Harvesting

Pick leaves to use fresh as required. There is no good way of preserving them.

CONTAINER GROWING

If the Romans could do it, so can we. Houseleeks do look good in containers and shallow stone troughs. The compost must be poor and very well drained. Use the bark, grit, peat mix but change the ratio to 50 per cent grit, 25 per cent peat, 25 per cent bark. No need to feed, and do not over-water.

CULINARY

The leaves can be added to salad dishes. I think it would be polite to say that it is an acquired taste.

CULTIVATION

Propagation
Seed

Most species hybridize readily, so seed cannot be depended upon to reproduce the species true to type. When you buy seed it often says, 'mixture of several species and varieties' on the packet. It can be good fun to sow these as long as you do not mind what you get; it is even more fun trying to name them as they develop.

The seed is very small, so start off in a seed or plug tray in spring. Sow on the surface. Do not cover except with a sheet of glass. No need for bottom heat. Use the bark, grit, peat compost (see p.591).

Offsets

All the houseleeks produce offsets that cluster around the base of the parent plant. In spring gently remove them and you will notice each has its own root system. Either put straight into a pot, using the bark, grit, peat mix of compost, or plant where required. Plant 23cm (9in) apart.

Pests and Diseases

Vine weevil, this scourge of the garden, is very destructive to a number of plants and they like houseleeks. You will know they have been when you see the rosette lying on its side with no roots. See page 606 for methods of destroying the pests.

Maintenance

Spring Sow seeds. Pot up or re-plant offsets.

MEDICINAL

The leaves are an astringent and when broken in half can be applied to burns, insect bites and other skin problems. Press the juice from the leaf onto the infected part. My son, when he goes on hikes or is building dens, always has some in his pockets – great for clothes washing – for when he gets stung by nettles they are much better than dock when rubbed in.

To soften skin around corns, bind one leaf for a few hours, soak foot in water in attempt to remove corn. Repeat as necessary.

Infuse as a tea for septic throats, bronchitis and mouth ailments. It is also said that chewing a few leaves can ease toothache.

Solidago virgaurea

GOLDENROD

Also known as Woundwort, Aaron's Rod, Cast the Spear and Farewell Summer.
From the family Asteraceae.

This plant is widely distributed throughout Europe including the British Isles, and North America. It is common from the plains to the hills, but especially where the ground is rich in silica.

Its generic name, *Solidago,* is derived from the Latin word 'solido', which means 'to join' or 'make whole', a reference to the healing properties attributed to goldenrod.

The plant, originally called Heathen Wound Herb in Britain, was first imported from the Middle East, where it was used by the Saracens, and it was some time before it was cultivated here. In Tudor times it was available in London but at a price, its expense due to the fact that it was still available only as an import. Gerard wrote, 'For in my remembrance, I have known the dry herb which comes from beyond the sea, sold in Bucklesbury in London for half a crown an ounce,' and went on to say that when it was found growing wild in Hampstead wood, no one would pay half a crown for 100cwt of it, a fact which the herbalist felt bore out the old English proverb, 'Far fetch and dear, bought is best for ladies.'

From Culpeper, around the same time, we know that goldenrod was used to fasten loose teeth and as a remedy for kidney stones (which it still is).

SPECIES

Solidago odora
Sweet Goldenrod
Also known as Aniseed-Scented Goldenrod, Blue Mountain Tea, Common Goldenrod and Woundweed.
Perennial. Ht 60cm–1.2m (2–4ft), spread 60cm (2ft). Golden-yellow flowers on a single stem from mid-summer to autumn. The green leaf is linear and lance-shaped.

Solidago nemoralis
Grey Goldenrod
Also known as Dyer's Weed, Field Goldenrod and Yellow Goldenrod.
Perennial. Ht 60cm–1m (2–3ft), spread 60cm (2ft). Yellow flowers on large terminals on one side of the panicle. Leaves greyish-green or olive-green.

Solidago virgaurea
Goldenrod
Also known as European Goldenrod.
Perennial Ht 30–60cm (12–24in), spread 60cm (2ft). Small yellow flowers from summer to autumn. The green leaves are lance-shaped.

Solidago 'Goldenmosa'
Golden Mimosa
Perennial. Ht 1m (3ft), spread 60cm (2ft). Sprays of mimosa-like yellow flowers from summer to autumn. Lance-shaped green leaves. Attractive border plant. Has no herbal use.

Goldenrod *Solidago virgaurea*

CULTIVATION

Propagation
Seeds
Sow in plug or seed trays in spring. As seed is fine, sow on the surface and cover with perlite. Germination within 14–21 days without bottom heat. Prick out, harden off, and plant out into prepared site in the garden at a distance of 45cm (18in). Remember, the plant will spread.

Division
Divide established plants in spring or autumn. Dig up the plant, split into required size, half, third, etc., and replant in a prepared site in the garden.

Pests and Diseases
This plant rarely suffers from pests or diseases.

Maintenance
Spring Sow seeds.
Summer Enjoy the flowers. If you have rich soil, the plants may become very tall and need support in exposed sites.
Autumn Divide mature plants.
Winter No need for protection.

Garden Cultivation
It is an attractive plant and has been taken into cultivation as a useful late-flowering ornamental. It is ideal for the herbaceous border, as it spreads rapidly to form clumps.
  In late summer, sprays of bright yellow flowers crowd its branching stems amongst sharply pointed hoary leaves. When planting in the garden, it prefers open conditions and soils that are not too rich and are well drained. It tolerates sun, semi-shade and shade, and being a wild plant it can be naturalized in poor grassland.

Sow seed thinly in spring or autumn in the chosen flowering position, having prepared the site, and cover lightly with soil. When the seedlings are large enough, thin to 30cm (12in) distance apart. (The plant will spread and you may have to do a second thinning.) If sown in the autumn, the young plants may in very cold temperatures need added protection. Use a mulch that they can grow through the following spring, or which can be removed.

Harvesting
Collect the flowering tops and leaves in summer. Dry for medicinal use.

Golden mimosa
Solidago 'Goldenmosa'

MEDICINAL

Goldenrod is used in cases of urinary and kidney infections and stones, and catarrh. It also helps to ease backache caused by renal conditions because of its cleansing, eliminative action. It is used to treat arthritis.
  A cold compress is helpful on fresh wounds because of its anti-inflammatory properties.
  Sweet goldenrod is used as an astringent and as a calmative. The tea made from the dried leaves and flowers is an aromatic beverage and can be used to improve the taste of other medicinal preparations. Native Americans applied lotions made from goldenrod flowers to bee stings.

CONTAINER GROWING

Goldenrod can be grown in containers, but being a tall plant, it looks much more attractive in a garden border. Use the bark, peat, grit mix of compost (see p.591) and in the summer only give it liquid fertilizer and water regularly. In winter, as the plant dies back, place the container in a cool airy place protected from frost, but n[ot] warm. Keep the compost o[n] the dry side.

Stachys officinalis (Betonica officinalis)

BETONY

Also known as Lousewort, Purple Betony, Wood Betony, Bishop's Wort and Devil's Plaything. From the family Lamiaceae

This attractive plant is native to Europe and still found growing wild in Britain. Betony certainly merits inclusion in the herb garden, but is thought by some to be one of the plant world's frauds. There are so many conflicting stories, all of which are well worth hearing. I leave it to you to decide what is fact or fiction.

The Ancient Egyptians were the first to attribute magical properties to betony. In England, by the 10th century, the Anglo-Saxons had it as their most important magical plant, claiming it as effective against the Elf sickness. In the 11th century it was mentioned in the *Lacnunga* as a beneficial medicinal plant against the Devilish affliction of the body. Later, Gerard wrote in his *Herbal*, 'Betony is good for them that be subject to the falling sickness,' and went on to describe its many virtues, one of them being 'a remedy against the biting of mad dogs and venomous serpents'.

In the 18th century it was still considered of use in the cure of diverse afflictions, including headaches and drawing out splinters, as well as being used in herbal tobacco and snuff. Today, betony retains an important place in folk medicine even though its true value is seriously questioned.

We owe the name to the Romans, who called the herb first *Bettonica* and then *Betonica*.

Betony *Stachys officinalis*

Betony *Stachys officinalis*

SPECIES

Stachys officinalis
Betony
Hardy perennial. Ht 60cm (24in), spread 25cm (10in). Dense spikes of pink or purple flowers end-spring through summer. Square hairy stems bear aromatic, slightly hairy, round, lobed leaves.

Stachys officinalis 'Alba'
White Betony
Hardy perennial. Ht 60cm (24in), spread 25cm (10in). White flowers end-spring through summer.

CULTIVATION

Propagation
Seed
Grows readily from seed, which it produces in abundance. Sow late summer or spring in planting position and cover very lightly with soil. Alternatively, sow seeds in trays and prick out seedlings into small pots when large enough to handle.

Division
Divide roots of established plants in spring or autumn, replant at a distance of

30cm (12in) from other plants. Alternatively pot up using the bark, peat mix of compost (see p.591).

Pests and Diseases

Apart from the occasional caterpillar, this plant is pest and disease free.

Maintenance

Spring Sow seeds. Divide established plants.
Summer Plant out spring seedlings.
Autumn Cut back flowering stems, save seeds, divide established plants
Winter No protection needed.

Garden Cultivation

A very accommodating plant, it will tolerate most soils, but prefers some humus. Flourishes in sun or shade, in fact it will put up with all but the deepest of shade. A wild plant, but it has for centuries been grown in cottage gardens. In the wild flower garden it is a very colourful participant and establishes well either in a mixed bed or in grassland. It is also excellent for the woodland garden.

Harvesting

Collect leaves for drying before flowering in late spring/early summer. Use leaves fresh either side of flowering.

Pick flowers for drying and for use in potpourris just as they open. Collect through flowering season to use fresh.

Save seed in early autumn. Store in dry, dark container.

CONTAINER GROWING

Betony grows to great effect in half a beer barrel and combines well with other wild flowers e.g. poppies, oxeye daisy, chamomile. I do not advise it for growing indoors or in small containers.

OTHER USES

The fresh plant provides a yellow dye. A hair rinse, good for highlighting greying hair, can be made from an infusion of the leaves.

WARNING

Care must be taken if it is taken internally because in any form the root can cause vomiting and violent diarrhoea.

Betony makes a good yellow dye

Betony *Stachys officinalis* **in flower**

MEDICINAL

Today opinions differ as to its value. Some authorities consider it is only an astringent while others believe it is a sedative. It is however now chiefly employed in herbal smoking mixtures and herbal snuffs. As an infusional powder, it is used to treat diarrhoea, cystitis, asthma and neuralgia. Betony tea is invigorating, particularly if prepared in a mixture with other herbs. In France it is recommended for liver and gall bladder complaints.

Symphytum officinale

COMFREY

Also known as Knitbone, Boneset, Bruisewort, Knitback, Church Bells, Abraham, Isaac-and-Jacob (from the variation in flower colour) and Saracen's Root. From the family Boraginaceae.

Native to Europe and Asia, it was introduced into America in the 17th century, where it has naturalized.

Traditionally known as Saracen's root, common comfrey is believed to have been brought to England by the Crusaders who had discovered its value as a healing agent – mucilaginous secretions strong enough to act as a bone-setting plaster, and which gave it the nickname Knitbone.

The Crusaders passed it to monks for cultivation in their monastic herb gardens, dedicated to the care of the sick.

Elizabethan physicians and herbalists were never without it. A recipe from that time is for an ointment made from comfrey root boiled in sugar and liquorice, and mixed with coltsfoot, mallow and poppy seed. People also made comfrey tea for colds and bronchitis.

But times have changed. Once the panacea for all ills, comfrey is now under suspicion as a carcinogen. In line with its common name America 'Bruisewort', research in has shown that comfrey breaks down the red blood cells. At the same time, the Japanese are investigating how to harness its beneficial qualities; there is a research programme into the high protein and vitamin B content of the herb.

SPECIES

Symphytum 'Hidcote Blue'
Comfrey Hidcote Blue
Hardy perennial. Ht 50cm (20in), spread 60cm (2ft). Pale blue flowers in spring and early summer. Green lance-shaped leaves. Very attractive in a large border.

Symphytum ibericum
Dwarf Comfrey
Hardy perennial. Ht 25cm (10in), spread 1m (3ft). Yellow/white flowers in spring. Green lance-shaped leaves. An excellent ground cover plant, having foliage through most winters. This comfrey contains little potassium and no allantoin, the crucial medicinal substance.

Symphytum officinale
Comfrey (Wild or Common)
Hardy perennial. Ht and spread 1m (3ft).

White/purple/pink flowers in summer. This is the best medicinal comfrey and can also be employed as a liquid feed, although the potassium content is only 3.09 per cent compared to '**Bocking 14**'s 7.09 per cent. It makes a first-class composting plant, as it helps the rapid breakdown of other compost materials.

Symphytum x uplandicum
Russian Comfrey
Hardy perennial. Ht 1m (3ft), spread indefinite. Pink/purple flowers in summer. Green lance-shaped leaves. This is a hybrid that occurred naturally in Upland, Sweden. It is a cross between **S. officinale**, the herbalist's comfrey, and **S. asperum**, the blue-flowered, prickly comfrey from Russia. A very attractive form is **S. x uplandicum 'Variegatum'**, with cream and green leaves.

Dwarf Comfrey
Symphytum ibericum

Symphytum x uplandicum 'Bocking 4'
Hardy perennial. Ht 1m (3ft), spread indefinite. Flowers near to violet in colour, in spring and early summer. Thick, solid stems. Large green lance-shaped leaves. Not a particularly attractive plant but it contains almost 35 per cent total protein, the same percentage as in soya beans. Comfrey is an important animal feed in some parts of the world, especially in Africa.

Symphytum x uplandicum 'Bocking 14'

Hardy perennial. Ht 1m (3ft), spread indefinite. Mauve flowers in spring and early summer. Thin stems. Green oval leaves, tapering to a point. This variety has the highest potash content, which makes it the best for producing liquid manure.

Russian Comfrey
Symphytum x *uplandicum*

CULTIVATION

Propagation
Seed
Not nearly as reliable as root cutting or division. Sow in spring or autumn in either seed or plug trays. Germination slow and erratic.

Root Cuttings
Dig up a piece of root, cut into 2cm (1in) sections, and put these small sections into a prepared plug or seed tray.

Division
Use either the double spade method or simply dig up a chunk in the spring and replant it elsewhere.

Pests and Diseases
Sometimes suffers from rust and powdery mildew in late autumn. In both cases cut the plant down and burn the contaminated leaves.

Maintenance
Spring Sow seeds. Divide plants. Take root cuttings.
Summer Cut back leaves for composting, or to use as a mulch around other herbs in the growing season.
Autumn Sow seeds.
Winter None needed

Garden Cultivation
Fully hardy in the garden, all the comfreys prefer sun or semi-shade and a moist soil, but will tolerate most conditions. The large tap root can cause problems if you want to move the plant. When doing this make sure you dig up all the root because any left behind will reappear later.

Harvesting
Cut leaves with shears from early summer to autumn to provide foliage for making liquid feed. Each plant is able to give four cuts a year if well fed. Cut leaves for drying before flowering.
Dig up roots in autumn for drying.

CONTAINER GROWING

Comfrey is not suitable for growing indoors, but it can be grown on a patio as long as the container is large enough. Situate in partial shade and give plenty of water in warm weather.

CULINARY

Fresh leaves and shoots were eaten as a vegetable or salad and there is no reason to suppose that it is dangerous to do so now, although it may be best to err on the side of caution until suspicions are resolved.

LIQUID MANURE
A quickly available source of potassium for the organic gardener. One method of extracting it is to put 6kg (14lb) of freshly cut comfrey into a 90 litre (20 gallon) tapped, fibreglass water butt. Do not use metal as rust will add toxic quantities of iron oxide to the liquid manure. Fill up the butt with rain or tap water and cover with a lid to exclude the light. In about 4 weeks a clear liquid can be drawn off from the tap at the bottom. Ideal feed for tomatoes, onions, gooseberries, beans and all potash hungry crops. It can be used as a foliar feed.

The disadvantage of this method is that the liquid stinks, because comfrey foliage is about 3.4 per cent protein, and when proteins break down they smell.

An alternative is to bore a hole into the side (just above the bottom) of a plastic dustbin. Stand the container on bricks, so that it is far enough off the ground to allow a dish to be placed under the hole. Pack it solid with cut comfrey, and place something (a heavy lump of concrete) on top to weigh down the leaves. Cover with lid, and in about 3 weeks a black liquid will drip from the hole into a dish.

This concentrate can be stored in a screw-top bottle if you do not want to use it immediately. Dilute it 1 part to 40 parts water, and if you plan to use it as a foliar feed, strain it first.

MEDICINAL

Comfrey has received much attention in recent years, both as a valuable healing herb, a source of Vitamin B_{12} and self-proliferate allantoin, and as a potential source of protein.

Comfrey is also useful as a poultice for varicose ulcers and a compress for varicose veins, and it alleviates and heals minor burns.

WARNING

Comfrey is reported to cause serious liver damage if taken in large amounts over a long period of time.

OTHER USES
Boil fresh leaves for golden fabric dye.

Comfrey is a good feed for racehorses and helps cure laminitis. For curing septic sores on animals, make a poultice between clean pieces of cotton and tie to the affected places.

Comfrey dye

Tanacetum cinerariifolium (Chrysanthemum cinerariifolium)

PYRETHRUM

From the family Asteraceae.

This plant is native to Dalmatia but is now cultivated commercially in many parts of the world, including Japan, South Africa and parts of central Europe.

It has been grown for many years for its insecticidal properties. The derivative was originally known as Dalmatian insect powder but is now better known as Pyrethrum insecticide. I list the two species to contain this natural insecticide.

SPECIES

Tanacetum cinerariifolium (Chrysanthemum cinerariifolium)
Hardy perennial. Ht 30–37cm (12–15in), spread 20cm (8in). Daisy-like flower, white petals with a yellow centre. Leaves green/grey, finely divided, with white down on the underside.

Tanacetum coccineum (Chrysanthemum roseum)
Hardy perennial. Ht 30–cm (12–24in), spread 30cm (12in). Large flowerhead which can be white or red, and sometimes tipped with yellow. Very variable under cultivation. Vivid green leaves. Native of Iran.

CULTIVATION

Propagation
Seeds
In spring sow into a prepared seed or plug tray and cover with perlite. Germination is easy and takes 14–21 days. In late spring, when the young plants are large enough and after a period of hardening off, plant out into a prepared site in the garden 15–30cm (6–12in) apart.

Division
Established clumps can be dug up in the spring and divided.

Pests and Diseases
In the majority of cases this plant is free from pests and diseases.

Maintenance
Spring Sow seed. Divide established plants.
Summer Dead head flowers to prolong season if not collecting seed.
Autumn Divide established plants if necessary.
Winter Fully hardy.

Pyrethrum
Tanacetum cinerariifolium

Garden Cultivation
Pyrethrum likes a well-drained soil in a sunny spot; it is drought tolerant and fully hardy in most winters.

Harvesting
The flowerheads are collected just as they open and then dried gently. When they are quite dry, store away from light. The insecticide is made from the powdered dried flower.

CONTAINER GROWING

This herb is very well suited to be grown in containers, especially terracotta. Use the bark, peat, grit compost (see p.591). Water well during the summer months, but be mean on the liquid fertilizer, otherwise the leaves will become green and it will stop flowering.

MEDICINAL

This herb is rarely used medicinally. Herbalists have found the roots to be a remedy for certain fevers. Recent research has shown that the flowerheads possess a weak antibiotic.

OTHER USES

This is a useful insecticide because it is non-toxic to mammals and does not accumulate in the environment or in the bodies of animals. It acts by paralysing the nervous system of the insects, and can kill pests living on the skin of man and animals. Sprinkle the dry powder from the flowers to deter all common insects, pests, bed bugs, cockroaches, flies, mosquitoes, aphids, spider mites and ants.

To make a spray, steep 28g (1oz) of pyrethrum powder in 28ml (1fl oz) of methylated spirits and then dilute with 14 litres (3 gallons) water. The solution decomposes in bright sunlight. Therefore for maximum effect and to reduce the risk to pollinating insects and bees, spray at dusk.

WARNING

Kills helpful insects and fish.
Wear gloves when processing flowers for insecticide use, as it may cause allergies. When the active ingredient Pyrethrum is extracted it is toxic to humans and animals.

Tanacetum balsamita

ALECOST
(COSTMARY)

Other names: Bible Leaf, Sweet Mary and Mint Geranium. From the family Asteraceae

Alecost originated in Western Asia and by the time it reached America in the 17th century, Culpeper wrote of its use in Europe that 'Alecost is so frequently known to be an inhabitant of almost every garden, that it is needless to write a description thereof.'

Since then, in America it has escaped its garden bounds and grows wild in eastern and midwest States, while in Europe it has become altogether rare. Only recently has interest revived among propagators as well as horticulturalists who, in the space of twenty years, have reclassified alecost twice, from *Chrysanthemum* to *Balsamita* and now to *Tanacetum*.

The first syllable of its common name, alecost, derives from the use to which its scented leaves and flowering tops were put in the Middle Ages, namely to clarify, preserve and impart an astringent, minty flavour to beer. The second syllable, 'cost', comes from *kostos*, Greek for 'spicy'. Literally, 'alecost' means 'a spicy herb for ale'.

The alternative, costmary, by introducing a proper name symbolic of motherhood, conveys another of the plant's traditional uses in the form of a tea.

Religious connotations extend to one other nickname, 'Bible Leaf', which grew out of the Puritan habit of using a leaf of the herb as a fragrant Bible bookmark, its scent dispelling faintness from hunger during long sermons.

Camphor plant *Tanacetum balsamita* subsp. *balsamitoides*

SPECIES

**Tanacetum balsamita
(Balsamita major)**
Alecost (costmary)
Hardy perennial. Ht 1m (3ft), spread 45cm (18in). Small white yellow-eyed daisy flowers mid- to late summer. Large rosettes of oval aromatic silvery green leaves.

Tanacetum balsamita subsp. balsamitoides
Camphor plant
Hardy perennial. Ht 1m (3ft), spread 45cm (18in). Appearance and habit very similar to alecost, but unlike the latter it is not palatable as a culinary herb. Its leaves are an effective moth repellent.

Alecost *Tanacetum balsamita (Balsamita major)*

Alecost *Tanacetum balsamita*
(Balsamita major)

CULINARY

Use only the alecost leaf
and very sparingly as it has
a sharp tang which can be
overpowering. Add finely
chopped leaves to carrot
soups, salads, game,
poultry, stuffing and fruit
cakes, or with melted
butter to peas and new
potatoes. Its traditional
value to beer holds good
for home brewing.

Alecost with new potatoes

OTHER USES

Both alecost and camphor
leaves, which are sweet
scented like balsam, serve to
intensify other herb scents
and act as an insect
repellent. Add to potpourris
or to linen bags or with
lavender to make nosegay
sachets, or infuse to make a
final scented rinse for hair.

Fresh or dried leaves of
alecost can be added to
baths for a fragrant and
refreshing soak.

Alecost potpourri

CULTIVATION

Propagation
Seed
The seed is fine and thin
and cannot be propagated
from plants grown in cool
climates (the seed not being
viable). Obtain seed from a
specialist seedsman. Sow in
spring onto the surface of a
seed or plug tray and cover
with perlite. Use low warmth
to encourage germination,
and be patient! The
seedlings may emerge in
10 days or 2 months, depending on the freshness of the
seed. Pot on or plant out
into the garden when they
are large enough to handle.

Division
The best way to propagate is
by division either in spring
or autumn. Take a portion
of the creeping root from an
established plant, and either
plant out or pot up using a
bark, peat, grit mix of
compost (see p.591). If
taking offsets in autumn, it
is better to winter the pots
in a cold frame.

Garden Cultivation
Plant 60cm (2ft) apart and, if
possible, in a sunny position.
Both alecost and camphor
plant will adapt to most
conditions, but prefer a rich,
fairly dry and well-drained
soil. Both species will grow in
shade but may fail to bloom.
But that is no great loss as
the flower is not striking.
Both die back in winter.

Pests and Diseases
Leaves of both are aromatic,
so pests are not a problem.

Maintenance
Spring Divide established
plants. Sow seed if available.
Feed established plants.
Summer Plant out seedlings
early into permanent
positions. Dead head.
Autumn Trim back flowers.
Remove offsets from
established plants to prevent
them encroaching into
others' territory.
Winter Tidy up dead leaves;
they spread disease if left to
rot. Bring in potted up
offsets.

Harvesting
Pick the leaves for fresh
culinary use any time. Both
alecost and camphor leaves
dry well and retain their
sweet aroma. Pick for drying
just before flowering for the
strongest scent.

The flowers are not worth
harvesting for drying.

Only in a warm climate is
it worth collecting seeds. Do
it when flowers turn brown
and centre eye disintegrates
on touch. Sow the following
year (see 'Propagation').

CONTAINER GROWING
Neither species lends itself
to container growing. They
grow soft, prone to disease,
are untidy when in flower
and tend to be blown over
by the wind. If there is no
other course, dead head to
prevent from flowering and
do not over-feed with liquid
fertilizer.

MEDICINAL

Traditionally in the form of
a tea (Costmary or Sweet
Mary Tea) to ease the pain
of childbirth. It was also
used as a tonic for colds,
catarrh, stomach upsets and
cramps. Rub a fresh leaf of
alecost on a bee sting or
horse fly bite to relieve pain.

Tanacetum parthenium (Chrysanthemum parthenium)

FEVERFEW

Known in America as Featherfew and Febrifuge Plant. From the family Asteraceae.

Feverfew was probably a native of south-east Europe and spread via the Mediterranean to many parts of the world, including Britain and North America. It is an attractive and robust, vigorous plant, and is found growing in the wild on dry, well-drained soils.

Its common name suggests that the herb was used in the treatment of fevers. It is said to be derived from the Latin 'febrifugia', meaning a substance that drives out fevers. The old herbalists even call it a febrifuge. However, strange as it may seem, the herb was hardly ever employed for the purpose.

Gerard, the Elizabethan herbalist, advised use of the dried plant for 'those that are giddied in the head or have vertigo'. In the 17th century Culpeper advised its use for pains in the head and colds. In the late 18th century it was considered a special remedy for a body racked by too much opium. Nowadays it is used in the treatment of migraines.

SPECIES

Tanacetum parthenium (Chrysanthemum parthenium)
Feverfew
Hardy perennial. Ht 60cm–1.2m (2–4ft), spread 45cm (18in). White daisy-like flowers from early summer to early autumn. The leaf is mid-green, and a typical chrysanthemum shape.

Tanacetum parthenium 'White Bonnet'
Double-Flowered Feverfew
Hardy perennial. Ht 30cm (12in), spread 45cm (18in). Double white flowers, otherwise as **T. parthenium**.

Tanacetum parthenium 'Aureum'
Golden Feverfew
Hardy perennial. Ht and spread 20–45cm (8–18in). Gold green leaves that remain colourful all year. Otherwise as **T. parthenium** Growth and colour make golden feverfew popular as an edging plant in formal herb gardens and as a parterre filling. Particularly conspicuous in winter.

Feverfew *Tanacetum parthenium*

CULTIVATION

Propagation

Seeds

Fine, thin and fairly small, they tend to stick together especially if they get damp. Mix a very small amount of seed with an equally small amount of perlite or dry sand to make sowing easier. Sow very thinly in spring or early autumn, directly into pots or plug trays. Cover with a final thin layer of perlite. Germination is usually very rapid, 7–10 days. No need for extra heat. Plant out 30cm (12in) apart, as soon as the seedlings are large enough to handle and hardened off. If sown in autumn, the young plants will need to be wintered under protection.

Division

Dig up established clumps in early autumn. Ease the plants apart, and either replant directly in the positions required or pot up in a standard pot or fancy container for flowers in late spring. Winter in a cold greenhouse or cold frame. Use the bark, peat compost (see p.591).

Cuttings

Take stem cuttings in the summer, making sure there are no flowers on the cutting material.

Pests and Diseases

Unaffected by the majority of pests and diseases, golden feverfew can suffer from sun scorch; if this occurs cut back and the new growth will be unaffected.

Maintenance

Spring Sow seeds.
Summer As flowering finishes cut plant back to restore shape, and remove all flowering heads to

Feverfew in sachets makes a good moth repellent

minimize self-seeding.
Autumn Divide established clumps. This is the best time for sowing if edging plants are required. Winter young plants in a cold frame.
Winter No need to protect, fully frost hardy.

Garden Cultivation

Feverfew, while tolerant by nature, is an invasive plant, so choose the site with care. It will grow anywhere, in nooks or crannies, but likes best a loam soil enriched with good manure in a sunny position. Seeds can be sown direct into a prepared site in late spring. When the seedlings are large enough to handle thin to 30cm (12in) apart.

Harvesting

Pick leaves before the plant flowers; dry if required for use medicinally. Pick the flowers just as they open; dry hanging upside down.

CONTAINER GROWING

Grown indoors, the plants get stretched and leggy. However, in containers outside all the feverfews flourish. Golden feverfew, having the most compact

habit, looks very effective in a hanging basket, tub or window box. Use the bark, peat mix of compost. Keep the plants regularly watered and feed during flowering. Cut back plants after flowering as this will help maintain their shape.

CULINARY

The young leaves of feverfew can be added to salads, but be warned they are very bitter so add sparingly.

MEDICINAL

That feverfew has a propensity to overcome melancholy has been known by herbalists for centuries. However, its ability to soothe headaches was not given much attention until the 1970s when it was thoroughly investigated scientifically, following claims that it reduced migraines. Many clinical trials were held and results, over a six-month period, showed a 70 per cent reduction in migraines, and

43 per cent of the patients felt other beneficial side-effects, including more restful sleep and relief from arthritis. 18 per cent had unpleasant side-effects. Golden and double-flowered forms have not been tested, though experience suggests that they will react similarly.

Eat 3 to 5 fresh leaves between a slice of bread every day to reduce migraines. As mentioned before, this is very bitter, so put the leaves in a sandwich (brown bread, of course). To make it more palatable, you could add a sprig of mint, marjoram or parsley. Do NOT eat more.

OTHER USES

A decoction or infusion of the leaves is a mild disinfectant, and the leaves in sachets make a good moth repellent.

WARNING

One side effect associated with taking feverfew is ulceration of the mouth.

Tanacetum vulgare (Chrysanthemum vulgare)

TANSY

Also known as Bachelor's Buttons, Bitter Buttons, Golden Buttons, Stinking Willy, Hind Heel and Parsley Fern. From the family Asteraceae.

Tansy is a native to Europe and Asia, and it has managed to become naturalized elsewhere, especially in North America. The name derives from the Greek *athanasia*, meaning immortality. In ancient times it was used in the preparation of the embalming sheets and rubbed on corpses to save them from earthworms or corpse worm.

SPECIES

Tanacetum vulgare
Tansy
Hardy perennial. Ht 90cm (3ft), spread 30–60cm (1–2ft) and more. Yellow button flowers in late summer. The aromatic leaf is deeply indented, toothed and fairly dark green.

Tanacetum vulgare var. crispum
Curled Tansy
As **T. vulgare** except Ht 60cm (24in) and the aromatic leaf is crinkly, curly and dark green.

Tanacetum vulgare 'Isala Gold'
Tansy Isala Gold
As **T. vulgare** except Ht 60cm (24in) and the leaf is golden in colour.

Tansy *Tanacetum vulgare*

Tanacetum vulgare 'Silver Lace'
Tansy 'Silver Lace'
As **T. vulgare** except Ht 60cm (24in) and the leaf starts off white-flecked with green, progressing to full green. If, however, you keep cutting it, some of the variegation can be maintained.

CULTIVATION

Propagation
Seed
Sow the very small seed in spring or autumn in a prepared seed or plug tray and cover with perlite. Germination takes 10–21 days. Plant out 45cm (18in) apart when the seedlings are large enough to handle. If sown in the autumn, overwinter under protection.

Division
All species produce root runners, so divide in spring or autumn.

Pests and Diseases
Tansy is rarely bothered with pests or disease.

Maintenance
Spring Sow seed. Divide established clumps.
Summer Cut back after flowering to maintain shape and colour.
Autumn Divide established clumps. Sow seeds.
Winter The plant is fully hardy and dies back into the ground for winter.

Garden Cultivation
Tansy needs to be positioned with care as the roots spread widely. The gold and variegated forms are much less invasive and very attractive in a semi-shaded border. They tolerate most conditions provided the soil is not completely wet.

Harvesting
Pick leaves as required. Gather flowers when open.

CONTAINER GROWING

Because of its antisocial habit, container growing is recommended. Use a soil-based compost and a large container, water throughout the growing season, and only feed about twice during flowering. In winter keep on the dry side in a cool place.

OTHER USES

Rub into the coat of your dog or cat to prevent fleas.
Hang leaves indoors to deter flies. Put dried sprigs under carpets. Add to insect repellent sachets. Sprinkle chopped leaves and flowers to deter ants and mice.
It produces a yellow/green woollen dye.

MEDICINAL

Can be used by trained herbalists to expel roundworm and threadworm.
Use tansy tea externally to treat scabies, and as a compress to bring relief to painful rheumatic joints.

WARNING

Use tansy only under medical supervision. It is a strong emmenagogue, provoking the onset of a period, and should not be used during pregnancy. An overdose of tansy oil or tea can be fatal.

Curled tansy
Tanacetum vulgare var. *crispum*

Taraxacum officinale sativum

DANDELION

Also known as Pee in the Bed, Lions Teeth, Fairy Clock, Clock, Clock Flower, Clocks and Watches, Farmers Clocks, Old Mans Clock, One Clock, Wetweed, Blowball, Cankerwort, Lionstooth, Priests Crown, Puffball, Swinesnout, White Endive, Wild Endive and Piss-a-beds. From the family Asteraceae.

Dandelion is one of nature's great medicines and it really proves that a weed is only a plant out of place! It is in fact one of the most useful of herbs. It has become naturalized throughout the temperate regions of the world and flourishes on nitrogen-rich soils in any situation to a height of 2,000m (6,500ft).

There is no satisfactory explanation why it is called Dandelion, Dents Lioness, Tooth of the Lion in medieval Latin, and Dent de Lion in French. The lion's tooth may be the tap root, the jagged leaf or the parts of the flower.

The Arabs promoted its use in the 11th century. By the 16th it was well established as an official drug. The apothecaries knew it as *Herba taraxacon* or *Herba urinari*, and Culpeper called it Piss-a-beds, all referring to its diuretic qualities.

Dandelion
Taraxacum officinale sativum

Dandelion *Taraxacum officinale sativum*

SPECIES

Taraxacum officinale sativum
Dandelion
Perennial. Ht 15–23cm (6–9in). Large, brilliant yellow flowers 5cm (2in) wide, spring to autumn. The flower heads as they turn to seed form a fluffy ball (dandelion clock). Leaves oblong with a jagged edge.

Taraxacum kok-saghyz Rodin
Russian Dandelion
Perennial. Ht 30cm (12in). Similar to the above. Extensively cultivated during the Second World War: latex was extracted from the roots as a source of rubber.

Taraxacum mongolicum
Chinese Dandelion
Perennial. Ht 25–30cm (10–12in). Similar to the above. Used to treat infections, particularly mastitis.

CULTIVATION

Propagation
Seed
Grow as an annual to prevent bitterness developing in the plant. Sow seed in spring on the surface of pots or plug trays. Do not use seed trays as the long tap root makes it difficult to prick out. Cover with a fine layer of perlite. Germination will be in 3–6 weeks, depending on seed freshness and air temperature. Plant out when large enough to handle.

Root
Sections of the root can be cut and put in either pots, seed or plug trays. Each piece will sprout again, just like comfrey.

Pests and Diseases
Dandelion is rarely attacked by either pest or disease.

Maintenance

Spring Sow seeds for use as an autumn salad herb.
Summer Continually pick off the flower buds if you are growing dandelion as a salad crop.
Autumn Put an up-turned flower pot over some of the plants to blanch them for autumn salads. Sow seed for spring salad crop.
Winter No protection is needed. For salad crops, if temperatures fall below −10°C (15°F), cover with agricultural fleece or 8cm (3in) of straw or bracken to keep the leaves sweet.

Garden Cultivation

If the dandelion was a rare plant, it would be thought as a highly desirable garden species, for the flowers are most attractive, sweet smelling and a brilliant yellow, and then form the delightful puff balls. Up to that point all is fine. But then the wind disperses the seed all over the garden. And it is very difficult to eradicate when established since every bit of root left behind produces another plant. So, it finds no favour at all with gardeners.

In general, details on how to grow dandelions are superfluous. Most people only want to know how to get rid of them. The easiest time to dig up the plants completely is in the early spring.

Harvesting

Pick leaves as required to use fresh, and flowers for wine as soon as they open fully. Dig up roots in autumn for drying.

CONTAINER GROWING

Dandelions do look attractive growing in containers, especially in window boxes, if you can stand neighbours' remarks. But in all seriousness the containers will need to be deep to accommodate the long tap root.

CULINARY

Both the leaves and root have long been eaten as a highly nutritious salad. In the last century, cultivated forms with large leaves were developed as an autumn and spring vegetable. The leaves were usually blanched in the same way as endive. Dandelion salad in spring is also considered a blood cleanser owing to its diuretic and digestive qualities. The leaves are very high in vitamins A, B, C and D, the A content being higher than that of carrots.

The flowers make an excellent country wine and dandelion roots provide, when dried, chopped and roasted, the best known coffee substitute.

Dandelion wine

Dandelion and Bacon Salad
Serves 4

225g/8oz young dandelion leaves
100g/4oz streaky bacon, diced
1cm/½in slice white bread, cubed
4 tablespoons olive or walnut oil
1 tablespoon white wine vinegar
1 clove garlic, crushed
salt and freshly ground pepper
oil for cooking

Wash and dry the leaves and tear into the salad bowl. Make a vinaigrette using olive oil and vinegar, and season to taste, adding a little sugar if desired. Fry the bacon, crushed garlic and bread in oil until golden brown. Pour the contents of the pan over the leaves and turn the leaves until thoroughly coated. Add the vinaigrette and toss again and serve at once.

Dandelion and bacon salad

MEDICINAL

It is one of the most useful medicinal plants, as all parts are effective and safe to use. It is regarded as one of the best herbal remedies for kidney and liver complaints. The root is a mildly laxative, bitter tonic, valuable in treating dyspepsia and constipation. The leaves are a powerful diuretic. However, unlike conventional diuretics, dandelion does not leach potassium from the body as its rich potassium content replaces what the body loses.

The latex contained in the leaves and stalks is very effective in removing corns and in treating warts and verrucas. Apply the juice from the plant daily to the affected part.

The flowers can be boiled with sugar for coughs, but honey has a greater

OTHER USES

As a herbal fertilizer dandelion is a good supply of copper. Pick 3 plants completely: leaves, flowers and all. Place in a bucket, pour over 1 litre (2 pints) boiling water, cover and allow to stand for 30 minutes. Strain through an old pair of tights or something similar. This fertilizer will not store.

A dye, yellow-brown in colour, can be obtained from the root and dandelions are excellent food for domestic rabbits, guinea pigs and gerbils. There is one thing for which they are useless, however – flower arrangements. As soon as you pick them and put them in water their flowers close tight.

Teucrium chamaedrys

WALL GERMANDER

**Also known as Ground Oak and Wild Germander.
From the family Lamiaceae.**

This attractive plant is a native of Europe, and is now naturalized in Britain and other countries in the temperate zone. It is found on dry chalky soils. The Latin *Teucrium* is said to have been named after Teucer, first king of Troy. It is the ancient Greek word for ground oak, its leaves resembling those of the oak tree.

In medieval times, it was a popular strewing herb and a remedy for dropsy, jaundice and gout. It was also used in powder form for treating head colds, and as a snuff.

SPECIES

Teucrium fruticans
Tree Germander
Evergreen hardy perennial. Ht 1–2m (3–6ft), spread 2–4m (6–12ft). Blue flowers in summer. The leaves are aromatic, grey/green with a white underside.

Teucrium chamaedrys L. 'Variegatum'
Variegated Wall Germander
Evergreen hardy perennial. Ht 45cm (18in), spread 20cm (8in). Pink flowers from midsummer to early autumn. The leaves are aromatic, dark green with cream/yellow variegation, small, shiny and oval.

Teucrium x lucidrys
Hedge Germander
Evergreen hardy perennial. Ht 45cm (18in), spread 20cm (8in). Pink flowers from midsummer to early autumn. The leaves are dark green, small, shiny and oval. When rubbed, they smell pleasantly spicy.

CULTIVATION

Propagation
Seed
Sow the small seeds in spring. Use a prepared seed or plug tray and the bark, peat, grit compost (see p.591). Cover with perlite. Germination can be erratic – from 2–4 weeks. When the seedlings are large enough to handle, plant in a prepared site 20cm (8in) apart.

Cuttings
This is a better method of propagating germander. Take softwood cuttings from the new growth in spring, or semi-hardwood in summer. Ensure compost does not dry out or become sodden.

Division
The teucriums produce creeping rootstock in the spring and are easy to divide. Dig up the plants, split them in half, and replant in a chosen site.

Pests and Diseases
Wall germander hardly ever suffers from pests or disease.

Maintenance
Spring Sow seeds. Take softwood cuttings. Trim established plants and hedges.
Summer Trim plants after flowering, take semi-hardwood cuttings.
Autumn Trim hedges.
Winter Protect the variegated form when temperatures drop below −5°C (23°F).

Garden Cultivation
Wall germander needs a well-drained soil (slightly alkaline) and a sunny position. It is hardier than lavender and cotton lavender, and makes an ideal hedging or edging plant. To make a good dense hedge, plant at a distance of 15cm (6in). If you clip the hedge in spring and autumn to maintain its shape, you will never need to cut it hard back.

It can also be planted in rockeries, and in stone walls where it looks most attractive. During the growing season it does not need extra water, even in hot summers, nor does it need extra protection in cold winters. The variegated variety is more temperamental, and will require cosseting in the winter in the form of a mulch or agricultural fleece.

Harvesting
For drying for medicinal use, pick leaves before the plant flowers, and flowering stems when the flowers are in bud.

CONTAINER GROWING

Both wall germander and the variegated form look good in containers. Use the bark, peat, grit mix of compost. Only feed during the flowering season. Keep on the dry side in winter.

CULINARY

This plant is used extensively in the flavouring of liqueurs.

MEDICINAL

Its herbal use today is minor. However, there is a revival of interest going on, and some use it as a remedy for digestive and liver troubles, anaemia and bronchitis.

Teucrium scorodonia

WOOD SAGE

Also known as Gypsy Sage, Mountain Sage, Wild Sage and Garlic Sage. From the family Lamiaceae.

This plant is a native of Europe and has become naturalized in Britain and other countries in the temperate zone.
There is not much written about wood sage apart from the fact that, like alecost, it was used in making ale before hops were introduced. However, Gertrude Jekyll recognized its value and with renewed interest in her gardens comes a revival of interest in wood sage.

SPECIES

Teucrium scorodonia
Wood Sage
Hardy perennial. Ht 30–60cm (12–24in), spread 25cm (10in). Pale greenish-white flowers in summer. Soft green heart-shaped leaves, which have a mild smell of crushed garlic.

Teucrium scorodonia 'Crispum'
Curly Wood Sage
Hardy perennial. Ht 35cm (14in), spread 30cm (12in). Pale greenish-white flowers in summer. The leaves are soft, oval and olive green with a reddish tinge to their crinkled edges. Whenever it is on show it causes much comment.

CULTIVATION

Propagation
Wood sage can be propagated by seed, cuttings or division. Curly wood sage can only be propagated by cuttings or division.

Seed
Sow the fairly small seed under protection in autumn or spring in a prepared seed or plug tray. Use the bark, peat, grit compost (see p.591), and cover with perlite. Germination can be erratic, taking from 2–4 weeks. When the seedlings are large enough to handle, pot up and winter under cover in a cold frame. In the spring, after a period of hardening off, plant out in a prepared site in the garden at a distance of 25cm (10in).

Cuttings
Take softwood cuttings from the new growth in spring, or semi-hardwood cuttings in summer.

Division
Both wood sages produce creeping rootstock. In the spring they are easy to divide.

Pests and Diseases
Wood sages are, in the majority of cases, free from pests and disease.

Maintenance
Spring Sow seeds. Divide established plants. Take softwood cuttings.
Summer Take semi-hardwood cuttings.
Autumn Sow seeds.
Winter No need for protection, the plants die back for the winter.

Garden Cultivation
It grows well in semi-shaded situations, but also thrives in full sun on sandy and gravelly soils. It will adapt quite happily to clay and heavy soils, but not produce such prolific growth.

Harvesting
Pick young leaves for fresh use as required.

CONTAINER GROWING

I have grown curly wood sage most successfully in containers. The plain wood sage does not look quite so attractive. Use the bark, grit, peat mix of compost, and plant in a large container – its creeping rootstock can too easily become pot-bound. Only feed twice in a growing season, otherwise the leaves become large, soft and floppy. When the plant dies back, put it somewhere cool and keep it bordering on dry.

MEDICINAL

Wood sage has been used to treat blood disorders, colds and fevers, and as a diuretic and wound herb.

CULINARY

The leaves of ordinary wood sage have a mild garlic flavour. When young and tender, the leaves can be added to salads for variety. But go steady, they are slightly bitter.

Wood sage salad

Thymus

THYME

From the family Lamiaceae.

This is a genus comprising numerous species that are very diverse in appearance and come from many different parts of the world. They are found as far afield as Greenland and Western Asia, although the majority grow in the Mediterranean region.

This ancient herb was used by the Egyptians in oil form for embalming. The Greeks used it in their baths and as an incense in their temples. The Romans used it to purify their rooms, and most probably its use spread through Europe as their invasion train swept as far as Britain. In the Middle Ages drinking it was part of a ritual to enable one to see fairies, and it was one of many herbs used in nosegays to purify the odours of disease. Owing to its antiseptic properties, judges also used it along with rosemary to prevent gaol fever.

Common thyme
Thymus vulgaris

Silver Posie thyme *Thymus vulgaris* 'Silver Posie'

SPECIES

There are so many species of thyme that I am only going to mention a few of interest. New ones are being discovered each year. They are eminently collectable. Unfortunately their names can be unreliable, a nursery preferring its pet name or one traditional to it, rather than the correct one.

Thymus caespititius (Thymus azoricus)
Caespititius Thyme
Evergreen hardy perennial. Ht 10cm (4in), spread 20cm (8in). Pale pink flowers in summer. The leaves narrow, bright green and close together on the stem. Makes an attractive low-growing mound, good between paving stones.

Thymus camphoratus
Camphor Thyme
Evergreen half-hardy perennial. Ht 30cm (12in), spread 20cm (8in). Pink/mauve flowers in summer, large green leaves smelling of camphor. Makes a beautiful compact bush.

Thymus cilicicus
Cilicicus Thyme
Evergreen hardy perennial. Ht 5cm (2in), spread 20cm (8in). Pink flowers in summer. The leaves are bright green, narrow and pointed, growing close together on the stem with an odd celery scent. Makes an attractive low-growing mound, good between paving stones.

Thymus x citriodorus
Lemon Thyme
Evergreen hardy perennial. Ht 30 cm (12in), spread 20cm (8in). Pink flowers in summer. Fairly large green leaves with a strong lemon scent. Excellent culinary thyme, combines well with many chicken or fish dishes.

Wild creeping thyme *Thymus polytrichus* subsp. *britannicus*

Thymus x citriodorus 'Golden King'
Golden King Thyme
Evergreen hardy perennial. Ht 30cm (12in) spread 20cm (8in). Pink flowers in the summer. Fairly large green leaves variegated with gold, strongly lemon scented. Excellent culinary thyme, combines well with many dishes, like chicken, fish and salad dressing.

Thymus x citriodorus 'Silver Queen'
Silver Queen Thyme
Evergreen hardy perennial. Ht 30cm (12in) spread 20cm (8in). Pink flowers in the summer. Fairly large leaves, grey with silver variegation, a strong lemon scent. Excellent culinary thyme, combines well with many dishes, like chicken and salad dressing.

Thymus Coccineus Group
Coccineus Thyme
Also known as Creeping Red Thyme. Evergreen hardy perennial, prostrate form, a creeper. Red flowers in summer. Green small leaves. Decorative, aromatic and good ground cover.

Thymus doerfleri
Doerfleri Thyme
Evergreen half-hardy perennial. Ht 2cm (1in), spread 20cm (8in). Mauve/ pink flowers in summer, grey, hairy, thin leaves, which are mat forming. Decorative thyme, good for rockeries, hates being wet in winter. Originates from the Balkan Peninsula.

Thymus doerfleri 'Bressingham'
Bressingham Thyme
Evergreen hardy perennial.

Ht 2cm (1in), spread 20cm (8in). Mauve/pink flowers in summer. Thin, green, hairy leaves, which are mat forming. Decorative thyme, good for rockeries, hates being wet in winter.

Thymus 'Doone Valley'
Doone Valley Thyme
Evergreen hardy perennial. Ht 8cm (3in), spread 20cm (8in). Purple flowers in summer. Round variegated green and gold leaves with a lemon scent. Very decorative, can be used in cooking if nothing else is available.

Thymus 'Fragrantissimus'
Orange-Scented Thyme
Evergreen hardy perennial. Ht 30 cm (12in), spread 20cm (8in). Small pale pink/white flowers in summer. The leaves are small, narrow, greyish green, and smell of spicy orange. Combines well with stir-fry dishes, poultry – especially duck, and even treacle pudding.

Thymus herba-barona
Caraway Thyme
Evergreen hardy perennial. Ht 2cm (1in), spread 20cm (8in). Rose-coloured flowers in summer. Dark green small leaves with a unique caraway scent. Good in culinary dishes especially stir fry and meat. It combines well with beef.

Thymus 'Peter Davis'
Peter Davis Thyme
Evergreen hardy perennial. Ht 8cm (3in), spread 20cm

(8in). Pink/mauve flowers in summer. Thin grey/green leaves, mild scent. Very attractive, good in rockeries or formal herb gardens.

Thymus polytrichus subsp. britannicus
Wild Creeping Thyme
Also known as Mother of Thyme and Creeping Thyme.
Evergreen hardy perennial. Ht 2cm (1in), spread 20cm (8in). Pale mauve flowers in summer. Small dark green leaves which, although mildly scented, can be used in cooking. Wild thyme has been valued by herbalists for many centuries.

Thymus 'Porlock'
Porlock Thyme
Evergreen hardy perennial. Ht 30cm (12in), spread 20cm (8in). Pink flowers in summer. Fairly large green leaves with a mild but definite thyme flavour and scent. Excellent culinary thyme. Medicinal properties are anti-bacterial and anti-fungal.

Thymus pseudolanuginosus
Woolly Thyme
Evergreen hardy perennial. Ht 2cm (1in), spread 20cm (8in). Pale pink/mauve flowers for most of the summer. Grey hairy mat-forming leaves. Good for rockeries and in stone paths or walls. Dislikes wet winters.

Thymus pulegioides
Broad-Leaved Thyme
Evergreen hardy perennial. Ht 8cm (3in), spread 20cm (8in). Pink/mauve flowers in summer. Large round dark green leaves with a strong thyme flavour. Good for culinary uses, excellent for ground cover and good in hanging baskets.

Thymus pulegioides 'Archer's Gold'
Archer's Gold Thyme
Evergreen hardy perennial. Ht 10cm (4in), spread 20cm (8in). Pink/mauve flowers

Lemon thyme
Thymus x citriodorus

in summer. A mound of green/gold leaves. Decorative and culinary, it has a mild thyme flavour.

Thymus pulegioides 'Bertram Anderson'
Bertram Anderson Thyme
Evergreen hardy perennial. Ht 10cm (4in), spread 20cm (8in). Pink/mauve flowers in summer. More of a round mound than 'Archer's Gold' and the leaves are slightly rounder with a more even golden look to the leaves. Decorative and culinary, it has a mild thyme flavour.

Thymus pulegioides 'Aureus'
Golden Thyme
Evergreen hardy perennial. Ht 30cm (12in), spread 20cm (8in). Pale pink /lilac flowers. Green leaves that turn gold in summer, good flavour, combining well with vegetarian dishes.

Pink Chintz thyme
Thymus serpyllum 'Pink Chintz'

Thymus serpyllum var. albus
White Thyme
Evergreen hardy perennial, prostrate form, a creeper. White flowers in summer. Bright green small leaves. Decorative aromatic and good ground cover.

Thymus serpyllum 'Annie Hall'
Annie Hall Thyme
Evergreen hardy perennial, prostrate form, a creeper. Pale pink flowers in summer. Small green leaves. Decorative, aromatic and good ground cover.

Goldstream thyme
Thymus serpyllum 'Goldstream'

Thymus serpyllum 'Goldstream'
Goldstream Thyme
Evergreen hardy perennial, prostrate form, a creeper. Pink/mauve flowers in summer. Green/gold variegated small leaves. Decorative, aromatic and good ground cover.

Thymus serpyllum 'Lemon Curd'
Lemon Curd Thyme
Evergreen hardy perennial, prostrate form, a creeper. White/pink flowers in summer. Bright green lemon-scented small leaves. Decorative, aromatic and good ground cover. Can be used in cooking if nothing else available.

Thymus serpyllum 'Minimus'
Minimus Thyme
Evergreen hardy perennial, prostrate form, a creeper. Pink flowers in summer. Tiny leaves, very compact. Decorative, aromatic and good ground cover. Ideal for growing between pavings and alongside paths.

Thymus serpyllum 'Pink Chintz'
Pink Chintz Thyme
Evergreen hardy perennial, prostrate form, a creeper. Pale pink flowers in summer. Grey green small hairy leaves. Decorative, aromatic, good ground cover. Does not like being wet in winter.

Thymus serpyllum 'Rainbow Falls'
Rainbow Falls Thyme
Evergreen hardy perennial, prostrate form, a creeper. Purple flowers in summer. Variegated green/gold small leaves. Decorative, aromatic and good ground cover.

Thymus serpyllum 'Russetings'
Russetings Thyme
Evergreen hardy perennial, prostrate form, a creeper. Purple/mauve flowers in summer. Small green leaves. Decorative, aromatic and good ground cover.

Thymus serpyllum 'Snowdrift'
Snowdrift Thyme
Evergreen hardy perennial, prostrate form, a creeper. Masses of white flowers in summer. Small green round leaves. Decorative, aromatic and good ground cover.

Thymus vulgaris
Common (Garden) Thyme
Evergreen hardy perennial. Ht 30cm (12in), spread 20cm (8in). Mauve flowers in summer. Thin green aromatic leaves. This is the thyme everyone knows. Use in stews, salads, sauces etc. Medicinal properties are anti-bacterial and anti-fungal.

Thymus vulgaris 'Lucy'
Lucy Thyme
Evergreen hardy perennial. Ht 30cm (12in), spread 20cm (8in). The thyme sometimes does not flower, and if it does, it is a very pale pink flower and not very prolific. The leaves are very small green. Excellent culinary thyme. Medicinal properties are anti-bacterial and anti-fungal.

Coccineus thyme *Thymus* Coccineus Group **and Snowdrift thyme** *Thymus serpyllum* 'Snowdrift'

Thymus vulgaris 'Silver Posie'
Silver Posie Thyme
Evergreen hardy perennial. Ht 30cm (12in), spread 20cm (8in). Pale pink/lilac flower. The leaves have a very pretty grey/silver variegation with a tinge of pink on the under-side. This is a good culinary thyme and looks very attractive in salads.

Thymus zygis
Zygis Thyme
Evergreen half-hardy perennial. Ht 30cm (12in), spread 20cm (8in). White attractive flowers. Small thin grey/green leaves which are aromatic. This is an attractive thyme which is good for rockeries.

Originates from Spain and Portugal, therefore does not like cold wet winters.

Upright Thymes
Up to 30cm (12in): Caespititius, Archer's Gold, Bertram Anderson, Peter Davis.

30cm (12in) and above: Camphor, Lucy, Lemon, Orange Scented, Golden King, Porlock, Common (Garden), Golden, Silver Posie, Zygis.

Creeping Thymes
Cilicicus, Doerfleri, Bressingham, Doone Valley, Wild Creeping, Woolly, Broad-Leaved, White, Annie Hall, Coccineus, Goldstream, Lemon Curd, Minimus, Pink Chintz, Rainbow Falls, Russetings, Snowdrift.

CULTIVATION

Propagation
To maintain the true plant, it is better to grow the majority of thymes from softwood cuttings. Only a very few, such as common and wild creeping thyme, can be propagated successfully from seed.

Seed
Sow the very fine seed in early spring using the cardboard technique on the surface of prepared trays (seed or plug), using the bark, peat, grit compost (see p.591) and a bottom heat of 15–21°C (60–70°F). Do not cover. Keep watering to the absolute minimum, as these seedlings are prone to damping off disease. When the young plants are large enough and after a period of hardening off, plant out in the garden in late spring/early summer, 23–38cm (9–15in) apart.

Cuttings
Thymes are easily increased by softwood cuttings from new growth in early spring or summer. The length of the cutting should be 5–8cm (2–3in). Use the bark, peat, grit mix of compost. Winter the young plants under protection and plant out the following spring.

Division
Creeping thymes put out aerial roots as they spread, which make them very easy to divide.

Silver Posie thyme
Thymus vulgaris 'Silver Posie'

Layering
An ideal method for mature thymes that are getting a bit woody. Use either the strong branch method of layering in early autumn or mound layer in early spring.

Pests and Diseases
Being such an aromatic plant it does not normally suffer from pests but, if the soil or compost is too rich, thyme may be attacked by aphids. Treat with a liquid horticultural soap. All varieties will rot off if they become too wet in a cold winter.

Maintenance
Spring Sow seeds. Trim old plants. Layer old plants.
Summer Take cuttings of non-flowering shoots. Trim back after flowering.
Autumn Protect tender thymes.
Winter Protect containers and only water if absolutely necessary.

Garden Cultivation
Thymes need to be grown in poor soil, in a well-drained bed to give their best flavour. They are drought-loving plants and will need protection from cold winds, hard and wet winters. Sow seed when the soil has warmed and there is no threat of frost. Thin on average to 20cm (8in) apart.

It is essential to trim all thymes after flowering; this not only promotes new growth, but also stops the plant becoming woody and sprawling in the wrong direction.

In very cold areas grow it in the garden as an annual or in containers and then winter with protection.

Harvesting
As thyme is an evergreen it can be picked fresh all year round provided you are not too greedy. For preserving, pick before it is in flower. Either dry the leaves or put them in a vinegar or oil.

Annie Hall thyme
Thymus serpyllum 'Annie Hall'

CONTAINER GROWING

All varieties suit being grown in containers. They like a free-draining poor soil (low in nutrients); if grown in a rich soil they will become soft and the flavour will be impaired. Use the peat, grit, bark mix of compost; water sparingly, keeping the container bordering on dry, and in winter definitely dry – only watering if absolutely necessary, when the leaves begin to lose too much colour. Feed only occasionally in the summer months. Put the container in a sunny spot, which will help the aromatic oils come to the leaf surface and impart a better flavour. Trim back after flowering to maintain shape and promote new growth.

WARNING

Although a medical dose drawn from the whole plant is safe, any amount of the volatile oil is toxic and should not be used internally except by prescription. Avoid altogether if you are pregnant.

CULINARY

Thyme is an aid to digestion and helps break down fatty foods. It is one of the main ingredients of bouquet garni; it is good, too, in stocks, marinades, stews; and a sprig or two with half an onion makes a great herb stuffing for chicken.

Poached Trout with Lemon Thyme
Serves 4

4 trout, cleaned and gutted
Salt
6 peppercorns (whole)
4 fresh bay leaves
1 small onion cut into rings
1 lemon
1 sprig lemon thyme
1 tablespoon chopped lemon thyme leaves
100ml (4fl oz) white wine
2 tablespoons fresh snipped garlic chives
75g (3oz) butter

Place the trout in a large frying pan. Sprinkle with salt and add the peppercorns. Place one bay leaf by each trout. Put the onion rings on top of the trout, cut half the lemon into slices and arrange this over the trout, add the thyme sprig, and sprinkle some of the chopped thyme leaves over the whole lot. Pour in the wine and enough water just to cover the fish. Bring it to the boil on top of the stove and let it simmer uncovered for 6 minutes for fresh trout, 20 minutes for frozen.

Mix the remaining chopped lemon thyme and garlic chives with the butter garlic chives with the butter in a small bowl. Divide this mixture into 4 equal portions. When the trout are cooked lift them out gently, place on plates with a slice of lemon and the herb butter on the top. Serve with new potatoes.

MEDICINAL

Thyme has strong antiseptic properties. The tea makes a gargle or mouthwash, and is an excellent remedy for sore throats and infected gums. It is also good for hangovers.

The essential oil is anti-bacterial and anti-fungal and used in the manufacture of toothpaste, mouthwash, gargles and other toilet articles. It can also be use to kill mosquito larvae. A few drops of the oil added to the bath water helps ease rheumatic pain, and it is often used in liniments and massage oils.

Tropaeolum majus

NASTURTIUM

Also known as Garden Nasturtium, Indian Cress and Large Cress. From the family Tropaeolaceae.

Nasturtiums are native of South America, especially Peru and Bolivia, but are now cultivated worldwide.

The generic name, *Tropaeolum*, is derived from the Latin 'tropaeum' meaning 'trophy' or 'sign of victory'. After a battle was finished, a tree-trunk was set up on the battlefield and hung with the captured helmets and shields. It was thought that the round leaves of the nasturtium looked like shields and the flowers like blood-stained helmets.

It was introduced into Spain from Peru in the 16th century and reached London shortly afterwards. When first introduced it was known as *Nasturcium indicum* or *Nasturcium peruvinum*, which is how it got its common name Indian cress. The custom of eating its petals, and using them for tea and salads, comes from the Orient.

Nasturtium Alaska
Tropaeolum majus Alaska Series

SPECIES

Tropaeolum majus
Nasturtium
Half-hardy annual. Ht and spread 30cm (12in). Red/orange flowers from summer to early autumn. Round, mid-green leaves.

Tropaeolum majus Alaska Series
Nasturtium Alaska (Variegated)
Half-hardy annual. Ht and spread 30cm (12in). Red, orange and yellow flowers from summer to early autumn. Round, variegated (cream and green) leaves.

Tropaeolum majus 'Empress of India'
Nasturtium 'Empress of India'
Half-hardy annual. Ht 20cm (8in), spread 30cm (12in). Dark red flowers from summer to early autumn. Round, mid-green leaves.

A few special species of interest:

Tropaeolum peregrinum
Canary Creeper
Tender perennial. Climber: Ht 2m (6ft). Small, bright yellow flowers with 2 upper petals that are much larger and fringed from summer until first frost. Grey/green leaves with 5 lobes. In cool areas, best grown as an annual.

Tropaeolum polyphyllum
Hardy perennial. Ht 5–8cm (2–3in), spread 30cm (12in) or more. Fairly small yellow flowers from summer to early autumn. Leaves grey-green on trailing stems. A fast-spreading plant once established. Looks good on banks or hanging down walls.

Tropaeolum speciosum
Flame Creeper
Hardy perennial. Climber: Ht 3m (10ft). Scarlet flowers in summer followed by bright blue fruits surrounded by deep red calyxes in autumn. Leaves green with 6 lobes. This very dramatic plant should be grown like honeysuckle with its roots in the shade and head in the sun.

CULTIVATION

Propagation
Seed
The seeds are large and easy to handle. To have plants flowering early in the summer, sow in early spring under protection directly into prepared pots or cell trays, and cover lightly with compost. Plugs are ideal, especially if you want to introduce the young plants into a hanging basket; otherwise use small pots to allow more flexibility before planting out. When the seedlings are large enough and there is no threat of frosts, plant out into a prepared site in the garden, or into containers.

Cuttings
Take cuttings of the perennial varieties in the spring from the new soft growth.

Pests and Diseases
Aphids and caterpillars of cabbage white butterfly and its relatives may cause a problem. If the infestation is light, the fly may be brushed off or washed away with soapy water. Nettles soaked in rainwater make a good blackfly repellent.

Maintenance
Spring Sow seed early under protection, or after frosts in the garden.
Summer Deadhead flowers to enhance flowering season.
Autumn Dig up dead plants.
Winter Plan next year.

Garden Cultivation
Nasturtiums prefer a well-drained, poor soil in full sun or partial shade. If the soil is too rich, leaf growth will be made at the expense of the flowers. They are frost-tender and will suffer if the temperature falls below 4°C (40°F).

As soon as the soil has begun to warm and the frosts are over, nasturtiums can be sown directly into the garden. Sow individually 20cm (8in) apart. For a border of these plants sow 15cm (6in) apart. Claude Monet's garden at Giverny in France has a border of nasturtiums sprawling over a path that looks very effective.

Harvesting

Pick the flowers for fresh use only; they cannot be dried.

Pick the seed pods just before they lose their green colour (for pickling in vinegar).

Pick the leaves for fresh use as required. They can be dried, but personally I don't think it is worth it.

Nasturtium *Tropaeolum majus*

COMPANION PLANTING

This herb attracts blackfly away from vegetables like cabbage and broad beans. It also attracts the hover fly, which attacks aphids. Further, it repels whitefly, woolly aphids and ants. Altogether it is a good tonic to any garden.

CONTAINER GROWING

This herb is excellent for growing in pots, tubs, window boxes, hanging baskets. Use the bark, peat, grit compost (see p.591). Do not feed, because all you will produce are leaves not flowers, but do keep well watered, especially in hot weather.

MEDICINAL

This herb is rarely used medicinally, although the fresh leaves contain vitamin C and iron as well as an antiseptic substance, which is at its highest before the plant flowers.

WARNING

Use the herb with caution. Do not eat more than 15g (½oz) at a time or 30g (1oz) per day.

CULINARY

I had a group from the local primary school around the farm to talk about herbs. Just as they were leaving I mentioned that these pretty red flowers were now being sold in supermarkets for eating in salads. When a little boy looked at me in amazement, I suggested he try one. He ate the whole flower without saying a word. One of his friends said, 'What does it taste like?' With a huge smile he asked if he could pick another flower for his friend, who ate it and screamed, 'Pepper pepper...' The seeds, flowers and leaves are all now eaten for their spicy taste. They are used in salads also as an attractive garnish. The pickled flower buds provide a good substitute for capers.

Nasturtium Cream Cheese Dip

100g (¼lb) cream cheese
2 teaspoons tender nasturtium
  leaves, chopped
3 nasturtium flowers

Blend the cream cheese with the chopped leaves. Put the mixture into a bowl and decorate with the flowers. Eat this mixture as soon as possible because it can become bitter if left standing.

Urtica

NETTLE

Also known as Common Nettle, Stinging Nettle, Devil's Leaf and Devil's Plaything. From the family Urticaceae.

Common nettle *Urtica dioica* **in full flower**

This plant is found all over the world. It is widespread on wasteland especially on damp and nutrient-rich soil.

The generic name *Urtica* comes from the Latin 'uro' meaning 'I burn'. The Roman nettle *Urtica pilulifera* originally came to Britain with the invading Roman army. The soldiers used the plants to keep themselves warm. They flogged their legs and arms with nettles to keep their circulation going.

The use of nettles in the making of fabric goes back before history. Nettle cloth was found in a Danish grave of the later Bronze Age, wrapped around cremated bones. It was certainly made in Scotland as late as the 18th century. The Scottish poet, Thomas Campbell, wrote then of sleeping in nettle sheets in Scotland and dining off nettle tablecloths. Records show that it was still being used in the early 20th century in Tyrol.

In the Middle Ages it was believed that nettles marked the dwelling place of elves and were a protection against sorcery. They were also said to prevent milk from being affected by house trolls or witches.

Settlers in New England in the 17th century were surprised to find that this old friend and enemy had crossed the Atlantic with them. It was included in a list of plants that sprang up unaided.

Before World War II, vast quantities of nettles were imported to Britain from Germany. During the war there was a drive to collect as much of the home-grown nettle as possible. The dark green dye obtained from the plant was used as camouflage, and chlorophyll was extracted for use in medicines.

SPECIES

Urtica dioica
Stinging Nettle
Hardy perennial. Ht 1.5m (5ft), spread infinite on creeping rootstock. The male and female flowers are on separate plants. The female flowers hang down in clusters, the male flower clusters stick out. The colour for both is a yellowish green. The leaves are green toothed and have bristles. This is the variety that can be eaten when young.

Urtica pilulifera
Roman Nettle
Hardy perennial. Ht 1.5m (5ft), spread infinite on creeping rootstock. This looks very similar to the common stinging nettle, but its sting is said to be more virulent.

Urtica urens
Small Nettle
Hardy annual. Ht and spread 30cm (12in). The male and female flowers are in the same cluster and are a greenish white in colour. The green leaves are deeply toothed and have bristles.

Urtica urentissima
Devil's Leaf
This is a native of Timor and the sting said to be so virulent that its effects can last for months and may even cause death.

CULTIVATION

Propagation
Seed
Nettles can be grown from seed sown in the spring. But I am sure any of your friends with a garden would be happy to give you a root.

Division
Divide established roots early in spring before they put on much leaf growth, and the sting is least strong.

Pests and Diseases
Rarely suffers from pests and disease, well not ones that one would wish to destroy!

Maintenance
Spring Sow seeds, divide established plants.
Summer Cut plants back if they are becoming invasive.
Autumn Cut back the plants hard into the ground.
Winter No need for protection, full hardy.

Garden Cultivation
Stinging nettles are the scourge of the gardener and the farmer, the pest of children in summer, but are very useful in the garden, attracting butterflies and moths, and making an excellent caterpillar food. They will grow happily in any soil. It is worth having a natural corner in the garden where these and a few other wild flowers can be planted.

Harvesting
Cut young leaves in early spring for use as a vegetable.

CULINARY

Nettles are an invaluable food, rich in vitamins and minerals.
  In spring the fresh leaves

Nettle soup

may be cooked and eaten like spinach, made into a delicious soup, or drunk as a tea.

Nettle Soup
Serves 4

When cooked, I am pleased to say, nettles lose their sting.

250g/¹/₂lb young nettle leaves
50g/2oz oil or butter
1 small onion, chopped
250g/¹/₂lb cooked potatoes, peeled and diced
900ml/1¹/₂ pints/3³/₄ cups of milk
1 teaspoon each (mix, fresh, chopped) sweet marjoram, sage, lemon thyme
1 dessertspoon fresh chopped lovage
2 tablespoons, cream and French parsley, chopped, optional

Pick only the fresh young nettle leaves, and wear gloves to remove from stalks and wash them. Heat the oil in a saucepan, add the chopped onions, slowly sweat them until clear. Then add the nettles and stew gently for about a further 10 minutes. Add the chopped potatoes, all the herbs and the milk and simmer for a further 10 minutes. Allow to cool then put all the ingredients into a liquidizer and blend. Return to a saucepan over gentle heat. Add a swirl of cream to each bowl and sprinkle some chopped French parsley over the top. Serve with French bread.

MEDICINAL

The nettle has many therapeutic applications but is principally of benefit in all kinds of internal haemorrhages, as a diuretic in jaundice and haemorrhoids, and as a laxative. It is also used in dermatological problems including eczema.
  Nettles make a valuable tonic after the long winter months when they provide one of the best sources of minerals. They are an excellent remedy for anaemia. Their vitamin C content makes sure that the iron they contain is properly absorbed.

WARNING

Do not eat old plants uncooked, they can produce kidney damage and symptoms of poisoning. The plants must be cooked thoroughly to be safe.

Handle all plants with care; they do sting.

Nettle rinse and hair conditioner

OTHER USES

Whole plants yield a greenish/yellow woollen dye.
  Nettles make a good spray against aphids, especially blackfly. Pick a bucket full of nettles, pour (soft/rain) water over them. Cover the container and allow to soak for a week. Strain the liquid, and put it into a spray. Spray on infected plants.
  Nettles have a long-standing reputation for preventing hair loss and making the hair soft and shiny. They also have a reputation for eliminating dandruff.

Nettle Rinse and Conditioner
Use it as a final rinse after washing your hair or massage it into your scalp and comb through the hair every other day. Keep it in a small bottle in the refrigerator.

1 big handful-size bunch of nettles
¹/₂ litre/1 pint of water

Wear rubber gloves to cut the nettles. Wash thoroughly and put the bunch into an enamel saucepan with enough cold water to cover. Bring to the boil, cover and simmer for 15 minutes. Strain the liquid into a jug and allow to cool.

Valeriana officinalis

VALERIAN

Also known as All Heal, Set All, Common Valerian, Garden Heliotrope, Cut Finger, Fragrant Valerian, Cat's Valerian and St. George's Herb. From the family Valerianaceae.

Valerian is a native of Europe and West Asia and is now naturalized in North America. It is found in grasslands, ditches, damp meadows and close to streams.

The name may come from the Latin 'valere' to be healthy, an allusion to its powerful medicinal qualities. Or from an early herbalist, Valeris, who first used it medicinally.

Fresh valerian roots smell like ancient leather, but when dried they smell more like stale sweat. In spite of this, valerian is still used to add a musky tone to perfume. Cats and rats are attracted to the smell and the Pied Piper of Hamelin is said to have carried the root. A tincture of valerian was employed in the First and Second World Wars to treat shell-shock and nervous stress.

COMPANION PLANTING

Planted near other vegetables, it boosts their growth by stimulating phosphorus and earthworm activity.

OTHER USES

Infuse root and spray on the ground to attract earthworms. Add mineral-rich leaves to new compost. Use the root in rat traps.

MEDICINAL

The root is a calmative. Its sedative and anti-spasmodic effects are of benefit in the treatment of a wide range of nervous disorders and intestinal colic.

Decoct the root or, more effectively, crush 1 teaspoon (5ml) of dried root and soak in cold water for 12–24 hours. Drink as a sedative for mild insomnia, sudden emotional distress, headaches, intestinal cramps and nervous exhaustion.

SPECIES

Valeriana officinalis
Valerian
Hardy perennial. Ht 1–1.2m (3–4ft), spread 1m (3ft). Pale pink/white flowerheads in summer. Leaves deeply toothed and mid-green.

CULTIVATION

Propagation
Seed
Sow the fairly small seeds in early spring, either in seed or plug trays. Press the seeds into the soil but do not cover, as this will delay germination. When the seedlings are large enough to handle, transplant to the garden at a distance of 60cm (24in) apart.

Valerian *Valeriana officinalis*

Division
Divide the roots in spring or autumn. Replant after division in a prepared site.

Pests and Diseases
Valerian is mostly free from pests and disease.

Maintenance
Spring Sow seed. Divide roots.
Summer Cut back after flowering to prevent self-seeding.
Autumn Divide establish plants if needed.
Winter A very hardy plant, no need for protection.

Garden Cultivation
Valerian is one of the earliest flowering, tall, wetland plants. As long as its roots are kept cool (which is why it prefers to be near water), it can be grown successfully in almost any garden soil in sun or deep shade. You can sow seeds direct in spring, leaving uncovered, but for a more guaranteed result start off in plug trays. Remember that cats love the scent when choosing the planting site

Harvesting
Dig up complete root in late autumn of the second and third years. Wash and remove the pale fibrous roots, leaving the edible rhizome. To dry this rhizome, cut it into manageable slices (see pp.609–10).

WARNING

Valerian should not be taken in large doses for an extended period of time.

Verbena officinalis

VERVAIN

Also known as Holy Herb, Simpler's Joy, Pigeon's Grass, Burvine, Wizard's Herb, Herba Sacra, Holy Plant, European Vervain, Enchanter's Plant and Herba the Cross. From the family Verbenaceae.

This herb is a native of Mediterranean regions. It has now become established elsewhere within temperate zones or, for that matter, wherever the Romans marched.

It is a herb of myth, magic and medicine. The Egyptians believed that it originated from the tears of Isis. The Greek priests wore amulets made of it, as did the Romans, who also used it to purify their altars after sacrifice. The Druids used it for purification and for making magic potions.

Superstition tells that when you pick vervain, you should bless the plant. This originates from a legend that it grew on the hill at Calgary, and was used to staunch the flow of Christ's blood at the Crucifixion.

In the Middle Ages it was an ingredient in a holy salve, a powerful protector against demons and disease: 'Vervain and Dill hinders witches from their will.'

Vervain *Verbena officinalis*

SPECIES

Verbena officinalis
Vervain
Hardy perennial. Ht 60–90cm, spread 30cm (12in) or more. Small pale lilac flowers in summer. Leaves green, hairy and often deeply divided into lobes with curved teeth. This plant is not to be muddled with Lemon Verbena, **Aloysia triphylla**.

CULTIVATION

Propagation
Seed
Sow the small seeds in early spring in a prepared seed or plug tray. Cover with perlite. No need for extra heat. When the seedlings are large enough, and after a period of hardening off, plant out in a prepared site, 30cm (12in) apart.

Division
An established plant can be divided either in the spring or autumn. It splits easily with lots of roots.

Pests and Diseases
If the soil is too rich or high in nitrates, it can be attacked by aphids.

Maintenance
Spring Sow seeds. Divide established plants.
Summer Cut back after flowering to stop it self-seeding everywhere.
Autumn Split established plants.
Winter No need for protection; fully hardy.

Garden Cultivation
Vervain can be sown direct into the garden in the spring in a well-drained soil and a sunny position. It is better to sow or plant in clumps because the flower is so small that otherwise it will not show to advantage. But beware its capacity to self-seed.

Harvesting
Pick leaves as required. Cut whole plant when in bloom. Dry leaves or whole plant if required.

CONTAINER GROWING

Vervain does nothing for containers, and containers do nothing for vervain.

MEDICINAL

Vervain has been used traditionally to strengthen the nervous system, dispel depression and counter nervous exhaustion. It is also said to be effective in treating migraines and headaches of the nervous and bilious kind.

Chinese herbalists use a decoction to treat suppressed menstruation, and for liver problems and urinary tract infections.

CULINARY

In certain parts of France, a tea is made from the leaves. Use with caution.

WARNING

Avoid during pregnancy.

Viola tricolor

HEARTSEASE

Also known as Wild Pansy, Field Pansy, Love Lies Bleeding, Love in Idleness, Herb Trinity, Jack Behind the Garden Gate, Kiss Me Behind the Garden Gate, Kiss Me Love, Kiss Me Love at the Garden Gate, Kiss Me Quick, Monkey's Face, Three Faces Under a Hood, Two Faces in a Hood and Trinity Violet. From the family Violaceae.

Heartsease is a wild flower in Europe and North America, growing on wasteland and in fields and hedgerows.

In the Middle Ages, due to the influence of Christianity and because of its tricolour flowers – white, yellow and purple – Heartsease was called Trinitaria or Trinitatis Herba, the herb of the Blessed Trinity.

In the traditional language of flowers, the purple form meant memories, the white loving thoughts, and the yellow, souvenirs.

SPECIES

Viola arvensis
Field Pansy
Hardy perennial. Ht 5–10cm (2–4in). The flowers are predominantly white or creamy, and appear in early summer. The green leaves are oval with shallow, blunt teeth.

Viola tricolor *Heartsease*

Viola lutea
Mountain Pansy
Hardy perennial. Ht 8–20cm (3–8in). Single-coloured flowers in summer vary from yellow to blue and violet. The leaves are green and oval near the base of the stem, narrower further up.

Viola tricolor
Heartsease
Hardy perennial, often grown as an annual. Ht 15–30cm (6–12in). Flowers from spring to autumn. Green and deeply lobed leaves.

CULTIVATION

Propagation
Seed
Sow seeds under protection in the autumn, either into prepared seed, plug trays or pots. Do not cover the seeds. No bottom heat required. Winter the seedlings in a cold frame or cold greenhouse. In the spring harden off and plant out at a distance of 15cm (6in).

Maintenance
Spring Sow seed.
Summer Dead head flowers to maintain flowering throughout the season.
Autumn Sow seed for early spring flowers.
Winter No need to protect.

Garden Cultivation
Heartsease will grow in any soil, in partial shade or sun. Sow the seeds from spring to early autumn where they are to flower. Press into the soil but do not cover.

Harvesting
Pick the flowers fully open – from spring right through until late autumn. Use fresh or for drying.

The plant has the most fascinating seed capsules, each capsule splitting into 3. The best time to collect seeds is midday when the maximum number of capsules will have opened.

CONTAINER GROWING

Heartsease look very jolly in any kind of container. Pick off the dead flowers as this appears to keep the plant flowering for longer.

CULINARY

Add flowers to salads and to decorate sweet dishes.

MEDICINAL

An infusion of the flowers has long been prescribed for a broken heart. Less romantically, it is also a cure for bed-wetting.

An ointment made from it is good for eczema and acne and also for curing milk rust and cradle cap.

Herbalists use it to treat gout, rheumatoid arthritis and respiratory disorders. An infusion of heartsease leaves added to bath water has proved beneficial to suffers of rheumatic disease.

Warning: In large doses, it may cause vomiting.

OTHER USES

Cleansing the skin and shampooing thinning hair.

Viola

VIOLET

From the family Violaceae.

There are records of sweet violets growing during the first century AD in Persia, Syria and Turkey. It is a native not only of these areas but also of North Africa and Europe. Violets have been introduced elsewhere and are now cultivated in several countries for their perfume.

This charming herb has been much loved for over 2,000 years and there are many stories associated with it. In a Greek legend, Zeus fell in love with a beautiful maiden called Io. He turned her into a cow to protect her from his jealous wife Juno. The earth grew violets for Io's food, and the flower was named after her.

The violet was also the flower of Aphrodite, the goddess of love, and of her son, Priapus, the god of gardens. The ultimate mark of the reverence in which the Greeks held sweet violet is that they made it the symbol of Athens.

For centuries perfumes have been made from the flowers of sweet violet mixed with the violet-scented roots of orris, and the last half of the 19th century saw intense interest in it – acres were cultivated to grow it as a market garden plant. Its main use was as a cut flower. No lady of quality would venture out without wearing a bunch of violets. It was also customary in gardens of large country houses to move the best clump of violets to a cold frame in late autumn to provide flowers for the winter.

Common dog violet *Viola riviniana*

SPECIES

Viola odorata
Sweet Violet
Also known as Garden Violet Hardy perennial. Ht 7cm (3in), spread 15cm (6in) or more. Sweet-smelling white or purple flowers from late winter to early spring. The leaves are heart-shaped and form a rosette at the base, from which the long-stalked flowers arise. **Viola odorata** is one of the very few scented violets. It has been hybridized to produce Palma violets, with a single or double flower, in a range of rich colours. Recently there has been a revival in interest in this plant and it is being offered again by specialist nurseries.

Viola reichenbachiana
Wood Violet
Hardy perennial. Ht 2–20cm (1–8in), spread 15cm (6in) or more. Pale lilac/blue flowers in early spring. Leaves are green and heart-shaped. The difference between this plant and the common dog violet is the flowering time; there is also a slight difference in flower colour but it is difficult to discern.

Viola riviniana
Common Dog Violet
Also known as Blue Mice, Hedging Violet, Horse Violet and Pig Violet. Hardy perennial. Ht 2–20cm (1–8in), spread 15cm (6in) or more. Pale blue/lilac flowers in early summer. Leaves are green and heart-shaped. This violet does not grow runners.

CULTIVATION

Propagation
Seed
The small seed should be sown in early autumn in prepared seed or plug trays. Use a soil-based compost; I have found violets prefer this. Water in and cover with a layer of compost, and finally cover with a sheet of glass or polythene. Put the trays either in a corner of the garden or in a cold frame (because the seeds germinate better if they have a period of stratification, though it will still be erratic). In the spring when the seedlings are large enough to handle, prick out into pots. If grown in cells allow a period of hardening off. Plant out as soon as temperatures have risen at a distance of 30cm (12in).

Cuttings

These can be taken from the parent plant, with a small amount of root attached, in early spring and rooted in cell trays, using the bark, peat mix of compost (see p.591). Harden off and plant out into a prepared site in the garden in late spring when they are fully rooted. Water in well.

When using runners to propagate this plant, remove them in late spring and replant in a prepared site in the garden, 30cm (12in) apart. Plant them firmly in the ground, making sure that the base of the crowns are well embedded in the soil; water in well.

Runners can be grown on in pots in early autumn. Remove a well-rooted runner and plant in a pot of a suitable size (see 'Container Growing' for further information). Over-winter in a cool greenhouse, watering from time to time to prevent red spider mite. Bring into the house in the spring to enjoy the flowers. After flowering, plant out in the garden into a prepared site.

Division

Divide well-established plants as soon as flowering is over in early summer. It is a good idea to plant 3 crowns together for a better show and as an insurance policy against damage when splitting a crown. Replant in the garden in exactly the same way as for runners.

Pests and Diseases

The major pest for container-grown violets in mild weather is red spider mite. A good way to keep this at bay is to spray the leaves with water. If it is persistent, use a liquid horticultural soap (again, as per manufacturer's instructions).

In propagating violets, the disease you will most probably come across is black root rot, which is caused by insufficient drainage in the compost.

Young plants can also be affected by damping off root rot, which is caused usually by too much water and insufficient drainage.

Maintenance

Spring Take cuttings from established plants. Remove runners, pot or replant in the garden.
Summer Divide well-established plants, and replant.
Autumn Sow seed. Pot up root runners for wintering under cover.
Winter Feed the garden with well-rotted manure.

Garden Cultivation

Violets thrive best in a moderately heavy, rich soil in a semi-shaded spot. If you have a light and/or gravelly soil, it is a good idea to add some texture – a mulch of well-rotted manure – the previous autumn. In spring dig the manure in.

Plant out in the garden as soon as the frosts have finished, allowing 30cm (12in) space between plants. When they become established, they quickly create a carpet of lovely sweet-smelling flowers. There is no need to protect any of the above-mentioned violets, they are fully hardy.

Harvesting

Pick the leaves in early spring for fresh use or for drying.

Gather the flowers just when they are opening, for drying or crystallizing.

Dig up the roots in autumn to dry for medicinal use.

CONTAINER GROWING

Violets make good container plants. Use the bark, peat, grit mix of compost. Give them a liquid feed of fertilizer (following the manufacturer's instructions) after flowering. During the summer months, place the container in partial shade. In winter they do not like heat, and if it is too warm they will become weak and fail to flower. So, it is most important that they are in a cool place with temperatures no higher than 7°C (45°F). There must also be good air circulation, and watering should be maintained on a regular basis.

CULINARY

The flowers of sweet violet are well known in crystallized form for decorating cakes, puddings, ice-cream and home-made sweets. They are also lovely in salads, and make an interesting oil – use an almond oil as base.

The flowers of common and dog violet can also be added to salads and used to decorate puddings. Their flavour is very mild in comparison to sweet violet, but they are just as attractive.

Sweet violet *Viola odorata*

MEDICINAL

Only sweet violet has been used medicinally. Various parts are still used, most commonly, the rootstock. It is an excellent, soothing expectorant and is used to treat a range of respiratory disorders, such as bronchitis, coughs, whooping cough and head colds. It also has a cooling nature and is used to treat hangovers.

Made into a poultice, the leaves soothe sore, cracked nipples. Also they have a reputation for treating tumours, both benign and cancerous. Strong doses of the rhizome are emetic and purgative.

The flowers have a reputation for being slightly sedative and so helpful in cases of anxiety and insomnia.

OTHER USES

The flowers of sweet violets are used in potpourris, floral waters and perfumes.

Zingiber officinale

GINGER

**Also known as Stem Ginger, Canton Ginger.
From the family Zingiberaceae.**

Freshly dug hand of ginger, Gaylephug, Bhutan

Ginger has been grown in tropical Asia for at least 3,000 years and was one of the first spices brought to Europe along the Silk Road from China. Arab merchants controlled the trade in ginger and other spices for centuries until explorers like Marco Polo reached the Indian Ocean. The Portuguese took ginger to their colonies and the Spaniards introduced it to the New World; in 1547 they exported over 1,000 tons of rhizomes to Jamaica and Mexico, and by the end of the century had a thriving trade with Europe. Fresh ginger is cultivated throughout the tropics and is freely available.

The creeping, branched rhizomes growing near the surface, with pale yellow flesh beneath a thin, buff-coloured to dark brown skin, look like knobbly fingers and are often referred to as 'hands'. The stems can grow up to 120cm (4ft) tall, with narrow, lance-shaped leaves; the short-lived flowers are yellow-green and purple, marked with spots and stripes.

VARIETIES

Each centre of cultivation has its own forms. Several clones are found in India and three in Malaya. Two found in Jamaica are the high-quality white or yellow form and 'flint ginger', with tougher, fibrous rhizomes.

CULTIVATION

Propagation
Propagate in late spring just before growth begins, using sections of rhizomes. Lift parent plants carefully to avoid rhizome damage, shake off the soil and break off sections about 5cm (2in) long with at least one good bud. Dispose of older sections, keeping the young growth and trim the ends with a sharp knife. Plant, buds uppermost, 5–10cm (2–4in) deep with 15cm (9in) between rows. Water thoroughly with tepid water after planting.

Maintenance
Spring Plant rhizomes under cover.
Summer Water, feed and keep weed-free. Maintain high temperatures and humidity.
Autumn Lift rhizomes carefully.

Garden Cultivation
Ginger needs an annual rainfall of at least 150cm (45in), high temperatures and a short dry season for part of the year.

The soil should be rich, moisture-retentive and free-draining; add well-rotted organic matter where necessary. It is essential that the ground is not compacted and all debris is removed, otherwise the rhizomes become deformed.

Water plants thoroughly during dry periods and keep them weed-free throughout the growing season. In the humid tropics, ginger can be planted at any time.

If rhizomes remain unused, they will sprout and rapidly develop

Protected Cropping

Ginger can be grown under cover, but as it needs high temperatures and humidity, this is not normally practical, and for optimum productivity it is better planted outdoors.

As a 'novelty crop' under glass, plant the rhizome just below the surface in peat-substitute-based compost in a 20cm (8in) pot. Keep it constantly moist, and feed with a liquid general fertilizer every 3 weeks during the growing season.

Harvesting and Storing

Younger tender rhizomes are harvested for immediate use and for preserving; they become more fibrous and pungent with age.

Harvesting can begin from 7 months after planting. Rhizomes for drying should be lifted about 9–10 months after planting.

Fresh 'root' can be stored in the refrigerator for several weeks wrapped in paper towels, foil or any container which allows it to 'breathe'. It can also be wrapped and frozen.

PESTS AND DISEASES

Soft rot can appear as dark patches at the base of the shoots. To prevent, handle rhizomes with care and avoid waterlogging.

Cultivated ginger flourishing near Transvaal, South Africa

CULINARY

Ginger is used throughout the world as a flavouring for sweet and savoury dishes; it plays a starring role in foods like gingerbread, but is also an integral part of many spice mixes, appearing in biscuits, cakes, soups, pickles, marinades, curry powder, stewed fruit, puddings, tea, beer, ale and wine.

It is the most important spice in Chinese cookery. In Japanese cookery it is used as a side dish called 'gari' to accompany sushi. Besides being used fresh, dried and in powdered form, ginger is pickled, preserved in syrup, candied and crystallized.

Rhizomes should be lightly scraped or peeled to remove the tough skin before use.

MEDICINAL

Ginger has been used for centuries in Chinese medicine. In the Orient fresh ginger is a remedy for vomiting, coughing, abdominal distension and fever. Many Africans drink ginger root as an aphrodisiac, while in New Guinea it is eaten dried as a contraceptive and in the Philippines it is chewed to expel evil spirits.

In the Middle Ages it was believed to possess miraculous properties against cholera. Culpeper in his *Herball* of 1653 says: 'It is profitable for old men; it heats the joints and is useful against gout; it expels wind.' It can be rubbed on the face as a 'rouge', stimulating circulation. Ginger is said to cleanse the body and lower cholesterol; it can be chewed to alleviate sore throats, is a digestive, relieves dyspepsia, colic and diarrhoea and prevents travel sickness.

Ginger tea

FRUIT

In this section, fruit is defined as plant flesh that we are induced by the plant to eat, in order to distribute its seeds. Included is the closely allied group of nuts, which are in fact the seeds themselves. Presumably the plants are satisfied if a small percentage of the nut seeds are distributed to grow elsewhere.

The fruits covered in the three chapters Orchard Fruits, Soft, Bush and Cane Fruits and Tender Fruits are determined by the manner in which we most usually grow them in temperate gardens. Those that require some protection or cover, such as the annual, perennial and tender fruits, are mostly fruits that are not hardy enough outdoors for the UK and northern European gardener, but are achievable in southern Europe, Australia and much of the USA. Of course we commonly grow many of these, such as melons, grapes and even lemons, quite easily with the aid of a greenhouse, in cooler regions. I've also included many exotic tropical and sub-tropical fruits on sale in supermarkets and abroad which may be grown (or eaten!) out of curiosity and interest. Most of these were once grown and fruited in Victorian stovehouses, and can often be fruited at home with a modest heated glasshouse or conservatory. Failing that, most of these make spectacular, educational and decorative houseplants. (Please bear in mind, however, the potential final height and size of your humble date palm seedling before you start dreaming of ever ripening a crop!)

The chapter on Shrub and Flower Garden Fruits includes those forgotten and unsung heroes that are only called upon in times of shortage and famine, and by those country folk who appreciate the sharp, strong flavours these piquant fruits offer. The potential of these fruits has often been overlooked; many of them are worthy of deliberate cultivation, and with only a little breeding and selection they could become sweet and tender attractions for our delectation. The strawberry today is gigantic and succulent compared to those of two centuries ago; we can only imagine what new fruits we may conjure from nature's raw materials in the future.

ORCHARD FRUITS

When fruits are mentioned, these are probably the first that come to mind: apples, pears, plums and cherries – the tree-hard or top fruits as they are known. They consist of two main groups: the pome fruits, which are the apple- and pear-like members, and the stone fruits, which are the plums, cherries, peaches and apricots. The pomes have small seeds in a core around which the 'stalk' from immediately behind swells, enclosing them with flesh. The stone fruits have a single seed in a hard shell around which the flesh forms. Both of these groups are related as they are both members of the Rosaceae family. Mulberries and figs come from different families. Nonetheless all are similar in hardiness, size and manner of cultivation to orchard trees.

Most of these fruits have been cultivated since ancient times. They were nearly all known to the Romans, who spread them throughout their empire. However, much knowledge of their cultivation was then lost during the Dark Ages. The monasteries, and a few noblemen, maintained fruit gardens and orchards, but the common people reverted to farming and cropping from the wild with little interest in fruit cultivation.

Indeed fruits were often seen as poor fare compared to meat, and more suited for animal feed. If it was not for the ease with which many of these fruits could be fermented to make intoxicating beverages, they would probably have been even more neglected. After the Norman Conquest of England the new lords proved to be more interested in fruit than the Saxons they had defeated, bringing many of their own improved varieties with them from France. Orchards became more widely planted, and the wealthy vied with each other in collecting the greatest number and variety and in having the earliest and longest-lasting fruits.

In the sixteenth century, Henry VIII brought many new fruit varieties from the Netherlands and France, and the streets of London became full of home-grown and imported favourites. The impetus of completely different and new fruits from the New World caused more interest in horticulture, reviving interest in the old fruits as well as the new discoveries. As old trusted varieties were exported to the colonies, new species and varieties were imported. These produced new varieties, which followed the old abroad at the same time as descendants of the first wave were already returning.

By the Victorian era the number of varieties in cultivation had escalated from a few hundreds to many tens of thousands, if you counted local varieties worldwide. The great cities were served by the immense orchards and market gardens that surrounded them. Every gentleman aspired to a house with grounds that would include an orchard at least, if not a grouse moor.

In the 20th century, after the two World Wars, the labour to maintain great gardens and orchards was not available and the land was needed for more basic crops. Orchards were grubbed up for cereals and more exciting fruits became available from abroad. The British orchard all but disappeared from many counties. Houses with grounds and orchards were demolished to make way for executive hutches at ten to the acre.

However, the green movement combined with people's increasing awareness of the utility of trees, the value of fruit, and the ecological advantages of permanent culture as opposed to annual crops, have all caused a reawakening of interest in orchard fruits. More are now being planted than for nearly a century.

Malus domestica from the family *Rosaceae*

CULINARY AND DESSERT APPLES

Tree up to 10m (33ft). Life span: medium to long. Deciduous, hardy, sometimes self-fertile.
Fruits: up to 15cm (6in), spherical, green to yellow or red. Vitamin value: vitamin C.

Malus domestica apples are complex selections and hybrids of *M. pumila* with *M. sylvestris* and *M. mitis.* Thus the shape of the fruit varies from the spheres of **'Gladstone'** and **'Granny Smith'** to the flattened buns of **'Bramley'** and **'Mère de Ménage',** or the almost conical **'Spartan'**, **'Golden Delicious'** and **'Worcester**

Granny Smith

Pearmain'. The colour can be green, yellow, scarlet orange or dark red to almost purple. The texture can vary from crisp to pappy and they may be juicy or dry, acid or insipid, bitter, bland or aromatic. All apples have a dent in the stalk end, the remains of the flower at the other and a central tough core with several brown seeds. These are edible in small amounts though there is a recorded death from eating a quantity as they contain small amounts of cyanide.

The trees will often become picturesque landscape features, particularly when seen in an orchard. They frequently become twisted or distorted when left to themselves. They have soft downy or smooth leaves, never as glossy as pear leaves. The flowers are often pink- or red-tinged as well as snow white.

Apples are native to temperate Europe and Asia. They have been harvested from the wild since prehistory and were well known to the ancient Phoenicians. When Varro led his army as far as the Rhine in the first century BC, every region had its apples. The Romans encouraged their cultivation, so although Cato had only noted a half dozen varieties in the second century BC, Pliny knew of three dozen by the first century AD. The Dark Ages caused a decline in apple growing in Britain and only one pomerium (orchard), at Nottingham, is mentioned in the Domesday book. However, interest increased after the Norman invasion. Costard and Pearmain varieties are first noted in the twelfth and thirteenth centuries, and by the year 1640 there are nearly five dozen varieties recorded by Parkinson. By 1669, Worlidge has the number up to 92, mostly cider apples. *Downing's Fruits*, printed in 1866, has 643 varieties listed. Now we have over 5,000 named apple varieties, representing about 2,000 actually distinguishable clones. Several hundred are easily obtainable from specialist nurserymen, though only a half dozen are grown on a commercial scale.

This sudden explosion in numbers was most probably due to the expansion of the colonies. The best varieties of apple trees from Europe mutated and crossed as they were propagated across North America, and then later Australia, and these then returned to be crossed again.

Orleans Reinette

Apples are now grown extensively in every temperate region around the world. The first apples in North America supposedly were planted on the Governor's Island in Boston Harbour, but the Massachusetts Company had requested seeds in 1629, and in 1635 a Mr Wolcott of Connecticut wrote he had made 500 hogsheads of cider from his new apple orchard.

Golden Delicious

'Spartan'

VARIETIES

The oldest variety known and easily available is **'Court Pendu Plat'** (midwinter, dessert) which may go back to Roman times and is recorded from the sixteenth century. It is still grown because it flowers late, missing frosts. **'Nonpareil'** and **'Golden Pippin'** also come from the sixteenth century and keep till midspring. However, they are rarely available, though there are a dozen and a half part-descendants all called **'Golden Pippin'**. **'Golden Reinette'** (midwinter, dessert) is still popular in Europe and dates from before 1650. The large green **'Flower of Kent'** (1660) has nearly disappeared. This was the apple that prompted Sir Isaac Newton in his discoveries of the laws of motion and gravity. **'Ribston Pippin'** (midwinter, dessert) has one of the highest vitamin C contents and superb flavour. It was bred in 1707 and is not happy on wet heavy soils. From 1720 comes **'Ashmead's Kernel'**, one of the best-tasting, late-keeping dessert apples, but it is a light cropper. **'Orleans Reinette'** (midwinter, dessert) is known from 1776. It is juicy, very tasty

with a rough skin and is not very good on wet cold sites. 1785 saw the birth of the rare but choice **'Pitmaston Pine Apple'** (midwinter, dessert). This has small fruits with a rich, honey-like flavour. **'Wagener'** is a mid- to late winter, hard-fleshed keeper, which was raised in New York State in 1791.

'Bramley's Seedling' (midwinter, culinary) raised in 1809, has one of the highest vitamin C contents of cooking varieties. It grows large, so have it on a more dwarfing stock than others. The **'Cornish Gillyflower'** is a very tasty, late-keeping dessert raised in 1813.

'Cox's Orange Pippin'

Unlike many other apples, it will flourish in a mild wet climate. It is unsuited to training or cordon culture. One of the best dual-purpose apples is **'Blenheim Orange'** (midwinter), a wide, flat, golden russeted fruit and a large tree. Raised in 1850, **'Cox's Orange**

Pippin' (late autumn) is reckoned the best dessert apple. However, it is not easy to grow as it is disease-prone, hates wet clays and does best on a warm wall. **'Sunset'**, raised in 1918, and **'Suntan'**, in 1955, are more reliable offspring. **'Beauty of Bath'** is one of the best-known earlies, fruiting in late summer with small, sharp, sweet and juicy, yellow fruits stained scarlet and orange. It was introduced in 1864. It is a tip bearer and not suitable for training.

'Egremont Russet' (late autumn), bred in 1872, is one of the best russets, a group of apples with scentless, roughened skin and crisp, firm flesh, which is sweet and tasty but never over-juicy or acid. Just a century old is **'James Grieve'** (mid-autumn, dessert). It is prone to canker, but makes a good pollinator for **'Cox'** and is a good cropper of refreshingly acid, perfumed fruits. The ubiquitous **'Golden Delicious'**, so much grown commercially in Europe, is a conical yellow. It actually tastes pretty good when grown at home, but

must be waxed for keeping as otherwise it wilts. It was found in West Virginia in 1916. **'George Cave'** is a modern (in horticultural terms), early dessert variety from 1945. It crops in late summer. Better flavoured than **'Beauty of Bath'**, it can be pruned normally, though it is inclined to tip bearing. **'Discovery'** was introduced in 1962. It is an early scarlet fruit with creamy white flesh that comes in late summer to early autumn. The flowers are fairly frost tolerant and it is scab resistant. It is rapidly dominating the early apple market because it will keep better longer than most other early varieties.

It is interesting to note some varieties have much more vitamin C than others that grow in the same conditions. **'Ribston Pippin'** typically has 31mg/100g, **'Orlean's Reinette'** 22.4mg, **'Bramley's Seedling'** 16mg, **'Cox's Orange Pippin'** 10.5mg, **'Golden Delicious'** 8mg and **'Rome Beauty'** 3.6mg. Maybe the famous saying should go 'A Ribston Pippin a day keeps the doctor away'.

'Egremont Russet'

CULTIVATION

Apples are much abused trees. They prefer a rich, moist, well-drained loam, but are planted almost anywhere and yet often still do fairly well. What they will not stand is being water-logged, or growing on the site of an old apple tree or near to others that have been long established, and they do not thrive in dank frost pockets. Pollination is best served by planting more than three varieties, as many apples are mutually incompatible, having diploid or triploid varieties with irreconcilable differences in their chromosomes. A 'Cox' and a 'Bramley' will not fruit on their own, but if you add a 'James Grieve' all three bear fruit. Crab apples usually prove good pollinators for unnamed trees.

Growing under Glass

Apples do not like being under glass all the time as they need a winter chill, and they are more susceptible to pests and diseases, especially if hot and dry, but the usual remedies apply. Some French varieties, such as the classic 'Calville Blanche d'Hiver', can only be grown to perfection under cover in Britain.

Growing in Containers

On very dwarfing stocks apples are easily grown in large pots. They need hard pruning in winter and in summer the lengthening shoots should be nipped out, thus tip bearing varieties are not really suitable. Special varieties have been developed for containers, which supposedly require little pruning.

Ornamental and Wildlife Value

The pink and white blossom is wonderful in late spring. The flowers are valuable to insects and the fruits are important to birds.

Maintenance

Spring Weed, mulch, spray seaweed solution monthly. *Summer* Thin fruits, summer prune, spray with seaweed solution, apply greasebands. *Autumn* Use poor fruits first, pick best for storage. *Winter* Hard prune, add copious compost, remove mummified fruits.

Propagation

Apple pips rarely make fruiting trees of value; however many of our best varieties were chance seedlings. Apples are grafted or budded on to different rootstocks depending on site

and size of tree required. Few grow them from cuttings on their own roots or as standards on seedling stocks as these make very large trees only suitable for planting in grazed meadows. Half-standards are more convenient for the home orchard and these get big enough on M25 stock at about 5.2m (17ft) high and 6m (21ft) apart. At the other extreme, the most dwarfing stock is M27, useful for pot culture but these midgets need staking all their lives and the branches start so low you cannot mow or grow underneath them. M9 produces a 2m (7ft) tree, still needing staking but good for cordons. On such very dwarfing stocks the trees do badly in poor soil and during droughts. M26 is bigger, growing to 2.8m (9ft) and still needs a stake but is probably the best for small gardens. It needs 3m (10ft) on each side. MM106 is better on poor soils, and on good soils is still compact at about 4m (13ft), needing 4.5m (15ft) between trees.

Pruning and Training

Apple trees are often left to grow and produce for years with no pruning other than remedial work once the head has formed. They may be trained and hard pruned summer and winter, back to spur systems, on almost any shaped framework, though rarely as fans. For beauty and productivity apples are best as espaliers; to achieve the maximum number of varieties as cordons; for ease and quality as open goblet-pruned small trees. Some varieties, especially many of the earliest fruiters, are tip bearers. These are best only pruned remedially as hard pruning will remove the fruiting wood. They can be grown on a replacement system as for peaches (see p.419) but it is hard work. As important as the pruning

This distinctive Ballerina 'Waltz apple tree dominates its contain

'Golden Delicious'

Trained apples underplanted with herbs

is the thinning. Removing crowded and congested, damaged and diseased apples improves the size and quality of those remaining and prevents biennial bearing. Thin after the June drop occurs and again twice after, disposing of the rejects to destroy any pests.

Weed, Pest and Disease Control

Apples are the most commonly grown fruit tree in much of the temperate zone. They have thus built up a whole ecosystem of pests and diseases around themselves. Although they have many problems they still manage to produce enormous quantities of fruit for many years, in often quite poor conditions. Vigorous growth is essential as this reduces many problems, especially canker. The commonplace pests require the usual remedies (see pp.602–7), but apples suffer from some annoying specialities. Holes in the fruits are usually caused by one of two pests. Codling moth generally makes holes in the core of the fruit, pushing frass out at the flower end. They are controlled by corrugated cardboard band traps, pheromone traps, permitted sprays as the blossom sets, and hygiene. The other hole-maker is apple sawfly, which bores narrow tunnels, emerging anywhere. They may then eat into another or even a third. They are best controlled by hygiene,

removing and destroying affected apples during thinning. Permitted sprays may be used after flower set, and running poultry underneath an orchard is effective. Many varieties are scab-resistant. If it occurs, it affects first the leaves then the fruits and, like brown rot and canker, is spread by mummified apples and dead wood. It is worst in wet areas. All of these problems, and mildews, are best controlled by hygiene, keeping the trees vigorous, well watered and mulched, and open pruned. Woolly aphis can be sprayed or dabbed with soft soap or derris. Sticky non-setting tree bands control many pests all year round, especially in late summer and autumn. Apples also get damaged by birds, wasps and occasionally earwigs, so for perfect fruits, protect them with paper bags.

'Winston' apples forming a decorative arch

A handy apple store

Harvesting and Storing

Early apples are best eaten off the tree. They rarely keep for long, going pappy in days. Most mid-season apples are also best eaten off the tree as they ripen, but many will keep for weeks if picked just under-ripe and stored in the cool. Late keepers must hang on the trees till hard frosts are imminent, or bird damage is getting too severe, then if they are delicately picked and kept cool in the dark they may keep for six months or longer. Thus apples can be had most months of the year, providing early- and late-keeping varieties and a rodent-proof store are available. They are best picked with a cupped hand and gently laid in a tray, traditionally padded with dry straw. (This may taint if damped so better use shredded newspaper.) Do not store early varieties with lates nor either near pears, onions, garlic or potatoes. The fruits must be free of bruises, rot and holes and the stalk must remain attached for them to store well. If apples are individually wrapped in paper they keep longer. Apples can be puréed and frozen, or juiced and frozen, or dried in thin rings, or made into cider.

COMPANION PLANTING

Apples are bad for potatoes, making them blight-prone. They are benefited by alliums, especially chives, and penstemons and nasturtiums nearby are thought to prevent sawfly and woolly aphis. Stinging nettles close by benefit the trees and, dried, they help stored fruits keep.

OTHER USES

Apple wood is used for mallet heads, golf clubs and in engraving. It is delicately scented when burnt, and is useful for smoking foods and as fire logs.

'Egremont Russet' apple blossom

CULINARY USES

Apples are excellent raw, stewed and made into tarts, pies and jellies, especially with other fruits which they help set. The juice is delicious fresh and can be frozen for out-of-season use, and made into cider or vinegar. Cooking apples are different from desserts, much larger, more acid and less sweet raw. Most break down to a frothy purée when heated and few retain their texture, unlike most of the desserts. 'Bramley's', 'Norfolk Beauty' and 'Revd Wilke's' are typical, turning to sweet froths when cooked. 'Lane's Prince Albert', 'Lord Derby' and 'Encore' stay firm and are the sorts to use for pies rather than sauces.

Flying Saucers
per person

1 large cooking apple
Approx. 3 dessertspoons mincemeat
Knob of butter
7g (¹/₄oz) sesame seeds
Cream or custard to serve

Wash, dry and cut each apple in half horizontally. Remove the tough part of the core but leave the outside intact. Stuff the hollow with mincemeat, then pin the two halves back together with wooden cocktail sticks. Rub the outside with butter and roll in sesame seeds, then bake in a preheated oven at 190°C/375°F/gas mark 5 for half an hour or until they 'lift off' nicely. Serve the saucers immediately with cream or custard.

Malus pumila from the family *Rosaceae*

CRAB AND CIDER APPLES

Trees up to 10m (33ft). Life span: long. Deciduous, often self-fertile.
Fruits: 1–7cm (½–3in), spherical, yellow, green or red. Value: make tonic alcoholic beverages.

Crab apples grow wild in hedgerows and have smaller, more brightly coloured fruits than cultivated varieties. The fruits vary from being unpalatable to completely inedible raw though they make delicious jellies. Cider apples are more like eating and cooking apples, with fruits in-between in size but similarly bitter and astringent. Selected crab apples are grown ornamentally and are useful pollinators for other apples, so they may be found on semi-dwarfing stocks as small trees. Cider apples were always grown on strong or seedling stock, gaining immense vigour which they needed to tower above animals grazing underneath.

Crabs have been used since prehistory and doubtless cider has been made for as long. It was probably brought to Cornwall initially by Phoenician tin traders.

Immature crab apples

Old varieties of cider apples from Sarah Bowen's orchard

VARIETIES

Many crabs are well-known ornamentals, such as **'John Downie'**, which has long golden orange fruits, and **'Golden Hornet'**, with bright yellow. Most are mixed hybrids of *Malus pumila* with the native *M. sylvestris*, which has sour, hard, green fruits and is sometimes thorny, and *M. mitis*, from the Mediterranean region, which has softer leaves and sweeter, more coloured fruits. *M. baccata*, the **Siberian crab**, and *M. manchurica*, from China, are widely planted for their bright red fruits. Cider apples are more improved and closer to *M. domestica* hybrids. Every local variety is rated the best. In trials, **'Yarlington Mill'** was thought outstanding. **'Sweet Coppin'**, **'Kingston Black'**, **'Tremlett's Bitter'** and **'Crimson King'** are also excellent.

CULTIVATION

Tougher than the finer apples, these may be grown almost anywhere not waterlogged or parched.

Growing under Glass
Neither crab nor cider apples are happy permanently under glass and do better in the open. They need a winter chill otherwise they crop badly. They are hardy enough for most places.

Growing in Containers
Crab apples can be fruited in pots; indeed they often do even in the small pots in which garden centres sell them. Cider apples are shy and less likely to produce heavy crops.

Ornamental and Wildlife Value
The crabs are very attractive in flower and many also in fruit. Cider apples are bigger and less pretty. Both are valuable to insects when in flower and to birds, rodents and insects with their fruit.

Maintenance
Spring Weed, mulch and spray seaweed solution.
Summer As spring.
Autumn Pick fruit.
Winter Prune, and spread the compost.

'Dabinet'

Propagation

Although some crabs can be grown from seed they are not reliable. Named varieties are grafted on to rootstocks suitable for the size and site intended. Neither crab nor cider apple varieties are usually available on the most dwarfing rootstocks, but on more vigorous stock they make large trees.

Pruning and Training

Crab apples are usually worked as half-standards on semi-dwarfing stock and are only pruned remedially in winter. Cider apples are worked as standards on strong growing stocks and make big trees. Likewise, cider apples should only be pruned remedially after forming a head.

Weed, Pest and Disease Control

Although these can suffer from the same problems as dessert and culinary apples, the crops are rarely badly affected. Crab apples are usually remarkably productive whatever care they get. For cider apples many problems such as scab are also mostly irrelevant.

Harvesting and Storing

Crabs can be picked under-ripe for jellying, but you can hang on, as the birds do not go for them as fast as softer fruits. Cider apples are left as long as possible to get maximum sugar and to soften. If they are shaken down they bruise, so the apples are then best pressed immediately, not stored in heaps to soften further before pressing.

COMPANION PLANTING

The plants that benefit dessert and culinary apples (see p.398) also associate well with these varieties. Both crab and cider apples are often grown in hedgerows and grazed meadow orchards. They seem content with grass underneath and old trees often have mistletoe growing in their boughs, to no obvious detriment.

'Michellin'

OTHER USES

Pressed apple pulp can be dried and stored till late winter for wild bird and livestock food.

Apple cider

CULINARY USES

Crab apples make delicious tart jellies by themselves, or mixed with other fruits which have less pectin and so do not set so easily. Cider apples are used solely to make cider. They are cleaned, crushed and pressed and the juice is fermented, often with the addition of wine yeast and sugar. After fermentation, cider may be flat, cloudy, sweet, or sparkling, green or yellow, depending on local taste. Ciders are made from several varieties of apple, to give a blend of acidity, sweetness and tannin. (Palatable cider can be made from a mixture of dessert and cooking apples.) Some cider is made into vinegar, deliberately.

Crab Apple Jelly
Makes approx 3.5kg (7lb)

2kg (4lb) crab apples
Approx.1.5kg (3lb) sugar

Chop the apples, then simmer them in water to cover until soft. Sieve or strain through a jelly bag and weigh the juice. Add three-quarters of its weight in sugar. Return to the heat and bring to boil, stirring to dissolve the sugar. Boil until setting point is reached, then skim and pour into warm, sterilized jars. Cover while still hot.

Pyrus communis from the family *Rosaceae*

CULINARY AND DESSERT PEARS

Tree up to 20m (65ft). Life span: very long. Deciduous, hardy, rarely self-fertile.
Fruits: up to 8x18cm (3x7in). Value: potassium and riboflavin.

'Conference'

Pears very closely resemble, and are related to, apples, but there are no known natural hybrids between them. Pears have a fruit that elongates at the stalk end, which stands proud, whereas an apple's stalk is inset in a dent in the top of the fruit. Some pears such as **'Conference'** and **'Bartlett'** will set fruit parthenocarpically (i.e. they fruit freely without pollination). However, these fruits are usually not as good as fertilized ones, being misshapen and of course lacking seeds. Pear trees resemble apples but have shiny leaves, more upright growth and the fat stems usually have a glossier brown hue and more angled buds than apple. Pears on their own roots make very big trees, too big to prune, spray or pick, and the fruit is damaged when it drops. Pears are thus usually worked on quince roots, which makes them smaller, more compact trees.

'Doyenne du Comice'

Pears are native to Europe and Asia. The first cultivated varieties were selected from the wild in prehistory. The ancient Phoenicians, Jews and pre-Christian Romans grew several improved sorts; by the time of Cato there were at least a half dozen distinct fruits, Pliny records 41 and Palladius 56. A list of fruits for the Grand Duke Cosmo III, in late medieval Italy, raises the number to 209, and another manuscript lists 232. In Britain in 1640 only five dozen were known. This rose to more than 700 by 1842. In 1866 the American author T.W. Field catalogued 850 varieties. The rapid increase in numbers and quality, from poor culinary pears to fine desserts, was mainly the work of a few dedicated breeders in France and Belgium at the end of the eighteenth century, who selected and bred most modern varieties.

'Durondeau'

VARIETIES

As pears are used more for eating raw than in cooking, and dessert pears can be cooked, but not vice versa, it is not worthwhile growing purely culinary pears. **'Doyenne du Comice'** (late season) is by far the best dessert pear. None other approaches it for sweet, aromatic succulence, and the fruits can reach a magnificent weight. These are very choice and deserve to be espaliered on the best warm wall. **'Bartlett'**/ **'Williams' Bon Chretien'** (early/mid-season) is widely grown for canning, but is an excellent table fruit – if a bit prone to scab. It is also parthenocarpic as is **'Conference'** (early/mid-season). This latter is a reliable cropper on its own and is scab-resistant. Raised in1770 in Berkshire, it is now very widely grown. **'Jargonelle'** is an old variety first recorded in 1600. It crops for me in early August in East Anglia, about the same time as **'Souvenir de Congress'**. These are the earliest with good flavour. **'Improved Fertility'** (mid) is very hardy and crops heavily and regularly. Other superb pears are **'Clapp's Favourite'** **'Dr Jules Guyot'** (both early/mid season); **'Glou Morceau'** and **'Durondeau'**

(both late) keep into the New Year. There are hundreds of other pear varieties, many of which are cooking not dessert, and several species which have more ornamental than edible value. The **Birch-leaved Pear**, *P. betulifolia*, comes from fourteenth-century China. Almost all parts were eaten, flowers and leaves as well as the small fruits. The **Nashi** is the most apple-like pear, brown green, russeted and crunchy, juicy, but a bit insipid, easy to grow, partly self-fertile and productive. Similar is the **Chinese Sand or Duck Pear**, *P. sinensis*. In Syria the **Three-lobed-leaved Pear**, *P. trilobata*, is popular. This may be the same as the native Turkish *Malus trilobata*.

'Beurre Hardy'

'Cattilac'

CULTIVATION

Dessert pears need a rich, well-drained, moist soil, preferably light and loamy. They can be cropped in the open in southern England, but need a wall further north. The blossom and fruitlets need protection from frosts as they flower early in spring. Pollination is best ensured by planting a mixture of varieties. Do not plant deep as pears are prone to scion rooting, which allows them to make big, less fruitful trees.

Growing under Glass
Pears appreciate a warm wall, but are not easy under glass as they do not like to get too hot and humid; they are thus difficult to grow in the tropics. Ideally plant in containers, keep indoors for flowering and fruiting, and put outdoors for summer and most of winter as they need some chill. They are hardy and can stand light frost, but the roots are most susceptible in pots.

Growing in Containers

Pears have often been fruited in tubs. They are amenable to hard pruning, and so respond better than most other fruits to this and to the cramped conditions of a pot.

Ornamental and Wildlife Value

Why plant an ornamental flowering tree when you can plant a pear? They are just smothered with blossom and buzzing with bees in early spring. The fruits are splendid, but soon eaten in autumn by insects and birds.

Maintenance

Spring Weed, mulch, spray with seaweed solution monthly, protect flowers against frosts.
Summer Thin fruits.
Autumn Pick fruit.
Winter Prune hard or not at all, compost heavily.

Propagation

Pears do not come true from seed, reverting to their unproductive forms. They may root from cuttings and can occasionally be layered, but get too big on their own roots. Normally they are grafted on to quince rootstocks, which are generally best. For heavy, damp soils and for big trees, pear seedling stock was always used, but there is little demand for this nowadays. Pears have been grafted on to apple stocks and even onto hawthorn. As some varieties do not bond readily with quince stock they are 'double-worked', or grafted onto a mutually compatible inter-graft on the quince. This takes more work and an extra year in the nursery.

A pear espalier

Pruning and Training

Grown as trees or bushes, pears can be left to themselves except for remedial pruning. They tend to throw twin leaders which need rationalizing. Alternatively they respond better than most fruits to hard winter pruning and are almost as amenable to summer pruning, thus they can be trained to an endless variety of forms. As they benefit from the shelter of a wall, they are commonly espaliered, and are more rewarding for less work than a peach in the same position. There are many specialized training forms for pears in addition to the cordon, espalier and fan, and equally intricate and specialized pruning methods. These include Pitchforks and Toasting Forks, with two or three vertical stems on short arms, the Palmette Verriers, with long horizontals that turn vertical at the ends, and the multi-curved L'Arcure. Pears will take almost any shape you choose, and you will not go far wrong if you then shear almost all long growths off by three-quarters in summer and then again by a bit more in winter. Take care not to let them root from or above the graft, which destroys the benefit of the rootstock!

Weed, Pest and Disease Control

Pears suffer fewer problems than apples. Providing the flowers miss the frosts and have a warm summer they usually produce a good crop of fruits despite any attacks. However, ripening is poor in

'Josephine Malines'

very cool or hot weather and results in hard or mealy fruits. Leaving the fruit too long on the tree or in storage causes them to rot from the inside out. Pear midge causes the fruitlets to blacken and drop off; inspection reveals maggots within. These are remedied by the hygienic removal and disposal of affected fruits; running poultry underneath in orchards is as effective. Fireblight causes damage resembling scorching. It usually starts from the blossoms. Prune and burn damaged parts immediately, cutting back to clean wood. Scab is a problem in stagnant sites. It affects the fruits before the leaves, which is the opposite from apples. Sprays are usually unnecessary with the more resistant varieties such as 'Conference'. Good open pruning and healthy growth, not overfed with nitrogen, reduce attacks. Always remove all mummified fruits and dead wood immediately. Leaf blistering is usually caused by minute mites. These used to be controlled with lime and sulphur sprays before bud burst. Modern soft soap sprays have also proved to be effective.

Harvesting and Storing
Early pears are best picked almost, but never fully, ripe. They should come off when lifted to the horizontal. Left on the tree they go woolly. Watch them carefully while they finish ripening. They will slowly ripen if kept cool, faster if warm. Late pears should be left until bird damage is too great, and picked with a stalk. Kept in a cool, dark place, late varieties last for months, ripening up rapidly if brought into the warm. Do not wrap them with paper as one does with apples, and take care not to store the two fruits near each other as they will cross-taint.

CULINARY USES

Pears are exquisite as dessert fruits and may be used in much the same way as apples, sliced and used in tarts, baked, stewed or puréed. They are delicious pickled with onions and spices in vinegar.

Pear Islands
Serves 4

4 large pears
90g (3oz) caster sugar
Half bottle sweet Muscat wine
2 level tablespoons cornflour
Splash of milk
Dark chocolate to taste

Peel, core and halve the pears. Dissolve two-thirds of the sugar in the wine over a gentle heat and poach the pears in this syrup. Place the pear halves on an oiled baking tray, dredge with the rest of sugar, pop under a hot grill for a minute or two until the tops caramelize. In the meantime, blend the cornflour with a little milk and stir it into the syrup. Return to the heat and cook gently, stirring, until thick. Pour the sauce into a serving bowl, grate on some dark chocolate and set the pear halves into this. Serve piping hot or chilled.

'Durondeau'

OTHER USES

The bark contains a yellow dye and arbutin, an antibiotic. The leaves have been used medicinally for renal and urinary infections. The wood is hard and uniform, so loved by carvers. It is beautifully scented and good for smoking foods.

COMPANION PLANTING

Pears are hindered by grass, so this should not be allowed near them in their early years. However, the pears may be grassed down later, especially if they are situated in rather too heavy and/or damp conditions.

Pear dye

Pyrus from the family *Rosaceae*

PERRY PEARS

Tree up to 20m (65ft). Life span: very long. Deciduous, rarely self-fertile. Fruits: up to 10x7cm (4x3in), variable, pear-shaped, yellow, brown or red. Value: make a healthy tonic beverage.

Perry pear fruits are smaller and hardier than their culinary and dessert cousins, while the trees are generally enormous. As these fruits were wanted in quantity for pressing, they were selected for large trees that would stand well above grass and the depredations of stock. The fruits are bitter and astringent, containing a lot of tannin even though they may often look very appealing. They are pressed for the juice, which ferments to an alcoholic beverage.

Perry pears may have been brought to Britain by the Romans, but they were introduced in force by the Normans. Normandy was by then well established as a perry-growing region and the Normans found parts of the West and Midlands of England equally suitable. Many of the original pear orchards would probably still have been planted for perry without the Norman influence, as early pears tended to be unpalatable raw anyway. The colonists of North America certainly did not start off without perry pears. By 1648 a booklet entitled *A Perfect Description of Virginia* describes a Mr Kinsman regularly making forty or fifty butts of perry from his orchard. Whereas cider has remained a popular drink, perry waned in the nineteenth century. It is now made rarely, except for one or two specialist brands and for local consumption.

A mature perry pear tree with a heavy crop of fruit

VARIETIES

There are some 200–300 perry pear varieties known, though these are called by twice as many names, each district having its own local variation. The **Thorn Pear** is recorded from 1676 and grows on a very upright tree. Other early varieties such as **'Hastings'** and **'Brown Bess'** could be eaten or made into perry. Later varieties such as **'Holmer'** are more single purpose and almost uneatable. In the nineteenth century, breeders thought dual-purpose pears would be useful and produced **'Blakeney Red'** and **'Cannock'**. The Huffcap group all make very big trees with fruits of a high specific gravity; Rock varieties make even stronger perry, but are still often called Huffcaps.

CULTIVATION

Perry pears are less demanding than culinary or dessert pears and will do quite well in fairly poor soils. They do not like shallow or badly drained sites.

Growing under Glass
These are fairly hardy and will make big trees, so are generally not likely to thrive under glass.

Growing in Containers
Although they would resent it by being short-lived and light-cropping, it should be possible to grow these in large tubs.

Ornamental and Wildlife Value
Perry pears make a mass of flowers and are tall attractive trees that live for several hundred years, making them very suitable as estate and orchard trees, but too big for most gardens except on modern dwarfing stock. The flowers are good for insects and the fruits are eaten by birds in winter.

Maintenance
Spring Cut grass, spray with seaweed solution.
Summer
Autumn Cut grass, collect fruits.
Winter Prune and spread compost.

Propagation
Perry pears were often grown from seed or grafted on to stocks grown from pips in order to get large trees. Now they can be had on dwarfing stocks, such as quince, and are more manageable.

Pruning and Training
Once the initial shape is formed these are only pruned remedially, though care should always be taken to ensure that such large trees are sound.

Weed, Pest and Disease Control
These suffer the same few problems as dessert and culinary pears which make little impression on the immense crops. Fireblight is a risk, but there is little one can do with such large trees.

Harvesting and Storing
Immense crops are produced; a ton or even two per tree is possible, after a wait of several decades. One tree in 1790 covered three-quarters of an acre and produced six tons per year. Perry pears do not keep and rot very quickly. Perry is usually pressed from one variety only, with sugar and yeast added. Dessert and culinary pears do not make a perry of any value, but can be made into a pear wine.

COMPANION PLANTING

Young trees were usually cropped between with cereals or hops and then grassed down as they matured, often grazed by geese.

OTHER USES

The wood is useful for carving and, as firewood, scents the room.

A standing cup made of pearwood, dating from the early seventeenth century

CULINARY USES

Perry pears are not normally very good for eating even when they are cooked, though 'Blakeney Red' was once considered a good baker.

Pressless Perry Wine

3kg (6lb) pears
1.5kg (3lb) sugar
4.5litre (1 gallon) water
Approx. 1 teaspoon wine yeast

Chop the pears, peel and all, into the boiling water. Stir in half the sugar, and bring back to the boil, then allow to cool to 22°C (7°F) before adding the yeast. Seal with a fermentation lock and keep warm for one week, then strain and add the remaining sugar to the liquor. Reseal with the lock and ferment in a warm place until all action has stopped. Siphon off the lees and store in a cool place for 3 months, then bottle and store for a year before drinking.

Cydonia vulgaris /C. oblonga from the family *Rosaceae*

QUINCES

**Tree up to 6m (20ft). Self-fertile, deciduous, hardy, long-lived.
Fruits: 7x12cm (2x5in), yellow and fragrant.**

'Portuguese' quince blossom

These are small, bushy trees, often twisted and contorted. There are two forms: a lower mounded one with lax branches, more suited to ornamental and wildlife use, and a stiffer, erect type, which bears larger fruits and is better for orchards. The leaves are downy underneath, resembling apple leaves more than pear. They turn a gorgeous yellow in autumn. The decorative pink and white flowers resemble apple blossom, but appear singly on short shoots, 12–15cm (6–8in) long, that grow before the flower opens, so they are rarely bothered by late frost. In some varieties the unfurled flower bud looks like an ice-cream cone with strawberry stripes, or a traditional barber's pole. The quinces are hard fruits somewhat resembling pears in shape and colour, often covered with a soft down when young, inedible when raw, but delicious and aromatic when cooked. Because they have long been used as rootstocks for pears and other fruits, they are sometimes found as suckers, surviving long after the scion has passed away.

Quinces are old fruits, still much grown in many parts of Europe though originally from Persia and Turkestan. Dedicated by the ancients to the Goddess of Love, they were promulgated by the Roman Empire as one of their favoured crops and were well known to Pliny and Columella. In AD 812 Charlemagne encouraged the French to grow more and Chaucer refers to them by the French name as coines. Their pulp makes *Dulce de Membrillo* or *Marmelo*, still popular in Portugal and Spain, and the origin of the marmalade we now make from citrus fruit.

Japonica quinces (see p.523) are almost identical to Cydonia

VARIETIES

The **'Portuguese'** is pear-shaped, vigorous, but slow to crop. **'Vranja'** (Bereczki) is from Serbia, large-fruited, pear-shaped and with erect growth. **'Meech's Prolific'** is also pear- shaped, early to bear and late keeping. **'Champion'** is rounder and mild-flavoured. Also available are **'Ispahan'** from Persia and **'Maliformis'** (apple-shaped). Also in the USA: **'Orange'**, **'Pineapple'** and **'Smyrna'**.

CULTIVATION

Quinces need a moist soil and flourish as waterside specimens. They prefer a warm site, doing rather badly in cold or exposed places. Plant them at least 3m (10ft) apart. Normally they will only need staking in their first years of life. They are self-fertile.

Growing under Glass and in Containers

There is little to be gained by growing quinces under glass. They can be grown against a wall with some success and could be grown in pots and taken indoors by those living in harsh climates, but the fruit hardly merits such efforts.

Ornamental and Wildlife Value

Quinces will make excellent small specimen trees as the flowers, fruits, autumn colours and then the knotted branches give year-round interest. The flowers feed beneficial insects while the fruits are relished by birds and other wildlife after all the apples and pears have long gone.

Maintenance

Spring Spray monthly with seaweed solution, weed and mulch well.
Summer Spray monthly with seaweed solution and weed.
Autumn Remove rotten fruit and pick best for storing.
Winter Prune out dead and diseased wood, add plenty of compost.

Propagation

Quinces can be had from seed or by suckers removed from pear trees as these are usually grafted on to quince stocks. Better fruits will always result from buying a ready-formed tree of an already named variety.

Pruning and Training

Quinces can be trained but the twisted contorted growth makes this difficult. They are best grown as bushes or standards, with pruning restricted to removing dead, diseased and crossing wood.

Weed, Pest and Disease Control

There are no widespread problems for quinces. Even the birds and wasps will ignore the fruits for most of the autumn.

Harvesting and Storing

Pick the fruits in autumn before they drop and keep them in a cool airy place. Do not store with apples or pears or vegetables as they may taint.

Quince fruits

COMPANION PLANTING

Like pears and apples, quinces may be expected to benefit from underplantings of chives, garlic and the pungent herbs.

OTHER USES

The wood is hard and prunings make good kindling. The fruits are excellent room perfumers and can be used as bases for pomanders.

CULINARY USES

Quinces can be made into aromatic clear jelly, jam or a pulpy cheese that goes well with both sweet and savoury dishes. Pieces of quince (if you can hack them off) keep their shape when cooked, adding both texture and aroma to apple and pear dishes.

Quince Cheese
Makes approx 2kg (4lb)

1kg (2lb) ripe quinces
1 unwaxed small orange
A little water
Approx.1kg (2 lb) sugar
1 or 2 drops orange flower or
  rose petal water (optional)

Roughly hack the quinces into pieces. Finely chop the orange and simmer both, with just enough water to cover them, until they are a pulp. Strain the pulp and add its own weight in sugar. Bring to boil and cook gently for approximately 1½ hours. Add the orange flower or rose petal water if liked. Then pot into oiled, warmed bowls, seal and store for three months or more before using. Turn the cheese out of the bowl and slice for serving with cooked meats or savoury dishes.

Prunus domestica from the family *Rosaceae*

PLUMS

Tree 6m (20ft). Long-lived, deciduous, hardy, slender, thorny, not usually self-fertile. Fruits: ovoid, usually 3–6cm (1–2in) in any colour. Value: rich in magnesium, iron and vitamin A.

Plums come in more variation than most other fruits. They differ in season, size, shape, colour and taste. We have mixed hybrids, descendants of plums originally selected from fifteen or more different wild species. The European plum, *Prunus domestica*, is thought to be predominantly a hybrid between *P. cerasifera*, the cherry plum or **Myrobalan**, and *P. spinosa*, the **sloe**. It is a small to medium, slender, deciduous tree with small white blossoms.

The European plum came from Western Asia and the Caucasus. It naturalized in Greece first and then throughout most of the temperate zone. Pliny describes cultivated varieties from Syria coming to Italy via Greece, and it is likely they were spread by the Roman Empire to Britain and Northern Europe. They were reintroduced in the Crusades. Henry VII is recorded as importing a 'Perdrigon' plum and Brogdale Fruit Research Station have a plum grown from a stone salvaged from the wreck of the *Mary Rose*, Henry VIII's splendid warship. Plum stones were ordered in 1629 for planting in Massachusetts, and plums became widely cultivated in the temperate parts of North America. In 1864 over 150 varieties were offered in nurserymen's catalogues. Some American plums returned to Europe; California, for example, became famous for exporting prunes – late, dark-skinned plums which are dried on the tree. Although unsuccessful in cool, damp climates, they can be dried with machinery. '**Fellemberg**' and '**Prune d'Agen**' are from Europe, but are more widely grown in California.

'Coe's Golden Drop'

VARIETIES

There are hundreds of good varieties, which ripen through the season. '**Victoria**' is fully self-fertile, pollinates many others and is always worth having. It has golden-yellow-fleshed, large, yellow, ovoid fruits, flushed with scarlet. '**Victoria**' ripens middle to late August in Sussex, where it was found around 1840. '**Coe's Golden Drop**' is a shy cropper, but superb. It needs a warm spot or a wall and closely resembles an apricot. '**Severn Cross**' is a delicious golden seedling from '**Coe's**' and self-fertile. '**Oullin's Gage**' is self-fertile. A plum with a richer, sweeter flavour, it flowers late, missing frosts. '**Czar**' has frost-resistant flowers and is self-fertile; it is for culinary rather than dessert use. '**Marjorie's Seedling**' is dual purpose, late cropping and self-fertile.

CULTIVATION

Plums like a heavier, moister soil than many other fruits. This means they often may be relegated to cold, damp sites and heavy soils, which they really do not like. Even on a shady wall some, such as '**Victoria**' or '**Czar**', do well.

Growing under Glass and in Containers
Because of their susceptibility to spring frost, brown rot and wasps, plums are worth growing under glass. However, they would be best confined to large pots so they can spend sometime outdoors, as they do not relish hot conditions.

'Victoria'

Ornamental and Wildlife Value

Plums are wonderful during their short blossoming. The flowers are loved by early insects and the fruits by birds, insects and rodents, who also chew the bark.

Maintenance

Spring Protect blossom from frost, weed, mulch, spray with seaweed solution, prune.
Summer Put out wasp traps.
Autumn Remove mummified plums.
Winter Protect buds from birds with cotton or nets.

Propagation

Graft on **'Pixy'** and other new dwarfing stocks, unless you have a big orchard and want immense quantities. Plums can be grown from stones, but take years to fruit and do not come true.

Pruning and Training

Plums make good high standards because, eventually, heavy fruiting branches weep, bringing the fruit down to a skirt. Overladen branches will need propping. Plums are usually grown as a short standard or bush. Leave them alone once a head is formed, except to cut out dead and diseased wood. Any work is best done in the growing season. They can be usefully trained on walls if on dwarfing stock, for example **'Pixy'**. Plums prefer herringbone not fan shapes.

Weed, Pest and Disease Control

Plums get a host of the usual pests and a few more besides, but when they avoid the frost and crop at all they are so prolific there is usually a surplus for private gardeners. They are susceptible to silver leaf disease, so should not be pruned in autumn, winter or early spring – only in late spring and summer and during dry weather.

Harvesting and Storing

Plums picked under-ripe for cooking will keep for days, but often have poor flavour compared to plums picked ripe off the tree. Many varieties can be quite easily peeled, and this avoids some of the unfortunate side effects of too many plums.

'Marjorie's Seedling'

COMPANION PLANTING

Avoid anemones which harbour plum rust. In the USA curculios are reportedly kept off by surrounding plum trees with garlic.

OTHER USES

Potent brandy is made from plums in Hungary and in central Europe.

CULINARY USES

Plums can be turned into jam, juice or cheese, or frozen if stoned first, and are Epicurean preserved in plum brandy syrup.

Prunes in Semolina
Serves 4

250g (8oz) dried prunes
100ml (4fl oz) plum brandy
100 ml (4fl oz) water
900ml (1½ pts) milk
Twist of lemon rind
½ teaspoon salt
7 dessertspoons semolina
2 dessertspoons honey
2 small eggs, separated
Grated nutmeg to taste

Soak the prunes in the brandy and water overnight. Strain off the juice and simmer it down to syrup. Put the fruits and syrup into the base of a pudding basin. Boil the milk, lemon rind, salt and semolina for 10 minutes, stirring continuously. Cool a little, remove the lemon rind and stir in the honey and egg yolks. Whisk the egg whites and fork them in. Immediately pour the mixture over the back of a spoon on to the fruit and syrup. Grate nutmeg over the surface and bake in a preheated oven at 200°C/400°F/gas mark 6 for 20 minutes, or until the top is browning.
  As delicious cold for breakfast as it is hot for dinner.

Double Victoria
Serves 6–8

500g (1lb) Victoria plums
50g (2oz) honey
25g (1oz) flaked blanched
  almonds

for the sponge:
100g (4oz) sifted self-raising
  flour
100g (4oz) vanilla-flavoured
  caster sugar
100g (4oz) softened butter
2 eggs, pinch salt

Wash, halve and stone the plums. Place in a buttered pudding dish and dribble the honey over them. Beat together the sponge ingredients in a mixer until creamy and light in colour. Dollop the sponge mixture over the fruit, smooth and garnish with almonds. Bake in a preheated oven at 190°C/ 375°F/gas mark 5 for 35 minutes or until golden brown and firm to the touch.

Prunes

Prunus italica from the family *Rosaceae*

GREENGAGES

Tree/bush 4–5m (13–16ft). Hardy, long-lived. Fruits: 2–4cm (1–1½in), green to red.

Greengages are like plums, fruiting in mid-season with sweet, greeny yellow or golden, lightly scented flesh. The fruits are smaller, firmer, more rounded and less bloomed than plums. They have a deep crease down one side and frequently russet spotting. The trees are sturdy, not often thorny, and bushier than most plums, though not quite as hardy.

Wild greengages are found in Asia Minor. Possibly introduced to Britain and Northern Europe by the Romans, they disappeared from cultivation during the Saxon period or Middle Ages and were not reintroduced until 1725. Originally known in France as the **'Reine Claude'**, the first greengage was brought to Britain by, and named after, Sir Thomas Gage, who lived in Bury St Edmunds, Suffolk – under 20 miles from where I now write. He was fortunate to live in East Anglia as the conditions suit greengages, which need a drier, warmer summer than plums. The original greengage almost always came true from seed, but there are some larger-fruited selections, and also some good crosses between gages and plums.

VARIETIES

The **'Old Greengage'** is original, but can be unreliable; an improved seedling is **'Cambridge Gage'**. The **'Transparent Gage'** is another old variety from France and is honeyed in its sweetness. It has almost transparent, golden-

'Early Transparent Gage'

yellow flesh and is heavily spotted with red. It fruits in late summer. The true **'Mirabelle'** is very similar, smaller fruited and of dwarf growth, but is rarely found except in southern France. (Sometimes the yellow Myrobalan plums may erroneously be called Mirabelles to make a sale!) **'Denniston's Superb'** comes

from the USA and is close to the original in flavour, but is larger fruited, hardier, regular cropping and most valuable of all, self-fertile. **'Jefferson'** is similar, later, but not self-fertile. **'Reine Claude de Bavay'** possibly has a plum as one parent. It fruits a fortnight or so after the previous varieties, in early autumn.

It makes a most delicious jam, a touch more acid and tasty if the fruit is picked a week or so early. **'Golden Transparent'**, another hybrid, is a large, round, transparent yellow. It ripens late and needs a wall in most cool areas, but is self-fertile.

CULTIVATION

Greengages need a lighter soil than plums but still need it to be rich, moist and well aerated. They are easiest to tend as standards at least 6m (20 ft) apart. In colder areas they need a wall. Some, such as 'Denniston's Superb', 'Early Transparent Gage', 'Jefferson's Gage' or 'Oullins Golden Gage', will fruit on a shady wall.

Growing under Glass and in Containers

Greengages, especially the choicer Mirabelle or Transparent varieties, are worth growing in pots as this is the only way to restrict their growth. They can then be taken under cover for the flowering and ripening periods. Greengages will need a rest in winter.

Ornamental and Wildlife Value

As for plums (see p.411).

Harvesting and Storing

Greengages are loved by the supermarkets green and hard, as in that condition they keep for weeks. Picked fully ripe off the tree they are delectable, but do not last, especially if wet. They can be jammed, turned into cheeses, juiced or frozen if stoned first.

Pruning and Training

They are usually grown as low standards or bushes with remedial pruning in late spring once the shape has formed. Overladen branches need propping, but not as much as for plums. As they also tend to irregular bearing, thinning of heavy crops is sensible, but not as effective as for most fruits. Gages are best worked like plums in a herringbone pattern on a wall, and summer pruned.

Maintenance

Spring Protect blossom from frost, weed, mulch, spray with seaweed solution, then prune.
Summer Put out wasp traps.
Autumn Remove mummified fruits.
Winter Protect buds from birds with cotton or nets.

Weed, Pest and Disease Control

As greengages are so sweet they suffer particularly from bird damage, and the buds are attacked as well as the fruits! The damage caused also allows dieback to get a foothold, so trees need netting or cottoning over the winter in bird-infested areas. Wasps also make a mess of the crop, so be prepared to be ruthless!

Propagation

Gages are usually grafted on to Myrobalan stocks, but newer dwarfing stocks mean that it is easier to fit them on to walls. Cuttings can be taken in late autumn with some success and the oldest varieties come nearly true from stones.

COMPANION PLANTING

Greengages benefit from being positioned on the sheltered, sunny side of the larger plums.

OTHER USES

Prunelle (left) is a liqueur from Alsace and Angers, made from Mirabelles. Slivovitsa, an *eau-de-vie*, comes from the Balkans.

CULINARY USES

They make the best plum jams. True Mirabelle jam is almost apricot flavoured, but even better.

Greengage jam
Makes 2kg (4lb)

1kg (2lb) greengages
1kg (2lb) sugar
A little water

Wash, halve and stone the gages. Crack a few stones, extract the kernels and add these to the fruit. Pour in enough water to cover the bottom of the pan and simmer until the fruit has softened. Add the sugar and bring rapidly to the boil, then carefully skim, jar and seal.

Prunus species from the family *Rosaceae*

DAMSONS
BULLACES AND JAPANESE PLUMS

Tree/bush up to 5m (16ft). Long-lived, some self-fertile.
Fruits: 2cm+ (1in), some vitamin value.

Bullaces (*P. insititia*) have globular, bluey-black or greeny-yellow fruits, which ripen in late autumn, at least a month later than most other plums. The fruits are small and generally too acid to eat raw, but make good preserves. The trees are sometimes thorny. Damsons (*P. damascena*) are closely related to bullaces, with larger, blue-black fruit which more closely resemble plums. However, they are more oval, with less bloom, and have a sweet, spicy flavour once cooked. Damson trees are compact and are reasonably self-fertile.

The **cherry plum** or **Myrobalan** (*P. cerasifera*) is less brittle and can be woven into hedges; it is often used as a windbreak. The white flowers open at the same time as the leaves which are glossier than those of other plums. They are self-fertile. The fruits are yellow, red or purple, spherical and a little pointed at the bottom. They have a sweet, juicy, if somewhat insipid, flesh and make good jam.

Japanese plums (*P. salicina* and *P. triflora*) are large, conical, orangey-red or golden fruits without much flavour. They blossom early and are vulnerable to cold, but they are also more productive and tolerant of a wider range of warm conditions than ordinary plums, so are extensively grown in Australia, South Africa and the USA. They have shiny, dark twigs, white flowers on bold spurs and leaves that turn a glorious red in autumn.

Bullaces are native to Europe and Asia Minor, but the current apparently wild stock has probably been inadvertently selected over the centuries. Damsons come from Damascus, or certainly that region, and were brought to Europe during the Crusades in the twelfth century, supposedly by the Duke of Anjou, after a pilgrimage to Jerusalem. Cherry plums come from the Balkans, Caucasus and Western Asia and were introduced to Britain in the sixteenth century. Some of these went to the New World and were interbred with American native species to cope with the harsher climatic conditions. Japanese plums, originally natives of China, were introduced to Japan about 1500 and only to the USA in 1870. Being rather tender they have never really expanded into Europe.

VARIETIES

The choice of Bullaces is down to the purpley-blue **Black Bullace** or the greeny-yellow **Shepherd's Bullace**. Though now difficult to find, the common wild plum of central Europe, **Zwetsche** or **Quetsche**, the source of many good liqueurs, has blue-black berries with golden-yellow flesh on a compact but twiggy tree. Damsons are now found in only three varieties: **'Farleigh'**, from Kent, is a heavy cropper if well pollinated and a sturdy bush often used as a windbreak; **'Merryweather'** has slightly larger fruits with greenish-yellow flesh, earlier in autumn; the **Shropshire**, or **Prune damson**, which ripens last, has the better flavour, but is a light cropper. **Cherry plums** are most often called **Red** or **Yellow Myrobalans**. There are several ornamental forms that may fruit; some have pink flowers, many are purple-leaved. Japanese plums, such as **'Burbank'**, may be available. Similar is **'Beauty'**, which is red with sweet, juicy, yellow flesh that clings to the stone.

Immature fruits and leaves of 'Merryweather'

A 'Merryweather' damson tree with tansy in foreground

CULTIVATION

Most of these are more tolerant of soil and site conditions than true plums, except for the Japanese, which require warmer conditions.

Growing under Glass and in Containers
As most of these plum types are hardy and culinary, it seems unprofitable to fruit them under cover. If only small quantities are required then these plums could be tried in pots.

Ornamental and Wildlife Value
The trees are not imposing until they flower, then they froth and foam. Later their displays of fruiting profligacy are quite stupendous. Great masses of fruits continue to feed the wildlife through many months.

Maintenance
As for plums (see p.411).

Propagation
Most types do well on Myrobalan stocks and many on their own roots. Japanese plums can bear in three years or so, the others maybe in five. Those on their own roots can be grown from suckers, and seedlings of most will come nearly true.

Pruning and Training
As for plums, these are best left alone except for remedial work.

Weed, Pest and Disease Control
These varieties of plums are generally not as susceptible to brown rot as true plums.

Harvesting and Storing
Bullaces and damsons are supposedly mellowed and taste better raw after frosts, but the birds will have eaten them by then.

CULINARY USES

Almost all of these fruits are now used culinarily only for jamming, jellying, fruit cheeses, winemaking and liqueurs.

Damson Cheese
Makes 2.5kg (5lb)

1.5kg (3lb) damsons
About 1kg (2lb) light brown sugar

Wash the fruit and then simmer till soft with just enough water to prevent burning. Sieve and boil the pulp with three-quarters its own weight of sugar. Cook until the scum has finished rising and the jam is clear. Pot the pulp in warmed oiled bowls and seal.

COMPANION PLANTING

Avoid anemones, which harbour plum rust.

OTHER USES

As hedges and windbreaks the bullaces and cherry plums are excellent. Damsons can be planted in sheltered sections.

'Merryweather' damsons with fruit

Prunus armeniaca from the family *Rosaceae*

APRICOTS

Tree, up to 6m (20ft). Hardy, deciduous, self-fertile. Fruits: 3x5cm (1½x2in), yellow/orange. Value: rich in vitamin A and potassium.

This small tree has white flowers (occasionally tinged with pink) very early in spring, well before the leaves emerge. These are spade-shaped and often glossy. The young shoots can also appear glossy as if varnished in red or brown. The leaves are more similar to those of a plum than those of a cherry or peach, and apricot fruits closely resemble some plums, but the stone is more spherical and the flavour distinct. Some think that **'Moorpark'**, one of the commonest varieties, is a plumcot (a plum-apricot hybrid).

The first apricots came from China or Siberia, not Armenia, where Alexander the Great found them. The fruits became loved by the Romans, but they never succeeded in transplanting any to northern Europe. Apricots reached Britain in the thirteenth century and were introduced again, more successfully, in the sixteenth. **'Bredase'** may be the oldest variety in cultivation; it closely resembles descriptions of Roman apricots.

'Moorpark' in flower

VARIETIES

'New Large Early' is the first, **'Alfred'** and **'Farmingdale'** ripen next and the latter has some dieback resistance. **'Moorpark'** is exquisite; the traditional variety, it ripens a little later. **'Hemskerke'** is early and worth trying on walls in cold areas. Also available are **'Breda'**, **'Bredase'**, **'Goldcot'**, **'Hongaarse'**, **'Shipley's Blenheim'** and **'Tross Orange'**. **Hunza** wild apricots of Northern India can be grown from the stones of dried fruits bought in natural food shops. They make large bushes with more ornamental than cropping potential. The **Japanese apricot**, *Prunus mume*, has scented flowers and sour fruit, usually eaten salted or pickled.

CULTIVATION

Like most stone fruits, apricots need a cold winter period to rest and warm summers to ripen the fruit. The plants themselves are tough, but the flowers are so early that they are always in danger from frost. The soil should not be heavy nor the site wet. In most cool areas they will only crop reliably against a wall.

Growing under Glass and in Containers

Grown under glass, apricots are more sure to crop if allowed a cold resting period, so do not plant in continuously heated greenhouses. A better plan may be to confine them in large pots. Keep these outside unless very cold, bring them under glass for flowering and take them back outside again once the weather is warm.

Ornamental and Wildlife Value

Apricots are not noticeable trees, though the flowers are pretty enough. Ornamental varieties and **Hunzas** are attractive but unfruitful. Their earliness makes the flowers useful to bees and beneficial insects.

'Moorpark' fruits well on a warm wall

Pruning and Training

The least work is to grow apricots as trees, only removing dead and diseased wood as necessary. Cut out all the dieback until no discoloration is seen. The wood is brittle, so watch for overladen branches and prop or prune early. On walls, build a fan of old wood with fruiting spurs. Prune the frame and any dieback in late winter, then prune again in summer to restrict the growth.

Weed, Pest and Disease Control

Apricots are not particularly bothered by pests. Ants may introduce and farm scale insects and occasionally caterpillars and aphids may be seen. Apricots do suffer from dieback and gummosis, however, the twigs dying back and resiny gum oozing out of the branches or, worse, the trunk. Both these conditions are symptomatic of poor growth and every effort should be made to improve the conditions; fewer weeds, more compost, more mulches, more water or better aerated roots, seaweed sprays and hard pruning should do it.

Propagation

Apricot trees are obtained budded on to suitable rootstocks, such as 'St Julien A' in the UK. This is better for wetter, heavier soils; seedling peach or apricot rootstocks suit lighter, drier ones. Successful trees have been raised from stones.

Maintenance

Spring Cover flowers on frosty nights, weed, mulch and spray with seaweed solution monthly.
Summer Thin the fruits early, summer prune, bag fruits against wasps and birds.
Autumn Keep weeded, tie in new shoots.
Winter Protect from very hard frosts, prune out dieback.

Harvesting and Storing

Apricots ripened on the tree are heavenly, but soon go over. Picked young enough to travel, they never develop full flavour. Thus they are best eaten straightaway, or jammed or frozen.

'Alfred' trees espalier-trained after fruiting

CULINARY USES

Apricots make scrumptious jam and can be preserved in brandy and syrup. Unlike the majority of *Prunus* fruits, most apricot kernels are sweet and edible and can be used to make ratafia biscuits.

Apricot Sponge
Serves 6–8

500g (1lb) apricots
Knob of butter
Coarse, light brown sugar

For the sponge:
55g (2oz) each of butter, fine, light brown sugar, white self-raising flour
1 large egg
A splash of milk
Real vanilla extract

Halve and stone the apricots (score or remove the skin if you prefer) and place in a buttered flan dish, cut side up. Sprinkle with coarse sugar. Cream together the butter and sugar, stir in the egg, then fold in the flour, together with the milk if the mixture is stiff, and the vanilla extract. Spoon the sponge mixture over the apricots and cook in a preheated oven at 190°C/375°F/gas mark 5 for about half an hour. When cold, turn out and serve with whipped cream.

COMPANION PLANTING

Do not grow tomatoes, potatoes or oats near apricots, but they benefit from *Alliums* nearby, especially garlic and chives.

OTHER USES

The wood is brittle, but of use as kindling.

Prunus persica from the family *Rosaceae*

PEACHES

Tree/bush up to 5x5m (16x16ft). Generally short-lived. Self-fertile, deciduous.
Fruits: 6–8cm (2½–3½in), yellow, orange, red. Value: rich in vitamin A, potassium and niacin.

Peach trees are small and resemble willows, with long, lightly serrated leaves. They bloom before the leaves appear. The smaller the flowers, the darker rose coloured they are, with the largest being lightest pink. Flowering a fortnight later than almonds, they are closely related, the almond having a tough, inedible, leathery skin over a smooth stone. The skin has a partition line along which it easily splits. Most peach stones are ribbed or perforated with small holes in the shell. In varieties known as clingstones the flesh clings to this shell; in others, the freestones, the fruit is free and easier to enjoy without having to tease it off the stone. The flesh may vary from white to yellow; there are even blood peaches with red staining. The texture varies with cultivar, soil and climate. The skin colour can be from dull green through yellows and orange to dark red. The most distinctive feature of peaches is the soft downy fluff on the skin.

The peach was known three hundred years BC to the Greek philosopher Theophrastus, who thought it came from Persia, and so it became named. Early Hebrew writings make no reference to it, neither is there a Sanskrit name, so it seems likely peaches did not reach Europe to any extent until shortly before the Christian period. Dioscorides mentions the peach during the first century, as does Pliny, who states that the Romans had only recently imported it from Persia.

Peaches are, in fact, of Chinese origin. They are mentioned in the books of Confucius from the first century BC, and can be traced back to the tenth century BC in artistic representations. The Chinese still have an immense number of varieties and these were initially spread by seed. The stones produce trees with ease, but of course do not come true. The variability may have accounted for the slow spread to Europe. However, this was more likely to have been because peaches were initially tried in hot countries at too low altitudes. Thus the trees did not get their winter dormancy and would have fruited badly, effectively discouraging further experiments. Pliny indeed mentions that peach trees were taken from Egypt to the island of Rhodes, but this transplantation did not succeed; they were then brought on to Italy.

It took till the middle of the sixteenth century for peaches to reach England and in 1629 a quantity of peach stones was ordered by the Governor of the Massachusetts Bay Colony of New England. The peach found its new home in North America highly suitable and spread abundantly. In fact it spread so rapidly through the wild that it was thought to be a native fruit. Peaches spread so widely that they conquered much of South America by Darwin's time. He spotted them on islands in the mouth of the Parana, along with thickets of similarly fugitive orange trees.

'Rochester' is a prolific fruiter

VARIETIES

'Amsden June' is early with greenish-white flesh, semi-freestone and a month behind its name. **'Duke of York'** has better-flavoured, creamy-white flesh and is also semi-freestone. **'Hale's Early'** has pale yellow flesh and is freestone. **'Peregrine'** is the best choice for a bush tree in the UK and has yellowish-white flesh of excellent flavour. It is freestone and comes mid-season. **'Rochester'** is my second favourite for a bush; it is not quite so well-flavoured and yellow-fleshed. **'Royal George'** comes late, has tasty, big, yellow fruits, flushed dark red with pale, yellowish-white flesh and a small free stone, but is prone to mildew. **'Bellegarde'** is a heavy free-stone cropper of beautiful red fruits, produced so late that in cooler areas the fruits will often not ripen. But with a wall, under glass, or in a warmer climate 'Bellegarde' can be excellent. Varieties also now available include: **'Alexandra Noblesse'**, **'Barrington'**, **'Dymond'**.

CULTIVATION

Peaches ideally need a well-enriched, well-aerated, but moist piece of soil. They prefer open gravelly soils to heavy, and need to be planted at least 6m/20ft apart. If they take (peaches do not always), they establish quickly and need no staking after the first year. They need copious quantities of compost annually and mulches are obligatory to ensure the constant moisture they demand. Where they are planted against walls, great care must be taken to ensure adequate water constantly throughout the season or the fruits will split. However, they are most intolerant of any waterlogging. Peaches also should not be planted near to almonds, as the two fruits may hybridize, resulting in bitter nuts.

Growing under Glass and in Containers
Peaches are often grown under glass where the extra efforts of replenishment pruning and tying in are repaid by gorgeous, succulent, early fruits free from the depredations of birds. The greenhouse must be unheated in winter to give peaches a dormant rest period. More problems occur under cover – the red spider mite can be especially troublesome unless a high humidity is maintained. Peaches are good subjects for large pots as they can take heavy pruning if well fed and watered. Pots enable them to be kept under cover during the winter and through flowering and then brought out all summer, thus avoiding peach leaf curl and frost damage. The flowers must be protected from frosts and so must the young fruitlets. The flowers are more susceptible to frost damage after pollination and the fruitlets likewise for a further fortnight.

Ornamental and Wildlife Value
The peach is a pleasure to have. The willowy leaves are held well into autumn and the sight of a good crop of fruits is magnificent. The blossom is wonderful too; peaches in bloom are a joy. The wildlife value of the tree is rather low in wet areas as the trees succumb to leaf curl, but in some drier areas peaches become weeds and are appreciated by birds, insects and rodents.

Pruning and Training
Peaches fruit on young shoots, thus it is essential to have plenty of these growths. They are best obtained by a partial pollarding operation late each winter. This makes the pruning more akin to that of blackcurrants than to that of most other tree fruits. Basically the top ends of the higher branches are removed to encourage prolific growth from the lower branches and stubs. This also serves to keep the peach bushes lower and more manageable.

On walls and under cover, peaches are usually fan-trained. Selected young shoots are allowed to spring from a main frame and then tied in to replace the previous growths once those have fruited.

Fortunately, if the pruning of peaches is temporarily neglected, healthy bushes respond to being cut back hard by throwing plentiful young growths. More important than pruning is thinning. Peaches are prone to overcropping, breaking branches and exhausting themselves. Thin the fruits hard, removing those touching or anywhere near each other. Do this very early and then again later.

'Duke of York' in a greenhouse

Ficus carica from the family *Moraceae*

FIGS

Tree/bush, up to 9x7m (30x20ft).
Hardy, self-fertile. Fruits: pear-shaped,
6x10cm (2x4in), browny green.

'Brunswick'

Fig leaves are large and distinctive, but vary in exact shape with each variety. Although figs are deciduous, young plants tend to be almost evergreen and are then more tender. Figs can be grown as trees or bushes, but are most often trained on walls. Almost all fig cultivars set the fruit parthenocarpically, without actual fertilization. However, some old and mostly inferior varieties in hot climates have female fruiting plants and male caprifigs that are separately and specifically cultivated to produce female fig wasps. These wasps will crawl through the minute end hole into the fruits to pollinate them.

Figs are indigenous to Asia Minor and were one of the first fruits to be brought into cultivation. They thus became an intrinsic part of the diet of the Mediterranean basin long before Classical times, though the Greeks claimed they were given to them by the goddess Demeter. Cato knew of six different figs, and two centuries later, in about AD 60, Pliny notes no fewer than 29 varieties! Figs were certainly brought to England by the Romans as remains have been found, though the plants were not officially introduced until the early sixteenth century. There are over 600 fig species. Many of the varieties that we encounter today are ornamentals such as the **India rubber plant** (*Ficus elastica*), the **weeping fig** (*F. Benjamina*) and the **fiddle leaf plant** (*F. lyrata*).

VARIETIES

In the UK figs ripen from mid-August. **'Brunswick'** produces large fruits that are most tasty a couple of days after picking; **'Brown Turkey'** is reliably prolific; **'White Marseilles'** has pale fruits. Also: **'Angelique'**, **'Black Ischia'**, **'Bourjasotte Grise'**, **'Castle Kennedy'**, **'Negro Large'**, **'Osborne's Prolific'**, **'Rouge de Bordeaux'**, **'St John's'**, **'Violette Dauphine'**, **'Violette Sepor'**, **'White Ischia'** and, in the USA, **'Adriatic'**, **'Celeste'**, **'Kadota'**, **'King'**, **'Magnolia'** (**'Brunswick'**), **'Mission'**.

'Brown Turkey'

CULTIVATION

Varieties vary in hardiness, but even if the tops are lost many will regrow from the roots if these are protected from the frost. Thus figs may be planted a little deep to encourage stooling. Often grown against a wall, they can be cropped in the open in southern Britain, their main enemy being the excessive wet rather than the cold. It is traditional to confine the roots of figs grown against walls to promote fruiting. This appears unnecessary if excessive feeding is avoided, but too much nitrogen will promote abundant undesirable soft growth.

Growing under Glass and in Containers

Figs fruit and ripen much more reliably under glass, and with heat and care three crops a year are possible. Figs can be grown confined in large pots and can make excellent foliage plants for house or patio, though they will need careful watering and training.

Ornamental and Wildlife Value

The very attractive foliage adds a luxuriant touch to a garden. Of little use to wildlife in colder climes, figs are much more valuable in hotter countries.

Maintenance

Spring Remove frost protection, weed, spray seaweed solution monthly, and thin the fruits.
Summer Protect the fruits carefully from wasps and birds, make layers.
Autumn Remove all fruits of all sizes before frosts arrive.
Winter Prune, take cuttings, protect from frost.

Wall-trained fig

Propagation

Layers can be made during summer. 20cm (8in) well-ripened or old wood cuttings taken during the early winter root, especially if given bottom heat. Seeds produce plants that are unlikely to fruit well.

Pruning and Training

The most fruitful wood is well-ripened, short-jointed and sturdy; long soft shoots are unproductive and better removed. Figs can be pruned any time during dormancy, but are best left until growth is about to start in spring. More importantly, remove any fruit or fruitlet in autumn to prevent these starting into growth, failing and thereby spoiling the second crop that could otherwise succeed.

Weed, Pest and Disease Control

Fig plants have few problems except birds and wasps. Weeding must be thorough near the trunks to prevent rodents nibbling the bark. Under cover, on walls or in pots they may suffer from red spider mites.

CULINARY USES

Figs are delicious fresh and they can be made into jams, jellies, cheeses and chutneys.

Savoury and Sweet Figs
Serves 4 as a snack or canapé

12 dried figs
90g (3oz) mild hard cheese
Pinch of celery seed
1 shallot
50g (2oz) marzipan
25g (1oz) each sultanas and raisins
25g (1oz) dark cooking chocolate
A little Cointreau or sweet liqueur
Honey

Stuff half the figs with some small chunks of cheese, a sprinkling of celery seeds and a thin slice of the shallot.
Grate the chocolate and marzipan. Mix in the dried fruit and liqueur, then stuff the remaining figs with this mixture. Smear all the figs with honey and put them in an oiled dish in a preheated oven at 180°C/350°F/gas mark 4 for 10 to 15 minutes. Serve the figs hot or cold.

Harvesting and Storing

The fruits are soft-skinned and do not travel or store well once ripe. In hotter regions figs can be dried and will then keep well.

COMPANION PLANTING

One of the few plants to get on well with rue.

OTHER USES

Figs are known by many for their syrup, administered as a laxative. Also valuable as a food, they contain nearly half their weight in sugar when dried.

Figs stuffed with mascarpone, glacé mixed peel, a little honey and brandy to taste are delicious

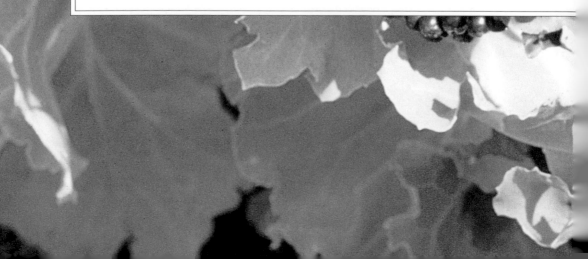

SOFT, BUSH AND CANE FRUITS

I prefer to group these fruits as fruitcage fruits because this accurately describes their most common factor: without a cage most of them cannot effectively produce fruits at all. The reasons for their other names are fairly self-evident: soft, because they are not hard fruits such as apples, bush is self-descriptive and cane refers to the slender branches. (The term vine is applied differently depending on region; in some places it is used solely for grapes, in others to plants with long, flexible branches, even cucurbits.)

The fruitcage members are grouped together by the gardener because they must be netted or grown in a cage. However, as with orchard fruits, most of them come from the *Rosaceae* family. They are shrubby perennials, not tree-like, and thus fairly compact, or can be kept so, quick to crop, and small fruited. Most are found growing naturally on the woodland's edge and thrive given moist root runs with plentiful humus-rich mould and thick mulches of leafy material. Most will grow and even crop in light shade, though of course they usually produce sweeter, better-tasting fruit given more sun. Grapevines will most obviously require much more sun than do the other plants of this group.

The majority of these fruits have been gathered from the wild native species since prehistory and their 'cultivation' will have

occurred inadvertently around sites of human habitation, from waste heaps and primitive latrine arrangements. (Both, of course, afford remarkably well-fertilized ground, and thus select for strains that could use such conditions.) Being fast-growing plants and quick to crop, the proximity and opportunity would have created more, but still inadvertent, selection. Such a process would have produced much improved 'cultivars', spread by migrating peoples, and these may well have influenced wild populations. Certainly now some wild fruits such as the blackberry are just such hybrids in most areas, and it may well be that some supposed native species are in reality escaped cultivars from our distant past.

Thus the cropping potential of some wild fruits may have been raised over the millennia by our own unintended selection. In any case, the wild forms of most of these fruits were so productive and available in such vast quantities that they were simply not brought into cultivation until the end of the Middle Ages, with the important exception of grapes, which have been tended since prehistory. Some, such as the strawberry, have undergone intense development and hybridization and so have improved dramatically, while others, such as aronia, have remained almost unaltered. Many closely related edible species are available, which could be crossed with cultivated forms, so improved fruits may be only be an experiment or two away. The Tayberry is the result of one such crossing, and is better by far than all its similar predecessors.

Fragaria hybrids from the family *Rosaceae*

SUMMER STRAWBERRIES

Herbaceous. 30cm (1ft). Life span: short. Self-fertile. Fruits: up to 5x5cm (2x2in), red, conical.
Value: some vitamin C and half as much iron as spinach

This most delicious of fruits really needs no introduction! Modern strawberries are hybrids based on *F. chiloensis*, the **Chilean Pine**, and *F. virginiana*, the **Scarlet Virginian**. The first contributed larger fruit with a pineapple tang and was brought to Europe in 1712; the latter, first mentioned in Massachusetts in 1621, provides the superior flavour, and is still grown commercially as **'Little Scarlet'** for jam-making. These two were first combined in the nineteenth century, with intensive development since. Every region has its favourite varieties.

VARIETIES

There are far too many to list and new improved ones are continually becoming available. My favourites are:

'Royal Sovereign' (mid-season), beautifully flavoured if light cropping, originally introduced in 1892; **'Silver Jubilee'** (mid) is tasty with some disease resistance; **'Cambridge Vigour'** (early) is a commercial variety, but has rich flavour; **'Late Pine'** is also simply delicious.

CULTIVATION

All preparation is well repaid. Strawberries need a very rich soil, full of humus, and benefit from slow-release phosphates, such as bone meal. Well-rotted manure or compost, and/or seaweed meal dressings, will be recouped with better cropping. The more space you give them the better they will do and the less work they will be! 60cm (2ft) each way is the minimum.

Growing under Glass

They do not like the hot dry conditions under cover, and these also encourage red spider mite. However, the advantages of protection from birds, prevention of rain damage and earlier crops mean that they are widely grown under glass and plastic. For winter cropping, the new Californian day-length indeterminate types are far superior.

Growing in Containers

Many containers, often tower shaped, are sold specifically for strawberries. While a good idea, the small amount of root run, hot in an above-ground position, and usually dry because of

low water-holding capacity, make these poor growing conditions for strawberries. The plants respond with low yields, all of which occur in a short period, which makes them neglected for much of the year.

However, strawberries can be grown successfully in pots and containers. They need regular feeding as well as copious automatic watering!

Ornamental and Wildlife Value

Rather too straggly to be considered decorative, they would make effective but short-lived ground cover and would not be very productive. By the losses, one must assume that they are valuable to birds!

Maintenance

Spring Weed, root first runners, spray seaweed monthly.
Summer Weed, straw, protect from birds and mould, pick.
Autumn Establish new plants, tidy up the best, eradicate old.
Winter Rake up old leaves and mulch and compost them well.

Propagation

Some special varieties can be grown from seed, but otherwise seed generally produces poor results. Runners are the obvious replacement, usually available to excess. These

'Cambridge Vigour'

'Tamella' strawberries displayed on a tiered stand

are best taken from quality plants that have been reserved for propagation and deflowered; half a dozen good ones, or many more poor, can be had thus. The first plantlet on an early runner is chosen, pinned or held to the ground – or preferably rooted into a pot of compost for an easier transplantation. Start new beds in late summer or early autumn to allow them to establish; they can then crop well the next summer. Late autumn or spring plantings should be deflowered the first summer to build up their strength for a massive crop the next.

Pruning and Training

Strawberries will become relatively unproductive after three or four years, so in practice a continual annual replacement of a quarter or a third of the plants is best. Replacing all every four years or so means years of gluts and years of shortages, as they are all the same age. Strawing up is essential for clean crops. Do not straw too early – only when the first green fruits are seen swelling. Remove surplus runners regularly.

Weed, Pest and Disease Control

Major losses are from birds and mould. Individual bunches can be protected from both with jam jars. Netting is usually obligatory. Mould can be decreased by strawing up and removing fruits that rot, preferably before the mould goes 'fluffy'. After fruiting has finished, tidy the plants, shearing back surplus runners and dead leaves, and in winter tidy them again, removing old straw as well for composting. Aphids spread the dreaded virus diseases, so you should buy in fresh clean stock every ten years or so.

OTHER USES

As for perpetual strawberries (see p.437).

Harvesting and Storing

Strawberries must be used quickly as they only keep for a day or so – they will last better picked with a stalk. They can be juiced and made into syrup, or jammed and jellied – the addition of apple, red- or whitecurrant juice will help with the setting. If frozen they will lose their delicate texture, but are still delicious.

COMPANION PLANTING

Before establishing a new bed, dig in a green manure crop of soya beans to help prevent root rots. Growing borage, any of the beans or onions nearby reputedly helps strawberry plants.

CULINARY USES

Wimbledon Fortune
Fresh strawberries, sprinkled with sugar, cream, a shortbread biscuit or two – and a small mortgage, unless enjoyed at home!

Fragaria hybrids from the family *Rosaceae*

STRAWBERRIES
PERPETUAL AND REMONTANT

Herbaceous. 30cm (1ft). Life span: short. Self-fertile. Fruits: up to 5x2cm (2x1in), red, conical.
Value: some vitamin C and half as much iron as spinach.

The remontant or perpetual strawberries are just as much a mixture of, and very similar to, summer strawberries, except that they fruit continuously through the autumn. In fact they start to set early crops even before the summer varieties, but these are normally removed to ensure bigger crops later when the summer crowd has finished. Some have extremely good flavour, probably due to some *F. vesca* ancestry.

This particular group of strawberries has been improved far more in continental Europe than in America or the UK. Their development has been parallel to that of the summer strawberries, but with different mixes of species used in the hybridization. Most of the strawberry family are greatly affected by the day length, and this group perhaps most of all. Most strawberry varieties respond to a change from their native latitude by producing primarily runners if they move north and fruits if they move south. It would thus seem that any variety would be a perpetual fruiter if cultivated at the 'right' latitude, and that perpetual fruiters are really just summer croppers enjoying a warmer latitude than nature intended.

Strawberries do well on window ledges in full sun

'Aromel'

VARIETIES

My favourite and one of the finest flavoured is **'Aromel'**; this also does well under cover. **'Mara des Bois'** is a new French variety and is extremely well flavoured and crops well. Both of these varieties runner well. **'La Sans Rivale'**, an old French variety, and **'Hampshire Maid'** produce few runners. The Dutch have some runner-forming, climbing, remontant varieties. (They do not climb, but have to be pushed!) **'Ostara'** and **'Rabunda'** are good autumn croppers, especially if the first flowers are disbudded in the early summer months.

CULTIVATION

Remontants need the same rich, moist conditions as summer strawberries. As they crop for longer and can give higher total yields they deserve even better treatment.

Growing under Glass
These are better value grown under glass than summer strawberries, as they use the space productively for longer. They benefit most from such cover at the end of autumn. They must have good ventilation or they mould rapidly, and they are prone to red spider mite attacks. Either use the commercial predators or suffer.

Growing in Containers

These perpetuals are often recommended for growing in containers, as they are productive for far longer than summer fruiters and make better use of limited space. However, they will do much better in the ground, especially if erratic watering is a possibility!

Ornamental and Wildlife Value

Climbing varieties can be trained well over trellis and can also be quite decorative, especially when in fruit. Their long flowering period makes these plants valuable to insects, and the fruits themselves are enjoyed by both birds and rodents!

Maintenance

Spring Weed, mulch, spray with seaweed solution and deflower.
Summer Deflower, root some runners, remove rest.
Autumn Straw up and pick the fruits.
Winter Tidy bed, de-runner, plant out in late winter.

Propagation

The perpetual fruited varieties cannot be reliably propagated by seed as they are such mixed hybrids. I have tried! Runners can be rooted in pots in summer and detached. They crop significantly more easily the first year than summer fruiters. This is because when planted out they have longer to establish before the fruiting commences, whether this happens in the preceding autumn, late winter or even early spring.

Pruning and Training

Remontants are grown similarly to summer strawberries, but it pays to give them a sunny spot so their later fruits can ripen.

Weed, Pest and Disease Control

Because they have such a long season, early mouldy fruits must be rapidly and hygienically removed, or later fruits will suffer exponentially. They are more prone to moulds because of the humidity in autumn and benefit from cloches. Bird damage is less as there are plenty of other attractive fruits around.

Harvesting and Storing

Because the remontants crop late into autumn they are juicier than summer varieties, but not always so sweet, and often rot before ripening. They can be picked green if there is a hint of colouring, and are then fine for culinary use.

COMPANION PLANTING

As with other strawberries, they do well with beans and are benefited by onions and borage. Most of all they love a mulch of pine needles.

OTHER USES

Eating strawberries will supposedly whiten your teeth. Strawberry leaves have been used as a tea substitute.

Strawberry tea

CULINARY USES

They can be used just like summer strawberries, but are conveniently fresh from summer till the frosts.

Baked Strawberry Apples
Serves 4

4 cooking apples
Punnet of strawberries
A few raisins
A little sugar and butter

Wash, dry and core the apples and smear with butter. Cut a thin slice off one end to ensure they sit flat in a greased baking dish. Setting aside the four best strawberries, eat some and pass the rest through a sieve. Fill the holes in the apples with strawberry purée. Push in raisins to bring the level over the top. Finish with the reserved fruits and a sprinkling of sugar. Bake at 190°C/375°F/gas mark 5 till the apples are bursting – for approximately 20 minutes. Serve hot with custard, cream or yoghurt.

Fragaria vesca semperflorens from the family *Rosaceae*

STRAWBERRIES
ALPINE AND WILD EUROPEAN

Herbaceous. 30cm (1ft). Life span: short! Self-fertile. Fruits: up to 1x2cm (½x1in).
Value: some vitamin C.

Alpine strawberries differ from the common garden strawberries in two distinct ways. The fruits and plants are smaller and they do not form runners. The alpines form neat clumps about 30cm (12in) across, with lighter green leaves, and flower all season almost from last to first frost. The other wild (European) strawberries, *F. vesca*, and **Hautbois**, *F. elatior*/**moschata**, are more like miniature versions of garden strawberries. With smaller fruits than even the alpines, they do make runners. Indeed some of the wild woodland forms only produce runners and rarely fruit.

'Alexandria'

These wild forms were the earliest strawberries cultivated and are native to Europe, but only north of the Alps. They were thus unknown to the Ancient Greeks, and although passing reference is given to them by Roman and early medieval writers, it is as wild, not cultivated fruits. In England the fruits are mentioned during the thirteenth century in the Countess of Leicester's Household Roll. By the reign of Henry VIII the fruit was highly esteemed and cost four pence a bushel. At the same time the **Hautbois** strawberry, *F. elatior*/**moschata**, was also popular, especially on the Continent. It was one of the most fragrant of all and made few runners. The species from the Americas arrived during this period, but were considered not as good as these native wild varieties. It was not until the nineteenth century that the natives became superseded by 'modern' hybrids.

VARIETIES

Alpines are grown from seed. They are little improved on the true wild form, though yellow and white-fruited versions are available. '**Baron Solemacher**' is a slightly larger-fruited selection; it needs nearly 60cm (2 ft) of space each way. '**Alexandria**' is tastier, juicier and does better in moist half shade. Wild, runnering strawberries, known as '**Fraises des Bois**', are obtainable on the Continent as seed or plants. The **Green Strawberry**, *F. collina*/*viridis*, has sadly vanished.

'Baron Solemacher'

CULTIVATION

Alpines are easier to grow, needing less richness and moisture than other types of strawberry, though they will do much better in improved conditions. They can be spaced at 30cm (12in) or so apart. Wild strawberries are better grown as ground cover in moist partial shade and allowed to run.

Weed, Pest and Disease Control
Alpine and wild species are much tougher plants than conventional varieties and rarely suffer from pests or diseases. The fruits are also less appealing to birds, so they can often be cropped without protection.

Pruning and Training
As with other varieties and species, it is best to replace the entire stock in stages normally running over a three- or four-year period.

Growing under Glass and in Containers
Alpines can be cropped under glass to extend the season, but become more prone to red spider mite. Other wild species resent being under cover more. In pots they are easier than more conventional varieties, however, as they need less water and do not run.

'Delight' is widely available

Alpine strawberry jam

Maintenance

Spring Weed, mulch, spray thoroughly with seaweed solution monthly. Sow seed, divide runners.
Summer Pick regularly all through summer.
Autumn Remove old, worn-out plants. Divide runners if they have become invasive.
Winter Sow seed in pots in coldframe in late winter.

Ornamental and Wildlife Value

Alpines make good ground cover and are more decorative than other strawberries, as they form neat mounds. The long flowering period makes them beneficial to insects and the almost evergreen clumps are good shelter and hibernation sites.

Harvesting and Storing

They can be picked under-ripe for culinary purposes. Pick and freeze them until sufficient quantities are gathered, then shake the frozen fruits in a dry cloth and many seeds can be removed. The fruits can be made into jams, jellies, sauces, syrups and compôtes.

Propagation

As true alpines make no runners, they are grown from seed. Rub the seeds off fruits that have been left in the sun to shrivel. Sow in late winter, early spring for plants to put out in spring. Do not cover. A bottom heat of 15°C (60°F) is helpful. Later in spring the seeds can be sown without heat.

Sometimes the crowns can be successfully divided. The new plantlets can be replanted where required during the growing season.

COMPANION PLANTING

Sixteenth-century poet Thomas Tusser said:
'Gooseberries, raspberries, roses all three
With strawberries under do trimly agree.'
In the wild strawberries are sometimes found growing with vervaine.

OTHER USES

The leaves and fruit of wild strawberries can be used for medicinal purposes.

CULINARY USES

Both alpine and wild strawberries are superlatively fragrant and delicious raw, if fully ripe. Cooking brings out even more flavour, from under-ripe fruits as well. These are less moist than ordinary strawberries, so require some water or redcurrant juice to make jam or jelly. They are also firmer after freezing and go well in compôtes.

Alpine Strawberry Tarts

Make individual sweet shortcrust pastry tart cases. Smear the insides with butter, then fill each tart with a mixture of both alpine strawberries and strawberry jam (alpine or otherwise). Bake in a preheated oven for ten minutes or so at 190°C/375°F/gas mark 5. Cool and top each with clotted cream before serving.

Vaccinium species from the family *Ericaceae*

BLUEBERRIES & BILBERRIES

Bush. 30cm–4m (1–15ft). Life span: medium to long. Deciduous, self-fertile. Fruits: 1cm (¼-½in), spherical blue-black. Value: some vitamins C and B.

Bilberries, blaeberries or whortleberries, *Vaccinium myrtillus*, are low shrubs native to Europe, found on heaths and moors in acid soils. They have slender, green twigs with myrtle-like leaves and spherical pink flowers followed by blue-black fruits in late summer. They are fiddly to pick and rarely cultivated. Highbush blueberries, *V. corymbosum*, and many near relations come from North America. The **Highbush** is a tall shrub up to 4m (15ft), so lower-growing cultivars for garden use have been bred, though commercial growers still prefer the tall. Many similar species are used as ornamentals because in autumn the leaves turn to some amazing reds and pinks. The **Rabbiteye Blueberries**, *V. virgatum/ashei* are similar. The **Lowbush Blueberry**, *V. angustifolium*, is different, only about 30cm (12in) high, and is much hardier than the **Highbush**. The berries are large, sweet and early so this has been crossed with the **Highbush**.

Bilberries were once highly popular. They would be picked from the wild and taken to market in the towns where they were esteemed for tarts and jelly. They were a staple food to the Scots highlanders who ate them in milk and made them into wine. Bilberries went into oblivion when the better fruiting blueberries from America became available. Blueberries are a traditional American fruit, with different regions favouring different species, such as **Highbush**, or **Swamp**, and **Rabbiteye Blueberries** in the warmer areas and the **Lowbush**, **Early** or **Low**, **Sweet Blueberry** further north. The last was particularly useful as it was easily dried for preservation for winter. The dried berries were beaten to a powder and made into cakes with maize meal. In the north-west they even smoke-dried them for extra flavour.

VARIETIES

Most of our garden varieties are of mixed American origin. Many of the better ones were bred in Maine, where the climate is similar to that of Britain. The early **'Earliblue'**, **'Goldtraube'** and **'Jersey'** are fairly compact bushes. **'Berkeley'** is a spreader, **'Blue Crop'** more upright. All are commonly available and need planting 1.5m (5ft) apart. Many of the species have edible berries. *Vaccinium ovatum*, the **Huckleberry** or **Box**

Blueberries

Huckleberries

Blueberry is a small, attractive, evergreen shrub with tasty berries and can be used to make a hedge. The **Red Huckleberry**, **Red Bilberry**, *V. parvifolium* is a large deciduous shrub which has red fruits. *V. membranaceum*, the **Big Huckleberry**, has big berries, is fairly drought resistant and is one of the tastiest. *V. hirsutum*, the **Hairy Huckleberry** is not very hardy and has hairy fruits.

CULTIVATION

An acid soil suitable for heathers or rhododendrons is essential; a substitute of peat and leaf mould will do. The tall species prefer wetter sites, the dwarfer ones suffer drier, but all crop better with moister positions. They prefer sunny sites though they will grow in partial shade. Partly self-fertile, they do better if several varieties are grown together.

Growing under Glass
They are sufficiently hardy almost anywhere, but glass protection may be worthwhile temporarily while they fruit to prevent losses to birds.

Growing in Containers
Blueberries have to be grown in containers in many areas as they die on lime soils. Ericaceous compost or a mixture of peat, sand and leaf mould is essential as is regular, copious watering with rain or acidic water. In limy areas avoid tap water!

Ornamental and Wildlife Value
Stunning colours in autumn. There are countless ornamental species and varieties. All berry and are valuable to birds.

Maintenance
Spring Weed and mulch.
Summer Make layers, pick fruit.
Autumn Take suckers and transplant once leaves fall.
Winter Prune if necessary.

Propagation
The species come true from seed but better varieties are layered in summer. Suckers can be detached in winter.

Pruning and Training
Bilberries and blueberries need little pruning except to remove dead or diseased growth, best done in winter.

Weed, Pest and Disease Control
Apart from the usual losses to birds, this is a remarkably pest- and disease-free family. Any distress will probably be due to an alkaline soil or lime in the water supply.

Harvesting and Storing
The berries should be picked when fully ripe and easily detached or they are too acid. They may be jammed, juiced, jellied or frozen; commercially they are obtainable dried.

Highbush

COMPANION PLANTING

As these are ericaceous they grow well near heathers.

OTHER USES

The leaves were used medicinally. Chewing dried bilberries was a cure for diarrhoea and mouth and throat infections.

CULINARY USES

Blueberries and bilberries can be used in pies, tarts, jams, jellies and syrups. Blueberry cheesecake and blueberry muffins are very popular American dishes.

Blueberry Grunt
Serves 4–6

500g (1lb) blueberries
50g (2oz) sugar
1 teaspoon allspice
1 small lemon
Maple syrup to taste
125g (4oz) white flour
Pinch salt
1½ teaspoons baking powder
50g (2oz) butter
300ml (½ pt) single cream

Simmer the washed blueberries gently with sugar, spice and the lemon's juice and grated rind. Add maple syrup to taste. Meanwhile rub the flour, salt, baking powder and butter into crumbs and blend in enough cream to make a smooth creamy dough. Carefully spoon the dough on top of the blueberries, cover the pan and simmer till the crust puffs and sets. Serve with the rest of the cream and more maple syrup.

Vaccinium species from the family *Ericaceae*

CRANBERRIES AND COWBERRIES

Bush. Prostrate to 60cm (2ft). Life span: medium to long, Evergreen, self-fertile.
Fruits: up to 2cm (³/₄in), reddish-orange. Value: some vitamin C.

Cranberries are very similar and closely related to blueberries and bilberries, the most noticeable differences being that cranberries have red berries and are evergreen.

V. oxycoccus, the **cranberry**, is a native of most northern temperate countries and is found on bogs and moorlands. The low-growing, evergreen shrub is tough and wiry with long, sparsely leafed stems. The leaves are longer and thinner than those of the blue-berried *Vaccinium* species. The flowers are tiny, yellow and pink, in early summer and are followed by the round, red fruits, which are pleasantly acid to taste. The **American Cranberry**, *V. macrocarpon*, is much the same, but larger in size and berry. The **Cowberry**, **Crane** or **Foxberry**, *V. vitis idaea*, is also similar, more densely leafed, with rounded ends and clusters of berries, which are more acid and less agreeable than cranberries.

The native cranberry has been gathered from the wild in most cool regions by native peoples throughout the northern hemisphere. The cowberry has not been enjoyed so widely as it is usually too acid to eat raw, though it is excellent after cooking. Strangely the British never much liked either, although both the cranberry and cowberry were very popular in Sweden. When better North American cranberries came as a sauce to accompany the new festive dish of roast turkey, cowberries were suddenly in demand – as now they could be sold to the unwary in London as 'cranberries'.

VARIETIES

Apart from those already mentioned, there are several other *Vacciniums* that fall between cranberries and blueberries and have edible berries; *V. floribundum*, the **Mortinia**, is the least hardy and comes from Ecuador but will survive in southern England. It is an attractive, evergreen shrub with heavy racemes of rose-pink blooms followed by masses of red berries. From East Asia and Japan comes *V. praestans*, a prostrate, creeping, deciduous shrub with sweet, fragrant, glossy, red berries. *V. nummularia* is one of the choicest little evergreens for an alpine house. It resembles a prettier cowberry, with arching, hairy stems and small black berries.

Cranberry fruit

The evergreen cowberry, *V. nummularia*

CULTIVATION

These really need moist boggy conditions, in lime-free soil and water. The best sites are made on the edge of a river or pond by slowly building up a layer of stones covered with a thick layer of peaty, humus-rich, acid soil. They must be moist but not drowned; they need to stand above the water! Most are small, needing as little as 60–90cm (2–3ft) each way and even tolerating some light shade.

Growing under Glass

As the usual varieties are hardy this is only worthwhile for bird protection. *V. floribundum* and *nummularia* benefit from cool cover, such as that afforded by an alpine house, and are very beautiful small shrubs.

Growing in Containers

Cranberries have to be grown in containers in many areas as they will die on lime soils. Ericaceous compost or a mixture of peat, sand and leaf mould is essential, as is regular and copious watering with rain or acidic water. Avoid tap water in limy areas!

Ornamental and Wildlife Value

On acid soils cowberries make excellent ground cover. Cranberries are not as dense, so they suppress weeds less well. The berries are loved by wildlife and, being evergreen, the plants will provide good shelter.

Maintenance

Spring Weed, mulch, make the layers.
Summer Keep well watered.
Autumn Divide plants, pick fruit before frost.
Winter Protect less hardy species from frost.

Propagation, Pruning and Training

The species can be grown from seed, or by dividing in autumn, or they can be layered in spring. Only remedial tidying is required.

Weed, Pest and Disease Control

Cowberries and most of the denser-growing species suppress weeds well. They are all pest- and disease-free in most gardens. Grown under glass they need to be kept cool or they suffer. Any problems are most often due to lime in the soil or water. Watering on sequestrated iron chelates will help but these are not available to organic growers.

Harvesting and Storing

Cowberries are made sour by frosts so must be gathered promptly. In Siberia they were kept under water through the winter, so that they gradually became less acid, and were then eaten in spring.

OTHER USES

The leaves and fruits of most of these berries have been used medicinally, Cowberries have been eaten as a cure for diarrhoea.

CULINARY USES

Invariably used for the jelly, but also in tarts and pies and added to many other dishes.

Cranberry Jelly
Makes about 3.75kg (7lb)

500g (1lb) cranberries
750g (1½lb) apples
Approx. 2kg (4lb) sugar

Wash the fruits, chop the apples and simmer both with enough water to prevent burning. Once the apples are soft, strain and add 500g (1lb) sugar to each 600ml (1pt) of liquid.
Bring the liquid back to the boil, stirring to dissolve the sugar. Cook briefly, skim and pour into sterile warmed jars. Seal at once. Serve with roast turkey.

COMPANION PLANTING

They are ericaceous and enjoy similar conditions, root bacteria and fungi as rhododendrons and azaleas so can be used as ground cover between these.

Coralling cranberries on the surface of a bog, Massachusetts, USA

Ribes grossularia from the family *Grossulariaceae*

GOOSEBERRIES

Bush up to 1.5m (5ft). Life span: long. Deciduous, self-fertile. Fruits: up to 3cm (1in), oval, green to purple.
Value: some vitamin C.

Gooseberries you find in the shops are green bullets, for culinary use, nothing like the meltingly sweet, well-ripened dessert varieties. Compared to other *Ribes*, gooseberries have bigger, hairy berries and sharp thorns. They are easy to grow but often handicapped by being grown as a stool. Given attention and good pruning, large, succulent berries can be had, in almost any colour and with delicious flavour, which can range from a clean, acid-sweet taste to vinous plumness.

Unnoticed by Classical writers but a European native, gooseberries, *Ribes grossularia*, are first mentioned in purchases for the Westminster garden of King Edward I in 1276. They became popular almost solely in Britain, and by the nineteenth century there were hundreds of varieties, and countless clubs where members vied to grow larger fruits, achieving berries the size of bantam eggs. One variety, '**London**', an outstandingly large, not so hairy, red was the biggest exhibited every year from 1829 to 1867, 37 years unbeaten champion! The wild relation is found in rocky terrain as a small shrub, variable in berry colour, size and in habit of growth, with some being inconveniently lax. American gooseberries/ Worcesterberries are derived from *R. divaricatum*. They have smaller berries and are resistant to the American mildew disease that can damage European varieties.

Worcesterberries

VARIETIES

'**London**' (mid-season) is biggest, and dark red. I love '**Langley Gage**' (mid-season) which has divine, bite-sized, syrupy sweet, translucent white globes hanging in profusion. '**Early Sulphur**' (very early) has golden yellow, almost transparent, tasty, medium-sized berries. For a substantial, dark olive green, strongly flavoured, large berry choose '**Gunner**' (mid), though it's not a heavy cropper. '**Leveller**' (mid) is, and has delicious yellow-green fruits. The **Worcesterberry** is even meaner-thorned and is really an American species with smaller black berries more like blackcurrants. '**Pixwell**' is an improved, green-fruited form. *R. hirtellum*, the **Currant Gooseberry**, is another edible American species with small reddish fruits.

'Langley Gage' in flower

CULTIVATION

Gooseberries love rich, moist, loamy soil and do not like hot, dry, sandy sites or stagnant air, doing better with a breeze.

Growing under Glass and in Containers

Gooseberries are so hardy they need no protection, and they are too thorny as well. They can be potted, but are easier in the ground.

Ornamental and Wildlife Value

The bushes are drab, the flowers inconspicuous and the berries not brightly coloured – the ideal landscaping plant to go with modern buildings! The flowers benefit early insects and the berries disappear.

Maintenance

Spring Weed, mulch, spray seaweed solution monthly.
Summer Thin and pick fruit, watch out for sawfly and mildew.
Autumn Take cuttings.
Winter Prune hard.

Propagation

Gooseberries are propagated by 30cm (1ft) long cuttings. Disbud the lower end to prevent suckers.

Pruning and Training

Often misgrown as a stool with many shoots direct from the ground, gooseberries are better hard pruned to spurs on a goblet-shaped frame with a short leg. I leave the pruning till late winter so that the thorns protect the buds from the birds, which perversely delight in disbudding gooseberries. To get larger berries or more varieties in a confined space, gooseberries may easily be grown as vertical cordons, fans or even standards.

Weed, Pest and Disease Control

American mildew is the worst problem, burning tips and felting fruits with a leathery coat that dries them up. Hygiene, moist roots, hard pruning and good air circulation reduce the damage. Sodium bicarbonate sprays and

'London'

sulphur-based ones (which burn some varieties) are available to organic growers. Occasionally, often in the third year or so after planting, gooseberries suffer damage from sawfly caterpillars. First appearing as a host of wee holes in a leaf, they move on to stripping the bush. However, vigilance and early action prevent serious damage.

Harvesting and Storing

Gooseberries do not have as much bird appeal as many fruits and can even be got unripe without protection. Birds and wasps do steal them once they're ripe, otherwise the fruits mellow and hang on till late summer if protected from such pests and damp.

COMPANION PLANTING

Tomatoes and broad beans nearby are reputed to aid them and I always grow them with *Limnanthes douglasii* as ground cover.

OTHER USES

Gooseberries make a powerful wine much like that of the grape.

CULINARY USES

Picked small and green, they make the most delicious acid jams and tarts – which turn red if overcooked. As they ripen they become less acid and fuller flavoured for dessert purposes. Ripe fruits for cooking combine well with redcurrants to keep up the acidity and are often jellied to remove the tough skins and seeds.

Gooseberry Fool
Serves 4

500g (1lb) ripe green gooseberries
Approx. 75g (3oz) light honey or sugar
300ml (½pt) thick cream
Dark chocolate and grated nutmeg to garnish

If the gooseberries are soft, press them through a sieve. If not, warm very carefully till soft first, or freeze and defrost first. Add sweetening to the puree to taste, and cool. Immediately before serving, whip the cream and fold in the purée. Garnish with grated dark chocolate and nutmeg.

Ribes nigrum from the family *Grossulariaceae*

BLACKCURRANTS

Bush, 1.5m (5ft). Life span: short. Deciduous, self-fertile.
Fruits: 1–2cm (up to ¹/₂in), black, spherical. Value: very rich in vitamin C.

Blackcurrants are quite different to the other types of *Ribes*, though they are often bundled in with redcurrants. They fruit on young wood, not old, and have dark purple, almost black, berries with a most distinct and unforgettable aroma, which is similar to that of the aromatic foliage and stems.

These, like other *Ribes*, seem to have been unknown to the Ancient Greeks or Romans and were only used medicinally, as quinsy berries, for curing colds and throat problems until the sixteenth century. Then they became more popular as a garden crop and are now very widely grown commercially in Europe, but not so much in the USA. Their rise in fame was due to their very high vitamin C content, and probably also to the fact that sugar, needed to make this naturally sour fruit palatable, became available more cheaply. The native plants can occasionally be found in wild wet areas of northern Europe and Asia, but are now more likely to be garden escapes. Improvement has been done mostly by selection rather than producing hybrids with other *Ribes*, though the **Josta** is a good example of what is possible.

VARIETIES

New varieties such as **'Ben Sarek'** (mid-season), **'Ben Lomond'** (late) and **'Ben More'** (very late) are numerous and generally more productive, with better disease resistance, than old favourites. **'Laxton's Giant'** (mid) is still one of the biggest, and **'Seabrook's Black'** (mid) is supposedly resistant to big bud. The **Josta** berry is a much larger hybrid, more like a thornless gooseberry, with heavy crops of large blackcurrant-flavoured berries. Some American species have been esteemed, such as the

'Ben More'

fragrant, bright-yellow-flowered **Buffalo Currant** or **Golden Currant**, *R. aureum/ odoratum*, which is also used as the stock for standard gooseberries. *R. americanum*, **American Blackcurrant**, has yellowish flowers and inferior fruit, but turns glorious colours in autumn.

CULTIVATION

Blackcurrants revel in rich, moist ground, the richer the better, and similarly respond to heavy mulching. They do not mind light shade. Late varieties are usually chosen to avoid frost damage during their flowering period.

Growing under Glass and in Containers
The bushes prefer to be cool so they are not happy for long under cover. They can be grown and fruited successfully in large pots.

Ornamental and Wildlife Value
Rather dingy plants of little decorative appeal, though the smell of foliage and stems is most pleasing. However the currants are as valuable to birds as to us and thus good subjects for wild gardens.

Maintenance
Spring Weed, mulch, spray seaweed solution monthly.
Summer Protect and pick fruits.
Autumn Take cuttings.
Winter Prune back hard and compost heavily.

Propagation
There are no easier cuttings! As blackcurrants are best grown as a stool, the main requirement is for multiple shoots from ground level. Thus cuttings have all buds left on and new bushes are planted deeper than is the standard practice for almost every other subject.

Pruning and Training
In order to provide as much young fruitful wood as possible, the optimum pruning is to remove annually all shoots from a one-third segment of the stool. The lazy and less effective way is just to cut back one third totally, preferably of three or more, of the bushes once every three years.

Weed, Pest and Disease Control
Weeds must be kept from encroaching on the stool, but rarely germinate there because of the intense shade. Birds are not so much of a problem, but will eat the currants eventually unless prevented. Mildew is aggravated by stagnant air and dry roots; hygienic pruning and vigorous growth is usually sufficient redress. Big bud is obvious. It is caused by microscopic pests that also carry virus diseases such as reversion. The simple solution is to replace old infected stock with new clean material after ten or fifteen years or when yields have dropped too far.

'Ben Lomond'

Harvesting and Storing
Blackcurrants will keep for several days once picked as they are so firm and tough-skinned. They can be frozen, jammed, jellied and turned into delicious syrups and juices.

COMPANION PLANTING

Nettles nearby benefit blackcurrants. In some parts of the USA blackcurrants may not be grown as they are host to white pine blister rust.

OTHER USES

The leaves have been used as tea for medicinal and tonic purposes and dried currants likewise, especially for throat infections.

CULINARY USES

The currants have too little liquid to simmer down on their own, so need water or other juices. Add redcurrant juice to make blackcurrant jams and dishes more pleasantly acid. Jelly is easier work than jam as de-sprigging the berries is tedious.

Bob's Cunning Blackcurrant Jam
Makes about 3kg (6½lb)

1.5kg (3lb) blackcurrants
500g (1lb) redcurrants
A little water
Approx. 2kg (4lb) sugar

De-sprig the best quarter of the blackcurrants and set aside. Simmer the rest with the redcurrants and just enough water to cover, till they are soft. Strain, reserving the juice. Cover the pulp with water, boil up again and strain off another lot of juice. Weigh the combined juices, add reserved blackcurrants and two-thirds of the juice's weight in sugar. Bring to the boil, stirring until the sugar has dissolved. Boil briefly, skim and pour into warm sterilized jars. Cover the jars immediately.

Aronia melanocarpa from the family *Rosaceae*

CHOKEBERRIES

Bush, up to 2m (7ft). Life span: medium. Deciduous, self-fertile.
Fruits: 2cm (½in), spherical, black. Value: very rich in vitamin C.

With a name like chokeberry you can be sure the fruits are astringent and sour raw, though fine cooked and sweetened. They are hard, red, ripening to purple or almost lustrous black. They closely resemble blackcurrants in appearance and even in taste, though are more acid and almost pine-flavoured, making them a useful substitute where blackcurrants may not be grown, such as in some parts of their native USA. The bushes are easy to grow, reliable, highly productive, and compact with a height and spread of about 1.5m (5ft). White, hawthorn-like flowers and brilliant autumn leaf colours make this a most decorative fruit bush.

Distantly related to the pear and *Sorbus* genus, these berries came from eastern North America in 1700. They were relished by native Americans who would mix the dried fruits with others to make 'cakes' for winter storage, but it was the autumn colouring that recommended them to European plantsmen. The Royal Horticultural Society Award of Merit was eventually granted in 1972, but still rather for their ornamental appeal than their taste. They are a fruit with great potential. I'm sure they would do better if called the tastyberry!

The dramatic autumn foliage of the 'Brilliant' chokeberry

VARIETIES

Aronia melanocarpa, **'Viking'** is available as bushes for fruit production and is self-fertile. Another similar cultivar of *A. melanocarpa*, **'Brilliant'**, is available but for ornamental plantings because it has exceptionally good autumn leaf colouring. *A. arbutifolia*, the **Red Chokeberry**, also has good autumn colour and produces red berries that were eaten by native American children for their aroma rather than for their taste. There is also a more erect form.

CULTIVATION

Chokeberries are easy and do well on any reasonable soil other than very shallow chalk or in very boggy ground. Naturally they will respond to better conditions by becoming larger and more prolific, and are happier with well-mulched peaty conditions. The bushes need to be 2m (7ft) apart for effective cropping, but possibly closer for massed displays of berries and autumn colour.

Maintenance
Spring Weed, mulch and spray with seaweed solution.
Summer Net to keep birds off and pick the fruit.
Autumn Prune out dead and diseased growths, take cuttings.
Winter Mulch with compost and straw, leaf mould or bark.

Propagation
The species come true from seed but named varieties are best reproduced from early autumn cuttings or division.

Pruning and Training
They can tend to sucker, turning them into a stool, but cultivation is easier if they are kept to a single stem. Pruning is mostly remedial, removing suckering, low growing,

'Viking'

congested and diseased growths. I suspect chokeberries would be good trained on wires or a wall – they would certainly be most decorative.

Weed, Pest and Disease Control

Other than the usual hazards of choking weeds and losses to the birds, these plants are remarkably free from problems. One reason chokeberries are coming into cultivation is that they are as good a source of vitamin C as blackcurrants, but also more productive, with none of their potential problems of big bud, reversion or mildew.

Growing under Glass and in Containers

There seems no need to grow chokeberries under glass as they thrive outdoors and are of little value fresh, only tasty once preserved. However, it is worth growing them in a container if you need a rich source of vitamin C and have no garden space available.

Ornamental and Wildlife Value

The tough reliability, the profusion of spring flowers, immense quantities of glossy black berries and the colour of the autumn leaves make this an essential plant for any area, ornamental or wild, especially if you like birds.

Harvesting and Storing

Chokeberries ripen in midsummer but the flavour improves if they are left to hang. They will need good bird protection. The best and only sensible means of storage is turning them into preserves.

Chokeberries ripening on the bush

COMPANION PLANTING

No good or bad companions are yet recognized as they have been little cultivated. I grow mine in a bed with rhubarb and seakale.

OTHER USES

The berries can be used for an edible dye and I can vouch for their being a high-vitamin self-service food for my poultry, who head for them whenever they get out.

CULINARY USES

They can be used in the same way as blackcurrants and indeed taste not dissimilar, if more piney and aromatic. However their preserve goes better with savoury dishes in the manner of cranberry jelly.

Chokeberry preserve

1kg (2lb) chokeberries
500g (1lb) whitecurrants or redcurrants if white unavailable
1 small lemon
A little water
Approx.1kg (2lb) sugar

Thoroughly wash the berries and currants, chop the lemon and simmer all three with just sufficient water to cover. Simmer till soft then sieve out the skins and pips, weigh the juice and return it to the pan with three-quarters of its weight in sugar. Bring to the boil. Skim well, then pot in small jars. Store for six months before use. Serve with gammon steak, new potatoes and peas.

Ornamental and Wildlife Value

Cultivated raspberries are not very ornamental themselves and the fruit does not last long enough to be called a display! Some of the species are more decorative, and scented, so are worth considering, but are nowhere near as productive as modern fruiting varieties. The birds adore raspberries and will get to them anywhere, so they are good in wild gardens. However, you have a duty to others to eradicate the berries when they become virus-infected. The flowers are very beneficial to bees and other insects.

Maintenance (Summer Fruiters)

Spring Weed, mulch heavily, spray seaweed solution at monthly intervals.
Summer Protect and pick fruit, thin shoots.
Autumn Cut out old canes, tie in the new.
Winter Add copious quantities of compost.

A spray of raspberry flowers

Maintenance (Autumn Fruiters)

Spring Weed, mulch heavily, spray seaweed solution monthly, thin the shoots as they emerge.
Summer Tie in canes.
Autumn Protect and pick the fruit.
Winter Cut all canes to the ground, add copious compost to soil.

Propagation

Varieties are multiplied by transplanting any piece of root with a bud or young cane in the autumn. Pot-grown ones may be planted in spring. Summer fruiters should not be cropped the first year but built up first; autumn fruiters may be cropped if they were well established early in the previous autumn. I have found seed can provide very vigorous and productive, if variable, plants, but it is a better plan to buy new, named cultivars.

Pruning and Training

Too lax to be left free, they are best restrained by growing between pairs of wires or winding the tips around horizontal ones. Alternatively, they can be grown as tripods, with three well-spaced stools being joined to an apex. Pruning for summer raspberries is done in autumn; remove all old canes that have fruited or died and fix the new ones in place, selecting the biggest and strongest at about 12cm (5in) apart. (It helps to pre-thin these when the shoots emerge in early summer.) Autumn fruiters are easier still: just cut everything to the ground in late winter. (Pre-thinning the canes in spring is again quite advantageous.)

Japanese wineberry (see pp.462–3), a raspberry/ blackberry hybrid

The 'Malling Jewel' raspberry – training canes

Weed, Pest and Disease Control

Weeding must be done carefully because of their shallow roots. Thick mulching is almost essential. Birds are the major cause of lost crops – no protection, no fruit! The raspberry beetle can be controlled with hygiene and mulching (methodically rake thick mulches aside in winter to allow birds to eat the pupae) or the use of permitted sprays if necessary. These maggots are rarely a problem with autumn fruiters. Virus diseases may appear, mottling the leaves with yellow and making the plants less productive. Replacing the stock and moving the site is the only practical solution, but wait till the yields have dropped.

Interveinal yellowing is a reaction to alkaline soils; seaweed solution sprays with added magnesium sulphate are a palliative. Compost and mulching provide the most effective cure.

Harvesting and Storing

Pick gently, leaving the plug; if it won't come easily, do not force it! They do not keep for long if they are wet, and less still if warm. If you want to keep them longest, cut the fruiting stalks with scissors and do not touch the fruits. They must be processed or eaten within a matter of hours as they are one of the least durable or transportable fruits. Those sold commercially are the toughest – and obviously also the least meltingly sumptuous!

COMPANION PLANTING

They reputedly benefit from tansy, garlic or marigolds and strawberries may be grown close by but not underneath them. Do not grow potatoes nearby as they will then become more prone to blight.

OTHER USES

Raspberry canes are bristly if not thorny. They have little strength or heat value but can be useful for wildlife shelters. I find short lengths, bundled together, then 'Swiss rolled' in newspaper and jammed into a cut-open plastic bottle, will make superb dry but airy ladybird hibernation quarters which I hide in evergreen shrubs. Raspberry leaves and fruits have been used medicinally, and have often traditionally been used as a tea.

Raspberry tea

Interwoven raspberry canes are easy to net and need no wires

CULINARY USES

Raspberries make wonderful juices, jellies, drinks and sorbets. They are often combined with redcurrant juice to add tartness. Their wine is delicate and beautifully coloured. Raspberries can be frozen, but have poor texture afterwards.

Kitty Topping's Raspberry Conserve
Makes about 2kg (4lb)

1kg (2lb) freshly picked raspberries
1kg (2lb) caster sugar

Pick fresh raspberries and hurry straight to the kitchen. Wash them and immediately heat them in a closed pan, rapidly but gently, swirling the pan to prevent sticking and burning. Once most berries have softened, but before they break down totally, add the same weight of pre-warmed caster sugar. Stir while heating. One minute after you are absolutely sure all the sugar has completely dissolved, pour into small, heated jars and seal. Keep in the cool and use quickly once opened as the aim of this recipe is the stunning flavour, not keeping quality. Try to use freshly picked fruit!

Growing under Glass and in Containers

They are so easy outside it would be bizarre to grow them under cover. Blackberries do not like the cramped conditions pots afford, and as most of them are thorny they are seldom grown this way. The thornless ones are still too vigorous to thrive in any reasonable pot.

Ornamental and Wildlife Value

The fruiting species are delightful in flower, with a mass of blossom in early summer, and there are many ornamental varieties and species though most are too vigorous for modern gardens. Their vast quantity of blossom is valuable for bees and other insects and the fruit is an immense feast for wildlife, fattening up the bird population for the winter. The thicket of the bushes makes a snug, dry home for many small creatures, from ladybirds and beetles up to small rodents and birds.

Maintenance

Spring Weed, mulch, spray seaweed solution.
Summer Tie in new shoots.
Autumn Root tips or cut off, pick fruit.
Winter Prune, add copious amounts of compost.

Weed, Pest and Disease Control

Remarkably tough and reliable, blackberries pose few problems. Even the birds find it hard to eat them as fast as they are produced. Weeds can get into the stool but rarely succeed for long as the brambles are so vigorous a weed themselves.

Propagation

Seedlings come up everywhere, but are variable. The tips readily root and form new plants in the few weeks at the end of summer and into autumn. At this time, make sure the tips go into pots of compost if you want extra plants, or cut them off if not.

Pruning and Training

Blackberries can fruit on wood older than one year old and the canes do not always die, as with raspberries. However the new wood is better and carries fewer pests and diseases so it is best to cut all the old and dead wood out and tie in the new. The canes are much longer and carry heavier loads than raspberries so strong supports are necessary. The young canes need tying in during summer. If new plants are not needed they are best de-tipped in late summer to stop them from rooting wherever they hit the ground.

Harvesting and Storing

Traditionally blackberries are picked as they ripen, from late summer up until Michaelmas, or the first frost, when the Devil was supposed to have spat on them and made them sour. They are unusable red but turn soft to the touch as they blacken. 'Bedford Giant' ripens one berry in each bunch way ahead of the others. The berries are fairly tough-skinned, so can travel and last longer than raspberries if picked dry and not so overloaded that they pack down. They are best used as soon as possible or frozen; the spoilt texture when they defrost is no problem if they are to be used in cooking anyway.

COMPANION PLANTING

Blackberries benefit from tansy or stinging nettles nearby and they are a good companion and sacrificial crop for grapevines.

Blackberry flowers and fruits

CULINARY USES

Blackberries are often too sour to eat raw but once cooked they are much tastier and do not have such a deleterious effect on one's insides. They make excellent jams, though, as they are rather seedy, the jelly is more often made. Frequently apples are included in blackberry dishes, especially jams and jellies, to aid setting and also because the flavours combine so lusciously. Blackberry wine is made by country folk everywhere and the berries used to be added to wines and spirits to give a distinctive colour, such as with the Red Muscat of Toulon.

Bob's Blackberry and Apple Pancake Supreme
Serves 4

*Approx 300ml (¹/₂pt) pancake
  batter*
250g (8oz) blackberries
Golden syrup to taste
Water
30g (1oz) cornflour
A little milk
2 apples
Knob of butter
*Sugar, lemon juice, lots of cream
  or yoghurt*

Prepare the pancake batter and set aside. Wash the blackberries and simmer with golden syrup till soft. Strain, reserving the juice, and keep the fruit warm. To the juice add enough water to make it up to 200ml (6fl oz), return to the heat and bring to the boil. Cream the cornflour in a little milk, pour it into the boiling blackberry juice, stirring all the time, and cook until the juice thickens. Set aside.
  Peel, core and chop the apples into chunks. Heat them rapidly with a little butter till they start to crumble at the edges, then

remove from the heat and keep warm. Next preheat a grill and a frying pan. Oil the pan. Once it is smoking, pour in all the pancake batter. As the bottom sets, but while the top is still liquid, take the pan off the heat, rapidly spoon in apple chunks, blackberry blobs and stripes of sauce. Swirl slightly so that the liquid batter blends a little but does not mix or cover completely. Sprinkle sugar generously over the top, then lemon juice and put under the red hot grill. Serve immediately the top has caramelized. This goes well with yoghurt or cream.

OTHER USES

Brambles make a secure and quick barrier to many four-legged animals, and to

Bob's Blackberry and Apple Pancake Supreme

two-legged rats. There are few in the world who will try to come over or through a fence or hedge clothed in any of this thorny bunch. 'Himalayan Giant' is so big and tough it will stop almost anything between the size of a rabbit and that of a tank! The prunings are vicious but do burn well and fiercely.

Rubus hybrids from the family *Rosaceae*

LOGANBERRIES

BOYSENBERRIES AND TAYBERRIES

Bush/vine. Life span: medium. Deciduous, mostly self-fertile.
Fruits: 6x2cm (2x³/₄in). Value: some vitamin C.

The loganberry resembles a blackberry in manner of growth, but the fruits are more like raspberries: cylindrical, dull red and firm, with a more acid flavour than either, making them sour raw but exquisite cooked. Boysenberry fruits are sweeter, more blackberry-like, larger and reddish-purple. They can be savoured raw with cream but also make the celebrated jam. The tayberry is bigger and sweeter than either, with an aromatic flavour. When fully ripe, the enormous loganberry-like fruits are dark wine red or purple and nearly three times the size of most other berries.

Loganberries were reputedly a hybrid of American dewberry and raspberry, raised by a Judge Logan of California in 1882. Introduced to Britain in 1897, loganberries have remained the supreme culinary berry for nearly a century. The boysenberry has a similar history. It is believed to be another hybrid dewberry but in fact is probably a youngberry x loganberry. It is not as hardy as other hybrids and does better in a warmer site than the rest. The **Medana Tayberry** was developed by the Scottish Crop Research Institute who crossed the Oregon blackberry **'Aurora'** with a tetraploid raspberry to produce this excellent fruit. It is outstandingly the best of all hybrids so far.

Tayberries

VARIETIES

There are several varieties and many other similar hybrids. The **Thornless Loganberry 'LY59'** is often thorny; the fruit does not pull off the plug easily, but it is a very heavy cropper and has a good flavour. The totally thornfree **'L654'** is better picking but is not quite as productive. I similarly find the **Thornless**

Boysenberry not as good a cropper as the thorned. There is now a thornfree **Tayberry**. The **Tummelberry** is like a late tayberry. The **Marionberry** and the **Youngberry** have the habit and appearance of blackberries but the fruits have more flavour. The **Youngberry**, sometimes called the **Young Dewberry**, is available as a thornless version. The **Black Loganberry** is a New Zealand variety; it has cylindrical, tapering fruits, and is slow to establish and crop. The **Black Raspberry** is close to the **American Black Raspberry**, *R. occidentalis*, in habit and fruit. The **Laxtonberry** has a round, raspberry-like fruit and is not self-fertile. The **Veitchberry** is a blackberry crossed with an autumn-fruiting raspberry, more mulberry-like, with a later fruiting season than that of other hybrids and large sweet fruits.

Thornless loganberries

CULTIVATION

The hybrids all need much the same, cool conditions and rich moist soils. The boysenberry will cope with drier sites and indeed prefers some shelter. They are generally quite happy on a cool shady wall if they have a moist root run.

Growing under Glass and in Containers

They prefer cool, shady positions so find the dry heat under glass too much and become prone to pests such as red spider mite. Generally needing a bigger, cooler root run than can be afforded in a pot, they will resent the confinement, sulk and crop poorly.

Ornamental and Wildlife Value

Not very useful ornamentally, and thorny, but their flowers and fruits are valuable in the wild garden, bridging the gap between raspberries and blackberries well.

Maintenance

Spring Weed, mulch and spray seaweed solution at monthly intervals.
Summer Protect and pick fruit, tie in new canes.
Autumn Root tips in pots or cut them off.
Winter Cut out old canes and tie in the new, add copious compost.

Propagation

As these are hybrids, they will not come true from seed, though interesting results may be had. Tips can be rooted in late summer and early autumn and occasionally the roots can be successfully divided.

Pruning and Training

They grow much like blackberries but can have more brittle canes, like raspberries, so care must be taken when bending them. They mostly fruit on young wood which dies and is cleared completely after the second year. Canes may produce again a third year, as blackberries might, but are usually unproductive, so annual replacement of all the old by new is generally considered a better policy.

Weed, Pest and Disease Control

The only common major problem is bird losses, which are high as these plants mostly crop after the summer fruits but before the wild blackberries. Weeds choking the stool can reduce their vigour more than with blackberries.

Tayberries

Boysenberries

COMPANION PLANTING

Tansy, marigolds and alliums are all beneficial.

OTHER USES

These canes will make good additional barriers with fences and hedges.

CULINARY USES

Generally best flavoured when fully ripe, these fruits are not very acid and benefit from the addition of redcurrant juice to many recipes. Varieties from which the plug is not easily removed, or which even detach a thorny stalk with the fruit, are best used by straining or juicing them first. These fruits make excellent jams, jellies, tarts and pies. The juices are delicious as drinks and make wonderful sorbets.

Summerberry Squash
Makes about 2.5l (4pts)

1kg (2lb) mixed berries
500g (1lb) redcurrants
1kg (2lb) sugar
1l (1³/₄pts) water

Wash the fruits and simmer them down with half the water till soft, then strain. Cover the fruit pulp with the rest of the water, bring almost to boiling point, and strain again. Combine the strained juices and the sugar, heating gently if necessary to make sure the sugar dissolves completely. Cool, then pour into plastic bottles when cold and freeze till required. Defrost and dilute with water to taste.

Rubus species from the family *Rosaceae*

JAPANESE WINEBERRIES
AND RUBUS SPECIES

Bush/vine. Life span: medium to long. Deciduous, self-fertile.
Fruits: variable. Value: some vitamin C.

Rubus phoenicolasius, the Japanese wineberry is the best of the vast raspberry/blackberry clan. This delicious and highly ornamental cane fruit resembles a vigorous raspberry covered with russet bristles and thorns. Unlike blackberries, these prick rather than jab so are more pleasant to handle and pick. The fruits are smaller than blackberries, orange to cherry red, and they are generally far more palatable.

Japanese wineberries are not a hybrid but a true species coming from North China and Japan. They certainly do come true, as you will find as they appear all over the garden once the birds spread the seed. Introduced to Britain around 1876, Japanese wineberries were considered worth cultivating and won a First Class Certificate from the Royal Horticultural Society in 1894. During the century since, however, they have not proved popular except with children of all ages who are lucky enough to find them.

VARIETIES

There are no named varieties of any of these species, though there is some variation in leaf and fruit colour so there is scope for improvement. *R. leucodermis*, **Blackcap**, has thorny, bluish stems with light green leaves, white underneath, on a medium-size bush, small white flowers and purple-black sweet fruits with a plum-like bloom. Yellow- and red- fruited forms occur in its native North-west America. Another, *R. parviflorus*, the **Thimbleberry**, has large, fragrant, white flowers on strong, thornless stems and large, flattened, insipid, red berries. *R. parvifolius*, the **Australian Bramble**, was fruited in England in 1825 and has small, pink, tasty, juicy berries. The **Salmonberry**, *R. spectabilis*, has maroon red flowers on prickly erect stems and acid orange-yellow fruits. Apparently native Americans ate the cooked young shoots. *R. arcticus*, the **Arctic** or **Crimson Bramble**, has amber-coloured fruits that are said to taste of pineapple. Very unusual is the **Rock** or **Roebuck Bramble**, *R. saxatilis*, which grows just like strawberry plants, and is eaten in much the same way. The Russians used to distill a spirit from the berries.

CULTIVATION

Although they will grow almost anywhere, the biggest berries come from plants growing in rich, moist soil well enriched with compost and leaf mould. They will grow in moderate shade or full sun and are self-fertile.

Best grown on a wire fence or wired against a wall, after the manner of blackberries, they need a spacing of at least 3–4m (10ft) apart and wires to at least 2m (7ft) in height. Like most fruits, they do best when grown in well-mulched, clean soil, but will still produce when grassed down around.

Growing under Glass

These are mostly so easy to grow outside that there is little advantage to having them under glass except to extend the season.

Growing in Containers

Growing them in pots will shorten their life and give greatly reduced yields, but it may be well worthwhile for both their snack and their garnishing value.

Ornamental and Wildlife Value

Japanese wineberry leaves are a striking light green, with russet bristled stems, bright orangey-red fruits and a star-shaped calyx left afterwards. They are highly decorative – probably the best fruiting plant to train against a whitewashed wall or up a pole for all-year-round interest and colour. Their value to wildlife is as immense as that of the whole clan.

Maintenance

Spring Weed, mulch, spray seaweed solution.
Summer Protect and pick fruit, tie in canes.
Autumn Pick the fruit and tie in canes.
Winter Cut out old canes, tie in the new, add copious quantities of compost.

Propagation

These are species, so they come true from seed and the tips can be layered in late summer and early autumn. Remove the old canes and tie in the new each autumn. Plants have a long life if cared for. Prune out any infections early.

Weed, Pest and Disease Control

Choking and climbing weeds such as nettles and bindweed must be well controlled. There are no major problems other than the birds.

Harvesting and Storing

Japanese wineberries are one of the most delicious of all fruits eaten fresh and also in quantity, though they will keep for a while in the cool of a refrigerator.

COMPANION PLANTING

Tansy, garlic and French and pot marigolds are all potential good companions.

OTHER USES

Their dense growth and prickly bristles make them attractive but impenetrable informal boundaries.

CULINARY USES

Very valuable as garnishing for sweet and savoury dishes and simply eating off the plant. Some berries can be frozen to add to mixed fruit compôtes. Japanese wineberry jelly does not set, but forms a treacly syrup, ideal to accompany ice-cream.

Wineberry Ripple
Serves 6

1kg (2lb) Japanese wineberries
Approx 500g (1lb) sugar
1kg (2lb) superb vanilla ice-cream

Freeze a few berries for garnishing. Simmer the rest till soft with just enough water to prevent sticking. Strain and weigh the juice. Thoroughly dissolve three-quarters of the juice's weight in sugar in the warm juice. Leave to cool completely. Once cooled, interleave scoops of ice-cream with the syrup, pressing it all down into a new container. Freeze the new rippled block and then scoop as required, garnishing with the frozen berries.

A cluster of Japanese wineberries

Vitis vinifera from the family *Vitaceae*

GRAPEVINES

Vine, up to any height. Life span: long. Deciduous, self-fertile.
Fruits: 2–3 cm (1in), ovoid, white, black, red. Value: generally beneficial.

These scrambling vines have smooth, peeling, brown stems, large lobed leaves and bunches of grapes in autumn. The flowers are so insignificant they are rarely noticed but are white and sweet scented. The leaves colour well in autumn; red-berrying varieties tend to go red and white ones yellow.

Grapes have been with us since Biblical times; Noah planted a vineyard. The Egyptians show full details of vineyards and wine-making in their relics from 2440 BC. The Romans spread vines all over Europe until, in the first century AD, Emperor Domitian protected his home market and ordered the extirpation of the grape from Britain, France and Spain. Two centuries later, Emperor Probus restored the vine and long after the Roman Empire collapsed the monasteries kept vineyards going. By the time of the Domesday Book, in the eleventh century, there were still thirty-eight vineyards in Britain. But the climate was cooling and the last UK vineyards disappeared in the eighteenth century. During the nineteenth century grapes were widely grown in glasshouses and the Victorians raised grape cultivation to perfection, almost year round, in hothouses. Without the cheap labour and even cheaper fuel of Victorian times these hothouse grapes disappeared – though some survived, unproductive, on the sunny walls left when the glass had long gone. Since the Second World War there has been a revival of British viticulture and the vineyards are returning. Of course in Europe the grape has remained part of life, and in 1494 was already being grown in the New World. Over the last centuries the vine spread to almost every part of the world. Now most grapes are grown on American roots to prevent *Phylloxera* root aphids.

'Golden Chasselas'

'Boskoop Glory'

VARIETIES

Specific grapes for growing under glass or for wine-making are recommended in the next sections. The **Zante** or **Currant grape** is nearly seedless. Introduced in 1855, it helped to make the Californian fruit industry, but is unsuitable in cooler regions. The hardiest and best grapes I have found for growing outside in a cool English climate are **'Boskoop Glory'**, a delicious, large-berried, dark purple grape; the **'Strawberry Grape'**, which produces rose-purple bunches in abundance, with a hint of American foxiness to them; and **'Siegerrebe'**, which has a rosé fruit with a sweet muscat flavour.

CULTIVATION

Grapevines are very easy to grow. They are usually too vigorous and do not need rich conditions to crop well. They need a hot, dry autumn to ripen well and thus are usually best grown on walls in cooler regions.

Ornamental and Wildlife Value

Grapevines are quick to climb over and hide objects and turn bright colours in autumn, so they are valuable where space allows them to ramble. In the wild garden grapevines are useful in both flower and fruit.

Growing under Glass and in Containers

These are so advantageous there is a further section on pages 468–9.

Maintenance

Spring Weed, mulch and spray with seaweed solution at monthly intervals.
Summer Tie in and later nip out ends of shoots.
Autumn Protect and pick the fruit.
Winter Prune back hard.

Propagation

In the UK we have no *Phylloxera* so we can grow grapes on their own roots; any ripe cutting will root in autumn. Otherwise they are budded on resistant rootstocks.

Pruning and Training

There are many ways to prune grapes and many sub-variations, enough to fill a book on their own. Left to themselves vines often produce rank growth and exhaust themselves with overcropping; see sections on pages 467, 469 and 471.

Netting is essential to keep birds off the grapes

Weed, Pest and Disease Control

Birds are the main cause of losses! Mould can be common in damp ripening seasons and mildews in dry ones. There are organic sprays to combat these but often the more resistant varieties crop unaided. The vine weevil may appear and is best treated with traps and by applying a parasitic nematode solution.

Harvesting and Storing

Kept cool and dry, the grapes hang on the vines well. Cut bunches with a stalk, place the stalk in a bottle of water and keep the grapes in a cool, dry cellar for weeks. The less they are handled the better they will keep!

COMPANION PLANTING

Traditionally grown over elm or mulberry trees, grapevines are benefited by blackberries, sage, mustard and hyssop growing nearby and inhibited by cabbages, radish, Cypress spurge and even by laurels.

'Strawberry Grape'

CULINARY USES

The best are excellent dessert fruits. They are easily juiced and the juice can be frozen for year-round use. They make good jellies and any surplus can be used for wine.

Love Nests
Per person

Individual meringue case
Approx 6 large dessert grapes, preferably muscat

Marzipan, apricot conserve, clotted cream and dark chocolate to taste

Peel and seed all but one grape per portion and fill each with a pellet of marzipan. Smear the meringue bases with apricot conserve, then a layer of cream. Press in the filled grapes, cover with more cream, top with grated black chocolate and the perfect grape. Serve the nests immediately.

Vitis species from the family *Vitaceae*

GRAPEVINE SPECIES

Vine. Life span: long-lived.   Deciduous, sometimes self-fertile.
Fruit: up to 2cm/³/₄in, in bunches, red or black

There are hundreds of true grapes, or *Vitis* species, which are mostly ornamental climbing vines. (Very closely resembling them are the *Ampelopsis* and *Parthenocissus*, of which the most common are known as **Virginia Creepers**. These resemble grapevines and even form bunches, which are not edible.) These *Vitis* species are much grown for their covering capacity as they soon hide eyesores, and for their spectacular autumn colour. The fruits are often considered a bonus, but offer different and exciting flavours.

Although the *Vitis vinifera* varieties are almost exclusively used for commercial purposes and wine-making there are countless other *Vitis* species grapes eaten throughout the world, and have been since time immemorial. Their blood has also influenced the *V. vinifera* varieties on many occasions. These are but a few.

VARIETIES

Vitis aestivalis, the **Summer**, **Bunch** or **Pigeon Grape** is from North America. It has heart-shaped leaves, downy underneath, scented flowers and early black grapes. It was first seen in Europe in 1656. *V. labrusca*, the **Plum**, **Skunk** or **Fox Grape** is another first brought to Europe in 1656. Its young shoots are covered in down and the leaves are thick, dark green on top, ageing to pink underneath. The fruits are rounded, blackish purple and have a distinctive musk or fox flavour which some dislike. I enjoy it but not in wine! It has given rise to several good cultivars such as **'Concord'**. *V. vulpina* is similar, with glossy leaves. Both have sweet-scented flowers. *V. rotundifolia* is the **Muscadine** or **Southern Fox Grape**, widely used for wine in southern USA. It produces only half a dozen large fleshy grapes per cluster, usually black, though there are cultivated local white varieties. The **Winter**, **Chicken** or **Frost Grape** berry, *V. cordifolia* is very hardy and does well on lime soils. The dark purple fruit has to be frosted before it is edible and is used for wine. Some local cultivated varieties have sweeter,

Grapes on the vine

tastier, red or black fruits. *V. riparia* is the high climbing **Riverbank Grape** from North America, with large, glossy, deeply lobed leaves and big panicles of male flowers that smell most distinctly and sweetly of mignonette. The fruits are black or amber and very acid. *V. coignetiae* comes from Japan and Korea. It has enormous leaves up to 30cm (1ft) across. It is strong-growing and the leaves turn crimson and scarlet in autumn so it is much used ornamentally, but the black grapes with a bloom are not very tasty. *V. davidii*, once called **Spinovitis** because it has spines on the shoots, stems and leaves, was brought from China for its glorious, rich crimson, autumn colouring. It also has edible black fruits. *V. californica* was originally cultivated by the native American Pueblo Indians. It must have been good because, to quote Sturtevant, 'The quantity of the fruit that an Indian will consume at one time is scarcely credible'.

CULTIVATION

Most species require much the same treatment as *V. vinifera* grapes. Over-rich conditions should be avoided. For most, a warm site is better, but they do not like warm winters and do best with some chilling in winter.

Growing under Glass
The freedom from frost, rain and birds is valuable but vines grown under glass become more susceptible to pests and mildew.

Growing in Containers
Like *vinifera* grapevines, the species do not enjoy cramped conditions, but they can be grown in large pots. This shortens their life and gives small crops but conveniently controls their vigour, allowing many to be grown in a small area.

Ornamental and Wildlife Value
These are of the highest value as ornamentals and are useful for quick screens and coverings, though they can be too vigorous for small gardens unless hard pruned. Their bountiful flowers and fruit make them very good for wildlife gardens.

Maintenance
Spring Weed, mulch and spray seaweed monthly.
Summer Tie in shoots, protect fruit, cut off tips.
Autumn Pick fruit.
Winter Prune well.

Propagation
As these are species they can be grown from seed. Ripe wood cuttings, taken in late autumn, are best, and budding or grafting is possible.

Weed, Pest and Disease Control
As these are species, they are generally resilient to most of the common grape pests and diseases. However birds are still as much, if not more, of a problem.

CULINARY USES

Most of these grapes are too small and pippy or sour to be used raw as dessert. They are best juiced or turned into jellies. The strong flavour of some such as the Fox Grape can make them unsuitable for wine.

Grape Jelly
Makes approx. 2kg (4lb)

1kg (2lb) grapes
Approx.1kg (2lb) sugar

Simmer the grapes with only just enough water to stop them sticking. When they are soft, strain and weigh the liquid. Add the same weight of sugar to the juice and bring to the boil, skim until clear, bottle into hot jars and seal.

Pruning and Training
See also sections on Grapes for Dessert and for Wine. There are many ways to prune grapes and many sub-variations, enough to fill a book on their own. The species are best treated much as regular vines which, left to themselves, often produce rank growth and nearly exhaust themselves with overcropping. For ornamental purposes that is no problem, but for fruit they are best hard pruned and trained on a wall on wires about 50cm (1½ft) apart, and on walls under cover for the more tender varieties. The main framework is formed the first years, covering the wires with stems furnished with fruiting spurs. Thereafter these shoot each spring and a flower truss appears between the third and fifth leaf. After another three or four leaves, each shoot is tipped, as are any replacements as they come. It is essential to thin the number of bunches, leaving no more than two per metre (yard) run of cane. In winter, all shoots are cut back to one bud out from each spur, except the leader shoots.

COMPANION PLANTING

Species grapevines are probably benefited by blackberries, sage, mustard and hyssop growing nearby and they are inhibited by cabbages, radishes, Cypress spurge and laurels.

OTHER USES

As with other grapes, the grapevine prunings make great kindling.

Vitis vinifera from the family *Vitaceae*

DESSERT GRAPES

UNDER GLASS

Vine. Life span: exceptionally long-lived. Fruits: up to 3cm (1in), oval or round, any colour.

Although most dessert grapes are grown in hot areas, the very best flavour, size and succulence come from grapes grown under glass in cooler regions. The varieties selected make bigger grapes with thinner skins than outdoor varieties. They are hardy, but depend on protection and warmth to ripen in time, so they will not crop outside except in favourable years.

Growing dessert grapes under glass was raised to an art by the Victorians who could afford the heat and labour to produce perfect bunches of fine grapes almost every day of the year. Now cheaper greenhouses and plastic-covered tunnels are within the reach of most gardeners and many varieties can be grown with little or no extra heat, so these gourmet fruits are once again achievable.

VARIETIES

'**Muscat Hamburg** is by far the best. It has oval, black bunches of firm, sweet grapes with a superb flavour. It is superior to '**Black Hamburg**', though this too is a fine old variety, with bigger grapes in larger bunches. The '**Black Hamburg**' planted at Hampton Court Palace in 1796 still produces hundreds of bunches every year. Neither will crop outdoors save in an exceptional situation. '**Buckland Sweetwater**' has small, white, sweet and long-keeping grapes. '**Chasselas Doré**'/ '**Golden Chasselas**' is early, with translucent yellow fruits. It is most reliable and will even crop outdoors on a warm wall. '**Perle de Czaba**' and '**Siegerrebe**' are both speedier still and may crop outdoors, but they are better and reliable only on a hot wall or indoors. They both have the spicy muscat flavour; the '**Perle**' is yellow and '**Siegerrebe**' a rosé. The latter is a shy cropper with very choice berries, but dislikes limy soils.

CULTIVATION

Amenable to almost any soil, they do not require rich conditions. The very best varieties need a long season with an early start. With Victorian heating they were started into growth in early spring. Heat was used to keep them frost-free through spring, and again in autumn to finish off a late crop. However, in a good season, many varieties can be cropped under glass just with the extra natural warmth afforded, the more so if they are grown in pots and brought in after chilling outside.

Growing in Containers
This is most sensible with grapes. They resent the confined root system and need careful watering and pruning, but become controllable. Several varieties can go in a greenhouse too small for one planted in the ground. They are also conveniently moved outside for winter chilling and brought under for an early start, and again for ripening in the warmth and protection.

Warm sun is needed to ripen the grapes

Ornamental and Wildlife Value
Well-pruned vines in pots or trained on walls are very decorative. The framework is easily manipulable so almost any form can be achieved as long as all fruiting wood is kept at roughly the same level and in the light.

Maintenance
Spring Bring in or heat greenhouse, spray with seaweed solution.
Summer Prune back tips, thin bunches, spray with seaweed solution.
Autumn Pick the fruits.
Winter Prune and put outside or chill glasshouse.

Pruning and Training
In pots, vines are grown vertically or wound as spirals around a central supporting post. Grown in the ground under glass they are best planted outside, trained in through a hole and then treated the same as on a wall. This means wires about 50cm (1½ft) apart and the same from the roof to allow enough space. The vine framework is formed over the first years, covering the wires with main stems furnished with fruiting spurs. Thereafter these shoot each spring and a flower truss appears between the third and fifth leaf. After another three or four leaves each shoot is tipped, as too are any replacements as they come. It is essential to thin the number of bunches, leaving no more than two per metre (yard) run of cane. In winter, shoots are all cut back to one bud out from each spur.

Weed, Pest and Disease Control
Grapes can suffer many problems but usually still produce. If the air is too humid when grapes are ripening they may mould. If they are kept too dry before then they get mildew and red spider mite. However, the permitted sprays and usual remedies work well with most problems. Vine weevils can be excluded from vines in pots by making a lid that fits snugly around the stem.

Harvesting and Storing
Under cover they ripen early and hang longer as they are less threatened by pests or weather. Late varieties protected with paper bags may keep almost until the New Year.

Vines in a pot need a central vertical support

'Muscat Hamburg'

COMPANION PLANTING

Grow French marigolds underneath the vines to deter whitefly.

OTHER USES

Pieces of old vine, detached when pruning, make good supports for climbers in pots.

CULINARY USES

The dessert fruit par excellence, their juice is delicious and freezes well.

For wine-making, the flavour and high sugar content go well in combination with outdoor grapes, which have lower sugar and higher acidity.

Recipe
Just eat them as they come, sun warmed.

Vitis vinifera from the family *Vitaceae*

GRAPES
OUTSIDE AND FOR WINE

Vine. Life span: long-lived. Deciduous, self-fertile.
Fruits: up to 2cm/1in. Some vitamin value.

'Miguel Torres'

Wine grapes are as sweet, or more so, than dessert varieties. They have been bred to produce many small bunches rather than large berries, and this suits the vine's natural habit. The grapes are every bit as tasty, just smaller, and if you don't want the wine the juice is still valuable. They are hardier than dessert grapes and many are cropped commercially.

Although wine is predominantly produced in the Mediterranean region and areas with a similar climate, vineyards have been and are successful in many cool regions. The wines are usually light whites, but new hybrids now produce reds as well. Unfortunately European legislation does not permit commercial plantings of the new, high-yielding, disease-resistant hybrids, but they are still available to the amateur.

CULTIVATION

Rich soils should be avoided as they will grow excessively. Obviously the warmer and sunnier the better; wires and supports should ideally run north–south, to give sun on both sides of each row.

Growing in Containers
Although crops are light they can be grown in pots, see page 469.

Ornamental and Wildlife Value
A vineyard is quite an accessory to any estate. Quote in bottles per year – it sounds bigger. The aim is two bottles per square metre/yard. The wildlife are certainly going to like your vineyard unless you invest in netting against rabbits, rodents and birds.

Maintenance
Spring Weed, spray with seaweed solution monthly.
Summer Thin and tie in new shoots, tip after flowering.
Autumn Protect fruit and pick when ripe.
Winter Prune back hard.

Weed, Pest and Disease Control
The major losses are due to bird damage. Wet summers cause mouldy crops with little sweetness – little can be done about this. Mildew is best avoided by growing the more resistant varieties.

'Pinot Blanc'

'Chilean Riesling'

'Chilean Cabernet-Sauvignon'

VARIETIES

The classic wine grapes such as **'Cabernet'**, **'Chardonnay'**/**'Pinot Blanc'**, **'Pinot Noir'** and even **'Riesling'** are not suitable for cooler regions. **'Mueller Thurgau'**/**'Riesling Sylvaner'** is much planted for its excellent white wine, but mildew can be a problem, **'Seyve Villard 5/276'** is a white hybrid. It is more reliable but lacks the character, so often both are grown. **'Siegerrebe'** is a light cropper of rosé berries, which add flavour to blander grapes. The hybrids are by far the best croppers and most disease-resistant, **'Triomphe d'Alsace'**, **'Leon Millot'**, **'Seibel 13053'** and **'Marshall Joffre'** produce masses of dark black bunches, which make good red wine or juice. The **'Strawberry Grape'** and **'Schuyler'** produce well and easily but their flavour is not to everyone's taste. **'Boskoop Glory'** is the best outdoor dessert grape, a consistent producer of large, sweet black grapes.

Vine weevils are controlled by having clean cultivation and keeping chickens underneath, except when the fruit is ripening.

Pruning and Training
There are many different ways of treating vines outside. They can be grown with a permanent framework, as with indoor grapes or those on a wall, and this can be high or low, with benefits from air circulation or heat from the ground. You pays your money, and more for the higher methods! Strong posts and wires up to shoulder height are probably best, so the fruit is borne high enough up to avoid soil splash. Thus the bottom wire should not be less than 30cm (1ft) high. A modified form of Guyot pruning is often used instead of spur pruning. A short leg reaches to the bottom wire and supports a strong shoot, or two, of last year's growth tied down horizontally to fruit from the buds along its length. Two replacements are

allowed to grow from the leg and all other new shoots there are removed. Fruiting shoots are nipped out a few leaves after the flower truss, as with other methods.

Harvesting and Storing
When the fruit has finally ripened enough, but before losses to the birds and mould have mounted, pick the bunches. A dry day after a rainy period gives cleaner bunches. Cut out mouldy bits as you go and press as quickly as possible for juice for drinking or for white wine. White wines can be made from black grapes; only certain Teinturier grapes have red juice. With most varieties the colour only comes from fermenting the skin. Red wines are fermented entire, with the grapes merely mashed. The juice is pressed from the pips and skins later. Extra pips and skins of those squeezed for juice can be added with benefit to the red wine mix as they increase the tannins and sweetness.

Harvesting 'Pinot Blanc' grapes in Baden, Germany

COMPANION PLANTING

Asparagus is sometimes grown with the vines in France.

Vineyards by the Mosel in Germany

OTHER USES

The vine prunings make good kindling. Big stems are often made into corkscrew handles.

CULINARY USES

The juice is one of the most satisfying drinks. It can be used from the freezer throughout the year and is useful as a sweetener. The wine may be even better.

Fruit Salad Soup
Serves as many as you like

Chop and slice finely as many fruits as available and serve in copious grape juice with cream or yoghurt and macaroon biscuits.

TENDER FRUITS

This chapter covers a huge range of fruits, from annual tender fruits, such as melons, to perennial tender fruits, which are a much more diverse group, including citrus, olives and kiwi, to the sub-tropical and tropical fruits, such as pineapples, bananas and mangoes. All need warm conditions in which to ripen, and so in cool, temperate conditions, benefit from some protection for at least part of the year, if not all year round. A few tender perennial fruits also need a winter period of cooling so that they will fruit the following year. These can survive outside in temperate areas, though their fruit may not ripen.

The annual tender fruits are mostly very short-lived perennials in their native lands and are grown as annuals in cultivation. Most take longer to fruit than our short growing season permits, so we gain extra weeks at the beginning by starting them under glass, with heat. They were brought to Europe and then America by the exploratory voyages of the sixteenth century. The hybridization and development during the next centuries in both continents slowly made better, more hardy and productive varieties available. In the garden the availability of myriad varieties has made it possible to grow these fruits with only an amateur greenhouse and a sheltered garden or warm wall.

With the exception of *Actinidia*, all the perennial tender fruits have long been in cultivation and their use from wild stocks predates history so early on they spread well beyond their native lands. This is probably due to the fact that most of them possess thick, rind-like skins and thus have some ability to travel and store well, as compared

to other fruits anyway. The human desire for new tastes and flavourings made each of these fruits important items of commerce as they are all distinctly different to other fruits. Once sampled, they became desired, and as world trade started to increase in the seventeenth century, most of these fruits became expensive luxuries and thus indispensable for the developing European, and later the American, markets. They had become common by the Victorian era, as increased production in the warm temperate countries, such as around the Mediterranean basin and in California and Florida, displaced longer distance imports. These areas became so competitive that few of these fruits have ever become worth growing commercially under glass in the colder regions, despite the ease with which they can be cultivated.

Some of the tropical and sub-tropical fruits are the tastiest and most luscious in the world. Strong sunlight and hot conditions produce sweeter, stronger flavours than in temperate zones. The natural conditions change little during the year, rather than the fluctuating heat and light and winter chilling of cooler regions. Tropical plants therefore often set fruit several times a year, or continuously throughout it. They were grown on large estates in colder countries from the seventeenth century, but the advent of the stovehouse in Victorian times – a large glass greenhouse with a massive stove keeping the temperature tropical – allowed more success with fruiting these plants. Many were successful, but others could not be persuaded to fruit even with extra heat. Now we are more fortunate: with electric light to replicate sunlight we can give these plants the brightness and day length they need. We also have automatic heat and humidity control, so it is easy to grow many exotic fruits ourselves. And if they still will not fruit, they always make attractive houseplants.

Physalis species from the family *Solanaceae*

CAPE GOOSEBERRIES
AND GROUND CHERRIES

Herbaceous. Life span: annual or short-lived perennial. Fruits: up to 6cm (2½in), yellow to purple in papery husk. Value: rich in vitamin C.

The *Physalis* are all distantly related to tomatoes, peppers, aubergines and potatoes. Their best-known member is the perennial **Chinese Lantern**, or **Bladder Cherry**, *P. franchetii/ alkekengi*, which has straggling stems, heart-shaped leaves, inconspicuous flowers and bright orange, papery lanterns surrounding a red, edible but unpalatable fruit. The more palatable species are similar. The **Ground Cherry**, **Strawberry Tomato** or **Cossack Pineapple**, *P. pruinosa*, is low-growing, up to knee level, and has small, green fruits ripening to dirty yellow. Sweet and acid, they are vaguely pineapple-flavoured. *P. peruviana*, the **Cape Gooseberry**, **Ground** or **Winter Cherry**, is taller (about 1m/3ft) with yellower fruits. Both fruits are enclosed in similar, though duller, papery husks to those of the **Chinese Lantern**. Another similar fruit is the **Tomatillo** or **Jamberry**, *P. ixocarpa*, which is perennial, with much larger green or purplish berries filling the husk.

The first *Physalis* to be commonly eaten seems to be have been *P. alkekengi*, which was known to the Greek Dioscorides in the third century AD and was gathered from the wild. The annual *P. pruinosa*, which grows wild in North America, was popular with Native Americans and, apparently, also with Cossacks. It was introduced to England in the eighteenth century, but never caught on. The perennial **Cape Gooseberry**, *P. peruviana*, comes from tropical South America and became an important crop for the settlers on the Cape of Good Hope at the beginning of the nineteenth century. *P. ixocarpa*, the **Tomatillo** or **Jamberry**, comes from Mexico, but has become popular in many warm countries as it fruits easily and reliably and makes good sauces and preserves. Improved versions are now being offered for greenhouse culture elsewhere.

VARIETIES

No varieties of any species are widely available except for *P. ixocarpa*, which has an improved form, **'New Sugar Giant'**, with fruits up to 6cm/2½in across, yellow or green instead of the usual purple. Many other *Physalis* species are cultivated locally in warm countries, but seed or plants are rarely available.

Cape gooseberries

Leaves and fruit of the Cape gooseberry

CULTIVATION

The *Physalis* are all best started under cover and planted out. The perennials can ripen outdoors in a good season in southern England, but are far more reliable under cover. *P. pruinosa* is tough and may crop outdoors without protection. They all prefer a rich, light, warm soil and a sunny position. Little support is really necessary, though they do flop.

Growing under Glass
All the family give better and sweeter fruits grown under glass and present no major problems; indeed they seem to be designed for it.

Growing in Containers
P. pruinosa is easily grown in pots. The larger *Physalis* can be grown likewise, but do not do quite as well, preferring a bigger root run. The decorative *P. alkekengi* is worth having in a pot just for the show it provides.

Ornamental and Wildlife Value
Most of the productive species are nowhere near as attractive as their more ornamental cousin, the **Chinese Lantern**. They have small value to wildlife, though the flowers are popular with insects.

Maintenance
Spring Sow indoors, pot up and plant out once hardened off.
Summer Support lax plants.
Autumn Pick fruits once fully ripe, discard husks.

Winter Protect the roots of perennials well for another season.

Propagation
Normally grown from seed, the perennial varieties can be multiplied by root cuttings or division in the spring. Start them off early and pot up regularly to build up a large root system.

Pruning and Training
They need little attention other than tying in the lax growths and clearing away the withered stems after cropping. The roots of perennial varieties can be got through mild winters under protection for earlier crops the following year.

Weed, Pest and Disease Control
They are remarkably pest- and disease-free. The **Tomatillo** is especially useful as it can be used much like a tomato, but can ripen as early in cool conditions and does not suffer blight as tomatoes may.

Harvesting and Storing
The fruits must be fully ripe to be edible. They can hang on the plant till required as they are rarely attacked by pest, disease or bird. The husk is inedible and must be removed.

COMPANION PLANTING

There are no known companion effects.

OTHER USES

The ornamental Chinese lanterns can be dried for winter decoration and have been used medicinally.

CULINARY USES

Most *Physalis* berries are relatively tasteless and insipid raw but make delicious preserves, sauces and tarts. The **Cape gooseberry** often tastes best on first acquaintance and may rapidly lose its appeal after the initial elusive strawberry flavour. It was once imported in vast quantities from South Africa, when it was known as Tippari jam or jelly.

Tippari Jelly
Makes approx. 2kg/4lb

1 kg (2lb) Cape gooseberries
A little water
Approx. 1kg (2lb) sugar

Remove the husks from the fruit and boil them with just enough water to prevent the fruit from sticking. Strain the juice and add its own weight in sugar. Simmer till fully dissolved, skim off scum, then jar and seal.

Cucumis melo from the family *Cucurbitaceae*

MELONS

Herbaceous vine. Life span: annual. Self-fertile but requires assistance as separate male and female flowers. Fruits: 5–25cm (2–10in) spheres, whitish cream to green, netted or smooth. Value: rich in vitamins A and C, niacin and potassium.

Melons belong to a very wide family of tender, trailing annual vines, much resembling cucumbers in habit. They have broad leaves, softly prickled stems and small yellow flowers, followed by fruits that can be any size from small to very large, round or oval. Melons are characterized by a thick, inedible rind covering succulent, melting flesh, which encloses a central cavity and a battalion of flat, pointed oval, whitish seeds.

The tasty, sweet, aromatic melons we know were apparently unknown to the Ancients. They certainly grew similar fruits, but these seem to have been more reminiscent of the cucumber. Pliny, in the first century AD, refers to the fruits dropping off the stalk when ripe, which is typical of melons, but they were still not generally considered very palatable. To quote Galen, the philosopher-physician, writing in the second century AD, 'the autumn (ripe) fruits do not excite vomiting as do the unripe'. By the third century they had become sweeter and aromatic enough to be eaten with spices, and by the sixth and seventh centuries they were distinguished separately from cucumbers. The first reference to really delicious, aromatic melons comes in the fifteenth and sixteenth centuries, probably as the result of hybridization between many different strains. The seeds were left wherever humans ventured. Christopher Columbus returned to the New World to find melons growing aplenty where his previous expedition had landed and eaten the odd meal of melons, liberally discarding the seeds. Likewise, both deliberately and inadvertently, melons have reached most warm parts of the globe and are immensely popular crops for the home garden in many countries. The Victorians developed reliable varieties that were successfully cropped year-round under glass, though most melons are now imported to Britain from warmer countries.

Honeydew melon

VARIETIES

There are countless varieties, literally hundreds if not thousands, and many more go unrecorded world-wide. Most of those that are available, either as seed or commercially, fall into three or four main groups. **Cantaloupe** varieties usually have orange flesh. The fruits tend to be broadly ribbed, often with a scaly or warty rind, but not netted. The flesh is sweet and aromatic. A good typical variety is **'Charentais'**. They are the hardiest – well, least tender – of the

An Ogen variety of melon

melons and **'Sweetheart'** is one of the most reliable. **Ogen** melons are an Israeli strain. These resemble a much improved but more tender **Cantaloupe**. The fruits are smooth, broadly ribbed and yellow when ripe, with very sweet, green, aromatic flesh. **Musk melons** are netted or nutmeg melons and have distinct netting, lighter in colour and raised from the yellow or green rind. These are the typical hothouse melons – large oval or round fruits with very sweet and aromatically perfumed flesh from green to orange. A good old variety is **'Blenheim Orange'**. Winter melons are round to oval, yellow or green, smooth or with a leather-like surface and hard yellow flesh that is not very sweet or perfumed. Often called **Honeydews**, these are long keeping, up to a month or so, thus they are popular in commerce.

CULTIVATION

Melons are not difficult if their particular requirements are met. They need continuous warmth, greater than that needed for tomatoes, peppers or aubergines, and must have a much higher humidity. This makes them difficult to accommodate with the *Solanum* glasshouse crops. They grow most happily with okra and other cucurbits such as cucumbers, as these all prefer similar humidity and heat and likewise will thrive in slightly less light than the *Solanums*. Indeed, they do not like bright light and prefer diffuse to direct sun. The soil must be rich, very well drained and, like the air, kept continually moist. Melons really do best on hotbeds or heating-up compost heaps.

Growing under Glass

This is almost essential in all but hot countries where they can be grown in the open. In some sheltered parts of southern England, in a good

Galia melon growing intertwined with cucumber

year, the new hybrid varieties such as **Sweetheart** may be grown in the open with some hope of success. Cold greenhouses can produce light crops, heated ones far more. A cold frame or curtained area in the greenhouse is better still, and the ease of providing extra warmth and humidity more than makes up for the diminished light. A cold frame set on a hotbed, or with soil-warming cables, in a greenhouse or polytunnel, is the best environment attainable by the average gardener and can produce an impressive crop. Indoors, pollination is advisable as a precaution.

Growing in Containers

Melons are one of the easiest plants to crop well in a large pot, providing they are kept warm, well watered and fed regularly with a liquid feed. (I even grow them successfully in bags of fresh grass clippings topped off with a bucketful of sieved garden compost to seal in the heat and smell. The seed is sown direct in a mound of sterile compost set on top of that and covered with a plastic bottle cloche. The bag stands in my polytunnel, a self-contained mini hotbed. When the plant is growing, the bottle is reversed to make a useful watering funnel.)

'Sweetheart' melons in net supports

'Countess of Caernarvon', a Cantaloupe variety of melon

Ornamental and Wildlife Value

These are not really very decorative plants, but can impress with their luxurious growth. The scent of ripening melons is heavenly. The fruits are well liked by rodents and birds, making these useful for the wild garden in warmer countries.

Maintenance

Spring Sow as soon as warm conditions can be maintained, pot up, nip out tip after four true leaves, pollinate, reduce excess number of fruits, spray with seaweed solution weekly and mist frequently.
Summer Spray with seaweed solution weekly, mist frequently and support swelling fruits.
Autumn Continue as for summer.
Winter Melons can be grown throughout the year if sufficient heat is maintained.

Melons are highly suited to growing in pots

Propagation

Melons are normally started from seed, which does not come true when self-saved unless you are very careful, as cucurbits are promiscuous cross-pollinators. The seed needs warm, moist conditions to start and the plants need continuous warm, rich, humid conditions. Avoid the roots making a tight ball in the pot, but do not over-pot. The stems can be layered or even taken as soft cuttings to continue the season.

Weed, Pest and Disease Control

Providing the growing conditions are just right, melons usually suffer no major problems. The slightest drop in humidity and red spider mite may need controlling, as this can check the plants. It is worth introducing the commercially available predator *Phytoseuilis persimilis* if red spider mites are spotted. Aphids and whiteflies sometimes appear, requiring the usual remedies. Melons do suffer occasionally from neck rot where the stem enters the soil, usually during cold conditions. Sterile compost, warmth and clean, carefully applied water usually prevent any occurrence. Victorian gardeners always grew melons on little mounds to keep the neck dry. If neck rot appears, rub with sulphur dust and then earth up with moist, gritty compost to encourage rooting from the base of the stem. Rodents and slugs attack the fruits.

Harvesting and Storing

Their heavily perfumed, aromatic sweetness and luscious, melting texture make them divine when ripened to perfection – though too often they are taken young to travel and are then not sweet, but woody and never well perfumed. For sybarites, they really must be ripened on the vine until they are dropping – the nets are not there to support but to catch the fruits! Once they are ripe enough to scent a room, the fruits should be chilled before eating to firm the flesh and then removed from the refrigerator a short while before serving to allow the perfume to emerge fully.

COMPANION PLANTING

Melons like to ramble under sweetcorn or sunflowers, enjoying their shelter and dappled shade, even in English summers! They also get on with peanuts, but do not thrive near potatoes. **Morning Glory** seed sown with melons is said to improve their germination. Most of all, melons need the same hot, humid conditions as cucumbers and there seems little problem with their pollinating each other. However, there might be if you want to save seed.

OTHER USES

Melons accumulate a great deal of calcium in their leaves, making them especially useful for worm compost. The empty shells make good slug traps. *Cucumis melo dudaim*, **Queen Anne's Pocket Melon**, is grown for its strong perfume but the flesh is insipid.

Musk melon with flower and fruit

CULINARY USES

Quintessentially a dessert fruit, melons are nevertheless most often served as a starter in the place of savoury dishes. They may be combined with savoury or sweet dishes and are exquisite as chunks combined with Dolcelatte cheese and wrapped in Parma ham. Melons can be made into jam or chutney, added to compôtes, and used as bowls for creative cuisine.

Melon Sundae
Quantities to taste

Ripe melon
Vanilla ice-cream
Toasted flaked almonds
Sultanas
Honey
Dark chocolate
Glacé cherries

Remove balls of melon with a spoon. Layer these in sundae glasses with scoops of vanilla ice-cream, almonds and sultanas. Then pour over the melon juice thickened with honey. Top with grated dark chocolate and a glacé cherry.

Melon chutney

Melon sundae

Citrullus lanatus/vulgaris from the family *Cucurbitaceae*

WATERMELONS

Herbaceous vine. Life span: annual. Self-fertile. Fruits: variably large, green.
Value: rich in vitamins and minerals; a serving contains more iron than spinach.

Watermelons are scrambling, climbing vines. Their leaves are darker, more bluey-green, hairy and fern-like than melon leaves; the flowers are similar, small and yellow. Watermelon fruits vary in size from small to gigantic, from light green to dark green or yellow in colour. The thin, hard rind is packed with red flesh, embedded in which are small, dark seeds. Eating the very juicy flesh is like drinking sweet water.

This productive and nutritious, thirst-quenching fruit comes from Africa and India, but was first mentioned by botanists and travellers in the sixteenth century. The fruit became widely cultivated, but it appears to have been little improved until it reached North America. There it was developed to produce examples weighing over 45kg (100lb) and many varieties with different coloured flesh, rind or seed. These included a sub-group with ornamental 'painted', 'engraved' or 'sculptured' seeds.

Watermelon 'Sugar Baby'

VARIETIES

The flesh is always exceedingly juicy and sweet and red, but once it varied in colour with black, white, cream, brown, purple and yellow-fleshed forms. Now few varieties other than the reds are grown on any scale. **'Charleston Gray'** is long, oval and light-green-skinned with crisp red flesh. **'Sugar Baby'** is round, darker green and with very sweet red flesh, but needs an early start for maximum sweetness. I have unexpectedly grown good fruits from seed saved from tasty, ordinary, unnamed supermarket varieties.

CULTIVATION

Warm, well-aerated but moist soil is needed. Although copious water is needed at the roots to swell the large fruits, watermelons prefer rather less humid conditions than melons or cucumbers. They also do not need the same high degree of fertility and thrive in any reasonable sandy soil, as they benefit from watering as much as from feeding. In temperate areas with hot summers, the watermelon can be grown outdoors as it produces more quickly than the melon does.

Growing under Glass
This is absolutely essential anywhere other than in a country with hot summers. The vines do not mind light shade but need warmth and prefer a drier atmosphere to melons or cucumbers – although they do better with them than with the *Solanums*. They need plenty

A spray of watermelon leaves

of space; grow them a metre (yard) apart. Provide support and train them up if space is limited, but keep the fruits well supported.

Growing in Containers
Watermelons can be grown in large pots although they resent the restricted root run and lack of aeration. Be sure to use an open, gritty compost and ensure that religious watering and feeding are maintained throughout the season.

Ornamental and Wildlife Value
The vines are much more decorative than those of melons. The fruits are appreciated by wildlife in hotter countries.

Maintenance
Spring Sow as soon as warm conditions can be maintained, pot up, pollinate, reduce excess number of fruits, spray with seaweed solution weekly.
Summer Spray with seaweed solution weekly and straw under swelling fruits.
Autumn Continue as for summer.
Winter Save the seeds for spring sowing.

Propagation
These are readily started from seed, but need regular potting up. Watermelons are not as easy to layer as melons. They prefer clay pots to plastic ones and react very badly to over-watering or to compaction of the compost.

Pruning and Training
Watermelons do not need stopping like melons, but it

is a good idea to limit each vine to one fruit to ensure a decent size. The plants are best allowed to ramble. If they are trained up anything, provide support for the immensely heavy fruits. On the ground they are best laid on straw or a tile to keep them clean.

Weed, Pest and Disease Control
Very prone to attack by red spider mite under glass, so commercial predators should be introduced early before a major attack starts. Although watermelons like it as warm as melons, a similar degree of humidity does not suit them.

Harvesting and Storing
Watermelons are ripe when they sound taut and 'hollow' to a tap from the knuckle. If really ripe and well grown they split open as soon as the knife bites. However, if left intact, they will keep for a week or more.

A good watermelon curry with chilli, turmeric and coriander powders, cumin seeds and lime juice is traditionally made in Rajasthan

COMPANION PLANTING

Watermelons do not object to potatoes, as melons do, and may run amongst the plants to advantage in warm countries.

Young watermelon plants growing in an old deep-freeze

CULINARY USES

Watermelons are best eaten fresh. Their seeds may be eaten – they are oily and nutritious. The pulp can be made into conserves, or reduced to make a sugar syrup.

OTHER USES

The closely related *Citrullus colocynthis*, **Colocynth**, **Bitter Gourd**, is like a small, intensely bitter watermelon. It is used medicinally and occasionally pickled or preserved after many boilings.

Watermelon Ices
All quantities to taste

Watermelon
Melted chocolate
Grated desiccated coconut

Freeze bite-size cubes of watermelon on a wire tray. Once they are frozen solid, dip each quickly in cooling melted chocolate, sprinkle with grated coconut and freeze again. Serve them nearly defrosted, but still just frozen, with piped cream and macaroon biscuits if liked.

Citrus species from the family *Rutaceae*

LEMONS, ORANGES

AND OTHER CITRUS FRUITS

Tree/bush, up to 8m (25ft). Life span: medium to long. Evergreen, self-fertile.
Fruits: variable size, orange, green or yellow. Value: rich in vitamin C.

Lemon

Citrus fruits of the Rutaceae family are small, glossy-leaved evergreens with green stems that are occasionally thorny, especially in the leaf axils. Typical of this family, the leaves have glands which secrete scented oil. The small, white, star-shaped flowers are intensely and similarly perfumed, and are followed by the well-known fruits, which take up to a year to ripen. These swell to a size which ranges from that of a cherry to a human head, depending on the species. They are yellow or orange with light-coloured flesh inside a tough, bitter and scented peel. The flesh is sweet or sour, always juicy, and segmented. Each piece may contain a few small seeds.

Orange

Originally from China and South-East Asia, some species and closely inter-related cultivars have been in cultivation since prehistory. They moved slowly westward to India and then on to Arabia and thence to the Mediterranean countries. The Ancient Greeks seem not to have been aware of any citrus. The Romans knew the citron, which is recorded in Palestine in the first century AD, but probably arrived several centuries before. They were widely planted in Italy in the second and third centuries, becoming especially popular near Naples.

The Romans were such gourmands that they would hardly have failed to notice a delight such as an orange. These did not reach Arabia until the ninth century. It was recorded as growing in Sicily in the year 1002 and was grown in Spain at Seville, still famous for its oranges, while it was occupied by the Moors in the twelfth century. It is said St Domine planted an orange in Rome in the year 1200 and a Spanish ship full of the fruits docked at Portsmouth, England, in 1290; the Queen of Edward I received seven. These were probably bitter oranges, as many believe the sweet orange did not reach Europe till later. First seen in India in 1330, the sweet sort was first planted in 1421 at Versailles; another planted in 1548 in Lisbon became the 'mother' of most European sweet orange trees and was still living in 1823.

The lemon reached Egypt and Palestine in the tenth century and was cultivated in Genoa by the mid-fifteenth century. The new fruits were soon spread around the warmer parts of Europe, and then further afield, with the voyagers of the fifteenth and sixteenth centuries. Columbus must have scattered the seeds as he went, for they are recorded as growing in the Azores in 1494 and the Antilles in 1557. They had reached orchard scale in South America in 1587 and by then Cuba was covered in them. They are now mainly grown in Florida, California, Israel, Spain and South Africa, though every warm to tropical area produce its own and more.

Pink grapefruit

VARIETIES

The various types are of obscure parentage and were probably derived by selection from a distant common ancestor. *Citrus aurantium* is the **Seville**, **Bitter** or **Sour Orange**. Too sour to eat raw, this is the best for marmalade and preserves and was the first sort to arrive in Europe. *C. sinensis* is the **Sweet Orange**, often known by the variety such as **'Valencia Late'**, **'Jaffa'**, which is large, thick-skinned and seedless, or the nearly seedless and finest quality **'Washington Navel'**. **Blood Oranges**, such as the **'Maltese'**, are sweet oranges with a red tint to the flesh.

C. limon is the lemon. The fruits are distinctly shaped yellow ovoids with blunt nipples at the flower end and the characteristic acid taste. The commonest are **'Lisbon'**, **'Eureka'** and **'Villafranca'**; the hardiest and most convenient for a conservatory is the compact **'Meyer's Lemon'**.

C. aurantifolia is the lime. This makes a smaller tree of up to 3.5m (12ft). The small, green fruits do not travel well and are mainly consumed locally or made into a concentrate. Limes offered for sale are often

The beautiful flowers of the 'Valencia Late' orange

Lemon 'Lisbon'

small, unripe lemons, given away by the nipple, which a true lime does not have. Alternatively, they may be the similar *C. limetta*, **Sweet Lime**, which is insipidly sweet when ripe. True limes are grown mostly from seed and will require near tropical conditions.

C. paradisi is the grapefruit. Not as acid as a lemon, this is relished for breakfast by many. They may be a hybrid of the **Pomelo** or **Shaddock**, *C. grandis*, which is similar but coarser. **'Marsh's Seedless'** is the commonest variety of grapefruit, with greenish-white flesh; but some prefer the Texan varieties with pink flesh.

C. reticulata is the **Mandarin**, **Satsuma**, **Tangerine** or **Clementine**. These names are confused and interchanged for several small, sweet, easily peeled and segmented sorts of small orange. *C. medica* is like a large, warty lemon and is now mainly produced in a few Mediterranean countries for making candied peel. There are many other citrus species and hybrids, **Uglis**, **Ortaniques** and **Tangelos,** to name but a few. The **Kumquat** is not a citrus, but belongs to the similar genus *Fortunella*. The fruits are very like small, yellowish, tart oranges, and are especially good for making preserves.

Kumquats

CULTIVATION

Citrus need a warm, rich, moist soil, well aerated and never badly drained. They are all tender, though lemons and oranges have, despite the odds, been grown successfully outdoors in favourable positions on warm walls in southern England, and even cropped in some years. In warm countries they are spaced about 5–6m (15–20ft) apart each way and are in their prime at ten years old. Trees with fruits of orange size will give a crop of over 500 each winter; small fruits, such as lemons, will crop more than 500; while big fruits, such as grapefruits, will crop less.

Growing under Glass
Frost-free protection in winter is necessary in northern countries. Citrus do not like being under glass all year round. They are much happier outdoors in summer and enjoy a rest in autumn. Thus they are best grown in large containers and moved under glass only for the frosty months, which conveniently are the months that they flower and crop. Limes and grapefruits are among the least hardy sorts and need more heat than the others.

A grove of 'Jaffa' oranges growing in Kos, Greece

Growing in Containers

This is ideal for citrus as it keeps them compact and makes it easy to give them winter protection indoors. They must have a well-aerated, well-drained, but rich compost. Avoid plastic pots or give them extra perforation. The 'old boys' always reckoned that diluted, fresh urine was the best feed for citrus.

Ornamental and Wildlife Value

Very decorative in leaf, flower and fruit, all of which have a wonderful scent, these are ideal subjects for a conservatory and for a warm patio in the summer. The flowers are loved by insects; the fruits are less use to wildlife – which is fortunate for us.

Maintenance

Spring Prune, spray with seaweed solution weekly, move outdoors.
Summer Prune, spray with seaweed solution weekly.
Autumn Prune, spray with seaweed solution weekly.
Winter Prune, move indoors, pick the fruit.

Propagation

Commonly, commercial plants are grafted or budded, often on *Poncirus* stock to dwarf them. Cuttings can be taken. I find some succeed quite easily in every batch. Seedlings are slow to bear fruit and may not be true; however, citrus seeds occasionally produce two seedlings, one being a clone copy of the original plant and the other normal. Seedlings are often more vigorous and longer lived than worked plants, which may offset their slow development.

Pruning and Training

Once these have grown tall enough they are best cut back hard to form a neat cone or globe shape. Regularly remove and/or shorten straggly, unfruitful, diseased and long shoots, cutting back hardest before growth starts in spring. They generally need no support until they are in fruit, when heavy crops may even cause the branches to bend severely and tear.

Weed, Pest and Disease Control

All manner of pests bother these plants under glass, but when they go out for the summer most of the problems disappear. The usual remedies work and soft soap sprays may also be useful against scale insects, which can particularly bother citrus, especially if ants are about to farm them. Bad drainage will kill them more rapidly than cold weather will!

Harvesting and Storing

Usually picked too young so they can travel, they are of course best plucked fresh off the tree and fully ripe. They do not all ripen at once and picking may continue over many weeks. The rind contains the bitter oil which can be expressed to give a zest to cooking.

Carved limewood is from *Tilia* species rather than *Citrus*

The beautiful Citrus Allée at the Villa Carlotta, northern Italy

COMPANION PLANTING

In warm countries citrus are benefited by growing aloes, rubber, oak and guava trees nearby. However, they are also said to be inhibited by *Convolvulus* or possibly by the *Ipomoea* species.

Citrus cuttings are easy to grow in pots

OTHER USES

The leaves, flowers and fruits, especially of *C. bergamia*, the bergamot, are used in perfumery. The empty shells of the fruits make slug traps and firelighters if dried. *Citrus/Poncirus trifoliata* is hardier than the others and heavily thorned; it is used as a hedge in mild regions.

CULINARY USES

The fruits can be juiced – much of the world's crop is consumed this way – or jammed or jellied and made into marmalade. The peel is often candied or glacéed. Small amounts of lemon juice prevent freshly prepared fruits and vegetables oxidizing and give a delightful, sharp, clean taste to most things, savoury or sweet. The Victorians grew the seeds for the young tender leaves to add to salads. The peels are much used for liqueurs and flavourings.

Orange Sorbet
Serves 4

4 large unwaxed oranges
Mace
Sugar
Egg white
Parsley sprigs

Cut the tops off the oranges and scoop out the contents. Freeze the lower shells to use as serving bowls. Strain the juice from the pulp and weigh and measure it. Simmer the chopped tops of the oranges with the pulp and a small piece of fresh mace in half as much water as you have juice, then strain out the bits and add half the juice's weight in sugar. Once it has dissolved, mix this sweetened water and the juice and partially freeze. Take it from freezer and beat vigorously, adding one beaten egg white per 450g/1lb of mixture, refreeze then repeat the beating. Serve, partially thawed, in the reserved shells with a garnish of parsley.

Lemon jam

Orange flower water lends a wonderful perfume to the bath

Orange sorbet

Olea europaea from the family *Oleaceae*

OLIVES

Tree, up to 10m (33ft). Life span: long. Evergreen, self-fertile.
Fruits: up to 2.5cm (1in), ovoid, green to black. Value: rich in oils.

Cultivated olive trees are gnarled and twisted with long, thin, dark leaves, silvered underneath, though the wild species are bushier with quadrangular stems, rounder leaves and spines. The inconspicuous, sometimes fragrant, white flowers are followed by green fruits that ripen to brown or bluey-purplish-black, and occasionally ivory white, each containing a single large stone.

Found wild in the Middle East, olives have long been cultivated. They were amongst the fruits promised to the Jews in Canaan. According to Homer, green olives were brought to Greece by Cecrops, founder of Athens. They were certainly the source of its wealth. By 571 BC the olive had reached Italy and in the first century AD Pliny records a dozen varieties grown as far as Gaul (France) and Spain. These are still the major producing areas; olives are also grown in California, Australia and China.

Olives ripening on the tree

VARIETIES

There are up to several dozen varieties of olive grown commercially in different regions, but only unnamed species are usually available. **'Queen Manzanillas'** are the biggest of the green pickling olive varieties.

CULTIVATION

Olives grow well in arid sites that will not support much else. They prefer a well-drained, light, lime-based soil. They will grow, but rarely fruit well, outside Mediterranean climatic regions. Small strong trees, they need little support.

Olive branch and leaves

Growing under Glass
Olives are almost hardy but it is worth growing them in big pots so that they can be brought in for winter and put outside in summer. If kept indoors, they must not be too hot or humid.

Growing in Containers
Olives make good subjects for containers, though they are unlikely to be very productive. They must have a free-draining compost and then are fairly trouble-free.

Ornamental and Wildlife Value
Very attractive shrubs, these are worth having even if they never fruit, and they probably won't. The flowers are beneficial to insects, and some are fragrant. They are dense evergreens, making good shelter, and the fruits are rich in oils, so these are useful plants for wild gardens in warmer climes.

Maintenance
Spring Prune, spray with seaweed solution monthly.
Summer Spray with seaweed solution monthly.
Autumn Spray with seaweed solution monthly.
Winter Take indoors or protect from frost.

Propagation
Seeds may not come true, though they are often used, and the resulting plants can be slow to come into fruit. Cuttings with a heel can be taken in late summer, but like the seed need bottom heat to ensure success. Grow seedlings on for a year or two in large pots before planting out – they get tougher as they get bigger.

Pruning and Training
As olives bear on the previous year's growth, they must have only remedial pruning to remove the dead and diseased or crossing branches. This is best done in late winter or early spring. They can be trained as fans on walls for the extra protection. If the tops are frosted, they can still come again from the root and can be cut back very hard or pollarded. Old trees often throw suckers as replacements.

Weed, Pest and Disease Control
Olives have very few problems in private gardens, though scale insects can bother them occasionally. Protection from frost and good drainage are more important.

A ripe green olive

Nets are suspended below the olive trees to catch the ripe fruit

Harvesting and Storing
In the Mediterranean region the trees bear when they are about eight years old. They produce about 25kg (60lb) of fruit each, which reduces to about a quarter to half that weight in oil. The green fruits are ones picked unripe and pickled; the black fruits are ripe and ready for pressing for oil or preserving. The oil that is squeezed out without heat or excess pressure is called extra virgin (an interesting concept, rather typical of Latin thinking). Cheaper grades are produced by heating or adding hot water to the mass.

COMPANION PLANTING

Oaks are thought to be detrimental to olive trees.

OTHER USES

The oil has many industrial as well as culinary uses. Much is used in cosmetics and perfumery and it was once burned in lamps.

CULINARY USES

The oil is used in many ways – in Mediterranean countries it is used in preference to animal fats – and the fruits are added to various dishes. The fruits are also eaten as savoury accompaniments pickled in brine, often stuffed with anchovy or pimento, or dried. If beaten to a paste, olives will make a delicious savoury spread.

Olive Bread
Makes 1 loaf

500g (1lb) strong white flour
1 packet dried yeast
Water
60g (2oz) black olives, stoned
Olive oil
Poppy seeds

Mix the flour and yeast with enough water to form a dough. Knead and allow to rise until it is half as big again. Knead again and work in the olives. Rub the dough with olive oil; place it in an oiled tin to rise again with a sprinkling of poppy seeds. Once it has risen to half its size again, put it in a preheated oven at 220°C/425°F/gas mark 7 for 20 minutes or till brown on top. Serve as an entrée with a crisp green salad and a sharp dressing.

Passiflora from the family *Passifloraceae*

PASSION FRUIT

Herbaceous vine, up to 10m (3ft). Life span: short. Semi-deciduous, self-fertile. Fruits: from 2.5cm (1in) to 10cm (4in), spherical to cylindrical, yellow, orange, red, brown, black or green.
Value: rich in vitamin C.

Passion fruit are a family of perennial climbers with tendrils, deeply lobed leaves, amazing flowers and peculiar fruits. These vary in size from that of a cherry to a coconut, and in colour, coming in almost any shade from yellow to black. They are usually thick-skinned with a juicy, acid, fragrant, sweet pulp inside, almost inseparable from smooth, black seeds. The passion fruit, *Passiflora edulis*, is the most widely grown species. It has white or mauve flowers fragrant of heliotrope and purple-black fruits that are best when 'old' and wrinkled.

Passion fruit are native to America and were first recorded in Europe in 1699. The flowers caused quite a stir in European society, with many contemporary Christians claiming that they were a sign of Christ's Passion (the Crucifixion). The three stigmas represented the nails, the central column the scourging post, the five anthers the wounds, the corona the crown of thorns, the calyx the halo, the ten petals the faithful apostles, and the tendrils the whips and scourges of His oppressors. These delightful climbers, with their stunning flowers and delicious fruits, have now become popular in most warm countries. They are often grown in conservatories and in pots on patios for the flowers rather than the fruits.

Passion fruit and leaves

VARIETIES

Passiflora edulis is the tastiest variety and hardy enough to survive in a frost-free greenhouse. Improved varieties such as **'Crackerjack'** are available. The **Giant Granadilla**, *P. quadrangularis*, needs more tropical conditions, but can produce fruits weighing many pounds; these are often used as vegetables in their unripe state. *P. laurifolia* is the **Water Lemon** or **Yellow Granadilla**, much esteemed in Jamaica. *P. incarnata* **'Maypops'**, comes from eastern North America. It has

Banana passion fruit

attractive creamy flowers, ornamental, three-lobed leaves and tasty yellow fruits. It is not self-fertile and spreads by underground runners. It can survive outdoors, as it comes again from the roots. *P. caerulea* is the hardiest, with blue flowers and orange fruits which may be edible, but are not palatable, even after boiling with sugar. Dozens of edible-fruited passion flowers are grown locally, such as *P. antioquiensis*, with yellow, banana-shaped fruits, *P. foetida*, the goat-scented passion flower, *P. mixta* **Curuba di Indio** and *P. ligularis*, said by connoisseurs to be the most delicious.

The passion fruit and its extraordinarily beautiful flowe

CULTIVATION

A humus-rich, moist soil and a sheltered position on a warm wall suit the hardier varieties, with thick mulches to protect their roots. However, most of these plants are happier under cover.

Growing under Glass
For edible fruit production, and to grow most of the more tender varieties, glass is essential. Fortunately, they can also be grown in pots, making them less rampant and allowing some to be put outside for the summer.

Growing in Containers
Surprisingly, such rampant climbers take fairly well to pot culture, but require a lot of watering. They will crop in pots and, indeed, this is one of the better ways of growing them, so they can be taken indoors for winter. They need an open, free-draining, rich compost and regular feeding.

Ornamental and Wildlife Value
Amongst the most attractive of all climbers in flower, foliage, or when festooned with fruits. The flowers are enjoyed by many insects and the fruits contain plentiful seeds for the birds.

Maintenance
Spring Tie in new growth, spray with seaweed solution monthly.
Summer Tie in growths, spray with seaweed solution monthly.
Autumn Pick fruits after a long, hot summer.
Winter Prune before frosts and protect roots or take pots inside.

Propagation
Passion flowers can all be grown from seed, which can give good results for they are still relatively unimproved and most are true species. Propagate good varieties from heel or nodal cuttings in midsummer if they are given bottom heat.

Pruning and Training
Pruning is remedial, removing dead and surplus growth. Strong wires are needed, as these are quite vigorous and productive.

Weed, Pest and Disease Control
Passion flowers tend to form rather dense stools, which means they are prone to weed infestations which make the crown damp and short-lived. Occasionally they fail to thrive, but generally they are no problem save for frost damage: protect the roots and lower stems.

Harvesting and Storing
Best ripen the fruit on the vine till they drop, though picked young for transport they keep well. As they ripen they will shrivel, appearing old and wrinkled, and the flavour is then at its best.

Passion fruit vines are highly decorative and provide a dazzling splash of colour

OTHER USES

The empty shells make good slug traps for the garden.

Passion fruit in flower

CULINARY USES

Thirst-quenching raw, passion fruit are made into juice which is a popular drink in many countries, much like orange juice and squash are in others. They can be made into jams, liqueurs and sorbets.

Passion Fruit Sorbet
Serves 4–6

12 ripe passion fruit
Approx.120g (4oz) sugar
Mint sprigs

Scoop out the fruit pulp and seeds and sieve. Discard the seeds. To the juice, add half its weight in water and the same of sugar, stir till the sugar has dissolved and freeze. Partially thaw and beat vigorously, then refreeze. Serve partially thawed, scooped into glasses and decorated with mint sprigs.

Eriobotrya/Photinia japonica from the family *Rosaceae*

LOQUATS

JAPANESE MEDLARS OR PLUMS

Tree/bush, up to 10m (33ft). Life span: medium to long. Evergreen.
Fruits: up to 5cm (2in), pear-shaped, orange. Value: minor.

Loquats have very large, leathery, corrugated leaves, woolly white underneath, and fragrant, furry, yellowish flowers. The fruits are orange and pear-shaped with one or more big, brown-black seeds and sweet, acid, chewy pulp.

First reported in 1690, these were imported from Canton to Kew Gardens in London in 1787. Widely cultivated in the East, they are now popular in the Mediterranean countries and in Florida.

VARIETIES

Only the species is generally available, though improved sorts are now grown in Japan and China.

CULTIVATION

They grow outdoors well enough in northern Europe, but do not fruit. Any reasonable soil and a warm, well-drained site will suffice. They do best on a warm wall, but it needs to be a big one. They will crop only under glass or in countries with warm winters.

Growing under Glass
As they flower in autumn and the fruits ripen in late winter and spring, loquats need to be grown under glass if they are to fruit in any country that does not have a warm winter.

Loquats ripening on the tree

Growing in Containers
Loquats make big shrubs, so they are usefully confined in large pots.

Propagation
Loquats can be grown from fresh seed, or layers, or softwood cuttings taken in spring with bottom heat.

Ornamental and Wildlife Value
Very architectural plants with a lovely scent, they will also make good shelter for birds and insects.

Weed, Pest and Disease Control
Few problems with these.

Maintenance
Spring Prune if needed, spray with seaweed solution, pick fruit.
Summer Move outdoors for the summer.
Autumn Bring indoors.
Winter Protect outdoor plants from frosts.

Pruning and Training
Only remedial pruning is needed. They are best trained on a wall and allowed to grow out from it or grown as bushes in pots. Trim back any dead and diseased growths in spring.

Harvesting and Storing
The fruits need warmth and protection to ripen in late winter/early spring, so they must be grown under glass in cold countries.

COMPANION PLANTING

These are dense evergreens that will kill off any plants grown underneath.

OTHER USES

These shrubs make tall and attractive screens in countries with warmer climes.

CULINARY USES

Loquats are eaten raw, stewed, jammed or jellied. They are made into a liqueur in Bermuda.

Loquat Jam
Makes approx. 2.4kg (5lb)

1.4kg (3lb) loquats
Approx. 1kg (2lb) sugar

Wash and stone the loquats, then simmer till soft with just enough water to prevent burning. Weigh and add three-quarters of the weight in sugar. Stir to dissolve the sugar, then bring to the boil. Skim and pot in sterilized jars. Store in a cool place.

Opuntia ficus indica/dillenii from the family *Cactaceae*

PRICKLY PEARS

BARBERRY FIGS

Herbaceous, up to 2m (7ft). Life span: medium to long. Evergreen, self-fertile.
Fruits: 5–9cm (2–3½in), ovoid, red, yellow or purple. Value: minor.

These are typical cacti, with round or oval, thick, fleshy pads covered with tufts of long and short spines. The flowers are large, 5–7cm (2–3in), yellow, with numerous petals, stamens and filaments. These are followed by red, yellow or purple, prickly, oval cylinders which are the fruits. Under the skin the flesh is very acid and sweet.

These are natives of the Americas where they have long been used. They have naturalized in the Mediterranean basin and almost every hot, dry country, even flourishing on the lava beds of Sicily.

CULTIVATION

Opuntia need a well-drained, open, limy soil and a warm position. They are remarkably hardy, for cacti. Several survive outside at the Royal Botanic Gardens at Kew in England, and I have had them for many years in eastern England.

Growing under Glass and in Containers
Growing under glass is vital if fruits are to be produced, and you will also need extra artificial light. In large and free-draining pots, prickly pears are happy enough.

Ornamental and Wildlife Value
Very decorative and quite a talking point in a garden. They are more reliable under glass and just as attractive. The flowers are good for insects.

Pruning and Training
No pruning is required. When the pads become heavy they may need propping up.

Weed, Pest and Disease Control
Weed control needs to be good, as these are nasty to weed between. Slugs and snails may develop a taste for the pads.

Prickly pears thrive in arid, Mediterranean areas

Maintenance
Spring Keep weed-free.
Winter Protect outside plants during coldest weather.

Propagation
These can be grown from seed, but are slow. Detached pads or pieces root easily and are much quicker.

Harvesting and Storing
This is a thorny task. Wrap a piece of bark round to pick the fruit, which will keep for several days. The peel is best skinned off completely before the fruit is eaten.

COMPANION PLANTING

I grow them outside in front of evergreen hedges of leylandii and holly. They survive, but unfortunately, have never fruited.

VARIETIES

Opuntia maxima is very similar to *Opuntia*. **'Burbank'** raised a spineless variety.

CULINARY USES

Prickly pears are usually eaten raw in place of drink and are occasionally fried or stewed. The red varieties will stain everything.

OTHER USES

After ensilaging or pulping with salt, prickly pears make a useful animal feed.

Ananas comosus from the family *Bromeliaceae*

PINEAPPLES

Herbaceous, 1x1m (3x3ft). Life span: short-lived, perennial. Fruits: average 10x20cm (4x8in), dull orange or yellow. Value: rich in vitamins C and A.

Pineapples need little description; they are the most distinctive of fruits – there is nothing else like them. They are Bromeliads, like many houseplants. They resemble common garden yuccas, being nearly cylindrical with a tuft of narrow, pointed leaves emerging from the top. The skin of the fruit is green to yellow, with many slightly raised protuberances. Wild species have serrated, thorny-edged leaves and set seed. Modern cultivars are seedless, with smoother leaves and smaller fruits; those of traditional varieties weighed up to 8kg (20lb).

Cultivated and selected from the wild by the people of Central America for thousands of years, the fruits were sensational in 1493 to the crew of Columbus. The first fruit, surviving the voyage back, was regarded as nearly as great a discovery as the New World itself. Pineapple motifs appeared, sometimes distorted, throughout European art – often as knobs on pew ends. By 1550 pineapple was being preserved in sugar to be sent back to the Old World as an exotic, and profitable, luxury. By the end of the sixteenth century pineapples had been spread to China and the Philippines and were naturalizing in Java, and soon after were colonizing the west coast of Africa. An enterprising M. Le Cour of Holland succeeded in growing them under glass in 1686 and was supplying plants to English gardeners in 1690. Within a few years there was a craze for pineapples, with noblemen's gardeners growing them under glass on deep hot beds of horse dung and leather wastes as far north as Scotland. British-grown pineapples were sold in the markets at a guinea apiece. The Victorians raised the cultivation of pineapples to a high level with the regulated heat from steam boilers. A photograph of English pineapples from the turn of the century is a humblingly impressive display.

Pineapple fields in Hawaii

VARIETIES

There have been hundreds of varieties, but most have disappeared as a few commercial cultivars monopolized trade. Pineapples are now grown most intensively in Hawaii, but also in Australia, Malaysia and South Africa. **'Smooth Cayenne'**, or **'Kew Pine'**, was widely grown for many years, but connoisseurs preferred **'Queen'** and **'Ripley'**. Long gone is the favorite British hothouse variety **'Enville'**.

Pineapples grow on a central stem, which rises out of the crown of the fruit

CULTIVATION, GROWING UNDER GLASS AND IN CONTAINERS

A tropical plant, the pineapple is happiest in Hawaii. It needs very high soil and fairly high air temperatures, high humidity during the growing season except when ripening, as much light as possible and a very rich, open, fibrous compost in quantity. In plantations pineapples have about a square metre/yard of ground each, so generous pots are required! Never let them chill below 21°C (70°F) or 'cook' above 32°C (90°F).

Ornamental and Wildlife Value

They are easy to root and grow as houseplants, but require lots of heat and care to fruit well.

Maintenance

Spring Pot up cuttings and mature plants.
Summer Root cuttings or crowns.
Autumn Tidy plants for the winter.
Winter Keep warm!

Propagation

Suckers from healthy plants are best, fruiting in a year and a half or so. Gills, the shoots produced at the base of the fruit, seeds and even stem cuttings can be used, but take longer to grow and fruit. The crown from a fruit is easily rooted; cut it off whole with a thin shoulder, prise off the shoulder and pull off the lower withered leaves individually. Root over heat in a gritty compost. Keep the foliage moist in a plastic bag, but be careful of mould.

Pruning and Training

Young plants rooted in summer need potting up in spring, growing on for a year and repotting the following spring to fruit that summer or autumn. Pot up annually, and remove superfluous shoots and fruited stumps if you have any. If happy, pineapples may grow and produce for five to ten years.

Weed, Pest and Disease Control

The main pests are white scale and mealybugs, controlled by sprays of soft soap or commercial predators.

COMPANION PLANTING

A secret of success is apparently to grow them with a light top dressing of banana skins.

HARVESTING AND STORING AND CULINARY USES

Picked underripe and kept cool, they can be stored for several weeks. They make tasty jam, delicious juice and are best-known canned. Although a fruit, they add sweetness and texture to many savoury dishes, from Chinese to curry, and can even be fried with gammon.

Pineapple-baked Ham
Serves 4

1 canned ham
1 larger pineapple
Garlic (optional)

Carefully empty the meat from the tin in one piece. Sharpen the open end of the can and use it to extract the pineapple from its skin, first slicing off the top shoulder. Leave the skin intact. (Slice and chill the pineapple flesh for dessert, cutting out the tough central core.) Insert the ham in the hole created, pin the shoulder back on to seal, and bake for at least an hour in a pre-heated oven at 200°C/400°F/gas mark 6. (Garlic lovers may rub the ham over before insertion.) To serve, turn the pineapple on its side to cut circles of ham with a pineapple rind. Serve with puréed sweetcorn and baked sweet potatoes.

Musa species from the family *Musaceae*

BANANAS

Tree/herbaceous plant, 3–9m (10–30ft) and nearly as wide. Life span: perpetual as vegetative clones but sterile. Fruits: up to 30cm/12in, green to yellow or red. Value: nutritious and rich in starch.

Banana plants form herbaceous stools of shoots like small trees. Each enormous shoot unfurls sheaths of gigantic, oblong leaves up to 4.5m (15ft) long. A mature shoot disgorges one flower stalk, which hangs down under its mighty bunch of many combs or hands of bananas. The hands point upwards, sheltered by succulent, purple bracts the size of plates, along the length of the stalk, and a mass of male flowers adorns the end. One bunch can hold about a dozen combs, each with over a dozen fingers. Bananas are the most productive food crop, giving about forty times the yield of potatoes. The fruits are green, ripening yellow, sweet, notoriously shaped and unforgettably scented.

The Ancient Egyptians had the culinary Abyssinian banana (*Musa ensete*), but early travellers from Europe soon discovered sweeter, more edible bananas in most tropical and semi-tropical regions. The hardiest, the smaller Chinese banana, was brought from the East Indies for cultivation in the Canary Islands by 1516 – and, it has been suggested, was introduced to the Americas from there, but evidence of indigenous bananas discounts this. Most cultivated bananas are probably descendants of *M. sapientum*, *M. acuminata* and *M. balbisiana*, wild bananas thought to come from eastern Asia and Indo-Malaysia. *Musa maculata* and *M. rosacea* descendants are popular in parts of Asia and world-wide there exist many other species. In prehistoric cultivation, seed-bearing species were replaced by selected hybrids with big, seedless fruits propagated vegetatively. These superior sorts multiplied and by the nineteenth century there were countless local varieties of bananas in most hot countries. Many of these have now been lost and replaced by a few high-yielding commercial cultivars.

VARIETIES

Common cultivars are **'Robusta'**, **'Lacatan'** and **'Gros Michel'**, the latter pair being old varieties that survived the Panama disease which destroyed many. However, they are tall and need hot, moist conditions such as those of Jamaica, where **'Gros Michel'** was introduced in 1836. The **Chinese Banana** (*M. cavendishii*), also known as **Dwarf** or **Canary Island Banana**, is hardier, smaller and particularly tasty with shorter, delicate fruits, making it widely grown for domestic use, and well suited for greenhouse culture. A new, medium-sized and more productive hybrid, **'William'**, is taking over commercially.

Plantains are separate varieties, possibly descendants of *M. paradisiaca*, larger and slightly horn-shaped. Plantains are most often used for cooking, not dessert purposes; thus cooking bananas are sometimes referred to as plantains.

Bob's own Abyssinian banana, which thrives outside in Norfolk

CULTIVATION

In warm climates bananas need a rich, quite heavy, deep, well-drained soil with copious moisture. Freedom from strong winds is also essential. The smallest varieties are usually planted about 3m/10ft apart; the larger proportionately more.

Growing under Glass and in Containers

In cooler climates the Canary/Chinese/Cavendish is best, as it is very compact and fruits at less than 3m (10ft) high. Keep the temperature above 19°C (65°F) in winter and under 30°C (85°F) in summer. Potted plants can go out for summer.

Maintenance

Spring Pot up or top dress, thin and root suckers.
Summer Top dress, thin suckers.
Autumn Cut fruits, remove old shoot, thin suckers.
Winter Keep warm.

Banana trees need large pots, so growing them in the ground under cover is best

Propagation

Some ornamental and inferior varieties grow from seed. The best edible plants are bits of rhizome with a bud or sterile hybrids, propagated by suckers. Viable buds will resemble enormous, sprouting bulbs. They root easily in a gritty compost over heat in a moist atmosphere.

The medium-sized hybrid, 'William', is becoming popular

HARVESTING AND STORING, CULINARY USES

Bananas are best matured off the tree and kept in a warm room. Most are at their best when yellow. They can be dried, made into flour or fermented to produce a sweet liqueur.

In hot countries, bananas are a staple food, being used as a vegetable and a source of flour, as well as a fruit.

Banana Custard Pie
serves 4

175g (6oz) digestive biscuits
75g (3oz) butter
30g (1oz) strawberry jam
300ml (10 fl oz) milk
60g (2oz) honey
15g (¹/₂oz) cornflour
Dash of vanilla essence
3 or 4 bananas, sliced and chilled
Nutmeg

Crush the biscuits and mix with most of the butter. Press into a pie dish and freeze. Spread the frozen surface with the remaining butter, paint with the jam and refreeze. Heat the milk and honey, mix the cornflour with a drop of water and the vanilla, then pour the hot milk on to the flour mixture. Return to the heat, stirring continuously, till thickened, then allow to cool. Put chilled banana slices into the cooled custard, mix together and pour into the biscuit case. Top with grated nutmeg and chill till required.

Pruning and Training

Bananas fruit continuously if growing happily. A stem will flower and fruit in about a year and a half. Only one main shoot and a replacement are allowed; all others should be removed, and once the main shoot has fruited it is cut out. The clump or stool may live as long as a human being, but is replaced commercially every dozen years or so.

Weed, Pest and Disease Control

No major problems for private gardeners.

OTHER USES

Often used in beauty preparations and shampoos (below). The foliage will provide good animal fodder.

Persea americana from the family *Lauraceae*

AVOCADO PEAR

Evergreen tree or shrub. Tender. Value: very rich in vitamin E, average fat content, high in monounsaturated fatty acids.

This sub-tropical tree from Central America was originally introduced to Europe by the Conquistadors and has since been planted in many parts of the world. Its anglicized name is a corruption of the Aztec word *ahuacatl*, which was used to describe both its fruit and the testicle. There are three main races: Guatemalan fruits are large with a warty skin; Mexican ones are small; and large, smooth-skinned types come from the West Indies. All have been hybridized, producing hundreds of cultivars suitable for Mediterranean to tropical climates.

VARIETIES

'Ettinger' (Mexican x Guatemalan) produces oblong fruit with bright green, shiny skin. **'Fuerte'** (Mexican x Guatemalan) is the most common cultivar, producing large fruit with green, textured skin. **'Hass'** (Guatemalan) is self-fertile, the skin dark purple when it is mature.

CULTIVATION

Avocados flourish in shelter and sunshine.

The ideal soil is a slightly acid, moisture-retentive, free-draining loam. Improve sandy or clay soils by adding organic matter.

Temperatures should be between 20–28°C (68–82°F) with humidity greater than 60 per cent all year round. Some can withstand temperatures down to 10–15°C (48–58°F). Allow 6m (20ft) between the trees and the rows. In exposed areas, plant windbreaks to prevent damage.

During the growing season, apply 1.5–2kg (3lb 4oz–4lb 6oz) of general fertilizer in 2 or 3 doses. Mulch round the base to suppress weeds. Water during times of drought until trees are established.

Shape young trees to ensure a balanced crown. Remove diseased, damaged or crossing branches after fruiting. They withstand hard pruning. Plant several cultivars with overlapping or simultaneous flowering periods to produce fruit.

Growing under Glass

Grow in a greenhouse or conservatory, maintaining moderate temperatures and humidity according to the origin of the cultivar.

Flowers and fruit are rarely produced in cool temperate zones due to low light intensity and reduced daylight hours.

Growing in Containers

Repot young plants as the compost becomes congested with roots. Every 2–3 years repot established plants into a pot one size larger, using a loam-based compost with moderate fertilizer levels. Top-dress in the intervening years by removing and replacing the top 5–7.5cm (2–3in) of compost in spring. Apply a general fertilizer every 2–3 weeks when plants are actively growing.

Water as the compost surface dries out. Reduce watering in winter and do not feed.

In spring, prune side branches to encourage bushy growth. Containerized plants can be placed outdoors in summer in a warm, sheltered position when there is no danger of frost. During winter, they need a light, cool position with temperatures no lower than 16°C (60°F).

A cluster of fruits in South Africa, ripe and ready for harvest and the increasingly demanding export market

An avocado orchard in Transvaal, South Africa

PESTS AND DISEASES

Use resistant rootstocks against avocado root rot. Those grown indoors may be attacked by whitefly: use sticky traps, the predator *Encarsia formosa* or soft soap. Control red spider mite by maintaining humidity and

Avocados for sale, Costa Rica

remove mealybug by dabbing them with a paintbrush dipped in methylated spirits.

OTHER USES

The pulp of avocados makes an ideal natural ingredient for face masks and for skin moisturizers.

Maintenance
Spring Repot containerized plants.
Summer Feed, harvest and water as necessary.
Autumn Bring containerized plants indoors in cool temperate zones.
Winter Reduce watering and stop feeding avocados grown under glass.

Propagation
Avocados are propagated from seed, although the seedling may not come true (more reliable results are obtained professionally by grafting named cultivars on to disease-resistant rootstocks). Choose healthy seeds, cut 1cm (½in) from the pointed end and dip the wound in fungicide. Sow in a 15cm (6in) pot of moist seed compost, with the cut end just above the surface. Germinate in a glasshouse, propagator or place the pot in a clear polythene bag, lightly knot the end and put in a bright position away from direct sunshine at 21–27°C (70–80°F).

When the fourth leaf appears, remove the bag and leave the plant for 2 weeks to acclimatize. Do not force the stone from the roots; allow it to rot away. Pot on as the compost becomes congested with roots; when they outgrow 30–40cm (12–16in) pots, plant out into their final positions.

Harvesting and Storing
Seed-raised trees fruit after 5 to 7 years; grafted plants take 3 to 5 years.

Remove fruit carefully using secateurs. Discard damaged fruit. They are ready for eating if slightly soft when pressed. If unripe, store for a few days.

CULINARY USES

Coat cut surfaces with lemon or lime juice to prevent discoloration. Avocado is delicious simply with olive oil and vinaigrette. The flavour also blends well with prawns, crabmeat and other seafood or grapefruit and pineapple. Try it with bacon in a sandwich, or made into a fine salad. To create the Mexican dip, Guacamole, bake and then mash avocados with chillies, onions and garlic and serve with tortillas.

Cold Avocado Soup
Serves 2

This is a welcome alternative to vichyssoise.

Purée 2 avocados, peeled and stoned, with 300ml (½pt) crème fraîche or

low-fat yoghurt combined with double cream. Gently heat 1 litre (1¾pt) well-flavoured chicken stock and stir in the avocado purée, gently heating: do not boil.

Season with salt and freshly ground black pepper and a judicious squeeze or two of lemon juice to accent the flavour. Decorate with a dollop of yoghurt and sprinkle with fresh chives.

Avocado Mousse
Serves 4

Oded Schwartz gives this unusual dessert recipe in Reader's Digest *Fast and Fresh Cooking*.

225ml (8fl oz) double cream
1 tablespoon sugar
1 teaspoon orange-blossom water
2 avocados
2 tablespoons runny honey
3 tablespoons Grand Marnier
Grated rind and juice of 2 limes
Mint, to garnish

Whip the cream until stiff and add the sugar and orange blossom water. Chill

well. Meantime, scoop the pulp from the avocado shells and purée with all the remaining ingredients bar half the lime rind.

Transfer to a mixing bowl and stir in the cream. Serve in individual glass bowls and decorate with the remaining rind and a sprig of mint.

Nutrition
Avocados are high in protein, vitamin B complex and vitamin E, have low carbohydrate levels and no cholesterol.

Avocado Mousse

Mangifera indica from the family Anacardiaceae

MANGO

Tree, variable size. Life span: as long as a human being. Fruits: variable in size, flat ovoids, green/yellow or red. Value: rich in vitamins A, B and C.

Medium to large trees, with luxuriant masses of narrow leaves, these carry fruits that weigh anything from a few grams (ounces) to a kilogram (2lb). They have an inedible, tough skin and an enormous, flat stone to which the fibrous flesh adheres.

Mangoes are native to India and exist there in countless variety. Doubtless early Europeans came across them, but they were first recorded by a Friar Jordanus in about 1300. Mangoes have now spread to most hot regions, including Florida.

VARIETIES

India's favourite varieties are **'Alphonso'**, large and of fine quality and flavour, and **'Mulgoa'**, medium-large, green and blotchy. The West Indies prefer **'Bombay'** (**'Peters'**), round, flat, yellow when ripe and very juicy, and **'Julie'**. Cuba once exported one rated very highly called **'Biscochuelo'**.

CULTIVATION

Mangoes want a hot, dryish climate and deep, well-drained, rich soils. Excessive rain spoils pollination and drought spoils the quality of the fruit. They want exceptionally deep and wide planting holes dug about 10m (30ft) apart.

A well-developed mango tree in the sunshine of St Lucia

Growing under Glass and in Containers

As they are large when fruitful, the glasshouse would have to be big. They may be grown in pots for ornamental use but fruiting success seems unlikely.

Propagation

Mangoes raised from seed are often polyembryonic, giving several seedlings. Some are near-clones of the original, and some produce poor fruits with stringy texture and a turpentine taint! The best varieties are grafted or layered and will bear in about four years.

HARVESTING AND STORING, CULINARY USES

Mangoes soften and turn yellow or red as they ripen and do not keep. Picked unripe, they travel well and are fine for culinary use. They are very messy to eat raw! They are widely used for chutneys, jams, tarts, pickles and preserves.

Mango Chutney
Makes approx. 1kg (2lb)

1kg (2lb) green mangoes
175g (6oz) salt

Pruning and Training

Remedial pruning of thin and poor growth is necessary once a head has formed, plus root pruning if the tree persists with strong, unfruitful growth.

OTHER USES

The seeds have been boiled and eaten in famines. The wood is poor but used for packaging crates and firewood.

600ml (1pt) vinegar
75g (3oz) each peeled chopped garlic cloves; sultanas; chopped dates
50g (2oz) each chopped fresh ginger; chopped blanched almonds
2 teaspoons hot chilli powder
500g (1lb) brown sugar

Peel, stone and chop the mangoes, sprinkle them with salt and keep cool overnight. Rinse and drain thoroughly. Mix all the ingredients except the sugar and simmer for several hours till soft. Add the sugar, bring to the boil and bottle in clean sterilized jars. Store for six months before use.

Carica from the family *Caricaceae*

PAWPAWS
PAPAYA

Herbaceous, up to 6m (20ft). Life span: very short.
Fruits: up to 30x15cm (12x6in).
Value: rich in papain.

Pawpaws (also known as papaya) are small herbaceous 'trees' that resemble palms as they are unbranched with ornate, acanthus-like foliage clustered on top and up to fifty green 'melons' underneath. There are male, female and hermaphrodite plants. The fruits uncannily resemble melons, turning yellow-orange as they ripen. The flesh is usually pink with a central hole full of small round seeds and can weigh up to 2kg (5lb).

Although it is indigenous to Central America, the pawpaw has rapidly spread to every warm country. Seeds were sent to Nepal as early as 1626 from the East Indies.

VARIETIES

'Solo' is a commercial dwarf, but most pawpaws are local varieties selected from seed and varying considerably. Grow them from fruit you like. *Carica candamarcensis*, or the **Mountain Papaw**, is hardier with coarser leaves and smaller fruit, which have blunt ridges and an apple-like aroma. They are too acid to eat raw, but good cooked or as jam.

CULTIVATION

Pawpaws prefer deep, humus-rich soil, and to be about 3m (10ft) apart. They need support while young. You should eliminate most males and replace the whole lot every five years.

A pawpaw tree in fruit

Growing under Glass and in Containers
They are practical for tall heated greenhouses, and highly ornamental, so also well worth growing as pot plants, but they do not fruit well easily.

Ornamental and Wildlife Value
Their foliage is very attractive and they're so easy to grow they are worth trying anywhere frost-free and elsewhere as summer bedding!

Propagation
Variable from seed; usually grown by sowing several to a hole and eliminating the poorest seedlings. (Only one male is needed to fifty females, but in fact they can only be differentiated when flowering.) Fruiting occurs within a year.

CULINARY USES

Pawpaws are in season all year, and unripe ones keep for many days. Eaten as dessert or cooked as a fruit or vegetable, pawpaw is delicious, especially the first time. However, most importantly, the fruit and leaves contain papain, which tenderizes meats cooked with them.

Pawpaw Breakfast Juice
Serves 2

1 ripe pawpaw
1 small lime
honey or sugar to taste

Scoop out the flesh and sieve out the seeds of the pawpaw. Add lime juice and sweetener and liquidize. Serve immediately in frosted glasses with sugared rims as breakfast starters.

OTHER USES

Papain is used medicinally, and for chewing gum.

Durio zibethinus from family *Malvaceae/Bombacaceae*

DURIANS
CIVET FRUIT

Tree, 30m (100ft). Life span: fairly long. Fruits: about 25x20cm (10x8in), ovoid, green to yellow. Value: a little protein, a little fat; one quarter to a third is fat and starch

This is an infamous fruit, banned from airlines and loathed by most people on first acquaintance. It has an aroma similar to that of an over-ripe Gorgonzola cheese in a warm room. The flavour was long ago described as "French custard passed through a sewer pipe". The texture is like that of blancmange or custard, and the sweet flavour delicious and addictive. Once bravely tasted, the durian is unforgettable and 'the sensation is worth a voyage to the East'.

The trees are very large and upright with leaves not dissimilar to those of a peach. The fruits are round to ovoid, very large, weighing up to 4–5kg (10lb), green initially, yellowing as they ripen, with a long stalk. They are covered in short, sharp spikes and resemble some brutal medieval weapon. The pulp is white with up to a dozen big seeds.

Durians come originally from Malaysia and spread to South-East Asia in prehistoric times. Widely grown all over the region, they have never managed to become more than a curiosity elsewhere.

VARIETIES

Local varieties exist with variation in size, shape and flavour, but no widespread commercial clones are available.

Durian fruits taste delicious, but smell revolting!

CULTIVATION

The large trees need a deep, heavy soil to secure them, but they are not too difficult to please.

Propagation, Pruning and Training
Seeds, if fresh, germinate in about a week and come nearly true. Only remedial pruning work is necessary.

Growing under Glass and in Containers
Their size and their need for tropical heat and moisture make them difficult. They may make good pot specimens if fresh seed can be obtained.

Ornamental and Wildlife Value
Attractive trees in their native climate.

OTHER USES

Durians help get railway compartments to oneself. They are also reputed to be an aphrodisiac.

The Durian tree has a truly majestic stature

HARVESTING AND STORING, CULINARY USES

Durians must be eaten fresh and they quickly spoil due to a chemical change (and the aroma gets worse!). They are best eaten raw but may be made into ice cream or jam, or juiced and drunk with coconut milk. The large, fleshy seeds are boiled or roasted and eaten as nuts.

Durian Delight
Serves 6

225g (8oz) each unsweetened durian purée, honey, natural set yogurt, cream Dash of vanilla essence

Mix the ingredients and beat till smooth. Partially freeze, beat again and repeat this two or three times before freezing firm. Keep well sealed until immediately before eating!

Annona from the family *Annonaceae*

CHERIMOYAS
CUSTARD APPLES AND SOUR SOPS

Tree, up to 6m (20ft). Life span: short.
Fruits: variable in size, green and scaly.

A family of small trees, known as custard apples or sour sops, from the flavour and texture of the better fruits. Many have aromatic leaves and/or fragrant flowers. Despite the varying appearance of each species, the common names are often swapped or confused in different countries. The flesh is usually white, sweet and acid, with up to 30 black seeds embedded in it and covered with a thin rind, which breaks off like scales when ripe.

Natives of the Americas, they are most popular there but have spread to other tropical and warm zones. They are grown in Madeira and the Canaries for the European trade.

OTHER USES

Corossol tea, shown above, was traditionally made from the leaves of *A. muricata*.

HARVESTING AND STORING, CULINARY USES

Picked under-ripe they keep for up to a week or so. They are usually eaten raw or used to flavour drinks and ices.

Sour Sop Sorbet
serves 6

500g (1lb) sugar
1 large ripe sour sop
60g (2oz) crystallized ginger

Dissolve the sugar in 450ml (16 fl oz) boiling water and chill. Squeeze the juice from the sour sop pulp and strain. To each cupful add half a cup of sugar syrup. Partly freeze, beat and refreeze. Repeat twice. After the final beating, mix in the chopped ginger.

VARIETIES

Anona squamosa is the true **Custard Apple** or **Sweet Sop** and is most common in the West Indies. *A. cherimolia* is the **Cherimoya**. This is deciduous and more hardy, growing at high elevations in the hotter areas. The leaves are deliciously scented and downy underneath; the flowers are fragrant, fleshy, green and yellow; the fruit resembles a small artichoke with a banana/pineapple flavour. *A. muricata*, or **Sour Sop**, is evergreen with leaves that smell of blackcurrants and large (up to 3.5kg/8lb), green fruits with soft spines in ridges and a sourer taste . *A. reticulata* is the **Bullock's Heart**, so-called because of its ruddy color. It has firm, sweet, yellow pulp. Numerous other species are grown all over the Americas.

CULTIVATION

They will thrive in poor soils but give better crops with better treatment and prefer dryish, hilly conditions.

Growing under Glass and in Containers
The cherimoya is worth growing even if it never fruits and custard apples are probably worth trying. Sour sops may not crop, but all are good value as pot specimens.

A ripening cherimoya fruit

Propagation, Pruning and Training
They grow from seed, but best varieties are budded. Only remedial pruning and nipping out is required.

A cherimoya tree will grow well in a pot

Averrhoa carambola from the family *Oxalidaceae*

CARAMBOLAS

Tree, up to 11m (35ft). Life span: medium. Fruits: up to 5x15cm (2x6in). Cylindrical, star-shaped in cross section, yellow. Value: sugar, some oxalic acid.

Averrhoas are small trees with delicate, pinnate (walnut-like) foliage. A profusion of sprays of little white or pinkish flowers is followed by huge quantities of yellow, cylindrical, star-shaped fruits with five prominent angles, which weigh down the branches.

Natives of Indonesia and the Moluccas, averrhoas are still mostly grown in South-East Asia and the Indian subcontinent. However, because of their decorative value, and being quite robust, they are now exported and appear almost everywhere.

The distinctive, star-shaped Carambola fruit

VARIETIES

Carambolas are variable in taste. Some are much better than others, though they are all juicy. I have eaten them from European supermarkets, when they were like yellow soap, and also fresh, when they were amber and a joy. *Averrhoa bilimbi* or **Billings** are similar, resembling gherkin cucumbers, but are used more as vegetables and in curries, and for the popular billings jam.

CULTIVATION

Adaptable to most warm, moist climates, and any reasonable, well-drained soil, they fruit prolifically with little attention.

Ornamental and Wildlife Value
Burdened with yellow fruit, they are impressive.

Growing under Glass and in Containers
Carambolas are pretty plants, so make good specimens. If they fruit they will put on a terrific show.

Propagation
Usually they are grown from seed, but better varieties are grafted. Only remedial pruning is needed.

The delicate sprays of the flowers are very attractive

HARVESTING AND STORING, CULINARY USES

They travel fairly well if picked just under-ripe, and then keep for a week or two. **Carambolas** are more often used for making jelly and preserves than as dessert fruits. Their star shape makes excellent decorative garnishes in compôtes and fruit salads. **Billings** are used for pickles and preserves and billings jam is made after soaking overnight and straining to remove the acid bitterness. The flowers of both species were once made into conserves.

Camaranga or Carambola Jam
Makes approx. 2kg (4lb)

1kg (2lb) carambolas
1kg (2lb) white sugar

Cut the fruit up into finger-thick pieces and discard the sharp edges. Do not discard the seeds, as they improve the flavour of the jam. Add water to cover them and boil till the pieces are softening – about 15 minutes should be sufficient. Add the sugar and bring to the boil again for another 15 minutes, then bottle and seal.

OTHER USES

Carambola juice removes stains from linen and can be used for polishing brass. Billings also polishes brass.

Achras sapota/Manilkara zapota from the family *Sapotaceae*

SAPODILLAS
OR SAPOTA, NASEBERRIES, BULLY TREES, CHIKKUS

Tree, 4–16m (14–52ft). Life span: medium.
Fruits: about 6cm (2½in), rounded, brown.

Sapodilla makes a medium to big tree with glossy leaves. The fruit is a large, round berry with a rough, brown skin over luscious pulp similar to a pear's, containing a core with up to a dozen seeds much like an apple's – black, shiny and inedible. The tree's milky sap can be tapped in the same way as rubber. Once collected, it is coagulated with heat and the sticky mass produced is strained out and dried to form chicle gum. Still mostly grown in its native region of Central America, sapodilla is still found wild in the forests of Venezuela. Sapodillas were more extensively planted when chicle gum started to be used for a booming new commodity – chewing gum. Now it is an important crop for Mexico and Central American countries. The naseberry is Jamaica's national fruit.

Fruit on the sapodilla tree

VARIETIES

Local varieties are cultivated for fruit, but there is little commercial demand, as it must be eaten absolutely ripe. However, there is a big demand for chicle gum; varieties selected for sap production can give up to 3kg (6½lb) of gum per year.

CULINARY USES

Perfectly ripened, they are considered superb dessert fruit. The fruits keep up to a month or more in a cold refrigerator.

Chewing Gum

120g (4oz) each of chicle gum, glucose, caramel paste, icing sugar
225g (8oz) sugar
Spearmint or mint flavouring to taste

Melt the gum carefully in a bain-marie. Meanwhile boil water, 100ml (4 fl oz), the sugar and glucose to exactly 124°C (255°F).

Remove from the heat, add the caramel and boil again. Off the heat, mix the syrup into the melted gum, beating steadily and briskly. Add the flavouring and pour on to a cold surface thickly coated with icing sugar. Roll flat. When cold, cut into strips, wrap and label.

CULTIVATION

Sapodilla prefers very hot, moist climates with rich soil.

Propagation, Pruning and Training
Propagate by seed or preferably by grafting for better varieties. Only remedial pruning work seems necessary.

Growing under Glass and in Containers
The trees are variable in size and unlikely to crop well under glass, but they are attractive so should make good specimen pot plants.

Ornamental and Wildlife Value
Sapodilla has very attractive foliage and the fruits are enjoyed by wildlife.

Harvesting and Storing
Best finally ripened off the tree, when the fruit softens and mellows in a few days to a treacly, gummy consistency. Left on the tree, the fruits become veined with milk, which makes them too acid until bletted like medlars (see p.522).

COMPANION PLANTING

Sapodilla trees are normally grown for the first five years with underplanted legume crops.

OTHER USES

Sapodilla wood is hard and durable, so it is used for handles and tools.

Nephelium lappaceum and *N. chinensis/litchi* from the family *Sapindaceae*

RAMBUTANS & LITCHIS

Tree, up to 18m (60ft). Life span: medium to long. Usually not self-fertile; male and female flowers often on separate trees. Fruits: 2.5–5cm (1–2in), round, reddish or yellow.

Rambutan or ramtum trees are large and spreading, with pinnate leaves, and festooned with hairy, chestnut-like conkers. These fruits are apricot-sized, covered with red or orange-yellow, soft spines like tentacles. Underneath the skin the flesh is wrapped around the single, inedible, brown seed. The flesh is sweet, acid, almost like pineapple with a hint of apricot – shame there is so little, as it is one of the best fruits I've ever tried.

Very similar yet more perfumed are litchees, lychees or litchis. These have a prickly, crackly shell and grow on a smaller tree.

Originally from the Malay archipelago, rambutans are greatly appreciated in South-East Asia where they are often grown in gardens, but, surprisingly, have never proved popular anywhere else. Litchis have long been a Chinese speciality, so they followed their people to many other suitable areas, such as Florida.

VARIETIES

Many different varieties of rambutan and litchi are grown in their regions. The **Pulassan**, *Nephelium*

mutabilechryseum, is another species, native to Java. It is similar but covered with warts instead of tentacles. *N. longana*, the **Longan**, is popular in southern China. It is smaller, brownish-yellow and nearly smooth-skinned, with similar chewy flesh.

CULTIVATION

They need tropical conditions. Litchis prefer lower humidity, rambutans more.

Litchis have tiny, soft spines

HARVESTING AND STORING, CULINARY USES

Both will ripen if picked early off the tree, so they are often found in temperate country shops.

Growing under Glass and in Containers

Sadly they are too large. They may possibly do as pot specimens for foliage, but are unlikely to fruit.

Ornamental and Wildlife Value

Handsome trees, they are often planted in gardens and parks in South East Asia and the Indian subcontinent. The fruit is exceptionally attractive to birds and also bats.

Propagation, Weed, Pest and Disease Control

They come nearly true from seed, but the best varieties are budded. Bird and bat damage is a severe problem.

Litchis are often preserved in syrup or dried to perfumed 'prunes'. All the fruits are superb desserts. Litchis are often used to close a Chinese meal.

Litchi Sundae
Serves 4–6

1kg (2lb) litchis
600ml (1pt) real vanilla ice cream
60g (2oz) blanched toasted almonds
Nutmeg
30g (1oz) coarse brown sugar
4–6 glacé cherries

Peel and stone the litchis, then chill them. Layer the fruit in tall glasses with ice cream and almonds and top with a flourish of nutmeg, sugar and a cherry.

Garcinia mangostana from the family *Clusiaceae (Guttifereae)*

MANGOSTEEN

Tree, 14m (45ft). Life span: long. Fruits: 6cm (2.5in), round, brownish. Value: small amounts of protein, mineral matter and fat; approx. one seventh sugar and starch.

The trees are small to medium-sized, cone-shaped and have large, leathery leaves somewhat like a lemon's. The fruits are round, purplish-brown, about apple size, with a rosette of dead petals around the stalk and an odd 'flower'-shaped button on the other end. If you cut the rind around the fruit's circumference, the top can be lifted off to reveal about half a dozen kernels of melting white pulp, tasting between grape and strawberry, tart and sweet, almost syrupy and chewy. There is a seed contained in many kernels, which is not eaten.

Mangosteens are natives of Malaya and were described by Captain Cook in 1770 in detail, and with delight. They were introduced to Ceylon (now Sri Lanka) in 1800 and were successfully fruited in English greenhouses in 1855. Widely held to be the world's most delicious fruit, they may be found in gardens in every tropical area, but are nowhere grown on a commercial scale.

Mangosteen trees

Ripe mangosteens

VARIETIES

There are many local varieties and also close relations, most of which are found in the East Indies. *Garcinia cambogia* has a smaller, yellow-pulped, yellow fruit. *G. cowa* is the **Cowa-Mangosteen**. Bigger, ribbed and apricot-coloured, it is generally too acid for dessert but makes good preserves. Another, *G. indica*, the **Cocum**, **Conca** or **Kokum**, has a sour, purple pulp used to make a vinegar, and the seeds are pressed for cocum oil. *G. dulcis* is a yellow-fruited variety found in the Moluccas. *G. morella* is common in South-East Asia and the plant also provides an orange-red resin, gamboge.

CULTIVATION

Mangosteens need deep, rich, well-drained soil, a sheltered site, shade when young, a hot, moist climate.

Growing under Glass and in Containers
If it can be done in England in the mid-nineteenth century, it can be done now.

Propagation
They are slow and unreliable from seed. They are then slow-growing, reaching only to the knee after two or three years. The best varieties are layered.

COMPANION PLANTING

Mangosteens benefit from light shade, especially when young, preferring tropically bright but not direct light, so they are planted in the shade of taller trees.

HARVESTING AND STORING, CULINARY USES

Use a ladder to climb up and pick mangosteens as they bruise if they fall. They can be picked unripe and kept for a few days or may be made into conserves.

Mangosteen Ecstasy
If you are fortunate enough to have a mangosteen, just eat it!

OTHER USES

The thick rinds are rich in tannic acid and dyes.

TRAVELLER'S TALE
TROPICAL FRUITS

There are many more fruits the inveterate traveller may come across in tropical and semi-tropical countries. Some of these are of more practical or commercial interest, such as the spices, while others are of such purely local interest they are rarely if ever recorded. Many may be unknown, as they are unpalatable by 'modern' standards, or they may be delicious but hard to cultivate. As we move into a homogenized world of mass consumption, the numbers of varieties of even the most popular fruits are declining. Quaint, difficult and unusual fruits have already disappeared from all but local native markets and botanic and private gardens. If you travel far off the beaten track, you may come across the following, and others – but, when choosing to taste them, do not rely on my identification.

Tamarind pods

Blighia sapida, **Akee, Sapindaceae**.

A medium-sized tree from West Africa, grown in the West Indies, especially Jamaica, where the fruit, fried in butter, is considered excellent fare. The fruits are bright red, heart-shaped pods, which burst to reveal three glossy, black seeds the size of peas sitting in a yellowish cup, which is the tasty bit. The seeds are inedible, the pink flesh highly poisonous and even the edible bit is poisonous if under- or over-ripe. One wonders how this ever became popular!

Borassus flabellifer, **Borassus** or **Palmyra palm, Palmaceae**.

A tall palm like a date palm but with shorter, fan-shaped leaves. It is widely distributed in the drier regions of Africa and Asia. The fruits contain much sap. This is also tapped from the trunk for boiling down into sugar or for fermenting.

Aberia gardneri, **Ceylon Gooseberry, Bixineae**.

Native to what is now Sri Lanka, this is a small, shrubby tree with large, purple-brown, round berries mostly used for making jams and preserves. Closely related is *A. caffra*, the **Kai, Kau** or **Kei Apple** of South Africa, which is yellow and so acid it is used as a pickle, omitting the vinegar.

Baccaurea dulcis/Pierardia motleyana, **Rambeh** or **Rambei, Euphorbiaceae**.

Found in Malaysia, especially Sumatra, and China, this has long, hanging bunches of large, yellow berries that are reputedly sweet-tasting, juicy and luscious.

Bactris/Guillielma utilis, **Peach Nut** or **Pewa, Palmaceae**.

A native of Central America, similar to a date palm, this has fruits like large dates. Usually cooked in salted water before eating, they taste of chestnuts. The best varieties are seedless. Other relations are the **Prickly Palm**, *B. major*, and the **Tobago Palm**, *B. minor*.

The Borassus or Palmyra palm

Carissa grandiflora, **Natal Plum, Apocynaceae**.

This and *Carissa carandas* are large, thorny shrubs used as hedges in Natal. They have purple, damson-like fruits tasting of gooseberry which are widely used for tarts and preserves. *C. carandas*, which is also used for pickling, prefers

The exotic Natal plum

Chrysophylum cainito, **Star Apple, Sapotaceae**.

Noted by Cieza de Leon in Peru in 1532–50, this is a large, evergreen tree with purple-brown 'apples', which, when cut through, have a star shape in the middle with about half a dozen shiny, brown seeds in a sweet/acid pulp.

Coccoloba uvifera, **Seagrape, Polygonaceae**.

A colonizer of tropical shores, this is a very salt-tolerant, small, evergreen shrub or tree found from Florida to Venezuela. The 'grapes' are up to half an inch across, mild and sweet. They are eaten raw or jellied. The wood is hard and takes a polish well. It is often used as hedging or for good windbreaks.

This banana tree from the Canary Islands thrives in Bob's own garden

Eugenia caryophyllus, **Cloves, Myrtaceae**.

Cloves are the dried flower buds of this Indonesian tree. Other *Eugenia* species such as the **Malay Apple**, *E. Malaccensis*, the **Rose Apple**, *E. Jambos* and, the **Surinam Cherry**, *E. uniflora* have edible fruits varying from yellow to red or purple. They are eaten raw and made into jams and liqueurs in tropical and subtropical countries.

Mimusops elengi, **Sapotaceae**.

This large East Asian tree has fragrant flowers. The 2.5cm (1in) yellow berries are eaten when ripe and an oil is expressed from the seed. Other *Mimusops* are also grown for their similar fruits. *M. elata* of Brazil is the **Cow Tree**. Its apple-sized fruits contain a milk-like latex that resembles milk, when fresh, and is drunk with coffee, but soon congeals to a glue.

Pimenta dioica, **Allspice, Pimento, Myrtaceae**.

This small, evergreen West Indian tree has pea-size berries that are dried unripe for their mixed spice flavour.

Piper nigrum, **Pepper, Piperaceae**.

Black and white pepper are the unripe and ripe (and de-corticated) seeds of this Indian climbing vine.

Spondias, **Spanish, Hog** or **Brazilian Plum, Anacardiaceae**.

Distantly related to cashews and pistachios, the *Spondias* have edible fruits, most of them only when made into preserves, but some are eaten raw. They are purple to yellow, resembling a plum with a central 'stone'. The stone of the **Spanish Plum**, *Spondias purpurea*, is eaten by some people.

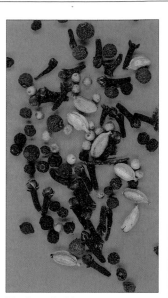

Black and white peppercorns, allspice, cloves and cardamoms

Tamarindus indica, **Tamarind Tree, Caesalpiniaceae**.

This large, handsome tree has brown pods containing very acid pulp used for beverages and in chutneys, curries and medicine.

Vanilla planifolia, **Orchidaceae**.

Vanilla is the fruit of an orchid that is native to Central America but is mostly grown in Madagascar. The bean-like pods are cured and dried for flavoring.

Zizyphus jujuba, **Jujube, Chinese Date, Rhamnaceae**.

An East Indian native, this reached China and was improved to dessert quality. In China it is popular dried or preserved in syrup. Jujubes resemble large, yellowish or reddish cherries with thick, tough skin, a hard kernel and a pithy, acid pulp, rich in vitamin C. The thorny, shrubby trees survive in cooler climates and have been in Mediterranean countries since biblical times. *Z. vulgaris*, a native of the Middle East, is similar but less agreeable. *Z. lotus* is like a sweet olive and is thought to be the lotus Odysseus had trouble with.

Shrub and Flower Garden Fruits

Wild Garden Fruiting Trees & Shrubs

Many of our familiar garden and countryside plants also bear fruit. Some of these are edible and can add variety and nutritional range to the diet. But first, I must insist that you never eat anything you are not sure of. Have it identified as safe by an expert on the spot. Also you must realize that although the fruits of some plants, such as yew, may not themselves be harmful, the foliage and seeds are deadly if ingested in quantity. Various parts may also be an irritant to some people.

However, such paranoid exclamations aside, there are many familiar plants that have edible, if not actually delicious, fruits. Although they might not seem at first glance very attractive or be popular with many of us today, some of these were once greatly esteemed by native peoples, and others were part of the country fare of our not-so-distant predecessors. With a little care and attention, these plants can provide us with fresh and unusual dishes, far exceeding in vitamins and flavour those made from the tired and flabby fruits usually offered for sale.

The plants at the beginning of this chapter are all excellent garden subjects, worthy of anyone's attention, which incidentally bear edible fruit. Some of the other plants with edible fruits are not attractive enough, or grow too big, for most gardens, but are of interest or value to insects or birds, and are more often planted in larger, public or wildlife gardens.

The ideal picturesque garden, often called the cottage garden, is typified these days by extravagant species at flower shows with odd mixtures of flowers, half of them out of season, grown elsewhere in pots and jammed full, with a camouflage of bark. The true cottager's garden was indeed a mixture of plants, but all with a purpose – to provide medicines, herbs, flavourings, fruits and, last of all, flowers.

Fruiting trees and shrubs can be easily cultivated with other plants underneath, and were the backbone of a true cottage garden. A mixture of plants that were found to grow happily together for both production and ornament was sensible, as it produced a mixed ecology so there were rarely pest or disease problems. In addition, the plants grown in flower, shrub and wild gardens are often innately more reliable than those especially cultivated for fruits, as they are closer to the wild forms, with natural pest and disease resistance.

The biggest handicap for some of these plants has probably been their very attractiveness. If they had been a little less pretty, they might have been developed further for their fruits and have remained part of our diet. Few of them are palatable raw, at least not to most people's taste, and all are better made into jams, jellies and preserves, but they have appealing and interesting flavours and are of inestimable value to the adventurous gourmet or those wishing to expand their dietary range. And for those interested in breeding, they offer plenty of opportunity for rapid improvement towards bigger, tastier and better fruits.

Amelanchier canadensis from the family *Rosaceae*

JUNEBERRIES

SNOWY MESPILUS, SHADS, SWEET/GRAPE PEARS

Tree/bush, up to 6–9m (20–30ft). Life span: medium. Self-fertile. Fruits: 1cm (½in), round, purple-black, rich in vitamin C.

Amelanchiers look beautiful covered in white blossom

The amelanchiers are small, deciduous trees or shrubs tending to suckering growth, most noticeable when absolutely covered with white blossoms. The fruits are purplish, spherical and about pea-size, but can be larger.

A. canadensis is the best species and a native of North America. Though there are relatives in Asia and Europe, these are not as palatable. *A. vulgaris* grows wild in European mountain districts and was long cultivated in England, as much for the flowers as the fruits.

VARIETIES

Amelanchier canadensis was a favourite fruit of Native Americans. It was adopted by the French settlers and became **Poires** in Canada and **Sweet** or **Grape Pear** in what is now the USA. It has small, purple berries which are sweet and tasty. *A. alnifolia*, or **Western Service Berry**, is larger and found wild in the states of Oregon and Washington. All cultivars are supplied for ornamental rather than fruiting purposes.

CULTIVATION

Amelanchiers do best in moist but well-drained, lime-free soil. They are slow-growing, tending to sucker.

Ornamental and Wildlife Value

Neat, compact, floriferous, good autumn leaf colours, excellent shrub border plants. The berries are much liked by birds.

Propagation, Pruning and Training

Sow seeds fresh for the species, but graft choice varieties in April onto *Sorbus aucuparia* stock. They may need to have suckers removed, otherwise prune only remedially.

Growing under Glass and in Containers

They are so hardy that they hardly seem worth the space under cover. They could be delightful small specimens in pots.

Weed, Pest and Disease Control

No particular problems affect these tough plants.

A spray of juneberries and leaves

HARVESTING AND STORING, CULINARY USES

They can be eaten raw, but are better as jams or tarts, or dried like raisins.

Snowy Mespilus Sponge Cakes
Makes about 10

60g (2oz) each butter, powdered sugar and white self-raising flour
1 large or 2 small eggs
Dash of vanilla essence
Splash of milk
120g (4oz) dried amelanchier berries

Cream the butter and sugar, beat in the egg and vanilla, fold in the sifted flour, then add enough milk to make a smooth mixture. Stir in the berries; pour into greased paper cups. Stand the cups on a metal tray and bake in a pre-heated oven at 190°C/375°F/gas mark 5 for 20 minutes or till firm.

OTHER USES

Can be used as rootstocks for pome fruits.

Berberis vulgaris from the family Berberidaceae

BARBERRIES
MAHONIAS, OREGON GRAPES

Bush, up to 4x4m (14x14ft). Life span: short.
Fruits: under 1cm (½in), white, yellow, scarlet, purple or black.

The *Berberis* family contains hundreds of small- to medium-sized, spiny shrubs that have masses of berries in many colours. The leaves of most deciduous varieties turn bright shades in autumn and the wood is usually yellow.

Various species are found all over the world. Our common barberry is now seldom relished, but was once widely popular. Indeed the settlers in Massachusetts grew so many that in 1754 the province had to forbid further planting.

VARIETIES

Berberis vulgaris is the **Common Barberry**, which once existed in a host of local forms and colours. One found in Rouen was seedless. Other species are enjoyed all over the world: *B. darwinii* is popular; *B. buxifolia*, the **Magellan Barberry**, is large and said to be the best raw or cooked. *Mahonia* is now a separate genus, but is very similar in many ways, only lacking the spines and having pinnate leaves. The flowers are yellow, usually scented, and the blue-black berries of *M. aquifolium* were made into preserves as Oregon grapes.

CULTIVATION

They will grow almost anywhere not actually dark, bone-dry or waterlogged, and are even fairly tolerant of salt spray. Cold hardiness depends on species.

Growing under Glass and in Containers
They are hardy enough not to need protection, but do make good plants in containers.

Ornamental and Wildlife Value
Some ornamental varieties are very attractive, though not as productive of berries, which are exceedingly well liked by birds. Most varieties are excellent when used for wildlife gardens.

Propagation, Pruning and Training
The species grows from seed, layered or grafted. They can usually be cut to the ground and will recover.

A cluster of barberries

Barberry flowers

WEED, PEST AND DISEASE CONTROL, COMPANION PLANTING

Barberries are an alternate host for wheat rust, so care should be taken not to plant them near wheat.

OTHER USES

They make good hedges and game cover. They were used for a yellow dye.

HARVESTING AND STORING, CULINARY USES

The berries can be pickled in vinegar, preserved in sugar or syrup, candied or made into jam. The leaves were once used as a seasoning.

Colonel Flowerdew's Bengal Chutney
Makes approx 1.4kg (3lb)

1kg (2lb) grated apples
120g (4oz) each of the following:
dried barberries, soft brown sugar, Demerara sugar, mustard seed, golden syrup
60g (2oz) each of the following:
chopped onions, chopped garlic, chopped fresh ginger and salt
15g (½oz) cayenne pepper
600ml (1pt) vinegar

Mix all the ingredients and simmer till soft, say 2–3 hours. Bottle in small jars for six months.

Mespilus germanica from the family *Rosaceae*

MEDLARS

Tree, up to 9m (30ft). Life span: medium. Self-fertile.
Fruits: 2.5–5cm (1–2in), green to russet.

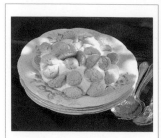

Medlars resemble pear trees but are smaller, have bigger leathery leaves, single, large, white flowers and fruits like giant, distorted rose hips. The brownish-green fruits have a rough 'leafy' end, which shows the seed chambers. Medlars seldom ripen fully on the tree in cool regions and were eaten 'bletted' – stored till at the point of decomposition. The taste is somewhat like that of rotten pear and they are now disdained.

Originally from Persia, medlars became naturalized over much of Europe. Theophrastus mentions them in Greece in 300 BC and Pliny refers to the Romans having three sorts. Once very popular, they are now planted infrequently.

Medlar flower and leaves

HARVESTING AND STORING, CULINARY USES

The fruits should be left on the tree till winter and then stored in a cool, dry place till they soften (blet). The pulp was once popular raw, mixed with liqueur and cream, but is better jammed or jellied.

Medlar Fudge
Makes about 2kg (4lb)

1kg (2lb) medlars
1 large or 2 small lemons
3 cloves
600ml (1pt) apple cider
Approx. 1kg (2lb) light brown sugar
Honey or maple syrup to taste, cream and macaroons to serve

Wash and chop the fruit, add the cloves and cider and simmer until the fruit is soft. Sieve and weigh the pulp. Add three quarters of its weight in sugar and bring back to the boil, then bottle and seal. When required, whip the fruit cheese with honey or maple syrup till soft, spoon into bowls and top with whipped cream and broken macaroons.

VARIETIES

There are only a few left. Generally the bigger the tree, the larger the fruit tends to be. **'Dutch'** and **'Monstrous'** are the largest, **'Royal'** and **'Nottingham'** the tastiest and smaller. The seedless **'Stoneless'** has disappeared.

CULTIVATION

Medlars are obliging and will grow in most places, generally preferring a sunny spot in a lawn or grass.

Medlar trees are beautiful in their autumn colours

Growing under Glass and in Containers
The tree is hardy, so it is a waste to grow it under cover, but the twisted framework and general attractiveness make it a good specimen plant for pot growing.

Ornamental and Wildlife Value
Pretty flowers, large leaves and gorgeous autumn golds make this a delightful specimen tree, with a twisted and contorted dark framework for winter

interest. The fruits are useful to the birds late in winter.

Propagation, Pruning and Training
Medlars can be grown from seed, but are usually grafted on pear, quince or thorn stock. They are best pruned only remedially, as they fruit on the ends of the branches.

Weed, Pest and Disease Control
Medlars rarely suffer from any problem.

Chaenomeles japonica from the family *Rosaceae*

JAPONICA QUINCES

Shrub, up to 3x3m (10x10ft). Life span: short. Self-fertile. Fruits: 2.5–5cm (1–2in), round, green/red/yellow.

A tangled mass of dark, occasionally thorny branches covered with red, white, orange or pink blossom in early spring. This is followed later in the year by hard, roundish fruits, green flushing red or yellow.

Often just called japonica, this shrub arrived in Europe from Japan as late as 1800. It was rapidly accepted and is now widely planted in many varieties and hybrids, for its flowers, not the fruits. There is opportunity for developing a better culinary or even a dessert form.

OTHER USES

Chaenomeles make good, sturdy hedges.

HARVESTING AND STORING, CULINARY USES

Inedible – well, impenetrable anyway – until cooked, when they have an aromatic scent similar to but different from Cydonia quinces. They can be used for tarts, baked or stewed or made into cheese or jelly.

Japonica Jelly
Makes approx. 4kg (8lb)

2kg (4lb) chaenomeles fruits
Approx. 2kg (4lb) sugar

Chop the fruit and simmer in 3 litres (5pt) water till tender, then sieve and weigh the pulp. Add 500g (1lb) of sugar per 600ml (1pt) of pulp and return to the heat. Bring to boil, bottle and seal. Store for three months before use.

CULTIVATION

Hardier than **Cydonia quinces**, these are easy almost anywhere, even on shady walls.

Growing under Glass and in Containers
Tough and unruly plants, they are better outdoors. However, I've found them dependable in pots to force for early flowers.

Ornamental and Wildlife Value
The displays of early flowers and long-lived fruit are exceptional, making these valuable shrubs. The flowers come in late winter, benefiting early insects, but the hard fruits often rot before the birds take them.

Propagation, Pruning and Training
Unlikely to come true from seed. Better varieties are

Japonica quince flowers provide a marvellous splash of colour

easily layered or can be grafted. Winter cuttings may take; softwood cuttings are better but trickier. The shrubs have a congested form and are best left alone or tip pruned in summer to control their size. I weave young growths like basket work to produce a tight surface that can be clipped.

Weed, Pest and Disease Control
Other than weeds and congestion, they have no common problems.

VARIETIES

The botanical *C. japonica* has orange flowers and is not common. The true japonica is *C. speciosa*. There are many ornamental hybrids and varieties that also fruit. **'Boule de Fer'** is my favourite and is a heavy cropper. A related species, *C. cathayensis*, is larger, with green fruits up to 15cm (6in) long, and is a thorny brute!

Fuchsia from the family *Onagraceae*

FUCHSIA

Semi-herbaceous shrub, to 2x2m (7x7ft). Life span: short.
Fruits: 1cm (½in), round/oval purple-black.

This gloriously flowered plant needs little description, and most of us must have noticed the roundish oval, purple fruits it occasionally sets. As I have always searched for new fruits from far places, I was amused when I first saw fuchsia jelly and learned that I had overlooked these berries, which are so close at hand, often edible and as delicious as many from distant shores.

The first fuchsia was recorded in 1703. Over the following century a few species arrived in Britain from South America with little remark, but in 1793 James Lee astutely launched his *F. coccinea*, the first with impressive flowers, and took the world by storm. Other species were introduced from New Zealand and now there is an amazing range of colours and forms of hybrids of many species.

Fuchsia flower and leaves

A mixture of royal ferns and fuchsia forms this rich Irish hedge

HARVESTING AND STORING, CULINARY USES

Some are tasty raw, but all are best jellied or in tarts.

Fuchsia Jelly
makes approx. 2kg (4lb)

1kg (2lb) fuchsia berries
Approx. 1kg (2lb) sugar
Juice of 1 lemon

Simmer the berries with sufficient water to cover. Once they have softened, sieve and weigh. Add the same weight of sugar and the lemon juice. Bring back to boil, then jar.

VARIETIES

Fuchsia species *corymbiflora* and *denticulata* were eaten in Peru and *F. racemosa* in Santo Domingo. Fuchsia clubs and societies often have jelly competitions. There appears to be no known poisonous variety – and I have tried many. As they are all bred for flowers, the berries are neglected and should be easily improved – there is enough variety to start with! *F. magellanica* is the hardiest, but rarely fruits.

CULTIVATION

Even many less hardy species can be grown in cold regions if the roots are well protected, as fuchsias usually spring again from underground to flower and fruit. Make backup plants to be safe and keep these indoors. Fuchsias are amenable to almost any soil but prefer a sunny site.

Propagation, Pruning and Training
Seed produces mixed results; cuttings are easy to train to any shape. Control growth by nipping out tips in summer; cut back in winter.

Ornamental and Wildlife Value
Fuchsias are appealing. They can support large numbers of unwanted wildlife.

Growing under Glass and in Containers
One of the ideal plants for a cool or heated greenhouse or conservatory. Can be grown for many years in large pots.

Weed, Pest and Disease Control
They suffer from common pests requiring the usual remedies (see pp.602–7).

OTHER USES

Fuchsias are used as hedges in mild regions.

Pinus pinea from the family Pinaceae

PINE KERNELS
PIGNONS, PINONS, PINOCCHI

*Tree, up to 25m (80ft). Life span: long. Evergreen, self-fertile.
Fruits: up to 1cm (½in) long, ivory-white seeds inside a cone.
Value: high in minerals and oils.*

Pine cones (above) contain the edible kernels (left)

Pine kernels are more nuts than fruits, as we eat the seed and not the surrounding part (in this case, the cone), but they are softer than true nuts. Most pine kernels come from the stone or umbrella pine. It is an attractive, mushroom-shaped tree with glossy, brown cones that expand in the sun, and drop the seeds. Each is in a tough skin that needs to be removed before it is eaten.

The stone pine is indigenous to the Mediterranean region. Loved by the Ancient Greeks, it was dedicated to the sea god Poseidon. The kernels of other species are eaten almost anywhere they grow.

Ornamental and Wildlife Value
Very attractive if the space is available. Pine kernels will provide excellent food for many species of birds.

Weed, Pest and Disease Control
Pines need companion bacteria and fungi, so do better if soil from around another pine is used to inoculate new sites.

Pruning and Training
Pines are best left well alone.

Propagation
They can be grown from seed or grafted (with skill).

A Colorado pine, Arizona, USA

OTHER USES

Pines are a source of turpentine and resin.

HARVESTING AND STORING, CULINARY USES

Pine nuts are roasted and salted in the same way as peanuts, and also used in marzipan, confectionery, salads and soups.

Pinon Truffle Salad
Quantities to taste

Pine kernels
Butter
Truffles
Walnut oil
Vinegar
Lettuce

Gently fry the kernels in butter till light brown. Remove from the heat; add finely sliced truffles, oil and vinegar. Cool the mixture and toss it with clean, dry lettuce leaves.

The brightly coloured Mexican stone pine flower and needles

VARIETIES

Pinus pinea grows happily in northern regions, but without enough sun the cones do not ripen. *P. cembra*, the **Arolla Pine**, is native to Central Europe and Asia and the seeds are a staple food in Siberia. *P. gerardiana*, **Gerard's Pine**, comes from the Himalayas. *P. cembroides* is a native of North America and has pea-sized kernels that taste delicious roasted. *P. edulis*, from Mexico, is the best variety, but unlikely to fruit in Britain. Likewise the **Araucaria Pine** or **Monkey Puzzle Tree**, *A. araucana*, which has edible kernels and grows but rarely fruits in cooler climates (see p.559). The **Parana Pine**, *A. angustifolia*, from South America, is not hardy and equally is too big for glass-house culture.

CULTIVATION

Stone pines will need shelter to fruit in cold regions. They prefer to grow in sandy soils and acid conditions.

Growing under Glass and in Containers
Most pines grow too large unless confined and are unlikely to crop. *P. canariensis*, however, is a particularly pleasing indoor pot plant.

Rosa from the family *Rosaceae*

ROSE HIPS

Clambering shrub, up to 9m (30ft). Life span: short to medium. Usually self-fertile. Fruits: up to 2.5cm (1in), ovoid, red, yellow or purplish black. Value: very rich in vitamin C.

There can be none of us who does not know roses and few who have never nibbled at the acid/sweet flesh of a rose hip. These are so rich in vitamin C that they were collected on a massive scale during the Second World War for rose-hip syrup for expectant mothers and babies. Rose stems are commonly thorny with a few exceptions such as the divine 'Zéphirine Drouhin'. The deciduous leaves vary from glossy to matte, the flower colour is any you want save black or blue, though wild roses are almost all white or pink. The **Eglantine** rose leaves smell of apples after rain.

Rose hips and flowers are eaten in countries all over the world. The brier or dog rose, *Rosa canina*, and eglantine or sweetbrier, *R. rubiginosa*, are natives of Europe and temperate Asia. Their fruits have been eaten by country folk since time immemorial, but are now regarded with some disdain. However, eglantine sauce was made at Balmoral Castle from sweetbrier hips and lemon juice and was considered good enough for Queen Victoria. Roses are bred for flowers, not for their hips, so most varieties have small hips. However, a little selective breeding could produce hips as large as small apples within a few generations.

VARIETIES

The **Brier** and **Eglantine** rose hips are the commonest varieties used for hips, though *R. rugosa*, the **Rugosa Rose**, offers larger hips, so is more rewarding. *R moyesii* has large flask-shaped hips and *R. omiensis* has pear-shaped, yellow and crimson fruits that ripen early. *R. spinosissima/pimpinellifolia*, the **Scotch** or **Burnet Rose**, is another European native, often found in maritime districts. It has a very sweet, purplish-black fruit.

Ripe rose hips are a glorious red

A spray of roses and leaves

CULTIVATION

Most roses are accommodating, but they prefer heavy soil, rich in organic matter, and need to be kept well mulched with their roots cool and moist, yet not wet.

Propagation
Some species can be grown from seed. Cuttings taken in early autumn are reliable for many varieties and most species.

Ornamental and Wildlife Value
Roses are *the* garden plant. At least one or more can fit into almost any garden anywhere to good effect. Single-flowered roses are valuable to insects and the hips are choice meals for winter birds and rodents.

A mixture of immature and ripe hips

Growing under Glass and in Containers

Only tender roses such as *R. banksiae* are happy under glass. Hardier varieties tend to become soft and drawn and suffer from pests. They must be kept moist at the roots, well-ventilated and shaded against scorch.

Maintenance

Spring Weed, mulch heavily and spray with seaweed solution often.
Summer Deadhead regularly, watch for aphids.
Autumn Take cuttings.
Winter Cut back or tie in.

Pruning and Training

This requires a chapter on its own just to list the methods. Basically, for most roses, plant them well apart, prune as little as possible and wind in growths rather than prune. Reduce tall hybrid bushes by a third to a half in height with hedge trimmers annually in late winter.

Weed, Pest and Disease Control

Roses suffer from a host of common diseases, but providing they are growing reasonably well the only real threat to flower and hip production is aphids. Control these with jets of water and soft soap.

COMPANION PLANTING

Underplantings of alliums, especially garlic or chives, help deter blackspot and pests. Parsley, lupins, mignonette and lavender are beneficial; catnip and *Limnanthes douglassii* are good ground cover underneath roses.

OTHER USES

Strong-growing roses such as *R. rubiginosa*, *R. spinosissima* or **'The Queen Elizabeth'** make excellent stock- and people-proof hedges. The flower petals are dried for potpourri and used in confectionery, medicinally and in perfumery. The seeds are covered in hairs that itch when put down the back of other children's collars . . .

A bowl of rose hip potpourri

HARVESTING AND STORING, CULINARY USES

The berries need to ripen fully on the bush before being eaten raw, but are best taken before they soften for culinary use. All seed hairs must be removed! Hips can be made into jellies, preserves and the famous syrup. The flower petals may be used as garnishes, preserved in sugar or syrup, used for rosewater flavouring, honeys, vinegars and conserves, pounded to dust for lozenges and they make good additions to salads. The leaves of *R. canina* have been used for tea (in desperation, one suspects).

Rose Hip Tart
Serves 6

for the pastry:
225g (8oz) self-raising flour
150g (5oz) butter
1 large egg yolk
30g (1oz) fine brown sugar
Pinch of salt
Splash of water

for the filling:
500g (1lb) rose hips
60g (2oz) each fine brown sugar, honey, chopped stem ginger preserved in syrup
1 saltspoon cinnamon
Sprinkling of sugar and grating of nutmeg

Rub together the ingredients for the pastry, making it a little on the dry side, and use it to line a tart dish. Wash, top, tail and halve the rose hips, extract every bit of seed and hairy fibre, rinse and drain. Mix with the sugar, honey, cinnamon and ginger and spoon on top of the pastry. Decorate with pastry offcuts and sprinkle with sugar and nutmeg before baking at 180°C/ 350°F/gas mark 4 for half an hour or until the pastry is light brown on top.

Cornus mas from the family *Cornaceae*

CORNELIAN CHERRY, SORBET

Tree/bush, up to 8m (25ft). Life span: medium to long. Deciduous, self-fertile.
Fruits: 1cm (½in), ovoid, red.

Cornelian cherry fruits resemble small, red cherries but are generally too sour to eat raw, except for the occasional better one. The trees or large bushes are tall, deciduous, densely branched and suckering, common in hedgerows and old grasslands. The stems are greyish and the leaves are oval, coming to a point with noticeable veins. The flowers are primrose-yellow and appear in small clusters early in spring before the leaves.

The Cornelian cherry is one of a genus of about a hundred, mostly small, shrubby plants up to 3m (10ft) high, but ranging from creeping sub-shrubs to small trees. One of the two species native to Europe and western Asia, *Cornus mas* was once widely cultivated and rated very highly, though now it is rarely eaten even by country folk. There are species from North America and the Himalayas and it seems a shame they have not been cross-bred for better fruits. The Cornelian cherry really is a fruit that has stalled in development and probably would not take much further work to improve immensely.

suecica used to be gathered by Native Americans, who froze them in wooden boxes for winter rations. *Cornus kousa chinensis* comes from China via Japan and is a smaller tree than *C. mas.* The flowers are greyish-purple backed by immense pale bracts, the fruits are more strawberry-like and juicy with better flavour. This species needs a moist, acid soil. *C. macrophylla* and the tenderer *C. capitata* come from Asia and the Himalayas and are eaten raw and made into preserves in India. *C. canadensis* (*Chamaepericlymenum canadense*), **Bunchberry** or **Dwarf Cornel**, is a different type altogether. A lime hater more resembling a soft dwarf raspberry in manner of growth, it has white flowers or low, soft shoots with vivid red fruits. These are pleasant enough, if tasteless, and can be added to summer puddings.

The distinctive primrose-yellow flowers of the Cornelian cherry

VARIETIES

The variety *C. mas macrocarpa* has somewhat larger fruits and is still available. There used to exist many other improved forms, now apparently lost. In France and Germany there are records of several varieties of

sorbets, as they were called – one that had a yellow fruit, some with wax-coloured fruits, white fruits and even one with a fleshy, rounded fruit. Other cornus such as *C. stolonifera*, the **Red Osier**, and *C. amomum*, **Kinnikinnik**, are found in North America and are edible. The former was eaten more in desperation than for pleasure; the latter, found in Louisiana, is said to be very good. The berries of *C.*

The flowers of the Cornelian cherry appear before the leaves in spring

CULTIVATION

C. mas is easy to grow almost anywhere but prefers calcareous soil. Some species need acid conditions. Generally they are among the most reliable of shrubs, requiring little attention.

Maintenance
Spring Cut back ornamental stemmed varieties, weed, mulch and spray with seaweed solution.
Summer Make layers.
Autumn Preserve fruit for winter.
Winter Take cuttings or suckers and prune.

Growing under Glass and in Containers
They are hardy, so are hardly worth growing under glass unless you wish to force them for their early flowers. They will grow well in pots.

Ornamental and Wildlife Value
Many species are liked particularly for their autumn colour and some species and varieties are grown for their brightly coloured stems. The flowers are early, benefiting insects, and birds and rodents love the berries. One of the best backbone shrubs of a wild garden.

Propagation
The species come true from seed with some variation, but are slow. Suckers taken in autumn are best, hardwood winter cuttings may take, but layering is more sure.

Pruning and Training
Generally only remedial pruning is needed – though, as these plants sucker, some root pruning may become necessary. Ornamental coloured-stem varieties are best sheared to ground level in early spring.

Weed, Pest and Disease Control
No common problems bother these tough plants

OTHER USES

Cornus sanguinea, the **Cornel Dogwood**, **Dogberry** or **Pegwood**, is a common European relation, not really edible, though the fruits were once used for oil and in brewing. *C. alba* varieties tolerate wet or dry situations and can be used to reinforce banks. Dogwoods grow stiff and straight, so were used for arrows.

HARVESTING AND STORING, CULINARY USES

In Germany the fruits were sold in markets to be eaten by children (who presumably liked them). They were widely made into tarts, confectionery and sweetmeats, even used as substitutes for olives. In Norway the flowers were used to flavour spirits and in Turkey the fruits were used as flavouring for sherbets. It is noticeable that fruits vary on different bushes and some are more palatable raw than others.

Sorbet Sorbet
Serves 4

1kg (2lb) cornelian cherries
1 small lemon
Approx. 600g (1¼lb) sugar
2 or 3 small egg whites

Wash the fruits, slit the cherries, chop the lemon and simmer them till soft, just covered with water, in a deep pan. Strain and measure the juice, then dissolve 200g (7oz) sugar per cup of juice. Bring back to boil, cool and partially freeze. Remove from the freezer and beat, adding one beaten white of egg for every two cups of sorbet. Repeat the freezing and beating one more time before freezing till required.

Crataegus azarolus from the family *Rosaceae*

HAWTHORN AND AZAROLE

Tree/bush, up to 8m (25ft). Life span: long. Deciduous, self-fertile.
Fruits: up to 2.5cm (1in), roundish, usually orange.
Value: rich in vitamins C and B complex.

The azarole is a more palatable relation of the well-known hawthorn and is cultivated in many of the Mediterranean countries for its cherry-sized fruits. These are usually yellow to orange, but can occasionally be red or white. They are larger than a hawthorn haw and have an apple-flavoured, pasty flesh with two or three tough seeds. Small, spreading trees or large shrubs, these are typical of the thorn genus, with clusters of large, white flowers that do not have the usual family scent.

Characteristic yellow azarole fruits on the tree

The thorn family are remarkably hardy, tough plants for wet, dry, windswept or even coastal regions. They are survivors and various species can be found in almost every part of the world, many of which bear similar small, edible, apple-like fruits. Native to North Africa, Asia Minor and Persia, the azarole, *C. azarolus*, may be the mespile anthedon about which Theophrastus wrote. More popular in the Latin countries, it was brought to Britain in 1640. In 1976 it got an award of merit from the Royal Horticultural Society, but it has never really caught on, most probably because other more floriferous varieties and species were readily available.

Red azarole fruits

The azarole is the more productive of the species and is grown commercially for flavouring liqueurs. It is probably the best choice for a tree for preserves. The Armenian *C. tanacetifolia*, the **Tansy-leafed Thorn** or **Syrian Hawberry,** is another good choice. The berries are almost relishable raw as dessert and have an aromatic apple flavour, which is surprising, as they also closely resemble small yellow apples. They are pale green to yellow, with slight ribs like a melon, and a tassel of 'leaves' at the end. The **Common Hawthorn** or **Quickthorn Haw**, *C. monogyna*, has one seed and is edible but not at all palatable, so is seldom eaten, save by curious children. Reputedly it was eaten raw when fully ripe by Scots Highlanders. The fruits are dark red and hang in immense festoons in autumn. The flowers have a sweet perfume when new, but go fishy as they age – on some trees more than others. Equally common, *C. oxycantha/laevigata* is very similar, usually with dark red flowers. There are several edible North American species. *C. tomentosa*, **Black Thorn** or **Pear Thorn**, has hard, orange-red, pear-shaped fruits; *C. flava* has yellow fruits; *C. douglasii* is a better species with small but sweet, black berries with yellow flesh. One identified as *C. coccinea* (now *mollis, sub mollis, pedicellata* or *intricata*) was very popular with Native Americans, who dried the large scarlet or purple fruits for winter use. Sometimes these fruits were mixed together with chokecherries and service berries before they were dried and pressed into cakes for storage.

A hawthorn or May bush in full flower

CULTIVATION

The thorns are all extremely easy to please and require little skill or attention. They tend to lean in the more exposed situations.

Growing under Glass and in Containers
Because they are so hardy they do not need protection, but several of the ornamental varieties can be grown in pots for forcing to produce early flowers.

Ornamental and Wildlife Value
The shows of blossom and masses of bright fruits make these an excellent choice for larger shrub borders and informal gardens. The flowers, fruit and foliage are useful to all manner of wildlife. The common thorn flowers attract over 150 different insect species.

Propagation
This is more difficult than for many fruits. The haws need stratifying for winter and a year before sowing the next spring, and may also produce mixed offspring unless they are from a true species grown far from any others. Cuttings are difficult, so choice varieties are best obtained budded in May or grafted in April onto common stock.

'Paul's Double Scarlet' hawthorn in flower

Maintenance
Spring Weed, mulch and spray with seaweed monthly.
Summer No maintenance.
Autumn Collect fruits before the birds do.
Winter Prune if necessary.

Pruning and Training
Very little is needed. Do not over-thin the branches, as thorns will naturally have a congested head.

Weed, Pest and Disease Control
Thorns rarely suffer badly from problems, though they are occasionally defoliated by caterpillar attacks. These attacks may be easily avoided by diligent observation and prompt action.

OTHER USES

Thorns make the best and most traditional hedge with a trimmed surface like fine tweed. The wood is heavy and hard and will burn with a good heat.

HARVESTING AND STORING, CULINARY USES

The flowers of common hawthorn once made a heady liqueur or wine. The young leaves and buds, known to schoolchildren as bread and cheese, had a nutty taste and made a welcome addition to salads. We are now told that both are slightly poisonous. However, the berries of azarole, common thorn, and especially the Armenian or Syrian, will make excellent preserves, wines and jellies.

Hedge Jelly
Makes approx. 3kg (6lb)

1kg (2lb) haws
500g (1lb) crab or cooking apples
225g (8oz) elderberries
Approx. 1.5kg (3lb) sugar

Wash the fruits, chop the apples and simmer the fruits together, just covered with water, for about 2 hours, till softened. Strain and weigh the juice. Add the same weight of sugar to the juice and bring back to a boil. Skim off the scum, jar and seal.

Sorbus aucuparia from the family *Rosaceae*

ROWAN, WHITEBEAM AND SERVICE BERRIES

Tree, up to 15m (50ft). Life span: short. Deciduous, self-fertile. Fruits: up to 1cm (½in), spherical, scarlet, in clusters. Value: very rich in vitamin C and pectin.

Rowans are most attractive, small trees with distinctive, pinnate leaves, dark green above, lighter underneath. They have big heads of foamy, cream flowers like elderflowers, but smell unpleasant. In autumn the branches bend under massive clusters of bright red to scarlet berries, which would hang through the winter if the birds did not finish them so quickly. The Latin name *aucuparia* means 'bird catching' and refers to the fruit's early use as bait.

The *Sorbus* family is large and includes dwarf shrubs and large trees. They are spread all over the world and the majority are quite hardy. They colour richly in autumn and are widely grown for their attractive shows of fruits, also in yellow and white. Many new ornamental species were introduced from China during the nineteenth century, but little advance has been made in fruit quality since *S. aucuparia edulis* (*moravica* or *dulcis*) was first introduced in about 1800.

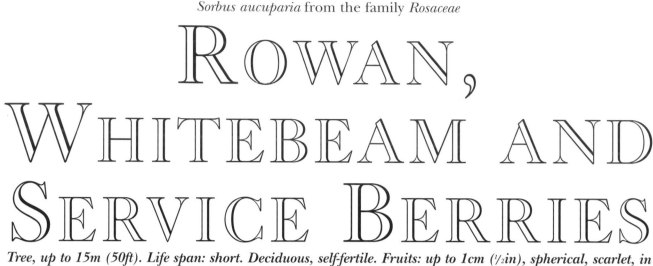

Sorbus is a native tree

VARIETIES

Sorbus aucuparia, the **Rowan** or **Mountain Ash**, has scarlet berries that birds love and which are generally too sour and bitter for our tastes. There are many other ornamental species and varieties, for example *S. aucuparia xanthocarpa*, which has yellow fruits. However, the common rowan is still the frequent favourite choice from the genus and much planted in metropolitan areas. The best variety by far for the gourmand is *edulis* which has larger, sweeter fruits carried in heavy bunches. *S. aria*, the **Whitebeam,** has similar red berries to a rowan and they were once eaten and used for wine. *Sorbus domestica*, the **Service Tree**, is a native of Asia Minor and was also once widely liked, but is now less common. It has smaller clusters of larger fruits of a brownish green, resembling small pears. They need to be bletted like medlars (see p.552) before they are edible. There were pear-shaped and apple-shaped versions; the flavour and texture were improved after a frost and they were commonly sold in London markets. In Brittany they were used to make a rather poor cider. The **Wild Service** or **Chequer Tree**, *S. torminalis*, has smaller, still harder fruits, that would pucker even the hungriest peasant's mouth, but were once eaten by children.

Rowan flowers and leaves

Fruits on the wild service tree

A mountain ash tree covered in berries

CULTIVATION

Mountain ashes are tolerant of quite acid soils and do not like chalky or limy ones, protesting by being short-lived. They generally prefer drier to wetter sites but, strangely, are commonly seen growing naturally by mountain streams and in wet, hilly country.

Growing under Glass and in Containers

They are hardy and rather too large for growing inside. They can be grown, and fruited, in pots if only a small crop is desired.

Ornamental and Wildlife Value

Almost all the species and varieties are very attractive to us in flower and fruit, turning glorious shades of crimson in autumn, but most unfortunately do lack a sweet scent. Rowans are valuable to the birds and insects and are pollinated by flies and midges.

Maintenance

Spring Weed, mulch and spray with seaweed solution.
Autumn Pick fruit before the birds get them.
Winter Prune as necessary.

Propagation

Seed from the species may come true if the tree is isolated, but it must be stratified over winter first. Cuttings are rarely successful, so selected forms are budded in midsummer or grafted in early spring onto seedling rootstocks. The fruits of rowans are thought to get larger if the trees are grafted on to service stock.

Pruning and Training

Pruning should be only remedial once a good head has formed, but watch for overladen branches and prop in time. The strongly erect growth of young trees can be bent down and into fruitfulness: pull them down gently with weights tied near the ends.

Weed, Pest and Disease Control

Apart from bird losses, and being rather short-lived on alkaline soils, the members of this genus need little care and rarely suffer problems. They are thus well liked for amenity planting.

OTHER USES

Rowan bark was used in dyeing and tanning. The wood is strong and was used for handles. Service wood is tough and resists wear well. The berries of the wild service tree, *S. torminalis*, were also used medicinally.

Rowan berries in autumn

Mountain ash jelly

HARVESTING AND STORING, CULINARY USES

Rowan berries make a delicious jelly, almost like marmalade, which goes well with venison, game and fatty or cold meats. They can be used in compôtes, preserves and syrups, and are sometimes added to apple dishes to liven them up. They have been used for fermenting and distilling liquor, and in emergencies the dried berries have been ground into meal to make a substitute for bread. Service fruits were used traditionally in quite similar ways.

Mountain Ash Jelly
Makes approx. 2kg (4lb)

1kg (2lb) firm ripe rowan berries
1 small lemon
Approx. 1kg (2lb) sugar

Wash and de-stem the berries, add the chopped lemon and 425ml (15fl oz) water and simmer till soft (for about an hour). Strain and add 450g (1lb) sugar to each 600ml (1pt). Bring back to the boil, skim and jar.

Prunus species from the family *Rosaceae*

SLOES, BIRD CHERRIES, BEACH PLUMS

Tree/bush, up to 9m (30ft). Life span: medium. Deciduous, self-fertile.
Fruits: up to 2.5cm (1in), ovoid, single stone, red to black. Value: rich in vitamin C.

Closely related to orchard plums and cherries, the wild *Prunus* species remain very much tough, hardy alternatives for difficult spots or wild gardens. Sloes are the fruits of the blackthorn, *P. spinosa*, which is a medium-sized shrub, many-branched, very thorny, with blackish bark. The fruits are black ovoids with a bloom that resembles plums, and hard, juicy, green flesh that is usually far too astringent to eat raw. However, like many children, I forever searched for a sweeter one.

Sloes are native to Europe, North Africa and Asia. The stones have been found on the sites of prehistoric dwellings, so they have long been an item of diet. They may be one of the ancestors of the damson and some of their 'blood' has probably got into many true plums. The bird cherry is a native of Europe and Asia, especially grown in the north of England. The sixteenth-century herbalist Gerard claimed it was in 'almost every hedge'. Many ornamental *Prunus* species were later introduced in the eighteenth and nineteenth centuries; *P. maritima* was introduced by Farrer in 1800.

Sloe berries and leaves

Ripe sloe berries have a sharp, bitter taste

VARIETIES

Prunus padus, the **Bird Cherry** or **Hag Berry**, is a small tree with white, fragrant flowers in late spring; the double-flowered form, *P. padus plena*, is more heavily almond-scented. The leaves and bark smell of bitter almonds and contain highly poisonous prussic acid. *P. maritima*, the **Beach Plum**, comes from the eastern seaboard of North America, from Maine down to the Gulf of Mexico. It is a small, compact shrub with masses of white flowers and red or purple juicy fruits up to 2.5cm (1in) across. These can be eaten raw, but are better if preserved. Another North American species is *P. virginiana*, the **Choke Cherry**. This is a tall shrub with glossy, green leaves and variable red to purplish-black berries. The **American Red Plum**, **Goose**, **August**, **Hog** or **Yellow Plum**, *P. americana*, was the Native Americans' favourite and is good for eating raw, stewing or jamming. It is reluctant to fruit in the British Isles, apparently preferring a more continental climate. *P. simonii*, the **Apricot Plum** from China, has large, attractive, red and yellow, scented fruits.

CULTIVATION

Sloes and bird cherries are very hardy and good for making windbreaks. They like an exposed site and thrive on quite poor soils, even one packed with chalk, while *P. maritima* does best in coastal regions, and is happy with salt winds and sandy soils. Do mulch these heavily; water well while establishing on very sandy soils as these hold little water.

Growing under Glass and in Containers

Most of these are hardy and not tasty enough to merit space under cover. *P. americana* may be more fruitful if pot-grown, wintered outside and brought in for the spring through to autumn.

Ornamental and Wildlife Value

All *Prunus* are good at flowering time, but few are worth space in most small, modern gardens. They are more use to the wild garden, as the flowers are early, benefiting insects, while the fruits are excellent winter fare for birds and rodents.

Pruning and Training

Minimal pruning is required and is best done in summer to avoid silver leaf disease. As hedges, blackthorn should be planted at forty-five degrees, staggered in two or three close rows, each laid in opposite directions. Most species can be trained as small trees, but leave beach plum bushes alone.

Bird cherry blossom

Flowers and leaves of the bird cherry tree

Maintenance

Spring Weed, mulch, spray with seaweed solution.
Summer Prune if any pruning is needed.
Autumn Protect fruits from the birds.
Winter Pick fruits.

Propagation

The species usually come true from seed. Choicer varieties have been developed for ornamental use and must be budded in summer or grafted in spring. Cuttings do not take.

Weed, Pest and Disease Control

These wildest members of the *Prunus* family suffer least from pests or diseases.

OTHER USES

Sloes are good hedging plants. Their leaves were formerly used to adulterate tea. Bird cherries do well in a hedge. Their wood is hard and used for carving and especially liked for rifle butts. Sloe bark was once used for medicinal purposes.

Blackthorn bush in flower

HARVESTING AND STORING, CULINARY USES

Sloe berries are much used for liqueurs, especially gin-based ones, and to add colour to port-type wines. All over Europe they are fermented for wine or distilled to a spirit. In France the unripe sloes are pickled like olives. They can be made into juice, syrup or jelly. Bird cherries have been used in much the same way but are inferior. The American species are used similarly. The apricot plum seems strangely under-rated.

Sloe Gin

Sloes
Brown sugar or honey
Peeled almonds
Gin, brandy or vodka

Wash and dry the sloes and prick each several times. Pack the sloes loosely into bottles. To each bottle add 120g (4oz) brown sugar or honey and a couple of almonds, then fill with gin (or brandy or vodka). Leave for several months before drinking.

VERY WILD FRUITS

A Hottentot fig in flower

There are many other edible, if not palatable, fruits in gardens and parks, just waiting for breeders to improve them. What could be more gratifying and worthy than to present the world with new and improved fruits that can be grown in almost anyone's backyard? The following are a few of the many that are occasionally eaten by some, but are not widely used. Please remember *not* to eat anything unless you are 100 per cent sure of it and you have had it identified on the spot by an expert!

Flower and leaves of the Hottentot fig

Asimina/Annona triloba, Northern Pawpaw, Custard Banana, Annonaceae

Introduced to Britian in 1736, the Custard Banana is a bottle-shaped fruit with fantastic potential. Closely related to the papaya, it is much hardier. In its native Americas it is found as far north as Michigan and New York. A large, attractive, long-leafed, suckering bush, it is pest-resistant with fragrant, purple flowers. It prefers moist, not wet soils. Male and female plants are needed; pollination is by flies. The fruits vary from 5–15cm (2–6in) long, are green, ripening yellow to bronze, with yellow pulp, big brown seeds and a resinous flavour, best cooked. Slow-growing, slow-bearing and long-lived, they are most likely to fruit under glass.

Carpobrotus edulis, Hottentot Fig, Aizoaceae

This resembles the mesembryanthemums, with which it was once classed. Native to South Africa, it is a low-growing succulent, found wild in maritime south-west England and southern Europe. Large, magenta or occasionally yellow flowers are followed by small, figlike fruits, which can be eaten raw or cooked, pickled or preserved. The fleshy, triangular leaves can be eaten as saladings as can those of the similar *Mesembryanthemum crystallinum*.

Ceratonia siliqua, Carob Tree, Leguminosae

The Locust Bean or St John's Bread is an edible, purple-brown, bean-like pod that tastes so much like chocolate it can be ground up and used as a substitute. The seeds are not eaten, but are so exact in size and weight they were used for weighing gold and were the original 'carat'. This tree is native to the Mediterranean region, and preserved pods have been found at Pompeii. Nowadays the pods are used as animal feed.

Elaeagnus umbellata, Autumn Olive, Elaeagnaceae

A strong-growing, spreading, deciduous shrub from Asia with fragrant, yellow flowers and small, orange or red berries used like redcurrants or dried to 'raisins'. Many species in this genus bear edible fruits, and most of these have fragrant flowers. *E. commutata*, the **Silver Berry**, has pasty, silver berries and silver leaves. *E. angustifolia*, **Oleaster** or **Wild Olive**, has sweet berries, and is still popular in south-eastern Europe.

Akebia quinata, Lardizabalaceae

A hardy climber from China with attractive, five-lobed leaflets and scented, chocolate-purple flowers in two sizes. These are followed by weird little purple sausage fruits, surprisingly edible – sweetish but pasty and insipid. This needs a warm spot to ripen the fruits, which have a yellowish pulp full of black seeds. *A. trifoliata/lobata* is similar.

Hovenia dulcis, Japanese Raisin Tree, Rhamnaceae

I remember having this as a child. Resembling brown, candied angelica, the 'fruit' is the dried, swollen flower stalk from behind the pea-sized seed of a small, attractive, Asian tree with glossy foliage.

Pods hanging from the carob or locust tree

Humulus lupulus,
Hop, Cannabidaceae

The common hop in flower

I have to include this strange fruit or I will never be forgiven by my beer-swilling compatriots! A rampant climber closely related to cannabis, this is a hardy native of southern Europe with maple-like leaves. Twining stems produce drooping, green-yellow, aromatic flower clusters that enlarge as they set. These are boiled to add their bitter, aromatic flavor to good ale and make it beer. The youngest shoots can be eaten in the manner of asparagus in early spring.

Rhus glabra,
Scarlet Sumac, Vinegar Tree, Anacardiaceae

This small, easily grown, hardy shrub was introduced to the UK from North America in 1622. It is often grown for its spectacular foliage, which turns scarlet in autumn. However, it can produce masses of fruits if both males and females are grown, and these were eaten by native Americans and children. They have a sour taste and were used as a substitute for vinegar. Dried and crushed, they were sprinkled over meat and fatty dishes as a seasoning. Some other members of the *Rhus* family have apparently had their fruits or foliage eaten, but as they are closely related to poison ivy, *R. toxicodendron*, great caution is advisable!

Taxus baccata,
Yew, Taxaceae

The foliage is deadly without cure, the seed may be poisonous, but for centuries children have eaten the red, fleshy aril. However, it is advisable not to try this one.

Yucca filamentosa,
Adam's Needle, Agavaceae

A well-known, spiky, garden perennial, this flowers occasionally in Britain and rarely sets fruit. This can be as large as a peach in the plant's homeland, south-western North America. Native Americans were fond of the fruit fresh or dried and ate the flower buds roasted or boiled.

Hippophae rhamnoides,
Sea Buckthorn, Elaeagnaceae

Often grown as an ornamental for its silver leaves, this tall, thorny shrub produces acid, orangey-yellow fruits if both sexes are planted. The fruits are too sour for most tastes, but have been eaten in famines and by children and are apparently widely collected in Russia, as they are very rich in vitamin C. They are used as a sauce with fish and meat in France, and in Central Europe they are made into a jelly that is eaten with fish or cheese.

Tilia species,
Limes, Lindens, Tiliaceae

These enormous, well-known trees have sweet sap which was formerly boiled down to sugar. The fruits were once ground into a 'chocolate', but this never caught on, as it kept badly.

Smilacina racemosa,
Treacle Berry, Convallariaceae

This delectable, herbaceous garden plant has scented, foamy, white flowers followed by apparently edible, sweet, red berries. One of the best of unknown fruits!

Harvesting lime flowers

Gaultheria procumbens,
Checkerberry, Teaberry, Ericaceae

A low-growing, evergreen native of North America with white flowers and red berries, needing moist, acid soil and partial shade. The berries are odd raw, but can be cooked for jellies and tarts and were once popular in Boston. Ironically the leaves were once used as 'tea'. *G. humifusa* was also used, as was *G. shallon*, another taller, shrubbier version with great clusters of purple berries which were eaten dried by Native Americans.

Colourful checker berries and leaves

NUTS

Nuts are different from fruits. We eat the seeds of nuts and usually not the coverings, though we often find uses for these as well. With fruits, plants are giving us, the animals and birds who consume them, a sweet pulp so that we will, inadvertently, help distribute their seeds. This trade-off is easy for the plant, as the seeds are the expensive items to manufacture and the sugary pulp takes little resource.

However, when we eat nuts, we eat big seeds that are very expensive for the plant to make, as they are rich in oils, minerals, proteins and vitamins. They have a high dietary value to us, but of course this does not serve the plant well. The trade-off is that the plant 'hopes' that if it produces a lot of nuts, some will escape the slaughter and be trampled underfoot or carried elsewhere and hidden but never recovered and thus start a fresh territory.

Squirrels are well known for assisting this process by burying nuts, but many other small mammals, particularly rodents, are also involved. Birds similarly hide nuts; there are plausible stories of birds that have filled attics with nuts, popping them in singly throughout the autumn through a small space such as a knot hole.

Because of their high oil content and nutritional value, nuts have long been gathered from the wild. The rise of industry created greatly increased demand for nuts as a source of oils for lighting and lubrication and for turning into margarines, soaps and cosmetics. The pulps that remained were rich animal feeds and helped to fuel the expansion of farming in the nineteenth century. Nuts were no longer wild crops, but had become cultivated crops on a vast scale.

Although nut trees generally require little work, they mostly grow too big for the garden and are best grown agriculturally. (Of course they then suffer from a build-up of pests and diseases – problems associated with all crops if they are grown as monocultures.) They are slow to come into production, though on the plus side they are mostly long-lived and make good timber. Many nut trees produce very hard or oily wood that lasts well. Walnut is one of the most prized of all timbers, so precious that it is mostly used only as veneer.

Nuts suffer different pests from those that attack fruits. Bigger birds and rodents are more of a threat and, as nuts are larger, they are harder to protect or grow under cover (indeed, except as bonsai, many are almost impossible to keep small). Also, they are unfortunately more tender and susceptible to frost damage than many fruits. This, plus the need for a hot summer and autumn to ripen the nuts, means that most nut trees are best grown in warmer countries than Britain.

One interesting connection between many of the nut trees covered in this chapter is how many of them have catkins and are wind-pollinated, even though these nut trees belong to entirely different families. This also means that they do not generally have scented flowers and give little nectar to insects, but they are, of course, a rich source of pollen.

From a commercial point of view, it is curious how almost all retail nut sales take place at Christmas, a period that serves to outsell the rest of the year put together.

Prunus dulcis/amygdalus from the family *Rosaceae*

ALMONDS

Tree, up to 6m (20ft). Life span: short. Deciduous. Fruits: 5cm (2in), pointed oval, in brown skin.
Value: rich in protein, calcium, iron, vitamins B2 and B3 and phosphorus.

Almond trees resemble and are closely related to peaches, with larger, light pink blossoms appearing before long, thin leaves. Flowering a fortnight earlier than peaches, they are often affected by frost. The wild varieties sometimes have spiny branches. The almond fruit has tough, inedible, leathery, greenish-brown, felted skin with a partition line along which it easily splits. The skin peels off a smooth, hard stone, full of small holes that do not penetrate the shell, containing the single, flat, pointed oval seed. Originally from the Middle East, almonds were known to the Ancient Hebrews and Phoenicians. Long naturalized in southern Europe and western Asia, they are now widely grown in California, South Africa and south Australia. Almond trees were introduced to England in 1548.

Almond blossom

VARIETIES

Prunus dulcis dulcis is the **Sweet Almond**, *P. dulcis amara*, the **Bitter Almond**. The former is the much-loved nut; the latter is used for producing oil and flavourings and is too bitter for eating. It contains highly poisonous amounts of prussic acid. In Spain, a light-cropping old variety, **'Jordan'**, is still grown and commercial varieties are available in some regions. The variety **'Texas'** is especially tasty roasted and salted with the skin on. Ornamental varieties rarely bear fruit.

CULTIVATION

Almonds want well-enriched, well-aerated, light soil, and to be at least 3m (10ft) apart. They need no staking after the first year. They want copious quantities of compost and mulches. Usually grown as a bush, they can be planted against walls. They should not be planted near peaches, as they may hybridize, resulting in bitter nuts. Hand-pollination is recommended. They are not completely self-fertile, so several trees should be planted together.

Growing under Glass
Almonds are rarely grown under glass because the necessary extra efforts of replenishment pruning and tying in are not usually well rewarded. The greenhouse must be unheated in winter to give them a dormant rest period. More problems occur under cover, and red spider mite can be troublesome unless high humidity is maintained.

Growing in Containers
Almonds can be grown in large pots, as they can take heavy pruning if well fed and watered. Pots enable them to be kept under cover during winter and through flowering and then brought out all through the summer, thus avoiding peach leaf curl and frost damage. The flowers must be protected from frosts and so too must the young fruitlets.

Ornamental and Wildlife Value
The almond is a real beauty – the fruiting tree as much as the many ornamental varieties. In hot, dry countries they are useful to birds, insects and rodents.

Propagation
Almonds can be raised from stones, but take years to fruit and may produce a

mixture of sweet and bitter fruits. Budded on to St. Julien A in the UK, for example, almonds will normally fruit in their third year. Seedling almond or peach rootstocks are better.

Maintenance

Spring Protect blossoms from frost, hand-pollinate, weed, mulch and spray with seaweed solution monthly.
Summer Thin fruits early.
Autumn Remove ripe and mummified fruits from the trees.
Winter Prune hard, spray with Bordeaux mixture.

Pruning and Training

Almonds fruit on young shoots, like peaches, but need to carry more fruits, so the trees are not pruned as hard. Commercially, every third year or so a few main branches are cut back hard and the top end of the remaining higher branches is removed to encourage prolific growth from the lower branches and stubs. This is best done in late winter, though it may let silver leaf disease in. It also keeps the bushes lower and more manageable. On walls and under cover, almonds may be fan trained, as for peaches (see p.419). Thinning the fruits is not essential, but prevents biennial bearing.

A grove of almond trees

OTHER USES

The wood is hard and makes good veneers; the oil is used in cosmetics.

Almonds ripening on the tree

Weed, Pest and Disease Control

Earwigs can get inside the fruits and eat the kernel, but are readily trapped in rolls of corrugated paper around each branch. Protect the bark from animals such as rabbits and deer. Almonds' main problem is peach leaf curl; see peaches (p.420) for treatment. Rainy weather in late spring and summer may cause fruits to rot. Dieback and gummosis are symptomatic of poor growth and are best treated by heavy mulching and hard pruning.

Harvesting and Storing

Once the nuts start to drop, knock them down, peel and dry. Commercially they are hulled, but the nuts will keep better intact. They can be stored in dry salt or sand for long periods.

COMPANION PLANTING

Almonds are benefited by alliums, especially garlic and chives. Clover or alfalfa and stinging nettles are also reputedly helpful.

CULINARY USES

The nuts are left with the brown skin on, or are blanched to provide a cleaner-tasting product. They may be eaten raw, cooked or turned into a milk, *Sirop d'Orgeat*.

Sirop d'Orgeat Milkshake
Quantities to taste

Sirop d'Orgeat
Ice-cold full-cream organic milk
Grated nutmeg

To one part Sirop d'Orgeat add approximately seven parts milk, mix well and top with the grated nutmeg.

Carya species from the family *Juglandaceae*

PECAN AND HICKORY NUTS

Tree, up to 30m (100ft). Life span: medium to long. Deciduous, partly self-fertile.
Fruits: up to 5cm (2in), green-skinned, hard-shelled nuts. Value: rich in oils and vitamins B1 and B2.

Pecans are very large, fast-growing trees with pinnate leaves, male catkins and insignificant flowers followed by pointed, rounded, cylindrical fruits. These have a leathery skin that peels off to reveal a reddish, smooth shell enclosing the walnut-like kernel. Hickories are similar, though not as large in tree or fruit, with non-aromatic leaves and peeling bark, while the pecan has grey, resinous leaves. Hickories also prefer more humid conditions than pecans.

Pecan nuts

These are natives of North America and have been long enjoyed by Native Americans. They are grown in Australia, but rarely crop well elsewhere, though they are widely grown for their timber. The first trees were introduced to Britain in 1629.

VARIETIES

Carya illinoensis is the **pecan**, a fruit much like a walnut in most ways save that the reddish shell is smooth, not embossed, and is also more cylindrical. The trees grow up to 21m (70ft) high, so are not very suitable for most modern gardens. Burbank developed new varieties of pecan with very thin shells, but these are not widely available. The hickories are similar to the pecan, with more flattened nuts. The trees generally grow up to half the pecan's height again, which is pretty big anywhere. The **Shellbark Hickory**, *C. laciniosa/alba*, and *C. ovata*, the **Shagbark**

Hickory, are the more popular and productive sorts. *C. tomentosa*, the **Mocker** or **Square Nut**, has a tasty nut, but is very difficult to shell. *C. cordiformis* is the **Bitternut Hickory**, and *C. porcina/glabra* is the **Pignut**. As their names suggest, these are suitable only for pigs and, of course, hungry children. *C. sulcata* is the **King Nut**, considered the best variety by Native Americans, but not yet developed commercially. Many other minor species are also occasionally eaten from the wild.

CULTIVATION

They will grow in the British Isles, but rarely fruit here. The pecan prefers a hotter, drier, more sub-tropical climate; the hickories prefer one that is warmer and wetter, so may produce crops in a favourable site in certain western regions.

Immature pecan nuts growing on the tree

The pointed, cylindrical pecan fruit contains the edible kernel

Growing under Glass and in Containers
There is little practical possibility of getting these huge trees under cover. They resent being confined in pots and are unlikely to crop, though they may make good bonsai subjects.

Ornamental and Wildlife Value
Given a suitable setting, these are large, attractive trees with decorative foliage that turns a rich yellow in autumn. Their nuts are of significant wildlife value.

Maintenance
Spring Weed, mulch, spray with seaweed solution.
Summer Prune, but only when needed remedially.
Autumn Collect nuts if it has been a long, hot summer.
Winter Cut out coral spot if any is seen.

Propagation
Normally grown from seed, they are best pot-grown and then planted out as soon as possible in their final site, as they do not like to be transplanted. They are slow to establish and then fast-growing. Improved varieties are grafted or budded on seedling stock.

Pruning and Training
Minimal pruning and training are required. Large specimens need staking for the first few years, as they are slow to take.

Harvesting and Storing
Ripe fruits are knocked down from the tree, peeled (if the peel has not dropped off already) and dried. They do not store as well as walnuts, though they may keep up to a year if they are stored in a cool, dry place. Commercially they are hulled before storage and will keep up to two years at −15°C (5°F).

WEED, PEST AND DISEASE CONTROL, COMPANION PLANTING

Very few pests or diseases are problems for the hickories in European gardens. The pecan finds Britain too cool to ripen its wood and suffers from coral spot, which needs pruning before it spreads. In America pecans suffer from many pests and diseases. No companion effects are known about for either tree.

OTHER USES

Hickories are planted for their tough, elastic timber and are renowned as fuel for smoking foods. Hickory bark was used for a yellow dye.

CULINARY USES

Pecan nuts taste much like mild, sweet walnuts and to my taste are preferable. They are used raw or cooked in savoury and sweet items, especially cakes and ice cream. Pecan pie is a legendary dessert. Hickory nuts are used similarly and can be squeezed to produce nut milk or oil.

Pecan Pie
Serves 4–6

175g (6oz) shortcrust pastry
60g (2oz) shelled pecans
90g (3oz) brown sugar
3 small or 2 large eggs
225g (8oz) golden syrup
30g (1oz) maple syrup
½ teaspoon vanilla essence
¼ teaspoon salt

Roll out the pastry and line a wide, shallow pie dish. Bake blind, weighed down with dried peas or similar, at 190°C/375°F/gas mark 5 for 20 minutes or until cooked. Cool and fill the case with pecans, arranged aesthetically. Beat together the other ingredients till the sugar is dissolved and pour over carefully without disturbing the nuts, which may float. Bake at 220°C/450°F/gas mark 8 for 10 minutes, then reduce the temperature to 180°C/350°F/gas mark 4 and cook for another 30 minutes. Cool and chill well before serving in slices with lashings of cream.

Juglans species from the family *Juglandaceae*

WALNUTS

Tree, 40m (135ft). Life span: long. Deciduous, partially self-fertile.
Fruits: up to 5cm (2in), green sphere enclosing nut. Value: rich in oil; the husks contain much vitamin C.

Walnuts are slow-growing, making massive trees up to 40m (135ft) eventually, with aromatic, pinnate foliage, silvery bark, insignificant female flowers and male catkins. All parts have a distinct sweet, aromatic smell. The fruits have a green husk around the nut, enclosing a kernel wrinkled like a brain.

Juglans regia, the common or Persian walnut, is native to western Asia. Introduced to the Mediterranean basin before the first century BC, it became an important food in many regions and was also grown for timber. Walnuts reached Britain in the sixteenth century, if not in Roman times. The black walnut, *J. nigra*, comes from north-east America and was introduced to Britain in 1686. It is even bigger than the common walnut and widely grown for timber. The nuts are large, very hard to crack and a valuable dietary source of phosphorus.

more you beat them the better they'll be' is advice that puzzles many. It is not to encourage fruitfulness, but rather to give the walnut a damaged bark which then produces a more valuable distorted grain in the timber. As to dog or wife, I suggest attention and treats probably develop better relationships with either.

Growing under Glass and in Containers

Huge trees, these can hardly be housed. I've a fifteen-year-old bonsai, but I doubt that it will ever fruit!

Ornamental and Wildlife Value

Very attractive and sweetly aromatic trees, they grow too big for most small gardens. They are not in general very valuable to wildlife, save to rodents and squirrels.

Maintenance

Spring Weed, mulch and spray with seaweed solution.
Summer Take young fruits for pickling.
Autumn Collect nuts, prune.

The fruit opens as it ripens to reveal the kernel inside

VARIETIES

Named varieties of common walnuts such as **'Franquette'** are hard to find in Britain, though may be available elsewhere. France had one called the **'Titmouse'**, because the shell was so thin that a titmouse could break in to eat the kernel! Black walnuts are usually offered as the species here, but there are several named varieties available from the USA. They can grow half as high again as common trees, up to 45m (150ft). Another American species, the **White Walnut** or **Butternut**, *J. cinerea*, introduced in 1633, is grown for timber and ornamental use. The nuts are half as big again as common nuts, strong-tasting and oily. *J. sieboldiana cordiformis* is the **Heartnut** from Japan. Fast-growing, fruiting after only five years or so, it has leaves up to 1m (3ft) long and small, easily shelled nuts which hang on strings.

CULTIVATION

Walnuts prefer a heavy, moist soil. They should not be planted where late frosts occur. As pollination is difficult, it is best to plant several together. The old saying 'The wife, the dog and the walnut tree, the

Walnut catkin

Propagation

The species can be grown from seed, but are slow. Improved varieties are grafted or budded, and still take a decade to start to fruit, finally maturing around the century. They are best started in pots and moved to their final site while still small, as they resent transplanting.

Pruning and Training

Walnuts must be pruned only in autumn, as they bleed in spring. Minimal pruning is required, but branches become massive, so remove badly positioned ones early. They need no stake after the first years.

The common walnut tree

Weed, Pest and Disease Control

There are few problems. Late frosts damage them, otherwise they are slow reliable croppers, each averaging 68kg (150lbs) annually.

Harvesting and Storing

The nuts are knocked down and the sticky staining peel is removed before drying. Walnuts can then be stored for up to a year. For pickling, pick the nuts green when a skewer can still be pushed through.

COMPANION PLANTING

Varro, in the first century BC, noted how sterile the land near walnut trees was. Walnut leaves and roots give off exudates that inhibit many plants and prevent their seeds from germinating. The American species are more damaging than the European and they are particularly bad for apples, *Solanaceae*, *Rubus* and many ornamentals.

OTHER USES

The foliage and husks have long been used as brown dyes and the oil as a hair darkener and for paints. The wood has always been valued for veneers and gun stocks, the more gnarled the better. Walnut trees were often planted near stables and privies, as their smell was thought to keep away flies. The walnut sap has traditionally been boiled to produce sugar.

CULINARY USES

Walnuts may be eaten either raw or cooked, often in confectionery or cakes, and associate particularly well with coffee or chocolate. They yield an edible, light oil. The young fruits may be pickled before the stone forms.

Walnut Aperitif

Young green walnuts
Brandy
Red wine
Sugar as required

Wash and prick enough nuts to fill a wide-necked bottle. Fill with brandy, seal and store in a cool, dark place. After a year, decant the brandy into another bottle, refill the original bottle with red wine and reseal. After another year, decant the wine into the brandy, refill the walnut bottle with wine and reseal. After another year decant again, fill the walnut bottle with white sugar and reseal. After a year (making four in total,) discard the nuts and add the sugar syrup to the wine and brandy. Serve in sherry glasses before meals.

Corylus species from the family *Corylaceae*

HAZELS, COBS AND FILBERTS

Tree/bush up to 6m (20ft). Life span: medium to long. Deciduous, partially self-fertile.
Fruits: up to 2.5cm (1in), pointed round, or oblong oval, brown nuts. Value: rich in oils.

These are shrubby trees, typical of woods and thickets, with dark stems, leaves rounded to a point and magnificent, yellow catkin male flowers in early spring. The gorgeous, carmine-red, female flowers are tiny, sea-urchin-like tentacles that protrude on warm days. The nuts are a pointed round or oblong oval. Hazels and cobs have a husk around the base, while filberts (full-beards) are completely enveloped by the husk. The shell is thin and the kernel sweet. Wild hazels are *Corylus avellana*, but, being wind-pollinated, these have often been influenced by *C. colurna*, cobs, also known as Turkish or Barcelona nuts, and *C. maxima* or filberts.

Hazelnuts of wild species were known in ancient times and filberts were introduced by the Romans from Greece. Pliny claims they came there from Damascus. The Romans may have brought filberts to Britain, but they were not noticed officially till introduced in 1759. Cob nuts were introduced earlier, in 1582, and the American hazelnut, *C. americana*, a similar, smaller nut with a thicker shell and heart-shaped leaves, arrived in 1798. Any appellation no longer signifies true breeding, as these all became interbred during the nineteenth century, giving us most of our current varieties.

Immature hazelnuts

planted severally to ensure pollination. They are an immensely easy crop for the lazy gardener, requiring even less effort than most.

Growing under Glass and in Containers

There seems no reason to grow them under cover and I suspect they would not like it anyway. They survive in pots quite well, looking attractive but seldom cropping.

Ornamental and Wildlife Value

These are not generally noticed, save when their catkins make a welcome display. The **Twisted Hazel** is attractively distorted and deformed and still crops well. The hazels will support many life forms, both large and small, and are also excellent plants for wild or native gardens.

Maintenance

Spring Weed, mulch and spray with seaweed solution at monthly intervals.
Summer Cut close underneath if grassed.
Autumn Clear mulch or cut the grass close to disclose any fallen nuts.
Winter Prune, mulch well if not under grass.

VARIETIES

I adore **Red-skinned Filberts**; they are certainly small and fiddly, with tight, russet husks, but they are so delicious. **'Cosford Cob'** is thin-shelled and a good pollinator of others.

'Kentish Cob' (**'Lambert's Filbert'**) is a prolific cropper of large nuts if pollinated by 'Cosford' or **'Pearson's Prolific'** (**'Nottingham Cob'**). This last is compact, a good pollinator and has large nuts. For the best flavour, however, you can't beat the wild hazelnut.

CULTIVATION

Hazels thrive in stony, hilly ground. A well-drained, loamy soil will do, but heavy, damp, rich soils cause too much rank growth and few female flowers. Hazels need no support and are best

Propagation

These can be grown from seed but do not come true. Layering or grafting is possible, but root suckers are best, detached in autumn and potted up or planted *in situ* or a nursery bed for a year before their final move.

Pruning and Training

Traditionally hazels were grown on a low, flat, cartwheel frame. They are probably best trained to spurs on goblets, but are often left to be bushes or thickets. It is worth keeping them on a single trunk, uncongested, and removing the suckers, to prevent losing any of the nuts.

Weed, Pest and Disease Control

Weedy growth underneath makes it hard to find nuts, so hazels are best planted in grass or mulched. In gardens they suffer few problems on a scale sufficient to damage crops, other than the attentions of birds, rodents, children and especially squirrels.

Male and female hazel flowers

Harvesting and Storing

The nuts can be eaten a little unripe, but have to be fully ripe to keep. Ideally they should be allowed to fall off, but many are stolen by wildlife. They need to be dehusked and dried to keep well, though I never dehusk my red-skinned filberts. They will keep best, and for years, if packed in salt.

COMPANION PLANTING

They seem to associate naturally with bluebells and primroses, and truffles can be grown on their roots.

OTHER USES

Hazels make good hedges and windbreaks. The foliage is eaten by many animals, including cows. The stems are tough and flexible, so are good for baskets and hurdles, and forked branches make divining rods. The wood is used for smoking fuel and I smoke my cheese with the shells.

Hazel growing in the wild

CULINARY USES

Hazelnuts of all varieties are used in savoury dishes, but more often in sweet dishes and confections. They are used for liqueurs and can be squeezed to express a light, edible oil.

Hazelnut Macaroons
Makes about 12

120g (4oz) hazelnuts
120g (4oz) light brown sugar
1 egg white
Drop of vanilla extract
Whipped cream to serve

Grind three quarters of the nuts in a food processor, then add the other ingredients and cream them together. Pour rounds of the mix on to rice paper on a baking tray, place the remaining nuts on top and bake for 15 minutes at 180°C/350°F/gas mark 4. Serve sandwiched with thick or clotted cream.

Castanea sativa from the family *Fagaceae*

SWEET OR SPANISH CHESTNUTS

Tree, up to 37m (120ft). Life span: long. Deciduous, rarely self-fertile. Fruits: 5cm (2in), prickly burrs containing two or three nuts. Value: rich in oils.

Sweet chestnuts make massive and beautiful trees. They have very large, serrated-edged leaves. The male flowers are long, yellow catkins, different from walnut or hazel catkins, as they are divided like pearls on a string. The fruits are brownish-russet, softly spiny burrs usually containing three brown nuts with thin, tough, leathery shells, flattened on one side and pointed.

Sweet chestnuts are native to the Mediterranean region. They were highly valued by the Romans for food and timber and became widely distributed. They fruit well only after hot summers in Britain, but are still capable of reaching a large size, so they have been planted for timber and were often coppiced. The major exporter of these nuts has always been Spain, though most southern European countries have their own production, as chestnuts have become a staple food. Madeiran nuts are said to be the biggest and traditionally served to sustain the peasants for months each year.

has been almost wiped out by a fungus, chestnut blight. Now American growers are breeding hybrids from the resistant *C. mollissima*, the **Chinese Chestnut**. *C. pumila*, the **American Chinquapin**, is rare in cultivation, and unlikely to fruit in Britain, but the nut is said to be very sweet. Other *Castanea* species are widely grown and the delicious nuts eaten with appreciation all around the world.

CULTIVATION

Sweet chestnuts are far too big for most gardens, rapidly reaching 30m (100ft) or even more. They do not like thin chalky soils, but are not calcifuges and will grow on an alkaline soil if it is also a light, well-drained loam or light, dry, sandy soil. They need no staking after the first year or so. If nuts are required rather than timber, plant on the sunny side of woodlands or windbreaks, ideally of yew or holm oak.

Maintenance
Spring Weed, spray with seaweed solution.
Summer Hope for hot weather.
Autumn Collect nuts if following a hot summer.
Winter Enjoy the nuts toasted over the fire.

VARIETIES

Castanea sativa is usually available only as the species or ornamental selections, though better varieties exist, such as *C. sativa macrocarpa*, **'Marron de Lyon'**, from France. *C. dentata* was the **American Sweet Chestnut**, with smaller, richly flavoured, sweeter nuts, but

Sweet chestnut leaves and ripening fruit

Ornamental and Wildlife Value

Sweet chestnuts make statuesque trees and the large leaves colour well in autumn. The nuts are often rather too useful to wildlife.

Growing under Glass and in Containers

Far too big to grow under glass, they resent being confined in a pot and they are unlikely to ever fruit in one, but there's a challenge.

Propagation

They can be grown from seed and are fast-growing but still slow to fruit. The best varieties are budded or grafted, but hard to find in the UK.

Pruning and Training

Minimal pruning is required and is best tackled in winter. Chestnuts get very large, so care must be taken to remove unsound branches.

The elegant shape of the sweet chestnut tree

Weed, Pest and Disease Control

Generally they are problem-free in Britain and will set crops in the south following hot summers. In America, chestnut blight wiped out their best species; so far this is no problem elsewhere. Rodents, birds (especially rooks and pheasants) and squirrels soon take the nuts.

Harvesting and Storing

The nuts are beaten down, the husks then removed and dried. They will keep for a year in cool, dry conditions; longer if totally dried first.

COMPANION PLANTING

Chestnuts are considered healthier when they are grown near oak trees.

The brown chestnut is contained within a tough, leathery shell

CULINARY USES

Chestnuts are not eaten raw, but are delicious roasted. They are made into *marrons glacés* (crystallized chestnuts), ground into flour and then made into porridge, puddings, breads, cakes, muffins and tarts and they are also much used for savoury dishes such as pâtés and in stuffing for meats. Sweet chestnuts are even made into liqueurs.

Chestnut Amber
Serves 4

225g (8oz) chestnuts
300ml (10 fl oz) milk
1 lemon
1 vanilla pod
60g (2oz) breadcrumbs
30g (1oz) butter
60g (2oz) caster sugar
2 eggs, separated
120g (4oz) shortcrust pastry

Roast the chestnuts for 20 minutes, cool and remove the skins. Simmer gently, with sufficient water to cover, until tender, then drain and sieve to a purée. Simmer the milk with the lemon peel and vanilla pod for 15 minutes, then strain on to the breadcrumbs. Blend the butter and half the sugar, mix in the egg yolks and lemon juice and stir in the puréed chestnuts, breadcrumbs and milk. Line a deep dish with pastry and fill with the mixture. Bake at 200°C/400°F/gas mark 6 for 25 minutes, or until firm and brown. Whisk the egg whites to a stiff froth, add a teaspoon of sugar, whisk again and spoon on top of the pie. Sprinkle with more sugar and then return to the oven until the meringue turns a delicious amber.

OTHER USES

Sweet chestnut has long been used for cleft paling. The wood is durable, but has 'shakes' or splits in it. Often used for rough or external timber, such as coffins and hop poles, it makes a poor firewood but superior charcoal. The nuts were traditionally esteemed for the self-service fattening of swine.

Anacardium occidentale from the family *Anacardiaceae*

CASHEWS

Tree, up to 12m (40ft). Life span: medium.
Semi-evergreen. Fruit: up to 8cm (3in) long, weird.
Value: kernels are nearly half fat
and one fifth protein.

Cashews are medium-sized, spreading trees with rounded leaves related to pistachios. The cashew comes attached underneath the bottom of the much larger and peculiar fruits, cashew apples, which are juicy and astringent. The nut is grey or brown, ear-shaped and contains a white kernel within the acrid, poisonous shell.

Indigenous to South America, cashews were planted in the East Indies by the sixteenth century and are now grown in many tropical regions, especially India and eastern Africa.

VARIETIES

Other cashews are eaten: *A. humile*, the **Monkey-nut**, and *A. nanum* are from Brazil and have similar nuts. *A. rhinocarpus* is the **Wild Cashew** of Columbia and British Guyana.

CULTIVATION

These are best grown by the sea in moderately dry tropical regions and will thrive in any reasonable soil.

The cashew (shown here in Kenya) looks like an English country park tree

Growing under Glass and in Containers

Plants dwarfed by large pots could probably be grown in a hot greenhouse or conservatory, if the seed could be found.

Ornamental and Wildlife Value

Cashews make interesting subjects for a collection or botanical garden.

Propagation

They are normally grown from seed, but this is difficult to obtain.

Pruning and Training

Only remedial pruning is necessary.

Weed, Pest and Disease Control

No problems are known. The trees exude a gum obnoxious to insects, which was used in book-binding.

Harvesting and Storing

Once the nuts are picked from underneath the fruits, they have to be roasted and shelled, which, despite mechanization, is labour-intensive. This is because all the shell must be removed, as it contains an irritant in the inner membrane around the kernel, though this is rendered harmless by heat.

OTHER USES

The shells of the nuts contain an oil used industrially. The 'apples' are then fermented to make a liquor. The sap makes an indelible ink.

CULINARY USES

Cashew nuts are popular raw, i.e., already partially roasted, or roasted and salted. They are used in many sweet and savoury dishes and can be liquidized to make a thick sauce. Cashews are fermented to make wine in Goa.

Cashew Tarts
Makes 12

225g (8oz) marzipan
A little icing sugar
120g (4oz) cashew nuts
60g (2oz) honey
1 teaspoon vanilla extract
A little milk
Glacé cherries

Roll the marzipan as pastry and form individual tart cases in a tray dusted with icing sugar. Liquidize the other ingredients, adding just enough milk to ensure success. Pour into the marzipan cases, set a cherry in each and chill them to set.

Macadamia ternifolia from the family *Proteaceae*

MACADAMIAS
OR QUEENSLAND NUTS

Tree, up to 18m (60ft). Life span: medium. Semi-evergreen.
Fruits: up to 2.5cm (1in), grey-husked nuts. Value: over 70% fat.

Macadamia trees are densely covered with narrow, glossy, holly-like, dark green leaves. The tassels of whitish flowers are followed by strings of small, hard, roundish, pointed nuts in greyish-green husks. The kernel is finely flavoured and of exquisite texture.

These nuts, despite the Greek-sounding name, are natives of north-eastern Australia. Not widely appreciated, they are mostly consumed in the United States from plantations in Hawaii. They were introduced to Ceylon, now Sri Lanka, in 1868.

The distinctive foliage of the macadamia tree

VARIETIES

No species or varieties are available in Britain.

Propagation
They are propagated by seed, but as they are usually sold roasted and salted this may be difficult to find.

Pruning and Training
Only remedial pruning is necessary and they will form bushy trees.

Harvesting and Storing
The shells are very hard to crack, so the bulk crops are collected mechanically and taken to factories to be de-husked, shelled, roasted and salted before packaging and storing, when they will keep for up to a year or so.

CULTIVATION

Macadamia nuts prefer tropical or sub-tropical, moist conditions. They are not particular as to soil and do best on the volcanic slopes of Hawaii. They thrive at medium elevations.

Growing under Glass and in Containers
If the seed could be obtained they might be grown under glass, in pots to constrain growth, though it is doubtful they would crop.

Ornamental and Wildlife Value
They are attractive, glossy, dark trees, but too tender for growing successfully outside sub-tropical zones.

CULINARY USES

Most macadamia nuts are eaten roasted and salted, but they are also used in certain baked goods and confectionery.

Macadamia Slice
Serves 8–10

120g (4oz) macadamia nuts
Icing sugar
225g (8oz) marzipan
1 dessertspoonful apricot
*   jam*
30g (1oz) chopped candied peel

Rinse and dry the macadamia nuts if they are salted. Dust a rolling board with powdered sugar and roll out the marzipan thickly. Coat thinly with jam and cut into two equally shaped pieces and an approximate third. On one piece spread a layer of nuts and peel, then place one third of marzipan on top, sticky side down. Smear the top with jam and add another layer of nuts and peel. Then put the last third on top (also sticky side down). Carefully press and roll this sandwich flatter and wider until the nuts almost push through. Trim, cut into small portions and sprinkle the mixture with powdered sugar before presenting.

Cocos nucifera from the family *Arecaceae*

COCONUTS

Palm, up to 28m (90ft). Life span: medium to long.
Evergreen, not usually self-fertile. Fruits: 30cm (12in) plus, green-brown, oval
husk containing the nut. Value: 65% oil.

These attractive palms, so typical of dreamy, deserted islands, are spread by their floating, oval-husked nuts. The thick, fibrous husk is contained in a rind and itself encloses a thick-shelled, oval nut with a hollow kernel that is full of milk when under-ripe.

Venerated in the islands of the Pacific as a sacred emblem of fertility, coconuts are distributed and known around the world.

VARIETIES

The **King Coconut** of Ceylon is esteemed for its sweet juice. The **Dwarf Coconut**, **Nyiur-gading**, of Malaysia has small fruits, but crops when young and at only about a metre (a few feet) high. The **Maldive Coconut** is small and almost round; the **Needle Coconut** of the Nicobar Islands is triangular and pointed.

The King Coconut

CULTIVATION

Coconuts thrive by the sea in moist, tropical heat and rich, loamy soils and are planted about 10m (33ft) apart.

Growing under Glass and in Containers

These are very attractive, easy plants to start with, rapidly outgrowing most places. The **Dwarf Coconut** may fruit, given good conditions, in only four years – thus while still small enough to stay indoors!

Ornamental and Wildlife Value

Very attractive trees, these can be used for indoor display until they grow too large.

Propagation

Ripe nuts that are laid on their side and barely covered with compost will germinate readily in heat.

Pruning and Training

Dead leaves need removing.

Harvesting and Storing

The nuts are used as they drop, but for milk, processing or cooking are picked by climbing or by using trained monkeys.

A coil of coir rope in Sri Lanka

COMPANION PLANTING

Coconuts are often grown in alternate rows with rubber trees, and with cacao while young. Climbing peppers, *Piper nigrum*, are grown up the coconut trunks.

OTHER USES

The trunks are used as timber, the leaves for thatch, the husk is coir, used for ropes and matting. The sap makes sugar or is fermented to toddy or distilled to arrack. Dried nuts are copra, used for oil for cosmetics, soaps and detergents. The pressed waste is animal food.

CULINARY USES

The milk is drunk fresh or fermented. The nut is eaten raw or cooked, often as desiccated, shredded coconut.

Coconut Biscuits
Makes approx. 10

1 egg white
150g (5oz) powdered sugar
75g (3oz) dried coconut
Rice paper
Glacé cherries
Crystallized angelica

Beat the egg white until stiff, then beat in the sugar and coconut. Spoon blobs of the mixture onto rice paper on a baking tray. Garnish each with a cherry and angelica and bake at 180°C/350°F/gas mark 4 for 15 minutes or until they are browning.

Bertholletia excelsa from the family *Myrtaceae*

BRAZILS
PARA OR SAVORY NUTS

Tree, up to 30m (100ft). Life span: long. Semi-evergreen.
Fruits: up to 15cm (6in), brown, spherical shell containing many nuts. Value:
65% fat and 14% protein.

The Brazil nut tree enjoys a warm tropical climate

These are tall handsome trees found on the banks of the Amazon and Orinoco Rivers. They have large, laurel-like leaves and panicles of white flowers, which drop brown, spherical bombs with thick, hard cases. These need to be smashed to reveal inside a dozen or more nuts shaped like orange segments, each with its own hard shell enclosing the oval, brown-skinned, sweet, white kernel.

Natives of Brazil, these are still mainly produced there and also in Venezuela and Guyana. They are grown ornamentally in other countries such as Ceylon, but rarely on a commercial scale.

Pruning and Training
These need no special attention, but are slow. They are often not cultivated, but are gathered from the wild, as they take fifteen years to start fruiting.

Propagation
The nuts can be started off in heat, but actually take months to germinate.

OTHER USES

The oil expressed from the kernels is used industrially; bark once caulked ships.

VARIETIES

Many consider the **Sapucaya Nut** superior; it is similar, though it comes from a different tree, *Lecythis zabucajo.*

CULTIVATION

Brazil trees thrive in deep, rich, alluvial soil in tropical conditions.

Ornamental and Wildlife Value
Very attractive trees, but too large and requiring too much heat and warmth for widespread use.

Growing under Glass and in Containers
These can be grown from seed and kept dwarfed in containers, making interesting specimens, but are unlikely ever to fruit.

Harvesting and Storing
The individual nuts are obtained by cracking the spherical containers, which are sealed with wooden plugs. Inside their shells the nuts will keep for up to two years.

CULINARY USES

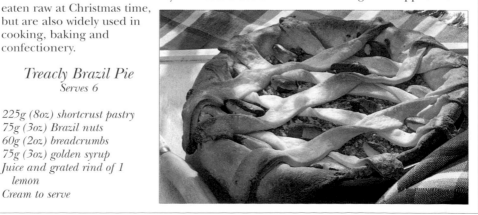

Most often Brazil nuts are eaten raw at Christmas time, but are also widely used in cooking, baking and confectionery.

Treacly Brazil Pie
Serves 6

225g (8oz) shortcrust pastry
75g (3oz) Brazil nuts
60g (2oz) breadcrumbs
75g (3oz) golden syrup
Juice and grated rind of 1 lemon
Cream to serve

Roll out three quarters of the pastry and line a pie dish with it. Use dried peas to weigh it down, and bake blind at 190°C/375°F/gas mark 5 for 10 minutes. Remove the peas and put a layer of nuts around the base of the case. Mix the other ingredients together and pour on top. Decorate with strips of pastry and then bake for 20 minutes at 190°C/375°F/gas mark 5. Serve the pie with lashings of whipped cream.

Arachis hypogaea from the family *Leguminosae*   **Groundnuts**

GROUNDNUTS OR PEANUTS

Herbaceous, 60cm (2ft). Life span: annual. Self-fertile.
Fruits: 1cm (½in) small oval seeds. Value: rich in oil, protein and vitamins B and E.

Peanuts are always known and used as nuts, although they are in fact the seeds of a tropical, pea-like, annual plant. After pollination of the yellow 'pea' flower, the stalk lengthens and pushes the seed pod into the ground, where it matures. The light brown husks shell easily to reveal a few red-skinned, whitish-yellow seeds.

Natives of tropical America, peanuts were brought to Europe in the sixteenth century and remained curiosities until the nineteenth. Useful for oil, animal feed and 'nuts', they are now grown worldwide.

VARIETIES

Spanish Bunch or **Virginia** varieties average fewer kernels than the better **Valencia** varieties, which have up to four. **Mauritius** peanuts are believed to be of superior quality.

CULTIVATION

Peanuts prefer loose, dryish, sandy soil. Cool, wet, British summers are unfavourable and they do better under glass, but can be raised indoors and planted out, and will then produce light crops. They are normally grown on ridges to make digging the crop easier.

Ornamental and Wildlife Value
Too pea-like to be attractive, they have curiosity value. The seeds are only too valuable to wildlife!

Pruning and Training
These require no care. The old, runnering varieties were more difficult.

Weed, Pest and Disease Control
On a garden scale these are problem-free, save for rodent thefts.

Harvesting and Storing
The pods are dug in autumn, thoroughly dried and shelled before storing. Commercially the bulk is pressed for oil and

Propagation
Sow in pots in heat for growing on in large pots to fruition, or planting out in favourable areas. In warm countries they are grown outdoors, sown 8cm (3in) deep, about 60cm (2ft) apart each way.

Growing under Glass and in Containers
Peanuts are good subjects for greenhouses, or in large pots, which can be kept under cover at the start and end of the season and put out on the patio during the summer months.

COMPANION PLANTING

Peanuts have been grown with rubber and coconuts.

OTHER USES

Peanut oil is used industrially.

CULINARY USES

Peanuts are commonly roasted and salted, and are much used in baking and confections, savoury sauces and for their butter and edible oil. They should be kept dry until required.

Roast Peanuts
Makes 1kg (2lb)

1kg (2lb) peanuts
30g (1oz) garlic
1x50g (2oz) can anchovies
7g (¼oz) oregano

Boil the peanuts for two minutes and slip off their skins, then dry the nuts. Blend the garlic, anchovies and oregano. Coat the peanuts with this mixture and roast at 180°C/350°F/ gas mark 4 for 10 minutes or so. Stir and cool.

OTHER NUTS

Araucaria araucana,
Monkey Puzzle or **Chile
Pine, Auracariaceae**
These well-known trees, with
spiny, overlapping, dark
green leaves festooning the
long, tail-like branches,
rarely fruit in the UK, it
seems, as they are usually
planted singly. Where they
have been planted severally,
as at a school in Sussex, they
reportedly set seed and the
nuts were shed most years.
In Chile the seeds are eaten
raw, roasted or boiled.
Closely related trees are
also grown in Brazil and
in Australia.

Castanospermum australe,
**Moreton Bay Chestnut,
Leguminosae**
These poisonous Australian
nuts are relished by native
Australians, who leach them
in water before drying and
roasting the nuts to render
them edible.

Coffea arabica,
Coffee, Rubiaceae
Small, evergreen trees, which
once grew wild in Arabia
and are now cultivated in
most hot countries. Coffee
'beans' are seeds from the
cherry-like berries, roasted
to oily charcoal, then
leached with hot water.

Cyperus esculentus,
Tiger Nut, Cyperaceae
Also called **Ground-almond**
or **Chufa**, this is not a nut
at all but the edible,
underground rhizome of a
small, perennial, grass-like
sedge. It is grown in dry,
sandy soils in western Asia
and Africa.

**An open, ripe cocoa pod
showing the beans and flesh**

Fagus sylvatica,
Beech, Fagaceae
A well-known tree that can
reach 30m (100ft) and
chokes out everything
underneath with heavy, dry
shade. Although parts of the
tree are poisonous and have
been used medicinally, an
edible oil can be extracted
from the seeds and they
have been eaten raw and
roasted to make 'coffee'. In
sheer desperation, beech
sawdust has been boiled,
baked and mixed with flour
to make 'bread'. A worthy
subject for parks on acid or
alkaline soil, but far too
large for most gardens!
The **American Beech**,
F. grandiflora, is similar.

Ginkgo biloba,
**Maiden Hair Tree,
Ginkgoaceae**
This 'prehistoric' plant is
grown ornamentally for the
strange, leathery, fan-shaped
leaves, which turn bright
yellow in the autumn. In the
UK the gingko rarely sets
fruits, which resemble
unpleasant-smelling, yellowish
plums, as it is usually
planted singly whereas both
male and female forms are
necessary. In the Far East
the seeds, which resemble
round, vaguely fishy almonds,
are eaten, especially by the
Chinese at weddings.

**Ripe coffee beans on bushes
in Costa Rica**

Myristica fragrans,
Nutmeg, Myristiceae
These nuts are only ever
used as a spice. They are
natives of the Moluccas
Islands in Indonesia and are
commercially grown in few
other places save Grenada
in the West Indies. The trees
reach 18–21m (60–70ft) and
have fruits resembling
apricots or peaches which
split, like almonds, revealing
a nut surrounded by a
reddish yellow aril. This is
the spice, mace. Inside the
thin shell is the brown
nutmeg kernel which rattles
when ripe. If still alive, they
will germinate in heat after
three months or so.

Pterocarya fraxiniflora,
**Caucasian Wing-nut,
Juglandaceae**
Native to the Caucasus and
Persia and introduced to
Britain in 1782, these are
strong-growing relations of
the walnut. They have large,
non-aromatic, pinnate

leaves, catkins and small,
edible nuts surrounded by
semi–circular wings. They
are hardy, though sustain
some dieback after hard
frosts, and succeed in damp
places. They could be
improved, perhaps by
crossing with other species
such as the **Japanese Wing-
nut**, *P. rhoifolia*, or the large-
fruited Chinese *P. stenoptera*.

Theobroma cacao,
Cacao, Sterculiaceae
The cocoa beans, known as
nibs in the trade, are
fermented, dried and
ground to make chocolate.
The trees, which are small
natives of the Americas, are
now mainly grown in West
Africa. The melon-like pods
are green, ripening to red
or yellow. They spring
directly out of the trunk and
main branches of the tree
after the delightful pink
flowers.

PRACTICAL GARDENING

PLANNING YOUR VEGETABLE GARDEN

Is there a more glorious site for a garden than the foot of the Alps?

Several factors determine the planning and layout of a vegetable garden and the species that can be grown:
• the locality and climatic conditions
• the size and shape of the plot
• the number of people to be supplied with vegetables
• the duration of cropping
• the skill of the gardener, and the time available for maintaining the plot
• whether the vegetables are intended for use when fresh, stored or both

It is a good idea to list the vegetables you like, then decide how and where they can be grown to achieve the best results. In large gardens a vast range and volume of tasty vegetables can be produced using crop rotation and protected cropping to extend the growing season. Smaller sites allow fewer opportunities for self-sufficiency, but it is still possible to grow a good selection or experiment with unusual varieties. Even the tiniest gardens, balconies or patios are suitable, particularly with the use of containers, while areas surrounded by buildings sometimes create favourable microclimates for tender vegetables such as okra. Protected cropping provides further opportunities to defy the cold weather.

Before preparing a planting plan it is important to be aware of the advantages and disadvantages of the site, considering everything from aspect and shelter to soil quality and drainage. Choose a design that suits your site and taste: traditionally, plots were planned in beds and rows, but you may prefer the potager (or 'edible landscape') developed by the French, or the raised bed system, which is ideal for intensive small or large-scale cropping. It is essential to provide the best possible growing conditions for optimum production and the old saying, 'the answer lies in the soil', is particularly relevant to vegetable growing.

Accurate timing is also a prerequisite. A cropping timetable should make full use of the ground all year round. It is advisable to plan backwards from the intended harvesting date to work out when crops should be sown. There is little advantage in having a garden full of vegetables that are cheap and plentiful in the shops; it is far better to plan your cropping dates for times when they are scarce and expensive.

Site and Soil

Most vegetables are short-term crops, which are harvested before they reach maturity. To achieve the necessary rapid growth, the ideal site is warm and light with good air circulation. This is particularly important for the fertilization of wind-pollinated crops such as sweetcorn, and to discourage pests and diseases, which flourish in still conditions. However, it is worth noting that strong winds can reduce plant growth by up to 30%.

On a gently sloping site facing the sun, the soil warms faster in spring than in other aspects, making such an area perfect for early crops.

It is more difficult to work the soil on steeper slopes, especially if machinery is being used: crops should be planted across, rather than down the slope to reduce the risk of soil erosion during heavy rain. On very steep slopes the ground should be terraced.

A sloping site is ideal for early crops   **Kitchen garden (opposite)**

ORNAMENTAL
VEGETABLE GARDENS

Small fruiting gourd – attractive as well as edible

Conditioned to believe that vegetables are functional, and flowers beautiful, many fail to appreciate the splendour and bounty of a vegetable plot with its contrasting colours, forms and textures, neatly framed by well kept paths.

The traditional design for a vegetable garden is based on a system of rows (see p.584). Large kitchen gardens were formerly attached to a 'great house', with the gardeners' task to cultivate a wide range of crops and supply the household with vegetables throughout the year. By way of contrast, most gardeners now have smaller gardens, and the basis for what they grow and how they grow it is more a matter of choice than necessity. This provides them with the opportunity to grow vegetables for their ornamental values as well as utilitarian ones. For the same reasons, it may also be preferable to grow small quantities of a wider range of cultivars.

Colour
Vegetables are not only eaten for their flavour and nutritional value but add welcome colour to a meal. Consider the range of colour and tonal variation in a salad; it is generally greater than the range of flavours.

There are tones of green in lettuce, endive and cucumber, yellow in peppers, purple in beetroot and leaf lettuce and red in tomatoes. For centuries, only the French potager capitalized on this display of colours, but vege-tables are at last more often used as design elements in ornamental planting. Vegetables in the flower border have in recent years become a familiar sight.

The contrasting red and green foliage of ruby chard is sumptuous, as is beetroot 'Bull's Blood', while purple-or yellow-podded French beans and the mauve leaves of Cabbage 'Red Drumhead' create their own exotic magic. Red-skinned onions like 'Red Baron' and the red-leaved lettuce 'Lollo Rosso' are equally stunning. Squashes impress with their bold shapes and colour (just look at 'Turk's Turban'), while tomatoes like the golden 'Yellow Perfection' and striped 'Tigrella' delight the eye. Flowers and fruits add other colour accents.

Form
A good many vegetables have appealing foliage or a distinctive habit. The bold

architectural leaves and sculptured form of globe artichokes are prized by garden designers, and a 'wigwam' of scarlet runner beans or trailing cucurbits makes a dramatic focal point. Members of the onion family, leeks, and chives have spiky, linear leaves, which contrast well with the rounded shapes of lettuce and the feathery, arching growth of carrot tops. Celery and Brussels sprouts naturally have a distinguished upright habit. Perhaps the most unusual of all, 'Rubine', the purple Brussels sprout, which is planted as a single specimen in a container, looks like an angular, alien sculpture.

Texture

The different colours and forms of vegetable foliage are underlined by their texture. Consider the solidity of a compact cabbage head, wreathed in glaucous, puckered leaves, or the soft, billowing effect created by the dissected leaves of fennel or asparagus foliage. Exploiting such contrasts provides a foliage display as interesting as a herbaceous border. Even after harvest the impact remains; the tall dried stems of sweetcorn look wonderful when frosted on a winter's day and the rustling sound as the wind blows through their dead leaves brings life to a desolate garden.

Vegetables as 'Bedding Plants'

Many vegetables are grown as annuals and, as each crop matures and is harvested, the appearance of the vegetable garden changes. Often, the only constant elements are the framework of paths and hedges and long-lived perennial crops.

Such intensively grown crops are easier to maintain when grown in a formal pattern as this provides the ideal opportunity to arrange crops in brightly coloured, bold patterns or emphasize their subtle qualities. Brightly

coloured chard, lettuce or kale or the shimmering foliage of carrots can be used to provide a foliage display rivalling any bedding.

Vegetables that have run to seed look particularly spectacular; lettuces are upright and leafy, beetroot display their red-veined leaves and bold flower spikes, while onions and leeks produce symmetrical globes of flowers, which are invaluable for attracting pollinating insects. Some gardeners allow a few plants to go to seed to enjoy such effects, but would you be daring enough to create a planting scheme featuring vegetables in their later stages?

One approach to creating a 'bedding' scheme is to group together plants with a similar life span, for a long-term display. Alternatively, with skilful planning, it is possible to plant crops taking different times to reach maturity, filling any gaps with suitable vegetables after harvest, to retain the impact of the design. The time scale can vary, with radishes taking a mere five weeks, and sprouting broccoli and winter cabbages remaining in the ground for several months. The rapid changeover of these annual crops means that plant colours as well as flavours are constantly changing within the scheme.

Perennial vegetables such as asparagus, globe artichoke and rhubarb can be grown in separate beds or used as permanent feature plants within the design. In smaller or irregularly shaped gardens, crop rotation allows a wide range of annual design patterns and planting arrangements.

The Potager

Their love of food and appreciation of aesthetics motivated French gardeners to create the potager, or ornamental vegetable garden, with a more obvious

Globe artichoke flowers are prime examples of attractive vegetables

visual appeal than the English kitchen garden. Simple, formal, geometric shapes such as four square-shaped raised beds dissected by straight paths form a permanent structure, enlivened with a succession of vibrantly coloured leafy crops chosen for their culinary and visual qualities.

Vegetables are placed according to their height and habit, larger vegetables forming centre pieces and smaller ones making up the rows. Climbing vegetables growing over ornamental tripods, arches or even canes provide height, and the whole area can be screened by trellis and include vegetables in containers.

To maintain the symmetry, harvest plants with an eye to pattern: work evenly from both ends and from the centre, or cut every other plant to keep the coverage balanced as far as possible. Make full use of successional cropping so that the soil is always utilized and the pattern maintained.

Random Systems

Scattering vegetables individually or in groups among ornamental borders is becoming more popular. They should be planted according to their ultimate height with lower plants near the front of the border, using brightly coloured vegetables strong enough to stand up to their brightly coloured neighbours. Grow purple-podded climbing French beans through shrubs instead of clematis, runner bean 'Painted Lady' instead of sweet peas and purple-leaved cabbage alongside nasturtiums. Mini vegetables can be grown in window boxes or hanging baskets; try tomato 'Tumbler' or grow climbers as trailing plants.

The only requirement for successful growth of vegetables among ornamentals is adequate soil or compost fertility, which can easily be maintained with well-prepared soil and careful feeding.

PLANNING YOUR HERB GARDEN

Herbs are so versatile that they should appeal to anyone, be they a cook, a lover of salads, or someone just wanting to enjoy the rich scents of plants and watch the butterflies collecting nectar from the flowers. And there are herbs for every space; they will grow in a window box or in a pot on a sunny window ledge; and some can be grown indoors as houseplants as well as outside in gardens, small or large. The best way to grow herbs is the organic way. Quite apart from the fact that if you use natural products, the soil remains clean and free from chemical pollutants, in organic herb gardens there is no chance of contaminating a plant before you eat it. Organic methods also encourage bees and other insects to the garden, which in turn helps maintain the healthy natural balance of predator and pest.

CONDITIONS

As herbs are basically wild plants tamed to fit a garden, it makes sense to grow them in conditions comparable with their original environment. This can be a bit difficult, for they come from all over the world. As a general rule, the majority of culinary herbs come from the Mediterranean and prefer a dry sunny place. But herbs really are adaptable and they do quite well outside their native habitat, provided you are aware of what they prefer.

CHOOSING THE SITE

Before planning your site, it is worth surveying your garden in detail. Start by making a simple plan and mark on it north and south. Show the main areas of shade – a high fence, a neighbouring house and any high trees, noting whether they are deciduous or evergreen. Finally, note any variations in soil type – wet, dry, heavy etc. Soil is one of the most important factors and will determine the types of herb you can grow. For different soil types, see pp.578–9.

USE

Next, decide what you want from your herb garden. Do you want a retreat away from the house? Or a herb garden where the scents drift indoors? Or do you want a culinary herb garden close at hand to the kitchen door?

STYLE

Then think about what shape or style you want the garden to take. Formal herb gardens are based on patterns and geometric shapes. Informal gardens are a free-for-all, with species and colours, all mixed together. Informal gardens may look un-planned, but the best have been well planned. This is worth doing even if it is just to check the final height and spread of the plant. It can be misleading buying plants from a garden centre – they are all neat, uniform and fairly small, and it is well worth investigating and trying to visualize their mature size.

The plants have to be accessible, either for using fresh or to harvest, so paths are a good idea. They also introduce patterns to the design and can help to define its shape. For convenience, herbs should be no more than 75cm (30in) from a path, and ideally the beds no more than 1–1.2m (3–4 ft) wide. If they are more than 1.2m (4ft) wide, insert stepping stones to improve access.

LAYING PATHS

There are a number of choices of materials you can use for paths.

Grass

A grass path is quite easy to achieve and looks very attractive. Another plus point is the minimal cost. Make it at least as wide as your lawn mower, otherwise you will be cutting it on your hands and knees with shears. It is a good idea to edge the path either with wood, metal or, more attractively, with bricks, laid on their side end to end. Disadvantages to this kind of path are that it needs mowing and will not take heavy traffic.

Gravel

Gravel paths really do lend themselves to being planted with herbs. Be sure to prepare them well otherwise a water trap will form, and the plants would be better off being aquatic.

First remove the topsoil carefully. Then dig out to a depth of 30 cm (12in), putting the soil to one side.

Back row, left to right: **Eau de Cologne Mint**, *Mentha* x *piperita* f. *citrata*, **English Mace**, *Achillea ageratum*, **Scented Pelargonium 'Mabel Gray'**, **Orange-scented Thyme** *Thymus 'Fragrantissimus'*; front row, left to right: **Creeping Savory**, *Satureja spicigera*, **Chives**, *Allium schoenoprasum*, **Lady's Mantle Conjuncta**, *Alchemilla conjuncta*, **Curry Plant Dartington**, *Helichrysum italicum* 'Dartington'.

It is advisable to put a wooden edge between the soil of the garden or lawn and the new path. This will stop the soil falling into the path, and keep the edge neat. Fill the newly formed ditch with 14cm (6in) hard core. Mix the topsoil with peat, bark and grit in the ratio 3:1:1:1, and put this mix on top of the hard core to a depth of 8cm (3in). Finish with 8cm (3in) gravel or pea shingle. There are many colours of gravel available, most large garden centres stock a good range, or if you have a quarry nearby it is worth chatting them up.

Roll the path before planting. Herbs that will grow happily in gravel are creeping or upright thymes, winter savory, and pennyroyal. The disadvantage of gravel is that you will find that weeds will recur, so be diligent.

Bricks
Paths made out of bricks have become very fashionable. There is now a subtle range of colours available, and varied and original patterns can be created. For standard-size bricks, dig out to a depth of 10 cm (4in). As with the gravel path, include a wooden edge. Spread 5cm (2in) of sharp sand over the base; level and dampen. Lay the brick on top of the sand in the desired pattern, leaving a 2–5mm (1/8-1/4in) gap between the bricks. Settle them in, using a mallet or a hired plate vibrator.

If you wish to plant the path with herbs, it is as well at this juncture to leave out one or two bricks, filling the gaps later with compost and planting them when the path has settled. When the whole path has been laid, spread the joints with a mix 4:1 of fine dry sand and cement, and brush it in. The mixture will gradually absorb the moisture from the atmosphere, so setting the brick.

Planning your planting

Paving stones
These can take up a lot of space and are expensive to lay over a large area. Garden centres now stock a large range in various colours and shapes. Also try builders' merchants, you may get a better deal, especially if you require large quantities. Paving stones are ideal for the classic chequer-board designs and the more formal designs.

If you want the paving stones to lie flush with the ground, dig out the soil to the depth of the slab plus 5cm (2in). Put 5cm (2in) of sharp sand on to the prepared area, level off and lay the slabs on top, tapping them down, and making sure they are level. If the chosen area is already level and you want the slabs to be proud, then lay them directly in position with only a small layer of sand underneath.

ALTERNATIVE PLANTING
Raised beds
If your soil is difficult, or if you wish to create a feature in the garden, raised beds are a good solution. Also, plants in raised beds are easier to keep under control and will not wander so much around the rest of the garden. Finally, they are more accessible for harvesting and stand at a good height for those in wheelchairs.

The ideal height for a raised bed is between 30cm (12in) and 75cm (30in). If you raise it over 1m (3ft) high you will need some form of foundation for the retaining walls, to prevent them keeling over with the weight of the soil. Retaining walls can be made out of old railway sleepers (which are not as cheap as they used to be), logs cut in half, old bricks, or even red bricks – leave the odd one out and plant a creeping thyme in its place.

For filling a 30cm (1ft) raised bed, the following ratios are ideal. First put a layer of hard core (rubble) on top of the existing soil to a depth of 8cm (3in), followed by an 8cm (3in) layer of gravel, and finally 4cm (6in) of topsoil mix – made up of 1 part peat, 1 part bark, 1 part grit or sharp sand, with 3 parts topsoil.

Lawns
Many herbs are excellent ground cover and can make a fragrant lawn but, as already mentioned under chamomile, beware of planting too large an area to begin with. It can be an error costly in both time and money. Small areas filled with creeping herbs give great delight to the unsuspecting visitor who when walking over the lawn, discovers a pleasant aroma exuding from their feet!

It may sound repetitious, but it is worth saying that preparing your site well is the key to a good garden. Given a typical soil, prepare the site for the lawn by digging the whole area out to a depth of 30cm (12in) and then prepare in exactly the same way as for the raised bed: 8cm (3in) hard core, 8cm (3in) gravel, 14cm (6in) topsoil mix – this time, 1 part peat, 2 parts sharp sand, 3 parts top soil. Apart from chamomile, other plants that can be used for a herb lawn are Corsican mint, *Mentha requinni*, planted 10cm (4in) apart, or creeping thymes – see pages 375–377 for varieties – and plant them about 23cm (9in) apart.

HERB GARDENS

The designs for six herb gardens included on the following pages can be adhered to religiously, or adapted to meet your personal tastes, needs and of course the space you have available in your garden.

It is with this last requirement in mind that I have specifically not included the exact size of the garden in the design and instead have concentrated on the shape, the overall layout and the

relationship between plants. I hope these plans give you freedom of thought and some inspiration.

FIRST HERB GARDEN

When planning your first herb garden, choose plants that you will use and enjoy. I have designed this garden in exactly the same way as the one at my herb farm. Much as I would love to have a rambling herb garden, I need something practical and easy to manage, because the nursery plants need all my attention.

It is also important that the herbs are easy to get at, so that I can use it every day. By dividing the garden up into four sections and putting paving stones round the outside and through the middle, it is easy to maintain and provides good accessibility.

For this garden, I have chosen a cross-section of

herbs with a bias towards culinary use, because the more you use and handle the plants, the more you will understand their habits. There is much contradictory advice on which herb to plant with which, but many of these are old wives' tales.

There are only a few warnings I will give: Do not plant dill and fennel together because they intermarry and become

fendill, losing their unique flavours in the process. Equally, do not plant dill or coriander near wormwood as it will impair their flavour. Also, different mints near each other cross-pollinate and over the years will lose their individual identity. Finally, if you plan to collect the seed from lavenders, keep the species well apart.

Aside from that, if you like it, plant it.

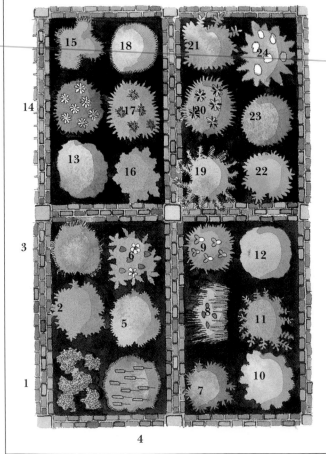

1   **Parsley** *Petroselinum crispum*
2   **Pineapple Mint** *Mentha suaveolens* 'Variegata'
3   **Fennel** *Foeniculum vulgare*
4   **Lavander Munstead** *Lavandula angustifolia* 'Munstead'
5   **Greek Oregano** *Origanum vulgare* subsp. *hirtum* 'Greek'
6   **Alpine Strawberry** *Fragaria vesca*
7   **Purple Sage** *Salvia officinalis* 'Purpurascens'
8   **Chives** *Allium schoenoprasum*
9   **Heartsease** *Viola tricolor*
10 **Golden Curly Marjoram** *Origanum vulgare* 'Aureum Crispum'
11 **Salad Burnet** *Sanguisorba minor*
12 **Lemon Thyme** *Thymus* x *citriodorus*
13 **Garden Thyme** *Thymus vulgaris*
14 **Roman Chamomile** *Chamaemelum nobile*
15 **Rock Hyssop** *Hyssopus offinialis* subsp. *aristatus*
16 **Buckler Leaf Sorrel** *Rumex scutatus*
17 **Bergamot** *Monarda didyma*
18 **Curry Plant, Dartington** *Helichrysum italicum* 'Dartington'
19 **Rosemary** *Rosmarinus officinalis*
20 **Borage** *Borago officinalis*
21 **Variegated Lemon Balm** *Melissa officinalis* 'Aurea'
22 **Apple Mint** *Mentha suaveolens*
23 **Winter Savory** *Satureja montana*
24 **Chervil** *Anthriscus cerefolium*

HERB BATH GARDEN

This garden may seem a bit eccentric to the conventially minded, but when my back is aching after working in the nursery, and I feel that unmentionable age, and totally exhausted, there is nothing nicer than lying in a herb bath and reading a good book.

The herbs I use most are thyme, to relieve an aching back, lavender, to give me energy, and eau-de-cologne to knock me out. Simply tie up a bunch of your favourite herbs with string, attach them to the hot water tap and let the water run. The scent of the plants will invade

both water and room. Alternatively, put some dried herbs in a muslin bag and drop it into the bath.

Remember when planting this garden to make sure that the plants are accessible. Hops will need to climb up a fence or over a log or pole. Again, quite apart

from the fact that the herbs from this garden are for use in the bath, they make a very aromatic garden in their own right. Position a seat next to the lavender and rosemary so that when you get that spare five minutes, you can sit in quiet repose and revel in the scent.

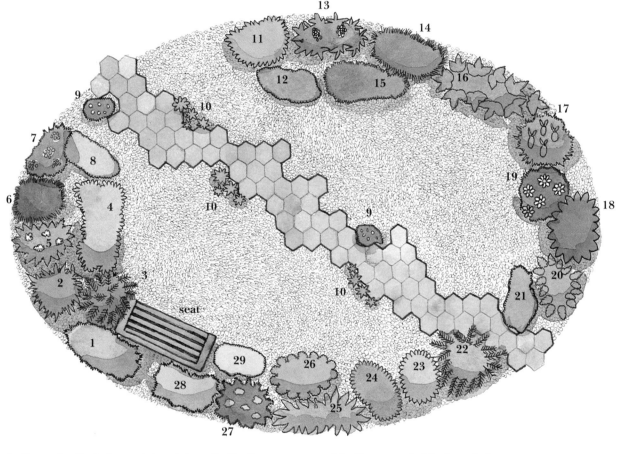

1 **Lavender Seal** *Lavandula* x *intermedia* 'Seal'
2 **Lemon Verbena** *Aloysia triphylla*
3 **Benenden Blue Rosemary** *Rosmarinus officinalis* 'Benenden Blue'
4 **Gold Sage** *Salvia officinalis icterina*
5 **Valerian** *Valeriana officinalis*
6 **Bronze Fennel** *Foeniculum vulgare* 'Purpureum'
7 **Tansy** *Tanacetum vulgare*
8 **Golden Lemon Thyme** *Thymus* x *citriodorus* 'Golden Lemon'
9 **Double-Flowered Chamomile** *Chamaemelum nobile* 'Flore Pleno'
10 **Houseleek** *Sempervivum tectorum*
11 **Peppermint** *Mentha* x *piperita*
12 **Orange-Scented Thyme** *Thymus* 'Fragrantissimus'
13 **Meadowsweet** *Filipendula ulmeria*
14 **Green Fennel** *Foeniculum vulgare*

15 **Pennyroyal** *Mentha pulegium*
16 **Hops** *Humulus lupulus*
17 **French Lavender** *Lavandula stoechas*
18 **Bay** *Laurus nobilis*
19 **Roman Chamomile** *Chamaemelum nobile*
20 **Lemon Balm** *Melissa officinalis*
21 **Porlock Thyme** *Thymus* 'Porlock'
22 **Prostrate Rosemary** *Rosmarinus officinalis* Prostrate Group
23 **Golden Marjoram** *Origanum vulgare* 'Aureum'
24 **Eau de Cologne Mint** *Mentha* x *piperita* f. *citrata*
25 **Comfrey** *Symphytum officinale*
26 **Lady's Mantle** *Alchemilla mollis*
27 **Yarrow** *Achillea millefolium*
28 **Lavender Grappenhall** *Lavandula* x *intermedia* 'Grappenhall'
29 **Silver Posie Thyme** *Thymus vulgaris* 'Silver Posie'

WHITE HERB GARDEN

This garden gave me great pleasure to create. For me, it is a herb garden with a different perspective.

It has a row of steps going from the road to the front door of the house. Either side of the steps is a dwarf white lavender hedge. In spring before the lavender, and just before the lily of the valley, are in flower, the sweet woodruff gives a carpet of small white flowers. This is the start of the white garden, which then flowers throughout the year through to autumn. It is a most attractive garden with a mixture of scents, foliage and flowers.

This planting combination can easily be adapted to suit a border. Even though it is not a conventional herb garden, all the herbs can be used in their traditional way. The garlic chives with baked potatoes, the horehound for coughs, the chamomile to make a soothing tea, and the lavender to make lavender bags or to use in the bath.

The great thing about a garden like this is that it requires very little work to maintain. The hedge is the only part that needs attention – trim in the spring and after flowering in order to maintain its shape.

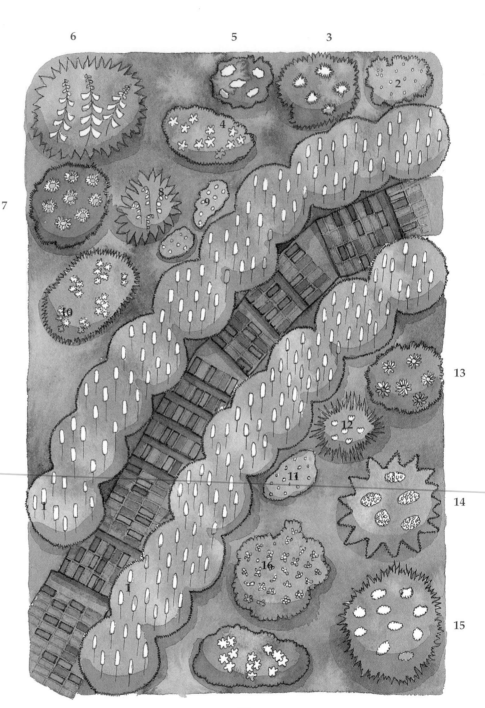

1	**White Lavender (dwarf)** *Lavandula angustifolia* 'Nana Alba'	
2	**Sweet Woodruff** *Galium odoratum*	
3	**Bergamot Snow Maiden** *Monarda* 'Schneewittchen'	
4	**Jacob's Ladder (white)** *Polemonium caeruleum* subsp. *caeruleum* f. *album*	
5	**Yarrow** *Achillea millefolium*	
6	**Foxgloves (white)** *Digitalis purpurea* f. *albiflora* (POISONOUS)	
7	**Roman Chamomile** *Chamaemelum nobile*	
8	**Lily of the Valley** *Convallaria majalis* (POISONOUS)	
9	**White Thyme** *Thymus serpyllum* var. *albus*	
10	**White Hyssop** *Hyssopus officinalis* f. *albus*	
11	**Snowdrift Thyme** *Thymus serpyllum* 'Snowdrift'	
12	**Garlic Chives** *Allium tuberosum*	
13	**Pyrethrum** *Tanacetum cinerariifolium*	
14	**Sweet Cicely** *Myrrhis odorata*	
15	**Valerian** *Valeriana officinalis*	
16	**White Horehound** *Marrubium vulgare*	
17	**Prostanthera** *Prostanthera cuneata*	

COOK'S HERB GARDEN

The best site for a culinary herb bed is a sunny area accessible to the kitchen. The importance of this is never clearer than when it is raining. There is no way that you will go out and cut fresh herbs if they are a long way away and difficult to reach.

Another important factor is that the sunnier the growing position, the better the flavour of the herbs. This is because the sun brings the oils to the surface of the leaf of herbs such as sage, coriander, rosemary, basil, oregano and thyme.

The cook's herb garden could be grown in the ground or in containers. If in the ground, make sure that the site is very well drained. Position a paving stone near each herb so that it can be easily reached for cutting, weeding and feeding and also to help contain the would-be rampant ones, such as the mints.

Alternatively, the whole design could be adapted to be grown in containers. I have chosen only a few of the many varieties of culinary herb. If your favourite is missing, either add it to the design or substitute it for one of my choice.

1	**Ginger Mint** *Mentha* x *gracilis*	15	**Garlic** *Allium sativum*
2	**Chervil** *Anthriscus cerefolium*	16	**Oregano Greek** *Origanum vulgare* subsp. *hirtum* 'Greek'
3	**Coriander** *Coriandrum sativum*	17	**French Tarragon** *Artemisia dracunculus*
4	**French Parsley** *Petroselinum crispum* French	18	**Lovage** *Levisticum officinale*
5	**Chives** *Allium schoenoprasum*	19	**Chives, Garlic** *Allium tuberosum*
6	**Corsican Rosemary** *Rosmarinus officinalis* 'Corsican Blue'	20	**Lemon Balm** *Melissa officinalis*
7	**Garden Thyme** *Thymus vulgaris*	21	**Moroccan Mint** *Mentha spicata* var. *crispa* 'Moroccan'
8	**Angelica** *Angelica archangelica*	22	**Dill** *Anethum graveolens*
9	**Fennel** *Foeniculum vulgare*	23	**Parsley** *Petroselinum crispum*
10	**Winter Savory** *Satureja montana*	24	**Lemon Thyme** *Thymus* x *citriodorus*
11	**Greek Basil** *Ocimum minimum* 'Greek'	25	**Sweet Marjoram** *Origanum majorana*
12	**Buckler Leaf Sorrel** *Rumex scutatus*		
13	**Bay** *Laurus nobilis*		
14	**Sweet Cicely** *Myrrhis odorata*		

SALAD HERB GARDEN

Herbs in salads make the difference between boring and interesting; they add flavour, texture and colour (especially the flowers).

Included in the design is a selection of salad herbs and salad herb flowers. There are two tall herbs in the middle, chicory and red orach (blue and red), which are planted opposite each other. Also, I have positioned the only other

tall plant – borage – on the outside ring, opposite the chicory so that the blue flowers together will make a vivid splash. To make access easy, there is an inner ring of stepping stones.

The herbs chosen are my choice and can easily be changed if you want to include a particular favourite. Remember to look at the heights; for instance, do not plant

angelica in the outside circle because it will hide anything in the inner circle. Equally, in the inner circle make sure you do not plant a low-growing plant next to a tall, spreading herb because you will never find it.

This whole design can be incorporated in a small garden or on the edge of a vegetable garden to give colour throughout the growing season. As the

majority of these herbs are annuals or die back into the ground, the autumn is an ideal time to give the garden a good feed by adding well-rotted manure. This will encourage lots of leaves from the perennial herbs in the following season, and give a good kick start to the annuals when they are planted out in the following spring.

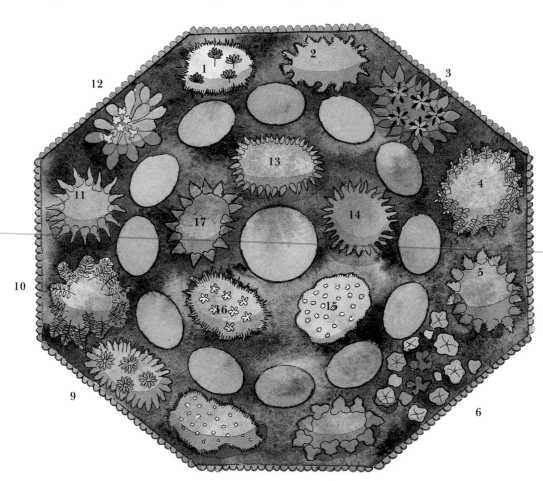

1	**Chives** *Allium schoenoprasum*	10	**French Tarragon** *Artemisia dracunculus*
2	**Caraway** *Carum carvi*	11	**Salad Rocket** *Eruca vesicaria* subsp. *sativa*
3	**Borage** *Borago officinalis*	12	**Cowslips** *Primula veris*
4	**Salad Burnet** *Sanguisorba minor*	13	**Spearmint** *Mentha spicata*
5	**French Parsley** *Petroselinum crispum* French	14	**Chicory** *Cichorium intybus*
6	**Nasturtium** *Tropaeolum majus*	15	**Lemon Thyme** *Thymus* x *citriodorus*
7	**Buckler Leaf Sorrel** *Rumex scutatus*	16	**Garlic Chives** *Allium tuberosum*
8	**Hyssop** *Hyssopus officinalis*	17	**Red Orach** *Atriplex hortensis* var. *rubra*
9	**Pot Marigold** *Calendula officinalis*		

MEDICINAL HERB GARDEN

I would like this garden, not just for its medicinal use, but for the tranquillity it would bring. The choice of herbs is not only for internal use but for the whole being. I can imagine sitting on the seat watching the dragonflies playing over the pond.

Some of the herbs included are certainly not for self-administration, for instance blue flag iris, but this is a beautiful plant and would look most attractive with the meadowsweet and the valerian. Chamomile, peppermint, dill and lemon balm are easy to self-administer with care as they all make beneficial teas. One should not take large doses just because they are natural, as some are very powerful. I strongly advise anyone interested in planting this garden to get a good herbal medicine book, see a fully trained herbalist, and always consult your doctor about a particular remedy.

1 **Blue Flag Iris** *Iris versicolor*
2 **Meadowsweet** *Filipendula ulmaria*
3 **Valerian** *Valeriana officinalis*
4 **Horseradish** *Armoracia rusticana*
5 **Sage** *Salvia officinalis*
6 **Lady's Mantle** *Alchemilla mollis*
7 **Rosemary** *Rosmarinus officinalis*
8 **Dill** *Anethum graveolens*
9 **Roman Chamomile** *Chamaemelum nobile*
10 **White Horehound** *Marrubium vulgare*
11 **Comfrey** *Symphytum officinale*

12 **Feverfew** *Tanacetum parthenium*
13 **Heartsease** *Viola tricolor*
14 **Lemon Balm** *Melissa officinalis*
15 **Garlic** *Allium sativum*
16 **Peppermint** *Mentha* x *piperita*
17 **Fennel** *Foeniculum vulgare*
18 **Pot Marigold** *Calendula officinalis*
19 **Seal Lavender** *Lavandula* x *intermedia* 'Seal'
20 **Garden Thyme** *Thymus vulgaris*
21 **Houseleek** *Sempervivum tectorum*

PLANNING YOUR FRUIT GARDEN

Planning your fruit garden means deciding your priorities – what do you want most? A little thought beforehand can save you a lot of wasted effort and ensure you actually get what you are after. With vegetables and bedding plants we have the luxury of burying our mistakes annually; with our trees and bushes we need to be more certain.

Although most of us get our garden fortuitously with our house, we usually have quite a wide choice of what we actually do with it, though the tendency is rarely to make radical changes. However if we spend as much time and effort planning and remaking the garden as we do on decorating and furnishing the rest of our home it will turn out a mighty fine place!

Obviously the soil, climate, large trees, buildings and the rest of the hard landscape have to be worked around. But with skill and cunning, and modern materials, we can have almost any fruit we desire. Which fruits we actually choose to grow must depend on our budget as much as our climate. Obviously growing fruit in the open garden is easiest and cheapest but a heated greenhouse allows for growing many more.

I think the first criterion for choosing fruit must be taste. After all, if you are growing for yourself, there is no point having poorly flavoured varieties or ones that are widely available commercially. Go for those

Apples grown as single-tier espaliers

with flavour and sweetness even if they are poor croppers. If you find you especially like a particular kind, you can always grow more.

Freshness is invaluable and one's own fruits are the most truly fresh. It makes sense to choose fruits and varieties that are best eaten straight off the plant and thus rarely found in shops. Likewise dessert are preferable to cooking varieties as we eat them with all their vitamins and flavour while culinary fruits lose some in the cooking.

Of course growing your fruit yourself guarantees freedom from unwanted chemical residues, and applying plentiful compost will ensure a good internal nutritional balance in the fruit. However, when choosing fruits, bear in mind that their dietary value

can vary as much with variety as with type or growing conditions. For example, **'Golden Delicious'** apples contain a third or less vitamin C than **'Ribston Pippin'** while **'Laxton's Superb'** has only one sixth!

Economy must always be considered. Fruit growing requires higher investment initially than vegetables but

running costs are lower. Similarly, soft fruit plants are cheaper than tree fruits individually, but require netting from birds in many areas. For maximum production, tree fruits produce as much weight from fewer plants per acre and usually require less maintenance, but are slower to crop, and live longer.

Dwarf peaches in a courtyard garden

Likewise vine fruits and cordons require more posts, ties and wires than trees or bushes. Any form of greenhouse or cover is costly, requiring upkeep, and of course heating uses much expensive energy.

The seasonal implications, and the time taken to maintain different fruits need to be considered, although in general fruit requires much less labour per yield than vegetable production. Initially the preparation and planting are heavy demands on time and energy but afterwards the workload is light, for the amateur if not for the professional. Fruit trees and bushes generally need mulching, thinning, picking and pruning, which are all light tasks and can be done upright in pleasant conditions. Growing the fruit is only half the battle though. After picking we need to process and store the fruit and this takes more time than the growing! Don't plan to grow fruits that mature just when you go away on your annual holiday!

Apples trained over interlocking arches leading to an apple tunnel

ORNAMENTAL FRUIT GARDENS

Trained fruit trees and bushes which can be bought ready-made in a host of interesting and architectural forms, such as espaliers and fans, create interest out of season as the framework of the plants becomes revealed. Attention to the appearance of the supports is essential as they are also disclosed for much of the time. Neatness and uniformity are thus of the greatest moment. Pergolas can look as beautiful clothed in grapevines as they do with any climber and even a fruit cage can be fashioned ornamentally from the right materials.

It is important in a fruit garden to allow for plentiful light and air, more than perhaps might be granted with a shrub garden. Wide paths aid such design and can be of grass sward where wear is light. Gravel is next choice for practicality and economy, and concrete or stone flags where the area is small or budget large.

More colour and interest, with benefit to the main planting, is obtained by having suitable companion plants to provide shelter, ground cover, flowers for nectar and pollen for the beneficial insects, and sacrificial plants that give up their fruits that others may not be eaten. However, vegetables are not easily mixed in. They do not grow well surrounded by vigorous competitors such as fruiting plants, but most of the culinary herbs can be grown to advantage and use.

Wildlife Fruit Gardens
Although these may be as stylized and neat as any purely decorative garden an accurate description of many so called wild gardens is 'unkempt'. Indeed the term is often used to justify total neglect.

However if the aim is truly to provide more and better habitats for endangered native flora and fauna then neglect is not enough. A wild garden needs to be managed so that we maximize the number and forms of life supported. The more fruiting and berrying plants we include the more wildlife we attract and we need to ensure other basic necessities for wild creatures.

The fruit helps immensely but shelter for nesting and hibernation, water and peace are also required. Dense brambles, shrubs and evergreens are mandatory, but do ensure the gardener can still gain access. Paths should be maintained to permit various tasks, but of course excess traffic will soon drive away most creatures.

Many garden soils are too rich for the more appealing wild flowers. To establish these it is frequently necessary to start them in pots and plant them out into sites prepared by removing the turf. Thus they should be kept away from the fruiting plants which require richer conditions.

Flowering espalier pear on the garden wall of a country house

ORCHARDS

Orchards are devoted to the production of top or tree fruits, most frequently, privately and commercially, for apples, pears and plums. Other fruits are less common, only being widely grown in suitable areas – for example cherries are little grown in wetter maritime regions but are common in drier zones such as Kent, in south-east England.

Orchards were always grassed down for convenience and soil preservation, though recent practice has been for bare cultivation, but this has been shown to be irresponsible. Initially weed-free conditions must be maintained in the orchard, but in general the preservation of bare soil is counterproductive. Most home orchard fruits will be best with a heavy mulch, ground cover or companion plants, or a grass sward.

For comfort and least cost, private orchards are still customarily planted with standard or half-standard trees on strong rootstocks. Though more intensive plantings with more dwarfing stock are more productive, they also require much more pruning and training and are difficult to mow underneath!

Grass clippings are an excellent mulch if put on in thin layers, and are a good fertilizer if returned to the sward. However orchards, and indeed most other swards, should not be composed solely of grasses, as these compete strongly for resources in the topmost layers and do not contribute much to the mineral levels. Include clovers, alfalfa and chicory seeds in your sowing mixture. Special blends are now available ready mixed.

Traditionally orchards

Mistletoe growing on an old apple tree in a cider orchard

were combined with grazing livestock. Though no longer done on a commercial scale, the practice is still useful for amateurs. Running chickens underneath adds interest and fertility, and almost guarantees freedom from most pest problems. Cynics might add, 'especially if you do not overfeed them!' Ducks control slugs and snails better than hens and do not scratch and damage so much, and the drakes do not crow so they are preferable from that point of view. Geese are superb lawnmowers, converting grass into fertilizer and eggs as well as being the most noisy watchdogs. Be warned though, as geese may damage young plants with

thin bark if they are hungry.

Other forms of livestock are more dangerous to the home orchard. I suggest that no four-legged herbivorous animals are allowed anywhere near valued plants unless each is individually and securely fenced and protected.

Orchards are also an enticement to two-legged rats and it has long been established best practice to surround them with a thick, impenetrable hedge of thorny plants such as quickthorn or blackthorn. This, and a narrow verge of long grass and native plants, simultaneously provides a good background ecology to help control all the other pests of the orchard. A

fence or wall does not contribute in the same way, and is usually more expensive and surmountable.

Groves of almonds, olives, oranges and lemons

SITE, SOIL, PREPARATION AND PLANTING

Commercial strawberry growing on polythene

Most old gardening books started off with instructions to make a garden on a well-drained, south-facing slope of rich loamy soil. If only we had such a choice! We must often take what comes. And as we get small gardens with modern houses we rarely have much choice of positioning within them.

SITE

Shelter is the most important aid we can give our plants – good hedges, fences, windbreaks, warm walls, cloches, plastic sheets and even old curtains on frosty nights. But be careful

not to overdo it and make the area stagnant. Drainage is occasionally necessary to prevent waterlogging, as few plants survive for long with drowning roots. But for most gardens, water is more often a problem in its absence. Growing on raised mounds is preferable to draining away the water in areas with dry summers.

SOIL

For most crops, a neutral to slightly acid soil with moderate fertility and organic matter content is ideal. There are basically four types of soil.

Chalk or Limestone Soil
This soil tends to be light and very well drained. But its inability to hold moisture can cause problems in a hot summer. It is alkaline in character and it is sometimes difficult to lower its pH level, so some plants become stunted and leaves go yellowish in colour, because the minerals, especially iron, become locked away. If you find the plants are not thriving, try a raised bed where you can introduce the soil you require.

Clay Soil
This soil is made up of tiny particles that stick together when wet, making the soil heavy. When dry, they set rock hard. Because it retains water and restricts air flow around roots, it is often known as 'a cold soil'. It may have a natural reserve of plant food, but even so it is better to work compost, sharp sand and horticultural grit into the top layer as this will help get the plant established and improve drainage. If you continue to do this every year, it will gradually become easier to cultivate.

Loam Soil
This soil is a mixture of clay and sand. It contains a good quantity of humus and is rich in nutrients. There are various types of loam: heavy, which contains more clay than loam and becomes wet in winter and spring; light loam, which has more sand

Sinking tree stake to support fruit tree

Young pear and apple trees protected by a hedge

than clay; and medium loam, which is an equal balance of clay and sand.

Sandy Soil
This is a very well drained soil, so much so that plant foods are quickly washed away. A plus point is that it warms up quickly in the spring so is ideal for early crops. For hungry plants you will need to build the soil up with compost to help retain moisture and stop the leaching of nutrients. Plants such as the Mediterranean herbs will thrive on this soil.

Soil Acidity and Alkalinity
The natural acidity of the soil must be taken into account. Find out whether your soil is acid or alkaline using a reliable soil-testing kit, available from any good garden centre. Soil acidity and alkalinity is measured on a pH scale ranging from 0 to 14; 0 is the most acid and 14 the most alkaline. Acid soils (0–6.5pH), on a

sliding scale from acidic to nearly neutral, include sphagnum moss peat, sandy soil, coarse loam soil, sedge peat and heavy clay. Alkaline soils (7.7–14 pH) tend to contain chalk or lime and are of a fine loam.

A reading that approaches either end of the pH scale indicates that the soil will tend to lock up the nutrients necessary for good growth. If it is very acid, you will need to add lime in the late autumn to raise the pH. Fork the top 10cm (4in) of the soil and dress with lime. Clay soils need a good dressing, but be careful not to over-lime sandy soils. It should not be necessary to do this more than once every 3 years unless your soil is very acid. Never add lime at the same time as manure, garden compost or fertilizer, as a chemical reaction can occur that will ruin the effects of both. As a general rule, either add lime 1 month before, or 3 months

after manuring, and 1 month after adding fertilizers. If the soil is alkaline, dress it every autumn with well-rotted manure to a depth of 5–10cm (2–4in), and dig over in the spring.

Soil pH also influences the number and type of benficial soil-borne organisms and the incidence of pests and diseases; worms dislike a low pH, but leatherjackets and wireworms are usually

more common in acid conditions, as is the fungal disease clubroot.

Some plants and plant families have quite specific pH requirements; others are more tolerant. On the whole, we have unwittingly selected plants that grow happily in the average, mildly acid to slightly alkaline soils most of us have. Herbs generally do best in a soil between 6.5 and 7.5pH (fairly neutral).

Fruit cage mulched with leaf mould

A few fruits such as blueberries need acid conditions. They resent lime in the soil and need to be cultivated in pots of ericaceous compost and watered with rain, not ground water. Brassicas benefit from a slightly alkaline soil to reduce the risk of clubroot.

PREPARATION

The more you plan in advance and the more carefully you prepare the site, the better the results and the more pitfalls avoided. Always work out schemes on paper. Draw a map of existing features and plan how you will fit in the new. For vegetables, plan your rotation (see p.582). For fruits and perennial herbs, imagine walking round after five years when all the plants have grown up.

A good soil structure can be easily damaged by cultivating when it is excessively wet or dry and by using heavy machinery – even walking on wet soil causes compaction and smearing. To reduce the impact, lay a plank on the soil to disperse the weight. Once the soil is under cultivation, aim to stick to the path rather than tread on the soil.

Eliminating Weeds

If you do this at the start, you will not have the hassle of trying to remove couch grass, bindweed or ground elder. Weeds do not emerge until the spring, and continue well into the season. If you wish to get rid of them successfully, it is best to cover the plot with black plastic the previous autumn. Dig a shallow trench around the area and bury the sides of the plastic in it to keep it secure. Starved of light, the weeds will eventually give up. This will take until the following spring, so if you do not like the sight of the black plastic, position a few paving stones (taking care not to make any holes because the weeds will find them and come

Potatoes are good ground-breaking crops

Double digging and filling a trench with green manure

through), cover the plastic with bark, and place terracotta pots planted up on top of the stones.

If you do not have the patience, use a weedkiller instead. There are NO organic weedkillers but you can use ammonium sulphamate, which is sold as white crystals in hardware shops. Read the instructions carefully, dissolve it in water and spray the weeds. It is effective against most perennial plants, so do not get it on any you wish to keep. You will notice the difference in about 1–2 weeks, but it is not safe to plant for 2–3 months. However, it is safer than modern weedkillers, both for the environment and for us, because as the plants die down the ammonium sulphamate breaks down to ammonium sulphate, which is a fertilizer used by gardeners. So, despite the fact that this is not totally organic it is beneficial in the end. But even this process does take time. There is no short cut to eradicating weeds.

Soil Cultivation
The soil structure essential for successful growth is created by incorporating different materials into the soil: well-rotted compost improves moisture and nutrient retention, creates an open structure and aerates the soil; sharp sand helps drainage; and 'green manures' improve the structure.

Digging is the most important method of cultivation prior to planting. In the vegetable garden it is an annual event. On heavier soils in cooler climates autumn digging is beneficial as the winter frosts that follow help to break down these wet, sticky soils into a workable tilth. Sandy soils can be lightly forked over and it is advisable to cover them with compost or green manure to reduce the loss of nutrients during the winter rains, or to leave the digging until spring. No matter what type of soil you have, it is beneficial to lay a good layer of well-rotted manure or garden compost over the surface in winter and dig it in the following spring.

Single digging consists of cultivating the soil to about 30cm (12in), a good spade's depth and the average rooting zone of many plants. Double digging is used on poorly drained and previously uncultivated land. It encourages deep rooting and promotes rapid drainage. 'Double' refers to the depth of cultivation, some 45–60cm (18–24in) deep or approximately two spades' depths. When double digging it is important to ensure that the topsoil and subsoil are not mixed.

There should be no need to add extra fertilizers to the soil if it has been well-prepared. Too much fertilizer causes lank, soft, disease-prone growth.

If necessary, in the vegetable garden you can gradually improve the soil by planting a ground-breaking crop such as potatoes or Jerusalem artichokes. Potatoes are so good for this because they need a number of cultivations to 'earth up' and cover the tubers, so preventing weeds from becoming established. Potatoes also produce large, leafy tops, blocking the light that is so essential for the germination of many weeds.

PLANTING
If this is a new garden, and you are planting fruit trees and bushes, herbs or perennial vegetables, it is worth laying the plants out on top of the prepared ground first, walking round and getting an overall view. Make any changes to the design now, rather than later. For details on buying plants, see page 593.

For trained, tall and lax subjects, the stakes or supports must be in place beforehand, and for trees and bushes they must be strong enough to do the job and must last for a reasonable number of years. It is false economy to be mean on these, as it will be hard to correct when the plants are grown.

Remember that once the planting is done, the future is determined. So do a good job and do not skimp on the digging or preparation of the ground. Dig a planting hole: bigger is always better! Mix in garden compost with the soil. Do not bury plants too deeply. Almost all wish to be planted at the same depth as they have grown. For grafted fruit trees, do not bury the rootstock. Keep their roots in their respective and different layers. Do not force them doubled up into a cramped hole and never pack them all down in a flat layer unless they grew like that. Gently pack soil around roots, filling and firming as you go. It is better to over-firm! Then attach the support if needed.

AFTERCARE
For fruit trees and bushes, herbs and perennial vegetables, use a mulch to retain moisture and suppress weeds. Try a thick layer of organic matter or a plastic sheet or carpet mulch.

In the fruit garden, whatever the final intention, do not allow a weed or grass within a circle as wide as the tree or bush is high for three years.

Good watering in dry spells is absolutely crucial! For long-term plants, water regularly for three years.

Raking in lime

CROP ROTATION

Rotation is a system whereby groups of vegetables are grown on a different section of the plot each year, so maintaining the balance of soil nutrients for successive crops. Growing crops in this way avoids the build up of pests and diseases, assists in weed control and prevents the soil deteriorating.

For crop rotation to be effective, a large area of ground is required, particularly when controlling soil-borne pests and diseases. White rot (which attacks the onion family), clubroot (which damages members of the cabbage family) and potato cyst eelworm remain dormant in the soil for many years and can survive on any weeds that are relatives. This makes good husbandry just as vital as crop rotation.

Planning

Before planting, first list the vegetables you want to grow and group them together according to their botanical relationship. Allocate each group to a plot, then compile a monthly cropping timetable for each space. The four rotational groups are as follows:

Legumes
Broad bean
French bean
Pea
Runner bean

Onion family
Bulb onion
Garlic
Leek
Salad onion
Shallot

Carrot and tomato families
Carrot
Celery
Pepper
Parsnip
Potato
Tomato

Brassicas
Cabbage
Cauliflower
Radish
Swede
Turnip

Next, allocate each rotation group to a plot of land ('plot A' etc), and draw up a month-by-month timetable for each space. The example below fully utilizes the land and provides continuity of cropping. As space becomes available, plant the crops due to follow immediately: for example, Brussels sprouts and leeks cleared in early spring should be followed by peas, salad onions and lettuce. Crops may come from different groups, which means that rotation from one plot to another is a gradual process, rather than a wholesale changeover on a set date.

	Year 1	**Year 2**	**Year 3**	**Year 4**
Plot A	*Legumes*	*Onion family*	*Carrot and tomato families*	*Brassicas*
	Broad bean	Bulb onion	Carrot	Cabbage
	French bean	Garlic	Celery	Cauliflower
	Pea	Leek	Pepper	Radish
	Runner bean	Salad onion	Parsnip	Swede
		Shallot	Potato	Turnip
			Tomato	
Plot B	*Onion family*	*Carrot and tomato families*	*Brassicas*	*Legumes*
	Bulb onion	Carrot	Cabbage	Broad bean
	Garlic	Celery	Cauliflower	French bean
	Leek	Pepper	Radish	Pea
	Salad onion	Parsnip	Swede	Runner bean
	Shallot	Potato	Turnip	
		Tomato		
Plot C	*Carrot and tomato families*	*Brassicas*	*Legumes*	*Onion family*
	Carrot	Cabbage	Broad bean	Bulb onion
	Celery	Cauliflower	French bean	Garlic
	Pepper	Radish	Pea	Leek
	Parsnip	Swede	Runner bean	Salad onion
	Potato	Turnip		Shallot
	Tomato			
Plot D	*Brassicas*	*Legumes*	*Onion family*	**Year 4** *Carrot and tomato families*
	Cabbage	Broad bean	Bulb onion	Carrot
	Cauliflower	French bean	Garlic	Celery
	Radish	Pea	Leek	Pepper
	Swede	Runner bean	Salad onion	Parsnip
	Turnip		Shallot	Potato
				Tomato

GROWING SYSTEMS

Vegetable gardens can be laid out in a huge variety of ways and the individual crops grown using different techniques. Select methods that suit your needs and the space available in your garden. Major paths between beds should always be wide enough for a wheelbarrow; access paths can be narrower.

spacing of plants in and between the rows. Plants may be set in staggered rows, creating a diagonal pattern. Pathways between the beds are slightly wider than those on the row system, but closer plant spacing means that more plants are grown per square metre and their growth and

Bed system, with paths separating each

Row of good-looking ball-headed cabbages

Rows
Traditionally, vegetables are grown in long straight rows, with plants close together within the rows, and paths to allow access. This has some drawbacks. Competition between plants for space in a row means that much of the plants' extension growth is into the pathways, causing leafy vegetables like cabbages, cauliflowers and lettuces to produce oval 'hearts' rather than round ones.

Beds
These are effectively multi-row systems, with equidistant

shape is more uniform. Close spacing ensures that weed growth is suppressed in its later stages and the soil structure remains intact, because there is less soil compaction when pathways are further apart.

Raised beds should be about 90cm (30in) wide so that it is easy to reach into the centre without overbalancing. After initial double-digging, and the addition of organic matter, they will not be trodden on, allowing a good soil structure to form. Layers of well-rotted compost added annually will

be further incorporated by worm activity. Worms are recommended for intensive vegetable production and are particularly advantageous in wetter climates.

Random Planting
Vegetables can be grown as 'edible bedding plants' scattered among flowering

plants and borders in the ornamental garden. Swiss chard, cabbage 'Ruby Ball', beetroot 'Bull's Blood', fennel and Brussels sprout 'Rubine' are particularly pleasing. See also page 565.

The Potager
This is the French tradition of planting vegetables in

Potagers can look extremely pleasing

formal beds; a practical and visually pleasing display. See also p. 565.

Long-term crops

Perennial vegetables such as asparagus are difficult to incorporate into a crop rotation programme. For this reason, they are often grown on a separate, more permanent site for several years before being replaced.

Sowing for Continuity

The greatest challenge is to have vegetables ready for harvest throughout the year.

sowing. Careful selection of cultivars also helps to achieve continuity; growing both rapidly maturing and slow-growing types extends the cropping period. The season for many root vegetables such as parsnips can be lengthened by growing a portion of the crop for eating fresh, and the remainder for storage. These can slowly be eaten over the winter period.

Successional Sowings

It is usually quick-maturing crops that are prone to gluts and gaps, often 'bolting'

seed when the first 'true' leaves of the previous sowing begin to emerge.

Intercropping

Spaces between slow-growing crops can be used as a seedbed for vegetables such as brassicas that will later need to be transplanted into permanent positions at wider spacings. This is only successful where the competition for moisture, nutrients, light and space is not too great. This can be partially solved by growing them between rows of deep-rooted crops, so that the roots are in different levels of the soil. To achieve this it may also be necessary to space crops a little further apart than the usual spacings. Radishes sown on the same day as parsnips will have germinated, grown and been harvested before the parsnips have fully developed, achieving the maximum possible yield, covering the soil with vegetation and suppressing weed growth. This intercropping requires some flexibility in the cropping plan.

Catch Crops

These are rapidly maturing vegetables and include radishes, lettuce and salad onions, all of which can be grown before the main crop is planted. Catch cropping is

useful when growing tender crops such as tomatoes, sweetcorn and courgettes, which cannot be planted until the risk of late frost is well and truly over.

Extending the Season

The season for vegetables can be extended by growing them under cover at the beginning or end of their natural season; sowing early under cover hastens maturity while protection later in the season extends the cropping period. See also pages 588–9 and 599.

Pot-raised Plants

Raising plants in pots or modules is useful for those that are frost tender and allows plants to mature while the ground is cleared of earlier crops. This saves time and space and gives more control over the growth and development of young plants. Brassicas, lettuces, leeks and onions can be grown in this way.

'The Hungry Gap'

Few vegetables mature from late winter to early sping – a period often referred to as 'the hungry gap'. Careful planning allows this gap to be bridged; spring cauliflower, winter cabbage, celeriac, kale and leeks can all be grown for harvesting during this period.

Runner beans interplanted with a row of lettuces

Some, such as asparagus, have only a short harvesting period, while vegetables like cabbage, cauliflower and lettuce are available at almost any time, provided that there is successional

and becoming inedible. To avoid this, sow sufficient seed for your needs a little and often, so that if something goes wrong, the problem is only a small one. a good guide is to sow a patch of

Vegetables in a random system, with aster, gladioli and plum

POLLINATION AND COMPANION PLANTING

Almost all of our fruiting plants require their flowers to be pollinated. Pollination usually occurs naturally, without intervention, but for some fruits. a few vegetables, and many plants grown under glass, you can improve the rate of pollination and thus fruit set. Many fruits are self-fertile and can set by pollinating themselves, but crop better if cross-pollinated. Some, such as figs, have varieties that produce fruit parthenocarpically, without pollination, thus they are often seedless. A few fruits such as 'Conference' pears are partly parthenocarpic – if not pollinated by another variety their fruits are different and oddly shaped.

Some plants do not have male and female flowers on the same plant and so we have to grow a non-fruiting male to pollinate every half dozen or so females. Kiwis and grapevines are good examples. For convenience, varieties have been bred that carry both sexes.

Some fruit trees, many nuts, and sweetcorn are wind-pollinated, while other plants are pollinated by bees and other insects. Under cover, neither of these natural pollinators exist and we have to assist. A rabbit's tail, a cotton ball or piece of wool lightly touched on each flower should suffice. We can lure more insects to help by growing attractant companion plants and this can also add a bit of colour and life as well. Commercial tomato growers even buy cardboard nests of bumble bees to pollinate for them.

Outdoors early in the year there are few insects about and for the earliest flowerers pollination is risky. Hand-pollination is effective but tedious. It is better to ensure insect pollination by increasing the numbers. Planting companion plants as attractants helps; taking up bee-keeping makes an enormous improvement.

It is well worth getting to know the pollination requirements of fruit trees. To pollinate each other, not only do varieties have to be compatible, they also have to be flowering at the same time. All good catalogues have a choice of suitable cross-pollinators indicated. When in doubt, the wild species is often the best pollinator for most of its varieties. Alternatively, simply plant more varieties. This is especially true for a few fruits that are not good pollinators themselves. For example the apples **'Cox's Orange Pippin'** and **'Bramley's Seedling'** never crop together, but if you add a **'James Grieve'**, all three fruit.

COMPANION PLANTING

Companion planting is of immense benefit to most edible plants as it brings in and supports pollinating and predatory insects, and maintains them throughout the rest of the year. Aim at having a continuity of flowers throughout the year as it is these that provide nectar and honey for the bees, hoverflies and other beneficial insects

Limnanthes douglassii **with gooseberries**

we want to encourage. Of particular usefulness is *Limnanthes douglassii*, the poached egg plant, which is a low-growing, self-seeding, weed-suppressing, hardy annual. It is especially beneficial under gooseberries and soft fruit. *Phacelia tanacetifolia, Convolvolus tricolor*, pot marigolds and clovers are all very good for beneficial insects.

Other plants can be good companions to our plants by repelling pests. French marigolds are one of the strongest and their smell will keep whitefly out of a greenhouse. Planted about the garden, they dis-orientate pests sniffing for their quarry. Other insect repellents include the herbs tansy, pennyroyal, nasturtiums, stinging nettle, hyssop, wormwood and southernwood. Fragrant herbs such as hyssop, thyme, marjoram and parsley also help maintain garden health.

Chives flourishing under apples

Alliums are valuable companions. Their smell deters many pests, yet their flowers attract beneficial insects. They seem to help protect the plants they grow with from fungal attack. Garlic and chives are the easiest to grow and use in quantity at the base of almost all fruit trees and bushes.

Many companion plants help access nutrients and make them available for our fruiting plants. Clovers, lupins and other leguminous plants are especially good as they fix nitrogen from the air and the surplus will feed our crops. *Alfalfa/ lucerne* is exceptionally deep rooted and brings up minerals from depths other plants cannot reach. It should be included in the seed mixture for orchard and wild garden swards. Similarly a few thistles and docks can be tolerated in those areas for the same purpose. Clovers and chicory should be included whenever grass is seeded as the sward produced will be richer and lusher.

In grass at the base of trees, dense shrubs and hedges, bulbous spring-flowering plants can be fitted in with no difficulty. These areas can remain uncut till the bulbs' foliage dies down and their flowers will be rich sources of pollen and nectar for the earliest pollinators and predators. Some ivy in the hedges provides late flowers for insects in autumn before they hibernate.

Ground-cover plants provide habitats for ground beetles and many other useful creatures, but may also harbour slugs, snails and over-wintering pests. On the whole it is better to have such habitats kept as far as possible from soft fruit and seed beds – after all the beetles, frogs and hedgehogs can walk further than slugs and snails! Particular plants that help or hinder others are noted with individual crop entries.

This attractive garden of herbs enjoys the semi-shade of a peach tree

CONTAINER CULTURE

Growing in containers is an ideal technique for fruits and vegetables that might otherwise be difficult, enabling you to control the size of the plant and conditions in which it is kept. Almost all herbs can be grown in containers. The individual plant entries give details of the best size of container for each crop and where to place it to receive the ideal growing conditions. This section provides more general information and advice on container growing.

ADVANTAGES OF CONTAINERS

With attention to feeding and watering, almost any plant can be coaxed to grow in a container. Where room is limited, containers offer an alternative to ground space. They can also offer different condtions to those found in the ground. Tomatoes and cucumbers have long been grown under glass in containers to prevent any contact with disease-infected soil. If you have a chalky soil, lime-hating plants can be grown in containers of ericaceous compost and watered with rain water.

Portable containers allow you to respond to weather conditions, moving plants outdoors once spring frosts end, and putting them under shelter again at the onset of colder weather.

For large fruit plants, a container cramps the root system, preventing them growing too large or too quickly. Allied with pruning, this allows us to dwarf plants we would find too large to handle. Often this restriction is resented by the plant and, perversely, may result in earlier fruiting.

The fruits may not be prolific, but a selection of containers can give several different varieties in a space otherwise occupied by one, allowing greater variety and a longer season.

Vegetables most suited to container culture are either rapidly maturing crops such as mini beetroot, carrots, lettuces, radishes and salad onins, or dwarf varieties of bush or climbing vegetables, including aubergines, beans, cucumbers, peas, peppers and tomatoes, as these need little support. Deep-rooted vegetables like sprouts, main-crop carrots and parsnips can be grown in containers at least 45cm (18in) deep.

CHOOSING A CONTAINER

Choose the container to suit the plant. If it is a tall plant, make sure the container has a base wide enough to prevent it toppling over, even outside in a high wind. For vegetables, the chance of successful cropping is improved with large containers; they allow for a greater rooting depth, dry out slowly and provide adequate anchorage for crops that need staking.

Plastic containers (with drainage holes) are more moisture-retentive than those of wood or terracotta, but the latter are preferred by some plants such as citrus.

If using unconventional containers – old watering cans, sinks, a half beer barrel – make sure they have drainage holes, and gravel or broken pots in the bottom of the container to stop the holes clogging up.

Herbs can suit hanging baskets, but the position is crucial. They dislike high wind and full sun all day. Also, they are mostly fast growers and if too cramped or over- or under-watered they will drop their leaves.

COMPOSTS AND FERTILIZERS

Choosing the right compost is essential for healthy plants. Composts for containers are either loam-based (soil-based) or loamless.

John Innes

This is loam-based and includes chemicals. On the plus side, it stays richer in nutrients longer, making feeding less critical; it holds water well and is a stable compost for a large, long-term plant. If it does dry out, it takes up water easily. The major watch point is that it is easy to over-water.

There are usually three different grades of compost, though some manufacturers combine No.1 and No.2. No.1 is for growing rooted cuttings, No.2 for seedlings and No.3 for final potting. The numbers indicate the amount of nutrients. You must choose the correct one for the job. Loam-based composts are generally ideal for vegetables and fruits in containers, and organic matter can be added if required. This is not a good compost for hanging baskets, because it is heavy when wet.

Own Soil-based Mix

If you wish to make a soil-based compost of your own this recipe is fairly reliable.

4 parts good weed-free garden topsoil
3 parts well-rotted garden compost
3 parts moist peat
1 part horticultural sharp sand

Multipurpose Potting Compost

This is usually peat-based with added chemicals. The bags are light and the compost is clean and easy to use. On the negative side, you will need to feed regularly as nutrients are soon depleted; also the compost is light, so watch out that large plants do not fall over. The most frequent problem is that it takes up water poorly if ever it dries out.

Own Mix Bark, Peat, Grit

This is ideal for many herbs as well as some fruits and vegetables. The open mix helps prevent over-watering; the bark retains water, which protects against under-watering and keeps the compost open to help absorb water if ever it dries out completely. It is suitable for containers and hanging baskets alike. Another plus is that you know what nutrients are in it, so will be able to feed in a balanced way.

Alternative Composts

Peat-free composts are increasingly available as we become aware of the need to conserve our diminishing peat fields. They are generally made of coir, a by-product of coconuts, or composted bark. Coir is very free-draining and so some composts include a jelly that retains water, releasing it gradually. Coir compost is light, so there may be a stability problem with tall or large plants. A final minus point – the nutrients are soon depleted so you will need to feed from the start.

Composted bark has similar drawbacks if used straight, with no peat or soil: watering and nutrient loss. If the bark has not been composted for long enough, it can leach the nutrients and starve the plants. However, mixed with peat or soil, bark is a great asset.

Fertilizers

Liquid seaweed contains small amounts of nitrogen, phosphorous, potassium, and it is also rich in trace elements. It not only makes a good soil feed but, as the elements are easily taken in by the plant, it can also be sprayed on as a foliar feed.

Calcified seaweed contains calcium, sodium, magnesium and numerous trace elements. It is ideal for adding to seed compost. Use according to the manufacturer's instructions.

MAINTENANCE

Most plants need moist soil but drown if waterlogged and wilt if dry. Water stress due to drought, even for short periods, can greatly reduce the potential productivity of plants. If you cannot maintain consistent watering, install an automatic system of irrigation. It is best to water containers in the early morning or the evening, especially in summer, as this reduces the amount lost through evaporation.

Repotting into a larger container helps provide new nutrients, but this may become difficult with larger plants. The alternatives are top-dressing with an enriched mix of compost and organic fertilizer, or feeding little and often with a diluted liquid feed such as seaweed, or comfrey and nettle extract.

Maintenance Calendar

Spring Pot on perennial plants if necessary (look for roots protruding from the bottom of the container). Use a pot the next size up. Carefully remove the plant from its old pot. Give it a good tidy up, removing any weeds and dead leaves. Place gravel or other drainage material in the bottom of the container and keep the compost sweet by adding a tablespoon full of granulated charcoal. As soon as the plant starts producing new growth or flowers, start feeding regularly with liquid feed. Prune fruits as needed.
Summer Keep a careful eye on the watering; make sure the pots do not dry out fully. Move some plants out of the midday sun. Dead head any flowers on herbs. Feed with liquid feed, on average once a week. Remove any pest-damaged leaves. Prune fruits as needed.
Autumn Cut back the perennial herbs. Weed containers and at the same time remove some of the top compost and re-dress. Bring any tender plants inside before the frosts. Start reducing the watering. Prune fruits as needed.
Winter Protect all container-grown plants from frosts. If possible move into a cold greenhouse, conservatory or garage. If the weather is very severe, cover the containers in a layer of sacking. Keep watering to a minimum. Prune fruits as needed.

Back row, left to right: **Lungwort**, *Pulmonaria officinalis, Prostanthera rotundifolia*, **Variegated Box,** *Buxus sempervirens* 'Elegantissima', **Rosemary Benenden Blue**, *Rosmarinus officinalis* 'Benenden Blue', **Box**, *Buxus sempervirens*; front row, left to right: *Prostanthera rotundifolia* 'Rosea', **Golden Curly Marjoram**, *Origanum vulgare* 'Aureum Crispum', **Rue Jackman's Blue**, *Ruta graveolens* 'Jackman's Blue', **Old Warrior**, *Artemisia pontica*

PROPAGATING AND BUYING PLANTS

One of the great joys of gardening is propagating your own plants. Success is dependent on adequate preparation and the care and attention you give in the critical first few weeks. This section provides general instructions for the main propagation methods. Individual guide-lines are given under each plant entry. Where space and time are short, or for larger perennial plants such as fruit trees and bushes, it may be easier to buy your plants.

SEED

Most vegetables, annual herbs and annual fruits are usually grown from seed. There is a huge range of seed available from seed catalogues, or you can save your own. Seed is not always advisable for perennials, particularly fruits; a fruit seedling will not fruit until mature, which may be quick for some but takes many decades for most trees. Until the fruit is produced there is usually no way of telling what it will be like – and it may not be very good. Most of the best varieties will not come true from seed.

Seed can be sown outside, either directly where it is to mature or into a seedbed for transplanting. Alternatively, starting off the seeds in a greenhouse or on a window-sill gives you more control over the warmth and moisture they need, and enables you to begin propagating earlier in the season.

Types of Seed

Seeds are usually bought as packets of individual 'naked'

seeds; but vegetable seeds in particular may be available in other forms.

Pelleted seeds are individual seeds coated in a ball of clay, which moistens and disintegrates in the soil. They are easy to handle and sow at precise spacings, reducing the need for thinning. Sow at a depth of about twice their diameter and keep the soil moist but not water-logged until germination.

Seed tapes and sheets are individual seeds encased at the correct spacing in tapes or sheets of tissue paper or gel. These substances are soluble when placed in moist soil. Tapes and sheets are quick to use and are precisely spaced so there is no need for thinning.

Primed seeds are in the

first stages of germination and are used for those that are hard to germinate or need high germination temperatures, such as cucumbers. They arrive by post in plastic packets to prevent moisture loss and are pricked out into pots or trays on arrival.

Preparation of Seed

Most seeds need air, light, particular temperatures and moisture to germinate. Some have a long dormancy, and some have hard outer coats and need a little help to get going. Here are two techniques. See individual plant entries for when to use these techniques.

Scarification
If left to nature, seeds that

have a hard outer coat would take a long time to germinate. To speed up the process, rub the seed between two sheets of fine sandpaper. This weakens the coat of the seed so that moisture needed for germination can penetrate.

Stratification (vernalization)
Some seeds need a period of cold (from 1 to 6 months) to germinate. Mix the seed with damp sand and place in a plastic bag in the refrigerator or freezer. After 4 weeks sow on the surface of the compost and cover with perlite.

Sowing Outside

In an average season the seed should be sown in mid-to late spring after the soil has been prepared and warmed. It is simplest to sow direct where the plants are to mature, and this is best for plants that resent root disturbance, such as many root vegetables. Alternatively you can use a seedbed if you need the space seedlings are to occupy for something else, and to save space as small plants are not at their final spacing until they mature.

Before starting, check your soil type (see pp. 578–9), making sure that the soil has sufficient food to maintain a seed bed. Dig the bed over, mark out a straight line with a piece of string secured tightly over each row, draw a shallow drill, 6–13mm ($\frac{1}{4}$–$\frac{1}{2}$in) deep (this will vary according to seed size), using the side of a fork or hoe, and sow the seeds thinly. For larger seeds, sow individually. If your soil is sticky clay, give the seeds a better start by adding a fine layer of horticultural sand along the drill. Do not

Misting unit

overcrowd the bed, otherwise the seedlings will grow leggy and weak and be prone to disease. For more precise details of seed spacing see individual plant entries.

Protected Sowing

Sowing under cover is expensive and often labour-intensive, yet it allows seeds to be sown whatever the weather. It is most often used in cooler climates for tender crops that cannot be planted out until there is no longer any danger or frost.

Start with a thoroughly cleaned container. Old compost also provides ideal conditions for damping off fungi and sciarid flies, so remove any spent compost from the greenhouse or potting shed.

Compost

It is best to use a sterile seed compost. Ordinary garden soil contains many weed seeds that could easily be confused with the germinating seed. The best compost for most seed sowing is 50 per cent propagating bark: 50 per cent peat-based seed compost. However, for plants that prefer a freer draining compost, or for those that need stratification outside, a 25 per cent peat-based seed compost: 50 per cent propagating bark: 25 per cent horticultural grit mix is ideal. And if you are sowing seeds that have a long germination period, use a soil-based seed compost.

Sowing in Seed Trays

Fill a clean seed tray with compost to 1cm (1/2in) below the rim and firm with a flat piece of wood. Do not press too hard as this will over-compress the compost and restrict drainage, encouraging damping off disease and attack by sciarid fly.

The gap below the rim is essential, as it prevents the surface-sown seeds and compost being washed over the edge when watering.

Water the prepared tray

using a fine rose on the watering can so as not to disturb the seed. Do not over-water. The compost should be damp, not soaking. After an initial watering, water as little as possible, but never let the surface dry out. Once the seed is sown, lack of moisture can prevent germination and kill the seedlings, but too much excludes oxygen and encourages damping-off fungi and root rot.

Sowing Methods

There are three main methods, the choice dependent on the size of the seed. They are, in order of seed size, fine to large:

1 Scatter on the surface of the compost, and cover with a fine layer of perlite.
2 Press into the surface of the compost, either with your hand or a flat piece of wood the size of the tray, and cover with perlite.
3 Press down to one seed's depth, cover with compost.

The Cardboard Trick

When seeds are too small to handle, you can control distribution by using a thin piece of card cut to 10cm x 5cm (4in x 2in), and folded down the middle. Place a small amount of seed into the folded card and gently tap it over the prepared seed tray. This technique is especially useful when sowing into plug trays (see below).

Sowing in Plug (Module) Trays (Multi-cell Trays)

These plug trays are a great invention. The seed can germinate in its own space, get established into a strong seedling, and make a good root ball. When potting on, the young plant remains undisturbed and will continue growing. This is very good for plants like coriander, which hate being transplanted and tend to bolt if you move them. Another advantage is that the problem of overcrowding is cut to a minimum, and

damping-off disease and sciarid fly are easier to control. Also, because seedlings in plugs are easier to maintain, planting out or potting on is not so critical.

Plug trays come in various sizes; for example, you can get trays with very small holes of 15mm (1/2in) x 15mm up to trays with holes of 36.5mm (1 1/4in) x 36.5mm. To enable a reasonable time lapse between germination and potting on, the larger are recommended.

Prepare the compost and fill the tray right to the top, scraping off surplus compost with a piece of wood level with the top of the holes. It is better not to firm the compost down. Watering in (see above) settles the compost enough to allow space for the seed and the top-dressing of perlite.

The principles of sowing in plug trays are the same as for trays. Having sown your seed, label the trays clearly with the name of the plant, and the date.

Sowing in Pots

Multi-sowing in pots speeds the growth of root and bulb vegetables. Sow up to six seeds (two for beetroot) into a 7.5–10cm (3–4in) pot, leave the seedlings to develop and then transplant the potful of plants, allowing extra space within the rows. Thinning is not needed. This technique works well for beetroot, cauliflower, turnips, kohlrabi, leeks and onions.

Fluid Sowing

This is useful when weather and soil conditions make germination erratic. Seeds germinated under ideal conditions are sown, protected by a carrier gel. To germinate the seeds, place some moistened kitchen towel in the base of a plastic container. Scatter the seeds evenly on the surface, cover with a lid or cling film and keep at 21°C (70°F). When the rootlets are about 5mm (1/4in) long they are ready to

sow. Wash them into a fine mesh strainer. Mix carrier gel from half-strength fungicide-free wallpaper paste, scatter the seeds in the paste, and mix. Pour into a clear bag, cut off a corner and force the mixture through the hole. Cover the seeds with soil or vermiculite.

Seed Germination

Seeds need warmth and moisture to germinate. In a cold greenhouse, a heated propagator may be needed in early spring for seeds that germinate at warm to hot temperatures. In the house you can use a shelf near a radiator (never on the radiator), or an airing cupboard. Darkness does not hinder the germination of most seeds, but if you put your containers in an airing cupboard check them daily. As soon as there is any sign of life, place the trays in a warm light place, not in direct sunlight.

Hardening Off

When large enough to handle, prick out seed tray seedlings and pot up individually. Allow them to root fully. Test plug tray seedlings by giving one or two a gentle tug. They should come away from the cells cleanly, with the root ball. If they do not, leave for another few days.

When the seedlings are ready, harden them off slowly by leaving the young plants outside during the day. Once weaned into a natural climate, plant them directly to where they will mature.

Seed Storage and Viability

Once seed is harvested from the plant, it begins to deteriorate; even ideal storage conditions can only slow down the rate of deterioration. Viability (the ability to germinate) usually declines with age. Always use fresh seed, or store in cool, dark, dry conditions (definitely not the corner of the greenhouse) in airtight containers.

CUTTINGS

Taking cuttings is the best way to propagate many fruiting plants and non-flowering herbs. This may be the only way to reproduce a particular variety or cultivar that will not come true from seed. For successful softwood cuttings it is worth buying a heated propagator, which can be placed in a greenhouse or on a shady windowsill. For successful semi-ripe, hardwood and root cuttings, a shaded cold frame can be used. For specific details, see under the individual entry.

Softwood Cuttings

Softwood cuttings are usually taken between spring and midsummer, using the new, lush, green growth. To produce successful rooting material from herbs, prune the plant vigorously in winter to encourage new growth, and take cuttings as soon as there is sufficient growth.

Prepare a pot, seed tray, or plug tray with cutting compost – 50 per cent bark, 50 per cent peat. Firm the compost to within 2cm (1in) of the rim. Collect the cuttings in small batches in the morning. Choose sturdy shoots with plenty of leaves. Best results come from non-flowering shoots with the base leaves removed. Cut the shoot with a knife, not scissors. Place the cutting at once in the shade in a polythene bag or a bucket of water; softwood cuttings are extremely susceptible to water loss.

To prepare the cutting material, cut the base of the stem 5mm ($^1/_4$in) below a leaf joint, to leave a cutting of roughly 10cm (4in) long. If the cutting material has to be under 10cm (4in), take the cutting with a heel. Remove the lower leaves and trim the tail which is left from the heel. Trim the stem cleanly before a node, the point at which a leaf stalk joins the stem. Remove the leaves from the bottom third of the cutting with a knife, leaving at least 2 or 3 leaves on top.

Make a hole in the compost and insert the cutting up to its leaves. Do not overcrowd the container or include more than one species, because quite often they take different times to root. Label and date the cuttings clearly, and only water the compost from above if necessary. Keep out of direct sunlight in hot weather. If it is very sunny, heavy shade is best for the first week.

Place in a heated or unheated propagator, or cover the pot or container with a plastic bag supported on a thin wire hoop (to prevent the plastic touching the leaves), or with an upturned plastic bottle with the bottom cut off. If you are using a plastic bag, turn it inside out every few days to stop excess moisture from condensation dripping onto the cuttings. Spray the cuttings with water every morning for the first week.

Average rooting time is 2–4 weeks. The cutting medium is low in nutrients, so give a regular foliar feed when the cutting starts to root. Harden off the cuttings gradually when they are rooted. Bring them out in stages to normal sunny, airy conditions. Pot them on using a prepared potting compost once they

compost should be freer-draining. Make the mix equal parts peat, grit and bark. Once the cuttings have been inserted in the compost, place the pot, seed tray or plug tray in a cold greenhouse, cold frame or cool conservatory, not in a propagator, unless it has a misting unit.

Fruit trees at a nursery

are weaned. Label and water well after transplanting. About 4–5 weeks after transplanting, when the plant is growing away, pinch out the top centre of the young cutting. This will encourage the plant to bush out, making it stronger as well as fuller. Allow to grow on until a good-size root ball can be seen in the pot, then plant out.

Semi-hardwood or Greenwood Cuttings

These are usually taken from shrubby herbs such as rosemary and myrtle towards the end of the growing season (from midsummer to mid-autumn). Use broadly the same method as for softwood cuttings, but the

Average rooting time for semi-hardwood cuttings is 4–6 weeks. If the autumn is exceptionally hot and the compost or cuttings seem to be drying out, spray once a week. Begin the hardening off process in the spring after the frosts. Give a foliar feed as soon as there is sufficient new growth.

Hardwood Cuttings

Taken mid- to late autumn in exactly the same way as softwood cuttings, but with a freer-draining compost of equal parts peat, grit and bark. Keep watering to the absolute minimum. Winter in a cold frame, greenhouse or conservatory. Average rooting time can take as long as 12 months. For hardwood cuttings of hardy

Young fruit plants in containers

A plastic bag to retain moisture

fruits, push cuttings into a slit trench lined with sharp sand in moist ground, firm well and keep them weed-free and protected from drying winds – a cloche is usually advantageous.

Root Cuttings

This method of cutting suits plants with creeping roots, such as bergamot, comfrey, horseradish, lemon balm, mint, soapwort and sweet woodruff. Dig up some healthy roots in spring or autumn. Fill a container with cutting compost – 50 per cent bark, 50 per cent peat, firmed to within 3cm (1in) of the rim. These cuttings lend themselves to being grown in plug trays. Water well. Cut 4–8cm (1½–3in) lengths of root that carry a growing bud. For comfrey and horseradish, simply slice the root into sections, 4–8cm (1½–3in) long, using a sharp knife to give a clean cut through the root. Make holes in the compost with a dibber. If using pots or seed trays these should be 3–6cm (1–2½in) apart. Plant the cutting vertically. Cover with a small amount of compost, and a layer of perlite level with the top of the container. Label and date. Average rooting time is 2–3 weeks. Do not water until roots or top growth appears. Then apply liquid feed. Slowly harden off the cuttings when rooted. Pot

on cuttings in seed trays and pots in a potting compost once they are hardened off. Label and water well after transplanting. About 2–3 weeks after transplanting, when you can see that the plant is growing away, pinch out the top centre of the young cutting. This will encourage the plant to bush out, making it stronger as well as fuller. Allow to grow on until a good-size root ball can be seen in the pot. Plant out in the garden when the last frosts are over.

LAYERING

Layering is a process that encourages sections of plant to root while still attached to the parent. Bay, rosemary, sage, and other evergreens suit this method. Blackberries root their tips anywhere they can in autumn, and many plants will root where they touch the ground to form natural layers, which easily detach with roots in autumn.

To layer a plant, cultivate the soil around it during winter and early spring by adding peat and grit to it. In spring trim the leaves and side shoots of a young, low vigorous stem for 10–60cm (4–24in) below its growing tip. Bring the stem down to ground level and mark its position on the soil. Dig a trench at that point. Roughen the stem at the point where it will touch the ground, and peg it down into the trench, then bend the stem at right angles behind the growing tip, so that it protrudes vertically. Return the soil to the trench to bury the stem. Firm in well and water. Keep the soil moist, especially in dry periods. Sever the layering stem from its parent plant in autumn if well rooted, and 3–4 weeks later nip out the growing tip from the rooted layer to make plant bush out. Check that the roots are established before lifting the layered stem. If necessary, leave for a further year. Replant either in open

A swollen graft point on a fruit tree

ground or in a pot. Label and leave to establish.

GRAFTING

Some fruit plants are only propagated by grafting or budding small pieces onto more easily grown rootstocks. Often this is done with special rootstocks simply to influence growth or to get the maximum number of plants from limited material. Budding and grafting techniques, although essentially simple, are profoundly difficult to master without much practice and are beyond the scope of this book.

BUYING PLANTS

Buying fruit, vegetable and herb plants has the advantage of ease and speed over growing them yourself, but is relatively costly and incurs a high risk of importing weeds, pests and diseases along with the plants, especially with pot-grown specimens.

To fill an average garden with plants does not require an immense investment but

it is still quite enough to warrant care and budgeting. For fruit, specialist mail order nurseries usually provide a greater choice, and are often cheaper than most local suppliers. Get several catalogues and compare them before ordering, and do so early.

For fruit trees and shrubs bare-rooted plants are easier to inspect than pot-grown ones for signs of health or disease. The root systems on well-grown, bare-rooted trees are usually more extensive than those of pot-grown plants. Furthermore, for larger growing trees, there is the danger of pot-grown specimens being root bound. However, for most smaller subjects, contain-erized plants from reputable suppliers are convenient and give good results.

Vegetables may be available pre-grown as seedlings, at the stage when they require pricking out; as plugs with three or four true leaves, which may need growing on; or as plants that are quite large (sold in strips or multi-

MAINTAINING THE GARDEN

Trained 'Catillac' pear tree

To ensure that plants are productive and the crops are of high quality, vegetables, herbs and fruit need careful nurturing and diligent husbandry. Vegetables require more constant attention than either herbs or fruit. However, all plants benefit from regular checking so that any problems can be spotted early. For watering, see pages 596–7; for pests and diseases, see pages 602–7.

PLANTING OUT

Plants that have been germinated or grown as cuttings in a greenhouse will need to be planted out after hardening off. The timing depends on the prevailing weather and soil conditions. All plants suffer a check in their growth rate after transplanting, caused by inevitable root disturbance and by the change in environment to somewhere cooler. Younger plants tend to recover rapidly while older ones take longer. To reduce stress, ensure there is plenty of water available, transplant on an overcast day into moist soil and provide shelter from strong sunshine until plants are established.

PLANT SUPPORTS

These should be positioned before they are required by the plants. Plants growing tall without a support can be damaged or suffer a check in growth. Select a support according to the plant being grown. Peas climb with tendrils, preferring to twine round thin supports such as chicken wire or spindly twigs, while runner beans hug poles or canes. Vegetables without climbing mechanisms need to be tied to stakes with garden twine in a loose figure-of-eight loop, positioning the stake on the windward side of the plant. Fruit trees trained against a flat surface need strong wires to which the branches can be tied.

PRUNING FRUIT TREES

We prune for two reasons: to remove diseased, damaged and ill-placed growths, and to channel growth into fruit production. We may also prune to reduce the size of a plant as it becomes too large for the space available.

Excessive pruning, especially at the wrong time, is counter-productive. In general, pruning even moderate amounts from a tree or bush in autumn and winter stimulates regrowth, proportionately as much as the amount removed. This is useful when the plant is young and we wish to form the framework by stimulating the growth of young, vigorous replacement shoots.

However such autumn and winter pruning is not so suitable for more mature fruiting plants whose structure is already formed and from which we wish to obtain fruit. Most respond much better to summer pruning, which is cutting out three-quarters of every young shoot, bar the leaders. This redirects growth and causes fruit bud production on the spurs or short side shoots formed. These may be further shortened and tidied in the winter but then, as only a little is removed, vigorous re-growth is avoided.

Although it may seem complicated, pruning is easy once you've done it a few times. Use clean secateurs, which have been sterilized with alcohol, rarely use a saw, and cover large wounds with a proprietary sealant to prevent water getting in.

Training the Basic Shape

The majority of our perennial woody fruiting plants can be trained and pruned to make a permanent framework which carries spurs, preferably all over. Growing just one such single stem, branch or cordon on a weak rootstock allows us to squeeze many varieties into the same space as one full-sized tree. Such single-stemmed cordons do not produce very much fruit, especially as they are hard to support if they reach more than head height. Sloping these cordons serves to make them longer without going too high.

Growing two, three, or more branches is a better compromise. These can be arranged as espaliers (in tiers), fans (radiating from the centre), or gridirons of almost any design. However, for the vast majority of trees and bushes, the actual shapes most commonly employed are the expanding head, and the open bowl or goblet arrangement, on top of a single stem or trunk.

This bowl shape maximizes the surface area of fruiting growth exposed to the sun and air. To achieve it the main leader is removed from the middle and the branches trained as a bowl with a hollow centre open to the sky. The number of main stems is customarily about five or six which divide from the trunk and redivide to form the walls of the goblet. The stem or trunk may be short, as is common with gooseberries, or taller, which is often more convenient.

Where the branches of a tree divide from the trunk on a short trunk they are termed bushes, at waist to shoulder height they are called half-standards, and standards where they start higher still. Bushes, especially those on the more dwarfing stocks, tend to be too low to mow underneath but can always be mulched instead.

Raspberries before pruning (top), and after (below)

A wall of Morello cherries

Half standards grow large, depending on stock, and are tall enough to mow underneath. Full standards make very big specimens and are only usually planted in parks and meadows.

Young unformed plants, maidens, can be bought more cheaply than those with a good shape or form already trained. It is very satisfying to grow your own espalier or gridiron from a maiden, but the result will depend on your skill and foresight.

Renewal Pruning

Some fruits need pruning on the renewal principle. Whole branches or shoots are removed at a year or two old after they have fruited. Summer raspberries are typical, the old shoots being removed at ground level as the young are tied in. Grape-vines can be constrained to two young branches emerging from the trunk, replaced each year. Peaches on walls also have young shoots tied in and old fruited ones removed. Blackcurrants have a third of growths from the ground removed annually.

Timing

A few plants are pruned only at certain times of year. Hollow-stemmed, tender and evergreen plants are pruned in spring once the hardest weather is over and *Prunus* are pruned in summer, as otherwise they

FERTILITY AND WATER MANAGEMENT

Plants have varying nutrient requirements according to the species. All need sufficiently fertile soil and water to grow and yield well. Fruits are ordinarily not as demanding as many vegetable crops; this is because they are mostly perennial. Growing in open ground, they make extensive root systems, which find the water and nutrients required. Annual and short-lived crops generally need much more attention to soil fertility and water provision because they have limited root systems. Plants in containers similarly require much care, and because of the confinement also readily suffer from any excess.

SOIL FERTILITY

Soil fertility is the source of essential nutrients needed for healthy growth. There is no precise definition of a fertile soil, but ideally it has the following characteristics: a good crumb structure; plenty of humus and nutrients; good drainange, moisture-retentive; a pH

that is slightly acid to neutral. Nutrients are absorbed in solution by the roots and transported through the plant's system. The major elements include nitrogen, phosphorus, potassium, calcium, magnesium and sulphur. Minor, or trace, elements include iron, manganese, boron, zinc, copper and molybdenum. These are needed in minute quantities yet are still essential.

Nutrients are present in the soil as a result of the weathering processes on the mineral particles and the chemical breakdown or decay of organic matter and humus by bacteria and other micro-organisms. These release nutrients in a form available to plants. To function effectively they must have an open, well-drained soil with adequate supplies of air and water. Extra nutrients in the form of compost and fertilizer may be needed to provide sufficient nutrients to sustain healthy growth.

Fertility is best provided

organically from materials that slowly convert to a usable form in the soil. Well-rotted farmyard manures, good compost, seaweed meal, hoof and horn meal, blood, fish and bone meal, bone meal, and fish emulsions are all eminently suitable.

If mineral shortages are suspected, then ground rock dusts provide cheap, slow-release supplies; potash, phosphate, magnesium (dolomitic) limestone, calcified seaweed and lime are all widely available, cheap and pleasant to apply. Wood ashes are extremely valuable to most fruiting plants. Seaweed extracts sprayed on the foliage can give rapid relief of mineral deficiencies.

Bulkier materials such as well-rotted manure and compost also provide much humus, which is essential for the natural fertility of the soil, its water-holding capacity and its buffering action (preventing the soil being too acid or alkali). The humus content is

conserved by minimal cultivation and refraining from soluble fertilizers.

More humus can be provided by growing green manures. These occupy the soil when other plants are dormant or if parts of the plot are empty throughout winter. Nutrients and water that would have leached away are combined with winter sunlight to grow dense covers of hardy plants. These also protect the soil surface from erosion and rain impaction. When the weather warms up, green manures are incorporated in situ by digging in or composting under a plastic sheet, or are removed and added to the compost heap.

Organic mulches such as well-rotted manures, composted shredded bark, leafmould, mushroom compost, straw or peat are all advantageous to most plants. They rot down at the soil surface aiding fertility and humus levels and suppress weeds if they are thick enough, but most

Freshly dug clay lumps will break up as weathering occurs

Freshly dug clay/loam soil

Watering cucumbers using a drip-feed system

importantly they conserve soil moisture.

Careful rotation in the vegetable plot can aid fertility. Plant 'hungry' crops such as celery, leeks and members of the cabbage family, which require plenty of nitrogen, after peas, beans and other legumes, which fix nitrogen from the atmosphere using nitrogen-fixing bacteria in swollen nodules on their roots and release nitrogen into the soil.

WATERING

Vegetables and fruits crop to their full potential only when water is plentiful. Yields are reduced when plants suffer from drought stress. The soil is a plant's reservoir and different soils are able to retain different levels of water. Clays retain water very efficiently, loams have a good balance between drainage and water retention, and sandy soils are very free-draining.

Water is lost from both soil and the leaves of plants and this loss is most rapid on hot, sunny days with drying winds. It is vital to reduce the loss of water from soil by:
• regularly incorporating well-rotted organic matter into the soil, to increase its moisture-holding capacity.
• deep cultivation to open up the soil and encourage

deeper rooting. This allows plants to draw water from a greater soil depth.
• covering the soil surface with organic or inorganic mulches such as well-rotted manure or black plastic to prevent moisture loss from the surface and upper soil layers.
• improving drainage on waterlogged soil; a high water table restricts root development, making plants prone to stress during drought. By improving the drainage system and lowering the water table, the roots are encouraged to penetrate to a greater depth, thereby leaving them more drought-tolerant.
• removing weeds, which compete with other plants for water. They should be removed at seedling stage.
• reducing plant density, particularly on dry, exposed sites, to allow each plant to draw water from a greater volume of soil.
• providing shelter, especially on exposed sites. Reducing wind speed reduces moisture loss from the soil and plants.
• being careful with accurate timing and frequency of application. Most plants have critical periods when adequate water supplies are very important for successful development and cropping.

Critical Watering Periods

Water before it is too late; if a plant is wilting it is already suffering badly!

Seeds and Seedlings
Water is essential for seed germination and rapid seedling development. Seedbeds should be moist, not waterlogged. Water seedlings using a fine rose on a watering can to provide a shower of tiny droplets and prevent plant damage.

Transplants
Plants often suffer from transplanting shock due to root damage after being moved, and the effects are more pronounced if the soil is dry. Water plants gently after moving them to settle moist soil around the roots. Water woody plants until they have been established for up to three years, particularly evergreens, which cannot drop their leaves when under stress and so survive dormant.

Fruiting Crops
Fruits and vegetables, such as peas, beans and tomatoes, with edible fruits have two critical periods for water availability once they have established: when flowering (to aid pollination and fruit set) and when the fruit begins to swell.

Leaf and Root Crops
These need a constant water supply throughout their cropping life.

Methods of Watering

It is vital to maintain rapid growth in the growing season, particularly in annual plants, otherwise plant tissues can harden and growth can be affected. Growth check in cauliflowers can cause young plants prematurely to form a small, poorly developed curd, while other annuals will 'bolt'.

Always water thoroughly, soaking the soil to a reasonable depth. It is bad practice merely to wet the

soil surface. This draws the roots up to form a surface mat while much is wasted by evaporation. A good soaking descends and draws the roots after it, thus they become deeper and more able to find other soil moisture on their own.

If you bury a length of hosepipe with the roots of a tree you can inject the water right where it is needed during the critical first few years. Likewise a pot or funnel pushed in nearby is a useful aid.

When time is limited and cash more abundant it is wise to invest in automatic watering equipment. Drip feeds and seeping hoses allow a constant and even supply of water close to the roots without the gardener's constant attention, and soon repay the investment. Overhead sprinklers are extremely inefficient as only about 20% of the water ever reaches the plant.

Mulching

Once the winter rains have drenched the soil a mulch prevents it evaporating away again. Any mulch helps, but the looser and thicker the better. Less than 5cm (2in) is ineffective, and initial applications always pack down, so be prepared to add more after a few months.

When organic material for mulching is in short supply, inorganic ones may be used. Sharp sand and gravel make excellent moisture-retaining mulches and are cheap and sterile.

Grass clippings are an excellent mulch, if applied in thin layers – though if applied too thickly in wet conditions they may make a nasty claggy mess. Clippings provide a rich source of nitrogen and encourage soil life. They soon disappear and need topping up. Continuous applications slowly make the soil less alkaline and more acid, which is often advantageous.

GROWING
IN GLASSHOUSES

There is no substitute for walk-in cover, which is more valuable if heated and frost-free, and even more so if kept warm or even hot. If maintained as warm as a living room all year round, many exotic fruits and vegetables become possible from oranges to aubergines. It is not only summer crops that benefit. Lettuce, spinach and other hardy winter salads produce more tender, better-quality crops in an unheated greenhouse than outside.

Exotics such as passion fruits are best grown under cover as they would not crop otherwise. The extra heat ripens the fruit and also the wood, which often cannot ripen outdoors. Some plants take many months to crop each year and without cover they would never ripen before frosts come. Extra warmth and shelter allows us to have tender or delicate plants that would not survive in the open, but it also means we can have the same crop earlier than outdoors – for example strawberries or tomatoes.

Often it is best to grow plants in containers that are to go under cover as this allows for more variety in the same area, though each plant will necessarily yield less than if it was in the ground. Containers not only control the vigour of the plants but also make them portable so they can be moved under cover and outside as convenient. This suits many fruits such as the citrus, which really prefer to be outside all summer but need frost protection in winter. By contrast, many varieties of grapevine are best under cover for an early start and for ripening, but need to be chilled in winter to fruit well.

This is why some plants are difficult. They need hot summers and warm autumns and also cold winters to go dormant. Without dormancy they do not ripen wood or fruit well and often just fade away. It is quite easy to chill a greenhouse in a cold area for the couple of months required, but not of course if other tender plants are kept there also.

The other requirement may be for extra light. Many plants need more light than can be had in winter through dirty glass. The physical barrier reduces light intensity by half. Fortunately, artificial lights are cheap to fit and run – compared to heating anyway. Some plants are very demanding; not only do they want more light and heat but they want enough hours of complete darkness every night as well. This requires the fitting of blinds to exclude daylight and light from any nearby streetlights, too! Similarly some plants find bright light too intense and need shading.

Fortunately most exotics are remarkably easy to grow. The biggest problems are usually the cost of heating and the eventual size of the plants.

Hygiene in the Glasshouse
Glasshouses should be cleaned annually in winter: wash thoroughly with disinfectant to kill overwintering eggs and fungal spores. If you have space, before introducing a new plant to the glasshouse, keep it in quarantine for a few weeks to prevent new problems being introduced.

Grapevine in conservatory

PROTECTED CROPPING

Many crops need protecting at some point in their life. In some cases they need protecting from the elements, to provide conditions more conducive to growth; they may also need protecting from predators such as birds and rodents.

Protection from the Elements

A few simple structures can extend the growing season in spring and autumn, accelerate growth and increase productivity.

Cold frames are ideal for raising seedlings or hardening off plants before transplanting outdoors. The lack of height limits the

floating film are flexible covers that can be laid immediately over the crop or suspended on hoops as 'floating mulches'. As the plants grow they are forced upwards. Fleece is lightweight, soft-textured spun polypropylene, which lasts for a year if it is kept clean, or sometimes longer if cared for. It is ideal for frost protection and for forcing early crops. Many crops, especially vegetables, can be grown under this, from sowing to harvesting, and it is an effective barrier against pests and diseases. More light and air can penetrate through this than

Fleece protecting newly planted sweetcorn

Cloches protecting spinach

crops that can be grown in them. Cloches of glass or plastic are easily moved to provide shelter to those individual plants or small groups that need it most. Low polythene tunnels are like small cloches, are cheap, portable and versatile, but are of limited use because of their flimsiness and lack of height. Crop covers or

through plastic film. Plastic film is usually perforated with minute slits or holes for ventilation, but the crop may overheat on sunny spring days. The film is laid directly over the plants; as they grow, the flexible material is pushed upwards, splitting open the minute slits and increasing ventilation. It is often used in the early stages of growth.

Plastic netting has a very fine mesh, filtering the wind and providing protection, but has little effect on raising temperature. It lasts for several seasons.

As many of these materials are manufactured in long, narrow rolls, the most effective way to use them is to grow crops in long, narrow strips. Insect-pollinated crops like courgettes, marrows, cucumbers and tomatoes should have the covering removed or opened as the crop develops.

Protection from Predators

Fruit cages are cover with netting. They are necessary to protect soft fruit in areas with many birds. The most troublesome birds, such as blackbirds and pigeons, can be excluded with coarse 2cm (1in) mesh, while smaller, insectivorous birds such as wrens and bluetits can still gain access. If all the net is wire, squirrels and rodents can also be stopped. If a finer mesh, down to about 1cm ($\frac{1}{2}$in) is used then bees can still enter but large moths and butterflies are excluded.

Fruit cages have other uses. The netting itself makes a more sheltered environment enjoyed by the plants. Light frosts are kept off, and chill

winds are reduced. In very hot regions, denser netting gives welcome shade and cooler conditions.

A fruit cage can even be reversed in principle to enclose all of a small garden and to confine ornamental seed- and insect-eating, but hopefully not inadvertently fruit-eating, birds. On a more prosaic level, it is practical to grow plants on a tall leg and then run chickens underneath for their excellent pest control. If you have chickens, they can be running in the cage during most of the year when the plants are not in fruit.

Fruit cages can be hand-crafted from second-hand materials or easy custom-made ones are available. In areas of high wind, obviously, the most substantial materials have to be used. Permanent sides of wire mesh and a light net laid on wires for the roof are most practicable. Make sure you can remove the roof net easily if snows are forecast as a thick layer on top will break most cages.

Most fruit cage plants are natives of the woodland's edge and do not mind light shade, but few of them relish stagnant air so do not overcrowd them.

WEED CONTROL

Any plant that grows in a place where it is not wanted is described as a weed. These compete with crops for moisture, nutrients and light, acting as hosts to pests and diseases, which can then spread to crops.

TYPES OF WEED

Knowledge of a weed's life cycle enables the gardener to control weeds effectively.
• Ephemeral weeds germinate, flower and seed rapidly, producing several generations each season and copious quantities of seed.
• Annual weeds germinate, flower and seed in one season.
• Biennial weeds have a life-cycle spanning two growing seasons.

• Perennial weeds survive for several years. They often spread through the soil as they grow, producing scores of new shoots and setting seed. New plants sprout from tiny fragments of root, rhizome or bulbils in the soil.

METHODS OF CONTROL

There are four main methods of weed control: manual, mechanical, mulching and chemical. Wherever possible, keep the garden weed-free and if germination occurs, remove weeds immediately, before they flower and produce seed. The old saying, 'One year's seed is seven years' weed' is, unfortunately, scientifically proven.

Complete elimination of weeds from an area before planting is invariably worth-while and is much easier than trying later to weed among the plants (see pp.580–81).

Manual Weeding

Digging, forking, hoeing and hand weeding, are often the only practical ways to eradicate weeds in confined spaces.

Digging cultivates the soil to a depth of at least 30cm (12in). Soil is turned over, burying surface vegetation and annual weeds. Perennial weeds should be removed separately and not buried among the surface vegetation.

Forking cultivates the soil around perennial weeds before they are lifted by

hand. If this is undertaken carefully, roots can be removed without breaking into sections and forming new plants.

Hoeing prevents weed seeds from germinating, reduces moisture loss and minimizes soil disturbance. Hoeing is best undertaken in dry weather and the blade should penetrate no deeper than 1cm ($^1\!/_2$in).

Hand-weed in dry weather when the soil is moist so that weeds are easily loosened from the soil; try to remove the whole plant. Remove weeds from the site to prevent them from rerooting.

Mechanical Weed Control

Machines with revolving rotary tines, blades or cultivator attachments are

Couch weeds flourishing among cabbages

useful for preparing seedbeds and can also be used to control annual weeds between rows of vegetables. They should be employed carefully to avoid root damage. When clearing the ground of perennial weeds, the blades simply slice through the roots and rhizomes. While this increases their number initially, several sessions over a period of time should gradually exhaust and eventually kill the plants. This is only viable when there is plenty of time.

Biological Weed Control

Mulching is the practice of covering the soil around plants with a layer of organic or inorganic material to suppress weeds, reduce water loss (see also p.597) and warm the soil. Choose your material carefully; straw harbours pests such as vine weevil and flea beetle and contains weed seeds, but is effective as an insulating layer over winter. It also draws nitrogen from the soil in the early stages of decay. Using rotted material like well-rotted farm manure or spent hops avoids this problem.

Organic mulches are also limited where crops need to be earthed up – a process that disturbs the soil. Inorganic materials like plastic sheeting, though effective, are unattractive but can at least be hidden beneath a thin layer of organic mulch.

Inorganic mulches suppress weeds and prevent seeds from germinating. They also conserve soil moisture by slowing evaporation; plastic films are the most effective for this purpose. They keep trailing crops clean. White plastic mulches hasten growth and ripening by reflecting light on to leaves and fruit; black plastic mulches warm the soil in spring. Sheet mulches are most effective when applied before the crop is planted,

and the young plants are then planted through small holes in the sheet.

Organic mulches improve soil fertility and conserve its structure by protecting the surface from heavy rain and being trodden on, encouraging earthworm activity and adding organic matter and nutrients to the soil. They insulate the soil, keeping it cooler in summer and warmer in winter. Weeds that push their way through are easily removed. For effective weed control organic mulches should be about 10cm (4in) deep, to block out the light.

In general, organic mulches improve soil fertility as they decay, while inorganic mulches are more effective against weeds as they form an impenetrable barrier.

Chemical Weed Control

Choose and use herbicides with extreme care and ensure they are suitable for the weeds to be controlled. FOLLOW THE MANUFACTURER'S INSTRUCTIONS CAREFULLY.
• Residual herbicides form a layer over the soil, killing germinating weeds and seedlings.
• Contact herbicides only kill those parts of the plant that they touch. They are effective against annual weeds and weed seedlings, but are not recommended against established plants.
• Systemic or translocated herbicides are absorbed by the foliage, travelling through the sap system to kill the whole plant, including the roots. Glyphosate is often the active ingredient. Individual weeds can be 'spot treated' using such herbicides in gel or liquid form.

Several chemical weed-control methods have been developed for use with vegetables and other edible plants but no single chemical is suitable for all crops. This gives the grower three options: stock a range of chemicals and change

the type regularly; use chemicals only as a last resort; or grow organically. For edible plants the latter is almost invariably the best.

Using and Storing Weedkillers Safely

Always wear adequate protective clothing, such as face mask, goggles, rubber gloves and old waterproof clothes when mixing weedkillers. Dilute weedkillers according to the manufacturer's instructions, and never mix different chemicals together. Never dilute chemicals in a confined space, as they may give off toxic fumes.

As for mixing, always wear the specified protective clothing when applying weedkillers. Follow the manufacturer's instructions carefully and use only as recommended on the product label. Do not apply weedkillers in windy conditions; nearby plants may suffer serious damage. Do not apply weedkillers in very hot, still conditions when there is a high risk of spray travelling on warm air currents. If you are using a watering-can to apply chemicals, ensure that it is obviously labelled and at no times use it for any other purpose.

Store chemicals in the original containers with the labels well secured so that the contents can be identified. Mark the container with the date of purchase, so that you know how long it has been stored. Never store dilute weedkillers for future use. Always store in cool, frost-free, dark conditions out of the reach of children and animals, in a locked cupboard in a workshop or shed.

Thoroughly wash protective clothing, sprayers, mixing vessels and utensils after use. Never use the same sprayer, mixing vessels and utensils for other types of chemical such as fungicides. The results could be disastrous!

GRASS MANAGEMENT

Under woody perennial plants such as fruit trees and bushes, the most convenient ground cover is usually grass sward. Grass competes vigorously, especially if kept closely mowed as a lawn. However grass sward is simple to maintain, ornamental, hygienic and prevents worse weeds. The clippings themselves are a free source of mulching material and can contribute much fertility to our plants.

Grass sward is most productive of useful clippings when the grass is cut often and not too closely. Long grass grows more quickly, is more drought-resistant and suppresses turf weeds better than closely cropped. Cut your grass regularly and frequently with slightly greater height of cut and the longer, more vigorous grass soon chokes out most weeds.

When grassing down, it is sensible to include clovers in the grass seed mix as they have the advantage of fixing nitrogen from the air to aid the grasses. A clover grass mixture also stays greener for longer in hot dry summers and, if left to flower, the clovers attract bees and other beneficial insects.

Providing you are not growing ericaceous plants or fine bowling green grasses you should lime all your turf every fourth year, even if you have lime in the soil. Most swards slowly become acid in the topmost layer; this encourages mosses and acid-loving weeds. If such weeds, say daisies, are increasing you need to add more lime, up to a couple of handfuls per square metre (square yard) per year. You probably also need to raise the height of your cut. If weeds that like wet acid soils such as buttercups appear, then lime is desperately needed and probably better drainage as well.

PEST AND DISEASE CONTROL

The control of pests and diseases is done to preserve the yield or appearance of our crops, but we must ensure that the costs incurred do not outweigh the gains. It is ironic that commercial apples are sprayed to prevent scabby patches on their skin, which is now peeled and discarded to avoid the very residues left by many such sprays. Herbs in general suffer from few pests and diseases and in fact many can be used to protect other crops (see pp.586–7).

For the home gardener the main causes of loss of crops most years is the weather. There is very little we can do to make the sun come out, the wind stop or the rain fall.

The second cause of loss is probably the gardener. We all leave action too late, skimp preparation and routine tasks, put plants in less than their optimum positions, and then over-crowd them as well. What we must remember is that our plants 'want' to leaf, flower

and crop. They are programmed as tightly as any computer, If we give them the right inputs they must produce the right output.

PREVENTING PROBLEMS

Organic gardeners avoid the use of artificial chemicals, relying on good management and natural predators to control pests and diseases, while working to create an environment in which they are unlikely to occur. If we give our plants the right conditions then they are also healthy and vigorous enough to shrug off most pests and disease. Healthy plants grow in a well-suited site and soil, with shelter and water when they are small, and are not overfed. Excess fertilizer makes plants flabby and prone to problems. Keep them lean and fit with well-made compost and mulches.

Working with Natural Defences

The most effective way to control pests is to persuade others to do it for you. The natural ecology always controls them in the long run. We can help it quickly reach a balance of more ladybirds, thrushes and frogs with fewer aphids, snails and slugs. Our allies require shelter, nest sites, food out of season, water and companion plants. If we provide these they increase in number and thus the pests decrease.

Timing can be of service. For example late raspberries usually escape the depredations of their fruit

Scab on apple fruit ('Golden Delicious')

maggot. Having many fruits that ripen at the same time also reduces damage. When successive plants ripen they are picked clean by small numbers of pests which are overwhelmed by a glut, as may be the gardener!

Check plants daily if possible. Instant eradication is often the best remedy: either remove the affected part of the plant or wipe off the pest or disease as with aphids.

General Hygiene

Plant debris is a logical host for pests and diseases, particularly over winter, allowing them to survive in preparation for reemergence and reinfection the following year. Do everything possible to keep plants healthy by cleaning your glasshouse and equipment regularly. Dispose of organic matter immediately; compost healthy material and get rid of infected plants at once by burning or placing in the dustbin. When buying plants,

ensure they come from a reputable source and, if possible, keep them in quarantine for a short while before introducing them to the glasshouse.

Winter is the perfect time to disinfect plant supports, particularly bamboo canes, which are hollow and often split with age, creating cracks and crevices which form suitable sites for fungi and insect eggs to overwinter. These can be sprayed or dipped in disinfectant.

Cultural Practices

Always use sterilized compost for seed sowing and potting. Seedlings are particularly vulnerable, especially when sown under cover. Sow seeds thinly, do not irrigate with stagnant or cold water, ventilate the glasshouse, but avoid chilling plants or seedlings and do not allow compost to become waterlogged. Promote rapid germination and continuous growth to reduce the risk of infection at the time when

Raspberry damaged by raspberry beetle

seedlings and young plants are at their most vulnerable. Inspect plants regularly, particularly if a variety is prone to certain problems. Grow pest- and disease-resistant cultivars where possible. Rotate vegetable crops and always keep the garden weed-free. Handle plants with care, particularly when harvesting, as this is a common cause of infection. Regularly check stored crops as rot spreads rapidly in a confined space.

CONTROL METHODS

Barriers and Traps

The simplest method of protection is to use a barrier to prevent pests or disease reaching the plant. For example, netting stops birds and horticultural fleece stops many insects.

On fruit trees, traps of corrugated cardboard, carpet or old sack can be made by rolling strips around trunk or stem. These attract pests by replicating creviced bark. They hide within and can be dislodged in winter. Non-setting sticky bands applied to aluminium foil wrapped tightly around trunk, branch or stem stop pests climbing up and down. Do remember to paint the support as well.

Sticky traps can be bought to lure flying pests to them with pheromone sex attractant 'perfumes'. Others use the smell of the fruit or leaf to entice the pest to a sticky end. Jars of water with lids of foil containing pencil-sized holes trap wasps when baited with fruit juice or jam.

Organic Sprays

Soap spray kills most small insect pests by suffocation and is remarkably safe for us and the environment. People used to employ ordinary household soap flakes but improved soft soaps are now sold specifically for pesticidal

Carrots covered with fleece to protect from carrot fly

use. Bordeaux mixture is an old-fashioned fungicide. It is wholly chemical, made from copper sulphate and lime, and is allowed to organic gardeners with moderation.

Derris and pyrethrum are insecticides made from plant products. They are the strongest allowed to organic gardeners and degrade fast, but kill pests immune to soft soap. Use them according to the instructions and spray at night when the bees have gone home!

Silver foil and other bird-scaring devices over cabbages

Biological Controls

Many predators are now available commercially. Apart from *Bacillus thuringiensis*, the bacterial control for caterpillars, few are effective outside the closed environment of a greenhouse. Most pesticides kill predators with the exception of insecticidal soaps and pirimicarb (against aphids) and so should be avoided. Particularly useful are *Phytoseiulus persimilis*, the predatory mite that controls two-spotted or red spider mite and *Encarsia formosa*, a parasitic wasp, controlling glasshouse white-fly. All biological control methods are relatively expensive when compared with chemical alternatives, and nearly all depend on warm temperatures to work efficiently.

Chemical controls

Chemicals offer a quick and simple solution to many pest and disease problems but, before using them, it is worth considering the following. Many chemicals are toxic and can be harmful to humans, pets and wildlife. They should be applied with extreme care. Chemicals may remain in soil and plant tissue for long periods, affecting predators. Many pests and diseases, particularly whitefly and red spider mite, can develop a resistance to chemicals that are used persistently for long periods, so rendering controls less effective. Applying a range of chemicals can overcome this. Government legislation may make some chemicals unavailable in the future.

Always follow instructions with regard to safety, mixing and application. Apply chemicals in still, overcast conditions, usually in the early morning or evening. Protect surrounding plants from the chemical solution. Thoroughly clean equipment after use. Dispose of unwanted chemicals according to the manufacturer's recommendations. DO NOT POUR THEM DOWN THE DRAIN.

Cutworms

SOIL-BORNE PESTS

Cutworms

These grey-green caterpillars, approximately 5cm (2in) long, appear from late spring until early autumn. They burrow into root crops including beetroot, carrot, parsnip and potato, and any plant with a soft taproot, eating through plant stems at soil level.

Plants grown under cover seem less prone to damage, and heavy watering in early summer often kills young caterpillars. To control them, incorporate a soil insecticide such as diazinon and chlorpyrifos or water pirimiphos-methyl into the top 5cm (2in) of soil.

Cabbage Root Fly

These white larvae, approximately 8mm (⅓in) long, are found from late spring to mid-autumn. They feed on the roots of brassicas just below soil level, stunting growth and causing plants to wilt, seedlings to die and tunnels to appear in root crops. As a preventive measure, grow under horticultural fleece. To control them, place a 12cm (5in) collar of cardboard, plastic, carpet underlay or similar around the plant bases. Alternatively, incorporate an insecticide such as chlorpyrifos and diazinon or pirimiphos-methyl into the top 5cm (2in) of soil.

Carrot Root Fly

These creamy-white maggots, approximately 8mm (⅓in) long, appear from early summer until mid-autumn. They are a common problem with carrots, but can also affect celeriac, parsnip, celery, parsley and other umbelliferous plants. Larvae burrow into the roots, causing stunted growth and reddish-purple coloration of the foliage.

Sow thinly and lift crops in late summer or in early autumn. Place a barrier 60cm (24in) high around crops or cover with horticultural fleece when young. Where plants are badly affected, pull them up and destroy them. Large herbs should overcome

Carrot Root Fly

attacks so just pick off dead leaves and boost with a liquid seaweed feed. A chemical control is to incorporate a soil insecticide such as pirimiphos-methyl into the top 5cm (2in) of the soil.

Leatherjackets

These grey-brown, wrinkled grubs, can be up to 3.5cm (1½in) long. They eat through roots and through the stems of young plants

Leatherjackets

just below soil level. Most crops are vulnerable, including Brussels sprouts, cabbage, cauliflower and lettuce. To discourage them, ensure the soil is well drained, dig over the ground in the early autumn, especially if it has been fallow in the summer. The problem is often worse on new sites and usually

Cabbage Root Fly

diminishes with time. A chemical solution is to water vulnerable plants with piriphos-methyl and treat soil with diazinon and chlorpyrifos.

NEMATODES (EELWORMS)

Potato Cyst Eelworm

These white to golden-brown, pinhead-sized cysts are found on roots in mid-summer. Each can contain up to 600 eggs which can remain dormant in the soil for up to six years. Potatoes and tomatoes are affected, with weak and stunted growth, small fruits and tubers, yellow foliage, with the lower leaves dying first followed by premature death of the plants.

Rotate crops and grow resistant varieties like 'Pentland Javelin', 'Pentland Lustre', 'Maris Piper' or 'Kingston'. Do not grow

potatoes or tomatoes on infected soil for at least 6 years.

Stem and Bulb Eelworm

These are microscopic pests that live inside the plant and move around on a film of moisture; most active from spring to late summer. The symptoms are weak, stunted growth, swollen bases on young plants, and later stems that thicken and rot. They affect a wide range of young plants from spring until late summer, particularly leek, onion, shallot and chives.

Rotate crops, practise good hygiene and management, and destroy infected crops.

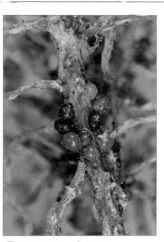

Potato cyst eelworm

grit, sand, eggshell or soot around plants or cut a 10cm (4in) section from a plastic bottle and place it as a

Dead potatoes after potato cyst eelworm attack

Do not grow potatoes or tomatoes on infected soil for at least 6 years, and any other vulnerable crops on the site for at least 4 years.

SLUGS

Slimy, with tubular-shaped bodies, up to 10cm (4in), from creamy-white through grey to jet-black and orange, slugs are voracious feeders, making circular holes in plant tissue; damaged seedlings are usually killed. They tend to feed at night. Most soft plant tissue is vulnerable. Slugs are more of a problem on wet sites and clay soils; keep the soil well drained and weed-free. Remove all crop debris. Grow less susceptible cultivars. Remove slugs by hand at night and destroy them. Create a barrier of

'collar' around plants. Make traps from plastic cartons, half-buried in the ground and filled with milk or beer, or lay old roof tiles, newspaper or old lettuce leaves or other tempting vegetation on the ground and hand pick regularly from underneath. Attract natural predators like toads to the garden or use biological controls.

Chemical controls include applying aluminium sulphate in the spring as the slug eggs hatch and using slug pellets, which contain metaldehyde.

WIREWORMS

These are thin, yellow larvae, pointed at each end, about 2.5cm (1in) long. They make holes in the roots and tubers, and can cause foliage to

collapse; seedlings are usually killed. A wide range of plants are attacked, particularly root crops and potatoes. Symptoms appear from spring until mid-summer. More of a problem on newly cultivated soil, wireworms

Wireworm

usually disappear after 5 years; avoid planting root crops until the sixth year. Lift root crops as soon as they mature. Cultivate the ground thoroughly well before planting and incorporate chlorpyrifos and diazinon into the top 5cm (2in) of soil.

SOIL-BORNE DISEASES

Clubroot

This is a soil-borne fungus that can remain in the soil for up to 20 years. It causes leaves to yellow and discolour, wilting rapidly in hot weather; the roots display swollen wart-like swellings, and become distorted. All members of the Brassicaceae family are vulnerable, including brassicas and weedy relatives. Clubroot is worse on acid soils, so lime to raise the pH and improve the drainage. Practise strict crop rotation, good management and hygiene, and grow your own plants instead of buying in, or at least purchase from a reputable source. Raise plants in pots. Swede 'Marian' has good resistance to clubroot.

If you wish to use a chemical control, dip the roots of transplants in a fungicidal solution such as thiophanate-methyl. Lift and dispose of affected plants immediately, and do not compost.

Common Scab

This fungus causes superficial damage to the underground parts of affected plants. Rough brown lesions appear on the surface of roots and tubers. It is more severe on alkaline soils and in dry summers. Common scab affects mainly potatoes, but can be found on radishes, beetroot, swede and turnips. Avoid liming, do not grow potatoes on soil recently used for brassicas, apply organic matter and irrigate thoroughly in dry weather. Grow resistant potato cultivars like 'Arran Pilot' and 'King Edward'. Avoid 'Majestic' and 'Maris Piper', which are very susceptible. Rotate crops.

Clubroot

Root Rot

This fungus is difficult to eradicate. It attacks beans and peas, causing shrivelled, yellowing leaves, stems and pods; roots rot and stems rot at the base. Plants collapse. Practise a minimum 3-year crop rotation; remove and burn infected plants. Sow seed dressed with an appropriate fungicide, or water seedlings with a copper-based fungicide such as cheshunt compound or Bordeaux mixture.

Stem Rot

This fungus is difficult to eradicate. It attacks aubergine and tomato, causing yellow-brown cankerous lesions with black dots in and around the lesions, occurring at soil level. Remove and burn infected plants and crop debris, disinfect anything that comes into contact with diseased material, including hands and equipment. Immediately after planting apply a fungicide such as captan to the bottom 10cm (4in) of the stem, repeating 3 weeks later.

White Rot

This fungus is almost impossible to eradicate. Common on onions and leeks, it also attacks chives and garlic, causing discoloured, yellowing leaves, which die slowly. Roots rot and plants fall over, becoming covered with a white felt-like mould. Do not grow susceptible crops for 8 years after an infection. Remove and burn infected plants immediately; do not compost any plant debris. Apply a fungicide such as thiophanate-methyl to the seed drills when sowing.

AIR-BORNE PESTS

Aphids

These are dense colonies of winged and wingless insects, from pale-green through pink to greeny-black. They attack soft tissue on a wide range of plants, including brassicas, beans and peas, lettuces, potatoes and root crops. Shoot tips and young leaves become distorted; they leave a sticky coating on lower leaves, often accompanied by a black sooty mould. Pinch the growth tips from broad beans, destroy alternative hosts, and take care not to overfeed with high nitrogen fertilizers. Treat small infestations by squashing or, on sturdy plants, washing off with a jet of water; spray with soft soap, derris, pyrethrum-based insecticide; encourage natural predators like lacewings, ladybirds and their larvae and small birds like blue tits. On larger woody perennials these are more of an inconvenience than a real problem.

Cabbage Caterpillars

These are small, hairy, yellow and black caterpillars up to 5cm (2in) long. Voracious feeders, the caterpillars eat holes in the leaves and in severe cases leave plants totally defoliated. They attack all brassicas, including horseradish, and are a problem from late spring to autumn. Inspect plants regularly, squash eggs or caterpillars as they are found, pick off caterpillars and grow crops under horticultural fleece or fine netting. Alternatively, spray regularly with derris, pyrethrum or permethrin when eggs are first seen.

Cabbage Whitefly

These small, white-winged insects are usually found on the leaf underside. Clouds of insects fly up whenever the leaves are brushed. The young leaves pucker and there is a sticky coating, often accompanied by a black mould. Whitefly attack all leafy brassicas. They can survive severe winter weather and are seen all year round. Remove and burn badly infected plants immediately after cropping. Spray with insecticidal soap

White rot on maturing onion crop

or pyrethrum-based sprays, dimethoate or malathion; concentrate on the leaf undersides.

Pea Thrips

These small, white to black-brown or yellow-bodied insects, usually on the leaf underside, are commonly known as 'thunder flies'. They cause distorted pods with a silvery sheen; peas fail to swell in the pod. The insects are often found on peas and also on broad beans. Remove and burn badly infected plants. Spray with a malathion or similar insecticide just as the plants start to flower.

Vine Weevils

The adult weevil is dark grey, beetle-like 1–2cm (½in) long, with a very long snout. It takes rounded bits out of leaves, but most harm is done by the grubs, which

are up to the same size with a grey-pink body and brown head. They destroy the roots of many plants. Adults can be trapped in rolls of corrugated cardboard, in bundles of sticks or under saucers, where they hide in the daytime. The grubs can be destroyed by watering on the commercially available predatory nematode.

Leaf Miners

These grubs are sometimes a problem on lovage, wild celery, certain sorrels and various mints. They eat through the leaf, creating winding tunnels in the leaves that are clearly visible. Pick off the affected leaves as you see them. If left, the tunnels will extend into broad dry patches and whole leaves will wither away.

Aphids

AIR-BORNE DISEASES

Blight

This fungus infects leaves, stems and tubers and is worse in wet seasons. Severe epidemics led to the Irish potato famine. In mid-summer brown patches appear on the upper and lower leaf surfaces, ringed with white mould in humid conditions; leaves become yellow and fall prematurely. In humid climates the fungus spreads rapidly over the foliage and stems which quickly collapse. Tubers show dark, sunken patches. The fungus attacks potatoes, tomatoes and closely related weeds. Remove and burn badly infected plant tops in late summer, avoid overhead watering and use resistant cultivars like 'Cara', 'Romano' and 'Wilja' potatoes. Do not store infected tubers. In wet seasons spray with fungicide before the disease appears. Spray in summer with copper-based fungicide or mancozeb, and repeat at regular intervals as soon as symptoms appear.

Botrytis

This fungus infects flowers, leaves and stems and usually enters through wounds. Discoloured patches appear on stems, which may rot at ground level; flowers and leaves become covered with woolly, grey fungal growth. It causes shadows on unripe tomato fruit called 'ghost spot'. Soft-leaved plants are particularly vulnerable including broad beans, brassicas, lettuces, potatoes and tomatoes. Maintain good air circulation, handle plants with care to avoid injury and remove infected material. If you wish to use chemicals, spray with thiophanate-methyl or carbendazim as soon as the disease symptoms are seen; remove and burn badly infected plants.

Cabbage caterpillar

Downy Mildew

This is a fungus that infects leaves and stems, overwintering in the soil or plant debris. It causes discoloured, yellowing leaves, which have grey/white mouldy patches on the lower surface; plants often die slowly in the autumn. Attacks brassicas including weed species, lettuce, spinach, peas and onions. Avoid overcrowding, remove and burn badly infected plants and maintain good air circulation. Spray with zineb, mancozeb or copper-based fungicide when the first symptoms appear.

Blight

Powdery Mildew

This common fungal disease can occur when the conditions are hot and dry, and the plants are overcrowded. Prevent it by watering well during dry spells, following the recommended planting distances, and clearing away any fallen leaves in the autumn. Adding a mulch in the autumn or early spring also helps. If your plant does suffer, destroy all the affected leaves.

Rust

Plants affected by rust should be dug up and thrown away. Alternatively you can, in the autumn, put straw around the affected plant and set it alight; this will sterilize the soil and the plant.

PESTS AND DISEASES UNDER COVER

Red Spider Mite

The spider mites like hot dry conditions and can become prolific in a glasshouse. Look out for early signs such as speckling on the upper surfaces of the leaves. Another telltale sign is cobwebs. At first sight, either use a spray of horticultural soap, or the natural predator *Phytoseiulus persimilis*, but not both.

Scale Insects

These are often noticeable as immobile, waxy, brown/yellow, flat, oval lumps gathered on the backs of leaves or on stems. These leaves also become covered with sticky black sooty mould. Rub off the scales gently before the infestation builds up, or use a horticultural liquid soap.

Whitefly

It is essential to act as soon as you see the small white flies, either by introducing the natural predator *Encarsia formosa*, or by spraying with horticultural soap.

OTHER PESTS

Birds

Birds damage many fruits and some vegetables. Netting is the answer. If the whole plant cannot be enclosed or moved under cover then protect each fruit or bunch with waxed paper or netting bags.

Botrytis

Things that flash, such as pieces of foil and humming tape, all work as bird scarers but only for a short time. Scarecrows rarely work at all!

Ants

A minor problem on their own, they farm aphids and scale insects, making these more of a threat. Put out some sugar, watch where they take it home, then pour boiling water down their hole.

Wasps

Wasps are valuable allies early in the year when they control caterpillars and other pests. Later they turn to fruit and need trapping with jars (see p.603). Dusting them with flour enables you to follow them home so the nest can be destroyed with derris dust puffed in the entrance as they all return in the evening.

Rabbits

Only netting the area will keep rabbits out. In case they get in, have a plank ramped against the fence so they are not trapped inside and eat even more. If the perimeter cannot be secured, surround or wrap each plant in wire netting.

HARVESTING AND STORING

One of the pleasures of a productive garden is picking your produce and cooking or eating it fresh. However, there are a myriad of means of storing many crops, thus extending the season, and avoiding unmanageable gluts. See also details under individual crops.

WHEN TO HARVEST
Vegetables
While the majority of vegetables are not harvested until they reach maturity, others, like some lettuces, are harvested while semi-mature and others still, such as rocket, are harvested while juvenile. Some vegetables, again like lettuce, cannot be stored for long and so must be harvested and eaten fresh. Many other leafy vegetables, such as Brussels sprouts and sprouting broccoli, are hardy, surviving outdoors in the ground in freezing conditions. The flavour of Brussels sprouts even improves immeasurably after they have been frosted. Some root vegetables with a high moisture content are easily damaged in winter, even when protected by the soil. This is usually caused by rapid thawing after a period of cold weather. Carrots, parsnip and swede are exceptions; they are very hardy and can be left in free-draining soils until required. In wet soils these crops would suffer winter loss by slug damage and rotting.

Herbs
Herbs can be harvested from very early on in their growing season. This encourages the plant to produce vigorous new growth and allows the plant to be controlled in shape and size. Most herbs reach their peak of flavour just before they flower. Snip off suitable stems early in the day before the sun is fully up, or even better on a cloudy day (provided it is not too humid). Cut whole stems rather than single leaves or flowers. Always use a sharp knife, sharp scissors or secateurs, and cut lengths of 5–8cm (2–3in) from the tip of the branch, this being the new, soft growth. Do not cut into any of the older, woody growth. Cut from all over the plant, leaving it looking shapely. Pick herbs that are clean and free from pests and disease. If herbs are covered in garden soil, sponge them quickly and lightly with cold water, not hot as this will draw out the oils prematurely. Pat dry as quickly as possible. Keep each species separately so that they do not contaminate each other.

Most annual herbs can be harvested at least twice during a growing season. Cut them to within 10–15cm (4–6in) of the ground, and feed with liquid fertilizer after each cutting. Give annuals their final cut of the season before the first frosts; they will have stopped growing some weeks before.

In the first year of planting, perennials will give one good crop; thereafter it will be possible to harvest two or three times during the growing season. Do not cut into the woody growth unless deliberately trying to prevent growth; again, cut well before frosts. There are of course exceptions: sage is still very good after frosts, and both thyme and golden marjoram (with some protection) can be picked gently even in midwinter.

Pick flowers for drying when they are barely open. Seed should be collected as soon as you notice a change in colour of the seed pod; if, when you tap the pod, a few scatter on the ground, it is the time to gather them. Seeds ripen very fast, so watch them carefully.

Roots of herbs are at their peak of flavour when they have just completed a growing season. Dig them throughout autumn as growth ceases. Lift whole roots with a garden fork, taking care not to puncture or bruise the outer skin. Wash them free of soil. Cut

Individual herbs laid out for drying

away any remains of top-growth and any fibrous off-shoots. For drying, cut large, thick roots in half lengthways and then into smaller pieces for ease.

Fruit
Without doubt most fruits are best, and certainly are enjoyed most, when they are plucked fully ripe off the tree or vine. Only a few, such as melons, are improved by chilling first. The majority are tastiest fresh and warmed by the sun. Some, such as pears, have to be carefully nurtured till they are fully ripe and need to be picked early and brought to perfection, watched daily, in a warm, not too dry, dim room. Medlars are similarly picked early and are then ripened, or bletted, to the point of rotting.

The best date for picking will vary with the cultivar, the soil, the site and the season, and can only be determined by experience as these factors all vary considerably. Of course, it will generally remain much the same in relation to other fruits nearby, which are also subject to the same conditions, i.e. in a late year, most fruits are late, which is pretty self-evident anyway.

On any tree, the sunny side ripens first. Fruit will also ripen earlier where extra warmth is supplied, so that growing sites next to a wall, window, chimney or vent, or close to the soil are good places for finding early fruits. Likewise, when all the rest have gone, you may find some hidden in the shade.

If you want to store fruits for home use, they need to

be picked at just the right stage. Most fruits store best when picked just under-ripe. They may keep much longer if picked even younger, but this is at the cost of flavour and sweetness.

STORAGE CONDITIONS

Vegetables

In colder areas, vegetables overwintering in the ground need further protection. This can be provided by spreading a layer of loose straw or bracken over them to a depth of 20cm (8in) and covering with a plastic sheet. While this is labour-saving, crops stored in this way are susceptible to attack by pests and diseases through the winter.

The traditional method for storing root vegetables is in a clamp or 'pie'. Low mounds of vegetables are laid on a bed of loose straw up to 20cm (8in) thick. The top and sides of the mound are covered with a similar layer of straw, and then with a 15cm (6in) layer of soil or sand. Clamps can be made outdoors on a well-drained site or under cover in a shed or outhouse; for extra protection outdoors, they can be formed against a wall or hedge. If crops are to be stored for a long period, find a site that receives as little sunlight as possible during the winter. Although storage conditions are very similar to those in the ground, harvesting from a clamp is much easier. However, losses from rodent damage and rotting can be high.

The length of time that vegetables may be stored depends on the type and cultivar as well as the storage conditions. When traditional methods are used, the main cause of deterioration is moisture loss from plant tissue; for instance, beetroot and carrot desiccate very rapidly. Fungal infection of damaged tissue is a common problem; onions and potatoes bruise very easily. Vegetables for storage should be handled carefully; only store those that are disease-free, check them regularly and remove any showing signs of decay immediately.

Fruits

Although we occasionally store some fruits, such as pears, for a period to improve their condition, predominantly we store fruit to extend the season so that we can enjoy them for as long as possible.

To be stored, all fruit must be perfect. Any blemish or bruise is where moulds start. Choose varieties that are suitable for storing – many early croppers are notoriously bad keepers!

Common, long-keeping fruits such as apples and quinces can be stored at home for months, or even up to a year. The major problems, apart from the moulds, are shrivelling due to water loss and the depredations of rodents and other big pests. A conventional store is too large for most of us and the house or garage is too warm, too cold or too dry. Dead deep freezers and refrigerators make excellent, compact stores. They are dark, keep the contents at the same constant temperature and will keep out night frosts easily. Most useful of all, they are rodent-proof.

Some ventilation is needed and can be obtained by cutting holes in the rubber door or lid seal. If condensation occurs it usually indicates insufficient ventilation, but too much draught will dry out the fruits. The unit can stand outdoors, as it needs no power. In a shed it is out of sight and better protected against the cold, but may then get too warm. In the UK, have it outdoors in the shade or in a cool shed.

When putting fruits in the store it is usually best to leave them to chill at night in trays and to load them into the store in the morning when they have dried off but before they have warmed up

Parsley stored in a bag for freezing, together with ice cubes for convenience

again. Similarly it is helpful to chill and dry off the fruits initially by leaving the store open on chill, dry nights and closing it during the day for a week or two after filling.

Most fruits are best removed from the store some time before use, so any staleness can leave them. Care should be taken not to store early and late varieties together or any that may cross-taint. Obviously it is not a good idea to site your store in the same place as strong-smelling things such as onions, paint or creosote! Likewise, although straw is a convenient litter, if it gets damp it taints the fruit. Shredded newspaper is safer, though it also has a slight whiff. Dried stinging nettles are reckoned good but dangerous to handle.

Always inspect stored fruits regularly. They can go off very quickly. Remember, if only one in ten goes off every month, you have to start with two trays just to have one tray left after six months. So do not store any fruit long just for the sake of it, but store well what you will use.

DRYING

Vegetables

Peas and beans can be harvested when almost mature and dried slowly in a cool place. Either lift the whole plant and hang it up or pick off the pods and dry them on a tray or newspaper. Beans can be collected and stored in airtight jars until required. They will need soaking for 24 hours before use. Storage areas should be frost-free. Chillies, green peppers, garlic and onions can be hung indoors where there is good air circulation. Peppers, tomatoes and mushrooms can be cut into sections and sun-dried outdoors where conditions allow, otherwise in the gentle heat of an airing cupboard or above a radiator.

Herbs

The object of drying herbs is to eliminate the water content of the plant quickly and, at the same time, to retain the essential oils. Herbs need to be dried in a warm, dark, dry and well-ventilated place. The faster they dry, the better the aromatic oils are retained. Darkness helps to prevent loss of colour and unique flavours. The area must be dry, with a good air flow, to hasten the drying process and to discourage mould.

Suitable places for drying herbs include: an airing cupboard; attic space immediately under the roof (provided it does not get too hot); in the oven at a low temperature and with the door ajar (place the herbs on a brown piece of paper with holes punched in it and check regularly that the

Grape vines growing in a glasshouse

herbs are not over-heating; a plate-warming compartment; a spare room with curtains shut and door open. The temperature should be kept at 21–33°C/ 70–90°F.

Herb leaves should always be dried separately from each other, especially the more strongly scented ones. Spread them in a single layer on trays or slatted wooden racks covered with muslin or netting. Place the trays or frames in the drying areas so that they have good air circulation. Turn the herbs over by hand several times during the first two days.

Roots require a higher temperature – from 50–60°C/120–140°F. They dry more quickly and easily in an oven and require regular turning until they are fragile and break easily. Seed should be dried without any artificial heat and in an airy place. Almost-ripe seed heads can be hung in paper bags (plastic causes them to sweat) so the majority of

seeds will fall into the bag as they mature. They need to be dried thoroughly before storing and the process can take up to two weeks.

An alternative method for flowers, roots or seed heads is to tie them in small bundles of 8 to 10 stems. Do not pack the stems too tightly together. Then hang them on coat-hangers in an airy, dark room until they are dry.

The length of drying time varies from herb to herb, and week to week. The determining factor is the state of the plant material. If herbs are stored before drying is complete, moisture will be reabsorbed from the atmosphere and the herb will soon deteriorate. Leaves should be both brittle and crisp. They should break easily into small pieces but should not reduce to a powder when touched. The roots should be brittle and dry right through. Any soft-ness or sponginess means they are not sufficiently dry and, if stored, will rot.

It is possible to dry herbs by microwave, but easy to over-dry and cook the leaves to the point of complete disintegration. Small-leafed herbs such as rosemary and thyme take about 1 minute, whilst the larger, moist leaves of mint dry in about 3 minutes. Add an eggcupful of water to the microwave during the process.

Herbs lose their flavour and colour if not stored properly. Pack the leaves or roots, not too tightly, into a dark glass jar with an air-tight screw top. Label with name and date. Keep in a dark cupboard; nothing destroys the quality of the herb quicker at this stage than exposure to light.

After the initial storing, keep a check on the jars for several days. If moisture starts to form on the inside of the container, the herbs have not been dried correctly. Return them to the drying area and allow further drying time.

Most domestic herb needs

are comparatively small so there is little point in storing large amounts for a long time. The shelf life of dried herbs is only about one year so it is sufficient to keep enough just for the winter.

If you have large, dark jars, thyme and rosemary can be left on the stalk. This makes it easier to use them in casseroles and stews and to remove before serving.

Fruit
Many fruits can be dried if they are sliced thinly and exposed to warm, dry air. Sealed in dark containers and kept cool and dry, they keep for long periods to be eaten, dried or reconstituted, when required. However, in the UK, and much of maritime Europe and North America, the air is too humid and so drying is not quick enough, not helped by the low temperatures in these regions. Solar-powered dryers – simply wire trays under glass – with good ventilation, allow fruit to be

Redcurrants preserve well

dried to a larger extent, but in the highest humidity regions the fruit may still go mouldy before it dries.

Slicing the fruit thinly and hanging the pieces, separated by at least half their own diameter, on long strings over a cooking range provides the dry warmth and ventilation needed to desiccate most within a day or two, or even just overnight for the easier ones such as apple.

Oven-drying with artificial heat is risky as it can cook the fruit. It is possible, however, if the temperature is kept down and the door kept partly open. It may be convenient to finish off partly dried samples in the cooling oven after you have finished baking. The dying heat desiccates fruit well with little risk of caramelizing.

FREEZING
Vegetables
Only the best-quality vegetables should be frozen, and they should always be thoroughly cleaned and carefully packed. Vegetables should be fast-frozen. Most freezers have a fast-freeze switch, and keep the freezer door closed during freezing. Do not open the freezer door regularly or leave it open longer than necessary. Many vegetables need to be blanched before freezing, and others need to be shredded, puréed or diced, or frozen when young. See under individual vegetables for details.

Herbs
Freezing is great for culinary herbs as colour, flavour and the nutritional value of the fresh young leaves are retained, and it is quick and easy. It is far better to freeze herbs such as fennel, dill, parsley, tarragon and chives than to dry them.

Pick the herbs and, if necessary, rinse with cold water, and shake dry before freezing, being careful not to bruise the leaves. Put small amounts of herbs into labelled, plastic bags, either singly, or as a mixture for bouquet garnis. Either have a set place in the freezer for them or put the bags into a container, so that they do not get damaged with the day-to-day use of the freezer.

There is no need to thaw herbs before use; simply add them to the cooking as required. For chopped parsley and other fine-leaved herbs, freeze the bunches whole in bags and, when you remove them from the freezer, crush the parsley in its bag with your hand.

Another way to freeze herbs conveniently is to put finely chopped leaves into an ice-cube tray and top them up with water. The average cube holds 1 tablespoon chopped herbs and 1 teaspoon water. The flowers of borage and leaves of variegated mints look very attractive frozen individually in ice-cubes for drinks or fruit salads.

Fruits
Most fruits freeze easily with little preparation. Obviously only the best are worth freezing as few fruits are improved by the process! Most fruits turn soggy when defrosted, but they are still packed full of sweetness, flavour and vitamins so are well worth having for culinary use, especially in tarts, pies, sauces and compôtes. A mixture of frozen fruits is marvellous if they are dechilled but not totally defrosted, so they retain their frozen texture like pieces of sorbet, served with cream.

For most fruits, merely putting them in sealed freezer bags or boxes is sufficient. However they then tend to freeze in a block. If you freeze them loose on open wire drying trays or greased baking trays, they can be packed afterwards and will stay separate. Fruits that are cut or damaged need to be drained first or, if you have a sweet tooth, they can be dredged in sugar, which absorbs the juice, before freezing them.

Stone fruits are best de-stoned before freezing as the stone can give an almond taint otherwise. The tough skins of fruits such as plums are most easily removed after freezing and before use. Carefully squeeze the frozen fruit under very hot water, when the skin will slip off.

Fruits lose value slowly in the freezer. The longer they are frozen the less use they are nutritionally.

JUICING
Not all fruits can be juiced, but the majority can be squeezed to express the juice, or heated or frozen to break down the texture then strained. Sugar may be added to taste as it improves the colour, flavour and keeping qualities. When the juice remains unheated, honey may be substituted, though it has a strong flavour of its own. Sweet juices such as apple can be mixed with tart ones like plum.

Fruit juices may be drunk as they are, added to cocktails, drunk as squashes diluted with water, and used in cooking. Grapes are the easiest to press and the most rewarding; they are best crushed first to break the skins. Most of the currants and berries can be squeezed in the same way. Apples and pears must be crushed first and then squeezed; they will go through the same juicing equipment as grapes, but more slowly than the more juicy fruits.

Pulpy, firm fruits such as blackcurrants and plums are best simmered with water till they soften then the juice can be strained off. If you repeat the process and add sugar to the combined juices you also have the basis for jellies. Raspberries, strawberries and fruits with similar delicate flavours are best frozen then defrosted and strained, to obtain a pure juice unchanged by heating.

Suitable equipment for processing large amounts of fruit is widely available if the quantities are too large for kitchen tools.

Commercially juices are passed through microfine filters or flash pasteurized. At home they will ferment rapidly in the warm, last longer if kept cool in the refrigerator, and keep for

OILS, VINEGARS AND PRESERVES

HERB OILS

These can be used in salad dressings, marinades, sauces, stir-fry dishes and sautéing. To start with, you need a clean glass jar, large enough to hold 500ml/³/₄ pint/2 cups with a screw top.

Basil oil

This is one of the best ways of storing and capturing the unique flavour of basil.

4 tablespoons/¹/₃ cup basil leaves
500ml/³/₄ pint/2 cups olive or
*   sunflower oil*

Pick over the basil, remove the leaves from the stalks, and crush them in a mortar. Pound very slightly. Add a little oil and pound gently again. This bruises the leaves, releasing their own oil into the oil. Mix the leaves with the rest of the oil, pour into a wide-necked jar and seal tightly. Place the jar on a sunny windowsill. Shake it every other day; and, after 2 weeks, strain through muslin into a decorative bottle and add a couple of fresh leaves of the relevant basil. This helps to identify the type of basil used and also looks fresh and enticing. Label.

Adapt for dill, fennel (green), sweet marjoram, rosemary and garden or lemon thyme. Garlic makes a very good oil. Use 4 cloves of garlic, peeled and crushed, and combined with the oil.

Bouquet garni oil

1 tablespoon sage
1 tablespoon lemon thyme
1 tablespoon Greek oregano
1 tablespoon French parsley
1 bay leaf
500ml/³/₄ pint/2cups olive or
*   sunflower oil*

Break all the leaves and mix them together in a mortar, pounding lightly. Add a small amount of the oil to mix well, allowing the flavours to infuse. Pour into a wide-necked jar with the remaining oil. Cover and leave on a sunny windowsill for 2–3 weeks. Either shake or stir the jar every other day. Strain through muslin into an attractive bottle. If there is room, add a fresh sprig of each herb used.

SWEET OILS

Good with fruit dishes, marinades and puddings. Use almond oil, which combines well with scented flowers such as pinks, lavender, lemon verbena, rose petals and scented geraniums. Make as for savoury oils above. Mix 4 tablespoons of torn petals or leaves with 500ml/³/₄ pint/2 cups almond oil.

SPICE OILS

Ideal for salad dressings, they can be used for sautéing and stir-frying too. The most suitable herb spices are: coriander seeds, dill seeds and fennel seeds. Combine 2 tablespoons of seeds with 500ml/³/₄pint/2 cups olive or sunflower oil, having first pounded the seeds gently to crush them in a mortar and mixed them with a little of the oil. Add a few of the whole seeds to the oil before bottling and labelling. Treat as for savoury oils and store.

HERBAL VINEGARS

These can be used in gravies and sauces, marinades and salad dressings. A time-saving recipe follows:

1 bottle white wine vinegar
*   (500ml/³/₄ pint/2 cups)*

4 large sprigs herb
4 garlic cloves, peeled

Pour off a little vinegar from the bottle and push in 2 sprigs of herb and the garlic cloves. Top up with the reserved vinegar if necessary. Reseal the bottle and leave on a sunny windowsill for 2 weeks. Change the herb sprigs for fresh ones and the vinegar is ready to use.

Seed vinegar

Make as for herb vinegar, but the amounts used are 2 tablespoons of seeds to 600ml/ 1 pint/2¹/₂ cups white wine or cider vinegar. Dill, fennel and coriander seeds make well-flavoured vinegars.

Floral vinegar

Made in the same way, these are used for fruit salads and cosmetic recipes. Combine elder, nasturtiums, sweet violets, pinks, lavender, primrose, rose petals, rosemary or thyme flowers in the following proportions:

10 tablespoons torn flower heads
*   or petals*
500ml/³/₄ pint/2 cups white
*   wine vinegar*

Pickled horseradish

Wash and scrape the skin off a good size horseradish root. Mince in a food processor or grate it (if you can stand it!). Pack into small jars and cover with salted vinegar made from 1 teaspoon salt to ¹/₂ pint cider or white wine vinegar. Seal and leave for 4 weeks before using.

SAVOURY HERB JELLY

Use the following herbs: sweet marjoram, mints (all kinds), rosemary, sage, summer savory, tarragon and common thyme.
Makes 2 x 350g/12oz jars

1kg/2lb tart cooking apples
*   or crab apples, roughly*
*   chopped, cores and all*
900ml/1¹/₂ pints/3³/₄ cups water
500g/1lb/2 cups sugar
2 tablespoons wine vinegar
2 tablespoons lemon juice
1 bunch herbs, approx 15g/¹/₂oz/
*   4 tablespoons chopped herbs*

Put the apples into a large pan with the bunch of herbs and cover with cold water in a preserving pan. Bring to the boil and simmer until the apples are soft, roughly 30 minutes. Pour into a jelly bag and drain overnight.

Measure the strained juice and add 500g/1lb sugar to every 600ml/1 pint fluid. Stir over gentle heat until the sugar has dissolved. Bring to the boil, stirring, and boil until setting point is reached. This takes roughly 20–30 minutes. Skim the surface scum and stir in the vinegar and lemon juice and the chopped herbs. Pour into jars, seal and label before storing.

SWEET JELLIES

Follow the above recipe, omitting the vinegar and lemon juice, and adding 150ml/¹/₄ pint/1 cup water. The following make interesting sweet jellies: bergamot, lavender flower, lemon verbena, scented geranium and sweet violet.

PRESERVES

Chutneys and pickles are a traditional method of preserving, and the perfect solution to harvest-time gluts in the fruit and vegetable gardens. Some recipes with regional and personal variations such as piccalilli, pickled onions and mango chutney have become legendary. Others, like runner bean chutney are reserved for small-scale production. They are the ideal accompaniment for cold meats, pies and other traditional fare, and are one of the best ways to maximize the variety and flavour from home-grown produce.

Coriander chutney

Makes 2 x 500g/1lb jars

1kg/2lb cooking apples, peeled, cored and sliced
500g/1lb onions, peeled and roughly chopped
2 cloves garlic, peeled and crushed
1 red and 1 green pepper, deseeded and sliced
900ml/1 1/2 pints/3 3/4 cups red wine vinegar
500g/1lb soft brown sugar
1/2 tablespoon whole coriander seeds
6 peppercorns tied securely in a piece of muslin
6 all-spice berries
50g/2oz root ginger, peeled and sliced
2 tablespoons coriander leaves, chopped
2 tablespoons mint, chopped

Combine the apples with the onions, garlic and peppers in a large, heavy saucepan. Add the vinegar and bring to the boil, simmering for about 30 minutes until all the ingredients are soft. Add the brown sugar and the muslin bag of seeds and berries. Then add the ginger. Heat, gently stirring all the time, until the sugar has dissolved, and simmer until thick; this can take up to 60 minutes. Stir in the chopped coriander and mint and spoon into hot, sterilized jars. Seal and label when cool.

JELLYING AND JAMMING FRUITS

These methods preserve the fruit in sugar gel. Jelly is made from the juice only, without the seeds and skins, while jam is made with and often also contains whole fruits or pieces thereof. A conserve is expensive jam, usually implying more fruit and less sugar or filler.

Almost any fruit can be jammed or jellied and many fruits are only palatable if so treated. The fruit is cooked to the point when the cells break up so that the juices run. The juice is then turned to a gel with sugar, which acts as a preservative as well. Most fruits need to have up to their own weight of sugar added to them to make a setting gel.

With jellies, the juice is often augmented with the squeezings of the fruit pulp reheated with some water. This thinner part then needs proportionately more sugar to set. Jellies are made from the strained juice and these washings, so they set clear and bright and are appreciated by many as there are no seeds etc. It is easy to pick and prepare fruits for jelly as the odd sprig, hard or under-ripe fruit or bit of leaf will be strained out.

Many prefer the textures (and the nutritional value) of jams with the seeds and skins etc. But these require much more careful picking and preparation.

White sugar is usually used for jamming and jellying unless a strong flavour is required. Honey is not really successful as the flavour is strong and it goes off when heated as much as is needed for jam. Concentrated juices can add too much flavour. The amount of fruit can be increased and the sugar decreased if your technique is good and you can eat the jam quickly!

Ideally, simmer down the fruit with the absolute minimum of water, strain if it is for jelly, add the sugar, bring to a boil, skim off any scum and pot in sterile conditions. Hot jars and clean lids put on immediately improve results. Store, once cold, in a dark, cool place.

Some fruits are difficult to set, particularly strawberries in a wet year. Adding chopped apples to the jelly fruits or their purée to the jams will supply the pectin needed to make any jam set. Extra acidity to bring out the piquant flavour of some jams is often achieved using lemon juice. Whitecurrant juice is a good substitute and redcurrant even better, especially where the colour is also an advantage. Adding white- or redcurrant juice also aids the setting of difficult jams. Their flavour is so tart yet mild that their jellies make good carriers for more strongly flavoured fruits in shorter supply, especially for raspberries and cherries.

A key tip: it is far quicker and easier to make four 2.5kg (5lb) batches of jam than one 5kg (11lb) batch – and the result is always better. Large batches have a low heating and evaporating surface compared to their volume and take much longer to process so the fruit degrades more.

Basil oil, coriander seed vinegar and coriander oil all make delicious additions to the store cupboard

NATURAL DYES

Herbs, vegetables and fruits have been used to dye cloth since the earliest records. In fact, until the 19th century and the birth of the chemical industry, all dyes were 'natural'. Then the chemical process, offering a larger range of colours and a more guaranteed result, took over. Now, once again, there is a real demand for more natural products and colours, which has resulted in a revival of interest in plants as a dye source.

Herbs offer the widest range of dyes, and the most common dyeing herbs are listed in the dye chart below. You will notice that yellows, browns and greys are predominant. Plenty of plant material will be required, so be careful not to over-pick in your own garden. To begin with, keep it simple. Pick the flowers just as they are coming out, the leaves when they are young and fresh and a good green; dig up roots in the autumn and cut them up well before use.

Few vegetables contain plant juices with residual colours; all must be used with a mordant and the colour varies according to the type used. There are three particularly worth trying. Juices of beetroot, although notorious for staining skin, produce drab brown or fawn when used for dyeing. The papery brown skins of onion bulbs are needed in large quantities for dyeing and produce colours ranging from pale yellow to a copper brown; although bold, these colours tend to fade rapidly when exposed to light. The 'flags' or foliage of leeks produce yellow and dull brown pigments.

Apple, pear and cherry barks yield dyes in shades of yellow, as do the roots and stems of berberis, while reddish-yellows come from pine cones. Walnuts stain everything they touch and need no mordant to help fix their dye, which can be obtained from the roots, leaves and husks. Elder bark with an iron mordant gives a black dye, the leaves with an alum mordant give a green dye and the berries produce shades of purple, blue and lilac, often used as hair dyes. Rowan berries give a black dye, plums and sloes a blue dye, and their bark yields a red-brown colourant, while junipers give an olive brown.

HERB DYE CHART

Common Name	Botanical Name	Part Used	Mordant	Colour
Comfrey	*Symphytum officinale*	Leaves and stalks	Alum	Yellows
Chamomile, Dyer's	*Anthemis tinctoria*	Flowers	Alum	Yellows
Chamomile, Dyer's	*Anthemis tinctoria*	Flowers	Copper	Olives
Elder	*Sambucus nigra*	Leaves	Alum	Greens
Elder	*Sambucus nigra*	Berries	Alum	Violets/purple
Goldenrod	*Solidago canadensis*	Whole plant	Chrome	Golden yellows
Horsetail	*Equisetum arvense*	Stems and leaves	Alum	Yellows
Juniper	*Juniperus communis*	Crushed berries	Alum	Yellows
Marigold	*Calendula officinalis*	Petals	Alum	Pale yellow
Meadowsweet	*Filipendula ulmaria*	Roots	Alum	Black
Nettle	*Urtica dioica*	Whole plant	Copper	Greyish-green
St John's Wort	*Hypericum perforatum*	Flowers	Alum	Beiges
Sorrel	*Rumex acetosa*	Whole plant	Alum	Dirty yellow
Sorrel	*Rumex acetosa*	Roots	Alum	Beige/pink
Tansy	*Tanacetum vulgare*	Flowers	Alum	Yellows
Woad	*Isatis tinctoria*	Leaves	Sodium dithionite, ammonia	Blues

FABRIC

Any natural material can be dyed, some are more tricky than others. It just takes time and practice. The following sections explain the techniques connected with dyeing wool, the most reliable and easiest of natural materials. Silk, linen and cotton can also be dyed, but are more difficult.

PREPARATION

First time, this is a messy and fairly lengthy process, so protect all areas. Best of all, keep it away from the home altogether. Some of the mordants used for fixing dye are poisonous, so keep them well away from children, pets and food.

The actual dyeing process is not difficult, but you will need a few special pieces of equipment, and space.

1 large stainless steel vessel, such as a preserving can (to be used as the dye-bath)

The flowers of St John's wort produce a beige dye

- 1 stainless steel or enamel bucket and bowl
- 1 pair of tongs (wooden or stainless steel; to be used for lifting)
- 1 measuring jug
- 1 pair rubber gloves essential for all but Jumblies – 'Their heads are green and their hands are blue, And they went to sea in a sieve.'
- Pestle and mortar
- Thermometer
- Water; this must be soft, either rainwater or filtered
- Scales

Dyeing comprises four separate tasks: preparation of the material (known as scouring); preparation of the mordant; preparation of the dye; dyeing process

PREPARATION OF THE MATERIAL

Prepare the wool by washing it in a hot solution of soap flakes or a proprietary scouring agent in order to remove any grease. Always handle the wool gently. Rinse it several times, squeezing (gently) between each rinse. On the final rinse add 50ml (2fl oz) of vinegar.

PREPARATION OF THE MORDANT

Mordants help 'fix' the dye to the fabric. They are available from chemists or dye suppliers. The list below includes some of the more common. Some natural dyers say that one should not use mordants, but without them the dye will run very easily.

Alum: Use 25g (1oz) to 500g (1lb) dry wool

This is the most useful of mordants, its full title being potassium aluminium sulphate. Sometimes potassium hydrogen tartrate, cream of tartar, is added (beware! this is not the baking substance) to facilitate the process and brighten the colour.

Iron: Use 5g (⅛oz) to 500g (1lb) dry wool

This is ferrous sulphate. It dulls and deepens the colours. It is added in the final process after first using the mordant alum. Remove the wool before adding the iron, then replace the wool and simmer until you get the depth of colour required.

Copper: Use 15g (½oz) to 500g (1lb) dry wool

This is copper sulphate. If you mix with 300ml (½ pint) of vinegar when preparing the mordant it will give a blue/green tint to colours. WARNING: Wear gloves – copper is poisonous.

Chrome: Use 15g (½oz) to 500g (1lb) dry wool

This is bichromate of potash and light-sensitive, so keep it in the dark. It gives the colour depth, makes the colours fast, and gives the wool a soft, silky feel. WARNING: Wear gloves – chrome is poisonous.

Dissolve the mordant in a little hot water. Stir this into 20 litres (4 gallons) of hot water at 50°C (122°F). When thoroughly dissolved immerse the wet, washed wool in the mixture. Make sure it is wholly immersed. Slowly bring to the boil and simmer at 82–94°C (180–200°F) for an hour. Remove it from the heat, then take the wool out of the water and rinse.

PREPARATION OF THE DYE

No two batches of natural dye will be the same. There are so many variable factors – plant variety, water, mordant, immersion time.

The amount of plant material required for dyeing is very variable. A good starting ratio is 500g (1lb) of mordanted wool in skeins to 500g (1lb) plant material.

Chop or crush the plant material. Place it loosely in a muslin or nylon bag and tie the bag securely. Leave it to soak in 20 litres (4 gallons) of soft, tepid water overnight. Slowly bring the water and herb material to the boil. Reduce the heat and simmer at 82–94°C (180–200°F) for as long as it takes to get the water to the desired colour. This can take between 1 and 3 hours. Remove the pan from the heat, remove the herb material, and allow the liquid to cool to hand temperature.

DYEING PROCESS

Gently add the wool to the dye mixture. Bring the water slowly to the boil, stirring it occasionally with the wooden tongs. Allow it to simmer for a further hour, then remove the pan from the heat and leave the wool in the dye-bath until it is cold, or until the colour is right. Remove the wool with the tongs and rinse in tepid water until no colour runs out. Give it a final rinse in cold water. Dry the skeins of wool over a rod or cord, away from direct heat. Tie a light weight to the bottom to stop the wool kinking during the drying process.

THE YEARLY CALENDAR

This calendar assumes that the garden is situated in northern Europe, the average date of the last major frost in spring being early April, and an average date for the first frost being mid- to late October. Gardeners with different frost dates can adjust this calendar accordingly. But as any gardener knows, you cannot be precise. Each year is different, wetter, windier, hotter, drier, colder. So use this calendar as a general guide.

JANUARY
Midwinter

Look back over the previous year, at successes and mishaps, and plan for the following season. Think about any structural changes as well as ordering seeds and plants. Keep an eye out for any weather damage in the garden, checking especially after heavy frost, snow and gales.

Vegetables
Prepare cropping plants. Lime autumn-dug plots if necessary. Place early seed potatoes in shallow boxes with 'eyes' uppermost, and store in a light, frost-free place. Towards the end of the month, plant out shallots if soil is moist enough.

Under cover, sow radishes and carrots in growbags or in the borders of a cold glasshouse; sow lettuce for growing under cloches, and leeks.

Herbs
This is one of the quietest months. Keep an eye on the degrees of frost and protect

Vines sprouting in spring from woody stock

tender herbs with an extra layer of agricultural fleece or mulch if necessary.

With a little bit of protection in the garden, bay, hyssop, rosemary, sage, winter savory, thyme, lemon thyme, chervil and parsley can be picked.

Start parsley seed with heat. Outside, if not sown in the autumn, sow sweet cicely, sweet woodruff and cowslip, to enable a period of stratification. Force chives, mint and tarragon in boxes in the greenhouse.

Keep watering of containers to a minimum. Clean old pots ready for the spring 'pot up'.

Fruit
Make a health and hygiene check and examine each plant in your care for pests, diseases and dieback. Check stores, remove and use any fruits starting to deteriorate before they go over and infect others.

FEBRUARY
Late winter

As the days lengthen, and if the weather is not too unpleasant, this is a good time to have the final tidy up before the busy season starts. If you want to get an

early start in the garden and you have prepared a site the previous autumn, cover the soil now with black polythene. It will warm up the soil and force any weeds.

Vegetables
Sow broad beans, early peas and spinach. Sow early-maturing cabbage and cauliflowers in pots from the middle of the month on. 'Chit' maincrop potatoes. Sow cabbages, carrots, lettuces and radishes under cloches or in a polytunnel.

Herbs
With a little bit of protection in the garden, bay, hyssop, rosemary, sage, winter savory, thyme, lemon thyme, chervil and parsley can be harvested. Chives start to come up if they are under protection, and mint can be available if forced.

Start borage, dill and parsley seeds with heat, and sow chervil in a cold greenhouse.

Herbaceous perennial herbs, including chives, lemon balm, pot marjoram, mints, oregano, broad-

Ladybirds on blackcurrants

leafed sorrel and tarragon, can be divided now, as long as they are not too frozen and are given added protection after replanting.

As the containers have been brought in for the winter, new life may be starting. Dust off, and slowly start watering.

Outside, check that any dead or decaying herbaceous growth is not damaging plants. Check for wind and snow damage.

Fruit
Check stores, remove and use any fruits starting to deteriorate before they go over and infect others. Spread a good layer of compost or well-rotted manure under and around everything possible and add a good layer of mulch, preferably immediately after a period of heavy rain.

Lime most grass swards one year in four, more often on acid soil, but not amongst ericaceous plants or lime-haters! Once ground becomes workable, plant out hardy trees and shrubs that missed the autumn planting. Sow the very earliest crops for growing under cover. Ensure good weed control, hoeing fortnightly or adding extra mulches on top.

Do major pruning work to trees and bushes missed earlier or damaged in winter (but not stone fruits or evergreens). Prune autumn-fruiting raspberries to the ground.

Spray everything growing with diluted seaweed solution at least once a month, and anything with deficiency symptoms more often. Spray peaches and almonds with Bordeaux mixture to protect against peach-leaf curl.

Examine each plant in your care for pests, diseases and dieback. Apply sticky bands and inspect the sacking bands on apple trees, and others if they suffered from many pests.

Check straps and stakes after gales. On still, cold nights protect the blossoms and young fruitlets from frost damage with net curtains, plastic sheeting or newspaper.

MARCH
Early spring
Gradually uncover tender plants outside and look for hopeful signs of life. Give them a gentle tidy.

Vegetables
Plant onion sets in prepared ground. Sow beetroot, cabbage, carrots, parsnip, lettuce and maincrop peas.

Plant lettuce under cloches or in plastic tunnels, sow salad onions in grow-bags in an unheated glasshouse for early crops. Sow early cabbages and cauliflowers under glass for transplanting in mid-April and tomatoes from late March to early April.

Herbs
Herbs available for picking include angelica, lemon balm, bay, chives, fennel, hyssop, mint, parsley, peppermint, pennyroyal, rue, sage, savory, sorrel and thyme.

Towards the end of the month start borage, fennel, coriander, sweet marjoram, rue and basil seeds with heat. In a cold greenhouse sow chervil, chives, dill, lemon balm, lovage, parsley, sage, summer savory and sorrel. Outside in the garden sow chervil, chives, parsley (cover with cloches), chamomile, tansy, caraway, borage and fennel.

Check seeds that have been left outside from the previous autumn for stratification. If they are

starting to germinate, move them into a cold greenhouse.

Take root cuttings from mint, tarragon, bergamot, chamomile, hyssop, tansy, sweet woodruff and sweet cicely. Divide mint, tarragon, wormwood, lovage, rue, sorrel, lemon balm, salad burnet, camphor plant, thyme, winter savory, marjoram, alecost, horehound and pennyroyal. This is a good time to start mound layering on old sages or thymes.

Tidy up all the pots, trim old growth to maintain shape. Start liquid feeding with seaweed. Re-pot if necessary. Pot up new plants into containers for display later in the season.

In the garden, clear up all the winter debris, fork the soil over and give a light dressing of bonemeal. If your soil is alkaline, and you gave it a good dressing of manure in the autumn, now is the time to dig it well in.

Remove black polythene, weed and place a cloche over important sowing sites a week before sowing to raise the soil temperature and keep it dry.

Towards the end of the month, if the major frosts are over, you can cut

lavender back and into shape. This is certainly advisable for plants two years old and older. Give them a good mulch. Equally, sage bushes of two years and older would benefit from a trim, but not hard back. Cut back elder and rosemary, neither of which minds a hard cutting back. Transplant the following if they need it: alecost, chives, mint, balm, pot marjoram, sorrel, horehound and rue.

Fruit
Continue to spread a good layer of compost or well-rotted manure under and around everything possible. Spread wood ashes under and around plants, giving priority to gooseberries and culinary apples. Plant out evergreen and the more tender hardy plants. Protect them from frost and wind the first season. Sow plants grown under cover or for later planting out.

Maintain good weed control by hoeing fortnightly or adding extra mulch on top. Cut the grass at least fortnightly, preferably weekly, returning the clippings or raking them into rings around trees and bushes.

Spray everything growing

Comfrey 'Goldsmith' nestling in a shady corner makes an attractive border plant

with diluted seaweed solution at least once a month, and anything with deficiency symptoms more often. Spray peaches and almonds with Bordeaux mixture against peach-leaf curl. Make a health and hygiene check on each plant in your care for pests, diseases and dieback.

Prune back tender plants and evergreens. Protect the new growth against frost afterwards. Pollinate early-flowering plants and those under cover by hand. On still, cold nights protect the blossoms and young fruitlets from frost damage with net curtains, plastic sheet or newspaper.

APRIL
Mid-spring
This is the main month for sowing outdoors, as soon as soil conditions permit. It is also now possible to prune back to strong new shoots the branches of any shrubs that have suffered in winter.

Vegetables
Dig plots occupied by winter greens and prepare for leeks; plant maincrop potatoes, cabbages and cauliflowers (sown under cover in March). Make further sowings of beetroot, radishes, spinach, carrots, cauliflower, maincrop peas, broad beans and parsnips. Sow iceberg lettuce, salad onions and seakale. From late April, sow winter cauliflower, Savoy cabbage, kale and broccoli into seedbeds. Transplant cabbages and cauliflowers sown in nursery beds in February. Pinch out the growing tips of flowering broad beans.

Tomatoes sown and pricked out in late March or early April should be transferred to a cold frame and hardened off. Sow marrows, squashes and sweetcorn at the end of the month. Prepare greenhouse borders or growbags for tomatoes, and plant towards the end of the month.

Herbs
Herbs available for picking include: angelica, balm, bay, borage, caraway, chervil, chives, fennel, hyssop, lovage, pot marjoram, mints, parsley, pennyroyal, peppermint, rosemary, sage, winter savory, sorrel, thyme, tarragon and lemon thyme.

Start basil seeds with heat. In the cold greenhouse sow borage, chervil, coriander, dill, fennel, lemon balm, lovage, pot marjoram, sweet marjoram, sage, summer savory, winter savory, sorrel, buckler leaf sorrel, horehound, rue, bergamot, caraway and garden thyme. Outside in the garden sow parsley, chives, hyssop, caraway and pot marigold. Prick out the previous month's sown seeds, pot on, or harden off before planting out.

Take softwood cuttings of rue, mint, sage, southernwood, winter savory, thymes, horehound, lavender, rosemary, cotton lavender and curry. Take root cuttings of sweet cicely, fennel and mint. Divide pennyroyal, chives, lady's mantle, salad burnet and tarragon.

You should be able to put all containers outside now; keep an eye on the watering and feeding. In the garden, if all the frosts have

finished, the following will need cutting and pruning into shape: bay, winter savory, hyssop, cotton lavender, lavenders, rue especially variegated rue, southernwood and thymes.

Fruit
Ensure good weed control, hoeing weekly or adding extra mulch on top. Cut the grass at least weekly, returning the clippings or raking them into rings around trees and bushes. Sow plants grown under cover or for later planting out. Plant out more tender hardy plants under cover or with protection.

Spread a good layer of mulch under and around everything possible, and spread wood ashes under and around fruit trees, giving priority to gooseberries and culinary apples. Spray everything growing with diluted seaweed solution at least once a month, and anything with deficiency symptoms more often.

Water all new plants established within the previous twelve months whenever there has been little rain. De-flower or de-fruit new plants to give them time to establish. Pollinate plants under cover by hand. Tie in new growths of vines and climbing plants. Make a health and hygiene check weekly and examine each plant in your care for pests,

diseases and dieback. On still, cold nights protect the blossoms and young fruitlets from frost damage with net curtains, plastic sheet or newspaper. Make layers of difficult subjects.

MAY
Late spring
Vegetables
Sow French and runner beans, Chinese cabbage, carrots, courgettes, outdoor cucumbers, lettuce, turnips, spinach and parsley. Plant out celeriac, celery, sweetcorn, and summer cabbage. Harvest asparagus, broad beans, cauliflowers, peas, radish and spinach. Earth up potatoes. Under cover, transplant aubergines, outdoor cucumbers, tomatoes, peppers and sweetcorn.

Herbs
Everything should be growing quickly now. The annuals will need thinning; tender and half-hardy plants should be hardened off under a cold frame or by a warm wall. A watch must be kept for a sudden late frost; basil is especially susceptible. Move container specimens into bigger pots or top-dress with new compost.

Nearly all varieties of herbs are available for picking. Outside, keep sowing coriander, dill, chervil, parsley, sweet marjoram, basil, and any other annuals you require to maintain crops. Prick out and pot on or plant out any of the previous month's seedlings.

Take softwood cuttings of marjorams, all mints, oregano, rosemarys, winter savory, French tarragon and all thymes. Containers should now be looking good. Keep trimming to maintain shape; water and feed regularly. In the garden, trim southernwood

Prepared seedbed with a measuring rod for spacing rows

into shape.

Cut second-year growth of angelica for candying. Cut thyme before flowering to dry.

Fruit
Maintain good weed control. Sow plants grown under cover or outdoors. Plant out tender plants under cover or with protection. Pollinate plants under cover by hand. Cut the grass at least fortnightly, preferably weekly, returning the clippings or raking them into rings around trees and bushes.

Water all new plants established within the previous twelve months especially whenever there has been little rain. De-flower or de-fruit new plants. Spray everything growing with diluted seaweed solution at least once a month, and anything with deficiency symptoms more often.

Examine each plant twice weekly for pests, diseases and dieback. Tie in new growths of vine and climbing plants. On still, cold nights protect the blossoms and young fruitlets from frost damage with net curtains, plastic sheet or newspaper. Make layers of difficult subjects. Protect almost every ripening fruit from the birds.

JUNE
Early summer
Vegetables
Sow French and runner beans, Chinese cabbage, carrots, courgettes, outdoor cucumbers, lettuce, turnips, spinach and parsley. Transplant celery, summer cabbage and tomatoes. Harvest asparagus, broad beans, cauliflowers, calabrese, peas, radish, spinach and turnips. Under cover, transplant aubergines and sweetcorn; pollinate tomato plants.

Herbs

This is a great time in the herb garden. All planting is now completed. Plants are beginning to join up so that little further weeding will be needed. Many plants are now reaching perfection.

All herbs are available fresh. Outside in the garden sow basil, borage, chives, coriander, dill, fennel, sweet marjoram, summer savory, winter savory, and any others you wish to replace, or keep going.

With all the soft new growth available this is a very busy month for cuttings. Make sure you use material from non-flowering shoots. Take softwood cuttings of all perennial marjorams, all mints, all rosemary, all sage, variegated lemon balm, tarragon (French) and all thymes. Also divide thymes and layer rosemary.

Plant up annual herbs such as basil and sweet marjoram into containers to keep near the kitchen. If you must plant basil in the garden, do it now. Nip out the growing tips of this year's young plants to encourage them to bush out.

Trim cotton lavender hedges if flowers are not required and to maintain their shape; clip box hedges and topiary shapes as needed. A new herb garden should be weeded thoroughly to give the new plants the best chance.

Cut second-year growth of angelica for candying. Cut sage for drying.

Fruit

Maintain good weed control. Plant out the tender plants or move them out for summer. Cut the grass at least fortnightly, preferably weekly, returning the clippings or raking them into rings around trees and bushes. Raise the height of cut of your mower. Spray everything growing with diluted seaweed solution at least once a month, and anything with deficiency symptoms more often.

Water all new plants established within the previous twelve months especially whenever there has been little rain. Examine each plant twice weekly for pests, diseases and dieback.

Start summer pruning.

This applies to all red- and whitecurrants, gooseberries and all trained apples and pears. From one third of each plant, remove approximately half to three-quarters of each new shoot, except for leaders. Prune grapevines back to three or five leaves after a flower truss. Tie in new growths of vine and climbing plants.

Also begin fruit thinning. To do this, remove every diseased, decayed, damaged, misshapen, distorted and congested fruitlet. This applies to all apples, pears, peaches, apricots, quality plums, dessert grapes, gooseberries, figs and especially to trained forms. Compost or burn rejected fruitlets immediately. Of course usable ones, such as the larger gooseberries, may be consumed.

Take softwood cuttings if you have a propagator. Make layers of difficult subjects. Protect almost every ripening fruit from birds.

JULY
Midsummer
Vegetables

Sow final crops of beetroot, carrots, lettuce, turnips, spinach and parsley. Sow salad onions, spring cabbage and seakale for overwintering. Sow keeping onions in a seedbed for transplanting the following March. In colder districts, plant leeks sown in cold frames in January at the beginning of the month. Remove basal suckers from early trench celery, water well and earth up.

Under cover, harvest cucumbers and tomatoes regularly to encourage further fruiting, and pinch out the growing point when each stem contains about 5 or 6 trusses of fruit.

Herbs

The season is on the wane, the early annuals and biennials are beginning to go over. It is already time to think of next year and to start collecting seeds. Take cuttings of tender shrubs as spare shoots are available.

All herbs can be harvested fresh. Outside in the garden sow chervil, angelica (if seed is set), borage, coriander, dill, lovage and parsley. Take softwood cuttings of wormwood, scented geraniums, lavenders and the thymes. Layer rosemary. Keep an eye on watering of containers as the temperatures begin to rise.

Cut all lavenders back

Back row: **Curly wood sage** *Teucrium scorodonia* 'Crispum'; **Lawn Chamomile** *Chamaemelum nobile* 'Treneague'; front row: **Variegated Meadowsweet** *Filipendula ulmaria* 'Variegata'; **Houseleek** *Sempervivum tectorum*; **Dwarf Marjoram** *Origanum vulgare* 'Nanum'

after flowering to maintain their shape. If this is the first summer of the herb garden and the plants are not fully established it is important to make sure they do not dry out, so water regularly. Once established, many are tolerant of drought.

Harvest and dry lemon balm, horehound, summer savory, hyssop, tarragon, thyme and lavender. Use lavender and rosemary for dyeing and potpourris. Harvest seed of caraway and angelica.

Fruit
Maintain good weed control. Cut the grass at least fortnightly, preferably weekly, returning the clippings or raking them into rings around trees and bushes. Raise the height of cut of your mower. Spray everything growing with diluted seaweed solution at least once a month, and anything with deficiency symptoms more often. Water all new plants established within the previous twelve months especially whenever there has been little rain. Examine each plant in your care for pests, diseases and dieback. Tie in new growths of vines and climbing plants.

Continue summer pruning. For red- and whitecurrants, gooseberries and all trained apples and pears, from the second third of each plant remove approximately half to three-quarters of each new shoot,

except for leaders. Prune grapevines back to three or five leaves after a flower truss. Blackcurrants may have a third to half of the old wood removed after fruiting. Stone fruits are traditionally pruned now to avoid silver-leaf disease.

Continue to thin fruits as in June. Take softwood cuttings if you have a propagator, and root tips of the black and hybrid berries. Protect almost every ripening fruit from the birds.

AUGUST
Late summer
Vegetables
Sow turnips for spring 'greens' and Japanese onions for overwintering. Sow spring cabbage in nursery rows. To prevent wind-rock in autumn and winter, draw soil around the stems of winter greens, particularly Brussels sprouts, kale and broccoli. Earth up trench celery. Harvest maincrop onions, ensuring that the bulbs' outer skins are well-ripened before storing. Under cover, harvest cucumbers and tomatoes regularly and self-pollinate tomatoes.

Herbs
Traditionally a month for holidays but it is also time to harvest and preserve many herbs for winter use. Collect and dry material for potpourris, and collect seeds for sowing next year.

All herbs are available

Protect your fruit from birds!

fresh. In the garden or greenhouse sow angelica, coriander, dill, lovage, parsley, winter savory. Take softwood cuttings of bay, wormwood, rosemary, the thymes and lavenders, scented geraniums, balm of Gilead, pineapple sage and myrtles.

If you are going away, make sure you ask a friend to water your containers for you. Give box, cotton lavender and curry their second clipping and trim any established plants that are looking unruly. Maintain watering of the new herb garden and keep an eye on mints, parsley and comfrey, which need water to flourish. There is no real need to feed if the ground

Apart from being beautiful, butterflies are a useful addition to the garden

has been well prepared, but if the plants are recovering from a pest attack they will benefit from a foliar feed of liquid seaweed.

Harvest thyme, sage, clary sage, marjoram and lavender for drying. Pick the mints and pennyroyal to freeze. Gather basil to make a basil oil. Collect the seed of angelica, anise, caraway, coriander, cumin, chervil, dill and fennel.

Fruit
Maintain good weed control. Plant new strawberry plants, if you can get them. Cut the grass at least fortnightly, preferably weekly, returning the clippings or raking them into rings around trees and bushes. Lower the height of cut of your mower. Spray everything that is growing with diluted seaweed solution at least once a month, and anything that

has deficiency symptoms more often. Water all new plants established within the previous twelve months especially whenever there has been little rain. Sow green manures and winter ground cover on bare soil that is not mulched; grass down orchards. Check for pests, diseases and dieback, and apply sticky bands and sacking bands to apple trees, and to others if they suffer from many pests.

Finish summer pruning. For red- and whitecurrants, gooseberries and all trained apples and pears, for the last, unpruned third of each plant, remove approximately half to three-quarters of each new shoot, except for leaders. Prune grapevines back to three or five leaves after the fruit truss.

Thin fruits as in June. Protect almost every ripening fruit from the birds. Root the tips of the black- and hybrid berries.

SEPTEMBER
Early autumn
Vegetables
Order seed catalogues for the following year. Plant out spring cabbages into permanent positions. Sow spinach for harvesting in April. Lift maincrop carrots, beetroot and potatoes, and store in a cool, dark place: later sowings may be left in the ground. Earth up celery before severe frosts. Lift tomato plants with fruits still attached and store; ripen on straw under cloches or in the greenhouse. Wrap green fruits in paper and store in the dark.

Plant thinnings from late-sown salads in frames or under cloches to provide crops during winter. Lettuces reaching maturity should be covered with cloches or frames; sow further crops in a cold frame. The autumn is a good time to lay drains through waterlogged sites.

Herbs
By mid-month, basil should be taken up and leaves preserved. Line out semi-ripe cuttings of box, cotton lavenders, etc, in cold frames, under cloches or in polythene tunnels for hedge renewal in the spring.

Herbs that can be picked fresh include: lemon balm, basil, bay, borage, caraway, chervil, chives, clary sage, fennel, hyssop, pot marigold, marjoram, the mints, parsley, pennyroyal, peppermint, rosemarys, sages, winter savory, sorrels and the thymes. Sow outside in the garden or greenhouse angelica, chives, coriander, parsley and winter savory. Take softwood and semi-ripe cuttings of rosemary, the thymes, tarragon, the lavenders, rue, the cotton lavenders, the curry plants and box. Divide bergamot.

At the beginning of the month give the shrubby herbs their final clipping (bay, lavender, etc). Do not leave it too late or the frost could damage the new growth. Put basil into glasshouse or kitchen. Top-dress bergamots if they have died back. If lemon verbena is to be kept outside make sure it is getting adequate protection. Towards the end of this month take in all containers, and protect tender plants like bay trees, myrtles, and scented geraniums. Harvest dandelion (roots), parsley, marigold, clary sage and peppermint for drying or freezing. Collect seed of angelica, anise, caraway, chervil and fennel.

'Malling Jewel' raspberries

Fruit
Maintain good weed control. Plant out pot-grown specimens and those that can be dug with a decent rootball or moved with little disturbance. Cut the grass at least fortnightly, preferably weekly, returning the clippings and fallen leaves or raking them into rings around trees and bushes. Sow green manures and winter ground cover on bare soil that is not mulched; grass down orchards. Spray everything that is growing with diluted seaweed solution at least once a month, and anything that has deficiency symptoms more often.

Make a health and hygiene check for pests, diseases and dieback. Apply sticky bands and sacking bands to apple trees, and to others if they suffer from many pests. On still, cold nights protect ripening fruits from frost damage with net curtains, plastic sheet or newspaper. Protect first the tops then the stems and roots of more tender plants before frosts come. Bring indoors tender plants in pots or protect them. Take cuttings of plants as they start to drop their leaves. Prune early fruiting raspberries and hybrids, and blackcurrants and other plants as they start to drop their leaves. Protect almost every ripening fruit from the birds. Root the tips of the black- and hybrid berries.

Alpine strawberries and thyme on a low bank

Winter trap

OCTOBER
Mid-autumn
Vegetables
Lift potatoes, beet and carrots for storing. Tie onions on to ropes when the skins have thoroughly ripened. Transplant lettuces sown in July to a well-drained, protected site to overwinter. Plant root cuttings of seakale in pots of sand and leave them in a sheltered place until the spring. Cut down asparagus foliage as it turns yellow. Tidy the vegetable plot, removing all plant debris. Double-dig, adding organic matter, and lime if necessary.

Sow lettuce in greenhouse borders or growbags for cutting in the spring. Continue harvesting green tomatoes, storing in a dark, frost-free place to ripen. Clear growbags used for cucumbers, peppers and tomatoes in the summer and replant with winter lettuce.

Herbs
The best time in all but the coldest areas to plant hardy perennial herbs.

Basil, bay, borage, chervil, fennel, hyssop, marigold, marjoram, parsley, rosemary, sage, winter savory, sorrel and the thymes can all be picked fresh. Sow parsley seed with heat. In the garden sow catmint, chervil, wormwood, chamomile, fennel and angelica.

Take softwood and semi-ripe cuttings of bay, elder, hyssop, cotton lavender, southernwood, lavenders, the thymes, curry and box. Take root cuttings of tansy, pennyroyal, the mints and tarragon. Divide alecost, the marjorams, chives, lemon balm, lady's mantle, hyssop, bergamot, camphor plant, lovage, sorrel, sage, oregano and pennyroyal.

Start reducing the watering of containers. Clear the garden and weed it well. Cut down the old growth and collect any remaining seed heads. Cut back the mints, trim winter savory and hyssop. Give them all a leaf mould dressing. Dig up and remove the annuals, dill, coriander, borage, summer savory, sweet marjoram, and the second-year biennials, parsley, chervil, rocket etc. Protect with cloches or agricultural fleece any herbs to be used fresh through the winter, like parsley, chervil, lemon thyme, salad burnet. Dig up some French tarragon, pot up in trays for forcing and protection.

Check the pH of alkaline soil every third year. Dress with well-rotted manure to a depth of 5–10cm (2–4in) and leave the digging until the following spring. Dig over heavy soils; add manure to allow the frost to penetrate.

Fruit
Ensure good weed control. Plant out bare-rooted hardy trees and bushes if soil is in good condition and they are dormant. Cut the grass at least fortnightly, preferably weekly, collecting the clippings with the fallen leaves or raking them into rings around trees and bushes. Spray everything that is growing with diluted seaweed solution at least once a month, and anything that has deficiency symptoms more often.

Check plants for pests, diseases and dieback. Top up the sticky bands and inspect the sacking bands on apple trees, and on others if they suffered from many pests. Check straps

Espalier-trained peaches on a red brick wall

and stakes before the gales. On still, cold nights protect ripening fruits from frost damage with net curtains, plastic sheet or newspaper.

Take cuttings of hardy plants as they start to drop their leaves. Prune early-fruiting raspberries and hybrids, and blackcurrants and other plants as they start to drop their leaves. Protect first the tops then the stems and roots of more tender plants before frosts come. Check stores, remove and use any fruits starting to deteriorate before they go over and infect others. Protect almost every ripening fruit from the birds.

NOVEMBER
Late autumn
Vegetables
Sow broad beans, and round-seeded peas in the open: protect with cloches if necessary. Remove dying leaves from winter greens,

allowing air to circulate between plants. Check stored vegetables regularly and remove any showing signs of decay. Use those that are slightly damaged immediately. Sow green manure. Lift and store crowns of chicory as well as seakale.

Herbs
The days are getting shorter and frosts are starting. Planting of hardy herbaceous herbs can continue as long as soil remains unfrozen and in a workable condition.

Basil, bay, hyssop, marjoram, mint, parsley, rosemary, rue, sage and thyme are available to pick fresh. Sow the following so that they can get a good period of stratification: arnica (old seed), sweet woodruff, yellow iris, poppy, soapwort, sweet cicely, hops (old seed), sweet violet. Sow in trays, cover with glass and

'Bedford Giant' blackberry

Runner bean 'Painted Lady' climbing a decorative frame

leave outside in a cold frame or corner of the garden where they cannot get damaged.

Cut back on all watering of container-grown plants. Give them all a prune, so that they go into rest mode for the winter. This is the time for the final tidy up in the garden. Cut back the remaining plants, lemon balm, alecost, horehound, and give them a dressing of leaf mould. Give the elders a prune. Dig up a clump of mint and chives, put them in pots or trays and bring them into the greenhouse for forcing for winter use.

Fruit

Keep on top of weeds. Plant out bare-rooted hardy trees and bushes if the soil is in good condition and they are dormant. Cut the grass at least fortnightly, collecting the clippings with the fallen leaves or raking them into rings around trees and bushes. Check plants for pests, diseases and dieback. Top up the sticky bands and inspect the sacking bands on apple trees, and on others if they suffered from many pests.

Check straps and stakes before the gales. Spread a good layer of compost or well-rotted manure under and around everything possible, preferably after a period of heavy rain. On still, cold nights protect ripening fruits from frost damage with net curtains, plastic sheet or newspaper. Protect first the tops then the stems and roots of more tender plants before frosts come.

Take cuttings of hardy plants as they start to drop their leaves. Prune late fruiting raspberries, hybrid berries, currants and vines, trees and bushes as the leaves fall. Check stores, remove and use any fruits

starting to deteriorate before they go over and infect others. Protect almost every ripening fruit from the birds.

DECEMBER
Early winter
Vegetables

Plan next year's rotation of vegetables, ordering seeds as soon as possible. Prepare a seed-sowing schedule. Lift and store swede and late-sown carrots. If heavy falls of snow or prolonged frosts are forecast, lift small quantities of vegetables such as celery, leeks and parsnips and store under cover in a cool, easily accessible place. Finish digging before the soil becomes waterlogged. On clay soils, spread sand, old potting compost or well-rotted leaf mould on the surface and dig in as soon as conditions are favourable, allowing the frost to break down the soil. Sow green manures on sandy soils or cover with compost to reduce leaching.

Herbs

Bay, hyssop, marjoram, oregano, mint (forced), parsley, chervil, rosemary, rue, sage and thyme are all available for picking fresh.

In the garden, remove all the dead growth that falls

into other plants, add more protective layers if needed. Wrap any terracotta or stone ornaments in sacking if you live in extremely cold conditions. Bring bay trees in if the temperature drops too low. Keep an eye on the plants you are forcing in the greenhouse.

Fruit

Maintain good weed control by hoeing or mulching. Plant out bare-rooted hardy trees and bushes if the soil is in good condition and they are dormant. Collect the fallen leaves and use them for leaf mould or rake them in rings around trees and bushes.

Examine plants for pests, diseases and dieback. Top up the sticky bands and inspect the sacking bands on apple trees, and on others if they suffered from many pests. Check straps and stakes before the gales.

Spread a good layer of compost or well-rotted manure under and around everything possible, preferably after heavy rain. Prune late-fruiting trees and bushes as their leaves fall and do major work to trees and bushes (but not to stone fruits or evergreens). Check stores and remove and use any fruits starting to deteriorate before they go over and infect others.

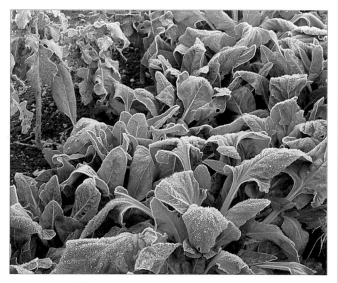

A covering of frost on a vegetable garden

GLOSSARY

Analgesic A substance that relieves pain.
Annual A plant completing its life cycle from germination to seed in one growing season.
Antidote A substance that counteracts or neutralizes a poison.
Aromatherapy The use of essential oils in the treatment of medical problems and for cosmetic purposes.
Astringent A substance that contracts the tissues of the body, checking discharges of blood and mucus.

Base dressing An application of organic matter or fertilizer, applied to the soil prior to planting or sowing.
Bed system A method of planting vegetables in close blocks or multiple rows.
Beta carotene The orange-yellow plant pigment and precursor of vitamin A, which protects against certain cancers and heart disease.
Biennial A plant completing its life cycle in a two-year period.
Blanch To exclude light from leaves and stems and prevent development of green coloration. In the culinary sense, to immerse in boiling water for the removal of skin or colour, often as a preparation for freezing.
Bolt To flower and produce seed prematurely.
Brassica A member of the cabbage family (Brassicaceae).
Broadcast To scatter granular substances such as seeds, fertilizer or pesticide evenly over an area of ground.
Bulb A modified plant stem, with swollen leaves acting as a storage organ.
Bulbil A small bulb rising above the ground in the axil of a leaf or bract.

Capping A crust forming on the surface of soil damaged by compaction, heavy rain or watering.
Carminative A substance that allays pain and relieves flatulence and colic.
Chitting Pre-germination of seeds before sowing. The same term is used for sprouting potatoes.
Clamp A structure made of earth for storing root vegetables outdoors.
Cloche A small portable structure, often made of plastic or glass, used to protect early crops grown outdoors.
Cold frame A low-lying square or rectangular unheated structure, with a glass or plastic lid.
Compost Decomposed organic material used as soil conditioner, mulch, potting or seed-sowing medium.
Cultivar A contraction of 'cultivated variety', a group of cultivated plants that retain desirable characteristics when propagated.

Damp down To wet the floors and benches in a glasshouse in order to increase humidity and lower high temperatures.
Deciduous Plants that lose leaves at the end of the growing season and redevelop them the following year.
Decoction An extract of a herb (when the material is hard and woody, i.e. root, wood, bark, nuts) obtained by boiling a set weight of plant matter in a set volume of water for a set time.
Diuretic A substance that increases the frequency of urination.
Dormancy Temporary cessation of growth during the dormant season.

Earth up To draw the soil around the base for support or to cover a plant for the purpose of blanching.
Emetic A substance that induces vomiting.
Essential oil A volatile oil obtained from a plant by distillation, and having a similar aroma to the plant itself.
Evergreen Plants retaining their leaves throughout the year.

F_1 Hybrid First-generation plants obtained by crossing two selected pure-breeding parents to produce uniform vigorous offspring.
Fanging A term to describe the forking of a root vegetable.
Fertilizer A chemical or group of chemicals applied to the soil or plants to provide nutrition.
Fleece Lightweight, woven polypropylene cover used for crop protection.
Floating mulch (floating cloche) Sheets of flexible lightweight material placed over plants to provide protection.
Fluid sow A method for sowing germinated seeds into the soil using a carrier gel.
Folic acid Part of the vitamin B complex, found in leafy vegetables. Deficiency of folic acid causes anaemia.
Friable Used to describe soil with a crumbly, workable texture, capable of forming a tilth.
Fungicide Chemical used for the control and eradication of fungi.

Genus A taxonomic classification used to describe plants with several similar characteristics.
Germination The chemical and physical changes that take place as a seed starts to grow.
Green manure A rapidly maturing, leafy crop grown for incorporation into the soil to improve its structure and nutrient levels.
Growbag A bag of compost used as a growing medium.

Half hardy Plants that tolerate low temperatures but not frost.
Harden off To acclimatize plants gradually, enabling them to withstand cooler conditions.
Hardy Plants that can withstand frost without protection.
Haulm The foliage of plants such as potatoes.
Heart up The stage at which leafy vegetables, like cabbage and lettuce, swell to form a dense cluster of central leaves.
Heavy soil A soil with a high proportion of clay particles, prone to waterlogging in winter and drying in summer.
Herbaceous Relating to plants that are not woody and that die down at the end of each growing season.
Herbicide A chemical used to control and eradicate weeds.
Homeopathy A system of medicine based on the supposition that minute quantities of a given substance, such as that of a medicinal plant, will cure a condition that would be caused by administering large quantities of the same substance.
Humus The organic decayed remains of plant material in soils.
Hybrid A variety of plant resulting from the crossing of two distinct species or genera.

Infusion An infusion is made by pouring a given quantity of boiling water over a given weight of soft herbal material (leaves or petals) and infusing.
Inorganic Term used to describe fertilizers made from refined naturally occurring chemicals, or artificial fertilizers.
Insecticide Chemical used to eradicate insects.

Inulin An easily digestible form of carbohydrate.

John Innes compost Loam-based growing medium made to standardized formulas.

Leaching The downward washing and loss of soluble nutrients from topsoil.
Leaf A plant organ containing chlorophyll essential for photosynthesis.
Leafmould Decaying leaves.
Legume The bean and pea family, which enrich the soil with bacterial nodules on their roots.
Lime Calcium compounds used to raise the pH of the soil.
Loam The term used for a soil of medium texture.

Maincrop The largest crop produced throughout the main growing season. Also used to describe the cultivars used.
Module A generic term describing the containers used for propagating and growing young plants.
Mordant A substance used in dyeing which, when applied to the fabric to be dyed, reacts chemically with the dye, fixing the colour.
Mulch A layer of organic or inorganic material laid over the ground which controls weeds, protects the soil surface and conserves moisture.

Nematacide Chemical used for the control and eradication of nematodes (eelworms).
Neutral Soil or compost with a pH value of 7 which is neither acid nor alkaline (see pH).
Nutrients Minerals that are essential for plant growth.

Organic Term used to describe substances that are derived from natural materials. Also used to denote gardening by encouraging the life in the soil and without the use of harmful chemicals.

Pan A layer of compacted soil that is impermeable to water and oxygen, and impedes root development and drainage.
Perennial A plant that survives for three or more years.
Perlite Expanded volcanic rock. It is inert, sterile and has a neutral pH value.
pH A measure of acidity or alkalinity. The scale ranges from 0 to 14, and is an indicator of the soluble calcium within a soil or growing medium. A pH below seven is acid and above, alkaline.
Pinch out To remove the growing tip of a plant to induce branching.
Pot on To move a plant into a larger pot.
Prick out To transfer seedlings, from a seedbed or tray, to a further pot, tray or seedbed.
Propagation The increase of plant numbers by seed or vegetative means.

Radicle A seedling root.
Rhizome A fleshy underground stem that acts as a storage organ.
Root The part of the plant that is responsible for absorbing water and nutrients and for anchoring the plant into the growing medium.
Root crops Vegetables grown for their edible roots, e.g. carrot and parsnip.
Runner A trailing shoot that roots where it touches the ground.

Salve A soothing ointment.
Saponin A substance that foams in water and has a detergent action.

Seed A ripened plant ovule containing a dormant embryo, which is capable of forming a new plant.
Seed leaves or *cotyledons* The first leaf or leaves formed by a seed after germination.
Seedling A young plant grown from seed.
Sets Small onions, shallots or potatoes used for planting.
Shoot A branch, stem or twig of a plant.
Shrub A plant with woody stems, branching at or near the base.
Sideshoot A branch, stem or twig growing from a main stem of a plant.
Species A taxonomic classification of similar closely related plants.
Spore The reproductive body of a non-flowering plant.
Stale seedbed method A cultivation technique whereby the seedbed is created and subsequent weed growth is removed before crops are sown or planted.
Stamen The pollen-producing part of the plant.
Stem The main axis of a plant, from which lateral branches appear.
Stigma The part of a pistil (the female organs of a flower) that accepts the pollen.
Subsoil Layers of less fertile soil immediately below the topsoil.
Sucker A stem originating below soil level, usually from the plant's roots or underground stem.
Systemic or *translocated* A term used to describe a chemical that is absorbed by a plant at one point and then circulated through its sap system.

Tap root The primary anchoring root of a plant, usually growing straight down into the soil. In vegetables this is often used for food storage.
Tender Plant material that is intolerant of cool conditions.
Thinning The removal of seedlings or shoots to improve the quality of those that remain.
Thymol A bactericide and fungicide found in several volatile oils.
Tilth The surface layer of soil produced by cultivation and soil improvement.
Tincture A solution that has been extracted from plant material after macerating in alcohol or alcohol/water solutions.
Tisane A drink made by the addition of boiling water to fresh or dried unfermented plant material.
Top-dressing The application of fertilizers or bulky organic matter to the soil surface, while the plants are *in situ*.
Topsoil The upper, usually most fertile layer of soil.
Transpiration The loss by evaporation of moisture from plant leaves and stems.
Transplant To move a plant from one growing position to another.
Tuber A swollen underground stem used to store moisture and nutrients.

Variety Used in the vernacular to describe different kinds of plant. Also used in botanical classification to describe a naturally occurring variant of a plant.

Vegetative Used to describe parts of a plant that are capable of growth.
Vermifuge A substance that expels or destroys worms.
Vulnerary A preparation useful in healing wounds.
Weathering Using the effect of climatic conditions to break down large lumps of soil into small particles.
Wind-rock Destabilizing of plant roots by wind action.

FURTHER READING

Bio-dynamic Gardening J. Soper, Souvenir Press 1983

Collins Guide to the Pests, Diseases & Disorders of Garden Plants S. Buczacki & K. Harris, Collins 1981

Complete Book of Herbs Lesley Bremness, Dorling Kindersley 1988

Complete Herbal Culpeper, J. Gleave & Son 1826

Complete Know and Grow Vegetables J. K. A. Bleasdale, P. J. Salter et al, OUP 1991

Complete New Herbal, The ed. Richard Mabey, Penguin 1988

Complete Cookery Course Delia Smith, BBC Books 1982

Contained Garden K. Beckett, D. Carr & D. Stephens, Frances Lincoln 1982

Diagnosis of Mineral Deficiencies in Plants HMSO 1943

Domestication of Plants in the Old World D. Zohary & Maria Hopf, Oxford Science Publications 1994

Dye Plants and Dyeing J. & M. Cannon, Herbert Press/Royal Botanic Gardens, Kew

Early Garden Crops F. W. Shepherd, RHS 1977

Encyclopedia of Garden Plants and Flowers ed. R. Hay, Reader's Digest 1978

Encyclopedia of Herbs and Herbalism ed. Malcolm Stuart, Black Cat 1979

Encyclopedia of Medicinal Plants Roberto Chiej, Macdonald 1984

Encyclopedia of Organic Gardening HDRA/DK 2001

English Gardener, The William Cobbett, 1833

Englishman's Flora, The Geoffrey Grigson, Paladin 1975

Evening Primrose Oil Judy Graham, Thorsons 1984

Food for Free Richard Mabey, Fontana/Collins 1972/75

Four-Season Harvest E. Coleman, Chelsea Green 1992

Gardener's Dictionary Philip Miller, 1724

Gardening on a Bed System P. Pears, Search Press/Henry Doubleday Research Association 1992

Gardening without Chemicals J. Temple, Thorsons 1986

Good Fruit Guide L.D.Hills, Henry Doubleday Research Association

Growing Under Glass K. A. Beckett, RHS/Mitchell Beazley 1992

Handbook of Insects Injurious to Orchard and Bush Fruits E.A. Ormerod, Simpkin, Marshall, Hamilton & Co. 1898

Herb Book, The John Lust, Bantam 1974

Herb Book, The Arabella Boxer & Philippa Black, Octopus 1980

Herb Gardening at its Best Sal Gilbertie with Larry Sheehan, Atheneum/smi 1978

Herbal John Gerard, 1636; Bracken Books 1985

Herbs for Health and Cookery Clair Loewenfeld & Philippa Black, Pan 1965

Herbs in the Garden Allen Paterson, Dent 1985

Hillier's Manual of Trees and Shrubs David & Charles

Hints for the Vegetable Gardener Gardenway Publications 1990

History and Social Influence of the Potato R. N. Salaman, CUP 1949

Jane Grigson's Vegetable Book J. Grigson, Penguin 1988

Kitchen Garden: a Historical Guide to Traditional Crops D. C. Stuart, Hale 1984

Maison Rustique, or the Country Farm Estienne, C. Liebault, 1570

Modern Herbal, A M. Grieve, Peregrine 1976

Nutritional Values in Crops and Plants Werner Schuphan, Museum Press 1965

Organic Bible Bob Flowerdew, Kyle Cathie 2001

Organic Gardening, Month by Month Guide to Lawrence D. Hills, Thorsons 1983

Organic Gardening R. Lacey, David & Charles 1988

Organic Growing for Small Gardens J. Hay, Century 1985

Organic Plant Protection R.B.Yepsen (ed.), Rodale 3rd printing 1976

Oriental Vegetables: The Complete Guide for Garden & Kitchen J. Larkcom, John Murray Ltd 1991

Ornamental Kitchen Garden, The Geoff Hamilton, BBC Books 1990

Oxford Book of Food Plants Peerage Books 1969

Pelargoniums Derek Clifford, Blandford 1958

Planning the Organic Herb Garden Sue Stickland, Thorsons 1986

Plant and Planet Anthony Huxley, Allen Lane 1974

Plant Finder 2002–3, The Dorling Kindersley 2002

Plant Physiological Disorders ADAS, HMSO 1985

Plants from the Past David Stuart & James Sutherland, Viking 1987

Pruning of Trees, Shrubs & Conifers George E. Brown, Faber & Faber 1972

Queer Gear: How to Buy & Cook Exotic Fruits & Vegetables M. Allsop & C. Heal, Century Hutchinson 1986

RHS Encyclopedia of Gardening ed. C. Brickell, Dorling Kindersley 1992

RHS Gardeners' Encyclopedia Oxford Press 1951

Salad Garden, The J. Larkcom, Frances Lincoln 1984

Science and Fruit Long Ashton Research Station, University of Bristol 1953

Seeds Jekka McVicar, Kyle Cathie 2000

Soil Conditions and Plant Growth Sir John Russell, Longmans 8th edition 1954

Sow and Grow Vegetables B. Salt, MPC 1995

Sturtevant's Edible Plants of the World ed. U. P. Hendrick, Dover Publications 1972

Successful Organic Gardening G. Hamilton, Dorling Kindersley 1987

Treatise on Gardening William Cobbett, 1821

Trees and Bushes of Britain and Europe Oleg Polunin, Oxford University Press 1976

Tropical Planting & Gardening H. F. Macmillan, Malayan Nature Society 1991

UK Green Growers' Guide, The S.G. Lisansky, S. Robinson, J. Coombs, CPL Press 1991

Vanishing Garden, The Christopher Brickell & Fay Sharman, John Murray 1986

Vegetable Garden Displayed, The J. Larkcom, RHS 1992

Vegetable Varieties for the Garden J. R. Chowings & M. J. Day, RHS/Cassell 1992

Vegetables R. Phillips & M. Rix, Pan Macmillan 1993

Vegetables of South East Asia G. A. L. Herklots, Allen & Unwin

Vegetarian Cookbook, The Sarah Brown, Dorling Kindersley 1984

Weed Control Robbins, Crafts & Raynor, McGraw Hill 1942

Your Kitchen Garden George Seddon, Mitchell Beazley 1975

USEFUL ADDRESSES

Organizations:
Biodynamic Agricultural
Association
Painswick Inn
Stroud
Gloucestershire

Centre for Alternative
Technology
Machynlleth
Powys
SY20 9AZ

Elm Farm Research Centre
Hamstead Marshall
Newbury
Berkshire
RG20 0HR

Friends of the Earth
26–28 Underwood Street
London
N1 7JQ

Henry Doubleday Research
Association (HDRA)
Ryton Organic Gardens
Coventry
Warwickshire
CV8 3LG

Horticultural Research
International (HRI)
Wellesbourne
Warwick
CV35 9EF

John Innes Centre
Norwich Research Park
Colney
Norwich
Norfolk
NR4 7UH

National Council for the
Conservation of Plants and
Gardens (NCCPG)
The Stable Courtyard
Wisley Gardens
Woking
Surrey
GU23 6QB

National Vegetable Society
5 Whitelow Road
Heaton Moor
Stockport

Northern Horticultural
Society
Harlow Carr Botanical
Gardens
Crag Lane
Harrogate
N. Yorkshire
HG3 1QB

Insititute of Arable Crop
Research (IACR)
Rothamsted
Harpenden
Hertfordshire
AL5 2JQ

Royal Horticultural Society
(RHS)
80 Vincent Square
London
SW1P 2PE

Royal Horticultural Society
of Ireland
Marley Park House
Grange Road
Dublin 16

Soil Association
40–56 Victoria Street
Bristol
BS1 6BY

WWOOF (Working
Weekends On Organic
Farms)
19 Bradford Road
Lewes
E. Sussex
BN7 1RB

Seed suppliers:
Chiltern Seeds
Bortree Stile
Ulverston
Cumbria
LA12 7PB

Dobies Seeds
Long Road
Paignton
Devon
TQ4 7SX

Fothergill Seeds
Gazeley Road
Kentford
Newmarket
Suffolk
CB8 7QB

Future Foods
Luckleigh Cottage
Hockworthy
Wellington
Somerset
TA21 0NN

Kings Seeds & Suffolk Herbs
Monks Farm
Kelvedon
Colchester
Essex
CO5 9PG

S. E. Marshall
Wisbech
Cambridgeshire
PE13 2BR

Suttons Seeds
Woodview Road
Paignton
Devon
TQ4 7NG

Thompson & Morgan
Poplar Lane
Ipswich
Suffolk
IP8 3BU

Unwins Seeds
Histon
Cambridge
CB4 4LE

**For citrus and conservatory
plants:**
Read's Nursery
Hale's Hall
Loddon
Norfolk
NR14 6QW

**For good quality hardy trees
and plants:**
R.V. Roger
The Nurseries
Whitby Road
Pickering
North Yorkshire
YO18 7HG

**For a very wide range of
hardy fruit:**
Deacon's Nursery
Moor View
Ventnor
Isle of Wight
PO38 3HW

Keeper's Nursery
Gallant's Court
Gallant's Lane
East Farleigh
Maidstone
Kent
ME15 0LE

Thornhayes Nursery
St Andrews Wood
Dulford
Cullompton
Devon
EX15 2DF

For sundries:
Chase Organics
River Dene Estate
Molesey Road
Hersham
Surrey
KT12 4RG

INDEX